May 27, 2000.

Happy Birthday Karl –

Love from

Dorothy &

Happy Birthday

May 27, 2000.

The DK Art School

AN INTRODUCTION TO
ART TECHNIQUES

The DK Art School

AN INTRODUCTION TO
ART TECHNIQUES

RAY SMITH
MICHAEL WRIGHT
JAMES HORTON

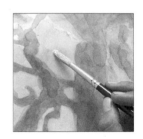   

DK PUBLISHING, INC
IN ASSOCIATION WITH THE ROYAL ACADEMY OF ARTS

A DK PUBLISHING BOOK

Senior managing editor Sean Moore
Deputy art director Tina Vaughan
US editors Laaren Brown, Constance V. Mersel,
Mary Ann Lynch
Editor Anna Kunst

First American Edition, 1995
4 6 8 10 9 7 5 3

Published in the United States by
DK Publishing, Inc., 95 Madison Avenue
New York, New York 10016

Copyright © 1995
Dorling Kindersley Limited, London

Visit us on the World Wide Web at
http://www.dk.com

A catalog record is available from the Library of Congress

ISBN 0-7894-0488-5

Colour reproduction by Colourscan in Singapore

Printed and bound in the United States

CONTENTS

6

AN INTRODUCTION TO
DRAWING

72

AN INTRODUCTION TO
PERSPECTIVE

138

AN INTRODUCTION TO
WATERCOLOR

202

AN INTRODUCTION TO
PASTELS

268

AN INTRODUCTION TO
OIL PAINTING

332

AN INTRODUCTION TO
ACRYLICS

398

AN INTRODUCTION TO
MIXED MEDIA

464

GLOSSARY

474

INDEX

AN INTRODUCTION TO DRAWING

Drawing	8	Form & Modeling	38
History of Drawing	10	Tonal Drawing	40
		Gallery of Form	42
MATERIALS		Layout & Construction	44
Pencils & Colored Pencils	14	Buildings & Architecture	46
Pens & Inks	16	Interiors & Exteriors	48
Chalks & Charcoal	18	Gallery of Composition	50
Pastel Types	20	Drawing Natural Forms	52
Drawing in Watercolor	22	Landscapes	54
Gallery of Drawing Media	24	Gallery of Landscapes &	
Paper	26	Natural Forms	56
Gallery of Paper	28	Figures & Drapery	58
		Life Drawing	60
TECHNIQUES		Portraits	62
Work Methods	30	Figures in a Setting	64
Getting Started	32	Gallery of Figures	66
The Basics of Drawing	34	Movements & Gestures	68
Linear Drawing	36	Drawing for Painting	70

DRAWING

A<small>S CHILDREN WE ALL DRAW</small> and paint – yet the older we become, the more we seem to ignore the significance of drawing as a vital source of communication and pleasure. Drawing is still one of the best ways to convey information directly, despite the increasing prevalence of photography. Scientists, and in particular archaeologists, actually prefer to draw many items because a detailed drawing can be more precise and informative than a photograph, since it involves a process of selection. Many natural history field guides rely on detailed drawings and paintings for identification purposes.

The best approach

As adults we see the world in a very different way than children do. The stumbling block for many of us is that with a more mature perspective we have a much greater sense of what is "correct" and what is "incorrect," (although this sense limits creativity and leads us astray), and this can often create inhibitions. There is, however, nothing that is intrinsically mysterious about the mechanics of drawing. Anyone can learn to draw if they adopt the right approach. Just as with any other subject, practice is essential for achieving good results.

Drawing well is all about how you perceive the world around you and interpret it into your own personal vision.

Interpreting what you see

Ultimately, drawing has far more to do with learning to see perceptively than with acquiring consummate skill with your hand. The quality of what you draw on paper stems from your imagination and the way you choose to interpret what you see. Look discerningly at objects, consolidating all the information you see, to give your drawings freshness and individuality. Don't be afraid to repeat lines or marks until a drawing looks right;

because of misconceptions about the process of drawing, people try to erase what they think are mistakes, believing that they will spoil the finished result. On the contrary, every mark you make reflects the progression of your drawing and often adds to its interest and vitality.

Problem solving

Drawing is perhaps the most direct of the arts, with an immediacy that allows you to record instantly what you see, and to draw from life can be both stimulating and rewarding. Anyone who gains satisfaction from solving crossword puzzles is likely to become absorbed by the practice of drawing; of discovering how to create, for example, perspective in a landscape, or how to foreshorten a reclining figure. Curiously enough, some of the best drawings are those in which an artist has struggled to resolve the most problematic aspects of a composition in order to create a tangible image.

Familiar materials

Many of the materials covered in this book have been available to artists for hundreds of years, so the equipment we use today is similar to that used by Renaissance artists five hundred years ago. Drawing with a piece of charcoal on paper still involves exactly the same process for us as it did for them. The basic pleasures and benefits of drawing will always remain, despite the burgeoning of modern technology and the sophisticated equipment that is available to artists today.

HISTORY OF DRAWING

T HE HISTORY OF DRAWING may be as old as the human race itself. Cave paintings have been discovered dating back as far as 10,000 years BC, so it seems that we have always been interested in creating images. However, it was during the Italian Renaissance that artists developed profound drawing skills and the art of drawing underpinned all other artistic disciplines.

ONE REASON WHY drawing reached such a high standard during this period was that it related directly to the great profession of painting; a sculptor or a painter had a distinguished position within society and good artists were constantly working. Renaissance artists such as Michelangelo *(1475-1564)* employed numerous assistants and ran a large workshop to cope with his many commissions. Unfortunately, most of the preparatory drawings these artists made for paintings – which today we would regard as important in their own right – were destroyed once the project had been completed.

More importantly, finished drawings were presented to clients as proposals for commissioned portrait work. Holbein *(1497/8-1543)* once had the precarious task of making a suitable drawing of a potential wife for Henry VIII so that she could be approved by the English king.

Pontormo,
Study for the Angel of the Annunciation,
c. 1525-30 *154 x 84 in (391 x 215 cm)*
Pontormo is generally acknowledged as one of the greatest Renaissance draftsmen and was highly regarded for his portraits. This study, with its subtle blend of chalk and wash, has a beautifully sensitive quality despite the solid form of the figure and the flowing drapery that tumbles about him.

Hans Holbein,
Charles de Solier,
Sieur de Morette,
c. 1534-35
13 x 10 in (33 x 25 cm)
Holbein was often commissioned to do life-like portraits. His fine quality of line both flatters the features of this figure and lends him a heavy sense of authority.

Northern Europe

Away from the high classical art of Italy, the Flemish painter Pieter Bruegel *(1525-69)* used drawing to depict the everyday world around him, and his realistic peasant scenes brought him great admiration. Bruegel was one of many artists in Holland and Flanders during the sixteenth and seventeenth centuries who cultivated a genre that was based upon the lives of ordinary people. Although this "Golden Age" of Dutch painting owed little to Italy,

an artist's training was based on figure drawing, which ultimately meant a pilgrimage to Italy.

One Dutch artist who never journeyed to Italy was Rembrandt *(1606-69),* who today is known particularly for his graphic work on

paper. As a portrait artist, he avidly drew anyone who interested him, from old beggars to noblemen, with astonishing perception – often in his favorite medium of quill, brush, and bistre wash (a transparent brown pigment made from soot).

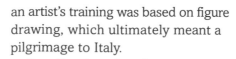

Pieter Bruegel the Elder,
Summer, **1568** *8½ x 11½ in (22 x 29 cm)*
This beautifully drawn study of peasant life in 16th-century Flanders is actually rather formal in its design, with the scythes of the two main figures creating diagonals that lead the eye into the middle and far distance of the composition. Bruegel also liked to convey a strong social message in his humorous depictions of life.

Artistic contemporaries

Rembrandt's great artistic contemporary in neighboring Flanders was Rubens *(1577-1640)*. As a draftsman, he was virtually unparalleled and was one of the few artists who appeared to make the process of drawing look easy. He drew copiously, working not only on preparatory studies for the vast number of commissions he fulfilled, but also on a much more intimate scale, depicting his family and servants with the freshness and immediacy that drawing allows.

Curiously, some of the greatest figures of the seventeenth century, such as Vermeer *(1632-75)*, Caravaggio *(1571-1610)*, and Velazquez *(1599-1660)*, left few if any drawings. Although it is improbable that these artists never drew at all, it is more likely that they preferred to solve their problems directly on the canvas in a painterly fashion.

Canaletto, *A View from Somerset Gardens Looking Toward London Bridge, c.* **1750** *23½ x 73 in (60 x 185 cm)*
Canaletto was renowned for his detailed paintings and drawings of architectural scenes. The wonderful clarity of this work was achieved by drawing the panoramic composition in pencil and then overlaying it with brown ink and gray wash.

Rembrandt, *Saskia at her Toilet,*
c. **1632-34** *9½ x 7 in (24 x 18 cm)*
Rembrandt was often at his best when he recorded a fleeting moment in time. This drawing reflects the precision of his observant eye as he worked adeptly, first with pen and ink, and then with a loaded brush. The result is a drawing that is both lucid and evocative in its depiction of a domestic scene.

Portrait drawing

While it did not produce many artistic giants, the eighteenth century did keep the commissioned portrait alive. In France, Watteau *(1684-1721)* produced fine studies of figures, heads, and drapery in his preferred medium of red, black, and white chalks, while in Italy, Giambattista Tiepolo *(1696-1770)*, arguably the greatest artist of his time, used pen and wash for drawings that remain unrivaled to this day.

11

Pencil drawings

The nineteenth century saw a great surge in artistic development, which in England began with Turner *(1775-1851)* and Constable *(1776-1837),* and in France with Delacroix *(1798-1863)* and Ingres *(1780-1867)*. Lead pencil was in use by this time, and Constable used the medium to draw many small images of rural Suffolk in his sketchbooks with great subtlety and expression. Turner began to develop almost unbelievable powers of observation and skill in his youth as he drew cathedrals and buildings with a lead pencil.

Portrait drawings were still fashionable, and studies drawn by the French Neo-Classicist Ingres were so real and lifelike that there was never any doubt as to their likeness to the sitter. Ingres' contemporary and great rival was Delacroix, who by contrast was a Romantic free spirit. He not only made studies in the traditional manner for grand historical pictures but also drew everything that caught his eye. In an age that preceded the advent of photography, drawing was the only way that Delacroix could record the trip he made to Morocco in 1832. Contemporary reports stated that he drew night and day, desperate not to forget the rich aspects of Arabian life.

The advent of modernity

Of the great draftsmen of the nineteenth century, one innovative artist assimilated everything that went before him. This was Edgar Degas *(1834-1917)*, whose life's work was based on drawing. Even as a middle-aged and well-established artist, he copied works by other artists to stretch his understanding of art and practice his techniques. Degas' enormous output of drawings, pastels, monoprints, and etchings represents an incredible achievement, but by the time he died in 1917, the modern art

John Constable, *Elm Trees in Old Hall Park, East Bergholt,* 1817
23¼ x 19½ in (59 x 50 cm)
Unlike Turner, who used a wide variety of media in his drawings, Constable preferred to use his materials separately to describe the countryside around him. He used a pencil expertly to capture the organic growth of these elm trees with incredible detail so that they are easily recognizable.

Eugène Delacroix, *Seated Arab,*
***c.* 1832** *15 x 18 in (38 x 46 cm)*
This study is typical of the sketches Delacroix made during his Moroccan tour. He probably drew the figure hastily from life and added washes of watercolor later.

movement was well under way and moving rapidly toward a language that he would not have recognized.

The history of drawing from this point is a checkered one, and it developed quite differently on the two sides of the English Channel. While France pursued modernism, spurred on by artists such as Henri Matisse *(1869-1954)*, England retained a basic attachment to drawing. The turn of the century in England saw the birth of several major art schools, all of which placed a great emphasis on drawing, and although

various modern movements came and went, drawing continued to underpin students' training. The work of artists such as Augustus John *(1878-1961)* and later Stanley Spencer *(1891-1959)* bear witness to the significance of drawing in England through the turbulent years of the early twentieth century.

One artist who has brought drawing to the forefront of the contemporary imagination is David Hockney *(b.1937)*. Inspired by Pablo Picasso *(1881-1973)*, who had an extraordinary breadth of style and "was not limited by 'form,'" Hockney takes pleasure in the lyricism and strength of pure line. Preferring the expressive beauty of drawings over more painterly approaches, Hockney has taken his drawing to a far wider audience than ever before.

Edgar Degas, *Woman in a Tub,*
c. 1885 *27½ x 27½ in (70 x 70 cm)*
Classically trained, Degas devised his own method of working with pastels. He built them up in layers, using strokes of color that blended optically to give an extraordinary richness.

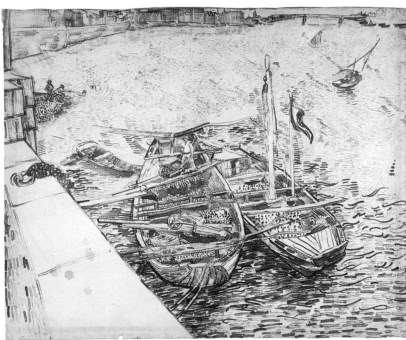

Vincent van Gogh, *Sand Boats,*
1888 *19 x 23½ in (49 x 60 cm)*
Van Gogh exploited the potential of pen and ink to its fullest in this work to produce an image alive with spontaneous line. A variety of marks and stippled effects together create a shimmering surface of movement that is heightened by the dynamic composition. The strong diagonal of the quayside and the horizon line that cuts into the top of the drawing create an arena for this scene of constant activity and motion.

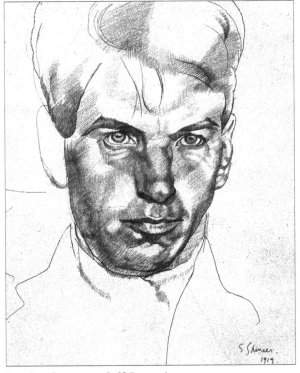

Stanley Spencer, *Self-Portrait,*
1919 *14 x 9 in (36 x 23 cm)*
The strong contours and subtle tones of this pencil study lend it an impressive sculpted quality. The solidity of line and sensitive tones belie the apparent simplicity of the medium.

13

PENCILS & COLORED PENCILS

PENCILS ARE THE SIMPLEST and most immediate of drawing media, enabling you to create a versatile range of strong or sensitive marks. What we call a "lead pencil" today is actually made of graphite – a mixture of clay and the mineral graphite – in the form of a rod that is usually encased in cedarwood. An array of grades exists from very hard to extremely soft, although artists seldom use the hardest varieties because they allow for so little expression when drawing. Colored pencils are a relatively recent innovation, and their waxy nature means that they retain their own distinct colors when drawn over each other.

Silverpoint study
Silverpoint, an original version of the pencil popular in Renaissance times, is a beautiful medium, as this 15th century study by Fouquet shows. The basic principle of silverpoint is to leave a metal deposit by dragging a piece of pure silver across paper previously prepared with Chinese White watercolor paint.

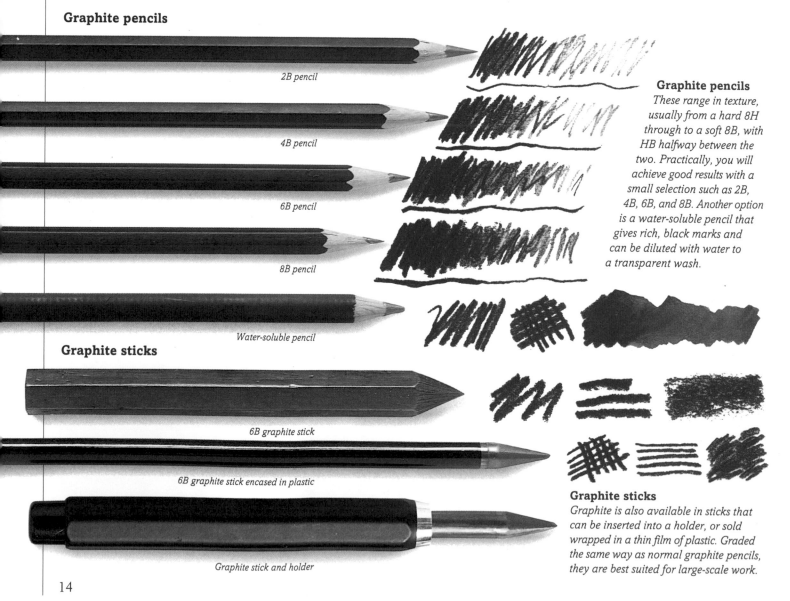

Graphite pencils

2B pencil

4B pencil

6B pencil

8B pencil

Water-soluble pencil

Graphite pencils
These range in texture, usually from a hard 8H through to a soft 8B, with HB halfway between the two. Practically, you will achieve good results with a small selection such as 2B, 4B, 6B, and 8B. Another option is a water-soluble pencil that gives rich, black marks and can be diluted with water to a transparent wash.

Graphite sticks

6B graphite stick

6B graphite stick encased in plastic

Graphite stick and holder

Graphite sticks
Graphite is also available in sticks that can be inserted into a holder, or sold wrapped in a thin film of plastic. Graded the same way as normal graphite pencils, they are best suited for large-scale work.

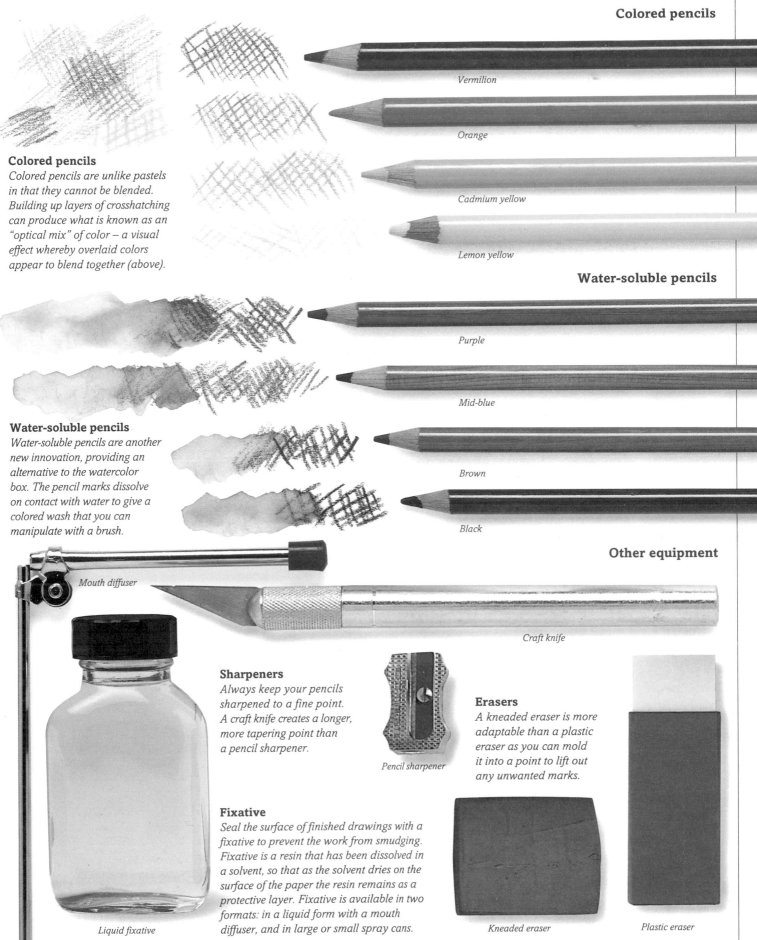

Colored pencils

Colored pencils

Colored pencils are unlike pastels in that they cannot be blended. Building up layers of crosshatching can produce what is known as an "optical mix" of color – a visual effect whereby overlaid colors appear to blend together (above).

Vermilion

Orange

Cadmium yellow

Lemon yellow

Water-soluble pencils

Water-soluble pencils

Water-soluble pencils are another new innovation, providing an alternative to the watercolor box. The pencil marks dissolve on contact with water to give a colored wash that you can manipulate with a brush.

Purple

Mid-blue

Brown

Black

Other equipment

Mouth diffuser

Craft knife

Sharpeners

Always keep your pencils sharpened to a fine point. A craft knife creates a longer, more tapering point than a pencil sharpener.

Pencil sharpener

Erasers

A kneaded eraser is more adaptable than a plastic eraser as you can mold it into a point to lift out any unwanted marks.

Fixative

Seal the surface of finished drawings with a fixative to prevent the work from smudging. Fixative is a resin that has been dissolved in a solvent, so that as the solvent dries on the surface of the paper the resin remains as a protective layer. Fixative is available in two formats: in a liquid form with a mouth diffuser, and in large or small spray cans.

Liquid fixative

Kneaded eraser

Plastic eraser

15

PENS & INKS

PEN AND INK has been for centuries one of the most common drawing mediums. In the past, pens were almost always made from quills, although reeds and bamboo were also used. Today, there is an abundance of pens to choose from, many of which can be used by artists, although the quality of ink in most commercially available pens is often poor and will fade over time. Drawing in ink is always a great challenge because the ink is impossible to erase and so, in many senses, embodies the spirit of drawing. Every mark made becomes a vital part of the evolution of a drawing and mistakes can often be used in a constructive and interesting way.

Quill pen

Traditionally made from goose feathers, the quill pen is still hard to beat in terms of flexibility and versatility. Each quill will vary in performance, depending on the strength and resistance of the shaft.

Choosing a pen

With so many different pens available, the only way to be sure of what suits your style is to test a random selection. A standard nib holder will take a variety of different width nibs, all of which give a variation of line depending upon the degree of pressure you exert. On the other hand, technical drawing pens, which also come in a range of sizes, are hard and inflexible and give a consistent width of line, regardless of pressure. Fountain pens are more convenient and give a good variety of line.

MAKING A NIB

1 *Reeds, bamboo, and goose feathers are all suitable to be made into nibs. Use a craft knife to cut cleanly through one end of a reed.*

2 *Cut a curved section out of the back and trim the front into a point with two 45° angle cuts. Make a small cut to split the nib.*

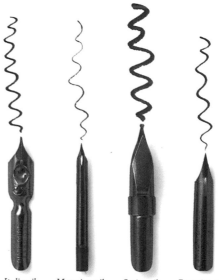

Italic nib   *Mapping nib*   *Script nib*   *Drawing nib*

Dip pens

Steel nibs all respond well to pressure to give a thicker or thinner line. Standard penholders take most nibs, but tubular mapping nibs need a separate holder.

Reed pen

The common reed (Phragmites) is normally used to make reed pens and, like quill pens, each makes its own distinctive marks. Pens made from natural fibers need a lengthways split in the tip of the nib to act as a channel to hold the ink.

Sketch pen
This pen has a flexible steel nib in a fountain pen format.

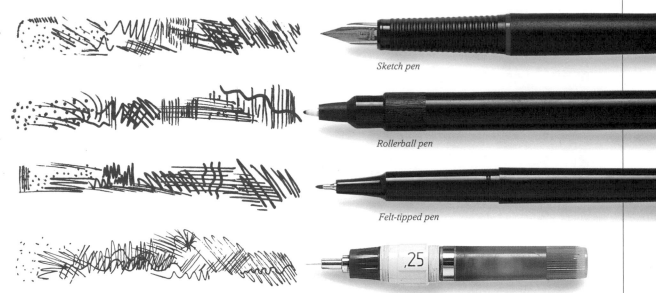

Sketch pen

Rollerball pen
Rollerball pens act like ballpoint pens to give a steady ink flow.

Rollerball pen

Felt-tipped pen
A felt tip allows the ink to flow smoothly in a thin line.

Felt-tipped pen

Technical pen
This pen gives both good control and consistency of line.

.25

Technical drawing pen

Chinese brush

Chinese ink
Use a Chinese brush and ink block (left) for eloquent yet controlled drawings.

Chinese ink

Using the right ink

Of the two basic types of ink – non-waterproof and waterproof – most non-waterproof inks will eventually fade if exposed to light. You can easily test for fading by drawing some lines in different inks on a piece of paper and then covering one half and leaving the other exposed to the light for several months.

Oak leaf drawn with oak gall ink

MAKING INK

You can make a permanent sepia ink with oak galls from oak trees. Crush the balls and boil the powder in water for two or three hours until the liquid is dark enough to strain.

Colored inks

Of the colored inks you can buy, the most common colors for drawing are black and a range of browns. In the past, ink was usually made with ground lampblack, or red ochre and a solution of glue or gum, molded into dry sticks or blocks to be mixed with water. Prepared in a similar way, India ink is a mixture of carbon black and water, stabilized by an alkaline solution such as gum arabic or shellac (a resinous substance used for making varnish).

Black ink   *Sepia ink*   *Raw Sienna ink*

CHALKS & CHARCOAL

WHITE CHALK IS ONE OF THE OLDEST drawing media, and has been used in its natural state to heighten artists' drawings for hundreds of years. Red chalk, known as sanguine, is a rust-colored earth, which can be found in areas such as central Italy. Today, processed colored chalks, or crayons, are produced by mixing limestone with pigment, water, and a binding medium. Charcoal, another natural material commonly made of charred willow, is a highly versatile medium that has also been used for hundreds of years. Today, the material is often compressed into solid sticks.

Sanguine
Sanguine – meaning a blood red color – can be used in its natural form by sharpening a piece of the red chalk to a point and inserting it into a holder. Processed sanguine is made up of iron oxide and chalk and then molded into bars, sticks, or pencils.

Charcoal
The rich, velvety black quality of charcoal makes it one of the boldest and most evocative mediums. It is sold in different degrees of hardness and thickness. Compressed charcoal has a more intense appearance than willow or vine charcoal sticks.

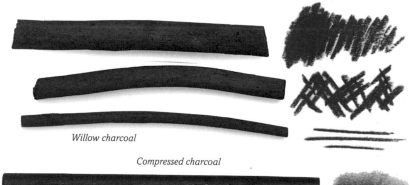

Willow charcoal

Compressed charcoal

Conté crayons
A hard version of chalk, these are less prone to breaking and come in a wide range of colors.

Drawing chalks
Similar in texture and appearance to pastels, these leave a finer deposit than crayons. White chalk is only effective on toned paper or over another color.

Sanguine Conté crayon

Brown Conté crayon

Blue drawing chalk

White drawing chalk

Charcoal pencils
Harder than charcoal sticks and graded, these pencils can be sharpened to a fine point for precise work.

6B charcoal pencil

4B charcoal pencil

Pastel pencils
Pastel pencils are ideal for creating fine lines and for delicate blending.

Sanguine pastel pencil

Drawing with Conté crayon

Conté crayons are a hard version of chalk, mixed with pigment and graphite and bound with gum and a small amount of grease. Their composition makes them harder to rub out than chalk or charcoal, so it is difficult to erase any accidental lines. They do, however, react in the same way as chalk when mixed with water; the pigment loosens on the paper so that it acts like a wash. Use a textured paper so that the distinctive qualities of Conté crayon will be heightened.

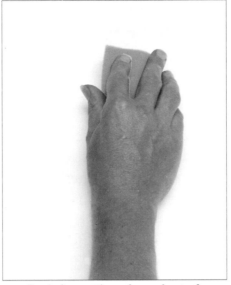

1 ▲ Begin by wetting a large sheet of paper with a household sponge. This damp surface will cause the crayon marks to absorb some of the water and appear thicker and heavier, giving a sense of solidity to the image of the figure.

2 ▲ Draw the outlines of the standing figure with a brown Conté crayon, sketching lightly at first and then reinforcing the lines once you are happy with the proportions. Don't worry about repeating lines if you need to alter a feature.

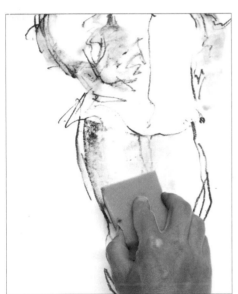

3 ▲ Now use the damp sponge to loosen the pigment in the lines of crayon. The pigment should disperse into a light wash that gives the figure a sense of shape.

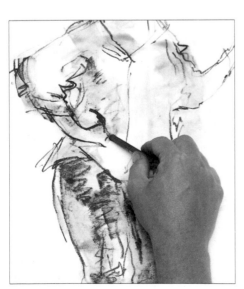

4 ◀ Use the tip of the crayon to illustrate the dark creases of the shirt and add details such as the fingers on the girl's hand.

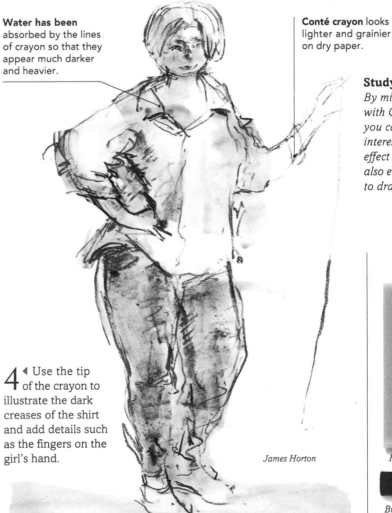

Water has been absorbed by the lines of crayon so that they appear much darker and heavier.

Conté crayon looks lighter and grainier on dry paper.

Study of a Girl
By mixing water with Conté crayon you can achieve an interesting drawing effect that should also encourage you to draw lucidly.

James Horton

Materials

Household sponge

Brown Conté crayon

PASTEL TYPES

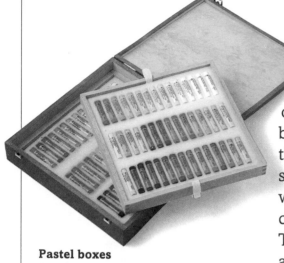

THE OPAQUE NATURE of soft pastels, and their ability to cover a surface easily, means that the medium may often be used in a paintlike fashion. However, pastels cannot be mixed in the same way that paint can, so they remain within the realm of drawing – that is, the artist must use the dry sticks of pigment individually to make a series of marks, which are then overlaid or blended. Pastels are essentially chalk that has been mixed with pigment and a binding medium. They vary in hardness depending on the particular pigments and the proportion of gum to chalk. The harder they are, the better suited they are to linear work.

Pastel boxes
Pastels are sold individually or in boxed sets that keep the colors clean and protect them.

Chalk pastels
These pastel sticks, with their brilliance of color and ease of handling, are the most popular form of pastel. The purity of pigment is retained by using just a small amount of gum solution to bind the various quantities of colored chalk into a solid form.

Pastel pencils
Pastel pencils are a harder version of the sticks. While their pencil format makes them ideal for detailed work and delicate modeling, they are less suited to covering large surface areas.

Protecting your work
The powdery composition of pastels makes them susceptible to smudging, so protect drawings with sheets of tracing paper.

Oil pastels
These pastels are made with oil rather than gum, which makes them more translucent and sticky. Their advantages over soft pastels: they adhere to paper easily, the colors can be blended, and they can be used for a variety of techniques such as sgraffito (p.38).

Water-soluble pastels
Similar in consistency and texture to wax crayons, these pastels can be used wet or dry and either drawn straight onto a damp surface, or softened with a wet brush that disperses the pigments.

Wax crayons
The waxy consistency of these sticks means that they are resistant to water. As a result, they can be combined with watercolor washes to provide interesting texture in a drawing.

Spray fixative
Because pastels smudge easily, the artist must always seal a finished drawing with fixative. If you use a spray, then pin the work to a vertical surface to prevent any drips from marking the surface.

Tortillons
Tortillons, or blending tools, are made of tightly rolled paper and are the thickness of a pencil. As the tip becomes soiled from pastel pigment, you can peel away a layer of paper to reveal a clean surface.

DRAWING WITH WATERCOLOR

USED INITIALLY IN THE WEST to "color" pen and ink drawings and heighten their descriptive qualities, watercolor has been a part of drawing media for hundreds of years. It mixes perfectly with traditional drawing tools such as pencil and ink, furnishing a linear drawing with an expressive rhythm and a pronounced spontaneity. Make sure you use permanent ink with watercolor washes or the water will dissolve the lines of ink. Watercolor is also useful because it can be blended into a smooth gradation of tones that increase the three-dimensional quality of forms in a subtle way. Using a sable brush also enables you to make the most sensuous of watercolor drawings; sable brushes offer the artist the flexibility to change instantly from a broad, bold brushmark to a fine, tapering line.

No. 4 sable brush

No. 9 sable brush

Watercolor box

Transparent watercolor
You can blend colors together or overlay separate washes.

Transparency and opacity
Watercolor is unique for its transparent light effects. The characteristic luminosity of the medium is caused by natural light penetrating a mix of pigment and water and reflecting back off the surface of the paper (*left*). The more colors you mix together, the less light can penetrate and reflect, creating a much darker color. You can also create stronger, heavier effects by mixing white with a color, or by using a watercolor paint known as gouache or body color. The opacity of gouache paint helps give solidity to an image (*below*) or create intense highlights if you are drawing on toned paper.

Watercolor boxes
Watercolor paint is available in a viscous form, in a tube, or in a solid block, called a pan. Pans are most convenient for drawing as they can easily be used and stored in a metal box. Pans are sold individually so that you can replace particular colors as they run out.

Sable brushes
Soft sable brushes give the best effects with watercolor, retaining their shape far longer than synthetic brushes. A small and a medium-sized or large brush are all you need for most drawings.

Opaque watercolor
Build up dark washes of color to create strong shadows.

Watercolor sketchbook

Working outdoors

Drawing with watercolor is almost synonymous with working outdoors or from life, because its fluency and ease of handling enable you to capture even the most fleeting of light effects. If you do decide to work outside, you can organize a simple travel kit of basic materials that takes up little room and is easy to handle. Use a protective canvas case or roll to store equipment such as pencils, a dip pen, and sable brushes safely. Take a hard surface, such as a wooden drawing board, and clips to secure the paper and support your hand as you draw.

Plastic tube

Canvas roll

Collapsible wooden stool

Transporting paper

When carrying paper, always protect it by using a folder or a plastic tube. You should also include a can or bottle of fixative in your kit to prevent finished drawings from smudging while they are stored together.

Canvas roll

A protective roll is the easiest way of transporting your drawing materials. The rolls are usually made from canvas with elastic strips sewn in to hold individual items securely. You may also want to take a small wooden stool if you are going to be working outdoors for any length of time.

Drawing board

Drawing board

Although it may be the bulkiest piece of equipment, a drawing board is one of the most important items to include in your kit and is a cheaper and more convenient alternative than a wooden or metal easel. Another option is to use a block of watercolor paper, which is sold with each sheet of paper lightly glued to the next to give a solid, flat surface on which to draw.

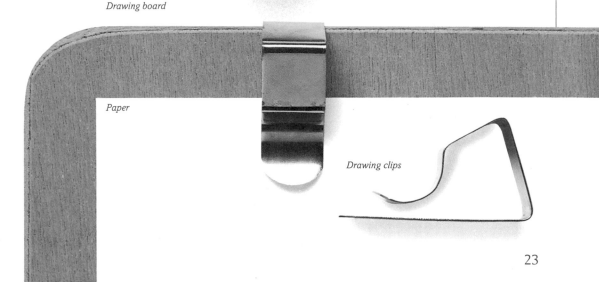

Paper

Drawing clips

23

GALLERY OF DRAWING MEDIA

O FTEN THE SUBJECT MATTER you draw will dictate what type of medium you use. A piece of detailed architecture can be drawn most precisely with a technical pen or a fine nib, and charcoal proves itself a superior medium for swiftly capturing the mood of a person. For an elegant, rhythmical drawing of a moving figure, brush and ink offers the widest range of expressive line. Occasionally mixing your media can introduce a whole new facet to your work, but the success of mixing different media together depends upon using each to its best advantage. A pencil sketch can evolve into a more substantial drawing if you add watercolor to strengthen the image, or add colored pencils or chalks to build up the texture in a series of hatched lines. Startling effects can be created by using a heavily textured paper with pastels and crayons in an array of vivid colors.

Karen Raney, *Les Planes Bedroom Window* *34 x 24 in (86 x 61 cm)*
The careful way in which these oil pastels have been applied in layers has resulted in a brilliance of color and a strong tonal pattern that enlivens the work.

A sgraffito technique has been used to scrape away some of the oil pastel color and produce bright highlights.

The oil pastels pick up the tooth of this textured paper so that tiny areas of white paper cause the colors to shimmer with light.

Paul Cézanne, *The Castle of Médan*, 1879/80 *12 x 18½ in (31 x 47 cm)*
Although the majority of Cézanne's watercolor drawings are quite slight, they are full of structure and power. In this study, pencil marks have been reinforced with watercolor to give a strong image that combines a lightness of feeling and a wide sense of space.

John Ward, RA, *Siena* *13 x 22 in (33 x 56 cm)*
In this picture, the artist has caught the dazzlingly bright light that shines on a bustling market square with a clever combination of watercolor and pencil. Rich, deep washes of watercolor have been drawn in shaded areas to heighten the contrast with the stark white paper, while clean pencil marks delineate the structure of the ornate Italian buildings precisely.

Jane Stanton, *Horace Shadow Boxing*

11 x 9 in (28 x 23cm)
This vigorous drawing in black and white chalks has been built up in a series of rhythmical marks. Interestingly, the white of the paper has been left untouched to depict the bandaged hands, while the highlights on the arm and shoulder have been produced by white chalk. This gives the figure a sense of solidity and heightens the tonal contrasts.

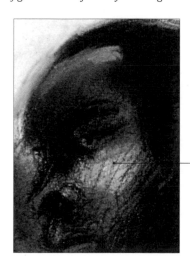

The contrast of intense black shading and lightly drawn linear marks creates a strong sense of movement.

PAPER FOR DRAWING

ORIGINALLY ALL PAPERS were handmade and tended to be of high quality. Paper was also quite scarce, so artists often drew on the reverse side for economy. Toned or colored paper, prepared by the artist himself with washes of watercolor, was a popular way of creating unusual effects. Today we have an enormous range of papers to choose from, which can make the choice a difficult one. Both handmade and commercially made papers have varying degrees of absorbency and are sold in different weights. Toned or tinted papers are also worth considering, and they are available in a selection of colors. Experiment with textures and weights until you find paper suitable for your technique.

Toned paper
Toned or colored paper can add an extra dimension to a work, providing a uniform tone and an underlying unity as well as influencing the mood of a drawing. Special artists' papers, such as Ingres paper, are best for this type of drawing.

Selection of colored pastel papers and toned watercolor papers

Commercially made smooth paper

Commercially made semi-rough paper

Cartridge paper

Handmade semi-rough paper

Texture
There are three types of commercially made paper: smooth or hot-pressed (HP); semi-rough or cold-pressed (NOT); and rough. Choose a texture that suits the medium you use; strokes of watercolor emphasize the grain of roughly textured handmade paper, while pen and ink requires a smoother surface to ensure that the ink flows smoothly. Try to buy acid-free paper so that it will not darken with age.

Commercially made textured paper

Roughly textured handmade paper

Making a sketchbook

Sketchbooks can be quite expensive to buy and may contain the wrong kind of paper for your drawing needs. By making your own sketchbooks, you can choose the size, weight, and absorbency of paper that best suits your style and media. Use wallpaper samples or wrapping paper to cover the outside of the book.

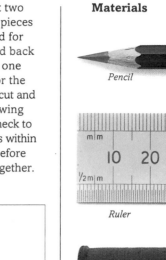

1 ◀ Cut out two identical pieces of cardboard for the front and back covers, and one long strip for the spine. Then cut and fold the drawing paper and check to see that it fits within the covers before binding it together.

Materials

Pencil

Ruler

Strong thread

Darning needle

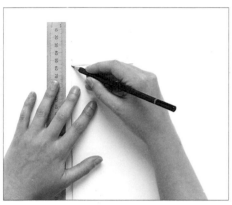

2 ◀ Measure the width of the binding tape first. Then place a ruler by the folded edges of the paper and divide the length into five. Mark the tape width at each section with a pencil.

3 ▶ Bind the pages with a needle and thread, leaving small loops along the edge of the folds.

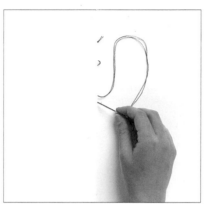

4 ▶ Slip small pieces of tape through each loop and then tighten and secure the thread. You can use any type of fabric tape so long as it is strong and adheres securely to the cardboard covers.

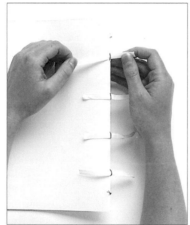

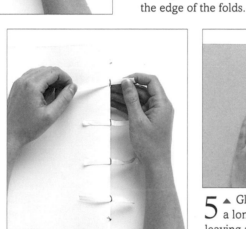

Fabric tape
Wallpaper
Strong material

5 ▲ Glue the pieces of cardboard onto a long section of strong fabric, leaving a slight gap on both sides of the cardboard strip to create a join.

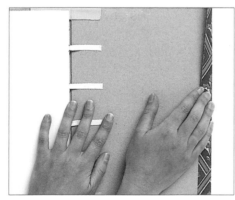

6 ▲ Secure each piece of tape to either side of the cardboard and glue the overlaps of the wallpaper down.

7 ▶ Neaten the inside covers by gluing a clean sheet of paper over the seams and tape.

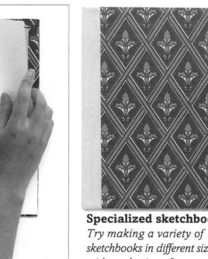

Specialized sketchbooks
Try making a variety of sketchbooks in different sizes with a selection of textured or colored papers.

Stiff cardboard
Textured paper

GALLERY OF PAPER TYPES

THE TEXTURE OF PAPER can easily affect the look of a drawing, and it is worth thinking about which type of paper to use for each particular medium. Using a smooth paper for pen work prevents the tip of the nib from scratching through the surface, while textured paper readily breaks up any lines or marks and suits media such as chalk and pastel. The absorbency and weight of a paper is important to note before using it with watercolor, as it determines the best way to handle the paint and how long a drawing should be worked on. Toned paper can also influence the look and mood of a drawing, serving either to heighten opaque highlights or to exist as a halftone.

Rembrandt, *A Girl Sleeping*, c.1655-6 *10 x 9 in (25 x 20 cm)*
Rembrandt's brush drawings have an almost unbelievably assured and spontaneous quality about them. This drawing in brown wash demonstrates how well the artist utilized his materials, producing a sensuous drawing of simple lines brought alive by the textured paper. The high absorbency of the paper meant that Rembrandt had to draw swiftly and confidently as the watercolor soaked into the surface; the paper's rough, grainy texture is emphasized by the dragged quality of each line as the paint catches on the tooth.

The resilient quality that gesso primer gives this paper has enabled the artist to rework details and scratch out areas to increase the rough texture of the drawing.

Karen Raney, *Mrs. Robb* *14 x 11 in (36 x 28 cm)*
This drawing relies heavily upon a particular technical approach, with the paper primed first with acrylic gesso to give a controlled, significant texture. This resistant surface allows the artist to explore her subject in a vigorous style, reworking the figure as needed with oil pastels in a series of lines and hatchings that are accentuated by the textured paper.

Kay Gallwey, *Spanish Dancer* *20 x 30 in (51 x 76 cm)*
This work is a fine example of how the quality and color of paper can influence a drawing; the pale gray tone of this surface heightens the opaque areas of white gouache while still allowing the more transparent strokes of watercolor to show up. Although it is as absorbent as the paper Rembrandt used, the smoother consistency of this paper allows the artist to draw lyrically, producing lengthy, more generous brushstrokes. The highlights on the cheek and hair are also highly effective against the subtle gray color of the paper.

The smooth, absorbent quality of the paper brings out the stylish strokes of watercolor.

Here the artist has utilized the colored paper as a halftone on the hand by building up tones of watercolor around an area of untouched paper.

Percy Horton, *Study of a Farmyard,* **1935** *12 x 18 in (30 x 46 cm)*
Drawn on fine Ingres paper, this study in graphite pencil and gray wash reveals the smoothness of the surface. The artist has used the gentle texture of the paper to help build up this drawing in an intricate style, incorporating finer details and precise information to produce a strong and interesting composition.

WORK METHODS

DRAWING IS A SKILL that improves with practice, and the more knowledge you have about your materials, the better your drawing will be. For example, your choice of pencil, pen and ink, or Conté crayon will affect the look of your drawing, and it may be that one medium suits your purpose better than another. You will need to work with the different materials to familiarize yourself with them, to discover what each is capable of, and to see which you feel most comfortable with. Pen and ink is ideal for fine, delicate lines, whereas a brush and ink can range from fine lines to broad sweeps of tone. Once you know the strengths and limitations of your materials, you can choose the appropriate medium for your subject matter and for the mood you wish to create. You will then be able to start a piece of work with a positive idea about how the subject relates to the medium.

Materials to suit your style

Of course each individual will view life differently, and two artists faced with the same subject would probably choose different media depending on how they perceive what they see and how they wish to portray it. Rembrandt, for example, used a loaded brush of ink to make rapid notations of fleeting effects and images. You can try to do the same, or make loose strokes with watercolor washes. Like ink, these will produce an effect very quickly, which can then be drawn over with a pencil or pen. You may be more methodical and analytical in your approach, and prefer the control that you can keep with a pencil. Many artists like to map out their drawings with great precision, and for this a pencil, a ruler, and an eraser are the perfect tools.

Choosing the right paper

Do not underestimate the importance of your paper. If you work on smooth paper your pencil will be able to flow uninterrupted over its surface. You will be able to modulate your lines without any unexpected effects. A disadvantage to smooth paper, however, is that large areas of tone may seem somewhat flat. A textured paper is just the reverse: used in conjunction with charcoal or chalks, it gives a lively, broken characteristic to lines or areas of tone. Take note of the weight of the paper too, so that if you use watercolors, for example, the paper will be heavy enough not to buckle.

Drawing with watercolor

The point at which a drawing ceases to be a drawing and becomes a painting is both a philosophical issue and a practical one. You can "draw" with color using colored pencils, pastels, or chalks, or you can add color to what are essentially linear drawings. You can essentially mix and match – start with pencil and add a watercolor wash, or start with watercolors and strengthen certain details later with pen and ink. By combining such media in this way, you can build up a more substantial drawing and create dramatic effects.

Procedures

Just as there are endless possibilities when mixing media, so too are there quite different procedures. There are no rules about what you can and cannot use, and no set order to how you work with your materials. For instance, you could start a drawing with a pencil, then perhaps add some watercolor. You could then refine the drawing with pen and ink and perhaps crosshatch over certain areas with chalks or pastels to create different textures.

Mixing media

Working in this way, you introduce a new medium at various intervals because it strengthens the previous one or creates a new, interesting look. On the other hand, you could make a decision from the outset to combine a selection of materials and use them in conjunction with each other. It is a question of what effect you wish to achieve and the best way to go about it. As with your drawing skills, learning to make the most of your materials is a matter of time, practice, and pleasure.

31

THE BASICS OF DRAWING

MUCH OF WHAT WE SEE around us can be simplified on paper into a series of very basic shapes. The most obvious shapes are cubes and spheres, and it is helpful to see objects in these terms when you begin to draw. Regular box shapes with parallel sides are quite easy to practice drawing, and a basic understanding of linear perspective and converging lines will enable you to create a better sense of structure and depth. Rounded objects are more complex as they should be constructed from a series of ellipses which can be quite hard to draw correctly at first. However, the best way to become comfortable with drawing solid objects is to gather a collection of household items and practice drawing their different shapes.

Copy the ellipses at the top and bottom of transparent objects.

Drawing ellipses

It is worth spending some time practicing ellipses so that you can gain confidence drawing round objects. Ellipses are in fact foreshortened circles and change their nature according to your eye level (*see below*). The principle of foreshortening is that the width of an ellipse remains the same, but its apparent height reduces the farther it tilts away from you. The easiest way to draw an ellipse is to sketch it roughly and then slice it in half, first vertically, then horizontally. You can then refine it until each quarter is the mirror image of its neighbor. Make sure each corner remains rounded

Drawing cubes
This chest of drawers is composed of straight, parallel sides that appear to grow smaller as they recede into space. Converging lines drawn as guides can help you get the right perspective.

and that the middle section doesn't look too flattened. Practice drawing an empty bottle or a glass so you can actually see the foreshortened ellipses through the transparent material.

Changing ellipses
Look at a glass from directly above, then below. The nature of its ellipses will change considerably. If you lean over the glass and view it at an angle, the ellipses will be quite rounded and circular; viewed from the side, they are at an extreme and are very foreshortened. Ellipses at the rim and the base of an object are never quite identical: the nearer an ellipse is to your eye level, the thinner it is; the farther away, the more circular it is. View the glass from below to see this effect.

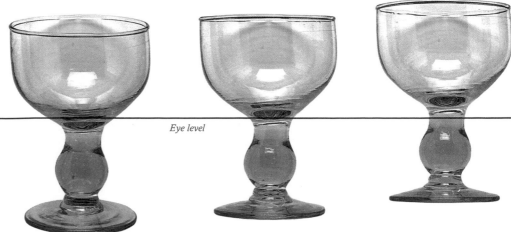

Eye level

Intersecting ellipses

To re-create the roundness of an object you need to imagine two ellipses, one horizontal, one vertical. The teapot, for example, is made up of a flattened circle for its basic form and then intersected at right angles by a second ellipse. The problem with drawing an object such as this teapot is its opaque nature, so you have to imagine the progression of the second ellipse through the back of the object and judge how foreshortened it actually is. This skill becomes easier with practice. Check your eye level and, if necessary, draw a faint guideline across the sketch to signify the angle from which you draw so that you create the right shapes.

Multiple ellipses
A complicated object such as this cocktail shaker, with sides curving in and out, should be constructed of several foreshortened ellipses at different angles and in varying sizes.

Obscured ellipses
Each ellipse has been fully drawn in this sketch of two opaque objects – even though in reality the back of the plate is obscured by the bowl. Once the subject has been drawn accurately, this line can be erased.

Guidelines
Use faint guidelines to establish the center of the drawing and the angle at which additional features should align.

Still life

Arrange an interesting collection of objects when you feel confident enough to draw several items together. If you want to draw imaginary ellipses through opaque objects, you may need to erase them when you have finished drawing, to give each object a better sense of solidity.

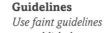

Concentrate on drawing the ellipses correctly rather than adding fine details or patterns.

Practice drawing a range of objects so that you learn to describe a variety of ellipses of different depths and widths.

LINEAR DRAWING

A LINE IS THE MOST basic form of representation in drawing, yet the power and versatility possible with the drawn line means that it has a wide range of descriptive possibilities. Linear drawing is essentially a technique that uses line, rather than the depth of color, as the main vehicle of expression. Lines can be drawn with great spontaneity, or they can be eloquent, economical, or even decorative. Shadows and highlights can also be suggested with a series of heavy or sensitive lines. A good line drawing will convey explicitly what the artist wants to express or describe.

Brush drawing
This canal scene is deftly developed with simple brushmarks. Notice the variation in strength and tone between the bold strokes on the poles and the gentle ripples of water.

The descriptive power of line

The drawn line can be very adaptable, providing the artist with a vast vocabulary when drawing. Strong, straight lines can be bold and dramatic; sensitive lines may evoke moods and atmosphere or convey lyrical qualities; and curved fluid lines can describe elegant contours. Once you have decided what you want to draw, choose the most suitable materials to either

Charcoal study
The soft, fluid lines of this charcoal drawing suitably capture the expression and the suppleness of this young child. Lines on the child's hair and dress are economically applied to suggest texture while other areas are weighted with thick line to give a sense of depth.

emphasize the illusion of solidity and weight or clarify delicate details and touches through lightly drawn lines. Experiment with different media until you find one that suits your style.

Technical pen sketch
You can create clear, well-defined lines with a technical pen. Here the figures are loosely sketched to capture the spontaneity of the scene. There is a roughness to the lines that evokes a sense of immediacy.

Drawing with pen and ink

Ink applied with a pen is a popular drawing medium. The ink comes in a range of colors, just as steel nibs come in a variety of thicknesses. It is best to use cartridge paper so that the nib does not become stuck in the fibers.

1 ▶ If you are unsure of drawing directly in pen and ink, start off with a light pencil sketch. This will allow you to make sure your proportions are correct and that you are happy with the composition. It will also train you to be observant.

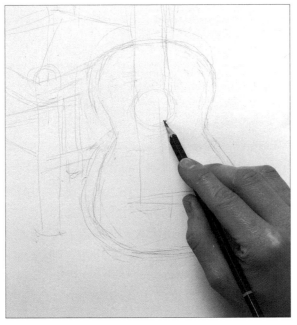

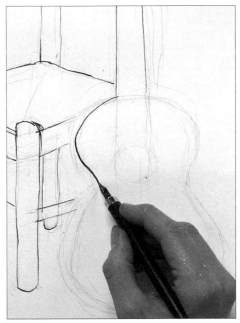

2 ▲ Define the shape of the chair with clean straight lines, and in contrast, draw the contours of the guitar with gently curved lines. You may have to apply more pressure to the nib when drawing curved lines to allow the ink to flow easily.

Guitar and Chair

This simple composition lends itself to an interesting interplay of straight and curved lines. The rigid form of the chair, drawn with vertical and horizontal lines, serves to accentuate the curvaceous outlines of the guitar. The overall effect is a pleasing balance of strong form and pure line.

You need a steady hand to draw these fine lines.

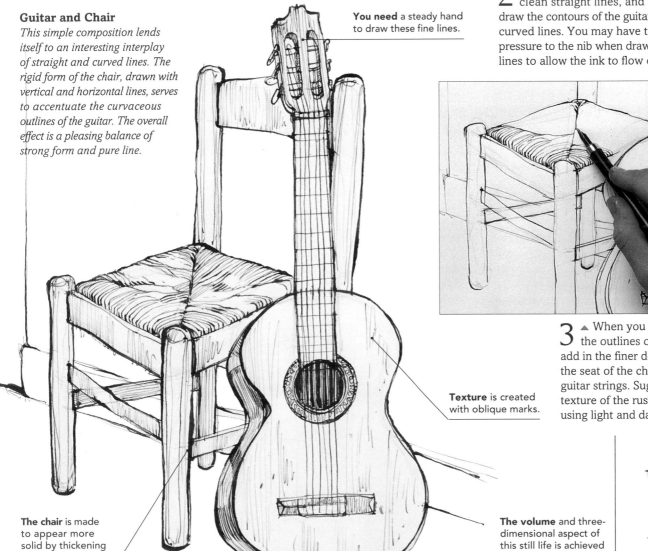

3 ▲ When you have drawn the outlines of both objects, add in the finer details, such as the seat of the chair and the guitar strings. Suggest the texture of the rush matting by using light and dark strokes.

Texture is created with oblique marks.

The chair is made to appear more solid by thickening the lines on the edge of the legs.

Karen Raney

The volume and three-dimensional aspect of this still life is achieved by applying a variety of thin and thick lines.

Materials

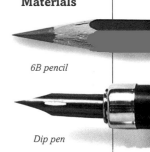

6B pencil

Dip pen

FORM & MODELING

FORM IS A TERM that is used to describe the visual appearance and shape of something. In a drawing, form can be represented with lines and as a series of tones (a range of values from light to dark) known as modeling. Modeling indicates the solidity and three-dimensional quality of a form, which is often enhanced or accentuated by light hitting the form and creating shadows. There are several different techniques to use for modeling, depending on which type of media you choose. Each medium gives a characteristic set of marks, but materials that cover the paper easily, such as pastels and watercolor, are good for large areas of shading, while colored pencils, which cannot be blended, are best used for feathering or crosshatching.

Solid shading
This sketch of a woman's back has been modeled into a three-dimensional form by lightly shading solid areas of tone with a pencil. The weighted contour lines also emphasize the volume of the figure. A less linear way of applying tone, this type of shading can be sensitive and subtle.

Describing form
Although the appearance and solidity of a subject can be suggested by drawing purely with line, a more substantial representation of its form can be achieved with modeling. Look for different textures and any deep tones before you start to draw so that you choose materials and techniques which best depict the smooth curves of a woman's back, for example, or a crumpled piece of material.

Solid shading

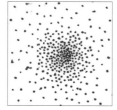
Stippling

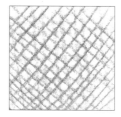
Crosshatching

Hatching

Mark-making
There are several ways to shade an image to create a sense of solidity. Hatching, crosshatching, and feathering are variations of a series of parallel lines drawn close to one another. Stippling is a technique whereby dots rather than lines form an image. Sgraffito, meaning scratched, can be similar to hatching.

Sgraffito

Bracelet shading

Feathering

Crosshatching
Crosshatching is a form of hatching, combining two or more sets of parallel lines that cross one another at an angle. They can be used to create a sense of form or, when using two or more colors, to produce secondary colors as the strokes intersect and mix optically.

The crosshatching on this leg gives it a much stronger sense of form and solidity than the outline of the other leg.

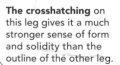

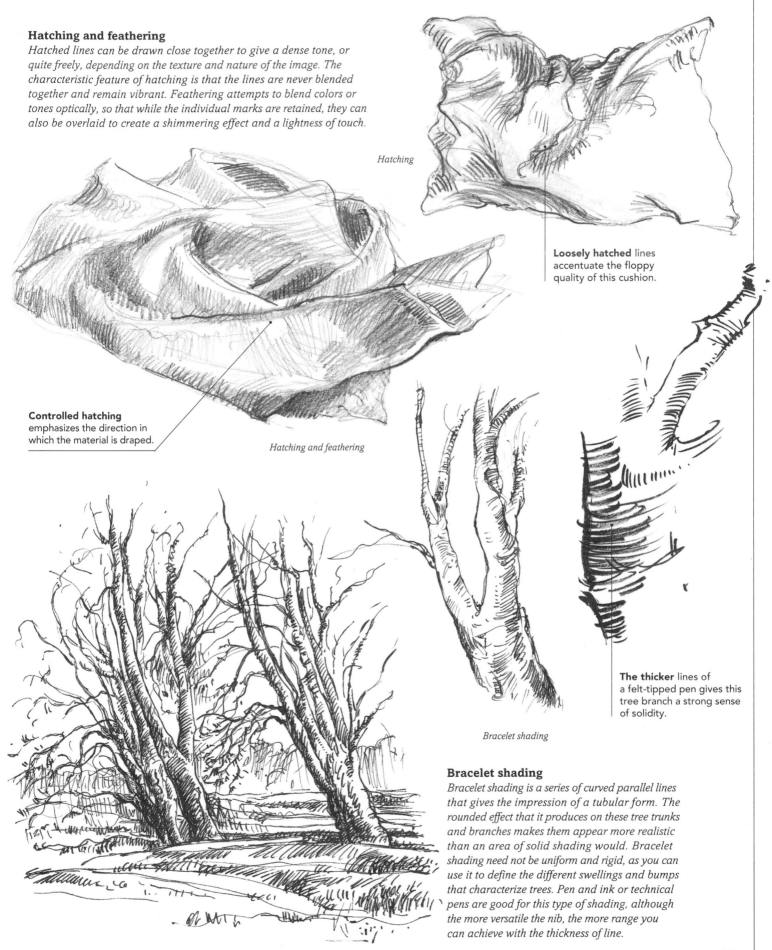

Hatching and feathering

Hatched lines can be drawn close together to give a dense tone, or quite freely, depending on the texture and nature of the image. The characteristic feature of hatching is that the lines are never blended together and remain vibrant. Feathering attempts to blend colors or tones optically, so that while the individual marks are retained, they can also be overlaid to create a shimmering effect and a lightness of touch.

Hatching

Loosely hatched lines accentuate the floppy quality of this cushion.

Controlled hatching emphasizes the direction in which the material is draped.

Hatching and feathering

The thicker lines of a felt-tipped pen gives this tree branch a strong sense of solidity.

Bracelet shading

Bracelet shading

Bracelet shading is a series of curved parallel lines that gives the impression of a tubular form. The rounded effect that it produces on these tree trunks and branches makes them appear more realistic than an area of solid shading would. Bracelet shading need not be uniform and rigid, as you can use it to define the different swellings and bumps that characterize trees. Pen and ink or technical pens are good for this type of shading, although the more versatile the nib, the more range you can achieve with the thickness of line.

39

TONAL DRAWING

TO UNDERSTAND THE VARYING degrees of darkness and light known as tonal values, it is essential to observe the effects of light and shadows falling on the objects you draw. You can then construct a drawing using areas of tone to describe shapes and to model forms so that they appear three-dimensional. Tonal drawings often tend to be more about mood and atmosphere, where whole areas can be suffused with light or submerged in deep shadows. A drawing may also be enhanced by using specific areas of contrast to create a tonal pattern throughout the composition. The important thing to remember about tonal drawing is to draw the minimum of lines and keep the emphasis on shapes and forms. Use tones as a painter would use colors to project images and to express a mood.

Lighting effects

To create the appropriate effects of strong light on a still life composition, it is important to set up the lighting at an angle that will maximize the presence of highlights and deep shadows. It is this contrast that will allow you the potential to explore tonal patterns in your arrangement. Use a soft dark pencil for shading the darkest forms and a kneaded eraser to create highlights by lifting out some of the tonal marks to reveal the brilliance of the white paper. The subtle shading of dark and light tones gives solidity to forms and atmosphere to your drawing.

Watercolor tones

This monochromatic watercolor sketch of the same still life illustrates how a similar effect of light and shade can be achieved by using just three tones. Limiting yourself to such a small selection of tones will help you look closely for strong shapes and effective tonal contrasts.

1 ▲ Begin by studying the shapes of the objects and also observe the play of light across their surfaces. With a soft pencil, make a series of loose marks to establish the scale of the arrangement of objects in relation to the size of the paper. Start with the largest object, the plate, so you can use it as a gauge to draw the other objects to scale.

2 ◀ Redefine the loose sketch with stronger lines once you are happy with the composition. At this stage use a lighter pencil to accentuate the contours, such as the spout of the coffee-pot. These outlines serve as a framework for modeling the objects by shading with light and dark tones.

3 ▶ Add a light gray tone by using gentle sweeping strokes with the side of the pencil. Once this is established you can deepen the tone for shadows and erase it for highlights. Explore the shapes that the shadows make between the objects: darkening the shadows will push the objects forward and make them look less flat. Develop the gradated tones on the objects, from the lightest to the darkest, to give them volume.

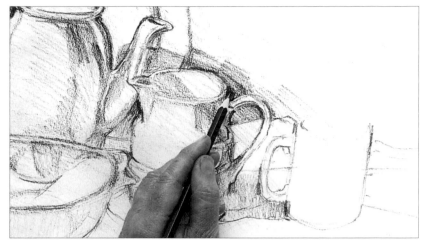

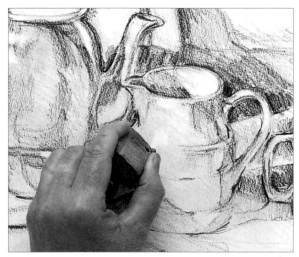

4 ▲ Now bring out the soft highlights on the pitcher by lifting out some of the tonal marks with the tip of a kneaded eraser. This is an effective way of "drawing" the light areas, using the white of the paper as the lightest tint in the tonal scale. These highlights will illuminate every object, as well as imbuing the drawing with a strong sense of light.

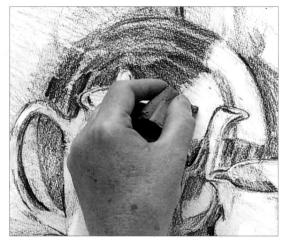

5 ◀ At this last stage refine the shadow edges on the plate with the kneaded eraser so that the darkest tones blend in subtly with the mid- and light tones to create a pleasing tonal effect. The shadows also enhance the sense of solidity of the plate.

Tonal Study
The three-dimensional quality of this still life drawing is achieved mainly by shading rather than by drawing with lines. The texture and form of each of the objects are developed and molded by employing a subtle range of tonal contrasts. An illusion of space and depth is also created by the careful positioning of shadows.

Main materials

7B pencil

Kneaded eraser

The light shading over the background creates an ambience and also serves as a unifying element in the compostion.

The sequence of shadows cast across the still life and the background forms a pleasing tonal pattern.

The highlights not only indicate the direction of light but also describe the smooth sheen of the ceramic objects.

Light tones and strong highlights capture the transparency of the glass dish and give the impression of reflected light.

Sue Sareen

41

GALLERY OF FORM

STRICTLY SPEAKING, the term *form* refers to the visual aspect and shape of an image, but within the realm of drawing it can also incorporate a sculptural quality: during the Renaissance and Baroque periods, the emphasis in art was on creating as solid and three-dimensional an image as possible. Michelangelo's work has a powerful feeling of shape and structure that goes well beyond a superficial rendering of the human body. This idea of sculpted form is still relevant to drawing today, although it is often interpreted differently. The quality of line may be more expressive and economical and may suggest movement more dramatically.

Michelangelo,
Drawing for a Late Pietà, c.1530s *15¾ x 9 in (40 x 23 cm)*
One of the greatest artists of the Renaissance, Michelangelo concentrated on the human figure almost exclusively and his anatomical knowledge was impressive. This perfectly proportioned image of Christ is caught by a diffused light that highlights the complexity of muscle and bone structure forming his body. The artist has modeled these features into a dynamic image that still exudes power in spite of the lifeless state of the figure.

Thomas Newbolt,
Study for "Bomb"
16 x 28 in (41 x 71 cm)
Even at first glance, this drawing has a wonderful sense of structure and strength. The artist has drawn the figures simply, with thick, heavy outlines so that they seem to create form collectively. He has kept details to a minimum, imbuing the scene with drama despite the anonymity of the figures.

Paul Lewin, *Penwith Coast,*
17 x 20 in (43 x 51 cm)
Rock formations, with their stark, craggy shapes and dramatic shadows, are a wonderful subject for studying form. The depth and drama of this drawing relies upon a bright light that picks out the eroding coastline as a series of unusual and abstract images. Deep shadows help build up a strong tonal pattern that combines with the highlights to give a three-dimensional form with a striking presence.

Donald Hamilton Fraser RA,
Dancer Rehearsing Juliet *18 x 20 in (46 x 51 cm)*
Watching dancers or acrobats is a good way to study the human form as it moves. Here the artist has made a sensitive yet elegant study of a dancer caught midway through a sequence. The essence of the power in this drawing is in the economy of line that describes the form of the body succinctly. Areas such as the hands and legs assume a sense of solidity despite the simplicity of line.

Thick, simple lines of chalk across the upper body suggest shadows and create a realistic sense of shape and depth.

A repeated line along the arm echoes the constant movement of the dancer.

LAYOUT & CONSTRUCTION

THE LAYOUT, OR COMPOSITION, of a drawing should provide a balanced order of shapes, colors, and forms. Use a viewfinder to choose the most appropriate scene and then draw the layout by measuring every feature carefully.

Measuring is an essential element in the construction of a drawing: it provides a scale by which to judge the relationship and proportions of different masses. Objects can be visually measured with the end of a pencil.

Adjust the two L-shapes of the viewfinder until you have selected the most suitable composition.

IT IS OFTEN DIFFICULT to select just a few elements of a landscape for a drawing, so use a viewfinder to crop the scene in front of you.

Using a viewfinder

A viewfinder made from cardboard (left) helps you select the part of a scene you wish to draw, and it can be adjusted to different proportions. The amount you see through the frame varies according to how close you hold it to your eye and how you adjust the two L shapes. Make a quick pencil sketch of this cropped image if you want to make sure the composition works well.

Measuring

If you work on a large composition, or from sketches and photographs, you may prefer to establish a scale to measure the different components of a scene. However, if you draw directly from life, try using a "sight size" technique. This involves measuring the size of an image exactly as you see it with the end of a pencil or a ruler. Transfer the measurement onto paper so that the image is an identical size.

Drawing a series of buildings from life

Drawing from life can be both stimulating and problematic, so plan your composition carefully and measure constantly until your eye becomes practiced at judging size and scale.

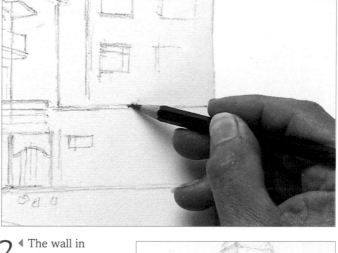

1 ▷ Draw the outlines of these buildings as a series of simple lines on a large piece of semi-rough paper with a soft pencil.

Deconstructing an image

A scene such as this group of buildings may at first appear quite complex and rather daunting, but if you can reduce it to a series of simple shapes and three-dimensional blocks in your mind, you will gain a better sense of perspective and structure as you begin to draw.

2 ◁ The wall in the foreground provides a strong sense of perspective, so draw it as a set of converging lines.

3 ▷ Add in the fine details, checking that doors and windows are in proportion to the size of the buildings.

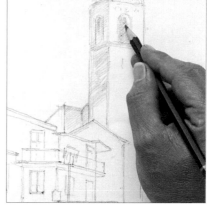

The Bell Tower

This simple pencil drawing has been constructed as a series of simple blocks and shapes that provide the basic substance of the drawing. The main features were all measured before they were drawn onto the paper. Then they were developed into more detailed structures once the proportions and balance of the picture had been established.

The three-dimensional appearance of these buildings creates a strong sense of depth.

Individual features have been measured carefully so that they have the right proportions.

This wall has been constructed with lines that tend toward one another to give a powerful sense of perspective.

James Horton

Materials

4B pencil

PLUMB LINE

A plumb line – a small weight on the end of a piece of string that gives a true vertical line – is vital if you need to check how straight and balanced a building actually is.

BUILDINGS & ARCHITECTURE

THE GREAT ADVANTAGE of drawing buildings is that they are permanent and stationary, so you can take your time to study the subject. Perspective – how an object with regular sides appears to diminish toward a vanishing point and so create a feeling of recession – is one of the most important elements to grasp if you want to draw a convincing architectural study. It is also vital to get proportions right so

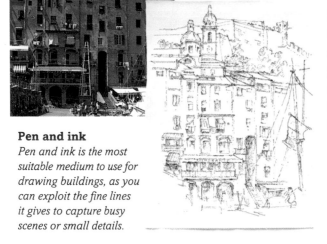

that the space occupied by windows and doors is in relation to the overall size of the building and the scale of any ornate or interesting features is exact. Modern buildings are usually quite simple in appearance, while older buildings such as cathedrals are likely to be more ornate and will adhere to classical rules of proportion. Watch for the changing effects of light on architecture as it can create interesting patterns of highlights and shadows, and try to describe a variety of textural surfaces to enliven your drawing.

Picking the right location

Once you have chosen an interesting building to draw, pick a quiet spot where you can easily view the whole structure – preferably at an angle so that you can draw more than one side of the building and give it a greater sense of solidity. The eye level from which you view it is also worth thinking about, especially if you want to emphasize the height of an imposing building.

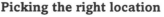

Pen and ink
Pen and ink is the most suitable medium to use for drawing buildings, as you can exploit the fine lines it gives to capture busy scenes or small details.

Simplifying details
You can easily simplify the buildings you draw if there are too many extraneous details, or omit unsightly objects such as parked cars. Such details can look too prominent and may compete unnecessarily with the architectural design.

1 ▲ Draw the basic structure of this building as a series of simple geometric shapes with a pencil on smooth Ingres paper; handmade paper is too rough and uneven when you start using pen and ink. This building is slightly curved at the top, so look for the way the light accentuates these different angles.

2 ◄ Mix up a pale brown wash of watercolor and apply it liberally over the drawing with a large sable brush to suggest the general tones of the building. Mix a deeper wash for areas with the darkest shadows, such as the overhanging trees to the left and the inside of the archway.

3 ◄ When the wash of color has dried, use a small sable brush to depict the textures and details of the building with a darker brown, describing the brickwork and the wooden slats of the window shutters with gentle dabs of color. Sable brushes, with their finely tapered points and ability to retain paint, allow you to draw far more precisely than other types of brushes.

4 ► For the finest details, use a brown sepia ink and a dip pen with a steel nib. Draw in the ornate wrought ironwork of the balcony carefully, trying not to put too much pressure on the nib – any heavy lines will detract from the delicate quality of the pen work.

5 ▲ Finally, emphasize any details that need to be made more prominent with the dip pen and sepia ink. The color of this ink serves to enhance rather than detract from the brown watercolor wash. Remember to select only those details that interest you or heighten the characteristic design of the building.

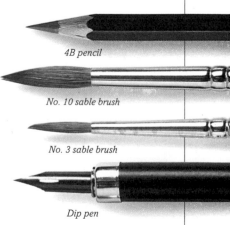

Tuscan Town House

A combination of pen and ink and watercolor wash on smooth paper turn this drawing into an attractive, detailed study. The artist has drawn the structure of the building accurately, noting the proportions of individual features and achieving a strong sense of perspective while ignoring details such as the TV antenna on the roof and the parked cars in front. This helps to give the drawing a timeless quality.

The very tip of the sable brush has been used to suggest textures such as the brickwork and the wooden shutters.

James Horton

Unnecessary details have been excluded or generalized.

Areas of light and shade help to increase the sense of perspective and enliven the drawing.

Materials

4B pencil

No. 10 sable brush

No. 3 sable brush

Dip pen

47

INTERIORS & EXTERIORS

THE MOST MODEST INTERIOR or garden can provide plenty of inspiration for an artist, particularly if the scene is familiar. The advantage of working in such immediate surroundings is that you can look for unusual shapes and interesting spatial relationships in simple objects such as chairs or tables. Combining an interior scene with an exterior view beyond can add an extra dimension to a work and prove a great challenge, particularly in terms of describing the contrasting quality of light inside and out. Select the amount of information you draw in each area to give a balanced composition.

The changing quality of light
The natural light that permeates interiors has a very different quality from that of light outdoors. A variety of suffused rays and deeper tones gives interiors a mellow, quiet atmosphere that provides an effective visual contrast with the strong, even light of outdoors.

1 ◀ Look for the rich, vivid colors of the view outside and the cool, muted tones of the interior. Sketch the scene in charcoal on mid-toned brown Ingres paper and then apply pale pastel tones to the tablecloth.

2 ▶ Contrast the pale pastels with deep purple and black on the door frame, using a hatching technique. The fine lines of color should appear to blend together optically.

3 ◀ Once you have decided on the basic areas of warm and cool color, begin to overlay the pale colors of the sunlit balcony with richer tones. Use a feathering technique to apply a strong pink over the pale mauve of the balcony floor. This combination of colors should produce a lively, sparkling effect. If you are at all unsure about using a particular pastel color on the toned paper, try it out first on a corner to see how it looks.

4 ◀ Emphasize the contrast between the balcony and the interior by drawing dark lines of charcoal in the deepest shadows of the doorway.

5 ▶ The interior is full of hazy, reflected light – light that bounces off objects in full sunlight. The angled ceiling above the doorway gives off this soft, shimmering light, so use a pale pink tone to draw it.

6 ▶ Finally, rework the fruit on the table with the brightest pastel colors. Then balance the strong hues of the still life by accentuating the details of the doorway with charcoal. Try to keep the background undefined and rather pale to increase the sense of distance beyond the balcony.

Main materials

Charcoal

Pastel selection for interior

Pastel selection for exterior

Still Life on a Balcony

This drawing is built up of color contrasts – with bright, vibrant pastels describing the scene outdoors and darker, more subdued hues evoking the shady interior. This pattern of highlights and shadows sets up a series of strong tonal values through the drawing, which also gives a good sense of aerial perspective. The doorway effectively frames the whole composition and leads the eye up easily to the active focal point of the fruit on the balcony.

Pastel marks have been left unblended so that the drawing has a sharp clarity.

Bright pastel colors, either pale or strong in tone, have been used for areas in sunlight.

The contrast between the light balcony and the dark interior increases the sense of atmosphere and the aerial perspective, or depth, in the drawing.

James Horton

KEEPING YOUR WORK CLEAN

Pastels and chalks generate a fine powder as you work with them, so use a sheet of paper to lean your hand on as you draw. This technique is also useful with lead pencils.

GALLERY OF COMPOSITION

A DRAWING CAN BE ANYTHING from a quick doodle in a sketchbook to a highly finished piece of work, yet composition is an important part of any drawing. Composition relies upon a variety of factors, such as the arrangement of shapes and forms and the degree of tone and color. The more complex a drawing becomes, the more you need to consider how individual elements will inter-relate to form a cohesive, interesting whole. An unusual viewpoint or angled composition can also produce an engaging work. You may find, after starting a drawing, that you want to explore areas beyond the existing confines of the paper, so add an extra sheet to develop the work into a larger composition.

Thomas Newbolt,
Study for the Bandstand III *24 x 18 in (61 x 46 cm)*
In this charcoal drawing the artist has used an ingenious vantage point – from a tree – so that he almost spies on the figures walking below him. As a composition, the drawing is simple but dynamic, with the figures held carefully in place by the diagonal path and the foliage of the tree that frames them.

Jon Harris, *King's Parade* *22 x 30 in (56 x 76 cm)*
This work has an extraordinary abundance of lines and marks, which the artist built up using a technical pen while actually sitting in the street. The powerful perspective that characterizes this composition is exaggerated by the road that engulfs the foreground and then converges rapidly to a vanishing point in the distance. The large, dissected road sign dominating the right of the picture increases the immediacy of the composition and gives it a less structured feel. A network of crosshatched marks helps give the picture tone and texture.

Jane Stanton,
Behind the Scoreboard *10 x 14 in (25 x 36 cm)*
This drawing is one of a series the artist made while sitting behind a cricket scoreboard. Although our attention is immediately drawn to the two seated figures, the artist is also fascinated by the shapes within the room – the intersecting lines of the walls, the repeated image of the doors, and the overhanging cupboards. By placing the figures at an angle, she intensifies our interest and heightens the sense of drama in the scene.

Anne-Marie Butlin, ***Two Pears*** *10 x 12 in (25 x 30 cm)*
This carefully thought out composition transforms a deceptively simple still life into a fascinating study. Viewed from a close angle, the edge of the table that cuts across the picture divides the composition in two so that our attention on the fruit is even more intense. The uneasy positioning of the pears also implies that the artist has sought to generate a certain degree of tension in this picture.

Boudin, ***Beach Scene, Late*** **19th century**
11½ x 28½ in (29 x 72 cm)
This delightful pastel captures the fun of people relaxing on a beach. Boudin has deliberately chosen a long, thin format to reinforce the sensation of gazing out at an endless stretch of coastline. The impressionistic suggestion of figures and shapes in colored pastels gives a spacious, indistinct feel to the drawing so that the scene appears to exist beyond the confines of the toned paper.

DRAWING NATURAL FORMS

DRAWING NATURAL FORMS tends to be a genre of its own, since it requires an investigative approach to record precisely and in detail the appearance and workings of an animal or a plant. You need to work methodically to capture the particular characteristics of your subject, rather than applying your own artistic interpretation. Select a medium that is sympathetic to the quality of the object – a bold medium for vigorous drawing and the clean lines of pen and ink for more exacting work.

Beachcombing is one of the best ways of finding interesting material to draw.

Crustaceans

Crustaceans are fascinating to look at, and the "mechanics" of a creature such as this lobster are intriguing. The longer you examine how the different joints are connected and the effects of the hard shell reflecting the light, the more realistic your drawing will be. Use a pencil first to establish the essential shape and features of the lobster before you move on to the permanent medium of pen and ink.

1 ▶ Arrange the lobster and sea shells in a corner where they can be left to enable you to take your time studying them. Sketch in the basic shape of the lobster with light, gestural strokes on smooth watercolor paper, using a pencil with a sharpened point.

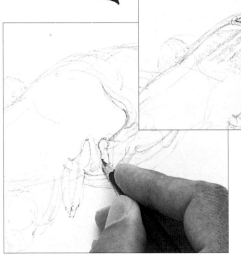

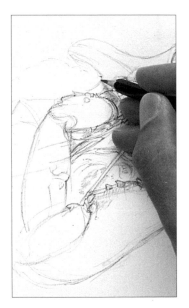

2 ▶ Describe the other objects around the lobster to establish the right proportions before you put in the finer details. You may want to rest your hand on a sheet of paper to avoid smudging the existing pencil marks.

3 ◀ With a medium-sized sable brush and a wash of pale yellow, begin to build up the form of the lobster. Apply the watercolor sparingly if you are worried about over-emphasizing any aspect of the work at this stage.

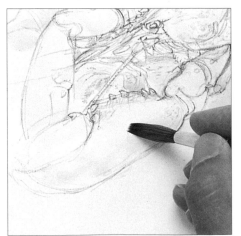

4 ▲ When the first wash of watercolor has dried, apply a scarlet-brown wash to the main body of the lobster in a series of dabs to echo the appearance of its mottled shell. The springy hairs of the sable brush should give you good control as you paint.

5 ▶ Lightly shade areas of the background with a thin wash of dark brown to give a sense of depth to the drawing and push the form of the lobster forward.

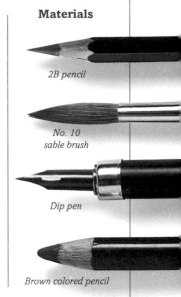

Materials

2B pencil

No. 10 sable brush

Dip pen

Brown colored pencil

6 ▲ Gently shade the side of the lobster shell with the pencil to build up a series of dark tones. This should help give the image a three-dimensional appearance.

7 ◀ Use a dip pen and sepia ink to redefine the shape and details of the lobster. Accentuate any shadowed areas with thick, dark lines, and highlights with thin, faint lines of ink. Hatched marks drawn in the darkest shadows will also push the image forward.

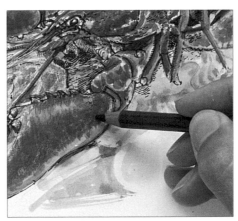

8 ◀ Deepen the tones of the shell and claws with a dark brown colored pencil. The pencil marks will also add texture to the drawing and help break up any areas of paint that look a little flat.

Lobster

The artist has taken his time studying this lobster, and the result is a beautiful and meticulous drawing with a wealth of detail. The layers of color and texture have been applied carefully to give the lobster a powerful sense of form, while the clean, crisp lines of ink define particular features that turn this drawing into a fascinating reference work.

Layers of watercolor have been built up into a series of subtle tones that mold the form of the lobster effectively.

A colored pencil breaks up the the flat areas of watercolor and provides texture.

Initial pencil lines that are technically incorrect add to the vitality of the drawing.

Richard Bell

LANDSCAPES

DRAWING LANDSCAPES is a relatively recent development in art, and it was not until the eighteenth century that the changing effects of light and weather on a landscape became such popular subject matter. It is always essential to be aware of the passage of the sun across a scene, as the definition of individual features and the length of shadows can change dramatically. Perhaps the greatest problem when you are drawing a landscape is choosing which features to include and which to leave out. A viewfinder is the best way of selecting one view from a broad panorama. Watercolor is one of the most suitable mediums to use for drawing landscapes – it enables you to capture the transient effects of the weather quickly.

1 ▶ Use a viewfinder to select an appealing composition. With a pencil, measure the proportions of the hill village and draw it in a series of blocks and triangles on rough watercolor paper. The slightly off-center positioning of the village creates an unusual composition and the vegetation surrounding it can be sketched in gradually to balance out the drawing.

2 ◀ Look for features in the foreground and middle ground, such as trees or a sloping hill, that give a sense of perspective; a diagonal line on the left helps lead the eye up to the village. Keep the landscape on the same scale as the village by measuring the different features carefully.

3 ▶ When you are happy with the scale of the composition, add some watercolor with a small sable brush to capture the effect of sunlight on the buildings. Use a wash of warm red for rooftops and cool purples for shadows.

5 ▶ Add some yellow highlights for buildings that catch the sunlight and draw in any small details, such as windows and doors, to give each building more of a three-dimensional form.

6 ◀ Use the pencil to suggest any shadows that are cast by the bell tower. Angle the pencil slightly so that you can gently shade the darkest areas. If the surrounding landscape still appears rather sparse, add more light, gestural strokes of watercolor to strengthen the composition of the drawing.

4 ▲ Describe the trunks and branches of the trees in the foreground with the sable brush and a pale brown wash. Apply the wash lightly to retain the clarity of line, and lift out any mistakes you may make with a piece of paper towel.

Mediterranean Hillside
The paper used for this drawing was quite absorbent, so that every mark made with the sable brush was linear and decisive, reinforcing the simplicity of the initial pencil drawing. The repeated watercolor marks also help to give the sensation of a large expanse of hillside stretching out around the small village.

The surrounding vegetation is merely suggested, rather than described in detail.

Trees in the foreground are used as identifiable landmarks and give a sense of perspective to the drawing.

Simple tones of color on the buildings evoke the sensation of bright sunshine hitting the village at an angle.

James Horton

Materials

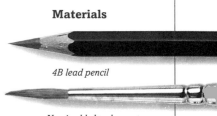

4B lead pencil

No. 4 sable brush

GALLERY OF NATURAL FORMS & LANDSCAPES

DRAWING NATURAL FORMS has often brought artist and scientist together. Many of Leonardo's drawings, for example, work equally well as drawings from life and as detailed scientific studies. Until the advent of photography in the mid-nineteenth century, drawing was used to illustrate all kinds of different subjects – resulting in a combination of images that were beautiful to look at and filled with relevant information. Drawing is all about the way we perceive the world around us, which is perhaps why artists turn so readily to landscapes and natural objects as a source of inspiration. Some interesting landscapes contain not only natural features; manmade buildings in a landscape can often strike a balance with the natural forms around them so that they seem to be subsumed into the environment.

Van Dyck, *Study of Trees, late* 1630s *8 x 9½ in (20 x 24 cm)*
The feathery texture of the trees in this lyrical pen and ink drawing illustrate van Dyck's concern for a stylistic interpretation of his subject rather than the identification of particular trees.

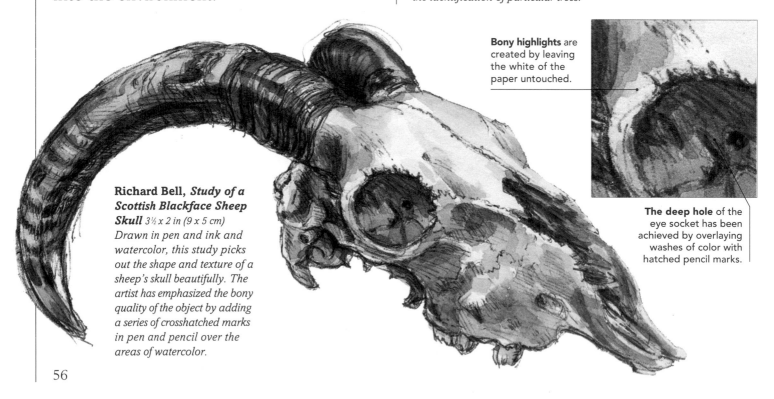

Richard Bell, *Study of a Scottish Blackface Sheep Skull* *3½ x 2 in (9 x 5 cm)*
Drawn in pen and ink and watercolor, this study picks out the shape and texture of a sheep's skull beautifully. The artist has emphasized the bony quality of the object by adding a series of crosshatched marks in pen and pencil over the areas of watercolor.

Bony highlights are created by leaving the white of the paper untouched.

The deep hole of the eye socket has been achieved by overlaying washes of color with hatched pencil marks.

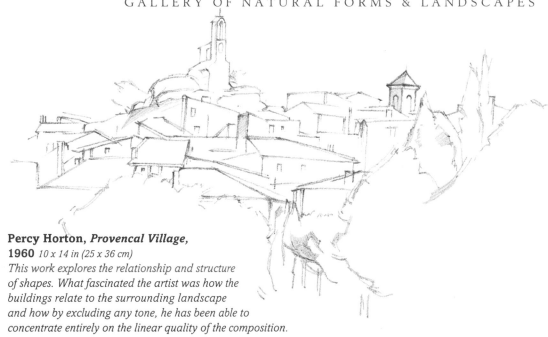

Percy Horton, *Provencal Village,*
1960 *10 x 14 in (25 x 36 cm)*
*This work explores the relationship and structure
of shapes. What fascinated the artist was how the
buildings relate to the surrounding landscape
and how by excluding any tone, he has been able to
concentrate entirely on the linear quality of the composition.*

Paul Lewin, *Seascape (After
Courbet)* *25 x 28 in (64 x 71 cm)*
*In this drawing the artist, rather
like Van Dyck, has concentrated
on a personal interpretation of
a natural scene. He has applied
pastel and charcoal vigorously to
develop a dramatic sense of mood
and atmosphere. Although the
picture has a low horizon point,
the sky is brought alive with strong
color and texture to form a
surface full of movement. This
work illustrates how a landscape
can be used as a springboard
for a personal vision.*

The lack of fine detail gives this
seascape an expressionistic feel,
which is heightened by the
limited use of color.

The dark, moody atmosphere of
this drawing has been heightened
by a series of deep tones and
heavy crosshatching.

FIGURES & DRAPERY

CLOTHES CAN DISGUISE and distort the real shape of our bodies, so it is important to understand how material behaves as it falls in folds around a figure. The simplest way to draw a clothed figure is to work out the proportions of the body first and draw it as a series of simple forms, ignoring the flowing shapes made by the drapery. Once you are satisfied with the shape of the figure, you can begin to explore the way the material hangs from particular areas of the body. Don't overwork the folds and gathers of the drapery or the image will look stiff and unnatural.

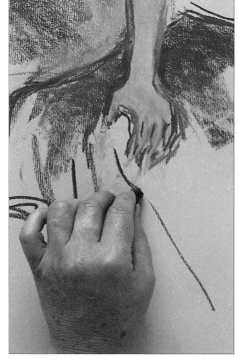

Sketching figures

People always make engaging studies. A good way to gain confidence in drawing people is with a sketchbook: make quick sketches of seated figures on buses or trains and note how their clothes hang and serve to accentuate the way they sit.

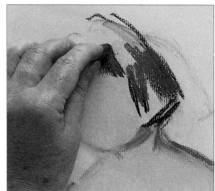

Moving figures

If you draw repeated studies of a moving figure, use a fast medium such as pencil or pen and watercolor to capture the most interesting features: look for the way their clothes behave as they twist and turn.

1 ◀ The folds made by drapery create interesting patterns on and around this figure. Draw in the proportions of the woman first with charcoal on lightly toned pastel paper, reducing the image to a series of simple shapes. Repeat lines or change the angle of the head until you have an accurate rendering of the figure.

2 ▲ Loosely block in the essential features and skin coloring of the figure with soft pastels until you have achieved a reasonable human likeness. Then concentrate on describing the varying rhythms and tones of the different materials.

3 ▲ Draw in the deep folds created by thedrapery thrown over the seat, looking to see how it hangs and catches the light. You will need to use a wide range of green pastels to re-create the strong lighting effects, so first establish the shapes of the drapery in one color.

4 ◄ Build up the tones of the woman's sarong, using dark colors for the deepest creases that help to shape her body. Then pick out the red pattern of the cloth and observe how its regularity is disrupted by folds and contours.

5 ▶ Use a deep blue pastel and charcoal for areas of fabric that cast the strongest shadows. This will give the material an intense, heavy feel and a sense of depth.

Main materials

6 ▶ Draw in the finer details of the figure with a pastel pencil: a slightly harder version of a soft pastel in a pencil format. This will allow you to work more precisely on smaller areas such as the face, capturing the final highlights and emphasizing any particular features.

Pastel selection for skin tones

Malaysian Woman in a Sarong
This richly colored study of a figure gives a strong visual description of the nature of drapery and the way it can echo and enhance the rhythms of the human body. The blended pastels on her sarong illustrate how the light strikes her body and gives it form, while layers of dark pastel on the bench fabric create the effect of a heavier, thicker cloth falling to the ground.

The shape of this figure is simple, yet strong enough to give a solid image on which to draw the hanging material.

The irregularity of the red pattern helps to identify the contours of the body and creases in the material.

Bold lines of dark color have been used for the deepest folds of cloth while the lightest tints pick up the direction of the strong light source.

Pastel selection for drapery

Pastel pencil

Sue Sareen

59

LIFE DRAWING

THE HUMAN BODY is generally thought to contain every aspect of form, visual complexity, and subtlety that an artist will encounter. Drawing a human figure regularly will help you to improve your powers of observation and drawing skills, but it is often hard for artists to find people willing to devote their time to sit as models. By joining a life-drawing class you can take your time studying figures and gleaning different ideas and techniques from observing other artists. While you should learn to pay attention to the anatomical proportions of the human body, a life-drawing class will also allow you the freedom to express a mood in the way a model sits or stands, or a certain characteristic feature in their personality.

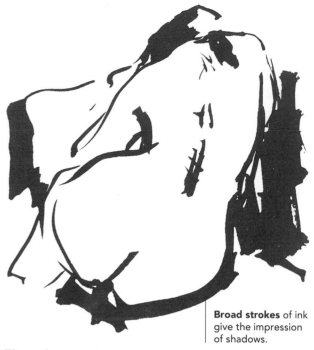

Broad strokes of ink give the impression of shadows.

Five-minute pose
This decisive yet eloquent study of a woman's back shows how a few expressive lines and the minimum of detail can create a convincing image. The study was drawn with a Chinese brush and ink, which encourages a lyrical style full of control.

The classroom
A life-drawing class provides a regular, disciplined period where the problems and complexities of the human figure can be tackled.

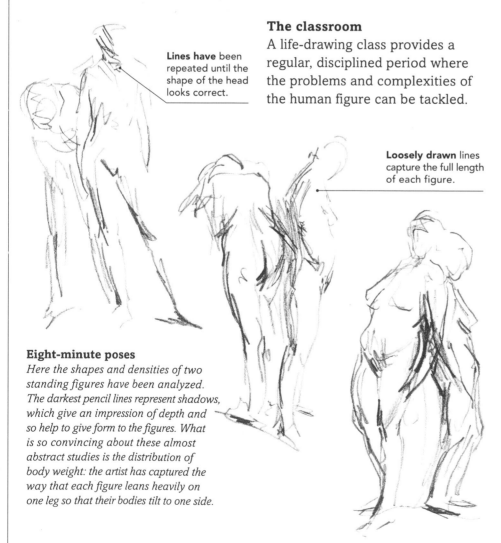

Lines have been repeated until the shape of the head looks correct.

Loosely drawn lines capture the full length of each figure.

Eight-minute poses
Here the shapes and densities of two standing figures have been analyzed. The darkest pencil lines represent shadows, which give an impression of depth and so help to give form to the figures. What is so convincing about these almost abstract studies is the distribution of body weight: the artist has captured the way that each figure leans heavily on one leg so that their bodies tilt to one side.

In order to get to know the different aspects of a model, it is useful to begin with a series of exercises that test your powers of observation rather than your ability to draw a lifelike figure.

By getting a model to do a series of timed poses, from about five minutes to several hours, you can develop a range of strategies and approaches with which to analyze and interpret the human figure. The quickest drawings, of five minutes or less, require a very swift, gestural style: you have to capture the essence of the model's stance by looking carefully for the strongest shapes and then distilling them into an impressionistic image. The most important aspect of this exercise is to draw the whole length of the figure and not waste time concentrating on incidental details.

Ten- and fifteen- minute poses still demand a certain speed, but they allow you to develop your style beyond the purely gestural. Take this extra time to look for the dynamic angles and planes of the body. Look also for the way that the model's stance affects the distribution of weight through the body, using a plumb line, if necessary, to determine the balance of the figure in relation to a true vertical line. With any short pose it is important to develop the drawing only as far as the time will allow and not to over-emphasize any individual characteristics.

Taking thirty minutes to an hour to draw a figure will give you the chance to develop more intricate aspects of character and study the form of the body in some detail. Work up a series of tones with solid shading or crosshatching and hatching to give the body a sense of depth and volume.

With poses of two hours or more, a different process evolves. The proportions of the body are more significant, so use the size of the head as a basic unit of measurement. The body should be approximately seven and a half times larger than the head. Think also about the light source: enhanced or distorted effects created by the light as it shines from different angles can create a fascinating study. Be aware of the patterns made by shadows across the body and how some areas are totally obscured, while other muscles or features are accentuated by an intense bright light. Describing the surroundings at this stage will help to put the figure in a more realistic context.

One-hour pose
Here the light hitting the back of the body illuminates some of the many planes and facets of the human figure. Such dips and curves, caused by muscles and bones beneath the skin, are important to depict – they give substance to the study. Although the shading is roughly executed, the effect gives a rugged realism.

The contrast of strong lights and darks gives this drawing atmosphere.

Two-hour pose
With more time to study his personal character, the artist has explored the mood of this man and generated a strong atmosphere of brooding contemplation. The wide range of tonal values drawn in charcoal gives the figure solidity, while the weight of his body pulls downward to give a forceful sense of gravity.

Four-hour pose
Subtle blending and a powerful perspective give this drawing a sensuous yet controlled feeling. The artist has taken his time modeling the figure, picking out the highlights with care so that the final impression is of a woman bathed in suffused sunlight. The treatment of the bed and the highlights that have been produced with an eraser add to the softness of the scene.

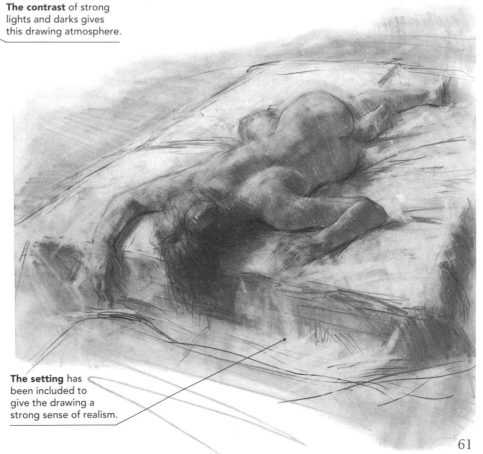

The setting has been included to give the drawing a strong sense of realism.

PORTRAITS

THE NEED TO DEPICT a person's individual characteristics sets portrait drawing apart from figure drawing. The best approach to take when you draw a portrait is to study the construction and form of the head, noting the proportions of particular features in relation to the size of the face. You may wish to experiment with the lighting to create an atmosphere or reflect the mood of the sitter, and such unusual effects may help you look at your subject in a fresh, interesting way. If you need practice capturing a reasonable human likeness, try drawing a self-portrait so that you can work at your own rate of speed.

Capturing a mood

Often the medium you use will reflect the mood of the sitter. A bold, heavy drawing in charcoal may signal an angry or defiant mood; a pencil drawing will enable you to describe a range of tones to give dimension to a portrait; a delicate pen and ink drawing can pick up the subtle nuances of a person's character.

Proportions

To draw a portrait successfully, you need to be able to produce a solid, lifelike image of a head with recognizable features that identify the sitter. Work out the symmetry of the face by dividing it roughly into three equal parts. The top section is from the crown to the brow; the central section is from the brow to the end of the nose; and the bottom section is from the end of the nose to the bottom of the chin. Draw the eyes approximately one eye's width apart, and measure the triangle made by the eyes and the end of the nose. These are important features and define the particular shape of the face most accurately.

Lighting

Lighting can radically affect the appearance of an individual. A full light shining straight onto the face will flatten the features and give you little chance to explore the depth of the head. Light shining on the side of the head creates a more interesting study, but if you want to exaggerate someone's personality or create an unsettling effect, try lighting them from below.

Self-portrait

Self-portrait studies are a good way to practice drawing human features, although they often portray a rather confrontational gaze as a result of your staring at yourself in the mirror. Select the most essential and interesting features as you draw – if you attempt to capture every detail you may end up with an overworked drawing.

1 ▶ Set up a mirror in a convenient place so that you can see yourself easily and, if possible, where the light will cast shadows for an interesting effect. Sketch the shape of your head and features in pencil on a broad sheet of textured paper, keeping the drawing as large as possible.

2 ▲ Block in the main areas of the face and hair with oil pastels, applying each color loosely to cover the paper effectively. Oil pastels give a rich, colorful effect and adhere to the paper easily. Use a cloth dipped in turpentine to wipe away mistakes or colors you may want to change.

Self-Portrait Study

Oil pastels give this self-portrait a richer, deeper effect than ordinary pastels would. The slight transparency of the oil pastels also allows separate lines of overlaid color to create an optical mix. The size of the paper is significant; it gave the artist confidence to draw boldly and capture the strong lighting effects cast across the side of her face.

Karen Raney

3 ▲ Use a finger or a piece of material to blend pastel marks together if you want to give a smoother texture to some areas of skin. Make sure the pastels are soft so that you can blend them easily on paper.

Main materials

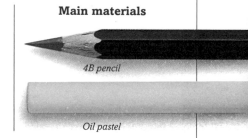

4B pencil

Oil pastel

Yellows and oranges have been used for warm lights, and cool mauves and grays for areas in shadow.

Pastel marks have been built up in layers to create an optical mix of color.

FIGURES IN A SETTING

Describe a background with just a few suggestive lines.

FIGURES ARE RARELY SEEN in isolation – usually they are situated against a backdrop, either indoors or outside. Invariably the background is a significant element in a drawing, but the most important thing to remember is that you should always relate the figures to their surroundings. The interaction between the two needs to be organized carefully within a composition to give a strong sensation of depth and create a series of spatial relationships. Try to avoid including too much background detail; this will keep the emphasis of the drawing centered on the figures.

Establishing a focal point

The human eye is similar to a camera lens in that it cannot focus on everything at once, so you will need to work systematically to establish the figure as a focal point first. Then go on to develop the background scene.

1 ▶ Sketch the figure lightly first in pencil on a toned, semi-rough watercolor paper. Then draw in the fountain and the most prominent features of the buildings. Once you have all the proportions drawn correctly, return to the figure and strengthen the image.

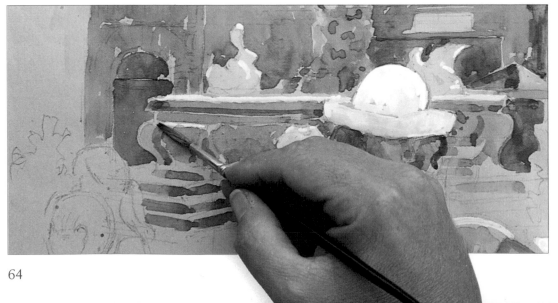

2 ◀ As this café scene is situated outside in a square, the quality of light is much stronger, casting short dark shadows and producing bright highlights. Mix some cool washes of watercolor for areas of the fountain and buildings that are in shadow and apply them with a small sable brush.

3 ▶ Represent the way the light defines the form of this figure with dark transparent washes for shadows and white gouache for the highlights. White gouache is essential for describing strong light and pale colors if you are working on toned paper. Redefine details, such as the hat, with a pencil. These subtle lines will give a better sense of form and shape and help push the figure farther into the foreground.

4 ▲ Use a charcoal pencil delicately to shade small features such as the stonework on the fountain. This refined form of charcoal retains the dark, heavy quality of the medium, while the pencil format allows you a greater degree of control and precision.

5 ◀ Use a dip pen and brown ink to draw in the final details, redefining any pencil marks that may have been covered by the washes of color.

Materials

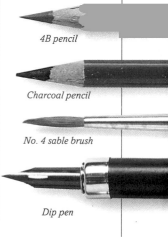

4B pencil

Charcoal pencil

No. 4 sable brush

Dip pen

Town Square

This figure and the setting behind her both complement and balance each other; the figure blends into the scene while still looking prominent enough as a focal point. The scale of the background also relates proportionally to the figure and the light cast across the whole scene links individual features in a series of strong tonal contrasts.

The strong sense of perspective gives the impression of a large area of space between the figure and the fountain.

The shape of the girl's hat provides an interesting feature against the fountain in the background.

James Horton

Opaque highlights are used to give a feeling of hot, bright light, while dark, transparent hues describe the short shadows of early afternoon.

Our attention focuses primarily on the girl, and then on the different features beyond.

GALLERY OF FIGURES

FIGURES HAVE ALWAYS been a fascinating subject matter for artists; after all, almost everyone is aware of, perhaps even intrigued by, the people around them and how they move and act. To draw figures successfully and understand your subject, you must capture not just the right proportions and shape of a human body, but the character of an individual. Details that may only be subconsciously observed on an everyday level, such as the color of someone's eyes or the way they dress, can be deliberately exaggerated in a drawing to transform the personality of a figure and emphasize their character. What all of these artists have achieved in their work is a convincing portrayal of human life that encapsulates each individual succinctly.

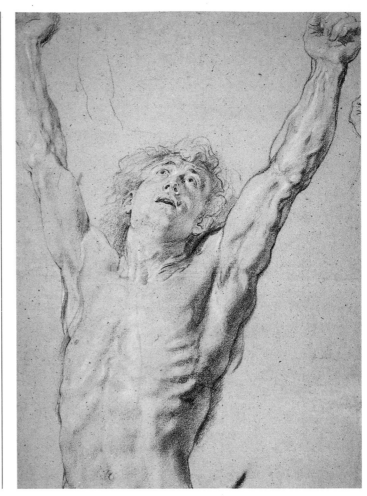

Rubens, *Study of a Crucified Man,*
c.1614-15 *21 x 14½ in (53 x 37 cm)*
This work in brown chalk is typical of the many studies Rubens would have made in preparation for a painting. Rubens used the drawing to familiarize himself with every aspect of this man's torso, bringing out the complexities of human form with remarkable subtlety. He describes the contours of the body and the muscles on the chest with precise yet evocative lines. His use of brown chalk is actually quite sparing and understated, though the tone of the paper and white chalk highlights generate a strong feeling of solidity.

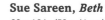

Sue Sareen, *Beth*
23 x 16 in (58 x 41 cm)
This portrait brings out the character of the sitter most sensitively. While not making a particularly detailed study, the artist has conveyed the personality of this figure effectively with small details, such as her posture and the position of her feet. The addition of color reinforces the loosely drawn image and accentuates the slumped position of this woman in her chair.

Diana Armfield RA,
Studying the Menu at
Fortnum's, London,
17½ x 10½ in (44 x 27cm)
In this pastel drawing the artist has cleverly arranged her composition so that the focus of attention is actually on the group of figures in the middle distance, in spite of the spacious foreground. The lack of finished detail in the foreground helps to lead the eye straight to the tables of seated customers, who appear more dominant than they really are. Although these figures are relatively small, their movements have been thoughtfully described and there is even a suggestion of their characters. Most importantly, they appear very much part of their environment, giving the work a strong sense of unity.

Norman Blamey RA,
St. Andrew, Fisher of Men *14 x 9 in (36 x 23 cm)*
This work is a study for a mural; the drawing has been squared up, ready to be transferred onto a wall. The most noticeable aspect of this study is the high viewpoint the artist has chosen. The rapid descent toward the foot, and the arms that appear too long for the body, are caused by an acute foreshortening of the whole figure. Again, Blamey has assiduously explored and studied his figure to create a profoundly fascinating drawing.

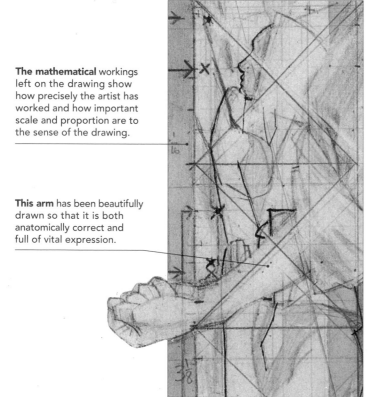

The mathematical workings left on the drawing show how precisely the artist has worked and how important scale and proportion are to the sense of the drawing.

This arm has been beautifully drawn so that it is both anatomically correct and full of vital expression.

67

MOVEMENTS & GESTURES

ONCE YOU HAVE gained confidence drawing people sitting still for you in a controlled environment, try drawing a scene full of movement and vitality. This type of subject matter requires a different approach: you need to be able to memorize a certain amount of information every time you look away from the scene, since it will change constantly.

This process depends upon assessing a fluctuating image and distilling it before you begin to draw. Dancers or animals are good subjects to begin with, as they often repeat movements or gestures, but try to adopt a loose style so that you can capture the essence of an image quickly. Working in this way, your drawings should have a freshness and immediacy that is difficult to achieve in a regulated situation.

Suggesting movement

The speed at which you need to draw a moving image means that you have to be adept at suggesting information and giving clues with the minimum of linear marks and shading. The best media to use for such fast work are those that enable you to cover the paper swiftly, such as watercolor or pastels.

Study animals such as lions and tigers and notice how they move.

Dancers, with their ability to move gracefully and powerfully, make fascinating subjects.

1 ▶ Choose a richly toned blue Ingres paper and capture this atmospheric evening scene on a balcony as quickly as possible with charcoal, reworking any lines swiftly and repeatedly until you are happy with the positioning of the figures.

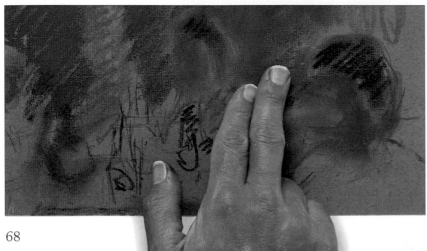

2 ▲ As this scene is full of movement and fleeting impressions, use your imagination to select interesting colors. Note any areas illuminated by the light with a bright orange-yellow pastel and loosely block in the background with deep, rich blues and purples.

3 ◀ To give a more impressionistic, hazy feel to the background, merge the blue and purple pastels by smudging the colors together around each figure with your fingers. Be sure to wash your hands afterward to avoid soiling the drawing.

4 ◀ Build up the form of each seated figure with a series of dark tones, using charcoal to redefine any outlines against the dark background. Try to capture the position or stance of the five diners – whether they are resting their elbows on the table, or leaning on the armrest of their chair – rather than attempting to discern facial expressions and small details.

Main materials

Charcoal

Selection of pastel colors

5 ▲ As these figures all face one another around a table, they should be linked by a focal point to give the composition some unity. The bright, magnetic light of the candles in the middle of the table provides this focus, so use a pale pastel color to delineate the flickering flames.

6 ◀ Once you have drawn in the main source of light, use a combination of light green, warm red, and deep yellow to pick out the soft highlights on each figure with loosely hatched marks.

Evening Meal on a Balcony

This night scene is full of fleeting impressions and suggested movement. Only the essential facts have been recorded with a series of gestural lines based upon a few glances and a good visual memory. The lack of attention to detail gives this impressionistic study a shifting rhythm and strong sense of mass.

Soft highlights help model the form of each figure.

James Horton

DRAWING FOR PAINTING

Analyzing the subject
In the charcoal work above, the artist John Ward has studied the anatomy of this figure intently so that he can describe her perfectly in "Zandra Rhodes Dress" (right).

HISTORICALLY, THE MAJORITY of artists' drawings were used solely as studies for later paintings. They were a means to an end rather than an end in themselves. Although drawing now has a much higher status and is accepted as an art form in its own right, drawings are still often used as preparatory studies for other works. A drawing, or a series of drawings, can help you familiarize yourself with your subject matter, investigating, for example, the play of light and assimilating all the information so that you have a precise visual reference as you paint. You can also combine several preparatory drawings into one painting by tracing each individual study and linking them in a strong composition.

Collating information

Making preparatory drawings for a painting is a good method of testing imaginative ideas visually on paper before you commit yourself to canvas. The images below are a mixture of sketches and detailed drawings that were drawn at different times. By scaling the figures down and trying them out in different areas of the room setting, you can establish where they work best to create the most harmonious relationship. If you include several separate drawings in one composition, you can prevent them from looking superimposed by making subtle tonal adjustments as you paint.

Standing figure
Figures should relate to their surroundings, so this image should be scaled to an appropriate size to look realistic within the interior.

Interior study
The essential details of this scene and the light streaming through the windows provide a good visual reference for a painting.

Seated girl at a window
In this pen-and-wash study the light hits the girl from the same direction as it does the standing figure. This creates a clear link between the two.

Creating a composition

1 ◀ Begin by copying the basic outlines of the interior study onto tracing paper with a soft pencil, keeping the sketch simple and well defined. Secure the tracing paper with masking tape to prevent it from moving.

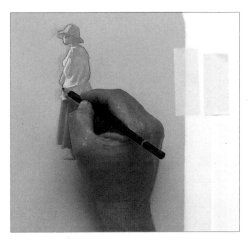

2 ▶ Scale down any image that is too large. Then trace around the outline of each figure.

3 ▶ Position the trace of the standing figure over the original interior watercolour study, moving it around until a suitable composition begins to materialize.

4 ◀ Transfer all the tracings onto paper, either by heavily shading the opposite side of the tracing paper and drawing the image again, or by using carbon paper.

Establishing a Scene
The artist has successfully placed these two figures in a strong composition in preparation for a detailed painting. Each figure has been accurately scaled to look realistic within the interior setting.

Each figure has been placed in an appropriate part of the setting.

The most relevant information has been included to give the composition clarity and interest.

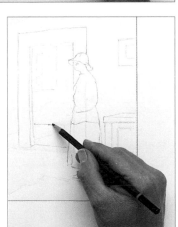

5 ▲ Once you have drawn in all the images, add the remaining features and details to give a comprehensive scene that can be transferred to canvas.

James Horton

Materials

6B pencil

Tracing paper

Masking tape

AN INTRODUCTION TO
PERSPECTIVE

Perspective	74	Three-Point Painting	110
A Brief History	76	Gallery of Landscape	
Starting Out	80	& Architecture	114
The Picture Plane	82	Reflections	116
Horizon Line or Eye Level	84	Sunlight & Shadows	118
Three Views on Perspective	86	Artificial Light	120
One-Point Perspective	88	Gallery of Shadows	
Curves & Circles	90	& Reflections	122
Atmospheric Perspective	92	Modern Devices	124
Detail & Definition	94	Gallery of	
Gallery of		Perspective Devices	126
Atmospheric Perspective	96	Anamorphosis	128
Two-Point Perspective	98	Curvilinear Perspective	130
Two-Point Painting	100	Gallery of	
Box Grid Construction	102	Curvilinear Perspective	132
Inclined Planes	104	Curvilinear Composition	134
Plans & Elevations	106	Gallery of	
Three-Point Perspective	108	Alternative Approaches	136

PERSPECTIVE

IN ITS MANY DIVERSE FORMS, perspective provides us with a means of arriving at a convincing two-dimensional visual picture of the complex three-dimensional world we perceive and inhabit. The idea of perspective is attractive to us because it is a system that allows us to enclose and contain the world, creating a two-dimensional scale model of reality. In this way, it renders the world accessible and helps us to come to terms with it. The main focus of this book will be on conventional linear perspective, though not at the expense of other equally important methods of projection. We need to retain a sense of the complexity of the way we actually see. This contrasts with the limitations of certain formalized systems of perspective. Linear perspective, for example, relies on a fixed rather than a constantly shifting viewpoint and on straight line projection to vanishing points. The more curvilinear reality

Egyptian fresco, *The Pool in Nebanum's Garden,* c.1400 B.C.
The ancient Egyptian method of representation showed the scene from above, from the side, and from the front at the same time. This opening out and flattening the space gives an extremely clear view of the subject. The different views are all shown on one plane.

of our perception is denied. Linear perspective is based on the notion that the world is perceived as if existing behind a rectangular pane of glass, like a display case at the museum. Such a system discounts the way we mentally

J. M. W. Turner, *Petworth Park,* **c.1828,** *24 x 57 in (60 x 146 cm)*
In this panoramic view, Turner has employed the conventions of one-point perspective. The lines of the shadows of the deer, the paving, and the line of dogs all converge to a central vanishing point on the horizon immediately beneath the light source. But because he has chosen such a wide angle of view, Turner has also incorporated curvilinear perspective in the sweeping curves that replace the horizontals in the foreground and in the arching sky.

enlarge what we are focusing on. In this book, we have concentrated on those aspects of perspective that will be of practical use to artists. So although there are pages that deal with some of the more technical aspects of perspective, this is not a strictly technical manual. We have tried to put perspective into context, to make the visual connection between a real image and whichever perspective construction is being featured. This includes the use of perspective drawing overlays on real images and, in the gallery pages, discussions of how artists have used perspective throughout history. The idea is to generate the confidence that helps us to recreate in the sketchbook or on the canvas what we see, after we understand its structure.

Ben Johnson, *Footfalls Echo in the Memory Down the Passage We Did Not Take Towards the Door We Never Opened,* **1993,** *54 in x 16 ft (1.37 x 4.88 m)*
Ben Johnson uses a computer to provide the perspective structure of his recreation of *The Ideal City*, attributed to Piero della Francesca.

Child's drawing
There is a link between this child's drawing and the Egyptian image. We look down on both from above, with the subjects flattened to the picture plane.

Norman Foster,
Drawing for BBC building
A good working knowledge of perspective comes into its own during the early stages of the design process. This sketch shows a confident facility in the freehand use of perspective that places the imaginary building within an existing context. It is important for an architect's client to be able to assess the scale of a building and the way it works within the available space. This is achieved here by the careful placing of figures. The foreground shading leads the eye into the focus of the sketch.

A BRIEF HISTORY

WHEN WE CONSIDER perspective historically, it is necessary to take a broad view. Within the various subdivisions of human history are a wide range of civilizations. Each has contributed to the ways in which we represent ourselves. No one system is more important or any more informative than another. Each approach adds to our understanding and to our ability to come to terms with the world as it changes.

Different perspectives

Today, there is a more raised awareness of the different approaches to representation within diverse cultures, both past and present around the world. Artists can develop a focus for their own work from a wide range of stylistic and interpretative approaches within many alternative systems of visual representation. This freeing of former constraints has generated an exciting diversity of approaches to representation in contemporary painting.

The images on these pages give an indication of some of the many diverse methods of representing space and narrative. They could broadly be described as incorporating projection systems other than linear perspective. Such methods are similar to the orthographic, axonometric, and isometric projection systems (*see* glossary) employed by architects and engineers. These methods are invariably favored over linear perspective drawing since they can provide such clear, self-explanatory images. There is no convergence to vanishing points and therefore none of the foreshortening that diminishes the size and detail of what you see. Such clarity can be seen in each of

David Malangi,
Mortuary Feast of Gunmirringgu the great ancestral hunter, **1963,**
27 x 17 in (69.5 x 43 cm)
In this modern aboriginal painting, narrative elements are shown as plans or elevations (side and front) on the same plane, which is the surface of the bark. Each element is clearly recognizable and has its own unique symbolism.

Assyrian Relief, ***The Battle of Til-Tuba,***
c.660–650 B.C., *58 x 69 in (1.47 x 1.75 m)*
The vigor and ferocity of this battle scene is a direct result of the system of representation adopted by the sculptor. We readily accept the convention that all the figures are projected the same size and from a similar viewpoint, and that the ground plane is the surface of the stone.

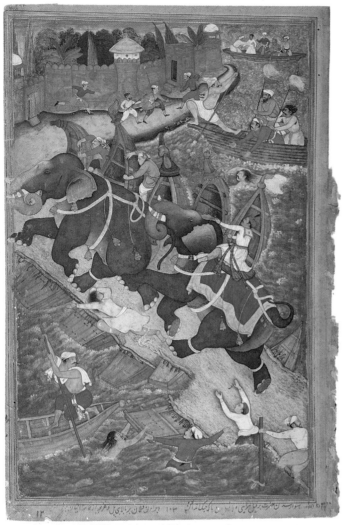

Miniature from the Akbar-nama of Abul Fazl, c.1595,
14 x 9 in (35 x 22 cm)
In this example of late Mughal painting, the main feature of the composition is the dynamic central diagonal of the two elephants thundering across the pontoon bridge. They are two-dimensional, but painted with great vivacity. If the viewpoint were the same for them as for the boats that are seen beneath the bridge, we would be looking at elephants lying on their side. However, we get a clear aerial view of the boats, which demonstrates their function perfectly, and a view of the elephants that gives us all the information we need. Unlike the Assyrian image, here the size of the figures diminishes with distance.

these works and particularly in the Japanese painting and Assyrian carving, where each of the figures is shown to the same scale and has equal weight in the composition. In the Mughal painting, while the image has a similar directness and immediacy, the structure of the work has not been defined solely by the conventions of its own culture. It has absorbed some perspective elements from Western painting – for example, the progressive diminution of the figures and boats into the distance.

The seeds of linear perspective
The ancient Egyptians and Assyrians were able to represent their world quite satisfactorily on one plane. Figures could be seen frontally, from the side, or in three-quarter view at the same time. They vary in size according to their importance. The correlation between size and importance also found expression, from the fourth century onwards, in Byzantine art, with its flat, iconic images.

According to the Roman architect and engineer Vitruvius *(first century B.C.)*, the ancient Greeks were the first to explore the notion of the recession and projection of images in order to give the illusion of buildings in painted stage scenery. There are a number of Greek and early Roman frescoes that show a considerable degree of spatial illusion and in which the sides of an object are shown receding at an angle, though they do not converge. The Room of the Masks on the Palatine in Rome is a fine example of the attempt to create a convincing architectural setting in parallel perspective on a two-dimensional wall. But in the West, the use of even rudimentary perspective died out for many hundreds of years until its revival in thirteenth-century Italy.

Tosa-Sumiyoshi School, *Entertainments in Kyoto,* **c.1661-72,** *8¼ x 12½ in (21.5 x 32 cm)*
This painting is a fine example of oblique projection. The front faces of the buildings are undistorted elevations, while the top and sides all project at the same angle. There is no convergence of parallel lines, so the figures retain the same size at any point in the painting.

The Western tradition

In the postclassical Western tradition, linear perspective was first clearly demonstrated in Florence during the early fifteenth century *(c.1413)* by Filippo Brunelleschi *(1377–1446)*. His paintings of the Baptistery and of the Palazzo de' Signori in Florence perfectly matched the proportions of the real buildings. Brunelleschi is said to have worked out his system through observation and the use of his surveying skills. He may even have projected his perspectives from plans and elevations. Leon Battista Alberti *(1404–72)* was the first to give a formalized account of a perspective system, known as the *costruzione legittima,* based on a *pavimento* (pavement) grid of perspective squares (*see* p. 88). Using Alberti's system, artists were able to put a grid over the plan of an object and transfer the lines of the object onto a similar grid in perspective. Heights could be established either by swinging a vertical up from the horizontal floor grid at the appropriate point in the perspective drawing or by using a vertical grid in addition to the horizontal one.

Artists like Paolo Uccello *(1397–1475)* and Piero della Francesca *(1415/20–1492)* were aware of the

Paolo Uccello, *The Flood,* c.1445
Uccello has exploited his mastery of the art of perspective by using it to show the vastness of the ark as it recedes on the left toward a central vanishing point on the high horizon line. In order to avoid a completely symmetrical image, Uccello has placed the wall on the right at a slightly different angle to the picture plane from that of the ark on the left, so that they do not share the same vanishing point.

Emanuel de Witte, *Interior with Woman at a Clavichord,* c.1665, *30 x 41 in (77 x 104 cm)*
In this fine example of one-point perspective, the eye is led through the house to a central vanishing point beyond the far window. The artist has used the patches of light from windows along the right of the house to break up the composition's symmetry and add visual interest along the ground plane.

limitations of the grid method. Painter and art historian Giorgio Vasari *(1511–74)* describes how Uccello preferred to work by projection from plans and elevations. Piero employed a complex system of projection based on Euclidean geometry. His paintings have a sense of order and serenity that stems from the spatial precision of their composition.

Among the artists who furthered study of the new art of perspective were the great German painter Albrecht Dürer *(1471–1528),* who wrote treatises on the subject, and Diego Velázquez *(1599–1660),* who held a significant collection of writings on

Gian Battista Tiepolo, *The Institution of the Rosary,* **c.1737–39**
From the sixteenth to the eighteenth centuries, illusionistic wall and ceiling painting developed toward the dazzling trompe l'oeil *works of Tiepolo. Perfectly foreshortened figures freewheel in space above settings of entirely convincing painted architecture.*

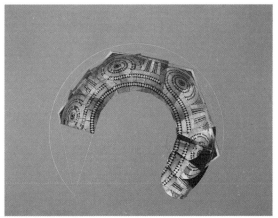

Jan Dibbets, *Spoleto Floor,* **1982,**
5 ft 7 in x 5 ft 9 in (170 x 175 cm) Jan Dibbets's seminal Perspective Correction *piece of the late sixties undermined the very notion of linear perspective. Here, the curvilinear or spherical approach to perspective representation gives a convincing view, though we are constantly aware of the flat surface of the paper.*

Fernand Léger, *Smokers,* **1911,**
51 x 38 in (130 x 96 cm) In this cubist work, the surface is a pattern of interlocking planes, but the scale of individual elements gives a sense of distance and movement. There is also a play between the clouds of smoke and the clouds in the sky. While the planes are broken up, there is still a genuine sense of perspective.

perspective. But it was Leonardo da Vinci *(1452–1519)* who made the greatest advances in the subject.

Leonardo is perhaps the one artist the extent of whose genius allowed him to explore the implications of perspective as it related to how we see and experience the world. He was the first to point out the anomalies of linear perspective, particularly in his observations on wide-angle views and the cone of vision.

It is possible to trace a growing sophistication in the use of perspective throughout the history of Western painting. From the experiments of Renaissance Florence to the complex Baroque illusionism of the late sixteenth century, perspective has been increasingly manipulated to convince the viewer of the truth depicted on the painted surface. A break in this process occurs with the abandonment of realist painting at the end of the nineteenth century and the advent of photography. With the spread of photography, many artists began to create paintings in which they aimed to break up the picture plane itself. In many cubist and futurist paintings, the fragmentation of the image is itself the means of creating meaningful perspective.

Curvilinear perspective
The idea of curvilinear perspective developed by Leonardo in his optical theories has appeared in the work of many artists. From the early fifteenth-century paintings of Jean Fouquet *(1420–81),* through nineteenth-century Romantic expressions of space in the landscapes of Turner *(1775–1851)* and John Martin *(1789–1854),* to the interiors of Van Gogh *(1853–90)* and the work of David Hockney *(b.1937),* curvilinear perspective is an approach to the depiction of space that many artists of our time have rediscovered.

STARTING OUT

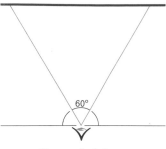

Cone of vision

To avoid distortion, any object we wish to draw must fall within a 60-degree angle of vision.

WHEN WE BEGIN drawing or painting, it can be difficult to decide just how much of what we can see should be put down on the paper or canvas. We focus on the scene in front of us, but at the same time we are aware of objects at the periphery of our vision. There is a sense in which we can see all around us. If we consider how much we can represent within the limitations of a conventional perspective approach, we will realize that it is extremely difficult to get the whole scene into our painting. We need to be selective, to narrow the angle of vision so that our painting might focus on only a fraction of what we see.

Selecting your subject

When standing in a landscape, we are conscious of the whole scene that surrounds us. We can focus on one part of the landscape, like the tree above left, and make a drawing or painting of something we can comfortably take in within a relatively narrow angle of vision, or we can attempt to give expression to a much wider view. In the photograph above right, we are aware of trees curving in toward us to the left and right at the periphery of our vision, and of the ground close to our feet. In the middle distance, a row of trees is clearly defined. Conventional linear perspective works without the distortion seen in the right-hand photograph because subjects or scenes are generally contained within a 60-degree angle or cone of vision.

Hallway scene

A hallway is usually a very narrow and vertical space. But here the artist has managed to fill the square format of her page with a convincing impression of all that the interior contains. The view is generally one of linear perspective, but at its edges the image begins to curve slightly as the limits of the cone of vision are reached.

Natural perspective

In this drawing of a large room, the artist has tried to represent the objects seen out of the corner of his eye to the left and right, in addition to the space in front. The sofa and chest (bottom left) *are in reality parallel to the table* (bottom right). *In certain types of perspective drawing, the back of the sofa and the edge of the table, which are at right angles to the floorboards, would be drawn along the same horizontal line. Here, they are at an angle to each other because that is how you actually see them. Similarly, the central beam across the ceiling is in reality straight and would be drawn so according to conventional perspective, but when you look at it, it appears curved.*

This section appears as it might in linear perspective before any distortion outside the cone of vision.

Wide-angle view

This simple sketch encompasses an extremely wide angle of vision. It could not be made using conventional linear perspective because the cone of vision is too wide, but it does demonstrate that a drawing taking in such a wide angle of view can generate a real sense of involvement and of place.

This tiny study shows a more conventional view through the car windscreen taken from the same position. In the larger drawing, the church can be seen above the girl's right elbow.

81

THE PICTURE PLANE

Start with a small subject

THE PICTURE PLANE IS THE CANVAS or sheet of paper on which you draw. It is possible to imagine the picture plane as a sheet of glass through which light rays from the object pass on their way to the eye. When you make a drawing in perspective, the objects that are marked on your canvas are shown as they would be seen when viewed through a transparent surface. If you make some drawings on a glass of the view seen through it, you will see for yourself some of the basic principles of linear perspective drawing.

Equipment

A sketching glass of around 8 x 10 in (20 x 25 cm) is suitable. You should hold the frame rigidly on the table and use a pigmented felt-tip pen, a brush, and ink or an all-purpose pencil to draw on the glass.

1 ▲ Close one eye and try to keep your head in the same position. As you draw, you may find that the image wobbles around; it is difficult to keep yourself and the glass still and draw at the same time.

2 ▶ If you use a sheet of glass in a frame you can hold, such as a small photo frame, you can alter your composition. The closer you move the frame toward the subject, the bigger the subject will appear on the glass.

Transferring your image

By laying a piece of damp paper on the glass, you can transfer a reverse image of what you have drawn.

Peeling back

Peel the paper off and you will find that the image has been transferred. To reverse the image, redraw the image on the back of the glass .

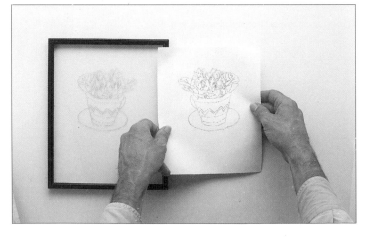

Composing your picture

Drawing on glass will help you to try out poses and angles for portraits, in addition to achieving reasonable likenesses.

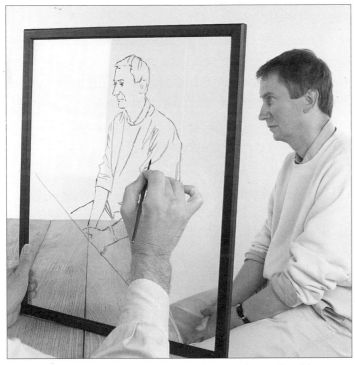

1 ▲ Place your subject so that he or she can sit comfortably without moving. The combination of your slight movements and those of the model can make it difficult to keep the image correctly lined up with the subject as you draw on the glass.

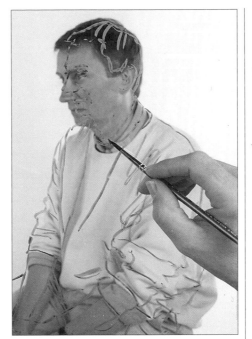

2 ▲ If you use a soft pointed sable or nylon brush with India ink, you will get the best results by tracing the lines and features of what you see through the glass freely and economically rather than being overly cautious in your approach. You can "print" the images as you draw them, using the technique described opposite. Out of a number of rapid sketches you will generally find one or two that work successfully.

Materials

Fine felt-tip pen

No. 4 round sable brush

Picture frame

Measuring your composition

You can use a pencil held out at arm's length to measure the size of a subject as you see it. A similar method with two rulers can be used to assess the angles of various parts of the image in relation to the picture plane. A simple rectangle of cardboard, with a smaller rectangle cut from the middle, is often used to define a composition and help show what might be included in a painting. Hold it in front of you and then try to draw what you see through the "window" in the cardboard. If you mark off a scale along the edge, it is relatively easy to see where a significant line, such as the horizon line or the top of a building, bisects the edge of the cardboard.

HORIZON LINE OR EYE LEVEL

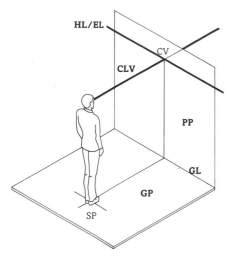

LINEAR PERSPECTIVE DRAWING is based on certain fundamental principles and a grammar of straightforward technical terms that relate the subject of the drawing to its image on the picture plane. These terms are important and useful to artists whether or not they wish to make technical perspective drawings. One of the first elements in a picture that the artist will need to establish is the Horizon Line (HL) or Eye Level (EL), which is the line at which the sea and sky appear to meet. It is important to know where it is, even if it is obscured by hills or buildings. The horizon line is always drawn straight, even though the earth is curved, as we are only ever drawing a small section of it.

Technical terms

The Ground Plane (GP) is the level ground upon which the artist is apparently standing in order to view a scene; it stretches to the horizon. The exact point where he stands is the Station Point (SP). The Ground Line (GL) represents the bottom edge of the picture plane where it cuts the ground plane. The Center Line of Vision (CLV) represents an imaginary line from the artist's eye to the horizon at 90 degrees to the Picture Plane (PP). It intersects the horizon line on the picture plane at the Center of Vision (CV).

View from a cliff

Whatever your position in the landscape, if you look straight ahead and do not tilt your head up or down, the horizon line will always be at your eye level. In this view from a high cliff top, you see considerably more of the ground below the horizon than if you were standing at sea level.

View from a beach

Here, you are standing on the beach at the edge of the sea, so the horizon line is low. You see a great deal more of the sky than in the image on the left. A distant figure of the same height standing on the same level would be bisected by the horizon line at the level of the eyes.

Normal viewpoint

These three paintings demonstrate how the position of the horizon line can affect our reading of a painting. Here, the artist's eye level roughly matches that of the children. The effect is to allow the viewer to participate in their experience – our eye is drawn with theirs to the distant horizon line.

High viewpoint

In this painting, the standing artist is taller than the children and his eye level is thus higher than theirs. The higher horizon line means we see more of the beach, while the girls themselves appear smaller and more vulnerable. The artist is more an observer than a participant.

Cone of vision

If you look at a scene from a fixed viewpoint without moving your head, your eye can only take in a certain proportion or segment of it without losing focus or encountering distortion at the edges of our angle of vision. For the purposes of linear perspective, we try to ensure that the subject comes well within an angle or, in three-dimensional terms, a cone of vision of up to 60 degrees. Anything seen from within that angle can be represented without perceived distortion. When drawing a tall building, we need to take particular care to set the station point sufficiently far away to ensure that its height comes well within the cone of vision.

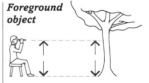

HL/EL

HL/EL

PP

GL

GP

SP

Converging rays

The diagram shows how a 60-degree cone of vision encompasses a beach scene. Where rays of light from the objects intersect with the picture plane, the scene would be depicted on the picture plane in linear perspective – the rays converge at the eye of the viewer. An artist would commonly choose to make a painting on a rectangular format from within the cone of vision.

Low viewpoint

Here, the artist has adopted a very low viewpoint and his eye level is much lower than that of the children. The image appears quite different from the previous ones and the children become much more independent and prominent. There is a sense of their ordering or controlling the scene.

ESTABLISHING THE HORIZON LINE

Since the horizon line is the principal location of vanishing points for objects on the ground plane, it is essential to know where to place it in your painting. You will not always be able to see the horizon – it may be concealed by a wall or a mountain range, for example. Below are two methods for establishing the horizon line. In the first, there is no object or surface in front of you to mark. In the second, there is.

Open space	***Foreground object***

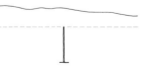

If there is nothing to physically mark your eye level on the scene in front of you, place a stick or cane in the ground and mark it at the level of your eyes.

Hold the edge of a sketchbook or credit card at eye level.

Plant the stick in the ground some distance in front of you. Be sure it is on ground that is level with that on which you are standing.

Make a chalk mark on the object – here, the trunk of a tree – at the same height as the card or book.

Note where the height of the stick corresponds with a distant feature and draw your horizon line.

The chalk mark will show where the horizon line would cut across the scene and where it will be in your picture.

85

THREE VIEWS ON PERSPECTIVE

PERSPECTIVE DIAGRAMS MAY APPEAR to bear little relation to the world we see. When an artist sets out to make a painting, it is unlikely that the subject will be a cube set parallel to the plane of the canvas, or at any specific angle to it. But once the principles of perspective have been absorbed, it is surprising how helpful they can be in constructing a framework on which to build a painting. It may be helpful to consider linear perspective construction as one-point, two-point, or three-point, based on the number of principal vanishing points in the construction.

One-point perspective

All lines at right angles to the picture plane and parallel with the ground plane appear to converge at the same vanishing point on the horizon; this point is also the center of vision.

A cube is viewed with one side parallel to the picture plane

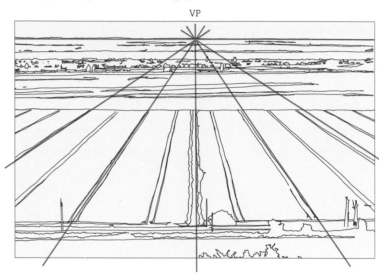

A cube is viewed at an angle to the picture plane (here each side is at 45 degrees)

Two-point perspective

Each side of this house is seen at an angle of around 45 degrees to the picture plane. Assuming the house is a regular cube, you see each side appearing to recede symmetrically towards a vanishing point on the horizon line on the left- and right-hand sides of the image. The vanishing points lie on the horizon line because the base of the house is on the level ground plane and the top edges of the walls are parallel with it.

If you are standing directly opposite the front edge of the cube, then the vanishing points are equidistant from the point you are facing (the center of vision). Find a simple building and try this out for yourself by making a simple drawing. Start with the vertical line of the front edge of the building and, using two rulers (see p. 83), assess the angles at which the sides of the building recede from it. Build up a complete image from these angles.

Two-point angular

The narrow boat has more of its stern facing the viewer than its side, so foreshortening in the long side appears to be greater. The vanishing point for this side is much closer to the center of vision than that for the stern. We are describing a rectangle, and if we were to look at the boat from above, we would see that the lines extending from these vanishing points to each side of the barge meet at an angle of 90 degrees. The subject, however, does not have to be rectangular; it need only have straight sides for a vanishing point to be established.

A cube is viewed at an angle to the picture plane

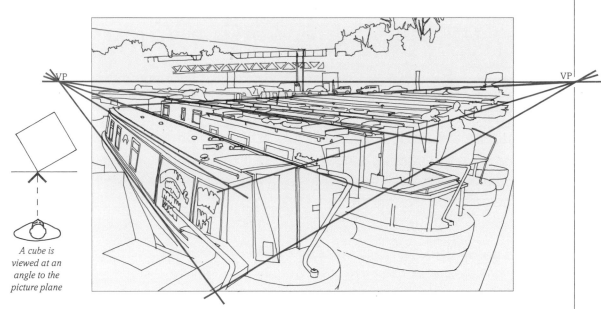

Further vanishing points

In any two-point construction, there can in fact be a number of vanishing points plotted in addition to the two principal ones that might be used – for example, to draw the front, back, and sides of a house set at an angle to the picture plane. In the case of a house, these additional vanishing points would be used to draw any feature – such as an open window – that is at an angle other than that of the walls of the house itself. In the image above, for example, the front doors of the barges are clearly at a very different angle to the vanishing lines that are drawn for the main body of the boats.

A cube is viewed with the picture plane at an angle to the viewer

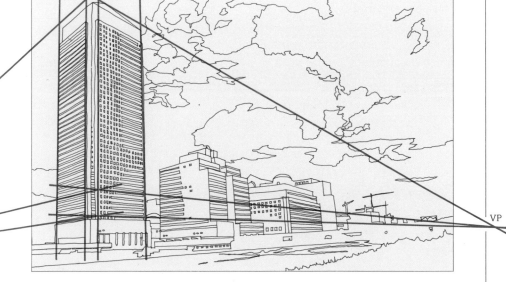

Three-point perspective

So far, either our images have had one side parallel with the ground plane or we have been sufficiently distant from them to be able to draw their vertical lines parallel with the left- and right-hand edges of the paper. But when the cube has none of its three planes parallel with the picture plane – like a box kite in midair, for example – we need to establish a further vanishing point for the third plane. When a building is so tall or we are so close to it that its vertical sides begin to converge, we plot its construction in three-point perspective. The basis of three-point perspective is that no side of the cube needs to be set at right angles to the picture plane or to be parallel with it. In the image above, if we were to extend the vertical lines of the building, they would eventually join at a third vanishing point.

ONE-POINT PERSPECTIVE

ONE-POINT PERSPECTIVE is based on a construction in which all parallel lines receding at right angles from the picture plane converge to a vanishing point at the center of vision. All lines that are parallel to the picture plane remain parallel in the drawing, so the box appears both to retain its true shape and to diminish in size as it recedes into the distance. If a cube is drawn with one face on the picture plane, the position of the back face of the cube on the ground plane must be established. This is usually done by constructing an additional diagonal vanishing point (or measuring point) on the horizon line.

Foreshortening

Imagine looking across a courtyard of square slabs in which two parallel sides of the slabs recede away from you in a straight line towards a central vanishing point and the other sides recede horizontally. The apparent distance between the lateral or horizontal edges will get progressively smaller. This is known as foreshortening.

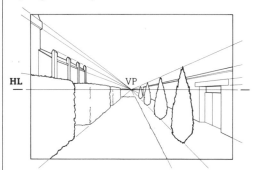

Convergence
The diagram at the left shows how parallel lines at right angles to the picture plane converge at a central vanishing point. Objects of equal height, such as the trees, look smaller the farther away they are.

Railway track
The farthest of the railway sleepers looks smaller because rays of light from each side of the sleeper begin to converge on the eye of the viewer from farther away. By the time they reach the picture plane, the distance between them is smaller than for the others.

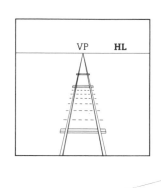

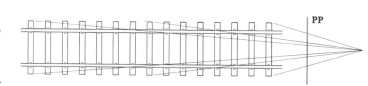

Pavement method

One-point perspective can be shown using a pavement or grid of squares. The front edge of this pavement is the ground line. Since this is the lower edge of the picture plane, the pavement can be used to establish scale. Draw the horizon line to scale at a suitable height (the height of a person). All parallel lines receding at right angles from the PP converge at the same VP on the horizon midway across the pavement. Join the point on the GL to the VP to give the orthogonals (*see* below).

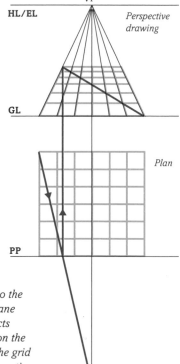

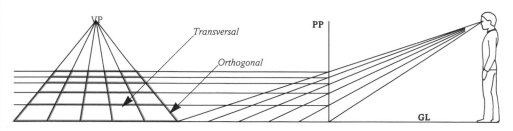

Alberti's method (*above*)
Alberti (see p. 78) constructed a side view showing the picture plane from the side, the viewer to the right and the pavement to scale along the ground plane. Rays of light pass from points on the pavement to the eye of the viewer. From the point of intersection with the picture plane, horizontal lines are drawn back to the original grid. Where they intersect the orthogonals determines the position of transversals (horizontals) on the grid.

Finding the transversals (*right*)
On a plan, project a line from the station point to the farthest corner of the grid, back to the picture plane and into the perspective drawing where it bisects the orthogonal at the appropriate place. A line on the perspective drawing drawn from one corner of the grid to another provides the remaining points of intersection where the transversals (horizontals) cross the orthogonals.

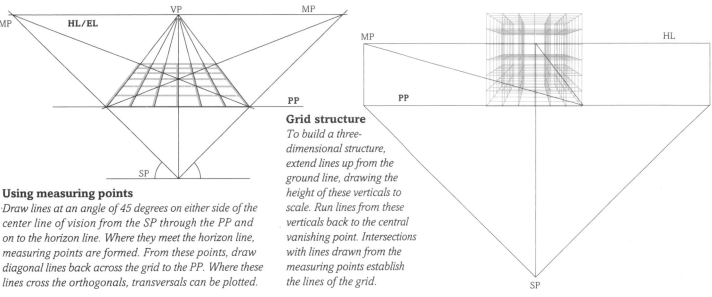

Grid structure

To build a three-dimensional structure, extend lines up from the ground line, drawing the height of these verticals to scale. Run lines from these verticals back to the central vanishing point. Intersections with lines drawn from the measuring points establish the lines of the grid.

Using measuring points

Draw lines at an angle of 45 degrees on either side of the center line of vision from the SP through the PP and on to the horizon line. Where they meet the horizon line, measuring points are formed. From these points, draw diagonal lines back across the grid to the PP. Where these lines cross the orthogonals, transversals can be plotted.

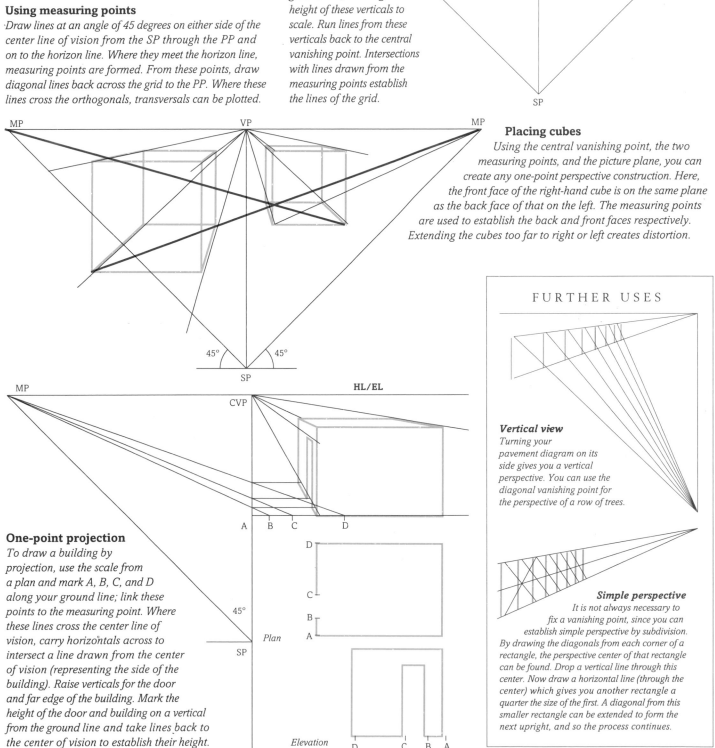

Placing cubes

Using the central vanishing point, the two measuring points, and the picture plane, you can create any one-point perspective construction. Here, the front face of the right-hand cube is on the same plane as the back face of that on the left. The measuring points are used to establish the back and front faces respectively. Extending the cubes too far to right or left creates distortion.

One-point projection

To draw a building by projection, use the scale from a plan and mark A, B, C, and D along your ground line; link these points to the measuring point. Where these lines cross the center line of vision, carry horizontals across to intersect a line drawn from the center of vision (representing the side of the building). Raise verticals for the door and far edge of the building. Mark the height of the door and building on a vertical from the ground line and take lines back to the center of vision to establish their height.

Plan

Elevation

FURTHER USES

Vertical view

Turning your pavement diagram on its side gives you a vertical perspective. You can use the diagonal vanishing point for the perspective of a row of trees.

Simple perspective

It is not always necessary to fix a vanishing point, since you can establish simple perspective by subdivision. By drawing the diagonals from each corner of a rectangle, the perspective center of that rectangle can be found. Drop a vertical line through this center. Now draw a horizontal line (through the center) which gives you another rectangle a quarter the size of the first. A diagonal from this smaller rectangle can be extended to form the next upright, and so the process continues.

CURVES & CIRCLES

PUTTING CIRCLES INTO perspective is simple. Just bear in mind that a circle fits perfectly into a square, with its edges touching the square at the midpoints of the square's four sides. It follows that you need only to put a square into perspective at the appropriate angle and then construct the circle within the square. A circle in perspective is an ellipse. The midpoint of an ellipse does not correspond to the midpoint of the same circle in plan, but is midway between the extremities of the ellipse on its major (longest) and minor (shortest) axes.

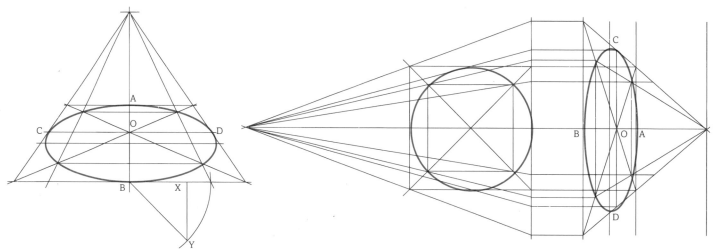

Putting circles in perspective

Put a square in perspective (see pp. 88-89). The center of your circle lies at the intersection of the diagonals (O). Draw a vertical line (AB) and a horizontal line (CD) through this point parallel with the edges of the square to establish four points (A, B, C, D) at which the circle touches the square. Measure a quarter the length of the square on the picture plane from its midpoint (BX). Drop a vertical line the same length (XY) and, using the midpoint as center, describe an arc to cut the front of the square on each side. From these points, draw lines back to the vanishing point. Where

they cut the diagonals from each corner, they will intersect with the line of the circle. The additional points of guidance for the drawing of a circle within a square are shown by measurement. They can be established by projection from a plan (see pp. 98-99, 106-107). The diagram on the left can be adapted to the requirements of your subject. In the diagram above, you are projecting across from the plan on the left to the perspective drawing on the right, as is the case with the motorbike below.

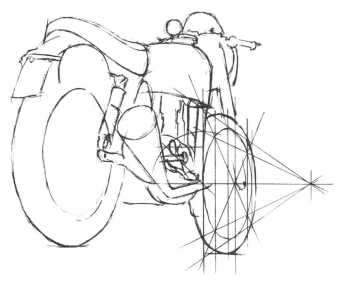

Placing ellipses

In this diagram for the acrylic painting on the right, the circle is on a receding vertical plane so the major axis of the ellipse is a vertical line, while the minor axis recedes to the vanishing point on the horizon.

Curves as straight lines

The perspective of a curve can be established, as it is here, by rendering it as a series of inclined planes (see pp. 104-5). If you were to look at this bridge from above, you would see the sides of the bridge are parallel. Whether the planes of the walkway and the angles of the handrails are ascending or descending, they all share the same vertical vanishing axis (left). You might continue the construction all the way around to show a waterwheel or a series of switchbacks like a roller coaster. The principle is that curves are often best represented by the use of straight lines.

CHANGING VIEWPOINT

The viewpoint adopted determines the angle of the ellipse and therefore the length of the vertical axis. Where the horizon line is level with the top of the glass, the circle will appear as a straight line.

Viewed from mid-point, the ellipse of the glass rim is very shallow. The smaller axis – here the vertical axis – corresponds to that with the greatest distortion.

A higher viewpoint produces a larger minor axis. Here, this is the vertical axis. The subject is further distorted by the refraction caused by the thick bottom of the glass.

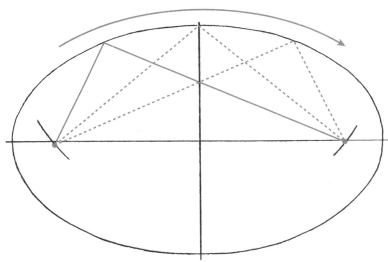

Drawing an ellipse

Draw the major axis of the ellipse and the minor axis at right angles to it. Open your compass to the length of half the major axis and, using the extremity of the minor axis as a center, describe an arc to cut each side of the major axis. Put a pin in each of these points and knot a circle of thread, looping it over the pins and pulling it taut to ensure that it reaches the end of one axis. With your pencil in the loop, draw the ellipse. A mechanical pencil also works well, as does a technical pen.

91

ATMOSPHERIC PERSPECTIVE

ATMOSPHERE AFFECTS the way we perceive tones and colors as they recede toward the horizon. An understanding of atmospheric or aerial perspective will give your work a greater illusion of depth not simply in relation to landscape but with any subject. Tones lighten and colors become cooler or more blue with distance. Warm colors advance, while cool colors recede. In misty weather, the lightening of tones in the receding planes of a landscape is particularly marked. Similarly, from a high vantage point on a sunny day, you can see how easily the green colors of a landscape become progressively blue toward the horizon.

Receding tones

You can imagine the landscape as a series of vertical, receding planes. Each of these planes is the same tone in nature, but the effects of atmospheric perspective mean that the farther they are from the viewer, the lighter they appear to be.

Landscape tones

If you look straight through them, you can see the effect of the receding tones as they appear in the landscape. Notice how in the diagram on the right your angle of vision can take in more of the landscape as it opens out toward the horizon.

Tonal watercolor

In this painting, based on the photograph at left, the dark tones of the foreground trees are continued in the pale gray tones of the distance. Similar, purely tonal paintings can be made in which you begin with the lighter, distant tones and end with the almost black silhouettes in the foreground. Here, the two distinct tones represent middle distance and foreground.

Tonal washes

A diluted wash is painted up to the line of the trees at the top. When dry, the darker tones of the trees can be painted over.

Receding color

These diagrams are set out in the same way as those opposite. They show how, together with the lightening of tone, colors become cooler as they recede. The same color green in each one of four receding fields appears to become more blue toward the horizon.

Atmospheric view

The photograph on the left clearly shows the effects of atmospheric perspective, from the dark tones of the village in the foreground to the lighter blue tones of the distant hills. This photograph has been used as the basis for a series of freely painted watercolor studies that explore the combined effects of tone and color in the landscape.

Color contrast

In this preliminary step, the artist has concentrated on color juxtaposing the yellow-blues of the distant hills with deeper-toned red-blues in the buildings. The effect is of sun in the distance with the foreground in cooler shadow.

Preliminary stage

Here, warmer ochres representing the town separate the grays of the foreground from those of the distant hills and create depth.

Changing brushstrokes

The effects of perspective can be accentuated by the use of different brushstrokes. Here, bold, deep-toned brushstrokes in the foreground move through smaller, more precise strokes in the middle ground to broad washes with no detail in the far hills.

Receding planes

Foreground roofs and tiles give way to middle-ground trees and distant slopes.

DETAIL & DEFINITION

THE CRISP BLACK LINES of technical perspective drawings may show the apparent diminution in the size of objects as they recede into the distance, but they do not show how the image becomes progressively less distinct. Of great importance to artists is the effect of atmospheric perspective on our perception of detail. Such changes have to be reflected in modifications to the techniques we use to represent objects over distance. The progressive diminution of tone and cooling of color with distance is a good general rule.

Here, aerial perspective is interrupted in the middle ground by brilliant sunlight

Loss of detail

The two photographs on the right show the same subject from two different distances. In that on the left, the subject is relatively close to the camera and as a result the image is very clear. In the image on the right, the blurring effects of atmospheric perspective have altered the definition of the face. The photographs below the two faces show the position of the camera in relation to the subject. Modern cameras are now sufficiently competent that the loss of detail is limited.

Facial features

A painter working close up to a model might want to record the clarity and fine detail that is plainly visible, but from a distance such details cannot be seen. The approach needs to be broader, reflecting the general shape and the overall tonal contrasts. One of the mistakes artists can make when starting out is to try to add detail to parts of an image in the middle ground or distance. This is particularly the case with images of people. It can look very odd where a head is too tightly painted in comparison to everything that surrounds it. You need to focus on what you actually see rather than what you think you can see. Often features can be marked with one or two light strokes.

Excluding detail

When depicting part of an image in which detail has been lost due to the effects of atmospheric perspective, you often retain a strong impresssion of the object seen. One of the simplest ways of overcoming the problem is to half-close your eyes to blur the focus a little. This will enable you to concentrate on only the basic forms.

Weight of line

The lightening of tone associated with distance in atmospheric perspective does not always have to be expressed in tonal shading. It is quite possible to show the effect by using line alone. In this line drawing of figures on a beach, the artist has used a lighter weight of line in the distance, giving a good sense of receding space. The detail below shows diminution of detail with distance. We accept that these are people far away even though we can barely make them out.

With watercolor, one way of softening the tones in the distance is to wash the whole painting, protecting certain areas with art masking fluid.

The effective contrast between blue and yellow enables the airplane to stand out from the background.

A few simple geometric touches of deeper blue or red-brown are enough to indicate the buildings in the village below.

Leaving out the middle ground

One of the ways in which artists can create a dramatic sense of perspective in the landscape is by losing the middle ground and simply showing foreground and distance. Here, the airplane is the foreground object, while the backdrop of landscape and sky provides a single distant plane.

Cloud effects

An essential feature of atmospheric perspective in relation to landscape is the treatment of clouds. The photograph clearly shows the diminution in the scale of the clouds as the eye moves towards the horizon. But it also shows how much they do to give a real sense of space above the land mass. You can use clouds to suggest substantial depth in a small area of canvas.

Clouds in perspective

The rules of perspective apply as much to clouds as to objects on the ground. There is a consistency in this mackerel cloud formation that makes the ridges appear uniformly closer and longer as they recede. Turn the page upside down and you could be looking at the ridges on mudflats.

GALLERY OF ATMOSPHERIC PERSPECTIVE

WHATEVER THE BROAD rules of atmospheric perspective may dictate, each situation is unique and has its own surprises. The diversity of these paintings shows how the effects of the atmosphere contribute to the illusion of perspective and how the artist can manipulate them to create a sense of structure and depth within quite small areas of canvas.

Nicolas Poussin, *The Burial of Phocion,* **1648,**
18½ x 28 in (47 x 71cm)
This idealized landscape has been composed with remarkable precision, taking the eye toward the center of the composition and the distant architecture in a series of flat curves. The light, which heightens a rise in the ground here or a part of the pathway there, breaks up the composition in a complex and intriguing pattern, sustaining our visual interest throughout the work. Toward the horizon, the artist has cooled the colors and lightened the tones almost imperceptibly in a classic example of aerial perspective.

The different sizes of the boats and subtle tonal variations beyond the waves reinforce the sense of receding space across the surface of the water.

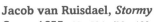

This detail is a miniature version of the whole composition. It also shows the care that the artist has taken with the surface.

Jacob van Ruisdael, *Stormy Sea,* **c.1655,** *39 x 52 in (98 x 132 cm)*
Here, the conventional view of a sky deepening in tone at the top and getting lighter toward the horizon is turned on its head. The depth of tone in the clouds toward the horizon gives a remarkable sense of the sky pushing down on the scene. The vertical post reaches up towards the sky, giving a sense of the huge expanse of space where a break in the clouds is visible. On the left-hand edge of the post, the white line indicates the light coming through these clouds and illuminating the seas just beyond the breakwater. The scene is pinned to the bottom edge of the painting by the heavy, dark tones of the silhouettes of the breakwaters in the foreground. One of the most remarkable achievements of this dramatic work is the sense of space the artist has managed to convey in the small area between the white waves and the horizon.

Caspar David Friedrich,
Moonrise over the Sea, **1821,**
53 x 67 in (1.35 x 1.7 m)
As you look at this painting, you share a similar eye level to the two men standing on the rock in the middle ground. Thus there is a link between the viewer's experience and theirs. They stand at the apex of a triangle that includes the seated women on the right and the driftwood sticking up on the left. This triangle is echoed above in an inverted and softened form by the arch of the clouds on each side of the moon, creating a quiet, almost elegiac atmosphere. Triangular elements in the composition form a stable structure within the painting, but they also relate to the vanishing lines of a perspective drawing and thus create a real sense of space. As the clouds approach the light of the horizon, they become gradually paler in tone and color, thus forming an important component of the atmospheric perspective.

Bill Jacklin, *Before the Hurricane,* **1988,**
78 x 78 in (1.98 x 1.98 m)
Jacklin's painting sets up a tension between surface and depth. The diagonals of rain shafting across the image are so evidently in the foreground that they seem to represent the picture plane, or the surface of the painting itself. Our awareness of this surface makes the sense of distance even more telling, as the street curves up and around into the painting. The sense of depth is reinforced by the the clouds in the far distance, which form reverse diagonals to those of the rain and echo that of the flagpole. The contrast between light and darkness, from left to right, is also a key element in the play of opposites.

The bright colors of the umbrellas lift them above the cooler tones of the figures, reflections, and pavement.

TWO-POINT PERSPECTIVE

TWO-POINT PERSPECTIVE can be drawn from observed reality, judging angles by eye, as shown in the project that follows (*see* pp. 100-1). A more accurate representation is achieved by the use of plans and projection – a method used by architects. As long as what is being drawn has its base on a flat ground plane and its verticals parallel with the picture plane, the side walls can be at any angle to the picture plane. A building can have four, five, or eight sides, with windows and doors open at any other angle. But whatever the angle, a line drawn from the station point to the picture plane, parallel with any of those sides, will intersect it at a point that establishes the vanishing point for that line and for any other line parallel to it.

Grids and projection

Probably the most common method of putting an image into two-point perspective is by projection from a plan. Heights are established from measure lines on the picture plane, where the height is true to scale (*below*). But there are other methods, including setting up a perspective grid and relating the heights and widths of the subject to the structure of the grid (*see* pp. 102-3). A combination of such methods can often be employed on the same drawing.

VP   VP

PP

SP

Constructing the pavement (*left*)

Draw lines from the VPs to the point O on the ground line. Take a line from the SP to the left corner of the pavement on the plan. Where this line intersects the PP, project it up vertically to intersect the line drawn from the left VP. These lines cross at the left corner of the pavement in the perspective drawing.

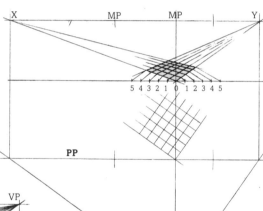

X   MP   MP   Y

5 4 3 2 1 0 1 2 3 4 5

PP

Using measuring points (*above*)

Two arcs drawn through the station point, with each vanishing point (X and Y) as its center, will give two measuring points at the horizon line. Mark evenly spaced points (1–5) on the ground line. A line from one of the MPs to any of these points will intersect with the line drawn from the vanishing point (O–VP). Draw lines from the points of intersection back to the respective VPs.

VP   VP

PP

SP

To station point

Elevations

Basic projection method (*left*)

Establish the eye level and where you wish to place the plan in relation to the picture plane. Here, the left-hand corner of the building lies on the picture plane. In the perspective drawing, measure up and mark from the ground line the height that the tower is shown on the elevation. Its intersection with a line from the left vanishing point will show the height of the towers along that face of the building.

Two-point projection method

However complicated the plan or elevation might appear to be, the principle of putting objects into two-point perspective according to the projection method remains the same. Take lines from the station point to the various points on the plan and, where they intersect with the picture plane, project them vertically into the perspective drawing. If part of the plan is behind the picture plane, the lines go back to the picture plane; if part is in front, they go forward to it. Measure lines at the picture plane establish the heights of the various parts of the building in perspective.

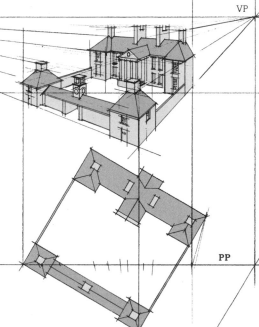

Elevations
Elevations are required only for those faces of the building that will be visible in the perspective drawing. Since the position of the vertical lines is established on the plan, it is the height to scale that needs to be measured from the elevations. Such measurements are made on the picture plane and taken back or forwards to the correct position in the perspective drawing.

Eye level
Remember that at the same scale, a change in the distance between the horizon line (eye level) and the ground line will show quite a different view of your subject. The ground line can be at the same level or below your eye level. Here, the high horizon gives a view looking down on the building similar to that on the left-hand page. The viewer might be imagined as standing on a hill.

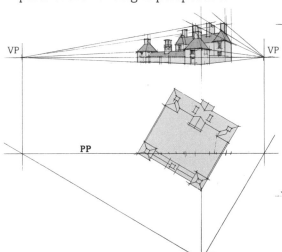

Lower viewpoint
In the drawing above, the plan is in exactly the same position relative to the picture plane as in the drawing on the right. The only difference is the lower eye level which is closer to that of a viewer standing at ground level. But as the perspective drawing shows, this single difference makes a massive change in the appearance of the building.

Enlargement
In the drawing on the right, the viewpoint, the eye level, and the angle of the building to the picture plane are the same as in the drawing above it. But the plan of the building has been placed in front of the picture plane rather than behind. The effect is to make the perspective image much larger.

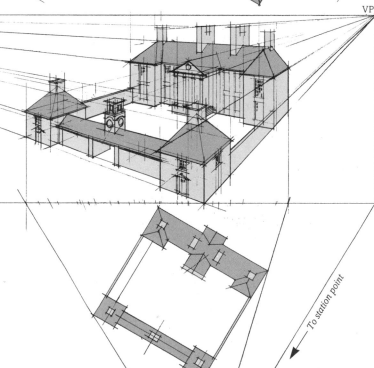

99

TWO-POINT PAINTING

AN UNDERSTANDING of the basic aspects of two-point perspective construction can help to inform the structure of your painting, so that what you represent looks credible within its setting. This old country house near Venice has windows at different levels and variously shaped chimneys, but the basic shape is a simple rectangle set at around 45 degrees to the picture plane. This is quite simple to draw in perspective. Once basic lines are set down, all the additional elements that give the house its character – such as the windows and doors and the rusticated surface of the walls – can be sketched in. You can then concentrate on the painting itself, fleshing out the structure with the tones and colors that give the image its special atmosphere without having to worry about the form.

1 ▲ Establish the horizon line. Fix the vanishing points and draw the vertical at the front edge of the building. It is now relatively simple to complete the overall shape and to establish the positions of doors and windows on the same plane as the sides of the house.

2 ▲ Use the bristle brush to block in the left-hand side of the house using Yellow Ochre; use a mixture of Titanium White and Ultramarine Blue for tones. Let these colors dry before adding the Chrome Oxide Green of the windows on the left and the browns of the doors. Add the shadow under the eaves with Burnt Sienna.

3 ▲ At this point, a strong horizontal line can be painted in across the left-hand side of the house, providing an anchoring feature for the more detailed side of the composition. A dark line of Burnt Sienna will make the porch stand out from the wall. A mixture of Cerulean Blue and Titanium White can be used for the sky.

4 ▲ On the left, add the foliage between the two floors and keep a similar angle for the shadows across the facade. Indicate the paving outside the house with a line of shadow in front, and add the sills to the windows. Shadows can be put in with Cobalt Blue.

Acrylics

Ultramarine Blue

Cobalt Blue

Cerulean Blue

Chrome Oxide Green

Burnt Umber

Burnt Sienna

Cadmium Red

Raw Sienna

Yellow Ochre

No. 4 flat bristle

5 ◀ Use the lines of the roof and those at the bottom of the wall to establish the angle of the brickwork, keeping the grapevine as a dividing line. You can create a grayish tone of Burnt Sienna by mixing in Titanium White and Ultramarine Blue. This will distinguish the softer brickwork from the jutting window sills. The corner wall forms a natural barrier between different tones and colors.

6 ▶ Keep a steady hand and paint in the electric and telephone wires with Chrome Oxide Green. This extends the composition beyond the house itself while fixing the subject firmly in its context.

7 ▶ The finished painting shows just enough detail to give a complete impression of the house, but not so much that it becomes tight and overworked. The relaxed, loose style of the painting benefits from the accurate underlying structure provided by the initial drawing. It may be bathed in sunlight, but with its shutters closed the house invites us to speculate on the identity of its owner. The image remains intriguing.

Jane Gifford

Two-point perspective drawing
A perspective drawing superimposed on the painting shows how closely the two images reflect each other. As painters, we can be intimidated by technical perspective drawings when they appear to be detached from the reality of what we see. But this image shows how far from the truth that is. The sequence illustrates how painting and perspective work together in the process of building up a painting.

No. 6 sable

No. 4 sable

BOX GRID CONSTRUCTION

ONE OF THE MOST common ways in which artists transfer images from a sketchbook or photograph to a canvas is by putting a grid of squares over the original drawing, putting a grid to the same scale on the canvas, and then transferring the image by working from square to square (*see* p. 128). You can use a transparent grid or tracing paper.

Of course, this is essentially a two-dimensional exercise. But you can use the same principle in order to put objects into three-dimensional perspective by constructing a perspective box grid. On this page, the construction of a simple one-point perspective box grid is shown; on the right, you can see the stages in the construction of a two-point perspective box grid.

Using the grid

On the ground plane in perspective, you can construct a pavement of squares on a grid and add vertical sides having a grid made in the same way and to the same scale. Once the box has been constructed, you can put objects inside it. Their height and width is assessed in relation to the height and width of the grid squares. You may think this is useful only when you are placing rectangular objects within the grid, but in fact you can use it to set up an image of any shape.

Setting up the grid (*right*)

Set up a ground line and a horizon line. Place the center of vision at an appropriate point on the horizon line. Here, it is a little to the right of a line halfway across the rectangle. Draw a rectangular framework on the picture plane appropriate to the scale of the box you wish to set up. At regular intervals around the edges, mark points where the edges of the squares of the grid, which are at right angles to the picture plane, will intersect with the picture plane. Draw lines from the central vanishing point radiating out through the points marked on the picture plane. This will give you the very basic lines of your grid.

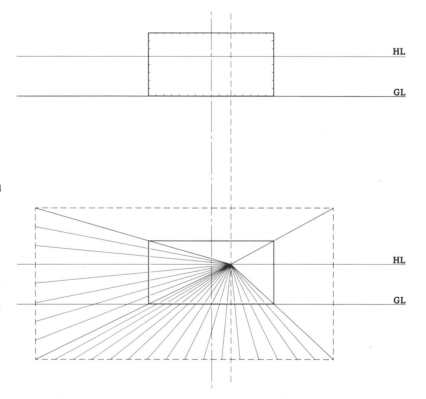

One-point grid

Set up a diagonal vanishing point on the right of the horizon line and draw a line from it through the bottom right-hand corner of the original rectangle. Where this line intersects the orthogonals you can draw the transversals, which should be parallel with the ground line and horizon line. The box can be extended backward or horizontally as far as is needed for the construction. Only two sides of the box are shown here, but the grid can be extended to the top, the back, the right-hand side and even internally.

Two-point perspective box grid

The following diagrams show the sequence for setting up a perspective box grid in two-point perspective, where the grid is at an angle to the picture plane. Any number of different objects can be placed in the composition using this method. More difficult or irregular shapes, such as curves or circles, can first be put in a square (*see* pp. 90-91) and then placed in the grid and scaled accordingly.

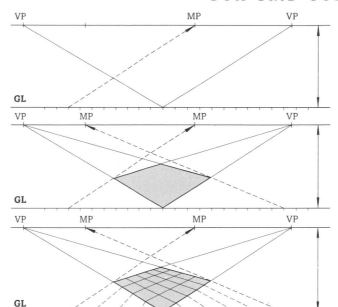

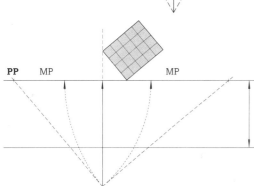

1 ▶ With the grid set at the appropriate angle, set up the station point in relation to the picture plane so that the grid comes within the 60-degree angle of vision.

2 ▲ Draw lines from the SP parallel with the sides of the grid to establish VPs for the grid. Mark MPs using the VPs as centers and a radius to the SP.

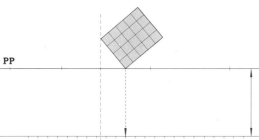

3 ▲ Assuming that you use the line on which you have set up the vanishing and measuring points as the horizon line, set up a ground line on the picture plane an appropriate distance below it and mark the widths of the squares of the grid to scale along this line. The distance between horizon line and ground line will determine the viewpoint of the finished grid.

4 ◀ Join the vanishing points to the ground line. In eight more squares, draw a line to the measuring point.

5 ◀ From the center, measure ten more squares and draw a line to the measuring point. The intersections of these lines mark the corners of the grid.

6 ◀ Having created the outline of the grid base, you can now draw the squares of the grid following the same method.

7 ◀ Draw a vertical measure or height line on the picture plane for the vertical face of the box grid.

8 ◀ Take lines back from the height line to the vanishing points. On the vertical faces of the box, establish the positions of the squares.

9 ◀ Once you have established a vertical and a horizontal plane, it is possible for you to start filling the grid with objects to scale.

10 ▶ The positions of the bases of the objects can be determined from a plan and drawn appropriately in perspective. The heights of objects can be determined in a similar way.

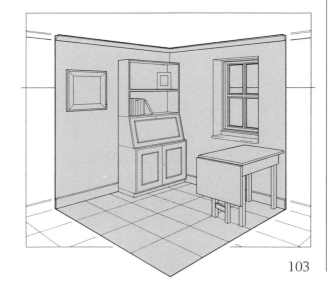

INCLINED PLANES

IT IS UNLIKELY that you will always be sketching vertical and horizontal planes on a level surface. Where you have to draw slopes, you can sometimes find the angles by completing the triangle of a vertical height line and a horizontal base line. More often you will need a vanishing point for the slope. Remember that all horizontal lines on a single vertical plane will recede to one vanishing point on the horizon. Any sloping lines on the same plane will recede to vanishing points on a vertical line above or below the vanishing point on the horizon.

THE PRINCIPLES FOR PLOTTING inclined planes can be used as the basis for drawing steps, as shown below. The diagrams on the right show a simple method for accurately plotting the intersection of sloping planes.

1 ▸ If you know the height of the vertical side of a right-angle triangle and the length of its horizontal base line, you can join these to create the third (sloping) side of the triangle. This is a basic step in creating sloping planes in perspective.

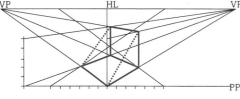

2 ▲ Put the vertical and horizontal planes of the triangle into perspective, using measurements on the picture plane and measuring points on the horizon line (*see* p. 103).

3 ▸ By carrying the lines of the slope in perspective back to their vanishing point, you will see that this point is situated on a vertical line above the vanishing point on the horizon.

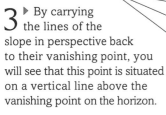

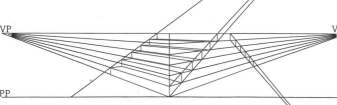

4 ▲ Set up a vertical on the picture plane with the height of steps marked off and take lines from these back to their vanishing points on the horizon. Choose an ascending vanishing point for the angle of the steps and draw lines from this to the top and bottom of the front step. The points where these lines bisect those already drawn show the position of the steps.

1 ▸ Draw the slope of the main roof by running lines back from the vanishing lines to an ascending vanishing point.

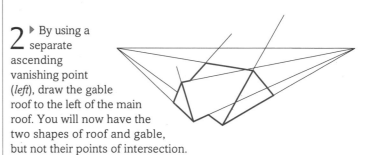

2 ▸ By using a separate ascending vanishing point (*left*), draw the gable roof to the left of the main roof. You will now have the two shapes of roof and gable, but not their points of intersection.

3 ▸ From the point X, drop a vertical to bisect the line AB. Join this point to the right VP. Where this cuts the bottom edge of the main roof, draw a line up the main roof using the ascending VP for the main roof until it intersects the point Y. This is the point at which the two sloping planes intersect. A line can now be drawn from this point to the intersection of the two roofs on the horizontal plane below.

Vanishing point for a set angle
Where you know the angle of a slope (X°), you may want to fix an ascending or descending vanishing point (A). First, establish a measuring point on the horizon line by describing an arc from the station point to the horizon line using the vanishing point on the horizon line as its center. A measured angle can be drawn to cut a vertical vanishing line from the vanishing point on the horizon at the ascending vanishing point for that particular angle.

Sloping street

You need to establish the angles of only two receding lines on a building to find the vanishing point on the horizon and, from there, the vertical axis for the ascending and descending vanishing points. Hold a pencil at arm's length in front of your subject or use tracing paper and a ruler with a photograph.

1 ▲ The vanishing point for the horizontals of windows of a house on sloping ground will be on the horizon line. But if you continue the line where the wall of the house meets the sloping ground, it will extend to a vanishing point immediately below that for the window because window and wall are on the same vertical plane.

2 ▶ As the front walls become more visible to the right, the angles of the cottages in relation to the picture plane change. Hence the vanishing point for horizontal features, such as the windows, doors, and roof line, moves to the right along the horizon line. The descending vanishing points also change with the angle of the cottages, but remain on a vertical axis below each of the vanishing points on the horizon.

View from a hill

The solid perspective structure underlying the oil painting gives strength to the image and, together with the warm orange-browns and ochres of the buildings, leads the eye from the near foreground through to the cooler greens and blues of the far distance. The strong sunlight and deep shadows emphasize the structure and tone of the trees on the right. They serve compositionally to prevent the row of cottages from sliding off the right-hand side of the painting.

The texture of the rough oil brush strokes used here conveys the layered structure of the clay roof tiling.

Details on the houses are put in with single strokes of thin color, following the basic perspective structure.

Noel McCready

105

PLANS & ELEVATIONS

BY USING THE PROJECTION METHOD, simple plans and elevations can be turned into complex two-point perspective compositions. The initial stages establish the angle of view required and its size. Subsequent stages involve transferring the points of intersection with the picture plane from a plan to a separate perspective drawing. Keeping the perspective drawing separate from the plan enables you to draw it directly onto your painting surface.

Elevations

Plan

1 ◀ Though it relates to a particular style of architecture, this house exists only in the artist's mind. It is not always necessary to rely on things we see. We can invent hypothetical plans and elevations and incorporate them as three-dimensional images into our paintings.

2 ▶ First, you need to decide from which angle you wish to view the building. From the three angles of 60 degrees shown here, the central one would be too two-dimensional and the one on the right, though similar to that on the left, would present a less interesting view of the veranda.

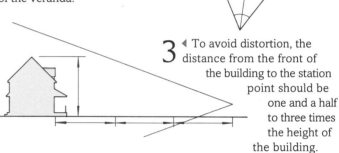

3 ◀ To avoid distortion, the distance from the front of the building to the station point should be one and a half to three times the height of the building.

Behind the picture plane

The position of the plan relative to the picture plane will determine the size of the image. In the drawing on the left, the house has been positioned behind the picture plane, with its front corner touching it. Lines are projected from the plan to the picture plane via each side of the house as shown. The width of the house as it would appear on the perspective drawing is shown between the two arrows.

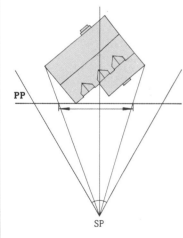

In front of the picture plane

In the drawing on the right, an alternative positioning of the plan is suggested from that drawn on the rest of these pages. The house is positioned so that most of the building stands in front of the picture plane. Constructed to the same scale, this drawing would produce a larger house than the finished drawing on the opposite page.

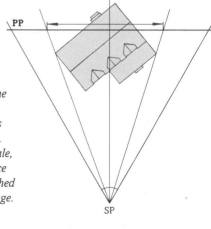

4 ▶ Placing the house behind the picture plane, you will need to establish two vanishing points for the sides of the building. Draw lines back from the station point parallel with the sides of the building. These will cut the picture plane on each side of the building at the vanishing points.

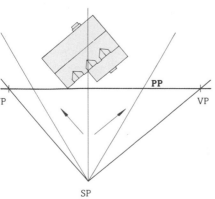

5 ▶ The position of the verticals of the building on the perspective drawing is determined by running lines from the station point to principal points on the plan (the corners of the building, the position of windows, etc.). You should mark the intersection of these lines on the picture plane.

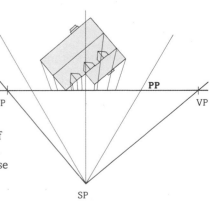

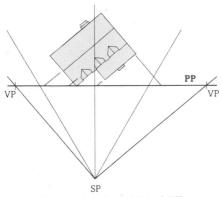

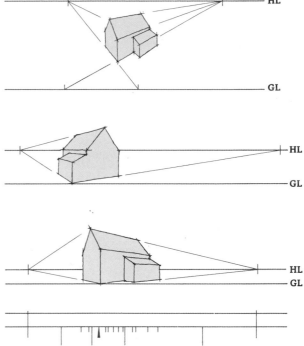

High viewpoint

A high viewpoint can give an interesting aerial view and can be particularly useful in an overview of several blocks, but the building itself may look less imposing.

Middle viewpoint

To start the perspective drawing, you need to draw only the ground line and the horizon line. Here, the horizon line lies across the eaves of the house, which may be confusing.

Low viewpoint

This is a more human view in that the distance between the horizon line and the ground line is equivalent to the height of a human being drawn to scale.

6 ▲ To establish the height of different points on the building, height lines will be drawn onto the picture plane. Mark the position of these height lines by extending lines from the principal axes of the building behind the picture plane to touch it at the appropriate position.

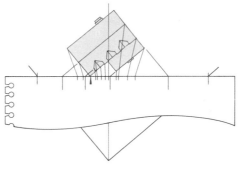

7 ▶ You will have marked the vanishing points and all the principal points where the vertical lines of the building and the height lines intersect with the picture plane. Now transfer these to a piece of paper as shown, so that when you set up the perspective drawing you do not need to draw the plan as well.

8 ▲ Transfer the reference points from the piece of paper to the ground line in the perspective drawing. These are the corresponding points on the picture plane for different elements in the composition and will be the points from which you draw up your verticals.

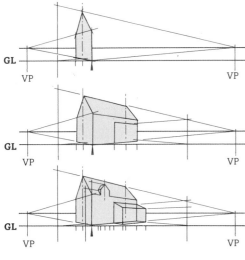

9 ◀ Establish height lines and the edges of the building by raising verticals from points on the ground line.

10 ◀ Draw lines from points on the height lines back to the relevant vanishing points to show the horizontal lines of the building.

11 ◀ Gradually build up details by working in a similar way from points on the ground line.

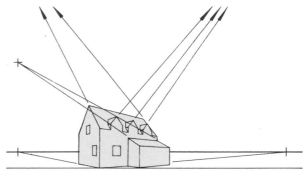

12 ▲ The vanishing points for the sloping planes of the roofs can be found on a vertical axis from each of the vanishing points on the horizon. But it is not necessary to use these here, since the slopes can be drawn by completing the third side of a triangle.

13 ◀ The finished drawing emerges with all its detail complete. Any element can be measured from the picture plane, taken back into the drawing and then worked up.

THREE-POINT PERSPECTIVE

WHEN WE TAKE photographs of buildings from close up, we see that the vertical sides of the buildings seem to lean in toward the middle of the picture from the vertical edge of the photograph. This is because they are subject to the laws of perspective like any other plane receding from our view. The addition of a third vanishing point in the vertical plane takes account of the convergence in the vertical sides of a tall building as well as that on the horizontal plane. It comes into play when we are looking up at a building or conversely looking down on a scene – in other words when the picture plane is tipped, or at an angle to the vertical.

Three-point projection

Three-point projection for plans and elevations is more complex than that for one- or two-point perspective. It can involve the incorporation of an inclined picture plane set at the correct angle to the ground plane. Some methods require a special plan of the object as seen from the inclined angle. This is prepared by projection from a tilted elevation.

Worm's-eye view

In this drawing, the three-point perspective is purposely exaggerated. The height of the buildings and the insignificant scale of the viewer are emphasized by placing the high vanishing point lower than it might be. The dramatic effect is like powerful uplighting along the vertical lines of the buildings.

Bird's-eye view

In the reverse of the drawing above, great plunging perspectives are produced by adopting a similarly dramatic viewpoint, but, in this case, looking down. So here the vertical vanishing point is located at the bottom of the drawing. An aerial view like this is considerably more common in the twentieth century and we are now quite accustomed to seeing such images taken from helicopters and airplanes. But there is also a particular feel to this kind of perspective that links it to the great romantic landscapes of the early decades of the nineteenth century (see p. 79). Generally, such steep views are too dramatic for any but the most imposing compositions. It is a quality which has been picked up in film and animation rather than in painting. In spite of this, some elements of three-point perspective are required in all but the simplest constructions, so it is therefore wise to consider this when establishing your basic structure.

Mountain landscape

As with any style of perspective drawing, the three-point system gives a particular appearance to an image. Artists use the system when looking down on a subject in order to draw the eye right into the center of the composition. When looking up, it creates an awesome sense of scale. This view of an imaginary landscape seen from a cliff top gives a sense of the whole scene opening out from a central core, like the petals of a flower. The effect is exaggerated by a vertical vanishing point that manages to stay within the borders of the composition. The images here show how three-point perspective can be adapted to suit the requirements of the artist's composition.

1 ▶ The three vanishing points can be set at the extremities of the composition, with the two horizontal vanishing points at the top on the horizon line and the vertical vanishing point at the bottom in the middle. The construction of the relatively simple village buildings is straightforward, using the intersections of lines from all three vanishing points to form the basis of the structures.

2 ◀ Block in the main areas of tone and color with an opaque acrylic. This creates an underpainting on which to build up form and color. Note the depth of tone used in the foreground. This acts to separate it from the distant view. Planes and levels are distinguished by different base colors. The warm and cool red roofs of the buildings are set up in complementary contrast to the blues and greens of the landscape.

The buildings are painted at angles to the vertical and appear to lean out of the center of the painting.

The vertiginous viewpoint of the artist is conveyed by the depiction of the cliff faces, which run at diagonals to the ground line.

Finished composition
During the subsequent stages of painting, the texture of the landscape itself is enriched and more detail is applied to the buildings. The angle and direction of light over the landscape is established, with shadows cast from the walls, trees, and buildings. Where the distant hills are in shadow, they are deepened in tone: the total effect is to make the viewer focus on the circular sunlit area at the center of the composition.

Julian Bray

109

THREE-POINT PAINTING

WHEN YOU LOOK UP AT a very tall building, or when you are standing so close to a smaller building that you have to look up to take it in, the effect of vertical convergence is considerably accentuated. Here, the artist has used a photographic reference, but at such a close range he has been unable to fit the subject in one shot and has combined four photos to provide information for a three-point perspective pencil sketch. The paradox with three-point perspective is that on the paper or canvas, the effect of the subject receding into the sky – away from the viewer – generates a sense of distance from the image. In reality, the viewer is particularly aware of the proximity of the building.

A montage of the photographs used for reference. The different lighting in each photograph is noticeable

Vanishing points
The two horizontal vanishing points are relatively close together on this narrow building. But the vertical vanishing point is far above the edge of the paper.

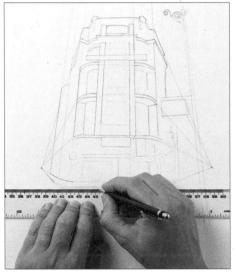

1 ▲ Making a perspective drawing of the image with a ruler and pencil creates a clear structure and a clean image on which to build up the acrylic washes.

2 ◀ A pale wash of Payne's Gray and Phthalo Blue around the top of the building gives an indication of the sky and lessens the stark contrast with the white of the paper, creating a sense of depth.

3 ▲ Float a wash down through the building, Phthalo Blue at the top, graduating to Yellow Ochre at the base. This gives an underlying tone on which the areas of shadow can be interposed.

Working tonally
By using very watery acrylic washes you can mimic the effects of watercolor. Recesses fall back as heavier tones are put in, while unpainted or lightly painted areas shine through, pulling these elements forward.

Faint washes of Burnt Sienna and Phthalo Blue bring the edges of the building forward.

Throughout this early stage the brush is kept very wet and colors remain largely unmixed.

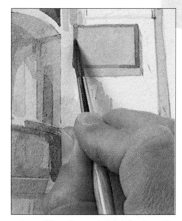

Acrylics

Deep Brilliant Red

Raw Sienna

Yellow Ochre

Payne's Gray

Olive Green

Phthalo Blue

Cerulean Blue

French Ultramarine

4 ▲ Use the point of the brush to paint a thin border of Raw Sienna around the street sign on the lamppost, in order to give it definition and bring it to the front of the composition.

5 ▶ The cool crimson red band of the sign is unmixed with other colors and works well as a bridge between the blue above it and the blue-gray underneath.

6 ◀ Build up detail in the storefront by adding more defined areas of wash. Although tones are dark in this area, their strength and subtlety arises from a buildup of thin washes rather than mixing a single dark tone.

7 ▶ Indicate the buildings to the right of the lamppost with firm vertical strokes of a flat bristle brush in a wash of Phthalo Blue. Use a mix of Titanium White and Phthalo Blue to paint in the sky.

8 ▶ Give the sky some body by using well-diluted Titanium White with a flat bristle brush. Do not worry about rendering clouds or sky accurately; if you keep the brush sufficiently wet, loose washes will bleed into one another, giving a convincing result. Be sure to allow the edge of the building and the lamppost to dry before applying the subsequent washes for the sky.

9 ▲ Define the forms of the distant buildings with a pale wash of Phthalo Blue. Details of the buildings on the right can be painted in with Burnt Sienna. Colors here must be painted subtly because paler washes will give a sense of distance. You should paint the more distant elements on this plane quite loosely; the viewer's perception of the architecture will lose detail as it recedes.

10 ◀ Try to establish a sense of perspective in the progressive diminution of detail, from the part of the building closest to the viewer to that which is farthest away. The nearer side of the windows can be painted in Raw Sienna, while the overall outline of the frame can be rendered in a paler wash of the same color. Architectural elements such as windows and doors are ideal for conveying a sense of recession and depth. Many of these features can be suggested with a single stroke.

11 ▲ Having established where the sun is in relation to the subject (here, it comes from the right), paint the shadows of the buildings on the right of the picture with the bristle brush using bold strokes of Burnt Sienna. Paint carefully around the lamppost in order to keep its pale shape against the brown background shadow. The foreground can be painted in with a wash of Yellow Ochre followed by a wash of Titanium White, the latter to convey the street's glaring white light.

12 ◄ With the point of the soft sable brush, using a thin mix of Cerulean Blue and Titanium White, sketch in the broad outlines of the man wheeling the cart. Use the vanishing points established for the horizontal lines of the building to work out the perspective of the cart. These faint lines can later be painted over.

13 ▲ The two foreground figures lead our eye into the space of the painting. Paint them in sufficient detail for them to be credible but do not overwork them. The painting needs to have an overall consistency of style. The shadows of man and cart have been painted in Burnt Sienna mixed with the white and yellow ground.

Corner building in Istanbul

The finished painting retains a fresh looseness of style with enough detail to establish a real sense of place. The perspective works well in the horizontal plane, where the man wheeling the cart leads the eye directly to the figures walking toward the vanishing point on the right-hand side of the image. There is a fine sense of space and light here. But it also works well in the vertical plane with the eye being led up the painting by the converging vertical sides of the building and then back down to the ground plane via the lamppost.

A mixture of Titanium White and Ultramarine Blue has been used to paint in the rest of the sky.

The two sides of the painting form an energetic interplay of light and shade.

The shadow of the man and cart, placed securely in the center of the large expanse of white road, provides a solid link with the ground plane.

Julian Bray

Apparently towering above the building itself, the lamppost indicates that the plane of the artist's viewpoint is tilted.

The angle of the cart draws the eye up to the street on the right.

The artist has felt confident to reinterpret his source. The car and some of the figures have been dropped to give the building greater prominence.

Materials

Mechanical pencil, 0.5 lead

No. 6 sable

No. 4 short flat bristle

GALLERY OF LANDSCAPE & ARCHITECTURE

IN THE DEPICTION of both landscape and architecture, an interesting viewpoint will change the whole nature of the composition. The tilted picture plane of Michael Smith's painting leads the eye up to the vertical convergence in the architecture, while the tilted-down picture plane of the Carline painting brings the horizon line close to the top edge of the image. All the images share a preoccupation with the depiction of space, whether in the panoramic exterior of David Prentice's work or the atmospheric interior of the Johnson painting. The latter is a beautiful example of two-point angular perspective.

Michael Smith, *Expo '92*, *4 x 6 ft (1.22 x 1.83 m)*
The vast awning that sweeps across this composition conveys a strong sense of space and atmosphere. It both transmits and reflects the bright Mediterranean light of Seville and emphasizes the low horizon, allowing us to focus on a skyline of plunging perspectives. An illusion of depth is created, an effect echoed in the cool gray and blue tones of the oil paint.

Sydney Carline, *The Destruction of an Austrian Machine in the Gorge of the Brenta Valley, Italy, 1918*, *30 x 36 in (76.2 x 91.4 cm)*
An important component in our understanding of perspective is the artist's ability to define space. Here, Carline articulates the volume of space within and above the landscape by the airplanes that circle around each other in the spaces between the distant landforms.

A sense of depth is created by painting the planes against contrasting grounds.

The peace of the scene is about to be shattered as the white plane is circled by its three red opponents.

Ben Johnson, *The Unattended Moment,* *6 ft x 7 ft 11 in (1.84 x 2.43 m)*
Johnson is outstanding among contemporary painters in his ability to
create atmosphere and meaning within images of uninhabited architectural
spaces. He uses complex preliminary work on a computer, and photo-
chemical methods to transcribe the perspective onto canvas. Here, the
surface of the pool is flat, mirrorlike, and undisturbed by any hint of
moving air. It is as if time has been suspended: the light takes on a living
dimension, filling voids, caressing surfaces, and inviting contemplation.

David Prentice, *Woman and Child,*
Worcester Beacon, Malvern,
22 x 33 in (56 x 84 cm)
In a landscape painting, it can be difficult to
establish the kind of scale needed to give the
viewer a real sense of the breadth or enormity
of the subject depicted. Here, the artist has
judiciously placed the path in perspective,
winding down the hill in the distance,
giving a sense of the journey of the two
foreground figures. Combined with the scale of
the buildings, this draws us into the painting
and provides a measure by which the size of
the hill may be judged. In the far distance
beyond the hill, the flat landscape continues
in progressively cooler tones to the horizon.

REFLECTIONS

THE INCLUSION OF SOME FORM OF REFLECTION in your painting can add a further dimension. The angle of the reflected image to the reflected surface will be the same as that of the object itself. In a plan, you can see that the distance from any point on the image to the reflective surface is equal to the distance from the same point in the reflection to the reflective surface. This is true of reflections both in glass and in water.

ABOVE, A VASE of flowers is placed on a horizontal mirror with vertical mirrors at 90 degrees. A ray of light from a corner of the vase, traveling on a line parallel to the picture plane to the mirror on the right, strikes the mirror at an angle of 45 degrees and is reflected at the same angle (*see* right).

Deceptive mirrors

You might think that the front faces of all the vases are the same, but in fact the front face of the right-hand vase is the (concealed) side face of the central (actual) vase. Similarly the front of the left-hand vase is the left side of the actual vase.

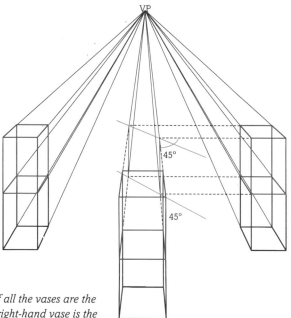

1 ▲ With the basic rules of reflections in mind, it is easier to understand the construction of an image and to sketch the preliminary structure for a painting. Keep pencil lines light so they can be erased later.

2 ▲ For the main areas of shadow within the broad pencil outlines, mix a single color and, with a soft hair brush, apply thin washes to serve as the underpainting.

3 ▶ Build up the tones and colors using thin washes. In order to keep the colors clean, ensure that the foliage is dry before painting in the flowers.

WHEN YOU ARE OUT sketching, you are more likely to come across reflections in water that are broken up by a surface that is disturbed by waves or wind, than to find clear reflections on completely smooth water. A reflection on disturbed water shows a fragmented image. The surface still acts like a mirror, so the angle of incidence equals the angle of reflection. As the water is disturbed, it reflects in many directions according to the angle of its surface. This can be seen in the diagram (*right*), where the viewer sees the sky reflected from one part of the wave and the building from another.

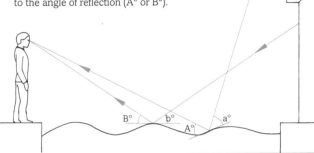

RIPPLE EFFECT

The uneven surface of rippled water creates a fragmented image. This is caused by the water reflecting different angles of the surrounding area. Here, the peak of the ripple reflects the side of the building while the trough reflects the sky, creating a striped effect on the water. Again, the angle of incidence (a° or b°) is equal to the angle of reflection (A° or B°).

Canal view, Venice (*left*)

In this characteristic view of a Venetian canal, the artist has used a watery acrylic wash to mimic the effects of watercolor. In order to create the ragged horizontal ripples, the brush is kept quite wet, as in watercolor technique. This allows the color to follow its natural course, giving the painting a relaxed, spontaneous feel. You can consider the perspective structure underlying the image as continuing within the reflection as if nothing on the surface of the water is affecting it. Then adapt the surface according to the nature of the ripples. Bear in mind that in Venice the movement of the water is often reflected on the sides of the buildings themselves.

Photo reference (*below left*)

The buildings are seen from an oblique angle. This has the effect of accentuating the verticals of the edges, windows, and doors of the buildings. The verticals are counterpointed by the ripples in the water, which give a horizontal look to the reflections.

Gondola in open water (*far right*)

On a smooth surface, the height of the gondola from the surface of the water would be reflected to an equivalent depth. The prow of the boat is raised well above the level of the water, so you would need to measure horizontally from where the boat actually touches the water toward the end of the prow and intersect with a vertical dropped from the prow. This vertical distance would need to be doubled to establish the depth of the prow in reflection. The water is undulating and the edges of the reflection are fluid.

Gondola at dockside (*right*)

The boats surrounding the gondola shown here have been omitted from the painting (*far right*). The use of thick acrylic in the painting was suggested by the circles of reflected light in the photograph and mimic the effects of oil.

SUNLIGHT & SHADOWS

FOR THE PURPOSES of perspective, we assume that the sun's rays are parallel, since the light source is so far away. When dealing with shadows cast by the sun, you must first establish whether the sun is in front of you, behind, or at the side. If at the side, to establish the length of the shadow, you follow the angle of the sun's rays through the top or corners of the object to the ground. This is the case whether the sun is to the left or right, and whatever its angle to the vertical. When the sun is in front, shadows appear to widen as they get closer to you.

The sun behind makes shadows appear to get smaller as they recede. In the latter two cases, establish the vanishing point for the sun's rays and the vanishing point for the sun's shadows. These are always on the same axis.

Achieving three-dimensions with light and shade

It is important to establish the direction of the light in order to understand how and where shadows are cast. On plans and elevations, architects often project rays of light at 45 degrees to the horizontal from top left to bottom right in elevation, and from bottom left to top right in plan.

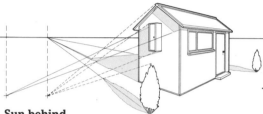

Sun behind
The vanishing point for the shadows lies on the horizon on a vertical line directly above the vanishing point for the sun's parallel rays, which appear to converge.

Sun to the side
When the sun is at the side, assess the angle of its rays and draw parallel lines from the topmost points of the objects to the ground plane, where the lengths of the shadows can be set. A pencil held at arm's length can easily establish the angle.

Sun in front
When the sun is up in front of you, the vanishing point for the sun's rays (the sun itself) is always above the horizon. The vanishing point for the sun's shadows cast on a horizontal ground plane is on the horizon line on a vertical below the vanishing point for the sun's rays.

Study in natural light

The sun is in front of the viewer around 30 degrees to the left; it is low in the sky, so it casts long shadows. The vanishing point for the shadows is just to the left of the top left corner of the image so the vanishing lines of the shadows all converge to that point.

Pencil study
In this vigorous pencil study, the artist explores the effects of light and shade monochromatically. The expressive tonal shading identifies areas in shadow and gives them depth and weight, making them almost as tangible as the chairs, table, and shrubs. By contrast, it also emphasizes the brightness of the sunlit areas.

1 ◀ In a painting that concentrates, as this does, on the effects of light and shade, it makes sense to define roughly the areas in shadow at a preliminary stage using a single color. As the sunlit areas will be predominantly yellow, underpaint the shadows in blue. This makes for a good color contrast. It also allows you to concentrate on getting the form and tone right before focusing on color. It is tempting not to do any more to a painting at this stage where all the main components of the image have been established with economy and fluent brushwork.

2 ▶ Flood the foreground with light by loosely painting in an overall warm yellow. This color is complemented by the various tones of purple in the table, the shrubbery, and the trunk of the tree. The depth of tone in the shadows is increased by the addition of a deep, cool green. This emphasizes the idea of the light establishing a pattern, which is every bit as important as the objects. The thin, cool red of the tubular steel chairs is set up as a contrast to the green foliage, while the pale shadows on the canvas seats and seat backs can be sketched in pale lilac.

Tea in the Garden

By careful reworking, the image moves from a diagrammatic-looking underpainting, where the tonal contrasts remain harsh, to a more fully resolved work with a richer, softer look. With the addition of sunlit foliage above the table and the softening and blending at the junction between sunlit areas and areas of shadow on the ground, the painting now has a more inviting atmosphere. It retains a relaxed spontaneity, held together by a strong perspective structure.

The cool lilac shadow on the seat complements the warmer yellow colors.

The tubular structure of the chair produces strong areas of negative space.

The sunlight on the table and on the foliage above lifts the light off the single plane of the ground, creating a sense of space between the table and grass.

Toward the left edge, the yellows become more orange-red, thus helping to frame the image.

Achieving three dimensions

When painting or drawing outside, your awareness of the position of the sun as outlined above will enable you to achieve an overall consistency in the orientation of shadows. This gives your painting real credibility. Above all, it is the effects of light and shade that give a painting the illusion of three dimensions. Bear in mind that there is not always a bright light source such as the sun on a clear day and that when the weather is overcast, for example, the effects described here are much more muted and the tonal contrast more subtle.

Sue Sareen

119

Preparatory studies
Make a few preliminary studies of parts of the composition before tackling the image as a whole.

ARTIFICIAL LIGHT

THE PERSPECTIVE OF SHADOWS cast from a single light source, such as a candle, is relatively straightforward. Light radiates in all directions from the source and the shadows cast by objects placed all around the light source converge at a vanishing point directly below that light source on the ground plane. (The ground plane is the vanishing point for shadows.) You can establish the length of the shadows by projecting lines from the light source itself via the top of the object to the ground plane. For an image that needs to express a warm intimate scene, such as this still life, pastel on warm orange-brown paper is a good choice of medium. Although the image is effectively tonal, the use of adjacent warm color harmonies fill it with life.

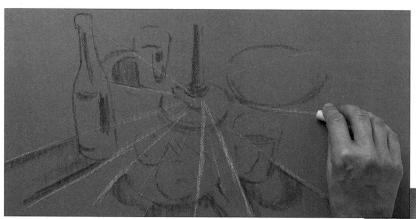

1 ▲ Draw the shapes of the objects using a single color. From this close position, with a wide angle of view, the vertical objects at the edges, such as the bottle, appear to lean outwards. Sketch a guide to the edges of the shadows like the spokes of a wheel.

ARTIFICIAL LIGHT

Unlike natural daylight, in the case of artificial light the light source is smaller than the subject and will cast shadows that flare from the base of the source. This is because the light source is smaller than the object that casts the shadow.

Test the truth of these rules with your own still life. In setting it up, try to create a composition and a viewpoint that gives its component parts clarity, allowing you to see clearly what is going on.

The edges of the shadows can be determined by lines taken from the light source past the top of the object to the ground plane. The vanishing point for the shadows is at the base of the candle.

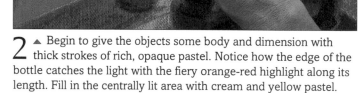

2 ▲ Begin to give the objects some body and dimension with thick strokes of rich, opaque pastel. Notice how the edge of the bottle catches the light with the fiery orange-red highlight along its length. Fill in the centrally lit area with cream and yellow pastel.

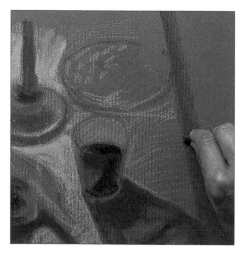

3 ◀ Draw the shape of the reflection in the wine glass and establish the tonal contrast between the cool dark brown and the warm bright red. Sketch in the edge of the cloth to act as a perspective framing device for the image. The red streak of the candle also contrasts well with the bright-toned central area of the tablecloth.

5 ◀ Deepen and extend the shadows on the bottle edge and the shadow on the table using the dark brown pastel. With the same pastel give definition to the rim of the glass, its shadow, and base. Similarly, heighten the contrast in the tones of the candle holder and candle and add highlights with light yellow.

4 ▲ Build up the shapes of the apples with broad tonal areas. Use the deepest brown for the base and bottom edges and for the indented top. The edges are drawn with a warm rich red similar to that used for the bottle and glasses. Be careful to avoid scuffing with your hand the colors you have already applied, especially in the highlighted areas.

6 ◀ Reestablish the pure white of the candle flame. This is the brightest area and a point of focus for the viewer; it contains the image and holds it together. Notice how the lighter yellows in the center are modified by the addition of this bright tone.

7 ▲ Add black to the edges of the glasses and bottle and retouch the white highlights. You should add the brightest and darkest tones at the end. This is especially true of pastel, where the blending of colors during drawing may neutralize tonal contrasts.

Still life with candle
The finished drawing has a charm and lack of pretension that makes it very accessible. The texture of the pastel on the paper is very evident and adds to the work's character.

When looking at an image, you can half-close your eyes to judge if the variation in tones is credible.

A streak of lighter tone in the shadow of the bottle gives a sense of the container's transparency.

A rather cold, crisp photograph has been transformed into a warmer image by the choice of medium and color.

Pastels

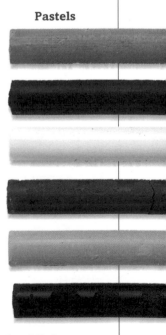

Jane Gifford

GALLERY OF SHADOWS & REFLECTIONS

THE ACCURATE DEPICTION of shadows gives credibility to the three-dimensional forms that we are painting and locates them within a particular space. The correct projection of shadows is therefore a crucial component in perspective. The nature and position of the light source illuminating our subject and the nature of the surface on which the light falls will determine how the light is perceived.

Edgar Degas, *Jockeys at the Stands,* c.1866, *18 x 24 in (46 x 61 cm) This painting shows how accurate shadows can define a setting and the nature of the surface on which they fall. The shadows on the track recede to a vanishing point on the horizon line immediately below the sun.*

Ian Cook, *Mission House, Georgia,* *24 x 20 in (61 x 51 cm) Strong tonal contrasts and the use of complementary colors in this painting give a clearly three-dimensional image of the chapel and trees. The artist has also incorporated warm and cool shadows: the warm orange hues of the field contrast with the blue shadows of the chapel. The long shadow cast by the spire suggests that it is either early morning or late afternooon.*

In this detail, rich, overhanging foliage bends heavily toward the water. The boughs are thick with paint as if to emphasize the textural contrast with the smooth, still water.

Ben Levene, RA, *Reverse Mirror Image with Japanese Vase,* *34 x 38 in (86 x 97 cm)*
Setting up a mirror behind a subject, as Levene has done here, opens out the space, deepens the background, and allows the artist to give a 360-degree view of the objects being depicted. This is apparent in the angle of the human figures reflected from the vase. The effect gives the painting a certain decorousness, as if the objects are politely holding their partners in a rather formal dance.

William Bowyer, RA, *The Golden Tree,* *48 x 48 in (122 x 122 cm)*
On still water, reflections are easy to work out. When a tree is set back from the water's edge, as it is here, try imagining the level water continuing through the bank to the point at which it would meet the tree trunk if the bank were not there. You measure up to the top of the tree from that point and then mark the same distance down for the extent of the reflection.

Claude Monet, *The Red Boats,* **c.1875,**
21½ x 25½ in (55 x 65 cm)
Here, the bright lines of the masts extend, by reflection, into the water, providing a vertical structure for the horizontal dashes of color.

In contrast to the William Bowyer painting above, here the surface of the water is disturbed. The reflection is broken up into a myriad of tiny mirrors at different angles that reflect different colors – greens, blues, and yellows – according to the slope of the ripples.

123

MODERN DEVICES

Any movement of the easel when using a projector will put the image out of alignment.

OVER THE CENTURIES there has been a wide range of devices to enable artists to draw images in perspective. These have included simple drawing frames and finders, including those with grids in wire, nylon, or thread. These remain useful tools for getting the perspective right on location. Another helpful device is the reducing glass. This looks like a magnifying glass, but gives a miniature image of the scene seen through it. The camera obscura and the camera lucida (*see* p. 465) were used in the past to project the image of a scene onto the canvas. They have now largely been replaced by the slide projector. Artists often take photographic slides of subjects that they want to paint and use these for reference.

1 ◀ The standard lens in cheap cameras is a relatively wide-angle one that does not allow you to zoom in as your eye can. For reference purposes, use a camera with a lens of variable focal length, from 28mm (wide-angle) to 260mm (telephoto), for example. This allows you to focus on whichever part of the scene you wish to include.

2 ▶ You will have to get used to working in subdued lighting in order to draw an image using the slide projector. You need enough ambient light to allow you to see what your pencil or charcoal is doing on the canvas, but not so much that you cannot see the projected image. Make sure that the slide projector is focused squarely on the canvas or paper to avoid any distortion of the image.

3 ▲ Here, the one-point perspective is relatively straightforward, yet there are many architectural details that are simply easier to draw by using a projector. Draw just enough detail to allow you to develop the painting in the way you want. Since your slide remains in the projector for some time as you draw, the slide projector should incorporate an electric fan in order to stay relatively cool.

Enlarging your image
If you use a slide projector with a lens of variable focal length, you can make the image bigger or smaller by rotating the lens rather than by moving the canvas forward or back, which can be rather awkward. Using a slide projector in this way, you can crop the image and establish the composition that suits your ideas for the painting. You can use any medium for capturing the essential components of an image. Here, the image is being drawn monochromatically on a canvas using a synthetic brush and thick acrylic paint.

Computer-generated images

There is now a widely available selection of computer software that allows you to draw plans and elevations and put them into whatever kind of perspective projection you choose. You can look at the resulting three-dimensional image from any angle, from close up or far away. This can be done without having to go through the laborious task of drawing everything with a pencil and set square.

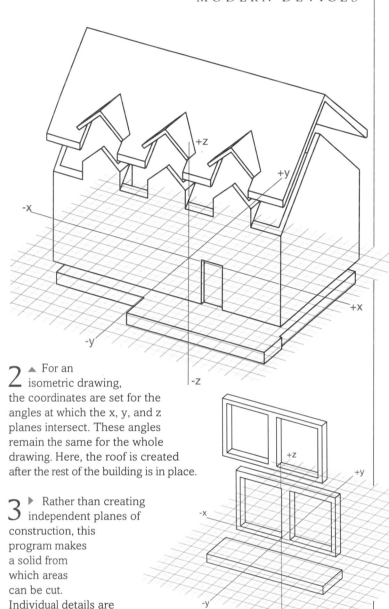

1 ▲ The computer can scan existing plans or create them from simple instructions. Here, the plan, as well as front and side elevations that are drawn to scale, are all the computer needs to set up the perspective model.

2 ▲ For an isometric drawing, the coordinates are set for the angles at which the x, y, and z planes intersect. These angles remain the same for the whole drawing. Here, the roof is created after the rest of the building is in place.

3 ▶ Rather than creating independent planes of construction, this program makes a solid from which areas can be cut. Individual details are constructed separately and slotted into holes cut for them.

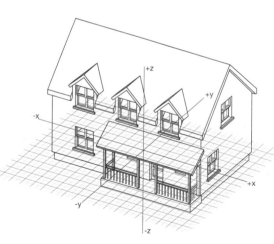

4 ▲ The completed isometric projection gives a clear image of the structure of the building in three dimensions. This projection is in perfect scale and can be used by the artist or architect to take measurements not given on the plan and elevations.

5 ▶ By pressing one command, the isometric building is rendered into linear perspective. The image can now be rotated and viewed from any angle, from close up (with the attendant distortion) or from farther away.

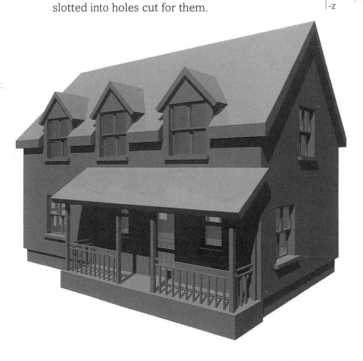

GALLERY OF PERSPECTIVE DEVICES

THERE IS A LONG TRADITION of artists using a wide range of mechanical or electronic devices as an aid to accurate representation, from a cardboard viewfinder to complex computer-generated methods. The accuracy of architectural detail in Canaletto's work and recent research into that of Vermeer indicate the use of the camera obscura. Both David Hockney and Gerhard Richter are among the many contemporary artists to have used slide projectors and other projection equipment.

Johannes Vermeer, *Woman Writing a Letter and her Maid,* 1671, *28½ x 23½ in (72.2 x 59.5 cm)*
Vermeer may not have needed a camera obscura for the simple one-point construction that underlies this painting. But the perfect placing of the characters, the heightening of the luminous contrasts, the economy of the painting style, coupled with the versimilitude, all point to the use of such a device.

Antonio Canaletto, *Venice: Piazza San Marco and the Colonnade of the Procuratie Nuove,* c.1756, *18 x 15 in (46 x 38 cm)*
In this wide-angle view of the Piazza San Marco, the tiny impasto touches of light opaque color showing the highlights are slightly overexaggerated, as though seen through the lens of a camera obscura.

The lines of the wall and those of the window to the left converge to a vanishing point at the center of vision where the woman's head is bowed as she writes the letter.

David Hockney, *Portrait of an Artist (Pool with Two Figures),* **1972,**
7 ft x 10 ft (2.13 m x 3.05 m)
Hockney is a prolific photographer. He has made a number of paintings where elements from different photographs are incorporated in a single unified composition. The subject here was suggested by two photographs lying on the floor of Hockney's studio in such a way that the standing figure seemed to be looking at the swimmer. The film A Bigger Splash *featured Hockney working on this painting and included a number of photographs of the swimmer to which the painter was able to refer. It showed how the photograph of the standing figure was projected onto the canvas so that Hockney could make an accurate sketch. The resulting painting has a remarkable clarity and freshness, with its contrast between the light and air of the hills and the clear blue water of the pool. The slope of the pool is unnerving, for the central vanishing point is in the sky at the top edge of the painting.*

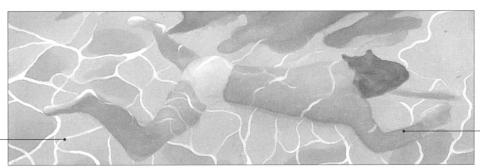

The pool is painted in transparent acrylic washes to give a watery look. The border of the pool is painted opaquely to emphasize its solidity.

The photograph of the underwater swimmer was taken in Hollywood in 1966. The reference has enabled Hockney to give an accurate image of the underwater distortion of the figure.

Gerhard Richter, *Meadow,* **1987,**
32 x 48 in (82 x 122 cm)
Richter's landscape oil paintings are transcriptions of photographs. They are initially sketched by projecting a slide onto the canvas. This allows the artist to stay close to the form of the original image. But in painting these images, Richter completely transforms them, painstakingly echoing the blurred edge of a form by the subtle blending of oil color. Oil is, of course, the one painting medium that stays wet for long enough to manipulate in this way. These strange landscapes have a self-contained quality – a kind of heartlessness that is nonetheless compelling.

ANAMORPHOSIS

Photo reference
By working from a photograph and on a flat surface, you can trace a grid more easily than by drawing from reality.

ANAMORPHIC PROJECTION is merely a reversal of Alberti's method of putting a grid into perspective (*see* p. 88). By using a simple grid system, the artist is able to create a highly distorted image of an object, which, when seen from an oblique angle, reverts to its original appearance. Anamorphosis has been popular for centuries as a means of concealing certain kinds of imagery from the uninitiated, of putting hidden messages into paintings and drawings, or simply to point out the very illusionistic nature of painting itself. Mastering the art of anamorphosis is a good introduction to the use of distortion, showing how perspective can be manipulated to achieve the painted image you require.

Other forms of perspective distortion

During the Renaissance, awareness of the illusionistic effects of perspective led to the use of alternative forms, such as accelerated perspective, in architecture and painting. Instead of being built parallel to each other, rows of columns on either side of a corridor might actually be built to converge, making the corridor appear longer than it is. The effects of counter perspective were well known to the ancient Greeks. Lettering on the side of a building is carved to a larger scale higher up than that carved lower down, if both are to be seen from the ground at the same size.

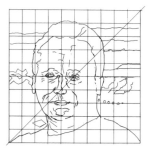

1 ▲ Construct a grid over your photograph and then transfer this image to a separate piece of paper, using the proportions of the squares to establish the proportions of the features. By drawing a diagonal through the grid, you can establish further center points, which will enable you to copy more difficult features such as the eyes.

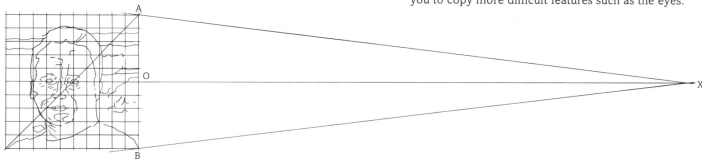

2 ▲ Once you have copied your image, extend the center line of the grid (O) to four times that of the width of the grid itself. Then draw diagonals from the right-hand corners of the grid (A and B) to join the farthest point of this center line (X). You can play around with the proportions depending on how distorted you want the image to be. The longer the line OX, the greater the distortion will be. The greater the distortion, the closer to the picture plane the viewer must be.

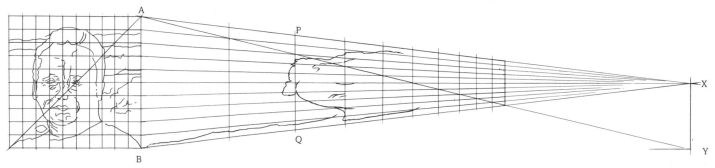

3 ▲ Join each of the grid points along the line AB to the point X. Plot a vertical line down through the point X measuring half the height of the grid (AB), then draw a line down from the top left-hand side of the grid (A) to the bottom of this new line (Y). The points at which the line AY cuts the horizontal lines will give you the points at which to plot your verticals (PQ, etc.). These divide the image according to the vertical lines of the grid but are spaced increasingly closer together as you move to the right.

4 ▶ Keep your gridded image on a separate piece of paper. You can then lay this over the area that you wish to distort. The grid can be drawn in colored pencil to avoid confusion. First, draw the main outlines of the face, such as the neck, the chin, and the sides. This will give you a good framework within which to work.

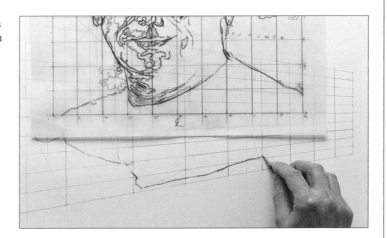

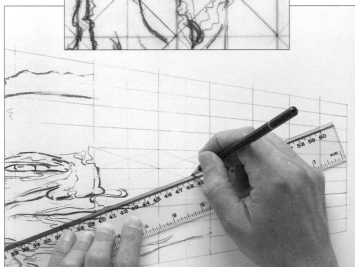

5 ▲ Divide the quadrilaterals of the distorted grid by drawing diagonals from corner to corner as you did earlier with the regular grid. When you are putting in the features, try to keep in mind the outline of the grid. You can erase these extra lines later on as you build up your image.

7 ▲ Start to fill in the skin tones with a light pink pencil. You can change the nature of the drawing's texture by altering the nature of your pencil strokes. In a loose portrait like this, differently angled stripes and shapes, and even curved lines for shading, will give an interesting surface and create texture and depth.

6 ▲ To draw the heavier details, use a solid graphite pencil; this smudges easily and is thus useful when working up areas of tonal shading. Remember that the right-hand side of your image will need to be heavier in tone than the left-hand side. Inevitably the features will be closer together, while the distortion will be greater in the left-hand side.

8 ▲ Seen head on, it appears as though the finished image has been pulled out to the right. When seen from the side, the image of the face comes back into proportion.

Side-angle view
The picture has been turned to the side to show the correct viewing angle of the picture. The tilted picture plane enables us to see the image of the face as in the original photographic reference.

Philip O'Reilly

CURVILINEAR PERSPECTIVE

LEONARDO DA VINCI'S observations leading to the idea of curvilinear perspective seem obvious when they are pointed out to us. We have all had the experience of standing under a long, high bridge and seen its two ends appear to curve down on each side, though we know the bridge is straight. But it is only relatively recently that artists seem to have rediscovered these ideas as forming the basis for a way of representing the world around us. The complex geometry of curvilinear perspective makes it more sensible for artists to use these ideas according to their actual experiences rather than to construct images along complex theoretical lines. In this respect, multiple sketches and photographs can be a great help.

Curved staircase

In this montage of black-and-white photographs, we are able to look up underneath the top steps of the staircase as well as peer down on the bottom ones. Defying the verticality of the central post supporting the structure, the composition curves back into the space away from the viewer at the top, and to a lesser extent at the bottom. Curvilinear perspective allows us to encompass much more of an image than would be possible using conventional linear perspective. In the latter case, the artist has to be a certain distance away from the subject to get everything in. We get a real sense of the whole structure in a way that seems to physically involve us in the space that is represented.

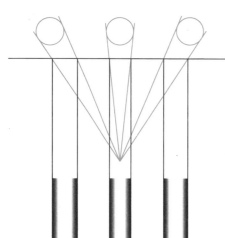

Straight picture plane

Leonardo drew three cylindrical columns of equal width, parallel with the picture plane (here, shown in red). He demonstrated that, according to linear perspective, the two outer columns would appear wider than the one in the center. Since the viewer was farther away from the two outer columns, they would not really be seen as wider.

Curved picture plane

In order for the outer two columns to look the same width, or smaller, the picture plane (here, shown in red) would have to be curved. This ties in with Leonardo's observations of wide-angle views in which he showed that a long, rectangular horizontal wall that ran parallel with the picture plane would need to be drawn converging both to left and right, either toward a center line or as a curved line.

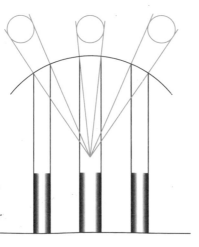

Woodland scene

Here, the montage sweeps around the space both horizontally and vertically, creating a circle in the center of the composition bounded by the curving line of the knoll against the sky, the waterfall on the left, and the track to the right. The structure of the landscape may be exaggerated *by this means, but it gives a sense of integration with the space that would be impossible using conventional perspective methods. Such an image is compelling in its own right, but could well form the visual source for a painting. A less obviously curved image would be achieved by moving the individual images farther apart.*

CURVILINEAR SPHERES

An image published by Hermann von Helmholtz in his *Handbuch der Physiologischen Optik (1856–66)* showed a circular checkerboard of black and white squares in which the lines curved progressively outward from the center. When this was viewed from a particular distance, the curved lines appeared to be straight. This confirms the idea that according to natural perspective, when we look at a subject with straight edges from close up, that is, with a wide angle of vision, its straight edges appear to curve. This is the basis of curvilinear perspective. The spheres (*right*) show Helmholtz's idea.

If you look at this checkered sphere from very close up with one eye, it looks like the sphere in the center when seen from a normal distance.

The image on the left, seen from close up with one eye closed, looks like the one above, which, seen close up, looks like the image on the right.

This is how the central image looks from close up. The edges of the image are distorted – it shows the effect of using curvilinear perspective.

Gallery of Curvilinear Perspective

IN RECENT TIMES artists have made paintings that attempt to go beyond the constraints of linear perspective in order to celebrate a wider angle of vision and the curving lines of the natural perspective we actually perceive in the world. The seeds of this new vision are evident in Edward Lear's watercolor, while the Carel Weight painting shows an understanding of how curvilinear perspective can be incorporated into a rectangular format. Other artists, such as David Hockney, show how we can dispense with the rectangle altogether in works which give an all-embracing sense of the subject.

Edward Lear, *Choropiskeros, Corfu*, 1856, *19 x 14 in (48 x 35 cm)*
Lear takes a multiple viewpoint that sweeps in a vertical line from the trunk of the tree in the foreground – where the artist is looking down – up through the middle distance to the distant hills and the high horizon at the top of the painting – where the artist is looking up. This gives a great sense of the breadth of the landscape, pushing against the confines of the rectangle.

David Hockney, *Sitting in the Zen Garden at the Rioanji Temple, Kyoto, Japan,* 1983, *57 x 46 in (1.45 x 1.17 m)*
Hockney's photomontages achieve their curvilinear effect by the artist minutely changing the plane of the camera with each shot that is taken.

This detail resembles a conventional perspective composition. When seen in relation to the whole, it is clear how much additional space is being depicted.

The composition radiates from the fountain like the spokes of a wheel.

Stanley Spencer, *Filling Water Bottles,* **1923–32**
Spencer compresses the imagery on the picture plane, pulling objects and figures into the painting from the edges of vision. The work here has a patternlike quality that makes the viewer very conscious of surface. But at the same time, parts of the imagery are pushed forward or back at varying angles, resulting in a strong sense of densely filled space. This panel comes from a series of images that decorate a chapel wall.

 A small part of the image works as an intriguing, though more conventional, composition in its own right.

Carel Weight, RA, *The Moment,* **1955,** *24 x 72 in (61 x 183 cm)*
The wide angle of view, with the curving of the wall and curb, creates the broad panoramic space in which the drama of the painting is enacted. Such a construction gives the viewer a heightened sense of the moment referred to in the title. At such moments, we retain a clear snapshot of the whole scene, and its very ordinariness becomes charged with meaning.

CURVILINEAR COMPOSITION

Fragmented reference
The photographic source for the painting is somewhat fragmented, but it contains much useful and clear visual information from which the pastel work can be constructed.

THE OFTEN CRAMPED SPACE around a busy market stall would make it very difficult to establish a sufficiently distant station point necessary to make an accurate drawing of it using linear perspective. In fact, conventional perspective would not give as good a sense of the bustle, the characters, the colorful, heaped piles of fruit and vegetables, and the feeling of integration within the locality that a curvilinear approach helps to provide. The artist has taken a preliminary series of photographs from a single standing position, moving the camera from left to right to create a miniature panorama that encompasses the whole scene. The pastel painting smooths out the disjunctions in the photographic reference and emphasizes the curvilinear sweep of the composition.

1 ◄ Establish the basic structure by drawing the two lines of the awning curving over the stall and the line of the front of the stall curving up and around. Mark these in faintly in charcoal so that you can brush them off again if you wish. Begin to sketch in the broad shapes of the figures.

3 ▲ Use the broad side of a deep, cool green pastel to fill in darker areas of tone between the figures at the front of the stall and on the ground. Here, a midtoned gray-blue retains a sense of color and is a good base for the darker tones that will be applied later. The dark colors create areas of negative space.

2 ▲ Once you are satisfied that your whole composition fits well on the paper, begin to firm up the structure of the figures and the stall. Do not use so much charcoal that you will soil the pastel.

4 ◄ Sketch in an indication of the colors for the hair and clothes of the figures. Lay a pale blue tone over the top of the awning.

5 ▶ Build up the forms by adding color. In each particular area, use adjacent color harmonies in order to keep the colors looking clean. In an area predominantly orange or red, for example, use only reds, oranges, and warm yellows. Avoid complementary blues in the shadows. For the woman's trousers in the foreground, use adjacent midtoned blue-grays, deeper blues, and purples. Rub colors with the fingers to blend.

6 ▲ When you have filled in the underlying color, as in the sky, draw the scaffolding using the broad sharp edge of the pastel.

7 ◀ Add the stripes to the awning. Keep the color clean by making the lines directly in single, bold strokes.

8 ▶ At this final stage, add the very darkest tones and the highlights. This will give the painting more effective contrasts.

Market Scene, Hackney, London
In the finished work, the purity of the bright colors has been retained, but not at the expense of the tonal contrasts, which remain sharp. The curvilinear perspective gives the feeling that we are seeing something completely and participating in a shared experience.

The artist has wisely avoided giving any real definition to the faces of the figures.

Jane Gifford

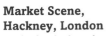

Materials

Pastels

Charcoal

135

GALLERY OF ALTERNATIVE APPROACHES

THE PLURALITY OF APPROACHES and styles in twentieth-century painting and other two-dimensional art forms has meant that artists no longer feel the need to rely on a particular form of conventional perspective. Artists may draw inspiration from any system or source that seems to offer the best way of solving a problem or expressing an idea. For many artists there is a great freedom in not being locked into a particular convention. It allows them to explore the techniques of other cultures and to invent new ones that may be more appropriate to new media. Here, each artist has adopted an approach that is appropriate to the context of the work, from the massive shifts in scale in the Gilbert and George work to the spatial compression of the painting by Mick Rooney.

Mick Rooney, RA, *Votive Offerings,* **1989,** *49 x 40 in (1.24 x 1.02 m)*
This painting takes a high viewpoint, with the horizon line well above the top edge of the painting and the ground plane practically parallel with the picture plane at the bottom. It encompasses a very wide angle of view and compresses the perspective so that we look at the narrative as though through the zoom lens of a camera with little depth of field. The result is a bold assemblage of forms, a busy, fecund work with an appropriate perspective framework for the scene it so vigorously portrays.

Umberto Boccioni, *The Laugh,* **1911,** *43 x 57 in (1.1 x 1.45 m)*
Along with his Futurist colleagues, Boccioni rejected what he saw as outmoded conventions of linear perspective. This work is a kaleidoscope of visual fragments – a mixture of diverse visual sensations in movement, complexity, and bright, saturated complementary colors.

Within the shifting planes of the painting, scenes of apparent realism are visible.

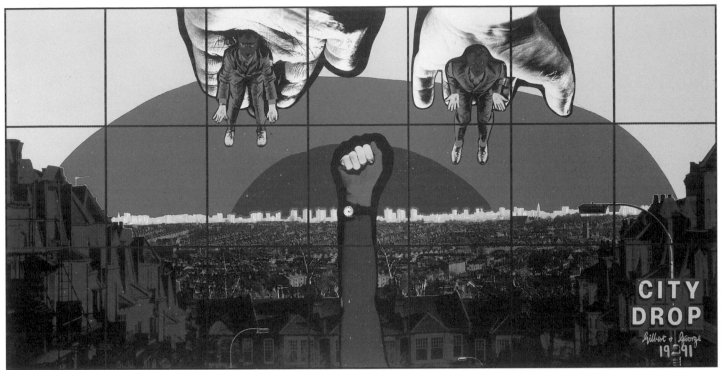

Gilbert and George, *City Drop,* **1991,** *8 ft 4 in x 16 ft 3 in (2.53 x 4.97 m)*
Just as Gilbert and George have reworked or subverted a traditional religious theme of apotheosis or ascension, so they have created their own version of a standard perspective. The artists themselves are featured precariously balanced on giant hands as if on some nightmare Big Dipper. At each side, the houses, like flats on a stage set, descend steeply in perspective to a central vanishing point below the arm and the bottom edge of the work. This has the effect of underlining the void below the figures perched high above. Their vulnerability is emphasized by the high viewpoint, as if seen from the height of the figures themselves. The feeling of vast space is echoed in the ground plane behind the houses that stretches to the horizon. It is an entirely built-up landscape, with its row upon row of terraced housing. The areas of foreground, middle ground, and distance are plainly delineated, each with its clear part to play in the drama.

Anthony Green, RA, *Paradise,* **1993,**
diameter 8 ft 7 in (2.62 m)
In this painting, the artist opens out the space, like the opening of the petals of a flower. The imagery shows an intimate domestic scene. We feel the painting could close up again on this personal encounter like a flower at night. Green has come up against the limitations of conventional perspective. He has used the shape of the canvas to suggest the opening out of two-dimensional space.

The shadows of the chair and dressing table are good examples of vertical oblique projection.

137

AN INTRODUCTION TO
WATERCOLOR

Watercolor   140
History of Watercolors   142

MATERIALS

Paints   146
Color Mixing   148
Mixing Primaries   150
Color Harmony   152
Light and Color   154
Gallery of Color   156
Watercolor Brushes   158
Brushmarks   160
Other Marks   162
Gallery of Brushstrokes   164
Paper   166
Stretching and Toning   168
Gallery of Paper   170

TECHNIQUES

Working with Method   172
Capturing an Image   174
Composing a painting   176
Drawing and Sketching   178
Laying a Wash   180
Washes   182
Gallery of Washes   184
Tone and Color   186
Building up Layers   188
Sponging Out   190
Scratching Out   192
Resist Techniques   194
Other Resist Techniques   196
Using Gouache   198
Gallery of Techniques   200

WATERCOLOR

OF ALL THE VARIOUS PAINTING MEDIA, including oils and acrylics, watercolor is by far the most convenient to work with. It has the range and adaptability for almost any kind of painting situation or style. All you need to get started is a small watercolor box, a couple of brushes, a pad of paper, and some water. When you look at a watercolor painting, you can see how it was painted, as well as getting a sense of the artist through the kinds of marks that have been made. This is because the nature of the watercolor painting method is such that almost nothing can be concealed in the painting. Unless you are using gouache paints (*see* pp.198-199), you cannot paint over something in order to conceal it, the way you can when you are painting in either oils or acrylics.

Picking up tips

What this means is that it is possible, just by looking at a painting carefully, to make a reasonably accurate guess at the means by which a particular effect was achieved. The implications of this are that anyone with a little experience and sense of how the medium works should be able to look at the watercolor paintings of artists they admire and pick up useful practical information. For this reason, each section of the book ends with a "gallery" of relevant paintings with examples of both historical and contemporary artists.

The power of transparency

What makes it possible to "read" a painting is that the watercolor medium is, above all else, a transparent painting medium. It relies for most of its effects on the fact that rays of light penetrate the watercolor paper and are reflected back to the viewer through the transparent paint film. The more the paint and the darker the washes, the less light is reflected back. In an opaque painting system, the rays of light would be reflected back off the surface of the paint itself rather than the paper, because the paint is too dense for the rays of light to penetrate. There is an opaque watercolor system based on gouache paint or bodycolor, and we shall be considering this later. There are also uses for bodycolor in largely transparent painting techniques where, for instance, the artist may be working on an off-white or colored paper and wishes to put in a white highlight. Purist watercolor painters have tended to avoid the use of bodycolor, favoring overlaid washes of transparent color, and using the white of the paper itself for highlights.

Drawings and color washes

At its most basic, the watercolor medium provides an effective and "clean" method of applying color washes to a pencil drawing. For many artists, this is the very first stage in the development of their practical knowledge of paint and painting. It is an excellent starting point because, used in this way, watercolor is not at all intimidating and, with a little practice, the results can look extremely competent. A simple drawing can be transformed by the addition of a couple of washes of color. It is important for beginners to realize that if they start in this way and follow a few basic guidelines, they can achieve a surprising degree of expertise in a relatively short time.

Getting started

This book is designed to introduce the medium, its tools, and techniques in a way that is practical and accessible. The Brief History that follows sets watercolor painting in its historical perspective, while the many "tips" boxes give you a handle on painting technique. The most essential element in all this is that you enjoy what you are doing. Always paint the things that you want to paint, not the things you imagine you ought to paint. You will no doubt get frustrated at times – all painters do – but keep practicing or try another approach until you get it right. Remember too that the quality of your materials is important – you cannot paint a fine line if your brush does not come to a point, and thin paper will buckle if it has not been stretched. Having said all that, it is time to look at some fine historical examples of watercolors, and start painting.

Good luck!

HISTORY OF WATERCOLORS

THE FLOWERING OF WATERCOLOR PAINTING in Great Britain toward the end of the eighteenth century tends to foster the idea that this was when watercolor painting began. In fact, artists had been using water-soluble binding materials with pigments for centuries. As early as the end of the fifteenth century, Albrecht Dürer *(1471-1528)* produced a remarkable series of landscape paintings that can rightly be called watercolors. Dürer used water-soluble paints on parchment or on paper, overlaying transparent colors and using the color of the paper for the lights.

Albrecht Dürer, *Lake in the Woods,* 1495-97
The brooding atmosphere of this famous early watercolor landscape gives it a particularly contemporary feel, with the trees on the left appearing to be blasted by war. The scene is deserted, as if not a human being is left alive.

THE SEVENTEENTH CENTURY saw a number of monochromatic drawings in pen and ink and wash, or simply in brush and wash, by such artists as Nicolas Poussin *(1594-1665)* and Claude Lorrain *(1600-82).* These studies may not be categorized technically as watercolors, yet they are very much the forerunners, in style and technique, of the work of later watercolor painters.

Toward realism

Wenceslaus Hollar *(1607-77)* was an artist from Prague who settled in England in 1636. His panoramic views of English towns and coastlines were an attempt to make faithful representations of places, rather than to create the kinds of imaginary classical landscape we associate with artists like Claude Lorrain.

Among other artists working in this way was Francis Place *(1647-1728)* who, in addition to his many panoramic works, produced a fine series of pen and wash drawings from nature – all characterized by a fluent and highly assured use of brush and wash.

The mid- to late eighteenth century saw the emergence of a number of painters who chose to concentrate on watercolor as their preferred medium. Paul Sandby *(1725-1809)* was one of the first British artists to recognize and fully exploit the potential of the medium in works that incorporated both transparent and bodycolor techniques. His architect brother Thomas *(1723-98)* was also a fine watercolor painter who had some skill in wash techniques.

J.M.W. Turner RA, *Venice: Looking East from the Giudecca, Sunrise,* 1819
This atmospheric study (left) is evoked with great economy of brushwork and color. The warm brown of the foreground creates a sense of distance across the lagoon.

Thomas Girtin,
Bamburgh Castle,
Northumberland,
1797-99
This strong, fully resolved landscape is painted on warm brown cartridge paper. In order to highlight certain details, Girtin has used touches of white bodycolor on the cows and on the gulls on the left, as well as on areas of the rock face.

Alexander Cozens *(c.1717-1786)* made a number of simple, economical studies from nature. His son J.R. Cozens *(1752-1797)* made landscapes characterized by their intensity and the power of the atmosphere they generate *(center)*. They have a breadth of scale in which tiny figures and buildings are dwarfed by huge mountains or vast city walls.

By contrast, but no less striking in their effect, are the paintings of Francis Towne *(1740-1816)*, whose almost diagrammatic style is immediately recognizable for its sense of form, design, and order.

For other contemporary artists such as Thomas Gainsborough *(1727-88)*, watercolor was primarily used to give color and tone to chalk drawings. His studies, with their loose, vigorous brushstrokes, demonstrate a remarkable spontaneity of approach.

John Robert Cozens,
Chamonix and Martigny, c.1776
The figures dwarfed by the overhanging rock and the apparent insignificance of the fir trees convey the immensity of scale in this vast mountain landscape.

John Constable RA, ***Landscape with Trees and a Distant Mansion,*** **1805**
This is a very relaxed study with the warm yellow browns of the trees and hedges set against the blues of the distant landscape and the sky. Constable liked to make direct studies from nature. The handling here is assured, with large, generous brushwork.

A new status

Toward the end of the eighteenth century, two of the great talents of watercolor painting emerged, J.M.W. Turner *(1775-1851) (bottom left)* and Thomas Girtin *(1775-1802) (top right)*. The quality, breadth, and directness of their work would bring a new status to the medium. It allowed watercolor paintings to be seen as works of art in their own right rather than merely as colored drawings or studies for oil paintings.

Thomas Girtin began to stretch the watercolor medium further than it had gone before. He made paintings on rough cartridge papers in order to work on a more mid-toned ground. He pared down his palette and found he could create all the effects that he needed with just a limited range of colors.

143

Ahead of his time

It was J.M.W. Turner, however, who came to grips with watercolor painting as no artist had done before. Not content with mere coloring-in exercises, he constantly experimented with ways of moving the paint around and with new pigments and papers. He used color very directly, working wet-into-wet, scrubbing off, sponging, and scratching out (*see* pp.190-193).

There were many contemporaries of Turner, working both in England and in France, who made significant contributions to the art of watercolor painting. John Constable *(1776-1837)* made direct studies from the landscape in a vigorous and very immediate style, often using scraping and scratching out techniques to build up a textured effect. John Sell Cotman *(1782-1842)* produced unique paintings of a quite different order. These are carefully designed works in which flat planes of color and tone build like a jigsaw over the surface.

The landscapes of David Cox *(1783-1859)* are often turbulent or brooding in spirit. The speed of execution is visible in the large, rich brushstrokes dragged across the rough paper.

19th century developments

The mid- to late nineteenth century saw work in watercolor by a number of interesting artists in England, including Samuel Palmer *(1805-81)* *(right)* and Alfred William Hunt *(1830-96)*. In France, Camille Pissarro *(1830-1903)*, Paul Gauguin *(1848-1903)*, and Paul Cézanne *(1839-1906)* were among the artists who used the medium. Cézanne painted more than 400 watercolors and experimented

with transparent effects on white paper and denser bodycolor effects on toned paper.

The diversity of movements and styles in the development of painting in the twentieth century has been reflected in the great variety of approaches to watercolor.

Camille Pissarro, *An Orchard,* **c.1890**
This delicate, watery study is one in which the colors are softly fused. But for all its delicacy and softness, it has great strength.

John Sell Cotman,
***Dolbadarn Castle,* c.1802**
Bathed in early evening light, this quiet atmospheric work displays Cotman's characteristic sense of order and design.

Samuel Palmer, *The Herdsman,* **c.1855**
Palmer's exuberant landscape is a celebration of nature, with its richly textured foliage and sense of sunlight. Using a variety of techniques,

Palmer has picked out the foreground highlights with white bodycolor, while in other areas he has scratched off the paint to get back to the white surface of the paper.

John Singer Sargent RA, *Santa Maria della Salute, Venice*, 1907-08
This is a loose and busy study by an artist who made many fluent sketches in watercolor. Here Sargent has juxtaposed elements of both color and design as the angular masts and spars of the heavily toned boats cut sharply across the pale, rounded domes in the background.

Edward Hopper, *Captain Kelly's House*, 1931
This painting shows Hopper's characteristic honesty. Nothing is concealed, and yet it remains hauntingly enigmatic.

Among the many groups of artists who were influential in reshaping attitudes to the medium were members of a Munich group, which included Wassily Kandinsky *(1866-1944)*, Franz Marc *(1880-1916)*, August Macke *(1887-1914)*, and Paul Klee *(1879-1940)* (*see* p.36). Kandinsky, born in Moscow, was one of the first to develop an abstract visual language, freeing watercolor from an overly pictorial truth and allowing images to float on the paper.

Klee made many experiments with the medium, working with thin, freely applied washes and also with densely pigmented gouache on a variety of surfaces. His works often have a magical, almost childlike, quality.

Across the Atlantic, artists such as Winslow Homer *(1836-1910)* and John Singer Sargent *(1856-1925) (top right)* were developing a distinctly American style. Sargent spent most of his life in Europe, adapting the skills he had learned as a portrait painter to a broad range of subjects. He echoed some of Homer's themes while becoming increasingly interested in the interplay of light and color.

Another American to become interested in the effects of light was Edward Hopper *(1882-1967) (left)*. His watercolors can seem disarmingly straightforward, but they are highly charged, demanding a response from the viewer.

One of the most impressive watercolor artists of this century was the German Emil Nolde *(1867-1956)* (*see* p.22). He would take his paints with him to the theater, working by feel in the dark. Like Turner a century earlier, he pushed the medium to its limits, constantly experimenting with techniques and materials. His vast body of work was a celebration of color and of form that brought a new richness to the medium.

PAINTS

Early watercolor paint box

Watercolor paints are made by first mixing and then grinding powder pigments with a water-soluble binding material such as gum arabic. The pigments used to make watercolor paints are, in general, the same as those used in other types of paint, such as oils or acrylics. Gum arabic is a natural sap taken from the African acacia tree that gets its name from the species *Acacia arabica*. The type most commonly used nowadays is Kordofan gum arabic, which comes from the Sudan.

Rose Madder root

Pigments
Earth substances and animal substances form the basis of many pigments.

Terre Verte

Cochineal insects

THE GUM IS PREPARED in gum kettles as a 30 percent solution in water and subsequently mixed into a paste with the pigment. The paste is then ground on granite triple roll mills and, for tube colors, put into tubes, or, in the case of pan colors, dried off in large round cakes before being rammed through a die and extruded in strings. These are then cut to the whole- or half-pan size before being wrapped. Certain

additional materials can be added to the basic pigment/gum arabic mixture to create a stable product. These include glycerine, a syrupy liquid used in very small amounts to aid the adhesion and flexibility of the paint as well as keeping it moist. In the past, honey was often used for this

purpose. A wetting agent, such as oxgall, is used to help disperse the pigment particles. A thickener is often incorporated when the mix with gum arabic alone is too thin and requires more body. Dextrin is often used for this purpose and is occasionally used as a replacement for gum arabic when a particular pigment will not

How paint is made
The crushed pigment and gum arabic mix are left to dry as slabs of color (below) before being forced through a die and extruded as strips (below right). These are then cut into segments to form pan colors.

French Ultramarine

Viridian

Yellow Oxide

Cadmium Yellow

Crushed pigments
Pigments are the solid separate particles in various colors that form the basis of watercolor paints. They each have certain characteristics, differing in their strengths, in their lightfastness, and in their degree of transparency.

Slabs of dry color

Lengths of pan color

flow out to a flat wash with gum arabic or reacts adversely with it. Dextrin is also used as a substitute for gum arabic in cheap watercolors. It is very resoluble, and this can affect the success of certain techniques, such as overpainting.

Artists' quality

Raw Sienna

Manufacturers also tend to add a preservative to prevent the growth of mold or bacteria. There is a great art to making the best-quality watercolor paints, since each pigment will require more or less of each of the ingredients in order for a stable and workable color to be made. With pan colors, the manufacturer has to ensure that the paint does not dry out in the box but, equally, that it does not absorb too much moisture and get soggy. The difference between artists' quality watercolor paints and the cheaper lines is marked. The pigment loading in the artists' paints is so high that it is the pigment that controls the

behavior of the paint. The differences between pan and tube watercolors vary from pigment to pigment, but the main overall difference between the two is that there is more glycerine in the tube colors and this makes them a little more soluble than the pans.

The soft or moist watercolors used today are somewhat different than the early prototypes. J.M.W. Turner, for example, would have used blocks of straight pigment and gum mixes with no added moisturizer – what are now known as "hard" watercolors. Once Turner's washes had dried completely, they would have been

Tube and pan colors
Tube colors contain slightly more glycerine than do the pans, but not noticeably so. For large washes of color, tubes are the better option.

Gouache
Gouache or bodycolor is a watercolor paint that is characterized by its opacity.

easy to overpaint without disturbing the color underneath (subject to certain differences in particular pigments). Nowadays, if a color already on the painting is at fairly full strength, for example, one can find difficulty in overpainting it without redissolving it to some extent.

Paints and palettes
Saucers and paint box lids are just two of the many options for mixing paints. Painted color swatches can provide a useful point of reference.

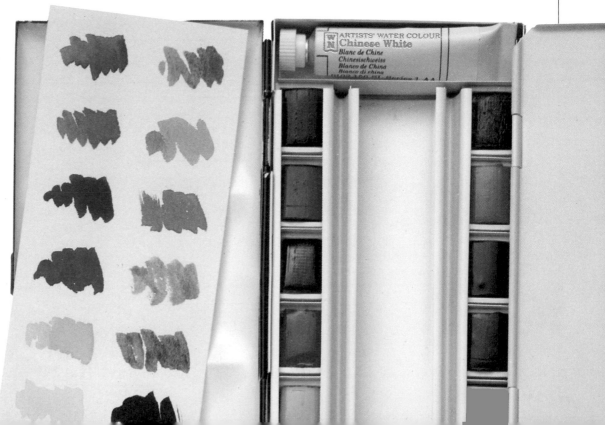

COLOR MIXING

IT IS THEORETICALLY POSSIBLE to mix any color you want from just three colors – red, yellow, and blue – known as primary colors. In practice, however, it can be difficult to find pigments pure enough to do this, although a cool yellow, a crimson or bluish red, and a pure greenish blue will make good greens and good purples when mixed together.

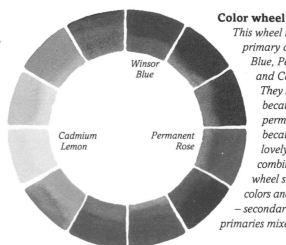

Color wheel
This wheel is based on the primary colors Winsor Blue, Permanent Rose, and Cadmium Lemon. They have been selected because of their permanence and because they make lovely colors in combination. The color wheel shows primary colors and secondary colors – secondaries being two primaries mixed together.

Winsor Blue

Cadmium Lemon

Permanent Rose

Secondary colors from Permanent Rose and Cadmium Lemon

Tertiary colors made from mixing all three primaries

OF THE THREE PRIMARIES, Permanent Red or Rose is a pure transparent color on the crimson side of red. It mixes very well with the other primaries to make violets or oranges. Cadmium Lemon is not as transparent as the red but, when reduced in washes, has a similar transparency on the paper.

Winsor Blue is a cool transparent blue with a high tinting strength, and its purity of color enables it to produce clean bright colors in mixtures. An alternative blue is French Ultramarine, which, like Winsor Blue, is very strong and can give deep-toned washes. It produces a lovely purple with Permanent Rose, but because it is a reddish blue, the greens it produces with yellow are grayish. Mixes made from two primaries are known as secondaries.

Secondary colors from Winsor Blue and Permanent Rose

Tertiary colors made from mxing all three primaries

Tertiary colors made from mxing all three primaries

Secondary colors from Winsor Blue and Cadmium Lemon

PIGMENT QUALITIES

Pigments vary enormously in their particle size and weight. Manganese Blue is a heavy pigment and gives a very granulated wash, while the highly diluted lighter Winsor Green here has a streaky effect known as flotation.

Flotation

Granulation

There is no doubt that it is best to work, initially at least, with a limited palette (range of colors). On this page are a number of pigments that are all excellent and from which you might make your selection.

Reds and browns

Light Red and Venetian Red are warm orange-reds, and Indian Red is a lovely cool purplish red. Burnt Sienna is a transparent reddish brown, while Raw Umber tends toward a greeny yellow, and Burnt Umber more toward a dark reddish brown.

Cobalt Blue   Cerulean Blue   Winsor Blue

Cobalt Violet   French Ultramarine

Light Red   Venetian Red

Indian Red   Cadmium Red

Permanent Rose   Alizarin Crimson   Rose Madder   Burnt Sienna

Yellow Ochre   Raw Sienna   Raw Umber   Burnt Umber

Blues

There are many permanent blues, of which these are highly recommended.

Yellows

Yellow Ochre and Raw Sienna are useful earth pigments, as are the brighter and permanent Cadmiums.

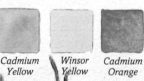

Yellow Ochre   Raw Sienna   Lemon Yellow Hue

Cadmium Yellow   Winsor Yellow   Cadmium Orange

Cadmium Lemon

Recommended palette

Your own palette or choice of colors will evolve naturally as you try out new colors and different kinds of painting, but these are some good ones to buy in terms of purity of color, pigment strength, and lightfastness. They also tend to work well in combination.

Cadmium Red *has good lightfastness and a little color goes a long way.*

Permanent Rose *is a modern lightfast pigment which can replace the less durable Rose Madder.*

Cadmium Yellow *is bright and acceptably permanent and has a high tinting strength.*

Cadmium Lemon *is slightly paler than Cadmium Yellow and is equally permanent.*

Winsor Green *is both strong and permanent, mixing well with colors like Burnt Sienna.*

Winsor Blue *is also very permanent and has largely replaced the less lightfast Prussian Blue.*

French Ultramarine, *like Winsor Blue, is very strong and gives deep-toned washes.*

Burnt Sienna *is an earth pigment, so it is very durable. It has a lovely transparency.*

Raw Umber *is another very useful earth pigment that will not fade over time.*

Greens

Terre Verte and Oxide of Chromium are permanent, low-key greens, Terre Verte being a transparent pigment, and Oxide of Chromium being more opaque. Viridian is durable but is weaker than Winsor Green.

Terre Verte   Oxide of Chromium   Winsor Green

Viridian

Permanent Rose and Winsor Green

Cadmium Red and Winsor Blue

MIXING GRAYS

There are a number of colors that make lovely grays in combination, as shown on the left. For a much darker gray, mix Winsor Blue with Burnt Sienna. Black should be used with caution in watercolors and is not needed to make gray.

MIXING PRIMARIES

Orange
Two ways of arriving at a color: left, laying one wash of color over another; right, mixing colors in a tray before painting.

IN WATERCOLOR TECHNIQUES, there are essentially two ways of mixing colors – you can mix them physically in your mixing tray, or you can mix them by laying one color on top of another on the paper. With the first method, you might add a small touch of blue to a yellow wash in your tray to create the color green. With the second method, you can paint a yellow wash onto your paper, let it dry, and subsequently overpaint a pale blue wash to arrive at a green. Whichever painting method you use, the effect is essentially the same, although overlaying a wash of a second color, if it is done well, can create a greater richness of hue. This is because your eyes should still be able to perceive the first color reflected up through the subsequent wash.

BOTH OF THESE FRUIT still lifes are painted by physically mixing three primary colors in a mixing tray before they are applied to the paper. The difference between the two versions is that the top one is painted with rather strong colors – what are known as high-key colors – while the bottom one is painted with muted, or low-key, colors.

Mixing colors

The mixing of two primary colors produces secondary colors, and the mixing of all three primary colors produces tertiary colors. Notice the range of colors that have been produced in each case with just three colors.

Range of colors produced from high-key primaries

High-key primaries
All the colors in this still life are created by mixing just three high-key primaries: Permanent Rose, Winsor Blue, and Cadmium Lemon. These colors produce a vast range of lovely hues; the swatches here are just a selection.

Range of colors produced from low-key primaries

Low-key primaries
This low-key study relies for its effects on mixing Indian Red, Cobalt Blue, and Lemon Yellow Hue. These more muted versions of the three primaries work well in combination, producing subtle ranges of reds, oranges, greens, and grays. The white highlights are created by the actual paper surface, rather than by an application of color.

Overlaying color

Here the tulips have been painted using three primaries, but the visual effects are created by overlaying washes of pure color, rather than by physically mixing the paint before applying it. Whichever way you choose to work, it is a good idea to do color swatches on a scrap of similar paper in order to try out each color on its own, as well as to see the effect when one color is overlaid onto another, dried color.

1 ◀ Starting with a pencil outline of the tulips, mix up a wash of Cadmium Lemon, and begin applying it to the drawing with a small round brush. Paint in most of the leaves, the stem, and the flowers, but be sure to omit any highlighted areas that you want to appear white in the final image.

Cadmium Lemon

2 ◀ Allowing the yellow wash to dry, mix up a wash of Permanent Rose and test it on a dried swatch of the yellow to make sure that it produces the right kind of red. Now overlay your rose wash on the body of the petals.

Permanent Rose

3 ◀ Again, allowing the paint to dry between layers, mix up some Winsor Blue and test it on a swatch of dried yellow. Using the tip of the brush, apply it to the darker areas of the stem and the leaves. Notice how the blue over the yellow creates an effective leaflike green, even though no green has been applied.

Winsor Blue

The darkest areas of the petals have touches of Winsor Blue over the other two colors.

The nature of overlaid color is clearly visible in the stem and the leaves.

Ceramic palette

The blue wash is stronger and denser in certain areas. This creates the shadows and gives the flower its three-dimensional form.

COLOR HARMONY

CONSIDER THE BALANCE OF COLORS in a painting. Are the colors bright, and do they seem to shout at you, or are they low-key and more subtle in their effect? If you are creating your own still life, you have the advantage of being able to select particular items and arrange them in a variety of ways until you are happy with the result. You can manipulate not just what goes into the painting, in terms of shapes and textures, but exactly where everything goes. You can play with the composition to make it crowded or sparse, vibrant or muted. You can create a subtle balance in the range of colors or go more for primaries and secondaries. But whatever arrangement you choose, whether it is dark or light, high-key and rich in color, or low-key and subdued, you will find yourself instinctively striving for a sense of balance.

High-key and low-key
The contrast in colors between the vibrant, manufactured objects of the beach ball and towels and the subdued, balanced tones of the pebbles and shells is striking. Here high-key and low-key are combined, the vibrancy of the stronger hues offsetting nature's more subtle offerings.

You can create interesting compositions by introducing bold primary colors into your still life.

Colors along the beach are generally low-key – soft muted creams, yellows, and browns.

IN JUGGLING THE ELEMENTS of sand, shells, and towels, you are making decisions about shapes, textures, and colors. Nature abounds with color, although along the seashore the colors are often muted, as pebbles, shells, driftwood, and sand provide a range of pale yellows and browns. But there are complementaries too – opposites on the color wheel – so that the yellows are balanced by the purples of the seaweed, as well as harmonious colors in which the tones or hues of color are similar and work well together.

Afterimages

If we look at an area of strong color for a long time and then look away at an area of white, we should perceive the complementary of the first color. So if we stare at an area of red and then look at a white wall we should, just for a moment, see a green shape. Similarly, if we focus on an orange-red color first and then look at a bright yellow, we might see the yellow as green because we are carrying the blue afterimage of the orange-red. These are the kinds of color effects that we should bear in mind when planning a painting.

Low-key colors
Here shells, pebbles, and starfish form a harmonious, low-key still life against the sand. The tones of the individual elements are roughly the same, with no single item vying for our attention.

Adjacent colors

Although technically the term adjacent color means one that is next to another on the color wheel, it is more commonly used to mean simply any color that is next to another as, for example, in a painting. Every color we use affects the appearance of the color next to it. We can take advantage of this by painting with complementaries as adjacent colors. The colors will then appear brighter and will irradiate against each other.

For example, putting orange/red next to violet makes it appear more orange because the violet induces its complementary yellow. The same orange/red placed next to orange will look more blue because the orange induces its complementary blue. Many modern watercolor painters have used the technique of isolating colors from each other by leaving a white or gray gap between the touches of pure color. This allows the individual colors to retain their clarity of hue.

Adjacent colors
The beach ball, with its vibrant primary and secondary colors, is offset by the equally strong towels. Note how the red of the ball reacts against its complementary green in the towel.

Isolated colors
The device of leaving unpainted edges around areas of bold color serves to heighten the intensity of the individual colors.

Complementary colors
This composition is made up of complementary colors – yellows and purples, with the shells highlighted against the purple towel. Opposite each other on the color wheel, complementary colors are mutually enhancing, with each one of a pair intensifying the effect of the other.

153

LIGHT AND COLOR

Warm lights / cool shadows

ONE OF THE MOST IMPORTANT aspects of watercolor painting is the way in which everything that we look at is affected by light, whether it be sunlight, moonlight, or artificial light. It can be tempting to paint something a certain color because that is the color we know it to be, for example, the pale yellow of sand on a beach. But at noon the sun can be so strong that the sand is virtually white, whereas in the late afternoon the sun may cast long, purplish shadows. You need to look carefully at the scene before you consider the color temperature of the light and how this affects the appearance of the ground onto which the shadows fall. A useful principle to follow is "warm lights/cool shadows," and conversely "cool lights/warm shadows." This principle holds whatever the subject and however subtle the effects.

Noon

Cerulean Blue

Burnt Umber with Black

Sap Green

Viridian with Chinese White

Lemon Yellow

Midday light

At noon, when the sun is bright in a cloudless sky, we see lights and darks and very little in between. In the brightly lit areas, the color is washed out by the hard, cool light, and the shadows are too dark to contain much color. If, instead, the light from the sun is partially diffused by clouds, the shadows will be less pronounced and the colors will be more evident.

Evening

Hooker's Green

Cadmium Yellow

Ultramarine

Magenta

Evening light

In the evening, when the sun is closer to the horizon and the light is less intense, the land can be bathed in a rich golden light. Here, a wash of Cadmium Yellow and Hooker's Green transforms the color of the grass, while Magenta and Ultramarine give the bluish / purplish tinge to the cricketers' white clothing.

NOT ONLY DOES LIGHT affect the colors that we see, but it gives form and life to shapes that might otherwise seem dull and flat. Objects in the foreground will be brighter and have more color than those farther back, so in a case where you can see a panorama of tree-covered hills, the trees in the foreground will appear much brighter and more vibrant than those near the horizon. In terms of both what you see and how you paint it, a general guideline is that so-called warm colors advance toward you and cool colors recede. You can test this when you paint by adding warm colors (such as orange/red) and cool colors (such as blue) and seeing which elements appear to advance and which appear to recede.

Monochromatic study
When you look at a landscape, you will notice how the quality of light changes noticeably from the foreground to the background, markedly affecting all the colors that you perceive. By starting with a tonal study of the scene, you can see quite clearly how the tones in the foreground are brighter and stronger than those in the background.

Chromatic study
In order to manipulate the way certain areas advance and recede in your painting, add warm colors such as yellows or reds to the foreground and cool colors to the background. Here you can see how the yellows have made the foreground trees stand out, while the cool, bluish purples, that have been added to the distant hills, make them appear even farther away.

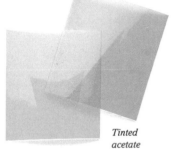

Tinted acetate

Adjusting the color
Painting in watercolors allows you to adjust the overall color of your painting by laying a wash over it. For example, you can make a painting warmer by overlaying a pale yellow wash over it, or cooler by overlaying a pale blue wash. Here, sheets of tinted acetate have been used to demonstrate the visual effects of overlaying warm and cool washes of color. You will find that, depending on the time of day, the weather, and the season when you are painting, you will need to adjust the intensity of the colors you use and the degree to which they seem warm or cool.

Although the painting is of a tropical landscape, the blue acetate makes the countryside seem almost English.

The central panel shows the actual painting, without any color adjustments.

The pale yellow acetate has the effect of bathing the scene in a wash of golden sunlight.

GALLERY OF COLOR

WATERCOLOR IS A HIGHLY appropriate medium for exploring the effects of color, as the pure colors of the pigments are seen in transparent washes against the white of the paper. Even when colors are overlaid, the translucent nature of the medium allows a subtle layering of color. But equally, striking color effects can be achieved by combining either high-key or low-key colors within a painting.

Sue Sareen, *Daffodils*
Sareen favors a limited palette. This painting shows the effects that can be achieved with just a blue, a yellow, and an ochre. Here she has worked with a very wet brush, allowing the background colors to merge while using the white of the paper to pick out the form of the flowers.

Philip O'Reilly, *San Giorgio at Dusk*
Painted as dusk set in, this striking image relies for its effect on the contrast between the dark solidity of the building against the intense blue of the evening sky. O'Reilly has used cream-colored paper to emphasize the warm hues of the Sicilian stonework and a granular blue-purple pigment to add texture and depth to the sky.

Paula Velarde, *Dining Room Brantwood*
Using candle wax to give a sense of texture, Velarde has overlaid bold washes of pigment with drier applications of color, capturing the drama of the setting by counterpointing the blue with threads of an equally strong yellow. The hints of red in this predominantly blue scene serve to balance the overall effect.

The eye is drawn back and forth from the interior scene to the view from the window, with the bright red sailboat forming a point of interest in the lake.

Jane Gifford, *Tourist at Indian Wedding*
In this high-key study, the traveler paints a view of herself as she photographs the bride and groom at a wedding. Choosing a range of fluorescent colors to capture the heat and feel of her surroundings, Gifford emphasizes the strength of the sunlight by painting yellow highlights around herself and on the clothes of the wedding party.

Emil Nolde (attr.), *Ruttebüll Tief* (c.1916–20)
Here Nolde displays his characteristic celebration of color, reveling in the power and purity of certain pigments. He has used washes of intense hue to create a highly personal non-naturalistic landscape. This vibrant painting demonstrates high-key color at its most dynamic; with a perfect balance between adjacent and complementary colors and between the warmth of the central middle distance area and the unexpected and yet perfectly controlled coolness of the foreground.

157

WATERCOLOR BRUSHES

THERE ARE TWO MAIN TYPES OF BRUSH: those with soft hairs, including red sable, ox hair, squirrel, and polyester brushes, and those with harder hairs, the bristle brushes. Soft hair and synthetic brushes are the more traditional in watercolor painting techniques, but bristle brushes are good for mixing up large amounts of color and also in scrubbing out exercises.

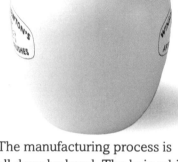

Earthenware vase for displaying brushes

THE ROUND SOFT HAIR BRUSHES, and in particular the sables, have been used to great effect in watercolor painting. They have excellent paint-carrying capacity, and they are springy and resilient. They come to a good point and can be used for fine work and also for laying in broader washes. Red sable is the tail hair of the Kolinsky, a species of mink. The soft wooly hairs are removed, and only the strong, "guard" hairs are used to make brushes. If you were to look at an individual hair through a microscope, you would see that, far from being smooth, it has a varying structure from root to tip, which allows it to retain the paint. Each hair has a "belly" – a wider section in the middle – and consequently it tapers above and below. The belly forms spaces in the brush that act as reservoirs for the paint.

The hairs are of varying lengths between 1 – 2½ in (25 – 60 mm). The long hairs are the rarest and the most prized and are around four times as expensive as the shorter ones.

The manufacturing process is all done by hand. The hair, which has previously been steamed under pressure and straightened, is put into a cannon, tapped, and combed out to remove short hairs.

Sable hairs

Ferrule

Sable brush

Anatomy of a brush
Brushes are made by hand; the lengths and quantity of the hairs are judged by eye.

The blunt "white" hairs are removed and the correct quantity taken to make an individual brush. The amount is judged by eye as just enough to fit snugly into the ferrule – the metal tube connecting the hair and the handle.

Made by hand

In the smaller sizes, the hair comes to a point naturally. In the larger sables, the hair has to be turned or twisted to form the shape of the brush. It is then tied with a clove hitch knot, trimmed, and cemented into the ferrule with epoxy resin for the larger sizes and shellac for the smaller sizes. The sable brushes are dipped into a weak gum arabic solution and individually sucked, so that they come to a point.

CARE OF YOUR BRUSH

● It is good practice always to paint with two jars of water, one for rinsing the dirty brush and the second for rinsing it again before mixing a new color. This way you will keep your brush and your colors clean. When you finish painting, wash your brushes with soap to remove all traces of paint and then rinse them thoroughly. Do not use hot water for this, as it may expand the ferrule, soften the glue, and make the hairs fall out.

● Brushes must be perfectly dry before being put away to avoid the possibility of mildew.

● You should keep your brushes clean and avoid building up deposits of paint at the ferrule, as this has the effect of splaying the brush open and ruining the point.

● You can judge a round soft-hair brush by its tip. A good one will always come to a point when dampened.

The toe (tip) of the brush

The heel of the brush

The synthetic soft-hair brushes are generally made from polyester monofilaments, which, unlike the sable hairs, do not have a scale structure or surface irregularities. They tend to suck up the paint and also release it more quickly than the sables would. Generally, however, they are fine substitutes for sables. Manufacturers also produce brushes that combine natural and synthetic fibers in sable/polyester ranges. While they do not have the characteristic springiness of the pure sable, they still do a perfectly reasonable job.

Round brushes
These come to a good point and, depending on the size, can be used for fine work or for laying in washes. The synthetic soft-hair brushes and the synthetic / sable blends are fine for most manipulations, although they are less springy than the sables.

Wash brush
This moplike wash brush is useful for laying down broad strokes of color over large areas.

Flat wash brush
The flat one-stroke brush is good for toning paper or for laying a wash. It can also be used to modify a wash that has just been laid down.

Large wash brush
Useful for laying down very broad strokes of color, this extra-wide wash brush comes into its own when covering large expanses of paper. The synthetic fibers have good paint-holding qualities and are excellent for laying washes and controlling the flow of paint.

Bamboo brush
Oriental soft-hair brushes are made of deer, goat, rabbit, or wolf hairs.

Bristle brush
This boar's bristle brush is good for mixing up color and also for scrubbing out techniques when it can be worked into the painted area with water. The shorter bristles aid control.

No.3 sable

No.6 sable

No.12 sable / synthetic

No.14b synthetic

1 inch sable / synthetic

2 inch synthetic

Japanese brush

Artist's boar's bristle
short flat

BRUSHMARKS

BRUSHES CAN BE USED in a number of ways, depending on the style or approach adopted by the artist. They can be used vigorously and expressively, for instance, to create brushstrokes of great energy and immediacy, or they can be used simply as the invisible tool that allows a wash to be applied evenly within a prescribed area. Between the two lies a world of different approaches. Factors that come into play are the amount of paint in the brush, the speed of the stroke, the angle of the brush, and the type of brush being used. The nature of the paper will also play a part. These pages show the variety of brushstrokes that can be made using just one brush.

Brushmarks from a single brush
All the strokes on these pages are made with a No.9 sable.

With a well-loaded brush, gradually increase the pressure until the full width of the brush comes into play.

Using lumps of pan paint, apply them to the paper with a very wet brush.

Using the tip of the brush in a circular motion, gradually increase the pressure to use more and more of the brush hairs.

A thin line can be drawn by just using the tip of the brush.

Rotate the side of the brush in a circular motion.

Roll a fully loaded brush on its side in complete revolutions.

Sponge the paper first, and then press the brush down firmly onto the dampened surface.

The tip of the brush can draw fine dots and outlines.

THIS SIMPLE PAINTING puts into practice some of the strokes that can be made with a single brush, again using a No. 9 sable. It is all a matter of control and of getting to know the nature of the brush, the paint, and the paper.

1 ▲ Wash in broad petal shapes with the body of the brush using Rose Madder and a touch of Ultramarine. Then, with a stronger mix, use the tip of the brush to dot in color. Where the petals are still wet, the dots will bleed.

2 ▲ Draw the stem in a thin line, using a mix of Rose Madder, Ultramarine, Sap Green, Viridian, Yellow Ochre, and Winsor Blue. Then, pressing harder on the brush, complete each leaf with a single brushstroke.

3 ▲ Using the finest point of the brush, draw in the filaments using Sap Green. If you are worried about being unable to control these fine lines, do a few practice lines on a rough scrap of paper before you begin, keeping your hand as steady as possible.

4 ▲ The anthers at the end of the filaments are Indian Red painted in dry brushstrokes. Applying the paint onto dry paper in this distinctive way creates a sense of depth and texture.

For fine lines just the tip of the brush comes into play.

To create a sense of depth, the background is painted in with a very dilute Yellow Ochre applied in broad brushstrokes.

You can make lines as fine as these with a No.9 brush by having just a touch of paint on the longest hairs.

The shadow from the vase is created by using the full body of the hairs to apply the paint both wet and dry.

The patterned surface is achieved by dipping the brush into a thick mixture of Winsor Blue and Ultramarine and then rolling the brush repeatedly on its side.

OTHER MARKS

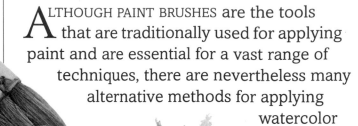

ALTHOUGH PAINT BRUSHES are the tools that are traditionally used for applying paint and are essential for a vast range of techniques, there are nevertheless many alternative methods for applying watercolor paint onto your paper.

It is largely a matter of trying out different implements and seeing which you prefer and which get closest to the effects you are after. But you do not have to buy lots of expensive equipment – there are any number of ordinary household items that you can experiment with. Artists have used such diverse materials as pieces of cardboard, sponges, wallpaper brushes, combs, paint rollers, and even squeegees, in order to achieve interesting effects. You will need to try different dilutions of paint and various types of paper to achieve the best results.

This bamboo brush, with its mix of animal hairs, creates broad, loose brushstrokes.

Blotting paper is used here. First apply paint with a brush. Then dip an edge of torn blotting paper into wet paint, and press it down. Draw the blotting paper along to create the pattern.

Dip an old sponge in masking fluid, press it onto the paper and let it dry. Paint over it and, while the paint is still wet, lift it off with a tissue.

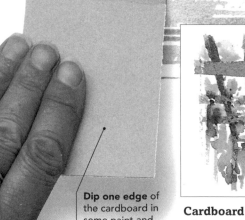

Dip one edge of the cardboard in some paint and drag it in vertical or horizontal strokes.

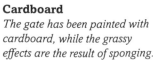

Cardboard
The gate has been painted with cardboard, while the grassy effects are the result of sponging.

Gum eraser
Gradually build up a ball of gum. It will have a mottled, uneven texture. Dip it into some paint and press it onto your paper. Repeat the process with other colors.

Old brushes have their uses. Here a worn, splayed brush has been dipped into a pale blue-gray wash and used to paint this tree.

This tree is painted with a fine sable brush. There is more control, particularly in the trunk, than can be achieved with the splayed brush.

The rigger, with its characteristic long, fine hairs, is capable of perfectly controlled lines and so is good for more detailed work.

Dip a natural sponge in masking fluid and apply it lightly to the paper. After it has dried, paint a wash of violet over it.

Use a comb for this effect. First paint the two colors in turn and, while each is still wet, draw the comb across the paint to create the blades of grass.

Sold in most art supply stores, this small sponge roller is good for laying strips of color. The tone will vary depending on how much paint the sponge has absorbed and on how hard you press down on it.

Natural sponge
The leaves are painted by dipping a sponge in light green and then dark green, and pressing it down on the paper. The irregular surface of the sponge creates interesting textures. For the trunk, dip the sponge in brown, squeeze it, and draw it down the page.

163

GALLERY OF BRUSHSTROKES

ONE OF THE PLEASURES of watercolor painting is that you really only need a couple of good-quality brushes to get started – a small round pointed sable for detailed work and a bigger, soft-hair round brush for washes and larger effects. Sables, with their characteristic springiness, are the traditional watercolor brush, but there are any number of excellent alternatives to choose from, including synthetic hair brushes and synthetic/sable mixes.

Julian Gregg, *Dieppe Harbor, Summer*
This study comprises a series of solid brushstrokes corresponding to areas of buildings in shadow and their reflections. Here the simple fluent line drawing was the essential starting point for the straightforward and economical brushstrokes. Gregg relied on just one or two brushes and a limited palette of colors, allowing the brushstrokes to remain clearly visible in the finished work. He built up the work swiftly and confidently, starting with the light areas and ending with the darkest reflections in the water.

Ian Cook, *Head of a Girl*
The intense color of the highly pigmented gouache shows in the thicker, dense brushstrokes, especially in the face and neck. The brushwork here is closer in feel to that of an oil painting with its rich, impasto effect.

John Pike, *Number 10 Fournier Street*
The artist worked from photos, sketches, and color notes to arrive at this degree of realism. The brushwork is relatively invisible so that nothing detracts from the final image. Pike built up the painting gradually, starting with overall washes and then filling in the details with a fine brush.

Raoul Dufy, *Nice, Le Casino,* 1936
This lovely loose study perfectly illustrates the artist's control over brushwork, with the figures, trees, and outlines of the building fluently touched in with the toe of a pointed, soft-hair brush.

These rapid and assured touches, balanced by the broader brushstrokes of some of the palm trees, are painted over sweeping washes of pinks, lilacs, and blues. The outlines of the buildings are similarly drawn in a wide range of colors.

**Gisela Van Oepen,
*The Sun Sets Behind the Tree***
Painted with confidence, the brushstrokes here are clearly visible, from the diagonal sweeps of the sky to the large frilly strokes used for the branches.

The bright rectangle in the lower left-hand corner of the window is light coming through from the far side of the building. Using a fine pointed brush, Pike painted carefully around this area, so that it is actually the paper, rather than any paint, that creates this bold shaft of light.

PAPER

Oriental sketchbooks
Unusual papers provide interesting textured surfaces.

WATERCOLOR ARTISTS REQUIRE paper in varying weights, of a quality that will not yellow with age, and with a range of surface types from smooth to rough. The paper should not buckle once it has been stretched and needs to be sufficiently strong to withstand rather severe treatment. Additionally, it should have the right degree of absorbency for the kind of painting the artist has in mind.

PAPER IS PRODUCED by the felting together of cellulose fibers, obtained from a variety of plant sources. In the West, most artists' papers are now produced from cotton fibers, while Oriental papers are made from a great variety of plant sources. These have fibers of varying length and strength, which impart very different characteristics to each type of paper.

The first stage of manufacturing is the pulping stage, during which the material providing the fibers is blended with water to produce a slurry. This is beaten

Cylinder mold machine
Here the pulped fibers are drawn over a wire mesh, arranging themselves in a random order.

and refined in order to produce fibers of the requisite quality. A neutral internal sizing is then added to the pulp. This, together with the additional surface sizing that may be added later, controls the absorbency of the paper.

Today, most watercolor papers are not made by hand but on a cylinder mold machine. From here the paper passes through a press on a woolen felt or blanket, which gives it a rough or a fine grain surface, depending on the weave used for the felt. The paper is still very wet, so it is passed

Waterford Rough

Waterford NOT

Waterford Smooth

Winsor & Newton Smooth

Mold-made paper
These are all standard machine-made watercolor papers. Note how the different surfaces affect the appearance of the paint, the blue looking much darker on the toned paper and much grainier on the Rough sheet at the back.

Winsor & Newton NOT

Bockingford White NOT

Bockingford Gray NOT

Bockingford Oatmeal NOT

through a press, and then around drying cylinders to remove the excess water. The paper is subsequently immersed in warm gelatin for surface sizing before being passed through squeeze rollers and dried. The function of the gelatin sizing is to decrease the paper's absorbency and make it harder. It allows it to withstand severe treatment such as constant repainting and scrubbing off.

Absorbency

This is determined by the amount of sizing used in the manufacture of the paper. (You can quite easily add a coat of gelatin sizing to make your paper harder and less absorbent.) A paper with no sizing is known as "Waterleaf". Many of the Oriental papers are very absorbent, taking up the brushstroke as it is made and not allowing any further manipulation.

Acidity is another factor you should consider. It is always preferable to use acid-free paper with a neutral pH. This ensures that the paper will not darken excessively with age.

Unusual papers
Oriental papers, such as the top two, are made from plant sources. Toned papers have a vegetable dye added to them.

Weight
This is measured in pounds per ream (480 sheets) or grams per square meter. Light, thin papers can be soaked through, if that is the desired effect, and can also be quite strong. Really heavy papers do not need stretching and so are ideal for vigorous painting techniques.

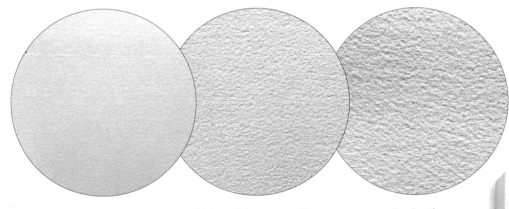

board   300 lb   260 lb   140 lb   90 lb

Blocks and pads
Watercolor paper can be bought in loose sheets, in spiral-bound pads, and in blocks. The blocks, which are bound on all four sides, have an advantage in that the paper does not need to be stretched before painting.

Hot-pressed or Smooth surface   *NOT or Cold-pressed surface*   *Rough surface*

Surface and weight

The three standard grades of surface in Western papers are Rough, HP (Hot-pressed) and NOT (Cold-pressed). Rough is just as its name suggests, a rough surface. Hot-pressed comes out very smooth, and NOT or Cold-pressed is a fine-grain or semi-rough surface – literally "not hot pressed". These categories vary enormously from one manufacturer to another, so look at several types before deciding which to buy. In terms of weight, both light and heavy papers have their advantages; it is largely a question of what you want to paint and which particular techniques you plan to use.

STRETCHING AND TONING

WATERCOLOR PAPER has to be stretched in advance to ensure that it does not pucker and buckle when you are painting on it but stays firm and flat on the drawing board. The procedure is quite simple: all you need is a board, masking tape, a sponge, and water. Once your paper has been stretched, you may want to tone it. Although you can buy toned paper, toning it yourself creates a somewhat different effect, since you are in fact laying a transparent color over white paper. Also, it allows you to create any color you desire.

Unstretched paper

Stretching paper

Unless you are going to use blocks of watercolor paper or very heavy paper, you should always stretch your paper before you start painting. You need to find a board that is about two inches wider than your paper on all four sides. It should be thick enough to withstand the tensions of the stretched paper without bending, and it should be slightly absorbent. Plywood, chipboard, particle board, or medium, density fiberboard make good surfaces and can be purchased cheaply from any lumber yard.

Materials for stretching

Sponges

Gum tape

Fiberboard
Chipboard
Plywood

1 ▲ Start by preparing four strips of heavy-duty masking tape of the right length, one for each side of the paper, and put them to one side. Next, wet your sheet of paper thoroughly with cold water to allow the fibers to expand. Don't use hot water, as this might remove the gelatin surface sizing of the paper.

2 ▲ Make sure the whole sheet is uniformly damp. You can wet the paper with a sponge or immerse it in a bath of cold water for a few minutes, depending on the thickness of the paper. Once the paper has expanded, moisten your lengths of gum tape with a sponge. If they are too wet, they will not stick properly.

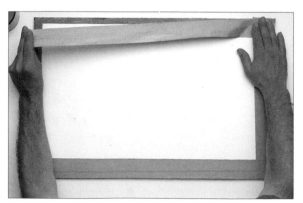

3 ▲ When your paper is thoroughly wetted, put it on the drawing board, smooth it out, and sponge off any excess water. Next, take the gum tape and stick the paper down firmly around the edges.

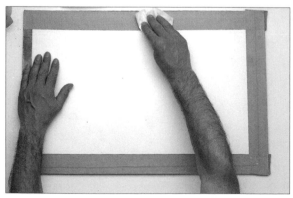

4 ▲ Now let the paper dry. You can speed up the process using a hair dryer on a low setting if you wish. When the water evaporates, the paper fibers contract, and the paper becomes hard and flat.

Toning paper

Most watercolor paper is white. While this suits those techniques that rely on the brightness of the ground to reflect light back through the color, the history of watercolor painting is full of works created on paper of widely varying tones. There are several advantages to toning paper yourself – it allows you to experiment with a wide range of different-colored grounds for your painting. Also, simple studies will look quite finished, with the color of the paper serving to unify the whole. One difficulty, however, is the problem of re-solubility – if you tone your paper with watercolor paint, you risk dislodging the color when you paint on it. Using well-diluted acrylic paints for toning will eliminate this risk.

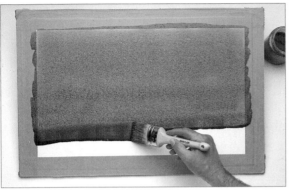

Materials for toning

Acrylic paint

1½ inch wash brush

1 ▲ Mix up sufficient paint – in this case well-diluted acrylics – to cover the whole sheet. Apply the mix using a large brush with the board at a slight angle to the horizontal. Pick up any drips with each successive brushstroke. The secret to toning paper evenly is to work quickly, making smooth horizontal brushstrokes.

2 ▲ Be sure to let your paper dry thoroughly before painting on it. The reason for using acrylics rather than watercolors for toning is that there is a slight danger that a watercolor base might dissolve when you paint over it. Acrylic paint will not be re-soluble after it has dried, so it will be fine to paint on.

Painting on toned paper
Although sketchy, the still life has quite a finished appearance because of the colored background. The artist has painted on the blue acrylic toned paper, using watercolors for the darker areas and white gouache for the highlights.

See how much lighter the background is once the paint has dried. You will need to allow for this when you tone paper yourself, whether you are using a watercolor base or an acrylic one.

The use of gouache for the highlights on the two fish and on the mushrooms is particularly effective. Pale watercolors would be lost against the strength of the background.

GALLERY OF PAPER

THE WAY YOUR WATERCOLOR PAINTING looks depends as much on the paper you use as on the way that you paint. A weakly sized absorbent paper will give a completely different look than will the same manipulation applied to a hard, surface-sized paper. The texture of the paper will similarly affect the appearance of the paint, with a rough surface giving a more textured look than that achieved with a smooth, hot-pressed surface, because the heavier pigments settle into the hollows of the paper. Another factor to consider is the color of the paper. The use of toned paper opens up a whole range of possibilities, including the use of bodycolor for highlights and a more low-key approach.

Although the paper is made by hand, there is nevertheless a regularity to the pattern that shows in the finished image.

The texture of the paper absorbs some of the paint and encourages a certain degree of bleeding of colors.

Jane Gifford,
Gathering Weed on Nagin Lake
Painted on rough handmade Indian paper, the water in this Kashmiri scene appears slightly choppier than that in the similar study on the right.

Sharon Finmark, *Portrait of Lia*
Many watercolor painters who enjoy the traditional transparent use of the medium tend to avoid toned paper, believing that it will adversely affect the appearance of the color. But, as with this sensitive study, the buff-toned paper actually creates a subtler and more effective backdrop than would a white ground. So in the areas that have been left unpainted, both to frame the girl and to act as highlights, it is the warmth of the paper that serves to harmonize and unify the whole.

Paul Klee, *Das Schloss*, c.1925
Throughout his life, Paul Klee was fascinated by the materials and techniques of painting, and his work reflects that interest. His constant experimentation with watercolors made him acutely sensitive to the innate quality of each new color and to the texture of a particular

Jane Gifford, *Two Shikaras on Nagin Lake*

This sketch, done on location in Kashmir, seems altogether more peaceful than the one on the left. Gifford uses the smooth surface of the paper to emphasize both the clearness of the sky and the glasslike quality of the water as the boats glide along its surface.

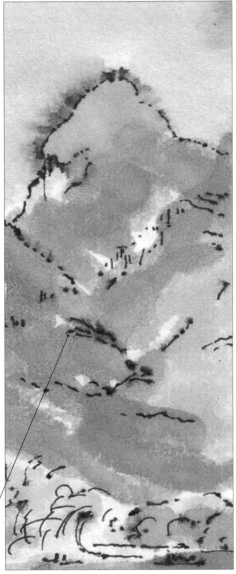

Here the unsized paper dictates the nature of the painting, creating a typically Chinese effect. The washes of paint are absorbed immediately into the paper, but even the ink lines, applied lightly with a fine drawing nib, bleed the moment the ink touches the paper.

piece of paper. It was factors such as these that led to the unique quality of his vision and his painting. Absolutely integral to the feel of this image is the heavy laid texture of the paper. The paint settles in its hollows and the scene is given a rough, grainy feel. The strong, scratchy ink line is the web holding this image together.

Jane Gifford, *Near Yangshuo, China*

An absorbent paper can give a softer, more diffused look than can a hard, surface-sized paper. This Chinese handmade paper automatically creates a Chinese-style painting. The quality of the paper prevents techniques such as washing off or masking.

171

WORKING WITH METHOD

IT IS USEFUL TO HAVE a certain amount of knowledge about the tools and materials of watercolor because this allows you to make appropriate decisions about which colors to use, for example, or which type of paper would be best in a given situation. But far more than this, you need to practice working with watercolor so that you get a real feel for the medium, rather than just understanding it intellectually.

Two basic brushes

An image made with a cow gum eraser

Gaining confidence

Essentially, the art of watercolor painting is about developing an ability to allow the paint to do its own thing while at the same time remaining in control of the process. Gradually you will start to recognize what is going on in your painting and will respond to it instinctively. What begins as a somewhat self-conscious process, as you attempt to make the right decisions about your painting – what colors to use, the degree of dilution, the type of brush, and so on – ends up becoming a much more intuitive one. You will start to recognize what your painting needs at any given moment without necessarily having to think about it. And with experience you will know both what particular colors or techniques are called for and also be able to put that knowledge into practice.

Controlling the medium

At its most complex, the watercolor medium can be extremely testing because it relies on such a high degree of control. It involves control over the amount and density of paint in the brush; control over how the brush applies the paint to the wet or dry surface of the painting; and control in modifying and moving the paint around on that surface. Many of the techniques associated with watercolor require the rapid and spontaneous application of color, and in some instances there is only one

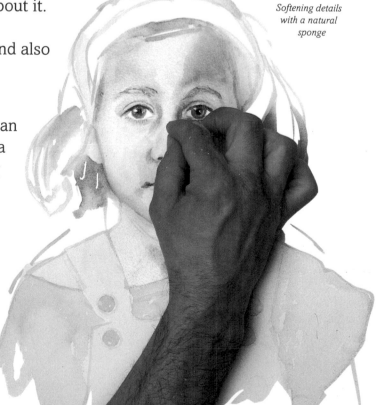

Softening details with a natural sponge

opportunity to get it right, if the whole thing is not to be washed off under cold water and begun again. But it also provides opportunities for artists who wish to create complex works involving, for example, building up layer on layer of thin washes of color using small and precise brushstrokes. In addition, there are a number of specialist techniques such as "stopping out" (*see* pp.194-5) and "wax resist" (*see* pp.196-7), in which different materials and skills are used in a painting to retain the original color of the paper or of a previous wash.

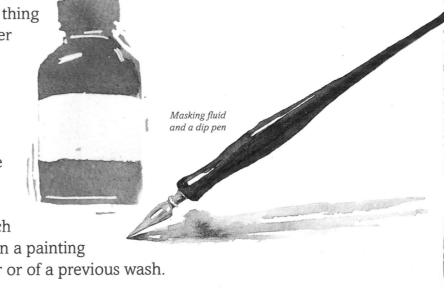

Masking fluid and a dip pen

A simple process

Crumpled paper towel

Natural sponge

Cow gum eraser

Toothbrush

Scalpel

In general, however, the materials and techniques of watercolor are straightforward. For the most part, for all their manipulations, both beginner and professional are simply using watercolor paints mixed with water. Most techniques are variations on a basic repertoire that involves the laying of washes, working wet-into-wet, and painting in layers. In the next section of our *Introduction to Watercolor,* we look at these various ways of working, starting with the basics of pencil sketches, drawing and composition, and moving on to the application of washes, the building up of color in layers, and the more advanced techniques of resist (*see* pp.194-7) and sgraffito (*see* pp.58-9).

Reaping the benefits

It may take time and practice to learn these skills so that the paint does what you want it to do and expect it to do, but the medium is rewarding right from the start. You will soon discover that watercolors can provide a satisfying and versatile challenge, as much to the beginner as to the more advanced artist.

Sandpapered surface

CAPTURING AN IMAGE

APART FROM MAKING PENCIL SKETCHES, artists today have a range of mechanical devices with which to record a scene, from simple drawing frames to cameras, camcorders, or slide projectors. Artists can project slides onto a screen and trace them or color-copy photographs, enlarging those areas that interest them the most.

Zoom lenses
Many cameras now have zoom facilities or wide-angle lenses so that you can get very close to a scene or record a much wider area, depending on what you want to record.

Drawing frame
You can use a drawing frame as a viewfinder, dividing the scene in front of you into manageable sections and then copying the grid onto a sheet of paper to guide you. You can make your own drawing frame by outlining a grid on a sheet of acetate.

Masking out
There may be details in your photo that you wish to exclude, in which case the simplest method is to mask them out. Here the artist wants to focus on the two girls with the rabbit, so she has "framed" the area she is interested in.

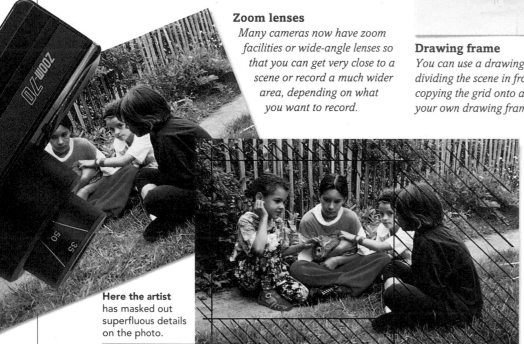

Here the artist has masked out superfluous details on the photo.

Color photocopies
The advantage of working from a photograph is that you can make a color copy of your print and then enlarge it (or a section of it) without losing quality. The larger of the two copies below has been blown up to 400 percent.

Tracing paper
If you lack the confidence to draw your image freehand, you can trace it from a photo. To tranfer it to your paper, copy the lines onto the back of the tracing paper, place it on your sheet and rub over the pencil lines.

THERE ARE NO RULES about how you should start your painting. If you feel sufficiently confident, you can do a pencil drawing directly on your sheet of paper, or even start painting immediately. But if you prefer to work from a photograph, or even to trace an image on your paper before you start, that is also fine. For centuries, artists have used whatever aids were at their disposal. Albrecht Dürer *(1471-1528)* illustrated a framed grid as a drawing device, and Vincent Van Gogh *(1853-90)* had a portable grid made up for him by a blacksmith. Today, with all the technological advances that have been made, there are even more tools to play with.

VIDEO CAMERAS

Artists of today can use home video cameras to record scenes they might wish to paint later. Often the camera lens sees more clearly than the eye, having the facility to take close-ups and focus in on the smallest details. Depending on the type of camera, video tapes can then be projected onto a screen or run through a television. Either way, it is generally possible to freeze-frame a scene and then trace or copy it onto a sheet of paper. You can then enlarge or reduce your image by using the grid method outlined below.

The grid method
This is the means of transferring an image onto your paper. You can either draw a grid of squares on your original or on a sheet of acetate that you place over your original. You then draw an identical grid on your sheet of paper, although it may be considerably larger if you want to scale the image up. You can then refer to the grid on the original and plot the outlines square by square on your paper.

Ruler and pencil

Painting by numbers

By numbering along one side of your grid and putting letters down the other, you can plot your picture more easily. Detailed areas of the original may need more squares. Here, for example, the girls' faces have more squares to make it easier to paint them.

175

COMPOSING A PAINTING

KNOWING HOW BEST TO COMPOSE your painting is often surprisingly difficult, but there are some guidelines that are worth following. The position of the horizon line is critical. Looking down from a high vantage point will give you a high horizon line, and consequently you will be able to map out the whole landscape or seascape like a carpet on your painting. A low horizon line, which allows you to look up at the scene in front of you, gives you an opportunity to make the most of the sky. It also means that large objects in the foreground will have the effect of towering above you. It is best to place points of visual interest slightly off-center and to avoid placing the horizon line right through the middle of the painting.

THE POSITIONING OF the main features of your composition does not have to follow a particular pattern, but artists generally try to achieve a sense of balance. This can be done intuitively – if it feels right, it probably is right. Such a balance can emerge from the fact that tones are deeper in the foreground and become progressively lighter toward the horizon. Or the sense of balance might be due to the relative weight of certain features in the painting. For example, an artist might feel that the massive shape of a tree on the left needs to be balanced by something on the right.

Sketching in pencil

A vast panorama
Here the artist wanted to capture the vastness of the scene in front of her. The focal point of the hilltop village is slightly off-center, and the rooftops lead the viewer in a meandering line, from foreground to background.

Playing with perspective
It is generally best to avoid placing the horizon line right through the middle of your painting. In the example above, the sky detracts from the points of interest; the low vantage point in the view on the right is far more dramatic.

Focal point

An alternative composition would be to place a large object, such as a tree, on a point off-center to the right or left, planted low but extending almost to the top edge. This would provide a focus or a pivot from which the rest of the composition would flow. Try looking at the painting and altering the edges with pieces of thick paper so that the tree is right in the center – you will see how much less subtle it is.

OPEN AND CLOSED COMPOSITIONS

In an open composition, the scene that you see is clearly part of a larger scene, while in a closed one what you see is all there is, like looking at a fish tank. Most compositions have elements of both. The important thing is not to let a key element of your composition slide off the page.

Closed composition

Open composition

The final painting

The artist selected this view for her finished painting, opting for the high horizon line to capture the sense of the village reaching heavenward. There is virtually no sky, and we are drawn up and down the scene in an upside-down "V" shape as we follow the line of the rooftops up and the trees back down again.

Here note both a visual harmony in the balance of shapes and forms and a color harmony in the balance of reds to greens. The background hills provide a resting point for the eye.

A sense of balance

In this composition, the artist has placed the focal point of the village slightly to the right of center, with the horizon line in the middle of the page. Although a centered horizon is something that should generally be avoided, it is not oppressive in this case because of the lightness of the sky. The viewer is led from the distant building on the summit of the hill, across the rooftops to the left of the page, and then on toward the nearest roof on the right. We are poised above the roof, looking out. The artist has achieved a sense of balance in the colors she has chosen, as well as with the positioning of the scene.

Shifting to the left

Here the points of interest are on the left-hand side of the painting. The horizon line has been moved up, so the sense of perspective is somewhat distorted as we look both down on the foreground buildings and up at the ones in the distance. The sun-drenched hills on the right tend to be more of a distraction than a harmonious counterpoint to the village.

DRAWING AND SKETCHING

DRAWING AND SKETCHING are an integral part of watercolor painting. Armed with just a sketchbook and a pencil, you can record the main features of a picture swiftly, or in greater detail. You can make notes about the particular colors and tones if you are going to translate your sketch into a painting later. Whatever your chosen method, making initial drawings gives you the space to reflect on what the focus of your painting should be and will tell you fairly quickly if something is going to work well as a final composition.

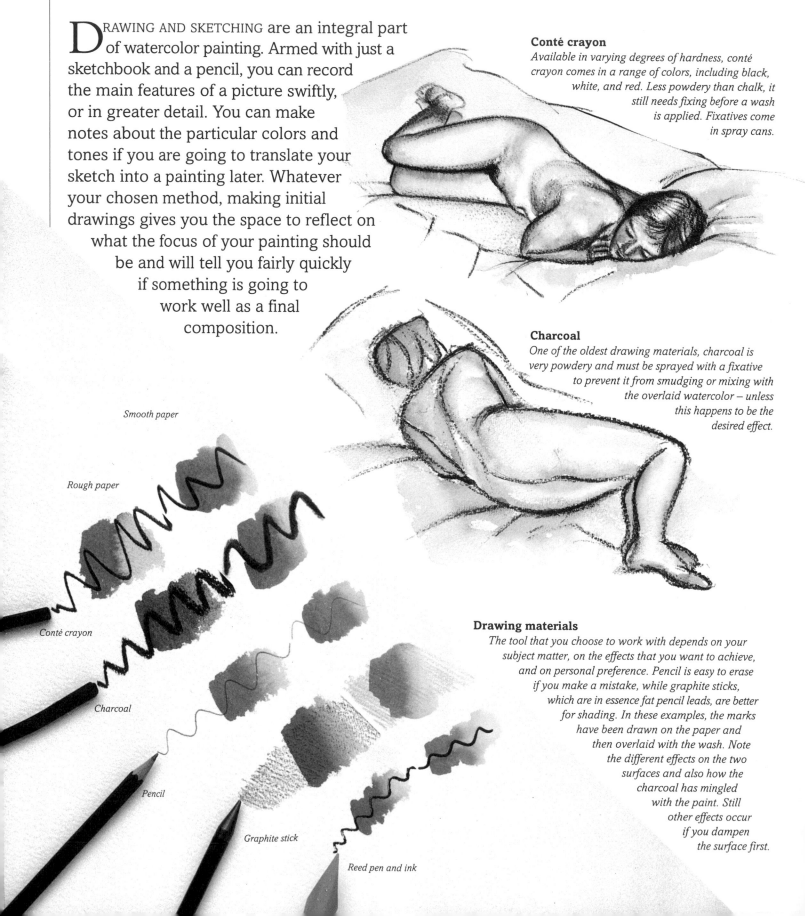

Conté crayon
Available in varying degrees of hardness, conté crayon comes in a range of colors, including black, white, and red. Less powdery than chalk, it still needs fixing before a wash is applied. Fixatives come in spray cans.

Charcoal
One of the oldest drawing materials, charcoal is very powdery and must be sprayed with a fixative to prevent it from smudging or mixing with the overlaid watercolor – unless this happens to be the desired effect.

Smooth paper

Rough paper

Conté crayon

Charcoal

Pencil

Graphite stick

Reed pen and ink

Drawing materials
The tool that you choose to work with depends on your subject matter, on the effects that you want to achieve, and on personal preference. Pencil is easy to erase if you make a mistake, while graphite sticks, which are in essence fat pencil leads, are better for shading. In these examples, the marks have been drawn on the paper and then overlaid with the wash. Note the different effects on the two surfaces and also how the charcoal has mingled with the paint. Still other effects occur if you dampen the surface first.

A PENCIL DRAWING can serve a variety of purposes, and different kinds of pencil are appropriate in each case. The traditional sketching pencil has a soft, fat lead that is good for tonal studies, but if you are making an essentially linear drawing you might prefer a clutch pencil with a relatively thin (.5 mm) lead no softer than about a B. Artists soon develop their own way of making drawings, but if you are not used to making pencil sketches, practice by making drawings of some small, simple objects. Before you begin, try to see the outline of the whole thing and then look to see how various lines and curves within the overall shape define the kind of object it is. It is best to start on a small scale before embarking on a larger picture.

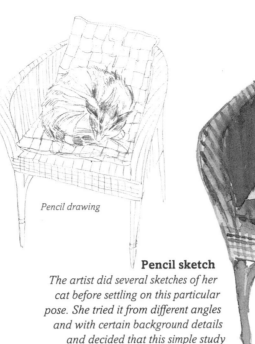

Pencil drawing

Pencil and wash

Pencil sketch
The artist did several sketches of her cat before settling on this particular pose. She tried it from different angles and with certain background details and decided that this simple study from a slightly raised perspective was the most successful.

Pen and wash
These two figures work well both as a simple pen and ink drawing and with the washes of watercolor. The latter has a greater solidity to it, but the line drawing has its own charm. Most drawing inks will not run or dissolve once they are dry, so there should be no problem in putting layers of paint over an ink sketch.

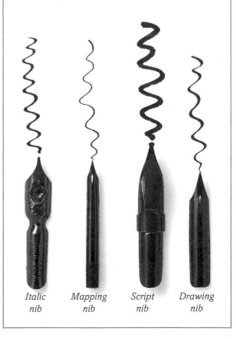

Ink drawing

Ink and wash

DRAWING NIBS

There are many types of steel nibs that you can use for drawing – it is largely a matter of personal preference. There are the standard drawing nibs and then the script pen nibs, which can also be used. These come in a variety of widths, with or without reservoirs. They all have a springiness in the steel that allows the artist to vary the width and the quality of the line while drawing. Mapping nibs are good for very fine lines, while italic nibs can be either fine or broad.

Italic nib *Mapping nib* *Script nib* *Drawing nib*

179

LAYING A WASH

WASH IS A THIN LAYER of watercolor paint, usually applied with a saturated brush over a fairly large area. It can be applied onto dry or damp paper, or it can be overlaid onto dry color already on the paper.

The wash can be manipulated wet, so that particular areas can be lifted and lightened, or other colors can be dropped into it while it is still wet. Alternatively, the wash can be adapted in various ways when it is dry.

How to lay a flat wash

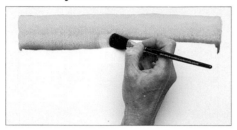

1 ◀ Mix up enough paint before you begin and make sure it is well stirred. You will not be able to stop halfway through to mix more. It is a good idea to use a bristle brush for mixing the paint, as this will break it down more easily. Then for applying the wash, use a soft-hair brush; either round or flat is fine.

2 ▶ With a saturated wash brush, keep a continuous line of wet color forming along the bottom edge. You may find it easier if the paper is at a slight angle. It is also easier to apply a flat, uniform wash onto a NOT or Rough surface than onto a smooth one, since the smooth surface will show up any streaks.

3 ▲ Pick up the paint with each succeeding stroke. Try to avoid any trickles, and apply the paint in a smooth, continuous motion. You can work left to right or in both directions.

Flat wash

This doorway has been created with washes of flat color, in this case a very dilute mix of Cobalt Blue and Permanent Rose. Note the granulation of the pigment on the NOT (semi-rough) surface.

Graded one-color wash

A graded wash is one in which the tone moves smoothly from dark to light. Mixing a light, a mid, and a dark tone of orange in separate saucers, apply the darkest tone first and proceed down the sheet.

Laying a variegated wash

1 ▲ To help the wash flow out, you can wet the area to be painted first, with a sponge or a brush. Then with a soft-hair wash brush, either round or flat, apply your wash of Winsor Blue to the paper.

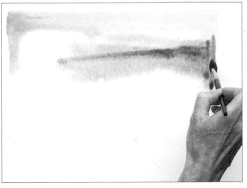

2 ▲ Remember to wash out your brush between colors. Then, starting at the right-hand side, wash in some Violet, touching the Blue in parts and allowing the Violet to diffuse across the page.

3 ▲ Working quite quickly, apply some brushstrokes of Lemon Yellow onto the wet surface, in the right-hand corner.

4 ◀ Here some areas of Carmine are added at the bottom. All the paints have been applied very wet, and the board has been moved around to allow the colors to flow in specific directions. Note how the different pigments react with each other and also with the surface of the paper.

TIPS

● Mix up enough paint before you begin, and make sure the mixture remains well stirred, since many pigments have a tendency to settle in the saucer.

● It is a good idea to mix your wash color with a different brush than the one with which you apply it. A bristle brush is best if you are mixing a fair amount of paint from a tube, as you can break the paint down into a well-diluted mix more easily than with a soft-hair brush.

● Many artists like to work with their paper at an angle when applying washes, as this allows them to control the flow of the paint more easily.

● To achieve a more uniform tone, you can dampen your paper before you apply your wash.

● Remember that a watercolor wash dries lighter in tone than it appears when you paint it on, so you should compensate for this in your mix.

Graded two-color wash
Running one tone into another can be done with two or more colors. Mix sufficient quantities of the colors you require and apply them swiftly, allowing them to mingle and diffuse if you wish.

Variegated wash
To wash several colors over areas of your painting, pre-mix the colors and then paint them rapidly up to the boundary of the neighboring color. The colors will then diffuse into each other along the join.

WASHES

WASHES WILL VARY depending on the pigments used, on how they are applied, and also on the quality of the paper. For example, on smooth paper there is a tendency for washes to appear streaky, while on a rough surface they may not penetrate the hollows of the paper. But washes can also be modified while they are still wet. Shapes can be sponged out of a wash, clean water can be dripped into them, or additional colors can be dropped in.

Smooth paper
The colors in the two studies are the same but appear deeper and more vibrant on the smooth paper. Washes should be applied in a continuous, even movement when a smooth paper is used.

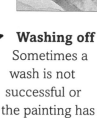

Rough paper
On Rough paper your brushstroke needs to be slower and firmer to ensure that the paint runs into the hollows. In this example, the Rough surface has created a sparkle effect.

Washing off
Sometimes a wash is not successful or the painting has become too dense with pigment to successfully overlay another color. If this happens, you can wash the whole thing off. You should use cold water to avoid removing the surface sizing on the paper. Very often a washed-off painting can look far better than it did before. It may only require minor adjustments to be complete.

The essential feature of a washed-off painting is that the texture of the paper is revealed more clearly since the process takes off the top surface. That is, the raised parts of a Rough or NOT surface will be left pale, while the pigment remains lodged in the deeper crevices of the paper. Washing off removes only part of a color. Once it is lodged in the fibers of the paper, watercolor is very tenacious. Some pigments have more staining power than others, but most resist the effect of washing off to some degree.

TIPS

Mixing up paint

● Use a bristle brush to mix up the paint, but use a soft-hair wash brush, either flat or round, to lay the wash. Make sure you mix up enough paint before you start, as you cannot pause to mix up more while you are in the middle of laying the wash.

● Smooth paper will show up any streaks that have been created by (a) not having stirred up the paint well enough, (b) taking too long to apply it, or (c) pushing down too hard with the brush.

● Rough paper will have a sparkle effect in which spots of white paper show through the wash. If you wish to avoid this, you may need to work back and forth over the same area several times to ensure that the paint gets into the dips in the surface.

Washing off and overlaying a second wash

Pink wash

1 ▲ Using a Rough paper, paint a blue wash over a section of it.

2 ▲ Wash the blue off under cold water, using a bristle brush to help dislodge the paint.

3 ▲ Paint a layer of pink over the washed-off blue. You will produce a grainy purple.

Wash techniques

Although we tend to think of washes as applications of paint that cover large areas of a painting, the technique is equally suitable for smaller areas. For these you simply use smaller versions of the same brushes, in particular, the small round sables. The following swatches are just a few examples of what you can do with washes of color. Some use the tip of the brush, others the toe, and still others involve two brushes being used simultaneously. The possibilities are endless.

A thick application *of Permanent Rose is dragged rapidly across a wet wash of Winsor Blue on a flat 1 inch brush.*

The toe *of a small, round, nylon brush with Permanent Rose is curled swiftly into the Winsor Blue wash to create this suffused vapor trail effect.*

Two drops *of Permanent Rose are dripped into the watery Winsor Blue wash and allowed to spread outward.*

Using a medium-size, *round, soft-hair brush, Permanent Rose is worked rapidly around the edge of this Winsor Blue wash.*

A band of *Manganese Blue and one of Winsor Green are allowed to fuse together. The granulated Manganese Blue wash contrasts with the more even green one.*

Curling a *dark tone of Winsor Green into the granulated Manganese Blue wash gives a very different effect.*

Working simultaneously *with two No.8 round brushes, fully charged with dense pigment, can give these rich effects.*

After the *Manganese Blue wash has been applied, the Winsor Green is scrubbed into the paper with a bristle brush.*

Two colors *have been applied onto a flat 1¼ inch wash brush before being dragged quickly across the paper.*

Separate blocks *of Violet and Rose have been applied and allowed to dry before being joined by using a clean, damp brush.*

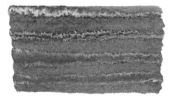

One thin stroke *of Violet is followed rapidly by another thin stroke of Winsor Green, to create this layered effect.*

The areas *of Winsor Green and of Violet are allowed to run together to create this densely textured, yet fluffy effect.*

APPLYING A WASH WITH A SPONGE

There are a number of ways of applying washes, from the traditional wash brush, for standard techniques, to small round brushes, for more confined areas, to household wallpaper brushes, for very large areas. Some artists, however, like to work with sponges because it allows them to cover large areas more rapidly and effectively. Try laying a wash with several types of sponges to see which you prefer.

1 *To sponge on a wash, mix up a large amount of color and soak your sponge in it. A small natural sponge is best, but you can use a household sponge for larger areas.*

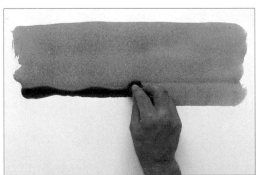

2 *Holding the sponge in your fingertips, rub it back and forth, catching the drips as you go. The technique is to work downward as if you were washing a window.*

GALLERY OF WASHES

SUCCESSFUL WATERCOLOR PAINTINGS depend, to a large extent, on the application of washes. Learning to lay washes is a skill that has to be acquired through practice, as it involves an understanding of the amount of paint required to be held in the brush, the degree of dilution of the paint, the nature and angle of the surface being painted, and the appropriate choice and handling of the brush itself. Washes can be free-flowing over a large area, with color blending into color and with variations of tone, or they can be tightly controlled in small or irregular shaped areas. In addition, they can be manipulated wet, so that particular areas can be lifted and lightened or altered by having additional colors dropped in.

Gisela Van Oepen, *Pays de l'Aude*
This painting clearly demonstrates the effect of working into very wet areas with dense color. This can be done either by laying a clear wash over chosen areas and then dropping in the deep colors or by applying color first and dropping in water or additional colors afterward.

Miles E. Cotman, *A Calm, c.1840-49*
This peaceful scene demonstrates great control in the application of washes. Notice how the uniformity of tone in the wash for the sky is sustained right up to the edges of the clouds. There are no dramatic sweeps of the brush – just the kind of consummate skill that allows the image to speak for itself.

Two washes of color, carefully controlled, are all Cotman needed to realize this sailing vessel in the distance.

Jane Gifford,
Street Scene,
Madras
In this simple yet effective study, the artist has carefully applied her washes in a form of "patchwork" to indicate the broad masses of color on the scene. She has allowed the washes to move around freely in areas where it is appropriate to the subject to do so, as on the dome.

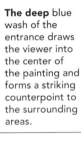

The deep blue wash of the entrance draws the viewer into the center of the painting and forms a striking counterpoint to the surrounding areas.

A couple of broad, loose brushstrokes is all that is needed to suggest this woman in her radiant sari, framed by the darkness of the doorway.

Julian Gregg, *Poppit Sands, Cardigan*
In this loosely worked sketch, there is practically no overpainting, and areas of the paper are left untouched. The artist has applied simple washes along the horizontal axis, allowing colors to bleed into one another wet-in-wet while relying on single, sweeping brushstrokes along the horizon.

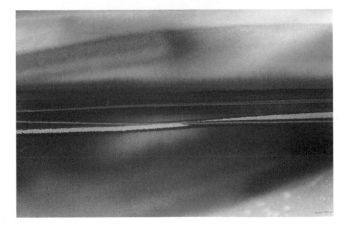

Robert Tilling, *Low Tide Light*
Using broad wash brushes, Tilling lays large areas of very wet color across his paper, skillfully controlling the paint. Here the washes are swept across the painting, softening in tone in particular areas to create the effect of the light. Certain colors are allowed to bleed into the next to create an evocative sense of space and mood.

185

TONE AND COLOR

AFTER LEARNING TO LAY WASHES, the next stage is to practice building up tone and color. The easiest way to approach this is to work initially in tones of one color. In the past, it was quite common for artists to paint monochromatic studies, using colors such as Sepia (a dark reddish brown), made from the ink sac of the cuttlefish, and red and brown earth pigments. Other good colors to practice with are dark green, blue and black.

Tonal values
Tone is the relative darkness or lightness of an image. If you look at the crumpled paper, you will see that, although it is white, the play of light over its surface creates a range of tonal contrasts from white to gray. It is these that give the paper its form.

1 ▲ After making a pencil sketch of the plant, apply the palest washes first, in this case a very dilute Indigo, and start filling in the leaves. Notice where the highlights are, and leave these areas white.

2 ▲ Look hard at the plant, trying to see the tones rather than the colors. A useful device is to half-close your eyes. Once you have distinguished the areas of light and dark, start building up the layers, remembering to let each layer dry before applying the next.

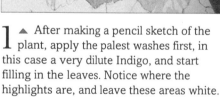

3 ◀ Start working in some of the details, remembering that the areas in shadow will be the darkest.

4 ▲ You may find you need a finer brush for the central area, with its intricate array of leaves and flowers.

The delicate flowers of the African violet are among the lightest areas of tone in this composition. See how the fine outline of the petals serves to throw them into relief.

5 ▲ When you apply very wet washes of paint, keep some blotting paper handy in case the color starts to run.

The sense of the roundness and solidity of the earthenware pot is created by the gradual darkening of tone from left to right, from the area where the light strikes it to the area of shadow.

6 ◀ As you work, you will notice that the color becomes considerably lighter as it dries. If you need a darker tone of blue, mix in some Payne's Gray with your Indigo. Use the darker mix for the veins in the leaves and for the areas that are in shadow.

If you look closely at this leaf, you can almost count the layers of paint that have been applied. It is the contrast between these very dark areas and the lighter ones that give the plant study its three-dimensionality.

Materials

Indigo

Payne's Gray

No.8 round

OVERLAYING A WASH

Although monochromatic painting is a rewarding technique in its own right, and one with a rich and celebrated history, watercolor painting is more traditionally associated with overlaid washes of color. To get a clearer idea of the nature of watercolor and the way in which each overlaid color affects the one below, do a simple painting in tones of one color and see what happens when you lay a wash of a different color over it. In the example below, the yellow landscape is transformed by the application of a Cerulean Blue wash. Note how the blue over the different shades of yellow results in a broad range of greens, even though no green was applied.

Range of yellows, Burnt Sienna, and Raw Umber

Swatches with overlaid blue

Effects of Cerulean Blue applied over yellows

BUILDING UP LAYERS

TRADITIONALLY, WATERCOLOR PAINTING is built up in stages. Since the watercolor medium is generally characterized by transparent color effects, with the color of the paper underlying all the painting, the overlaying of color is really a form of glazing. Any number of colors may be glazed over each other, and each will affect the look of the whole. The most important feature of the technique is that each color beneath must be completely dry before you paint over it.

Testing colors
It is good practice to try your colors out, both singly and by overlaying them, before committing them to your actual painting. These are the colors used for the painting of the lighthouse.

1 ▲ In this exercise, you will see how you can create a painting by building up washes of color. First, with a No.12 wash brush, fill in the sky, sea, and cliff areas with a mixture of Cobalt Blue and Payne's Gray.

2 ▲ Once the blue has dried, mix up a wash of Alizarin Crimson and fill in some of the sky area and more of the cliffs. See how the blue shows through the pink and how it is affected by this single layer of overpainting, taking on a purplish hue.

3 ▲ To warm up the color of the cliffs, add a wash of Raw Sienna. Use this color also for the basis of the lighthouse, the trees, and the grassy areas.

4 ◀ Again allowing the Raw Sienna to dry, add a layer of Prussian Blue over the trees and grass, building up those areas that need to be darker. Note how the blue over the yellow results in a green, the hue depending on the relative strengths of each.

COMPLEMENTARY COLORS

The balance of complementary colors plays an important part in painting techniques. If, for example, you are painting a predominantly green landscape, you can create a subtle balance in the color by laying a bright green wash, letting it dry, and overpainting it with a red one.

In the scene shown below, the sky as well as the foreground area have been overlaid with a red wash, with the poppies forming the final detail. The overall effect is to warm up the landscape, heighten the sense of perspective, and greatly enrich the feel of the work.

Landscape in blues and greens

Landscape with overlaid red wash

5 ◀ To strengthen the tone of the sea, add a second layer of Prussian Blue mixed with Indigo over some of the foreground waves. You will see that the colors appear brighter while the paint is wet, so you may need to deepen certain colors once your painting has dried.

Lighthouse study
Final touches of blue have been added to give definition to the windows and bring foreground areas into sharper focus.

Note how areas have been left so that the white of the paper forms the clouds and sides of the buildings.

Materials

Cobalt Blue

Payne's Gray

Alizarin Crimson

Raw Sienna

Prussian Blue

Indigo

No.8 sable/synthetic

No.12 synthetic

189

SPONGING OUT

FOR CERTAIN EFFECTS, you may need to modify your painting while it is wet, or even after it has dried. For example, you might want to create shapes that are lighter in tone in a certain area. In such a case, it is often easier to apply a broad wash of color over a complete section of a painting rather than trying to avoid or paint around certain areas.

You can subsequently sponge out or blot out those areas that need to be lighter, a technique known as lifting off. You can do this when the paint is wet or after it has dried, depending on which method is more convenient. The effect is largely the same, although lightening areas after the paint has dried may require some vigorous brushwork to dislodge the pigment.

1 ◄ To sponge out cloud shapes, apply a wash of Cerulean Blue plus Mauve with a medium-size brush. While the paint is still wet, dip a small natural sponge in water, press it onto the blue wash, and remove it in one movement. The sponge will lift off the blue wash.

2 ▶ To practice sponging out from dry paint later, lay a green wash for the bank of the river, making some of the hills in the distance a little darker. Once this has dried, fill in the tree and grass details with a rigger – a fine, pointed brush with long hairs.

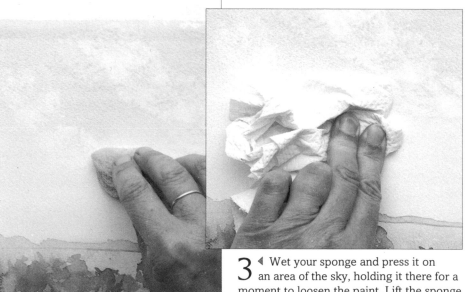

3 ◄ Wet your sponge and press it on an area of the sky, holding it there for a moment to loosen the paint. Lift the sponge off, and press a sheet of paper towel onto the area that has been wetted. Remove the paper towel to lift the paint off. The sponge will have created cloudlike forms.

4 ▲ To accentuate the shape of the clouds and build up the sky, mix up some Burnt Sienna and Cerulean Blue. With a medium-size brush, apply your blue wash to the sky, painting around the whited-out cloud areas in order to create shadows and give them a sense of three-dimensionality.

EXAMPLES OF LIFTING OFF

Lifting with brush from dry paint
Here the clouds have been created by working into the sky with a wet bristle brush until the paint has loosened sufficiently to be removed. To dislodge dry paint, you will need to use your brush quite vigorously. Some pigment may remain in the paper.

Lifting with paper towel from dry paint
A wet sponge has loosened the dried paint of the sky after which the clouds have been lifted with a paper towel.

Sponging out from wet paint
Here the clouds have been sponged out using a moistened sponge on wet paint. The sponge has been rubbed onto the blue wash and lifted off, taking some of the paint with it. Notice the soft, diffused effect the sponge creates, particularly in comparison to the other methods of lifting off.

5 ▶ In order to lighten the foreground grass, load your brush with clean water and draw it across the area of dry color you wish to modify. While the water seeps in, work your brush between the trees to create greater definition between them. The degree to which you can wash areas out of your painting will depend on the staining power of the pigments you have used.

6 ◀ Press a sheet of blotting paper onto the wet grass, and then remove it. A good deal of the paint will come off. Repeat the process between the trees, first wetting the area you wish to modify with a brush dipped in clean water and then blotting it off with the blotting paper. You may be able to lift a tree out completely in this way.

Riverside study
In this finished version, you can clearly see those areas that have been lightened – the clouds, the foreground grass, and the details between the trees. What you cannot tell is which areas have been modified while wet and which while dry. It does not make much difference which way you choose to work. It is largely a matter of personal preference and convenience. If you are doing a quick study outdoors, you might even sponge out shapes when you get back to your studio.

Materials

Rigger

No.6 sable

Natural sponge

Blotting paper

SCRATCHING OUT

Cornish graveyard

IN WATERCOLOR PAINTING, the technique of scratching out is a means of getting back to the white of the paper or to the dried paint film underneath the one that has just been applied. It can be used for highlights or for particular effects and is as applicable to wet paint films as it is to dry. With wet paint, the technique is to scrape the surface with the blunt blade of a penknife, taking care not to cut the paper. With dry paint, the method is to physically skin the dry paint off of the area you want to reveal. The way you handle your blade – using gentle strokes or vigorous ones – will determine the look of the technique.

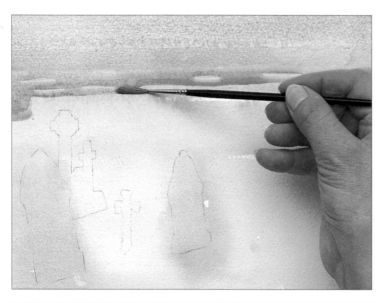

1 ◄ Using Rough paper, apply a wash of Raw Umber with a 1 inch brush, starting at the horizon. Dilute the paint as you work your way down; a somewhat patchy effect is fine. Once this has dried, draw a faint pencil outline of the gravestones. Next, take a small round brush and paint a wash of Cerulean Blue over all of the paper, taking care to avoid the gravestones. Apply the blue in loose horizontal strokes. You may have to go over certain areas since paint dries lighter than it appears when it is wet.

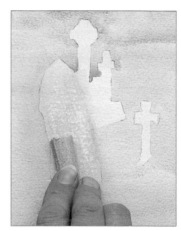

2 ▲ Once the paint has dried, cut a piece of medium grade sandpaper and wrap it around your pencil. Then, using the sandpapered surface, gently scratch the three front stones.

3 ▲ Build up the grass area by adding layers of Aureolin – a bright yellow – and more Cerulean Blue, always allowing the paint to dry between layers. You may use a hair dryer on cool to speed up the process. Next, take a craft blade and use it to scratch highlights in the sea, pulling the blade down in short vertical strokes (or horizontal ones for headland waves). Notice how the blade reveals the Rough surface of the paper.

4 ▲ Mix Cerulean Blue and Sepia and use your fine, pointed brush to build up the background details. Now take a wet sponge and rub it over an area of dried paint to sponge out another gravestone.

5 ▲ Take a scalpel and gently score around the side of the house, cutting just deep enough to remove the surface of the paper without cutting right through it. Using the blade or a pair of tweezers, lift off the sliver of paper.

6 ◀ Do the same on the second house. The act of skinning these surface layers raises the nap of the paper. You need to burnish (rub down) the paper that you have revealed with your nail or the flat of a paper cutter. This is particularly important if you want to overpaint the area later.

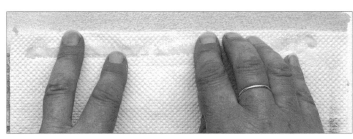

7 ◀ To lighten the blue of the horizon and create a feeling of distance in your painting, dip a flat wash brush in clean water and draw it over the area that you want to modify. Allow the water to seep in for a moment.

8 ◀ While the surface is still wet, press a paper towel over the area and then lift the towel off. You will see that the towel removes some of the loosened paint. If you want to make the horizon even lighter, roll a small piece of soft bread over it while the paint is damp. You will find that this picks up still more of the pigment.

Finished work
For the final touches, the artist has used the wooden end of the brush to "cut" blades of grass in the foreground area while the paint is still wet. She has also rubbed sandpaper over the dried paint film of the gravestones, to give them their characteristic coarseness.

Sanding down
certain areas of the grass reveals the roughness of the paper surface.

Materials

No.8 round brush

1 inch flat brush

Medium sandpaper

Craft blade

Scalpel

Natural sponge

Paper towel

RESIST TECHNIQUES

Pencil sketch

I F YOU WISH to protect certain areas of your painting so that you can paint over them without disturbing what lies beneath, you can use a method known as masking or stopping out – a "resist" technique. This involves applying masking fluid.

Once the fluid has dried and you have painted over it as much as you wish, you can rub off the masking fluid to expose the protected area of the painting. Masking can be used for highlights, as a means of keeping the paper white, or for safeguarding an area that is light in tone while you deepen the tones around it.

USING MASKING FLUID

1 *Do a pencil drawing of your fox and carefully mask around the edge. Here it has been done in two stages, first with masking fluid applied with a dip pen and then more loosely with a brush.*

2 *Let the masking fluid dry and then dampen the area inside it so that the colors will merge when you apply them. Lay down washes of Burnt Sienna, Cadmium Scarlet, and Payne's Gray.*

3 *Once the paint has dried, gently rub off the masking fluid. You can do this in a number of ways, either with a cow gum eraser, a putty eraser, or simply by using your fingers. You will find that the pencil lines are erased in the process.*

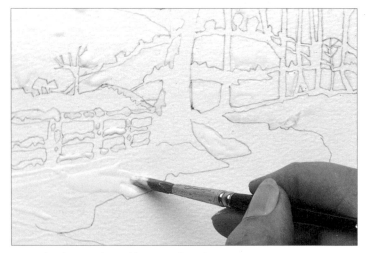

1 ▲ Again, starting with a pencil outline, mask out the areas you wish to protect. As the masking fluid tends to ruin the hairs, you can either use an old brush for this, or protect your brush by rubbing the hairs over a bar of soap before you start. Always wash the brush in warm soapy water as soon as you've finished.

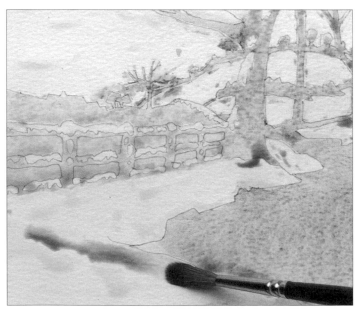

2 ▲ Let the masking fluid dry naturally or speed the process up with a hair dryer. Then, using a medium-size brush, apply a wash of Cobalt Blue and Burnt Sienna over the unmasked areas.

4 ▲ Dry the masking fluid with a hair dryer. You can test it to make sure it is dry by touching it lightly with your fingertips. Next, deepen the tones of the river with another Burnt Sienna and Cobalt Blue wash.

CARE OF YOUR BRUSH

Use an old brush for applying masking fluid and always wash it out in warm soapy water between applications. If you use a good brush, rub the hairs with wet soap before you start. This offers some protection as it prevents the masking fluid from clogging up the ferrule and adhering to the hairs. The lower brush was treated in this way, while the top one shows the effects of masking fluid having dried and coagulated on the hairs.

3 ▲ Apply more washes of Burnt Sienna and Payne's Gray to darken the tones of the trees and the fence, allowing each layer to dry between applications. Then mask out areas of reflection in the river using an old, smallish brush. Wash the brush in warm soapy water as soon as you have finished, to stop the masking fluid from ruining the hairs.

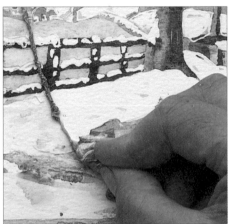

Masking fluid gives a hard edge to any shape that is masked out, a characteristic that can be seen most clearly in the snow-covered fence.

The sky is the final detail to be painted, having been masked from the outset.

5 ◀ Lift off the masking fluid with a cow gum eraser or a putty eraser. Once it has been removed, fill in the sky with a wash of Alizarin Crimson, Cobalt Blue, and Burnt Sienna.

Materials

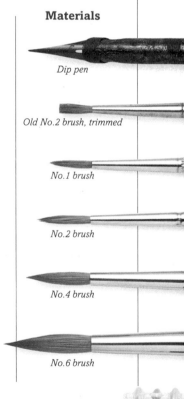

Dip pen

Old No.2 brush, trimmed

No.1 brush

No.2 brush

No.4 brush

No.6 brush

Masking fluid

Winter scene
With the removal of the masking fluid, several things happen: the whiteness of the paper is revealed and the original pencil lines are rubbed out at the same time.

OTHER RESIST TECHNIQUES

FOR MORE SUBTLE MASKING-OUT effects than those achieved with masking fluid, you can use gouache paint, wax, or gum arabic. The results are slightly different in each case, and the gouache and the gum arabic have to be washed off the paper in order to achieve the resist effect. This means that you are disturbing the color you have just painted on, so remember that when you paint over the masked-out areas, you must use a deeper tone than the one you want to end up with. The effect of washing off gives a slightly softer-edged feel to the masked-out area than you would achieve with masking fluid. If you opt for gouache, it is best to use white. It has the least effect on the colors when it is washed off.

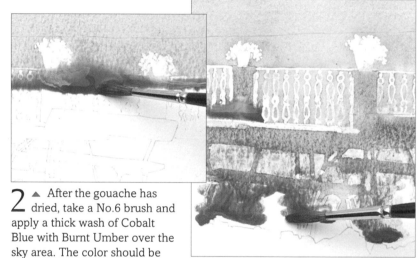

2 ▲ After the gouache has dried, take a No.6 brush and apply a thick wash of Cobalt Blue with Burnt Umber over the sky area. The color should be quite strong to allow for the fact that some of it will be washed off. See how the gouache paint repels the blue and umber wash.

3 ▲ Once the blue has dried, mix up a wash of Burnt Umber. Apply this smoothly and rapidly to the columns and benches so as not to disturb the gouache.

1 ▲ For gouache resist, draw an outline of the balcony details on a Rough paper and plan which areas will need to be masked out. Mix up some white gouache paint relatively thickly, like heavy cream. Then take a very fine brush and paint in the railings and the flower pots, and use a larger brush to paint the balcony floor.

4 ◀ For wax resist, use a sliver of a candle and draw in some foreground grass. Draw additional grass with olive green and light green wax/oil crayons. Both the candle and the crayons will repel washes of color.

5 ▲ Mix up a wash of Burnt Umber and Viridian Green and paint it thickly over the foreground area. Note how the wash refuses to adhere to the wax-resisted surface. Although the effects are quite subtle, if you look closely you will be able to distinguish individual blades of white and green grass once the wash has dried.

Materials

6 ▶ Add another layer of your blue and umber mix to deepen the color of the hills. Allow this to dry. Then lower your painting into water and gently sponge over the whole surface. The process will remove the gouache as well as dislodging some of the paint, but the candle wax and wax crayon will not be affected. Now stretch your paper on a board and leave it to dry.

7 ▲ For gum arabic resist, make sure your painting is completely dry and then draw the outline of the overhanging leaves in pencil. Next mix up a wash of Viridian and Cadmium Yellow with equal amounts of gum arabic and water and apply it to the leaves. You can block in large areas of color, since details of sky around the leaves can be lifted out later.

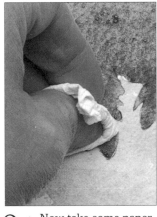

8 ▲ Allow the paint to dry. It will appear quite shiny because of the gum arabic solution. Now dip a fine brush, perhaps a No.1, in water and "paint" an area in the foliage which you wish to lift off later in order to reveal some sky. Allow the water to sink into the paint for a while.

9 ▲ Now take some paper towel, press it onto the moistened area, and lift off the green paint. Because of the gum arabic, it will come off quite easily, without disturbing the blue beneath it.

No.6 brush

No.1 brush

Wax/oil crayons

Wax candle

Natural sponge

Final touches
Because the washing-off process lifts off some of the paint, details have to be painted in or accentuated later. Here the flowers are painted in Cadmium Scarlet. The columns and the benches are darkened, and the shadows are then added as a final stage.

Gum arabic

The white gouache leaves no trace on the paper and yet effectively blocks out any color. It also creates a much softer edge than masking out with masking fluid.

The wax resist adds texture to the foreground grass.

USING GOUACHE

GOUACHE, OR BODYCOLOR as it is also known, is a watercolor – but it is characterized by its opacity rather than by the transparent effects normally associated with the medium. Because of its different properties, it has specific uses in watercolor painting, for example, to create highlights in a traditional watercolor painting, or to provide a matte and uniformly even tone when that is what is required. It is generally applied more thickly than a regular watercolor and can create a more impasto effect. Because of its opacity, gouache works particularly well, and economically, on toned or colored paper.

SINCE GOUACHE PAINT is used more thickly than traditional watercolor, the paint film needs to be a little more flexible. It also needs to flow well to ensure that it can be brushed smoothly out in flat, opaque tones. Although gouache colors are made in almost exactly the same way as other watercolors, there are certain modifications that make them marginally more soluble than watercolors, an effect that is noticeable when overpainting them.

Highlights
Gouache paints are traditionally used for highlights, specifically for picking out details on buildings. Their opacity makes them useful in conjunction with traditional watercolors. In the image on the left, the white gouache creates the sense of form on what might otherwise seem a rather flat, two-dimensional structure.

OVERLAYING GOUACHE

Gouache is, in effect, just another form of watercolor. The paints can be used in the same way as straight watercolor paints, provided they are sufficiently diluted. They can, however, also be used much more thickly, when, for example, a flat uniform tone is required in a particular area, or a more textured look is desired. Between these uses lies a wide range of possible manipulations and effects.

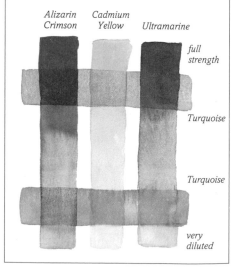

Alizarin Crimson   *Cadmium Yellow*   *Ultramarine*

full strength

Turquoise

Turquoise

very diluted

Toned paper
Gouache is particularly effective on lightly toned paper where the background color serves to unify the whole. To work in this way, begin by sketching in the main features. Then look for the lightest tones and paint them in by adding a touch of color to the white gouache. Next look for the dark tones and paint them using a more watery mix as above. Although similar to using oils as a technique, the finished appearance is quite different and displays a characteristic chalky matte quality.

High pigment loading

The opacity of gouache is often obtained by incorporating very high levels of pigmentation – far more than in watercolor. Gouache paints work well in washes, so they can represent good value for money as an alternative to watercolor.

The opaque nature of gouache means that for certain colors there is no other way to get a high level of brightness than to use brilliant but very fugitive pigments. Such colors may be fine for illustrators, whose work is designed for reproduction, but there is no point in using them in artwork that you wish to be permanent. It is a therefore advisable to check the durability rating before you purchase a gouache color.

Transparent and opaque

Gouache can be used in conjunction with transparent techniques or on its own, as in this nude study. Here the artist has exploited the diverse nature of gouache by using it both thickly, as in the face and neck area, and highly diluted, as in the legs. Generally, however, she has chosen to use it more like a traditional watercolor than as an opaque painting medium.

A versatile medium

Having said that, gouache, with its wide range of manipulations and uses, is somewhat more versatile than traditional watercolor paints while being equally easy to handle. It has been used for such a diverse range of subjects as small-scale Indian and Persian miniatures and large-scale studies for oils. When used on a large scale, gouache paints are generally applied with bristle brushes. These are particularly good both for breaking down the paint and for blending it.

Although gouache can be used on its own, either thickly or thinly as in the two examples on this page, it can equally be used in conjunction with traditional watercolors. Indeed, some contemporary artists have made a point of juxtaposing the transparent and opaque techniques of the two forms of watercolor paint in the same work, in order to exploit their different natures and effects.

Impasto effects

Gouache can be used thickly, much like oil paints, with the advantage that it dries far more quickly. Here the artist was fascinated by the colors in the water and wanted a water-based medium to capture the shimmering, elusive quality of the fish. The gouache gives the painting a richness and density of tone not possible with transparent techniques.

GALLERY OF TECHNIQUES

THE RANGE OF TECHNIQUES available to the watercolor painter is limited only by the imagination of the individual artist, so you will no doubt devise methods of your own for controlling and manipulating the way you apply the paint. But there are particular techniques associated with the medium that range from the way washes are applied, to sponging and scratching out, washing off, wet-in-wet manipulations, and various methods of masking out. Artists have tried everything from toothbrushes to windshield wipers to create interesting effects.

Note how pattern features throughout this painting, even down to the repeated elements on the rugs. The colors are both muted and vibrant, with an extraordinary richness due to a technique O'Reilly has devised. He has added certain inks and gums to the paint to heighten the textural effects and to give a sense of three-dimensionality to the kilims.

Philip O'Reilly, *Ali Baba Carpet Shop, Kusadasi*
This painting creates pattern through texture and vivid tonal contrasts. Contrary to conventional practice, O'Reilly likes to build up his paintings from dark to light, so that the view from the window here and the sun-drenched rug were his final touches.

Philip Fraser, *Glade in Wood*
This work relies entirely for its effects on the use of masking fluid. Here you can see the characteristic hard-edged shape that shows where the dried masking fluid has protected the paper from the paint, creating suffused areas of light and color.

The roof was painted later with a mixture of traditional watercolor and gouache. It is the gouache that gives the color its density.

**Eric Ravilious,
The Wilmington Giant, 1939**
Here a real sense of scale is created by showing the wire fence large in the foreground, then disappearing into the distance – at which point the massive figure of the chalk giant rises across the Sussex Downs of southern England. The work is characterized by the use of wax resist: the watercolor is repelled in those areas shaded by the wax.

The window details were masked at an early stage to retain the fine lines and clarity of outline.

**Paul Newland,
*Screen and Light***
This unassuming yet atmospheric study in low-key color explores the idea of pattern and shape. The technique involves floating simple flat color washes into designated areas of the painting. Other areas are left unpainted, so it is the paper itself that creates the strong sense of sunlight.

**Colin Kent,
*Evening Cottage***
Fascinated by textures and techniques, Kent chooses smooth paper so that he can create his own surfaces with the paint and with particular methods of application. In this painting he used a pen for the blades of grass, a wallpaper brush for the sky, and a paint-soaked rag for some other areas. He has even been known to use windshield wipers if they achieve the desired effect.

201

AN INTRODUCTION TO
PASTELS

Pastel	204	Composing with Pastels	234
Brief History	206	Gallery of Composition	236
		Sketching with Pastel	238
MATERIALS		Sketching with Tone	240
Soft Pastels	210	Blending Colors	242
Other Pastel Types	212	Warm Tints, Cool Shades	244
Equipment	214	Scumbling	246
Oil Pastel	216	Feathering	248
Selecting Colors	218	Dry Wash	250
Gallery of Pastel Types	220	Exploring Texture	252
Range of Papers	222	Gallery of Techniques	254
Textures and Colors	224	Using Oil Pastel	256
Texturing Paper	226	Soft Pastel and Water	258
Gallery of Supports	228	Charcoal and Soft Pastel	260
		Gallery of Mixed Media	262
TECHNIQUES		Thinking Big	264
Ways of Working	230	Preserving and Framing	266
Capturing an Image	232		

PASTEL

MANY ARTISTS CHOOSE to work in pastels rather than other painting media because of pastels' distinctive luminosity and ease of use. Pastel is unique in the way in which it combines the immediacy of drawing with a rich and painterly coloring power. It is ideal for a beginner wanting to make the transition from drawing and sketching into painting and equally valued by the professional artist who wants to develop an image simply and directly. Pastels are sticks of pure pigment that are made in a wide range of vivid colors and subtle tints. If you are using them for the first time, you may be surprised at how easily you master the essential techniques of handling them and the attractiveness of the imagery you produce. Pastels are suited to all types of images: they can capture a dramatic landscape or a quiet still life, a domestic scene or a moody portrait. Another advantage of the medium is that you don't have to organize a palette or prepare a painting surface before you begin work; there's no need for water or turpentine and no equipment to clean when you finish.

Morning still life

Range of colors

Because pastels are essentially dry painting sticks consisting of opaque pigment, they are not mixed in the ways that other media such as watercolor or oil paints can be mixed. Instead, manufacturers produce an enormous selection of colors for you to choose from. Pastels can, however, be mixed effectively by overlaying them or blending them directly on the pastel paper. This luminous, dry medium is easily effaced, reworked, and blended, allowing you to alter and develop a work without the complications of waiting for paint to dry.

One of the great advantages of pastel is that you can work quickly. It is perfect for catching the inspired moment, for translating transient images and spontaneous thoughts in full vibrant color. In addition, the portability and convenience of pastels make them excellent for working outdoors.

Autumn street scene

Far from being a fragile, delicate medium, pastel is as suited to large, ambitious compositions as it is to quick, lively sketches. You can develop it through many reworkings into vibrant layers or into a delicate surface of the most subtle nuances of color. The contemporary usage of the term "pastel" to describe light or soft colors belies the range and power of pastel as a coloring medium.

Peaceful landscape

Pastel types

You can buy boxed sets of pastels or select your own colors. Before choosing an extensive range, you should explore the different types of pastel for their suitability to your needs and perhaps try one or two from the different manufacturers. You will find that the quality of each of the pastel types varies considerably between the various brands, and it is likely that you will have strong preferences for a particular shape, size, texture or quality of color unique to a certain color company.

Gaining in confidence

Depending on how you hold the pastel and how much pressure you bring to bear, you can draw fine, delicate lines or bold blocks of color. Held in your fingertips, pastel is responsive and sensitive to every movement of your hand. As you become more familiar with the medium, you will be able to achieve the most startling range of colors and textures.

Getting started

The aim of this book is to introduce you to the pleasure of working with pastel and to show you the rich variety of materials and techniques available to the pastelist. The major differences between the pastel types are whether they are water- or oil-based and their varying soft, medium, or hard texture. Each pastel type has its particular qualities and suitability to a range of painting and drawing techniques, which will be explored through the following chapters.

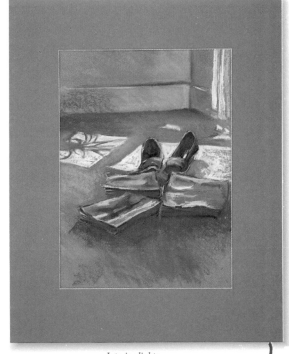

Interior lights

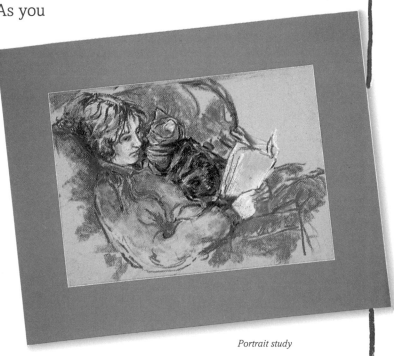

Portrait study

Brief History

Pastel as a painting medium became popular in the 18th century – relatively late within the scope of the history of art. It had been used prior to this but primarily to heighten chalk drawings by giving them a greater range of colors. The form of soft pastel that we are familiar with today was first invented by a minor French artist, Jean Perréal, in the early 1500s. Although he used it to enhance drawings of Louis XII's military campaigns in Northern Italy, it is for his method of mixing pigments with a binding agent that he is chiefly remembered. In Italy Leonardo da Vinci *(1452-1519)* was quick to recognize the value of this new, dry coloring method and used it for some of his studies of the Last Supper. Artists could now work swiftly and easily in full color without having to wait for their paints to dry.

Jacopo Bassano, *Old Man Standing, Arms Outstretched, Contemplating the Sky,* **c.1575** *20 x 15 in (51 x 38 cm)*
This dynamic study of an old man is an example of "pastel-heightening," which was most commonly used in portraits throughout the 16th century. Black chalk on a blue ground has been worked with pink pastel, lending a greater realism to the drawing.

From chalk to pastel

A method of drawing that grew in popularity throughout the 17th and 18th centuries employed a "three crayon technique." This involved using black, sanguine (red), and white chalk, usually on a toned paper. Chalks had been the common graphic medium at the end of the 15th century. Portraits and studies, which were traditionally done in these three colors, gradually started to be executed with the addition of pastel. Around 1665, the French artist Charles Lebrun used pastel for a solemn, regal portrait of Louis XIV, thereby imbuing the relatively fledgling medium with a royal seal of approval.

The first artist to work exclusively in pastel was the celebrated Venetian artist Rosalba Carriera *(1675-1758).* Starting her career by painting snuff-boxes, she graduated to painting portraits in pastels and found herself

Rosalba Carriera, *Portrait of a Young Girl,* **c.1727** *13 x 11 in (34 x 27 cm)*
Carriera's portraits have a lightness of touch and an immense subtlety of blending. Here, she has used very different treatments to portray the girl's face, the hair, and the soft lace neckerchief.

in great demand both in Italy and France. Her paintings were mainly of high-born women and are characterized by a delicate style and a surprising air of spontaneity. Carriera was spectacularly successful and was invited to undertake portrait commissions in pastel throughout the major cities of Europe. In 1720, she traveled to Paris and is reputed to have painted no fewer than 50 portraits in that year alone.

The French artist Joseph Vivian *(1657-1735)* had already established pastel as a portrait medium in Paris, but it was Rosalba Carriera who exerted a tremendous influence on the painters of the day. Fellow artists clamored to see her work and emulate her style, and even years after her death her influence continued to be felt. It is estimated that by 1780 there were more than 2,500 pastelists working in Paris.

Jean-Baptiste-Siméon Chardin, *Self-Portrait in a Green Eye Shade*, 1775 *18 x 15in (46 x 38cm)*
Chardin worked in pastel in his later years, as a result of failing eyesight. This powerful work evinces a realism and sobriety quite distinct from the frothy portraits of his day.

Maurice Quentin de La Tour, *Portrait of Mme. de Pompadour*, c.1752 *70 x 52in (177.5 x 132cm)*
This exceptionally ambitious pastel work is testament to La Tour's consummate skills. An initial portrait of Mme. de Pompadour's face was produced on an oval piece of paper and subsequently glued onto the composition, which is constructed of several sheets joined together.

Quentin de La Tour

Of the many French portrait painters in the 18th century, Maurice Quentin de La Tour *(1704-88)* was one of the most brilliant; along with Jean-Baptiste Perroneau *(1715-83)*, he was the most celebrated pastel portrait artist of his day. Converted to the medium by Carriera, La Tour pushed pastel to its technical limits. He prided himself on his ability to express the personality of his sitters, and indeed his portraits are characterized by psychological insight and a striking degree of animation. Speaking of his concern with the inner reality of his subjects, he commented, "I descend into the depths of my sitters and bring back the whole man." La Tour's sureness of draftsmanship made him the ideal artist to exploit the medium on a larger scale.

Other notable 18th-century pastelists are François Boucher *(1703-70)*, who epitomized the fashionable frivolity and facile elegance associated with this period, and Jean-Baptiste-Siméon Chardin *(1699-1779)*, who introduced new methods of building up color. It was Marie-Louise Vigée-Lebrun *(1755-1842)*, however, who was the court favorite. In Switzerland, Jean Etienne Liotard *(1702-90)* was influential in his treatment of highly finished portraits in Eastern costume.

With the French Revolution, the world of the aristocracy and wealthy patrons who commissioned pastel portraits collapsed, and the great age of portraiture was closed. During the first half of the 19th century the use of pastel declined, finding favor with few major artists until Jean François Millet's *(1814-75)* surprising and powerful use of the medium to evoke melancholy rural landscapes.

Jean François Millet, *Winter with Crows*, 1862-3 *28 x 38in (72 x 96cm)*
Millet's figurework relied on a monumental treatment of form in memorable images of rural labor. He also produced a series of landscapes without figures both in oil and in black chalk and pastel. This brooding and expressive piece is constructed out of small touches of pastel and is in striking contrast to the smooth treatment and blended form of the previous century, while foreshadowing the use of broken color associated with the Impressionists.

THE ADVENT OF IMPRESSIONISM heralded a new era for painting as artists started to focus on scenes of everyday life and experiment with capturing the effects of light. Pastel was a perfect medium for the Impressionists' aspirations toward a luminosity of color and a spontaneity of application. They introduced broken color effects using mixtures of primary and secondary colors juxtaposed in small strokes so as to blend in the eye of the viewer.

The towering figure of the early 19th century was Eugène Delacroix *(1798-1863),* a brilliant colorist who exerted a strong influence on many of the younger painters. He had used pastel in preparatory sketches for large-scale studio compositions and also for studies of landscape. Eugene Boudin *(1824-98),* who ran a small stationery and picture-framing business in Le Havre, was so impressed by Delacroix's use of pastel that he began producing delightful scenes of the Normandy coast, catching the varying effects of light and weather. Boudin, in turn, exerted a considerable influence on Claude Monet *(1840-1926).* Camille Pissarro *(1830-1903)* and Berthe Morisot *(1841-95)* produced notable works in pastel, but the major exponents were Edgar Degas *(1834-1917),* Édouard Manet *(1832-83)* and Mary Cassatt *(1845-1926).* Degas did the most to extend the creative use of pastel, having worked consistently with the medium throughout his long career. He was a brilliant draftsman whose concern with the effects of movement led him to work from theatrical scenes, ballet dancers, horses, and images of women at their toilette, exploring expressive arrangements of the figure, often in artificial light.

The Impressionists were aided in their search for a new approach to composition by the possibility of cropping afforded by photography. Japanese prints were another major influence because of their unconventional arrangements and use of clear, rhythmical outline surrounding flat areas of color.

Edgar Degas, *Woman Combing her Hair,* **c.1890-92** *32 x 22 in (82 x 57cm) Degas' pastels are characterized by inventive design and a restless experimentation. He worked pastel with other media such as gouache, alternating between drawing and painting techniques in the same work. His approach was to build up the surface in rich layers of color by steaming the support and spraying it with fixative between applications of color.*

Mary Cassatt, *Sleeping Baby,* **c.1910** *25½ x 20 in (64.8 x 52cm) Cassatt, born in the US, later studied in Paris. Degas so admired her drawing skills and approach to composition that he invited her to exhibit with the Impressionists. This particular work is typical of her unsentimental but sensitive observation of her favored subject matter of mother and child.*

Odilon Redon, *Ophelia and Flowers, c.*1905-8
25 ½ x 36 in (64 x 91cm)
Redon uses a recurring motif of a female head in profile. Here, it is placed alongside flowers in a dreamlike and evocative arrangement. If you view the painting from the right-hand side, it is immediately apparent that the composition began as a study of a vase of flowers. Redon subsequently turned the composition on its side and added the profile of the head.

Into the 20th century

In 1870 the Société de Pastellistes was founded in Paris, and the first exhibition of the Pastel Society was held in London in 1880. Among the many major artists who have used pastel are Pierre-Auguste Renoir *(1841-1919)*, Henri de Toulouse-Lautrec *(1864-1901)*, Edouard Vuillard *(1868-1940)*, and James Whistler *(1834-1903)*. Vuillard produced a significant number of works in pastel, and Whistler executed a series of pastel compositions from the female figure and a number of landscapes.

A major exponent of the medium was Odilon Redon *(1840-1916)*, who progressed to pastel relatively late in his career, producing many rich, mystical scenes. The Surrealists of a later generation regarded Redon's imagery as a precursor to their own explorations of the subconscious.

Many painters of the 20th century have used pastel as an extension of drawing but less frequently as a painting medium. The most notable exception is the contemporary R.B. Kitaj *(b.1932)*, whose powerful pastel paintings are concerned with the human experience and address inner realities with beauty and pathos.

Pablo Picasso, *Woman Seated at the Window,* 1937 *51 x 38 in (130 x 97cm)*
Picasso used pastel at several stages in his career, but seldom to such a degree of finish as in this delightful work. He has built the image on a ground of red-brown which can be seen through the scumbled application of pastel. The dramatic use of lighting creates a tonal play between the positive shape of the wall and the negative shape of the window. The rounded forms of the figure are colored in primary and secondary hues, creating a playful quality which complements the sophisticated structure of the composition.

R.B.Kitaj, RA, *Study for the World's Body,* 1974
12 x 7 ¾ in (30 x 20 cm)
Kitaj is a highly respected painter and draftsman. He has worked consistently with pastel, both from photographic source material and direct from life. There is frequently a sexual or political tension at play between the protagonists that people his images of contemporary life.

209

SOFT PASTELS

SOFT PASTEL IS THE ORIGINAL AND MOST popular form of the pastel medium. It is essentially pure pigment held lightly in a gum solution. Its soft fine-grained nature makes it ideal for painting techniques because of its ease of application, its surface-covering power and its amenability to blending. It provides you with an exciting breadth of surface qualities from delicate traces of overlaid colors to full, rich impasto. The first touch of soft pastel on paper reveals the beauty of the medium as the particles of pigment are dispersed and reflect light with a characteristic bloom.

THE TERM PASTEL comes from its Italian name *pastello*, a derivation of the word *pasta*, meaning paste. The name indicates the nature and style of manufacture of pastels, in which pigments are formed into a paste by mixing varying amounts of chalk and a light solution of a gum. The

The basic ingredients

Pastels are made up of dry pigments, precipitated chalk, and a binder such as tragacanth. The pigment is mixed into a stiff paste using a

paste is then fashioned into sticks and left to dry.

Soft pastel contains just sufficient binder to hold the pigment in stick

weak solution of gum dissolved in water. The chalk is added to the pigment in increasing proportion to create tints of the colors.

form and as a consequence retains the purity of hue of the original pigment. The tonal range of soft pastels is slightly restricted in the darker tones, but the artist is more than compensated by its extraordinary brilliance of hue.

There are a number of different companies that produce soft pastels of both artist and student quality. Artists' quality pastels use the finest pigments and are lightfast – they do not fade with time – and so they tend to be more expensive. A point to note is that soft pastels are not of a uniform consistency; you will find that, depending on the pigment you have chosen, some colors are much softer than others.

For example, some of the darker colors are considerably harder than the tints – the lighter versions of each color – which are uniformly soft. This is because the tints have a greater quantity of chalk in their makeup. It is therefore worth trying out the darker colors to test their relative softness.

Mortar and pestle

Boxed sets

Soft pastels are extremely fragile and must be stored carefully. A good solution is to buy boxed sets, as the pastels come in foam-filled trays. An added benefit of the foam compartments is that the colors stay clean. You can also buy empty pastel boxes with individual compartments if you prefer to make your own color selection.

Of the different pastel types – soft, hard, water-soluble, oil pastel, pastel pencil, and so on – soft pastel comes in the most extensive range of colors. Soft pastels are sold singly from cabinets or in boxed sets of various types and sizes. The very large sets have similarly impressive price tags. Some manufacturers produce more than 300 different colors.

Half pastels
These are sold in boxed sets of up to 60 and are favored by some artists for their shorter length.

Large pastels
Although quite costly, these chunky pastels are ideal for blocking in areas of color and for large-scale work. They come in a broad range of colors and are generally available from professional artists' suppliers.

Cleaning with rice
Soft pastels become dirty with use, making it difficult to recognize the different tints. It is good practice to clean them as you work by wiping them with a tissue. Alternatively, you can lay them in a tray of rice, which automatically rubs away the loose surface powder. Badly soiled pastels can be given a thorough cleaning by placing them in a jar of rice and gently shaking the jar up and down.

Pastel dust
By nature pastels are very soft and are likely to create a fine powder as you work with them.

Square pastels
Because of their sharp edges, these allow for more delicate lines than their round equivalents, but they are otherwise similar in their consistency and use. The color range, however, is more limited.

Blue over yellow
Here blue has been applied over yellow in broad strokes using the side of the pastel. Where the colors overlap they mix optically to create a green.

Making marks
Pastels allow you to vary your line by altering the angle of the pastel to the paper, by using either the edge, the tip, or the side of the pastel, or by changing the pressure with which you apply it.

OTHER PASTEL TYPES

A SURPRISING DIVERSITY of pastel types have been developed to accommodate a wide spectrum of creative uses. These "other" pastels are manufactured using similar fine ground pigments, but they are held together by different quantities or types of binding media. You can buy pastels in pencil form, and recent innovations have produced a water-soluble pastel that can be worked with a brush to create watercolor effects.

Pastel sticks can be either soft, medium, or hard, depending on the ratio of gum to pigment. After soft pastels, the most common type are hard pastels or Conté crayons. The brilliance of the color diminishes with the increase of gum, but the harder texture that makes this form of pastel ideal for detailed work compensates for the color loss. Hard pastels are more suited to drawing than painting techniques.

Similarities and differences
Hard pastel is compatible with soft pastel and is most commonly used in the early stages of a work when a certain degree of drawing is needed. It would then be overlaid with soft pastel. It is also used to put in fine line details in the latter stages of a soft pastel work.

Fine crayon mark
Hard pastels are square in section and can make a range of strokes, depending on how you hold them.

Crayons
These are medium-hard pastels that combine the facility for painting associated with soft pastels with the sharpness of line achieved by hard pastels. They come in a range of up to 80 colors and are popular for sketching and outdoor work as they are less bulky and less susceptible to breakage than soft pastels.

To aid detailed work, hard pastels can be sharpened using a blade, an emery board or small sheets of glass paper to gently pare the end to a point. When using the pastels, however, be careful not to exert too great a pressure since a sharpened hard pastel is likely to score the paper surface and reveal itself as a white line when you subsequently rework it with soft pastel. Conversely, it is also important not to fill the tooth of the paper with soft pastel as this prevents any further working with hard pastel.

Hard pastels come in a limited range of colors. Some makes have small amounts of black as an

Broad crayon mark
Hard pastels and crayons can be used on their side to create flat areas of color.

additional constituent, which gives them a slightly darker tone than soft pastels. The limited range of colors means that you are required to engage in frequent color mixing directly on the paper if you want to achieve a subtlety of color. You can blend the colors by working them over one another in strokes using a close weave of marks to mix the different colors optically, or blend the colors with your finger or a stump of pastel.

An advantage of hard pastels is that they do not fill the tooth of the paper as readily as soft pastels. However, they do not have the textural range of soft pastel, and you can damage the paper surface trying to achieve a dense color effect. If you press too hard with a hard pastel you effectively burnish away the tooth of the paper.

Pastel pencils
These are of the same consistency as pastel crayons, apart from being slightly softer and encased in wood. They are ideal for linear detailed work and can also be blended for delicate modeling of forms. Pastel pencils come in a range of around 80 colors. You can buy large boxed sets and replace the pencils as you use them or buy them singly.

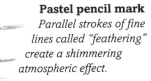

Cross-hatched marks
You can make fine lines with pastel pencils or gradations of tone if you increase the pressure.

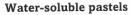

Pastel pencil mark
Parallel strokes of fine lines called "feathering" create a shimmering atmospheric effect.

Water-soluble pastels
These have a waxy consistency and can be used dry or wet. They are good for traditional drawing techniques but can also be washed over with a brush and water, transforming and softening the linear marks by dispersing the pigment into washes of color. Water-soluble pastels are sold singly and in boxed sets in a limited range of up to 48 colors.

Washing over pastel

Water-soluble pastel marks
Depending on the amount of water applied, it is possible to vary the degree of dispersion. Water-soluble pastels are suitable for the technique of "line and wash." You can also achieve interesting rich color effects by drawing into a damp surface.

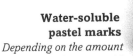

EQUIPMENT

A MAJOR ADVANTAGE OF working with pastels is their portability. Compared to other painting media, pastels are exceptionally straightforward to use. You will not need a palette to mix them on or thinners to dilute them. Usually the only equipment you will require are the pastels themselves, a support such as paper attached to a board, and the most subtle of all tools – your fingers.

In this respect pastel work is not dissimilar to drawing in its ease of use and utter simplicity of requirements. You can capture an image swiftly, anywhere, and in rich, velvety color. There are some additional tools and materials that you may be tempted to buy as you try the various techniques outlined in the following pages, but they do not cost a great deal and are readily supplied by most art supply stores.

Scalpel

A scalpel is used for creating pastel dust for dry wash techniques (see pp. 250-1), for paring hard pastels down to a point, and for cutting paper and mounts. In oil pastel techniques, you can use a scalpel to scrape away color, to create lines in your painting, or to make changes.

Masking tape

This is used to mask off the edges of an area to be painted and for taping work to a board. Its particular advantage over other types of tape is that it peels away easily without tearing any fibers from the surface of a work.

Fixative

Pastel paintings can easily be spoiled by smudging. To prevent this you can spray fixative onto the paper to "fix" the pastel. Fixative is also used when you build up a painting in layers by means of spraying and fixing each successive layer of color. Fixative comes in large and small spray cans and is also sold in liquid form.

Mouth diffuser

Used with liquid fixative. Place the long end of the diffuser into the bottle of fixative and blow through the shorter end. It is far less convenient than the spray cans as you need to blow hard to have any effect. Take particular care not to inhale the fumes.

Sandpaper

Sandpaper is used to file the blunt ends of hard pastels and pastel pencils to a point for delicate linear work. You can buy small artists' pads of pastel paper from art suppliers; the idea is the same. If you purchase sandpaper from a hardware store, be sure to buy one of the finer grades.

FIXING YOUR WORK

Fixative is essentially a resin dissolved in solvent. As you spray your work the solvent evaporates leaving the resin on the support. This is what holds the pastel pigment in place. When fixing an image, make sure that you pin or tape the paper to a vertical surface rather than spraying it flat; this avoids the danger of large droplets falling onto your work.

Ideally, spray outdoors or in a well-ventilated but wind-free area, using a sweeping movement across the surface from the top to the bottom of your work. Be careful not to overspray your painting as the fixative is likely to alter the colors slightly, darkening them and making them lose their purity of hue.

Cotton swab

Small tortillon

Larger tortillon

Blending tools

Tortillons are the traditional blending tools for pastel work. They are tight twists of paper of various sizes. As you dirty the end you can peel away a layer of paper to create a clean point for further work. An alternative to tortillons are cotton swabs, and cotton balls can be used for blending larger areas.

Cotton ball

Erasers

There are a wide range of erasers on the market, most of which are unsuitable for pastel work. Soft and hard pastels can be erased effectively using either a kneading eraser or some soft bread. Oil pastel, however, cannot be erased with an eraser.

Brushes

Brushes are used for both applying and removing pastel. They are not as efficient as bread or putty rubbers for lifting off color, but they are effective for retrieving the tooth of the paper surface if it has filled up with pastel pigment. To do this, use a soft but firm watercolor brush and gently flick away the pigment. You can then rework the area with a new color.

Stiff short hair brush
This is used to blend soft or oil pastel into a support and for dry wash techniques in which you blend the pigment powder in. You can trim an old hog hair or stiff watercolor brush to achieve the necessary short length.

Hog hair brush
Some pastelists prefer stiff bristle brushes for making corrections on larger works. The method used is known as "dry scrubbing" and is as it sounds. These brushes are also used for moving pastel on the support with water.

Bread
Surprisingly, the most thorough eraser of all is bread. If you knead some fresh bread into a soft ball it will be ideal for erasing areas of soft pastel. Dry bread is unsuitable as it does not lift the particles of pastel from the fibers of the paper and may also scratch the surface.

Kneaded eraser
This type of eraser is highly suitable for soft pastel work and lifts color off easily. You can shape it into a point with your fingers so as to remove tiny areas of pastel pigment.

Watercolor brush
This is used to flick away pastel dust from the tooth of a pastel work, although it will rarely remove the pigment completely. Its springy fibers are suitable to delicate corrections and also to detail wet work.

Wet wipes
These are a valuable addition to the studio and particularly practical when you are working outdoors. You can use them to clean your hands between colors and also to wipe down the pastels and minimize the amount of dust you inhale.

Plastic rubber
This tends to smear a pastel work but is good for thoroughly cleaning the paper surface after you have lifted an area of pastel off by using bread or a kneaded eraser.

Tracing paper
Tracing paper or "glassine" are used to cover a pastel work and protect the surface from accidental smudging. Both are available from art supply stores.

OIL PASTEL

OIL PASTEL IS markedly different in character than other forms of pastel as the use of oil rather than gum as a binder produces a rich depth of tone and a distinct degree of transparency. Initially, oil pastels feel sticky against the tooth of the support. Their performance, however, is altered by temperature, and they become less sticky and move more easily over the surface of the paper as they get warmer. Just the heat from your hand will soften them, so it is a good idea to keep the wrappers on them as you work. They can be used on any paper or canvas support with a slight tooth and are frequently used on textured oil paper or board. Like oil paints, they can be modified by using turpentine.

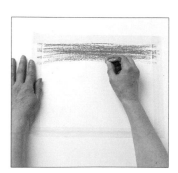

Seascape of softly blended colors

THE TOOTH OF THE PAPER surface soon fills with oil pastel and subsequent layers of color tend to slide on the surface. You can, however, make alterations to oil pastel in ways that you cannot with soft pastel. For example, you can scrape the oil pastel off with a blunt blade or work into it with turpentine or white spirit.

Fan of colors
Oil pastel comes in a less extensive range than soft pastel, numbering about 80 colors in all, but you can make subtle and attractive blends.

Blending two colors
You can see here that the oily texture of the pastel produces a transparent mix of red and yellow.

Pink blended into blue

Fine lines of color

LAYING A WASH

1 *Apply the oil pastel in an even and not too dense application across the surface of the support.*

2 *Wearing a glove, dip a cotton ball in turpentine to disperse the color in a gradated tone.*

3 *Repeat the same procedure for the ground, laying in green in sweeping horizontal strokes.*

4 *Use a brush to apply the turpentine. This disperses the color without removing it.*

Techniques

Oil pastels can be worked in an exciting array of techniques. They can be thinned to create luminous washes of color, they can be blended, and they can be applied quite thickly to create an impasto effect. They are also ideal for the technique of "sgraffito" where you can scratch lines through a dense layer of oil pastel to reveal the underlying color that stains the support. Because they involve the use of turpentine, it is best to work on textured oil paper or oil board rather than use watercolor paper.

SOFTENING EDGES

The addition of white spirit or turpentine makes the pastel more malleable, and this can be used to great effect. For example, it is easier to mix colors on the support by blending one color into another or to soften the edges of an image with a brush or cotton ball, or to make more subtle transitions between tones.

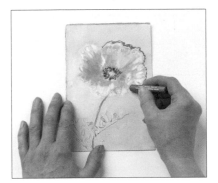

1 Lay a line of pastel around the edge of the flower to define the petals and accentuate their feathery texture.

2 With a cotton swab dipped in white spirit, go around the line to soften the mark. The cotton swab allows for precise blending.

Impasto

The stiff texture of oil pastel makes it particularly suited to the dramatic effect of impasto, in which the pastel is pressed hard onto the support so as to leave a thick and opaque deposit of pigment.

Sgraffito

The technique of sgraffito is particularly effective in oil pastel. Here the artist has laid down bands of color to create a sky and then scraped through to the underlying tone with a blunt penknife.

Sgraffito

In this image, a thick, opaque layer of black oil pastel has been applied to the support and a blunt penknife has been used to draw into the pastel. The artist has scraped away lines to reveal the lighter tone of the support, achieving different tones by varying the pressure with the blade.

Stippling

This is a technique of applying pastel in a broken pattern of small marks to produce an attractive play of colors. The various colors then mix optically.

Materials

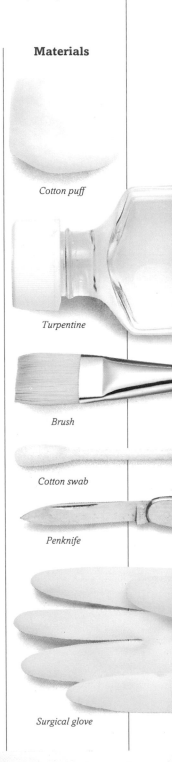

Cotton puff

Turpentine

Brush

Cotton swab

Penknife

Surgical glove

Oil paper

SELECTING COLORS

PASTEL WORK IS UNIQUE in that colors cannot be mixed on a palette in a conventional way. For this reason pastelists normally work with an extensive range of colors and tints. It is important to make a well-informed selection, as your choice will effectively become a ready-made palette of premixed colors. There are several ways to approach the selection of colors. You may find that a boxed set is entirely suitable to your needs. The smaller sets contain an adequate range of colors for sketching, but they can be frustrating when you cannot achieve a particular color that you want. If you intend to work with varied subject matter, it is preferable to select the widest range of colors. Ideally, you need a range of about 48 pastels to approach a broad spectrum of subjects with confidence.

IF YOU INTEND TO MAKE your own selection of colors, you need to feel that you have chosen the optimum breadth without buying unnecessary ones. Manufacturers produce charts of their colors and tints which present a delightful but often bewildering array of possibilities – sometimes up to 300 different colors. When you look at a color chart or a tray of pastels in a store you will find that there are full-strength colors, each of which has an adjacent set of up to eight tints that move progressively toward white. Start by selecting from the full-strength colors, and then buy one or two tints of your preferred choices.

Color wheel
The inner ring contains a warm and a cool pastel of each of the essential primary and secondary colors plus a single mid-orange. In addition, there are earth colors, a black, and a white. The outer ring consists of two tints of each of the full-strength colors. The total selection is 48 pastels and represents a good range of colors, although you may well prefer to make your own choice to work with.

Range of greens
The different types of pastels are sold in boxed sets or singly from selection trays where they are usually arranged in ranks of tints of colors. Soft pastels are sold in the most extensive range; this selection of greens gives an indication of the wealth of tints available just for one color.

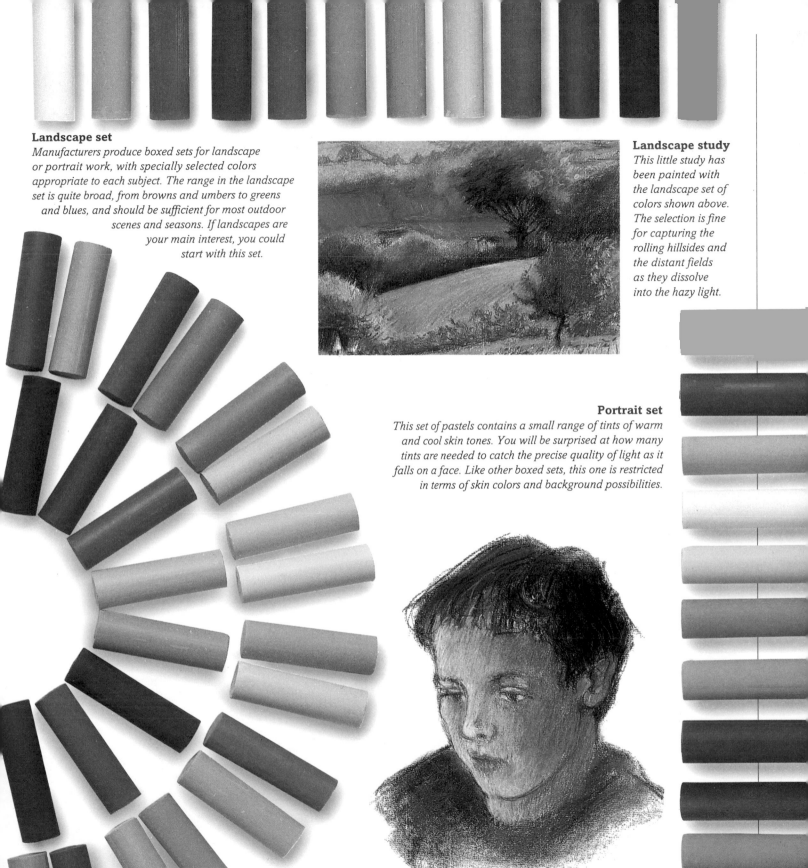

Landscape set

Manufacturers produce boxed sets for landscape or portrait work, with specially selected colors appropriate to each subject. The range in the landscape set is quite broad, from browns and umbers to greens and blues, and should be sufficient for most outdoor scenes and seasons. If landscapes are your main interest, you could start with this set.

Landscape study

This little study has been painted with the landscape set of colors shown above. The selection is fine for capturing the rolling hillsides and the distant fields as they dissolve into the hazy light.

Portrait set

This set of pastels contains a small range of tints of warm and cool skin tones. You will be surprised at how many tints are needed to catch the precise quality of light as it falls on a face. Like other boxed sets, this one is restricted in terms of skin colors and background possibilities.

Portrait

This small cameo of a child is painted with the full range of tints shown on the right. Note how many different colors are required to accomplish the subtle modulation of warm and cool tints in the boy's head from areas of full illumination to the cooler tones in the shadow.

GALLERY OF PASTEL TYPES

THE DIFFERENT TYPES OF PASTEL – soft, hard, oil, and water-soluble – have unique qualities that make them suitable to a particular range of techniques. In choosing one, the major consideration is whether you prefer the dry, powdery quality of the soft and hard pastels or the transparent, waxy colors of oil pastels and water-soluble pastels. Each of the works shown here has been executed with a different type of pastel, and together the paintings exemplify the enormous range of techniques which can be achieved.

Ian McCaughrean, *Koi Carp* *9 x 13 in (23 x 33 cm)*
The watery qualities of this painting have been achieved by using water-soluble pastels. The artist developed the composition by drawing the forms of the carp and lilies in a linear technique and then hatching in areas of dense color. He then washed over the colors with a wet paintbrush, turning the areas of pastel into washes of color. Water-soluble pastels are similar in texture to wax crayons when dry but take on the quality of a watercolor wash when reworked with water. The transformation into wash is particularly evident in the yellow highlights on the fish and the reflections on the water.

Paul Bartlett, *Father Reading Sunday Newspapers*
17 x 25 in (43 x 64 cm)
In this carefully worked portrait of his father, Bartlett has used dry pastel and three shades of pastel pencils – pink, brown, and black – to capture the sense of light and shadow within the room. The suitability of hard pastels to a detailed drawing technique is evident in this powerful composition, which relies for its effect on the strong shafts of light falling across the forms of the interior. Note in particular the fine lines in the top left-hand corner. The artist has used a warm, mid-toned paper with quite a pronounced tooth to create this grainy sense of reality.

The artist could only have rendered this extraordinary degree of detail by using pastel pencils; soft pastels would have been totally inappropriate for capturing such fine definitions of line and tone. The artist's attachment to his subject is evident in the care with which he has drawn the fingers and cuff of the sleeve.

Odilon Redon, *Profile, the Flag,* c.1900 *16 x 15 in (38.5 x 37.5 cm)*
In this very beautiful composition, you can see the full range of techniques that are possible using a combination of soft and hard pastels or chalks. Redon has employed a dark-toned chalk, honed to a fine point, to define the profile of the head, the eye, and the mouth, and to cross-hatch around the face. A fine gold highlights the headband and the nose and cheek. He has achieved the rich tones of the background, however, by skillful blending of soft pastel.

In this detail of the shoulder, you can see the range of marks Redon has employed, from the fine lines of black chalk to the open textural marks of the blue and the pink. He has applied the white more thickly, giving the work a contemporary feel of improvised abstraction.

Rosemary Saul, *Somerset Garden*
16½ x 23 in (42 x 59 cm)
This composition in pastel pencil presents a dreamlike and surreal landscape. There is a dramatic interaction between areas of light and shadow that invests the forms with a sculptural presence. Saul has used pastel pencils to blend warm and cool colors in a rich weave of parallel feathered and hatched strokes.

Jane Strother, *The Yellow House* *8 x 10 in (21 x 26 cm)*
The artist has created a highly dramatic composition in oil pastel from the bold use of contrasting colors. The luminous tone of the house is framed against the deep violet of the sky with its ominous storm clouds. Strother uses turpentine to loosen the oil pastel and create washes of color, as can be seen in the broad sweep of red in the foreground.

In this detail you can see the way the artist has combined the blending and drawing capabilities of pastel pencil, relying on the point of the colored pastels to create the range of textures and effects.

RANGE OF PAPERS

THE SUPPORT OR SURFACE YOU CHOOSE to work on is particularly significant with pastels because its texture and color will interact visually with the pastel colors, influencing your technique and affecting the appearance of the finished work. Paper, cardboard, and linen supports manufactured for pastel work have a distinctly textured surface that is referred to as the "tooth." This rubs away the pastel and holds the loosened pigment in its surface fibers. A wealth of supports are manufactured to suit the many different pastel types and techniques.

THE BEST QUALITY PAPER to work on is artists' quality watercolor or printmaking paper that is either hand- or machine-made. It is more expensive than ordinary paper but is heavy enough to sustain prolonged application of color. Such paper is usually embossed with the manufacturer's name and often has a watermark.

Pastel papers

For pastel work you need to choose a paper of artists' quality with sufficient tooth and weight to hold the pastel powder. Most watercolor papers are fine, but there are also papers which are specifically designed for pastel work. These are the Ingres and Canson papers that are sold as single sheets or pastel pads and come in an extensive range of colors and tints. They have a stippled or "laid" (ladderlike) texture of lines created by the manufacturing process of machine-rolling the paper.

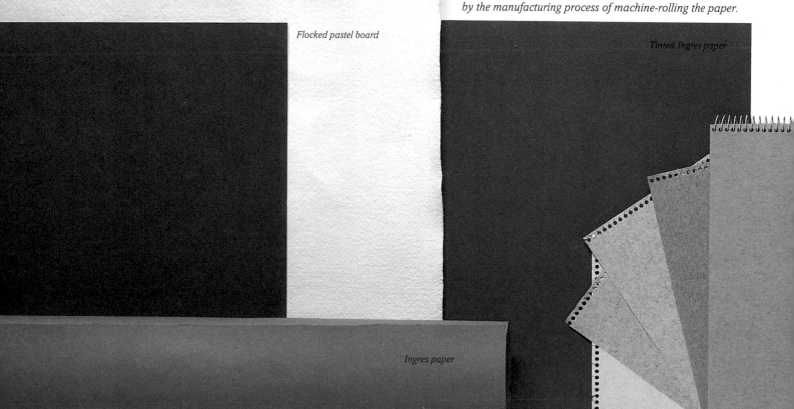

Canson paper

Flocked pastel cardboard

Watercolor paper

Flocked pastel board

Tinted Ingres paper

Ingres paper

THESE HIGH-QUALITY PAPERS are made from 100 percent cotton rag. Unlike wood pulp papers, which rapidly become brittle and yellow with age, these are made without bleaching agents and will not change over time. Artists' quality paper comes in various thicknesses and is graded according to the weight of a ream, which is approximately 500 sheets of paper. Thin paper is about 72lbs (150gsm); medium 90lbs (190gsm). The heavier papers are 140lbs (300gsm) and above.

Some of the heavier papers are available in a rough surface that has a distinctly coarse grain. Smooth paper is generally unsuitable for pastel work since it lacks sufficient tooth.

You can also buy other types of supports for pastel work. Pastel board, for example, has a pronounced texture that is created by spraying fine particles of cloth onto the surface of the board. The flocked surface produces a softening effect on the pastel marks and is suitable for subtle blending effects. Another form of pastel board, often known as glass paper, has a fine layer of grit which has an exceptionally high degree of tooth. This is suitable to impasto work, in which thick applications of pastel are made.

Large sheets and rolls

Artists' quality paper comes in a range of sizes, from standard sheets to extra-large sheets – roughly 5ft by 4ft (153cm by 122cm). You can also buy 33ft (10 meter) rolls, either 30in (75cm) or 60in (150cm) wide, which can be cut to length for large-scale compositions. They are costly, so before buying a roll try out a sheet of paper of the same weight and texture.

Pads and books

Spiral-bound pads come in a selection of warm and cool tints and are very convenient for pastel sketching. You can try out different colored pastels on the various grounds to see which works best for your composition. The better quality books and pads have sheets of "glassine" separating the individual sheets of pastel paper. Glassine is a glossy paper that protects the finished pastel sketch by insuring against accidental smudging.

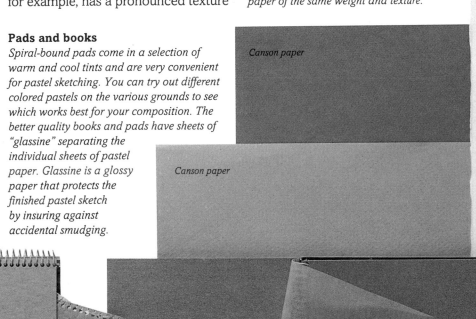

Canson paper

Canson paper

223

TEXTURES AND COLORS

YOU MAY BE SURPRISED at how the different textures and colors in supports can affect your paintings. You will need to select your support carefully to achieve the effect you want. The best way to gain a feel and an understanding of texture and color is to explore a simple subject composed of a few colors on a variety of different supports. You will notice that the same colors in your composition will be affected by your choice of background. One may really enhance the colors, while another may instead dull them. The different textures of your supports will also determine the way you apply the pastel.

THERE IS AN EXTENSIVE RANGE of textured papers and pastel boards for you to explore, from the soft surfaces that are almost like blotting paper, to the gritty surface of glass paper. Each of these surfaces is suitable for a particular range of techniques. An advantage of a heavily textured paper is that it will hold more pastel than a less textured one and allow you to build up a thick surface of color. A heavily textured support is tougher, so it is suitable for extensive overworking.

If you apply a pastel color lightly over a textured surface, the pastel will adhere to the high spots, creating tiny alternating particles of pastel that seem to sparkle. As you press harder you will achieve an even tone.

Textured paper
This fuchsia is drawn on a handmade watercolor paper. The impact of the image is rather feeble, as the white tone of the paper dulls the colors of the flower and the vase.

Watercolor paper
The even texture is suited to a more controlled blending than heavier textured papers.

Ingres paper
This is very popular, comes in an extensive range of colors, and has a pronounced texture of parallel lines.

Canson paper
This comes in an attractive range of colors and has a stippled texture on one side.

Flocked pastel board
This surface produces a softening effect which lends itself to subtle blending effects such as "sfumato."

Carborundum pastel board
The exceptional tooth on this makes it suitable for heavy impasto work, in which pastel is applied thickly.

Watercolor paper
Rough textured watercolor paper can sustain heavy treatment.

A selection of colored and tinted papers

COLORED PAPERS ARE PRODUCED by many paper mills and vary in quality and texture. Look for artists' quality pastel papers; ordinary colored papers are likely to fade over time and may not have sufficient tooth to hold the pastel. There is a vast selection of subtle warm and cool tints that are generally used for pastel work as well as a delightful range of strong colored papers.

A colored support will harmonize or contrast with the pastel colors of your composition, creating either a dominant atmospheric tone or a unifying element in your painting.

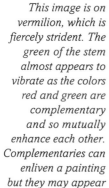

Mauve paper
This composition is similar to the one below: the dark tone of the purple makes the image appear luminous. The blue of the vase harmonizes with the support because they are both cool and purple contains blue. Purple also enhances the yellow in the stem and the flower.

Peach paper
This image is not as dramatic as the other three, but it possesses a more subtle and less overbearing play of complementaries. The key to this effect is in the blue vase. The blue and the peach enhance each other, and the tone of the paper is dark enough to highlight the head of the flower.

Red paper
This image is on vermilion, which is fiercely strident. The green of the stem almost appears to vibrate as the colors red and green are complementary and so mutually enhance each other. Complementaries can enliven a painting but they may appear crude if used to excess.

Green paper
This image is strikingly different from the image on white paper. The fuchsia is radically altered and appears luminous against the dark tone of the support. The olive green harmonizes with the lime green of the stem and throws the flower into sharp contrast against the melancholic ground.

225

TEXTURING PAPER

IT IS WELL WORTH EXPERIMENTING with texturing and coloring your own supports. You will be surprised at how simple the process is and what unusual, expressive effects you can achieve. Apart from the fact that you can create a far greater diversity of textures than those which are commercially available, you have the added benefit of being able to create exactly what you require for a particular subject matter or technique.

Both muslin and canvas can be stretched and glued onto board and make very stable surfaces with a strong texture suitable for pastel work. Alternatively, you can apply a layer of grit or sand or any other suitable material to board or paper using PVA glue or a gesso primer. These will provide interesting textures over which you can then add color by blending crushed pastel into the surface or by washing over it with a water-based paint.

COATING WITH GESSO is a very old method of preparing a surface for painting, and today's acrylic gesso is resistant to cracking and so is suitable for nonrigid supports such as canvas and paper. You can create an even and slightly textured support by applying gesso with a stiff hog hair brush. Paint a generous layer of acrylic gesso in downward strokes on the support. When this layer is dry, apply another layer in horizontal strokes. Alternatively, you can create a heavily textured surface by stippling the gesso onto the support in any configuration you choose. To create a textured surface with a greater degree of tooth you can mix powdered materials such as carborundum or graded sand into your gesso before you paint your support.

1 ▲ Tip orange pastel powder and fine carborundum into a dish containing acrylic gesso.

2 ▲ Start stirring the powders into the gesso with a stiff brush to gradually blend them in.

3 ▲ Continue working the mixture for a few minutes so that it attains the strength of the color.

4 ▲ Apply the mixture in parallel brushstrokes across the surface of the support to create an even texture.

The textured paper after drying flat

Materials

Large bristle brush

Soft round brush

STIPPLED TEXTURED GROUND

1 *A heavier texture is created by mixing a graded sand and a crushed dark brown pastel into gesso.*

2 *The mixture is applied using a loaded brush in short, stippling motions across the surface of the paper.*

Stormy landscape
The finished support has been used as a springboard for this abstract painting.

FROTTAGE

Frottage is a simple technique for creating a textured pattern on paper. Place a medium to thin sheet of paper on a textured surface such as unplaned wood or a wall, and rub the side of a pastel across the surface of the paper as you would in brass rubbing. You can use different pastel colors to create a varied effect or take multiple rubbings using the same sheet of paper at different angles on the one surface. The frottaged surface of the paper makes an exciting ground for subsequent reworking and is an excellent stimulus to improvised abstractions. Frottage is also an ideal method of creating sheets of varied textures for use in collage work.

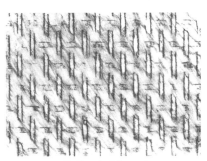

Frottaged wickerwork

Creating a textured support using carborundum

1 ▲ Dilute some PVA glue with water to make it more soluble and paint an even coat onto card- or art board with a wide brush.

2 ▲ While the glue is still wet, tip some carborundum powder into a small sieve and gently sprinkle the grit onto the surface.

3 ▲ Continue sifting the powder over the support to build up an even texture. Don't worry if some spills over the edge.

4 ▲ Tap the support to remove the surplus powder and place the board under weights to stop it from buckling as it dries.

Materials

Orange pastel pigment

Sand

Carborundum powder

Sieve

PVA glue

Acrylic primer

Canvas

Muslin

Sand and grit supports

These three boards have been dusted with different grades of grit. The bottom one is carborundum, which is the finest, smoothest grade. The middle is a slightly grainier sieved sand and the top one is a coarser, unsieved sand which creates a less even texture.

Muslin and canvas boards

The bottom sheet is a manufactured linen board. The other two are handmade: the middle one has muslin stretched and glued onto board, and the top one has a fine-grained cotton duck canvas stretched and glued onto board. Both of these supports have been treated with an acrylic primer.

Textured and colored supports

These supports have been colored and textured using, for the bottom one, a crushed orange pastel brushed on with PVA. Next is a mix of crushed orange pastel, carborundum and gesso; then comes a support painted in crushed charcoal and PVA. The top support is two stippled patterns of brown pastel and gesso.

Hardboard

Paper

227

GALLERY OF SUPPORTS

THE DECISION YOU MAKE as to the scale, format, texture, and color of your support will make a major contribution to the impact of your composition. For example, a large scale allows you to engage in an ambitious treatment of a theme. Texture will influence the quality of the marks and control the way the pastel sits on the support. The color and tone of the support will create a note that runs through the composition, harmonizing with some colors and throwing others into sharp relief. As you will see, each of the artists in this gallery has capitalized on a particular quality inherent in their chosen support.

Edouard Manet
Portrait of Méry Laurent, **1882** *21 x 13 in (54 x 34 cm)*
Here, as in the majority of his pastel compositions, Manet has worked in soft pastel on fine-grained linen canvas. The texture of the support allows him to exercise his extraordinary skills in blending colors, since the tooth of the canvas gently holds the pigment. The treatment in this portrait is typical of Manet's use of a dramatic tonal range and limited colors. There is a beautifully observed play of light in the cool shadow cast in the manner of a veil across the luminous face of the sitter.

Richard Cartwright, *Clevedon*
Bandstand at Night *29 x 39 in (74 x 99 cm)*
Cartwright uses a black pastel paper mounted on cardboard and starts working on his images by blending soft pastel into the surface of the paper. Here he evokes the mysteries of night and the yearnings of a solitary figure.

To achieve the moonlit quality, the artist has applied pastel in a spectrum of techniques that includes blending, dotting, and sprinkling pastel onto the surface of the support.

Shanti Thomas, *Sleeping Woman,* *5 x 4 ft (150 x 122 cm)*
It is possible to buy large sheets or rolls of watercolor paper which are of sufficient weight and texture for extensive work in pastel. Here, Thomas has used a full sheet to produce a portrait of monumental scale. By making it nearly life-size she has invested the figure with heroic proportions as testament to the often unrecognized labors of women in their nurturing role.

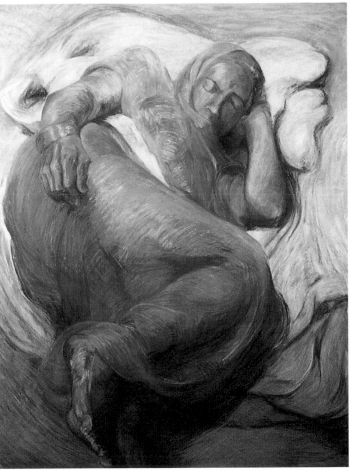

Margaret Glass, *Free Range* *9½ x 10 in (24 x 33 cm)*
The particular pastel paper used here is one which creates an even and dense texture. Known as glass or flour paper, it has exceptional hold and so is suitable to an impasto technique in which the color is built up thickly. In this painting the support itself secures the image without need of fixative, which lends the image its particular luminosity of color.

Diana Armfield, RA,
Campo S. Angelo, Venice, **1988** *9¾ x 8¼ in (25 x 21 cm)*
An accomplished pastelist, Armfield has relied on a warm-toned paper to offset the rich blue note of the sky and to create the effect of the sun's rays warming the buildings. She has left much of the paper unpainted so that the hue of the buildings is due more to the tone of the paper than to any overlaid pastel. The composition is organized on the principle of complementaries – blues set against salmon-pinks – and in the contrasting play of warm colors against cool.

In this detail the warm tones of the support shows through the broken marks of the buildings, the figures, and the paving stones, serving to link and unify the composition.

The movement of the figures is suggested by the rhythm and angle of the pastel marks.

Here, the figures are visually linked to the paving stones of the piazza by the same color range of cool blue-gray notes.

WAYS OF WORKING

ONCE YOU HAVE BOUGHT the basics – a set of pastels and some sketch pads is all you really need to get started – you may want to set up a studio arrangement in your home. Choose a light corner near a window and try to avoid direct sunlight, as this will cast strong shadows in the room. You can buy daylight bulbs that allow you to work in the evening in a light that does not alter the appearance of your colors. If you work very vigorously you should keep the window open to minimize the amount of pastel dust you inhale.

Choosing a work surface

You will need a hard surface to work on. The advantage of an easel is that it allows you to angle the pastel work so that the surplus dust falls away without sullying the purity of the colors. Choose one that is strong enough to hold a large drawing board but light enough to be carried and folded with ease. A cheaper alternative is to get fiberboard or plywood cut to size and work with the board angled in your lap. A piece of cardboard cut to the length of your drawing board, folded at an angle and held in place by thumbtacks or tape is a useful device to catch the dust that falls from the pastel work.

Keeping things clean

It is a good idea to keep some tissues for cleaning your hands between colors or even for cleaning the pastels. Pastel dust is very fine and can settle over a wide area of the room, so lay down a drop cloth before you start.

Storing your paintings

The best way to store your work is to attach a sheet of tracing paper over it and place it in a portfolio or a map chest. Never roll a pastel work as the tension will cause serious loss of pastel from the paper surface.

Felicity Edholm

CAPTURING AN IMAGE

THERE ARE SEVERAL techniques that you can use to capture an image, depending on the nature of your subject matter and how much time you have. As a general rule, it is better to start developing an image when you have the subject in front of you; however, often this is not possible. If, for example, you are trying to capture a child at play, your subject will be constantly moving. There are several ways of dealing with this, from making a series of quick sketches to taking photographs to use for reference later. Either method is fine, and you should practice them, either singly or in combination, so that you gain confidence in working in this way. When sketching from a changeable subject, choose a pastel pad that is big enough to develop a composition, and work with a limited number of colors. Try to select the most important features, as you will find that a few well-placed lines and colors will say a great deal about your feelings for what you are painting. The more you tackle different subjects, the more you will gain confidence in your ability to capture their essential character.

THE USE OF A CAMERA has a number of advantages, as you can photograph moving subjects in a rapid succession of shots and capture scenes that you would never be able to see with the naked eye. Also, a camera allows you to crop your subject using the viewfinder and make early decisions about how you wish to compose your final image. Alternatively, you may prefer to get ideas by cropping your finished photos in a variety of ways.

Series of snapshots

Cropping
An excellent method of developing a composition is to cut two pieces of cardboard into L-shapes to create a rectangular viewer. Use this to frame your subject or to crop a photo so as to achieve the most dynamic arrangement.

Greyhound racing
The painting is based on different views selected from the various photos. The fleeting passage of the greyhounds is expressed through the connecting rhythm of the legs, which contrasts with the blurred treatment of the shadows on the track and the surprisingly abrupt cropping created by the vertical edges of the support.

Blocking in

Working outdoors can be exciting but requires specific skills to catch an image in a particular quality of light when that light is constantly changing. You will find that you are forced to act decisively as you try to interpret a chosen scene. A good aid is to squint at your subject, which makes you focus on the major shapes and tones. Try this when you are working, and then block in the dominant tones in broad areas of color.

Working from a photograph

Initial blocks of color

Village street

Here the artist started by squinting at the photo to focus on the major shapes and tones and then did a preliminary sketch, blocking in the basic elements in broad areas of color. For the final image he chose to crop the left-hand edge off the photo and adapted and intensified the colors.

Sketching

Cats are ideal subjects for sketching, as they are capable of an extraordinary range of movements as they engage in their daily rituals of feeding, playing, and grooming. You will need to set down the essential shapes and relationships of the cat's form in rapid, decisive strokes. You can then work up a more finished painting by selecting the best of your sketches and either tracing your choice or copying it onto another sheet. Copying has the advantage that you can alter the size.

Quick sketches

Sebastian grooming

The finished composition has the cat on his favorite rug, preening himself. The sketches, with their limited tonal range, have been transformed by a far more vibrant range of colors.

233

COMPOSING WITH PASTEL

COMPOSITION FORMS THE HEART of painting. It is the art of organizing shapes and colors into a pleasing or expressive arrangement. When you look at a painting that you admire, you see a subject portrayed in a style that attracts you. More importantly, you experience the mind of the artist selecting, organizing, and inventing new shapes out of their subject. Successful composition requires a unifying theme – that is, a particular quality that recurs throughout the work, such as a dominant mood or visual rhythm. If you copy a subject faithfully, your composition will conform to certain predictable expectations – for example, the way gravity affects the objects in a room or how the quality of light is consistent. Deny these expectations and a composition soon takes on a disoriented feeling. However, we are easily bored by the predictable and often enjoy the surprise of unusual color arrangements or juxtapositions of shapes. Successful paintings frequently develop out of the search for both a recurring theme, which gives a work a sense of order, and a quality of the unexpected.

STILL LIFE is an ideal way to explore compositional issues. You can exercise complete control over the arrangement in a way that is not possible with other subjects. You can choose a specific range of colors to contrast or harmonize with one another; you can control the direction of the light, and you can position the objects in a variety of arrangements without fear that the set-up will alter while you paint. You will see that as you rearrange your chosen objects or alter the light or even view them from different angles you will immediately create entirely different compositions.

Standard view
Grouping objects is like the arrangement of players on a stage; each one will have its own character and will interact with the other players. Here, the vase dominates, creating the point of balance for the arrangement, while the surrounding forms echo one another in terms of shape and scale.

Horizontal arrangement
By translating a three-dimensional world of forms onto the two-dimensional world of the picture surface, you will create shapes that did not exist in your original subject. These new shapes are created by cropping and framing the subject by means of the vertical and horizontal edges of the support. In this horizontal composition, based on the format of a double square, the artist has invested the negative shapes between the positive shapes of the objects with as much interest and care as she has the objects themselves.

Balance

Consciously or unconsciously, we look for a balance of shape, color, tone, and directional lines within a composition. It is as if we place the painting on an imaginary fulcrum and intuitively find the balancing point. This is rarely in the exact middle of a painting but more often slightly off-center. Colors have different weights depending on how dark or how intense they are. For example, large, light, or weak-colored areas can be balanced by small, dense, and dark ones.

Vertical arrangement
Directional lines can create rhythmical connections within a composition and imbue it with a dynamic sense of movement and energy. Here the diagonal lines lead the eye on a zigzag route upward and across the width of the painting. They create a sharp impact that contrasts with the soft, rounded forms of the various objects within the arrangement.

Square format
Colors affect us deeply. They can lift or lower our spirits and will have many physical and emotional associations for us: blue for sky and water, green for grass and growth, red for blood and heat, yellow for sun and daylight, white for the moon and night light. Here the bold colors of the forms, balanced within the square, sing out against the red ground.

Vertical arrangement
The format of a support has a major impact on the way you arrange a composition. As a general rule, a vertical format is more dynamic and a horizontal format is more restful. Here, the artist has chosen a vertical format while striving for a sense of balance. She has placed her horizontal line across the lower third of the painting, instinctively recreating a visual formula known as the "Golden Section" that was considered aesthetically superior in the 19th century.

Arrangement with shadow
You can radically alter the appearance of a subject by changing the angle of the lighting or switching from daylight to artificial light. Here, a dramatic feeling of tension is created by the use of long diagonal shadows ascending from the base of the composition. The drama is increased by the steep angle of vision at which the objects are drawn. The theatrical lighting creates threatening and ambiguous shadows that invite imaginative interpretation.

235

GALLERY OF COMPOSITION

COMPOSITION IS ESSENTIALLY the art of selection and arrangement. The same subject viewed in a variety of ways will create entirely different compositions. One may seem balanced and generate a sense of calm while another may seem dramatic or even disturbing. For this reason, artists often paint a favored subject in a variety of ways. Composition requires you to be selective. It has as much to do with what you choose to leave out as what you choose to put in.

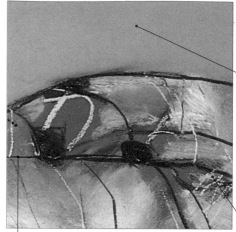

Blackburn blends pastel into the tooth of the paper, creating a rich surface of color that evokes a sense of light and atmosphere.

Divisions of fields and bushes are implied by luminous traces of lemon yellow and punctuating dark notes of deep blue.

The strong black lines suggest trees and saplings gripping the slopes of steep hills.

Joy Girvin,
Scala de Luce,
38 x 30 in (96 x 76 cm)
Girvin uses a vertical format, which amplifies the sense of enclosure created by the dense rhythm of the trees. The tangle of roots and branches creates a rich interplay of forms throughout the composition. The eye is drawn to the area of light along the diagonal line of the path as it winds its way through the cool shadows of the surrounding foliage to the promise of warmth and light beyond.

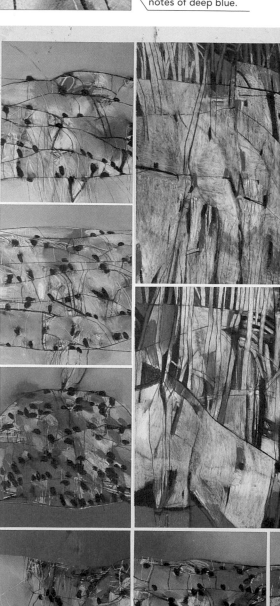

David Blackburn, *A Landscape Vision No. 7,* **1990** *60 x 65 in (153 x 165 cm)*
This highly inventive composition draws on memories and associations with landscape rather than portraying a series of literal views. The deliberate ambiguity engages the viewer in an imaginative interpretation not dissimilar to the experience of listening to music. The landscape is evoked rather than described as the mind reads the rhythm of shapes and colors, recalling experiences of journeys through woods and fields. The format is a symmetrical arrangement of rectangles forming a polyptych that has its roots in early religious altarpieces. Like an altarpiece, the image, with its small pieces clustering around the larger ones, seems designed as a focus for quiet meditation.

David Prentice, *Red Earl's Dyke, Malvern* *34 x 23 in (86 x 58 cm)*
Light transforms a landscape, creating atmosphere and visual drama.
The artist has made compositions from this subject through the changing
color and light of the seasons. This composition is constructed in a
striking, yet balanced, arrangement of contrasting shapes that amplify
the contours of the hill as it falls away from the afternoon light.

**The whiteness
of** the buildings
serves as a focal
point within the
composition.
Flat areas of
light balance
against the dark,
undulating sweeps
of the hillside.

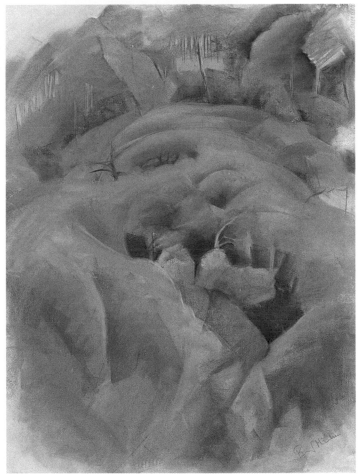

Bridget McCrum,
Autumn Landscape on the Dart *40 x 32 in (102 x 81 cm)*
Bridget McCrum is a sculptor who works from studies of animals.
In this powerful pastel piece, she has imbued the landscape with the
muscular flexings of a recumbent beast through the use of recurring
convex forms. The forbidding scale of the scene is implied by the
steep ascent of the orange and gold canopy of beech trees stretching
upward from the base of the picture. The forms merge and
separate, suggesting a hidden world beneath the surface.

SKETCHING WITH PASTEL

PASTEL IS AN IDEAL MEDIUM for sketching and is capable of an exceptionally wide range of mark-making. Depending on the pressure with which you apply the pastel to the paper, you can vary the texture of a mark from a grainy, faint trail to a thick line to a dense area of impasto. The expressive marks used in these sketches are created by a variety of gestures that do not attempt to copy the birds in precise detail so much as to record the artist's response to their mood, movement, and form. In this sense the act of sketching is a type of visual shorthand that translates the movement of the birds into an evocative language of lines and color.

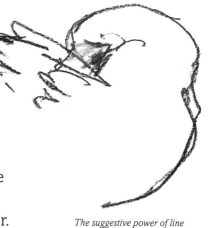

The suggestive power of line

THE DOMINANT USE OF LINE within a composition will lead the eye on a journey across and through the picture plane, and as a line is varied in pace, the eye of the viewer will automatically retrace the artist's response to the subject. For many people, linear marks have musical associations – lines can create a rhythm of movement and, depending on their strength or tension, can produce a sensation of energy or of relaxation. In addition to setting the mood, line acts as a boundary that defines shape. With practice you will be able to achieve an enormous variety of line simply by the way in which you manipulate the pastel. Hold the pastel with your fingertips, keeping the heel of your hand away from the paper surface so that you do not accidentally smudge your work.

A hint of color
There is a dramatic contrast created by the change in tone from the delicate light blue, used to describe the heads and bodies of the geese, to the black notes of their tail feathers. The complementary orange of their feet serves to root them quite firmly to the ground.

Defining form
This rapidly executed sketch has created a sense of energy, while the vigorous application of the marks suggests the presence of mass. Rather than simply outlining form, the curved lines imply the volume and solidity of the bird.

Foreshortened perspective
Even a few rapid lines can suggest a great deal about the character of a form. The perspective here allows you to imagine the ungainly gait of the bird as it waddles on dry land.

LINES DO NOT EXIST IN NATURE in the way that we represent them on paper; rather, they are an artificial device for directing the movement of the eye around the form of a subject and, depending on the character of the line, for suggesting qualities such as texture and mass.

As you work, you will find that you instinctively use the tip of the pastel to create fine lines and the side of the pastel to create areas of tone. You can suggest mass and volume by controlling areas of light and shadow so that you capture the way the light is falling on your subject. In addition, you can hatch or cross-hatch with the tip of the pastel to further define form.

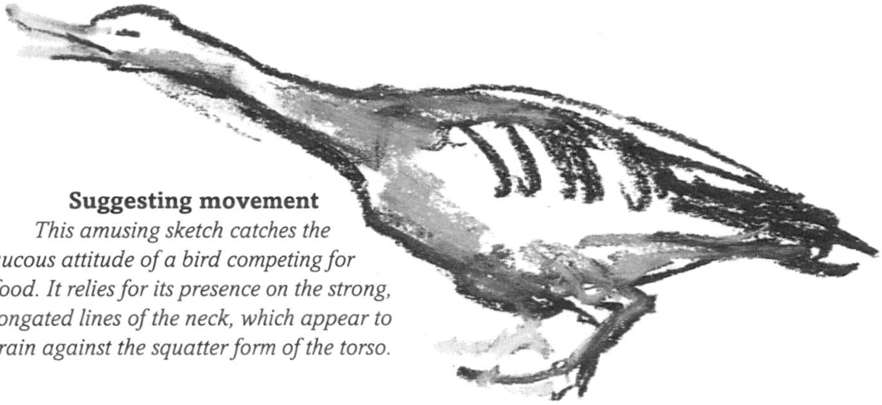

Suggesting movement
This amusing sketch catches the raucous attitude of a bird competing for food. It relies for its presence on the strong, elongated lines of the neck, which appear to strain against the squatter form of the torso.

Line and color
Here color, particularly the use of white, adds to the sense of mass. The thrust of the parallel forms of the torsos and feet in these birds implies the angle of vision from which each was observed.

Thumbnail sketch
This little sketch shows how a sharply observed contour can be invested with a convincing sense of mass by the addition of color and tone – and also by the omission of color. The broken texture of the application of pastel to the back implies the luster of the feathers.

Building up the form
Here line and tone are combined to suggest the arrangement of feathers in the wings and tail. The neat, volumetric form of the torso, however, is encapsulated in the few loose, suggestive marks that define the bird.

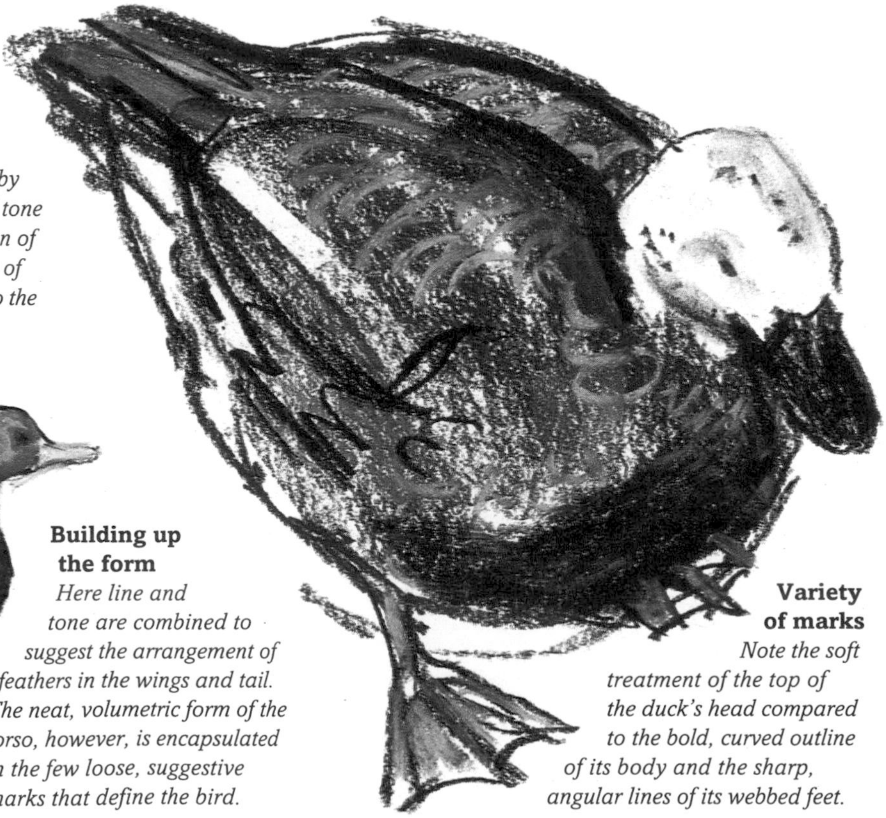

Variety of marks
Note the soft treatment of the top of the duck's head compared to the bold, curved outline of its body and the sharp, angular lines of its webbed feet.

239

SKETCHING WITH TONE

TONE REFERS TO THE DEGREE of lightness or darkness of a surface. To work tonally is an approach totally different from one relying largely on line, since it is all about describing forms in terms of light and shadow. Tone defines the surface qualities of a subject as it is affected by light. A particular feature of tone is the way it unifies a composition.

As light falls into a space, all the forms will be unified by a similar degree of illumination and shadow, and this is referred to as the "tonal key" of a composition. A good way of understanding this tonal key is to squint or half close your eyes as you look at a subject. What you will see are tones rather than sharply defined details. Most artists do this instinctively as they paint in order to see the underlying tonal relationships in a situation.

Sphere and cube

The best way to gain an understanding of tonal relationships is to work from simple forms that have no distracting surface patterns. Place the forms in a strong light source so as to create clear areas of light and shadow. Squint hard at each shape and use a single, cool, dark color to block in the shadow on the forms and the cast shadows. Compare the relative depth of each tone you lay in and build the forms out of the gradations of light and dark tone.

1 ◀ For this composition, use a warm, light-toned pastel paper which will serve to heighten the sense of sunlight. Start with cool, light colors and block in the main shapes of the room with the side of the pastel. Use an ice blue to define the edges of the windows, then a pale lilac to delineate items of furniture.

2 ▶ Gradually adding darker tones, build up blues, greens and purples, working over the image as a whole. Use the side of the pastel for broad areas and the tip for darker, sharper lines. The illuminated areas of the scene should be left unpainted so that the warm tones of the paper create a unifying sense of light.

3 ▲ Switching to a deep plum color, draw in the outline of the chair and start blocking in the window seat. As you strengthen the tones, you will automatically increase the sense of sunlight pouring in through the windows.

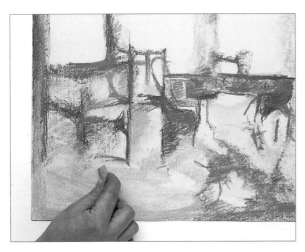

4 ◀ To capture the feel of the strong morning sunlight, start adding light, warmer tones to the painting – oranges and pinks and purples. Draw a pale peach color along its side to block in the areas of sunlight that are striking the floor.

5 ◀ You can alter the mood of the room by adjusting the colors or modifying the various tones. Here a warm, grassy green is overlaid onto the blues, pinks, and purples to give this rich blend of colors. The effect is to create a hazy, atmospheric painting rather than a literal rendition of an interior.

6 ◀ Always mindful of how the light strikes the objects in the room, continue to build up the areas of light and shadow. Use a rich blue to strengthen contours and deepen the tone of the shadows in the foreground. The addition of this blue helps to frame and balance the image.

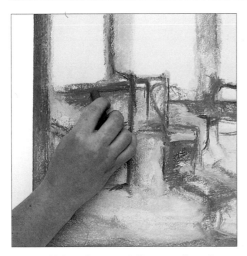

The shadow of the window frame and wall travels uninterrupted through the furniture onto the floor of the room.

The sewing machine is silhouetted against the light of the window, its tone and form contrasting sharply with the tone of its surroundings.

7 ▲ Although essentially a tonal study, the addition of line helps to sharpen certain forms. Here you can draw a very fine line with the edge of the pastel to help define the window seat and the chair.

Morning light

This tonal study explores the way that strong directional light determines the appearance of form, dividing the room into distinct shapes of light and shadow. The unpainted areas of the paper establish a recurring note for the sunlight as it floods the room.

Tamar Teiger

Light imparts a degree of warmth to all the surfaces it falls on, as in the color of the floor. The colors of the shadows here are conversely cool.

BLENDING

PASTELS DIFFER FROM OTHER PAINTING MEDIA in that they have to be mixed directly on the paper rather than in a palette. The pastel artist has several methods to choose from to achieve new colors. The most straightforward of these is simply to blend them. Blending is a technique of rubbing and fusing two or more colors on the surface of the paper into a unified tone. To do this, you can use your fingers, the side of your hand, or a blending tool, depending on the scale you are working in and which method you prefer. The pastel dust is held quite loosely by the tooth of the paper so that it is easy to spread adjacent colors into one another in this way.

Watermelon

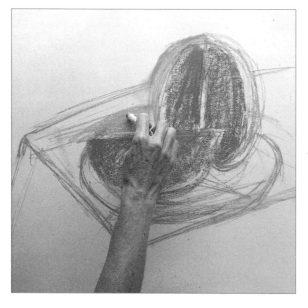

2 ◀ Blend in the flesh of the watermelon with your finger. Rubbing the surface in this way will distribute some of the loose pastel pigment over the paper.

1 ◀ Looking closely at your still life, sketch in the outlines of the watermelon, the platter, and the tablecloth using a yellow ochre soft pastel. Next, start blocking in areas of color using broad, loose strokes.

3 ▲ Continue to build up areas of color with loose strokes. Here, a pink pastel is used to add richness to the underlying color and to physically blend it in.

BLENDING TOOLS

Tortillons are the traditional tools for blending pastels. A tortillon is a tight roll of paper shaped like a crayon. You can use either the tip or the side to move and blend the pigment powder. Although tortillons afford a high degree of control, many artists prefer to use their fingers since the fibrous nature of tortillons – and similarly of rags and cotton swabs – tends to lift off some of the color instead of just blending it.

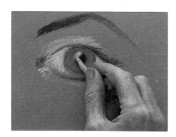

Kneaded eraser
Soften a lump of eraser in your hands and work it into a point. This forms a very fine blending and erasing tool, able to move tiny areas of pigment around or to lift pigment off completely.

Brushes
Soft brushes are good for larger areas, particularly where the desired effect is a gradual changing of tone. They can be used to disperse the loose pigment particles or to lift the color off.

Tortillon
Available in two sizes, the tortillon is useful for softening the edges of an image although it may also remove some of the pigment. When it gets dirty, unwind some of the paper from the tip.

Soft cloth
A soft cloth can draw pigment across the paper and so is ideal for altering larger areas of pigment or, as in this case, for forming wispy white clouds on a blue background.

4 ▲ Lighten the area closest to the rind with a cotton ball. Its fibrous nature will lift off some of the pastel.

5 ◄ Continue to work over the piece as a whole. After sharpening the contours of the platter and filling in broad areas of the tablecloth, you can concentrate more on the folds of the cloth, particularly the crease made by the edge of the table. Make a bold wavy line along this edge; once you rub along it with your finger or a tortillon it will soften considerably.

Materials

Cotton swab

Small tortillon

Large tortillon

Soft brush

Kneaded eraser

Soft cloth

Cotton ball

6 ▲ After adding the seeds, draw a line along the center of the melon. Run your finger along the line to gently blend that color into the surrounding area.

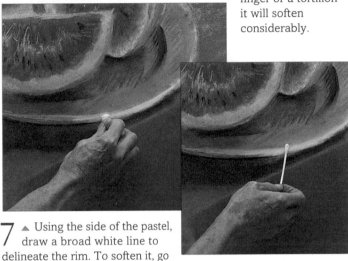

7 ▲ Using the side of the pastel, draw a broad white line to delineate the rim. To soften it, go over it with a cotton swab. Its size makes it ideal for working on small areas, allowing you more control than your finger would.

Note how blending the brown line at the point where the slice has been cut has dispersed some of the loose pigment into the pink, creating a greater sense of form and depth.

Melon still life
By building up the colors in the tablecloth, the artist has gradually filled in the tooth of the paper, creating what is known as an impasto effect. This creates a dense, unbroken area of color.

The rich color of the cloth is created by overlaying a range of blues, purples, browns and reds and blending them in with the pastels themselves.

Sharon Finmark

WARM TINTS, COOL SHADES

MODELING FORM REQUIRES an awareness of light and shadow, and an understanding of warm and cool colors. Just as you can divide up the different areas of a form into distinct light and dark tones as the form moves in and out of the light, so, too, you can divide a form into areas of warm and cool hues. The color of a form as it is perceived in an even white light is called the "local color." We rarely see a form in its true local color; what we see is how the form appears in a slightly colored light. Daylight and more extremely artificial tungsten light are generally biased toward yellow. This means that

as light falls on a form it will influence the local color and produce a yellowish cast. Conversely, the areas of local color in shadow will appear cool and biased toward blue-violet. When you are painting outdoors, the effect of light is particularly noticeable – you will find that the quality of light alters dramatically over a period of time, totally transforming what you see. Here, the artist has produced two portrait studies, one in direct frontal light and one in oblique lighting, exploring the way in which this indoor light alters the appearance of the form and changes the mood of a composition.

Directional light

1 ▶ Using a tinted flock pastel paper, map out the contours of the face in an earthy red. There is strong light coming in from the left, so start blocking in the shadows in a cool blue.

2 ◀ Look hard at the face and see which areas are thrown into shadow by the lighting and which are thrown into relief. Use a strong yellow to capture the highlights on the forehead, cheekbone, nose, and neck.

3 ◀ Start building up the tones, using light browns and reds for the warm lights in the hair, and purples and blacks for the shadow. The pastel clings to the textured surface of the paper, allowing for very little movement once the color has been applied.

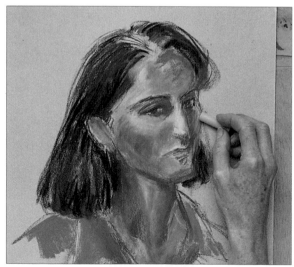

4 ▲ Continue adding the lights and darks, leaving the eyes for one of the final details so that the whites do not get muddied. Although one side of the face is in shadow, there is nevertheless a certain amount of light reflecting off that cheekbone.

Reversing the light

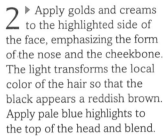

1 ◀ Using a tinted pastel paper, lay down the outlines of the face and start blocking in the areas of shadow. Because of the woman's dark skin tones, the areas in shadow veer toward the purple.

2 ▶ Apply golds and creams to the highlighted side of the face, emphasizing the form of the nose and the cheekbone. The light transforms the local color of the hair so that the black appears a reddish brown. Apply pale blue highlights to the top of the head and blend.

3 ◀ Draw in the eye and eyebrow with a dark brown and then use a greenish gray to define the contours of the nose and eye. Because of the quality of the flocked paper, you can lay down colors and blend them with your fingers to create areas of shadow.

4 ◀ To complement and heighten the warm colors of the head, lay down a cool background color. Apply strokes of turquoise around the side of the face and then blend the color outward with the side of your hand. This has the effect of softening the tone as the blue spreads outward, moving farther from the face.

Aspects of a woman

Light defines form as well as creating mood. Here the two images of the woman look quite different largely as a result of the way the light strikes her. In the image on the left, there is a sharpness to the contours on her face, with strong cheekbones and chiseled lips. Her blouse is a radiant blue, balancing and complementing the olive skin tones. The right-hand portrait appears softer, the tonal changes on the side of her face in shadow are more subdued and the blue of the blouse is almost bleached out by the light.

Sharon Finmark

245

SCUMBLING

THE TECHNIQUE OF SCUMBLING is a means of building up a pastel painting in layers. The side or blunted tip of a soft pastel is lightly drawn across the surface of the paper to create the effect of a delicate veil of color through which some of the underlying color is visible. Enough pressure is applied to impart grains of pastel to the raised tooth of the support without obscuring or lifting the previous layer of color. The characteristic quality of scumbling is a broken color effect where the newly laid color, interacts visually with the underlying color causing the colors to "sparkle." Because the technique involves applying layers of pastel, there is a tendency for the tooth of the paper to fill up. To counter this, fixative spray can be used to fix each successive layer of pastel and create a new surface for subsequent applications of color to adhere to.

Blue over pink

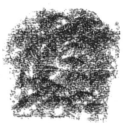

Pink over blue

Scumbled marks

Although the same two colors have been applied in the pairs above and below, the visual effect is quite different depending on which color has been scumbled first. See also how the randomness of the marks creates interesting textural and color effects.

Ultramarine over yellow

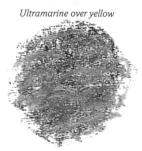

Yellow over ultramarine

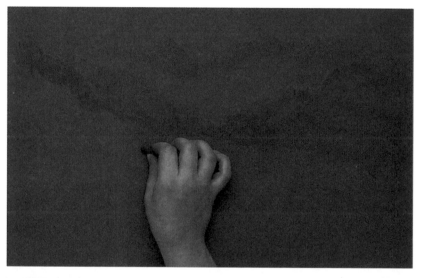

1 ▶ For this exercise the artist has studied a black and white photo of a landscape and used it as a springboard for her imagination. For a similar effect, use dark-toned paper and apply a bright blue in circular movements with the side of the pastel. The purple is then blocked in, defining the middle ground of the painting.

2 ▲ Taking a lighter blue, fill in a distant mountain and highlight some areas in the foreground. To start creating a point of interest, scumble in a line of fir trees along a diagonal ridge.

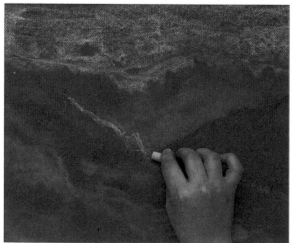

3 ▲ Take a cream-colored pastel and scumble the sky using the side of the pastel. Then use a broad line to define the point at which the mountains meet.

5 ◀ Following the principle that in a landscape warm colors appear to advance and cool colors appear to recede, use a warm yellow to define the area closest to the viewer. Notice how powerful the color is, drawing the eye immediately to the foreground.

4 ▲ Once the main details are in place, it is largely a question of strengthening the image and striving for a good color balance. Short, horizontal strokes of pink warm up the sky and appear to silhouette the distant hills.

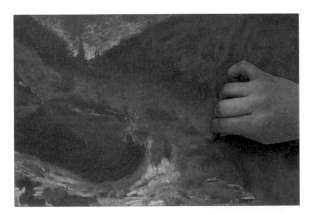

6 ◀ Always using the side of the pastel, overlay veils of gold, purple and a rich turquoise. The strength of the colors now vies with details such as the trees, which will need building up.

7 ▲ The final application of yellow to the sky creates a sense of depth and balances the vibrance of the foreground. Approximately six different colors have been scumbled over the sky to arrive at this rich density of color.

Distant hills

The scumbling of veils of color has produced a compellingly rich surface to this image. Layers mingle to create surprising new hues, and the darkness of the ground reacts with the pastels to strengthen certain colors and tone down others. Diagonals lead the eye back and forth over the picture, and colors appear to recede into the background.

The darkness of the trees is arrived at by overlaying strokes of blues, greens, and purples rather than applying black.

Notice how the original color of the paper is still visible even with this degree of overlaying.

The strength of the gold visually vibrates against the contrasting tone of the purple paper.

Tamar Teiger

FEATHERING

FEATHERING IS A TECHNIQUE of laying delicate parallel strokes of color with the point of a pastel, usually over an existing layer of pastel color. It is close to the technique of hatching in that the strokes serve to assert and clarify the planes of a form while creating a coherent surface of marks. And like the technique of scumbling, feathering is a means of enlivening a flat, even area of color and can be used to modify a tone in a pastel painting. When you add fine strokes over an existing color, the two colors appear to mix, which creates subtle color changes. This can be used to particularly good effect if, for example, you wish to capture the shimmering quality of light in certain atmospheric conditions.

Charcoal sketch

ENLIVENING COLORS

The technique of feathering in which short strokes of one color are overlaid onto another can greatly enrich the feel of a work. In the first example below, the blended colors of the jacket and the chair produce a realistic image but one that is nevertheless somewhat flat. The shadows give it a certain sense of form, but not nearly as much as in the lower feathered example. Here the overlaid colors create a far greater richness, particularly in the folds of the jacket and the seat of the chair.

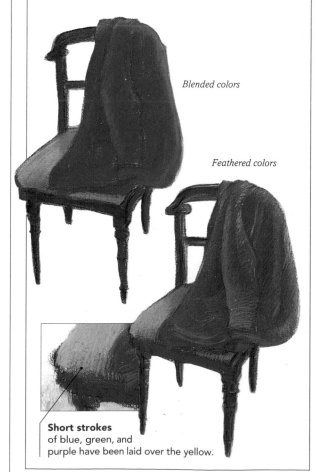

Blended colors

Feathered colors

Short strokes
of blue, green, and
purple have been laid over the yellow.

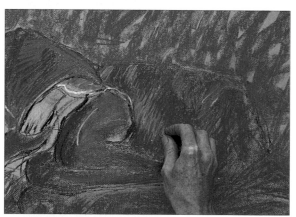

1 ◀ Block in the main areas of color, using the tip and the side of the pastels. You will need several shades of each color to capture areas of light and shadow. Here downward strokes with the side of the pastel create a sense of the folds in the fabric.

2 ▶ Start by feathering the fabric of the chaise longue. Overlay parallel strokes of ochres, reds and gold. Each additional color serves to modify the overall effect.

3 ◀ Complementary colors placed next to each other create a powerful effect. In this case the addition of green counterbalances the richness of the oranges in the folds of the fabric, just as the purple in the trousers works against the strokes of yellow.

4 ◄ The original purple of the background has been scumbled on in loose, circular movements. To achieve a more muted effect, tone down the color with a paler hue such as lilac and start blending it in with your fingers. If the background still appears too dominant, blend the pastel with some cotton balls to lift a little of the color.

5 ► Following the principle of implementing complementary colors for creating shadows, overlay a cool green to counterbalance the warm pinks of the flesh tones in the areas of the hands and neck.

6 ▲ To counteract the flatness of the trousers, apply short strokes of blue, purple, and brown over the original color. These feathered strokes create a greater richness of hue in the areas of shadow.

7 ▲ By feathering pale blues and pinks over the darkness of the blue, you arrive at this very strong quality of light, which accentuates the sense of form.

Woman reclining
The finished picture is bathed in a glowing light that has been achieved by feathering strokes of high-key colors into the rich local colors of the figure and drape. There is a pleasing balance between the relaxed pose of the figure and the gentle curves of the chaise longue.

See how shades of green have been feathered into the orange of the drape to create the sense of folds and shadows.

The flatness of the background is achieved by blending the colors.

The rhythmical curve of the shoulder is echoed in the shape of the chaise longue.

Short strokes of blues, oranges, browns, and lilacs add to the sense of form in the legs.

249

DRY WASH

THE TECHNIQUE OF DRY WASH is a method of laying a broad area of color in a uniform, unbroken tone. It is a way of achieving seamless transitions of two or more colors and so is particularly suited to creating subtle atmospheric effects in landscape painting. To prepare a dry wash, simply scrape or crush a pastel into a fine powder. You can then either tip the powder directly onto areas of the support to create dense areas of color or pick up the powder using a brush, rag, fine sponge, or cotton ball and then work the powder into the support. Whichever method you choose, you can then blend the powder into the support with your fingers or any of the other blending tools, depending on the effect you desire (blending with your fingers creates the strongest tone). You can achieve subtle and precise blending of dry washes by either mixing different powdered pastels together before you apply them or overlaying individual colors directly on the support.

1 ◀ With a scalpel, scrape the end of a dark olive green pastel onto your paper. Try not to apply too much pressure as you do this – you could find yourself with chips of color rather than fine pastel powder, or even break the pastel completely.

2 ▶ Now work the powder into the paper with your fingers. You will be surprised at how far a small amount goes.

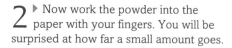

3 ▲ Another way of laying a dry wash is to scrape pastel powder into a dish and apply it with a cotton ball. The effect will be less dense than when you use your fingers, since the cotton ball fibers retain some of the pigment.

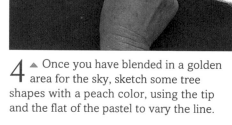

4 ▲ Once you have blended in a golden area for the sky, sketch some tree shapes with a peach color, using the tip and the flat of the pastel to vary the line.

5 ◀ Complete the trees using a combination of dry wash techniques for the foliage and conventional drawing techniques for the trunks and outlying branches. Now sprinkle pastel powder onto the sky to create cloud shapes and blend them in with your fingers.

RECONSTITUTING PASTELS

Inevitably, pastels will break as you work and you will find yourself with dozens of fragments, too small to use. Don't throw them away. Save them, sorting them into groups of similar colors, and use them to make new pastels later. The process is extremely simple and you can create your own rich colors from your various bits and pieces. You can use skim milk to bind particularly soft pastels and give them a slightly harder texture. Most pastels, however, contain enough binder to be reconstituted by simply adding water to the powder and mixing it.

Pastel fragments

1 *Take your yellow pastel fragments and grind them into a fine powder with a muller on a glass slab.*

2 *Grind the blue pastel fragments in the same way. Once they are finely ground, you can start to mix the colors.*

3 *Use a palette knife to mix the colors into each other. After a period of time, the blue and yellow will form a green.*

4 *Add a spoonful or two of skim milk, mixing it in with the knife until you arrive at a fairly dry paste.*

5 *Fashion the paste into a roughly oblong mass, first with the palette knife and then with your fingers.*

6 *Place the pastel on absorbent paper and roll it with your fingers. Leave it to dry at room temperature for 24 hours.*

Chunky new green pastel

6 ◀ Finally, to enliven the foreground color and create a greater sense of depth, sprinkle some bright blue pastel powder onto certain areas of the green and blend it in with your fingers. The combination of magenta and this bright blue blended into the green creates a richly varied surface.

The dry wash technique is ideal for creating the subtle, hazy feel of the sky.

Materials

Small dish

Scalpel

Cotton ball

Hampstead Heath

The dense tones achieved by the dry wash technique have been used to create an image of both striking tonal contrast and subtle color modulation. The artist has balanced the positive shapes of the hillside with the negative shape of the sky.

The broken silhouette of the branches, scumbled with the side of a pastel, relies for its effect on the tooth of the paper showing through.

If you look closely you can see distinct layers of blue, magenta and green in this area.

See how the dry wash has filled in the tooth of the paper.

Felicity Edholm

EXPLORING TEXTURE

Dried flowers

THE ADAPTABILITY OF soft pastel to both drawing and painting techniques makes it an ideal medium for exploring textural qualities. The pastelist can apply a striking variety of marks ranging from delicate traces of line to full impasto (rich, thick applications of paint), and from loose, open scumbling to smooth, blended transitions of tone. As can be seen below, the versatility of pastel provides an exciting opportunity to exploit a diversity of textures. Here the artist has chosen an imaginative combination of textural materials that evoke a surreal and dreamlike association with the sea. The luminous arrangement of disparate forms appear to float as jetsam and contrast with the dark folding waves of deep green velvet.

TRANSPARENCY

Painting glass presents particular sets of problems since it is both a transparent material and a reflective one. Light plays on its surface and also through it, altering the tones of what lies within. Here, as light passes through the glass there are subtle changes of tone from a warm orange-red to a cooler magenta, as well as highlights where the glass reflects the light source.

Painting glass
To capture the essence of liquid within glass, start with a pencil drawing. Study the different tones of the wine and apply first the mid-tones, blending them in a circular motion with your finger. Build up the darker tones and then add white to the rim and sides of the glass for highlights. Overhead light passing through the glass casts a pink-violet tone.

1 ▲ Here a trumpet, dried flowers, and a fish are laid on velvet to create an interesting range of textures. As the composition is quite complex, start with a pencil sketch and then block in the main areas of color using the side of the pastels. It is a good idea to start with mid-tones and then gradually build up the lights and darks.

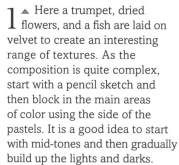

2 ▲ For the velvet, apply broad swathes of green with the side of the pastel and then overlay similar swathes of a dark blue. The velvet is soft, so you should draw the side of the pastels across the paper in fairly soft, broad sweeps. Blend the blue into the green with your fingers, following the lines in which the color has been applied.

3 ▶ The flowers with their spiky shoots and leaves demand quite different treatment. Draw in some of the stems in bold, continuous movements using the tip of the pastels, pressing down quite hard, and use short spiky lines to outline the flower heads. Next, return to the deep turquoise to outline some of the shapes and define their forms against the velvet.

4 ◀ For the reflection of the velvet on the trumpet, apply a range of blues, greens, and yellows, following the line of the bell. The shiny effect is achieved by blending each color in turn with a finger. Be sure to clean your hands between colors to avoid smearing one color over another.

5 ◀ Continue building up lights and darks, adjusting areas as you work. If you are worried about disturbing areas you have already painted, lay a sheet of paper on the image and rest your hand lightly on your work.

6 ◀ For the shiny, somewhat wet surface of the fish, draw lines of different colors along its body – blues, grays, pinks, and muted yellows – taking care not to fill the tooth of the paper. By not pressing down too hard with the pastels you can take advantage of the texture of the paper to create the impression of the fish's scales.

A musical composition
The artist has chosen a large sheet of watercolor paper – 22 x 30 in (56 cm x 76 cm) – in order to be able to work in considerable detail. She finds that the pastels are simply too large to execute finely detailed work on smaller-sized sheets.

The bell of the trumpet forms the focus of the composition, acting as the still point of a vortex of lines of movement.

The lustrous skin of the fish has been achieved through a mixture of scumbling and blending techniques. The delicate blues and gray-greens have been scumbled, while the pink and white highlights have been blended with a finger.

The smooth form of the trumpet has been modeled by means of a careful blending of the warm tones of the brass reflecting the cool tones of the light and the surrounding velvet cloth.

The cool deep turquoise of the velvet has been highlighted with warmer notes of green along the folds.

The dry strokes of pastel used to define the spiky forms of the dried flowers contrast with the blending technique used to achieve the wet and shiny forms of the fish and trumpet.

Jane Gifford

GALLERY OF TECHNIQUES

THE MOST IMPORTANT FEATURE to appreciate about pastels is that they are open to a diversity of drawing and painting techniques. Each of the pastel works in this gallery shows how the artists have selected a particular technique that is appropriate to the interpretation of their subject matter. For the majority of artists, the development of their particular solution has been arrived at through experimentation, which has evolved through trusting their creative instincts and enjoying the many possibilities of this exciting and promising medium.

Ken Paine, *Mrs. Groffes* *25 x 21 in (64 x 54 cm)*
In this moving portrait, Paine has used a limited palette of colors and a range of techniques to invest the composition with emotional presence. He has concentrated on the face, modeling the woman's features delicately to create this dreamy, soft-focus effect. He has treated the woman's dress quite differently – with vigorous open hatching and long, bold strokes – so as to balance the composition and not distract from the essential quality of the portrait.

Sally Strand, *Eggs under Water*
36¼ x 48½ in (96 x 123 cm)
Sally Strand's work is characterized by an exceptional sensitivity to the blending properties of soft pastel. Here she demonstrates the use of blending and feathering as techniques of modeling form and as a means of controlling the delicate transitions between light and shadow.

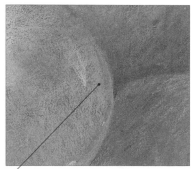

In this detail, you can see the subtle blending of warm and cool hues that establish the light reflected by the eggs and refracted by the surrounding water.

Sophie Aghajanian, *Mirror Image* *22 x 30 in (56 x 77 cm)*
Sophie Aghajanian works on Fabriano paper in a technique called sfumato (smoky), and achieves a dreamlike quality in her painting by means of a dry wash. For this, she scrapes pastels into a fine dust, which she then works into the support using her hands, a cloth or tortillons. This composition is a striking example of how a simple subject can be transformed by the way in which it is arranged. The dramatic tilt of the mirror is counterbalanced by the downward movement of the flamelike flower heads.

The forms of the jam jar and the flowers emerge out of darkness and are invested with unexpected associations of flight. The intensity of the petals comes from the purity of the pigment powder.

Ken Draper, RA, *Nile, Last Light*, 1993 *18 x 20 in (46 x 51 cm)*
Much of Draper's work develops from a highly imaginative interpretation of landscape using a technique which frequently combines the dry quality of soft pastel with the dense impasto of oil pastel. Here he has blended areas of dusky blue-violet over darker tones, building up areas of pastel and scratching back to achieve a great richness of texture. In this evocative composition, the pale evening sky is suspended between the silhouetted landscape and the majestic canopy of dense black clouds.

This detail shows Draper's mastery of techniques as he creates vibrant, pulsating areas of red against the subtly blended darker tones.

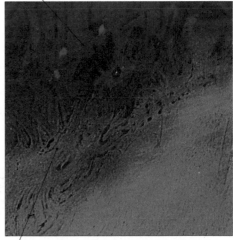

Here Draper creates ripples on the painting surface by dragging dark, rich tones of oil pastel over hazy, blended areas of soft pastel.

255

USING OIL PASTEL

OIL PASTEL HAS DISTINCT qualities that require a different approach than the other pastel types. It is suitable for bold, colorful composition as it adheres vigorously to the support, rapidly filling the tooth of the paper, but at the same time it can be dissolved by turpentine and used more like a wash. Its range of hues is more limited than with soft pastels but this is compensated for by the way transparent colors can be overlaid on the support. The performance of oil pastels is altered by temperature; they become softer and more fluid as they warm up. Because of this, it is best to keep them in their original wrappers to prevent them from sticking to your fingers.

Basket of silk flowers

1 ▶ Using oil paper, sketch in a rough composition with some yellows, blues, and greens. When you are happy with the basic arrangement of forms, start building up the color. With a cotton swab, wet an area of the paper with turpentine, draw in some blue lines and blend the blue with the wet cotton swab. Note how some of the color soaks into the paper.

RANGE OF EFFECTS

This simple sketch of the artist's daughter shows the variety of effects you can achieve with oil pastel, from lines of varying thicknesses to subtle washes of color to dense areas of pigment. Here, the tip of the pastel has been used to draw in the outlines and to suggest areas of shadow. The smooth tones of the background are the result of laying down light strokes of turquoise and then blending them with a cotton ball. The flower in the girl's hair is suggested by a thicker, impasto application of colors.

Hayley sketching

2 ◀ For the background, apply strokes of turquoise using the tip of the pastel and then blend the area with a dry cotton swab. Blending on dry paper without the addition of turpentine creates a much more even effect than on the wet paper, as the oily color stays on the surface.

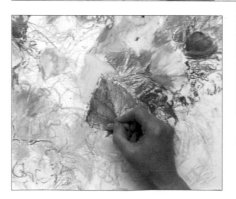

3 ◀ Turning to one of the leaves in the foreground, build up areas of light and shade with different tones of green. You may want to soften some of the darker green by blending strokes of pink into it.

Materials

Cotton ball

Turpentine

Penknife

4 ◀ Pressing quite hard with your pastel, lay a thick application of green and then scratch lines out of it with a blade. You can use this "sgraffito" method to draw veins into leaves or simply to get back to the paper if you wish.

5 ◀ For the aster with its rich cluster of petals, stipple the red onto the paper. Stippling involves laying a pattern of dots on the surface of the paper to create an impression of form. Viewed from a distance, the colors will appear to mix, in an effect known as optical mixing.

6 ▶ Cotton balls, either wet or dry, can be used to blend colors or model forms. Here a cotton ball lifts off some of the pink from the petal, creating a sense of light falling on it and giving it a greater three-dimensionality.

A riot of flowers
This composition demonstrates a diversity of oil pastel techniques and, in particular, the use of turpentine to dissolve oil pastel into transparent washes. By blending, stippling and scratching out, the artist has echoed the huge variety of shapes and textures visible in the many different flowers.

Note how the color of the strut in the wicker basket has been arrived at by overlaying a range of blues, pinks, purples, greens, and browns.

The artist has used the diagonal angle of the handle to contrast with the curvilinear forms of the flowers.

The anemone, with its stippled corona, draws the eye up toward the taller hollyhocks at the back.

The leaf forms a point of interest in the foreground area.

The impasto effect, with its blobs of white color, is clearly visible in the petals of the chrysanthemums.

Rosemary Saul

257

SOFT PASTEL AND WATER

THE USE OF WATER with conventional soft pastel techniques creates surprising and dramatic results. You will need to have a fairly heavy watercolour paper taped to a board to stop the paper from buckling or tearing. Block in areas of colour and then either spray water on to the pastel or work into the colour with a wet paintbrush. As the pastel particles absorb water they will temporarily darken in tone.

The absorbency of pastel can be used in another technique, which involves wetting the paper support with a brush, sponge or spray before working pastel on the surface of the paper. As the pastel touches the paper it is transformed into a thick, rich impasto. Alternatively, you can grind pastel to a powder state, add water, and then apply the paste in varying degrees of dilution as a wash.

1 ▲ Using the side of the pastel, block in areas of purple and red for the night sky and brown for the foreground figures. The drawing can be quite sketchy at this stage, since the addition of water allows you to make alterations later.

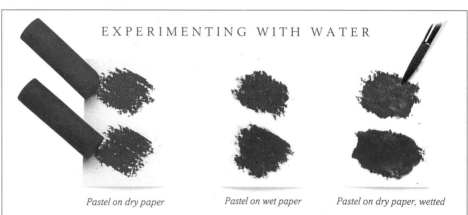

EXPERIMENTING WITH WATER

Pastel on dry paper *Pastel on wet paper* *Pastel on dry paper, wetted*

These swatches show the same soft pastel colours used in three ways. The first shows pastel applied in a normal way on to dry paper. The second shows marks made on to wet paper in which the pastel colours have absorbed some of the water and so seem thicker, more like gouache paint. And in the third the marks have been made on to dry paper and then wetted with a brush so that the pigment particles have dispersed on the support.

2 ▲ Scumble some red in loose strokes over the purple and then "paint" over the area with a large round paintbrush dipped in clean water. The red pigment particles will immediately be dissolved by the water and will wash over the page like a very strong watercolour paint.

3 ▲ Continue adding colour and washing over the composition with a wet brush in broad, loose strokes. Remember to dip your brush in clean water as you work on different areas, so as to preserve the vibrance of the individual colours.

4 ◀ To create a cascading firework, spray water on to the paper and apply short strokes of a bright blue on to the damp surface. The blue adheres to the paper in a rich, impasto effect. Now draw some of the blue down the painting with a sponge.

5 ▶ You can wash out an overworked area and start again. Here the artist wetted the sky and lifted off most of the paint with a paper towel. He then reworked the firework on the left and added the sparkler.

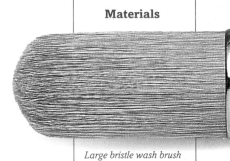

Materials

Large bristle wash brush

Synthetic brush

6 ▲ Apply more strokes of browns, pinks, and yellows, and paint over them with a wet brush. The colours will dry lighter than they appear while they are wet as the water evaporates from the pigment.

7 ▲ Once you are satisfied that the main elements of the composition are in place you should highlight any details that you want to emphasize. The addition of a bold yellow in the foreground creates an eerie sense of light in this bright night sky.

Natural sponge

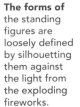

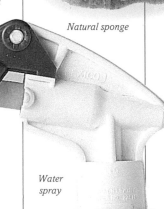

Firework display

The artist has tried to capture the ambiguous feelings induced by a firework display. The fascination with the dramatic light effects of the exploding fireworks is tempered by associated thoughts of war and man's ingenious destructiveness.

The forms of the standing figures are loosely defined by silhouetting them against the light from the exploding fireworks.

Michael Wright

Water spray

PASTEL AND CHARCOAL

Working sketch

CHARCOAL IS OFTEN USED as a starting point for a pastel painting and is valuable both for creating the structure of a work and for establishing a tonal balance. It is easily manipulated across the surface of the paper and can be altered without difficulty by using bread, a kneaded eraser or the heel of the hand. Although you can alter or obscure charcoal lines quite easily, it is not always desirable to do so, since the charcoal adds a depth of tone and acts as a visual scaffolding for the layers of color. You can also use it in the final stages of your composition for accentuating lines or strengthening certain areas. When you work with charcoal, you may need to fix it so that it does not blend into any subsequent layers of pastel.

TYPES OF CHARCOAL

Willow charcoal

Compressed charcoal

Willow charcoal comes, as it sounds, from the willow tree and is essentially just twigs, dried and fired, to be used as a drawing medium. It is particularly good at the initial drawing stage, since it is easily manipulated and altered. Compressed charcoal is made from Lamp Black pigment mixed with a binder and compressed into round or square sticks. It produces a denser, richer line than the willow charcoal and is harder to alter once on the paper.

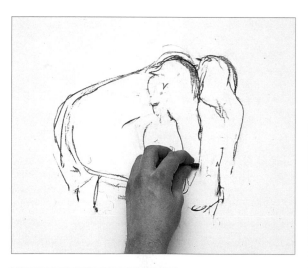

1 ◀ Use a piece of charcoal to sketch in the basic shapes. Here the artist has opted for compressed charcoal, which produces a deep, rich velvety black line. This is less easily displaced than willow charcoal.

Preliminary sketches
Spend some time studying the elephants, watching how they carry themselves, how they move, how they interact with one another.

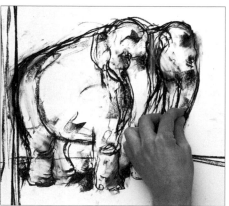

2 ◀ Continue building up the elephants, blending areas as you go along. Draw in some verticals and horizontals to place them within the composition.

3 ◀ Block some aqua into the background to create a sense of depth. The crimson highlights on the elephants' heads add a startling touch, drawing you into the picture to look more closely at their faces.

4 ▶ Using the flat of a pastel, start filling in some background details. Block in the red door at the right and lay in a corner of yellow. See how these few colors begin to give your painting some weight and solidity. It is now largely a question of adjusting the color balance in the composition.

5 ▸ Add colors in loose, broad strokes, scumbling blues and purples into the background. Zigzag a sharp turquoise line to build up the color on the right of the composition. Add areas of white to the bodies of the elephants and blend them in with your thumb. These highlights are in sharp contrast to the black of the charcoal and form a powerful counterpoint to the image.

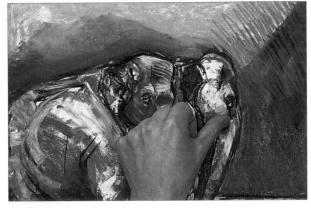

6 ▸ Returning to your charcoal, go over the violet of the railing to give it a greater sense of form, and draw in a gate on the left. Add layers of blue, purple and scarlet to the upright post to create an interesting texture. If you are not happy with the way the charcoal and the pastel mingle, spray the various layers with fixative.

7 ▴ Take your charcoal and redefine areas of shadow on the elephants, drawing in lines and then blending them. Charcoal can be used to add a depth of tone to your work, particularly in the darker passages of your composition.

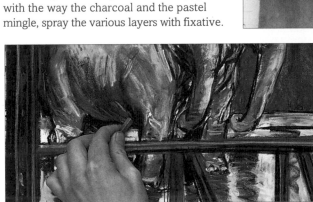

8 ◂ Continue building up the colors, working over the image as a whole. Here the belly of the elephant nearest to us is made up of a range of grays, a crimson, and a green. The various colors are applied in short, diagonal strokes and appear to mix optically.

Elephant house

The combination of charcoal and pastel has been used to dramatic effect in the play of light and shadows throughout this composition. The rhythmical, muscular forms of the elephants are contained by the severe geometry of their environment. As light falls into the enclosure, it creates cool tones and reflections on the wet concrete and serves to heighten the sense of confinement of the elephants.

The use of red here counterbalances the red of the door on the right-hand side.

The artist has used the red door set against strident black lines to amplify the theme of confinement.

The play of light across the elephant's head sharply defines the extraordinary structure of the beast's skull.

The barren environment has been given a vigorous treatment in the assertion of a contrasting rhythm of light and shadow across the floor and railings.

This corner of the composition shows how every surface is linked by a recurring theme of cool purple and blue shadows.

Ian McCaughrean

261

GALLERY OF MIXED MEDIA

ALL THE FORMS of pastel can be worked together or with other media. The most common technique is to lay down an acrylic, watercolor, gouache, or ink wash as a base for overworking in soft or hard pastel. Another option with startling effects is to use a "resist" technique in which an oil pastel drawing is overlaid by a water-based wash. The oil pastel resists the overpainting, emerging free of the wash.

Lucinda Cobley, *Palace on the Lake* 7 x 5in (18.5 x 12cm)
In this small but powerful composition, the artist has worked soft and oil pastel over an acrylic base. She has greatly simplified the architectural form so that the work relies for its impact on the striking and evocative contrast of warm and cool colors, and the unusual way the wet and dry media interact with the texture of the paper.

R.B. Kitaj, RA, *Red Eyes*, 1980 30 x 23in (76 x 60cm)
Kitaj is a superlative draftsman and has used charcoal here as an integral part of the pastel work rather than as an underdrawing. The strident line that defines the contour of the form and accentuates the visual details contrasts with the subtle modulation of the coloring. This surprising and moving diagonal composition displays Kitaj's consummate skill in portraying the human condition through drawing.

In this detail, a lilac soft pastel has been lightly scumbled over the orange to create a broken effect on the texture of the watercolor paper.

Here, an intense red has been encouraged to bleed into the surrounding lighter orange wash.

The strong lines of Conté crayon create the skeleton of the composition, defining the forms and leading the eye on a journey across the picture plane.

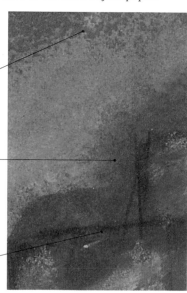

Frances Treanor, *Nude Study* 11 1/2 x 8 1/4 in (31 x 21 cm)
In this dynamic nude study, the artist has used a combination of oil pastel and felt-tip pen with great confidence, as both media require a surety of drawing and allow little scope for alteration. The work has been executed in a vigorous treatment of broad strokes of oil pastel that overlay and complement the tightly controlled black felt-pen line, which defines the contour of the form. The surrounding negative shapes of blue and violet add to the dramatic impact of the angular arrangement.

The broken areas of red pastel create a striking pattern of white shapes that jump against the dense violet-black mass of the model's hair while forming an anchor to the diagonal movements of the image.

Unlike the oil pastel, the black felt-tip produces a line of consistent strength and thickness, lending a clarity to the contours of the woman's face.

Paul Lewin,
Kenidjack Castle 22 x 17 in (55 x 43 cm)
Lewin is a contemporary landscape artist who has produced a series of works exploring compositional arrangements between the natural elements of sea and rocks. In this startling image, he induces a sense of vertigo as the rock face drops steeply into the shadowy chasm. The image has been worked through an inventive treatment of scraped, blended, and scumbled soft pastel over washes and spatterings of watercolor. The artist works his compositions on site, usually finishing a work in one day of intense activity, spraying the pastel work with fixative between layers.

The texture of the sea has been created through an inventive play of watercolor overlaid by rhythms of dense pastel work, the direction of the strokes suggesting the movement of the water. The impression of sunlight striking the water at the point where the rocks meet has been effected by laying a wash of pale blue watercolor.

The layers of color in the rock face reveal the interplay of washes of watercolor overlaid by bold strokes of soft pastel.

263

THINKING BIG

SOME PEOPLE THINK of pastel as a delicate, genteel medium, but it is as suited to robust, ambitious compositions as any other painting media. Indeed, in some ways it is especially suitable since the pastels are a dry painting medium and so large sheets of paper will not buckle or warp as you work on them. If you want to experiment with sizes and formats, you have a number of options: you can either work on several standard sheets of paper and then join them, use rolls of artists' quality watercolor paper or drawing paper cut to a specific size, or work on large sheets of canvas as a support. If you are working on individual sheets of paper you can add to them and build up a virtual tapestry of images.

Initial photos for reference

THE ARTIST HAS developed two radically different compositions exploring alternative means of building large-scale works in pastel. One is a multiple image brought together in the form of a "joiner," and one is a mixed-media composition that exploits the richly varied properties of pastel and collage.

Since working on this scale is impractical to attempt on site, the solution is to take photographs or make sketches which explore the compositional possibilities of your subject. If you work out a composition on a small scale, you can then translate this to a larger format. You can either draw a grid of squares onto your original or onto a sheet of acetate that you place over your original. You then draw an identical grid onto your large support, making sure the proportions match, and copy your image square by square.

Split images
Working from a series of photos of the scene, the artist settled on four separate panels to capture the expanse of the bridge and London's river panorama. Here, the panels appear more as a related group of images than as a single composition.

Panoramic view
Here, the panels create an extended composition punctuated by the rhythmical vertical notes of the bridge supports. The bridge spans the river and links the separate panels in a warm thread that runs through the heart of the scene. Its impact is complemented by the delicate panorama of buildings in the background.

Varanasi bull

In this striking composition, which is roughly 5ft by 4ft (155 by 125cm), the artist has engaged in a tour de force of imaginative interpretation. The large scale of the composition has encouraged her to exploit the use of collage as a means of laying extensive, flat areas of color. By including a range of colored and marbled papers, she has lifted the image into an imaginative realm rather than creating a facsimile of the original experience. She has used delicate lines of pastel to denote the door lintel and pick out the architectural details, and a much denser application of pastel within the shrine to lead the eye into the distance. The image has been worked on a length of paper cut from a roll of artists' quality watercolor paper and stapled to a sheet of soft board.

Hand-textured and colored sheets have been torn and cut to create contrasting edges that evoke the stonework of the building.

By scumbling color onto the collage of the bull the artist has created a leathery feel to the hide.

There is an inventive play between line and tone to describe the shapes of the hooves as they are framed against the strident red shadow.

PRESERVING AND FRAMING

GIVEN THE POWDERY NATURE of pastels, the surface of works executed in pastel is easily disturbed and needs to be protected from the effects of handling. The simplest method of caring for your work is to tape a sheet of glassine, wax paper, or tracing paper onto it so that it covers the image. These preserving sheets are nonabsorbent and so will not pick up or displace any of the pastel dust. Once you have covered your paintings in this way you can then safely store them on top of each other, either in a portfolio, in a map chest, or placed between two sheets of hardboard. If you decide to store them between sheets of hardboard, you need to tie the sheets together to prevent any lateral movement. Alternatively, you can attach your pastel work to a backing board, cover it with a suitable mat, and then frame it under glass. You need to use the mat in order to keep the surface of your work away from the glass. Apart from its attractiveness, framing has the additional advantage of protecting your work from the harmful effects of air pollution.

Materials

Glue

Brush

Rice paper

Masking tape

Museum board

Tracing paper

Mounting pastel works

It is a good idea to mount your pastel work, whether or not you plan to frame it, since the stiffness of the mounting board holds the paper firmly and protects against shedding of pastel pigment. It is best to buy acid-free backing board, also known as museum board. Measure your work and draw faint pencil lines to indicate where the corners of your picture will sit within the board you have chosen.

1 ◀ Lay the pastel work face down on a sheet of tracing paper. Cut lengths of rice paper, 2 by 1 in (5 by 2.5 cm). Fold the lengths in half and apply paste lightly to half of each hinge.

2 ▲ Place the hinges, glue side down, along the top edge of the back of the pastel work, just in from the sides. Be careful not to get glue on your artwork. Press down gently and allow the paper hinges to dry.

3 ▲ Put a little glue onto the remaining surface of the hinges, turn the pastel work over and place it centrally on the mounting board, pressing down lightly on the hinges to secure them.

4 ◀ If you are not intending to frame the work, you should attach a sheet of preserving paper to the back of the mat with masking tape so that it covers your painting.

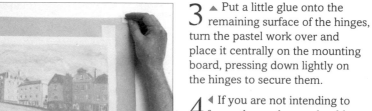
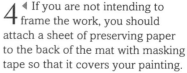

Framing pastel work

It is advisable to frame your work if you want to protect it permanently. Choosing the right frame and mat is largely a matter of taste, but you should consider the effect each will have on the appearance of your work. As a general rule, choose a frame that is at least 2 to 3in (5 to 7.5cm) wider than your work and reflects the color key of the composition.

There is a wide selection of ready-made frames and mats available.

1 ▲ Measure the inside dimensions of your frame and mark these on the mat. Cut the mat to fit, using a sharp craft knife and steel ruler.

2 ▲ Using a mat cutter, cut a window to fit your work and tape the mat to your board.

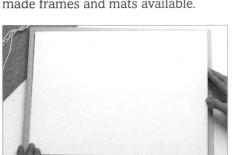

3 ◀ Making sure that the glass is free of any dust or smear marks, place your mounted work into the frame. Now place a backing board over it, cut to fit snugly against the edges of the frame.

4 ▲ Secure the board by placing a few brads at 4in (10cm) lengths along the inner edge of the back of the frame.

6 ▲ Make two holes with an awl, one on each vertical section of the wooden frame, a third of the way down the back. Screw in two eye hooks with rings.

5 ▲ Place lengths of masking tape along the back of the frame to seal the join. This stops moisture, dust, and insects from gaining access to the picture surface.

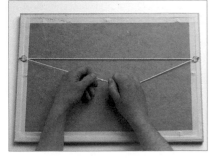

7 ▲ Finally, attach a length of picture-hanging cord to the rings. Your work is now ready to be hung.

Finished work

It is worth comparing this painting with the original version on page 233 to see the dramatic effects of mounting and framing.

Materials

Mat cutter

Steel ruler

Hammer

Awl

Brads

Eye hook with ring

String

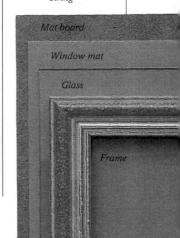

Mat board

Window mat

Glass

Frame

AN INTRODUCTION TO
OIL PAINTING

Characteristics of Oil Paint   270
History od Oil Painting   272

MATERIALS

Oil Paints   276
Equipment   278
Choosing Colors   280
Color Mixing   282
Low-key & High-key Color   284
Oil Colors   286
Brushes for Oil Painting   288
Blending & Dry Brush   290
Glazing & Impasto   292
Brushwork Effects   294
Gallery of Brushwork   296
Choosing a Support   298
Preparing Supports
   & Grounds   300

TECHNIQUES

Ways of Working with Oil   302
Creating a Composition   304
Composition   306
Gallery of Composition   308
Painting on a White Ground   310
Painting on a Toned Ground   312
Gallery of White
   & Toned Grounds   314
Alla Prima Painting   316
Working with a Painting
   Knife   318
Gallery of Alla Prima
   Paintings   320
Painting in Layers   322
Painting in Stages   324
Gallery of Painting in Layers   326
Experimental Techniques   328
Varnishing & Framing   330

CHARACTERISTICS OF OIL PAINT

ONE REASON WHY OIL PAINT has been so popular for hundreds of years is that it is an incredibly versatile painting medium that can be manipulated in many ways. Oil paint is so responsive because it dries slowly, allowing for colors to be modified and moved around on the surface of the painting for some time after they have been applied. This aspect of oil paint makes it an excellent medium for alla prima painting methods (pp.316-317), in which the paint itself can accurately reflect the immediacy of the artist's response to an image. Once oil paint has dried, it can be overpainted in a number of ways without disturbing or dissolving the original color beneath. This means that a complex layer structure of paint can be built up to create different effects.

A smooth board is overlaid with thin layers of transparent color

Changing the texture of oil paint

If oil paint is used directly from the tube, it can be painted thickly with bristle brushes in a rich, impasted style. It has sufficient body to hold the crisp shape made by a brushstroke or a painting knife, whether that shape is urgent or delicate. This can give painting a real sense of directness and establish an immediate link between the style of the painting and the artist. Oil paint can also be thinned down slightly to a creamy consistency, and brushed out to an enamel-like smoothness. If it is diluted very thinly with turpentine, or white spirit, the consistency of the paint is ideal for sketching a composition, or if mixed with an

This rough board emphasizes the thick strokes of rich color

oil painting medium it can be formulated as a glazing color. The painting medium enables the glaze to become a transparent stain that modifies the appearance of a color beneath. Oil paint can be used "stiffly," or unmixed, to create textured dry brush and scumbled techniques (pp.290-291) with bristle brushes, or it can be used in smoother manipulations with soft hair brushes. Of all the painting media, oil paint is the one best suited to blending techniques, in which one color or tone can be made to fuse smoothly and almost imperceptibly into another.

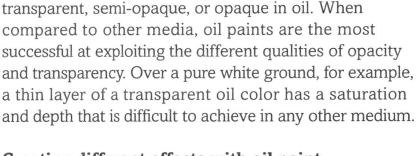

The qualities of oil paint

One characteristic of oil paint that differentiates it from other media is its richness and depth of color. This is because the pigments are ground in a drying oil that has a relatively high refractive index (the amount of light it reflects and absorbs). Chalk that otherwise appears opaque white becomes practically transparent when it is mixed with linseed oil. Pigments vary in their refractive index, which to a large extent dictates whether they appear transparent, semi-opaque, or opaque in oil. When compared to other media, oil paints are the most successful at exploiting the different qualities of opacity and transparency. Over a pure white ground, for example, a thin layer of a transparent oil color has a saturation and depth that is difficult to achieve in any other medium.

A rough colored canvas gives these dry strokes of color more texture

Creating different effects with oil paint

The four studies shown here demonstrate some of the characteristic effects of oil color, used in different ways on a variety of surfaces. The smooth board on the top left-hand side provides a hard, untextured surface on which the brushstrokes remain clearly visible and unblended. A thin, warm transparent glaze, painted over the various colors, deepens the tone of the portrait and makes the face appear more cohesive. The bottom panel on the left is a rough surface on which thick paint has been applied as impasted brushstrokes. The uneven texture of this surface automatically affects each brushstroke, and as a result, the style is much bolder and chunkier. The top right-hand section is a rough canvas that has been prepared first with a single tone of one color, applied over the whole surface and then left to dry. This colored canvas is visible between areas of paint on the face and hair, so that the canvas and paint appear to be integrated as one surface. Paint has been applied with a dry brush technique that picks up the ridges of the rough canvas, while scratches (known as sgraffito) on the hair have been made with the end of a brush handle. The bottom right section shows a smooth canvas over which paint has been carefully blended. Different tones and colors have been painted as areas of light and shade, and then blended together to create a smooth transition between colors.

This fine canvas allows individual strokes of color to be blended smoothly together

271

HISTORY OF OIL PAINTING

THE DEVELOPMENT of oil paint as the most common medium for painting in Europe evolved slowly in the fifteenth century. Before this, a popular medium for painting on panel had been egg tempera, but it did not have the flexibility of pigments bound with a drying oil. Oil paint also had the capacity to be blended and manipulated on the surface of the painting, and its transparency allowed for a far greater range of tones and resonant colors.

THE TRANSITION from egg tempera to oil paint in Northern Europe, and then in Italy toward the end of the fifteenth century, produced many examples of paintings in which the preliminary work was done in egg tempera, while later stages, such as thin transparent glazes, were applied in oil color. There are also examples of works in which egg and oil are contained in the same layer.

Although the Dutch van Eyck brothers are popularly credited with the discovery of oil painting in the early fifteenth century – Jan van Eyck *(b. before 1395-1441)* made progress developing the oil medium and using glazes – the use of oil-resin varnishes and drying oils is in fact quite well documented since the eighth century. Painters in Italy began to copy the Netherlandish way of modeling the underpainting in opaque colors, and then applying rich transparent glazes.

The progress of oil paint
Fifteenth-century Italy saw artists such as Piero della Francesca *(1410/20-1492)*, whose early work is predominantly in egg tempera, coming to terms with the new oil medium. In Venice, Giovanni Bellini *(c.1430-1516)* began to exploit the depth and richness of tone and color that could be had with oil

Jan van Eyck,
The Arnolfini
Marriage, **1434,**
32¼ x 23⅓ in (82 x 60 cm)
Oil has been used in this most famous of 15th-century portraits, though there may be egg tempera in the underpainting. With this new medium, van Eyck achieved an extraordinary range of tones, with deep shadows and clear bright lights.

painting. He often worked first on an egg tempera underpainting, with its characteristic cross-hatched modeling, but the use of oil in the later stages of painting gave his figures an almost tangible existence. Perugino *(c.1445/50-1523)* and Raphael *(1483-1520)* were among other artists of the time working in both media. Raphael sustained the purity of the whites and blues in his skies by using the less yellowing walnut oil as a binding medium, rather than the linseed oil he used with other colors. By the

Cosima Tura, *Allegorical Figure,*
mid-15th century *45¾ x 28 in (116 x 71 cm)*
Said to portray one of the Muses, this Italian work was painted initially in egg tempera and then extensively remodeled in oil. Transparent glazes enrich and deepen the colored drapery.

Titian, *The Rape of Europa*, 1559-62 *73 x 81 in (185 x 206 cm)*
This painting shows Titian moving toward the very loose style of his last paintings, where fluidly modeled forms in opaque colors are overpainted in transparent glazes. The work is alive with movement, with the turbulent figure of Europa echoed in the twisting figures above.

first decade of the sixteenth century, oil paint had become universally established as the prime painting medium in Italy.

It is with later Venetian painters, such as Titian *(c.1487/90-1576),* and then Tintoretto *(1518-94),* that we see a freeing up of composition and expression. That these artists were now using oil paint exclusively had much to do with this new freedom of expression, for its flexibility allowed them to take a looser approach, not only in initial stages, but throughout the whole painting process.

Economical painting

By the seventeenth century, it was common for painters to work in an economical style on a colored surface that provided the mid-tones, while opaque colors were added for lights, and thin transparent darks for shadows. Artists as diverse in style as Caravaggio *(1571-1610)* and Velásquez *(1599-1660)* used these dark "grounds" to emphasize any areas of high contrast and create dramatic lighting effects.

Rembrandt *(1606-69)* often used double grounds on his canvases, with an underlayer of red bole (clay), or red ochre and a layer of gray or brown on top. His images often seem to be sculpted in relief out of the dark ground. Rubens *(1577-1640)* worked similarly, but often prepared a warm yellow-brown layer that he applied with a bristle brush over a white priming. This underlayer helped him to create images more freely, giving more expression to his painting style.

Rembrandt van Rijn, *Self-Portrait at the age of 63,* 1669 *33⅛ x 27¾ in (86 x 71 cm)*
This painting was made in the last year of Rembrandt's life. The canvas was prepared with a dark brown ground, and the face modeled vigorously using thick Lead White. These impasted brushstrokes give vitality and texture to the face. There is a sense of composure and honesty in this self-portrait, and the sense of gravity is heightened by the flickering shadows that cross his features.

Rachel Ruysch, *Flowers in a Vase,* c.1800 *22½ x 17⅛ in (57 x 43 cm)*
Ruysch was an accomplished and successful still-life painter in 17th-century Holland. She adopted the popular technique of using a red-brown ground as a base, with opaque highlights and transparent darks on top. This ground has the effect of bringing the flowers out of their shadows and into bright focus. Each petal and leaf has been blended with exquisite finesse.

Unusual additions

Oil paintings from the seventeenth to the nineteenth centuries reveal some complex layer structures – and can include complicated materials. The British artist George Stubbs *(1724-1806)* used wax-resin mixtures with a drying oil in certain works. Some artists used what are now recognized as unstable materials; Sir Joshua Reynolds *(1723-92)*, for instance, incorporated oil, resin, and bitumen mixtures into his paintings. Gainsborough *(1727-88)*, on the other hand, generally painted fairly thinly, with a drying oil plus pigment mixtures thinned with a solvent.

Research on paintings from the eighteenth and nineteenth centuries is limited, but what we can learn from the state of many works in this period is that the more straightforward the painting techniques and materials are, the more reliable the results.

A change of direction

During the nineteenth century, many artists rejected the constraints of traditional academic practices and moved toward "plein-air" landscape painting from nature. This, combined with new ideas about color and the discovery and development of new pigments, led to the new movement known as Impressionism. Artists such as Monet *(1840-1926)* and Renoir *(1841-1919)* made paintings that were often no less complex than oil paintings of the past, but were characterized by a sense of freshness and immediacy that was quite new. Now the character and texture of the individual brushstroke was integral to the look of the work. Color became a focus of painting as never before, with new pigments available to artists and a greater use of bright, saturated primaries and secondaries.

The change in attitude and new approach to oil painting that was first initiated by the Impressionists led to further reevaluations during the Post-Impressionist years of Gauguin *(1848-1903)* and Van Gogh *(1853-90)*. The Cubists Braque *(1882-1963)* and Picasso *(1881-1973)*, and German Expressionists Kirchner *(1880-1938)* and Nolde *(1867-1956)*, for example, all used the adaptable medium of oil to make great stylistic and technical changes in art. The Surrealists Max Ernst *(1891-1976)* and Salvador Dali *(1904-89)* both used oil in dramatic new ways. Dali reworked the technique of blending oil into soft fluid forms to give expression to his interior thoughts and subconscious desires, while Ernst unlocked his imagination and invented or adapted techniques to give complex textural starting points for his works.

Claude Lorraine, *Echo and Narcissus*, 1644 *46½ x 37¼ in (95 x 118 cm) Like Titian, Claude incorporated stories from Ovid into his serene landscapes. While Titian's work is turbulent, Claude's is calm, suffused with a golden light. The poignancy of self-deception and the failure of human communication is underscored by this soft, warm Arcadian landscape.*

Claude Monet, *The Ducal Palace at Venice,* 1908 *32 x 38½ in (81 x 98 cm) Monet relied on color contrasts to create the* brilliant effects of light. Pure yellows and violets and blues and orange-red make this facade glow against the sky and shimmer on the water.

Twentieth-century style

With oil paint now used and adapted for a diversity of painting styles, its position at the forefront of painting media has been reinforced in the twentieth century. The German artist Gerhard Richter (b. 1932) has considered the relationship between painting and photography. His 1960s monochromatic paintings, based on newspaper photographs, exploited the way oil color could be blended. He found a correlation between oil techniques and the smooth, often blurred quality of photographs.

During the most recent decades, many artists have found distinctive ways of working with this painting medium to give us new insights and meanings. Works by the Italian artists Francesco Clemente (b. 1952), Enzo Cucchi (b. 1949), and Mimmo Paladino (b. 1948), although personal and individualistic, give expression to universal needs and aspirations. The cool, powerful works of British artist Lucien Freud (b. 1922) demonstrate the impact and intensity that can be achieved by painting directly from life, while the less direct approach of Howard Hodgkin (b. 1932) to his subjects has resulted in forceful works controlled by strong, energetic color. Paintings by artists such as Christopher Lebrun (b. 1951) appear to draw on myths and images from the past, but they remain utterly contemporary in their engagement with surface, texture, and color. In the US and elsewhere in the world, a number of artists have begun to find inspiration in new forms of abstraction that still draw on the same techniques and traditions used for over five hundred years.

Paul Cézanne, *Green Apples,*
c.1873 *10¼ x 12½ in (26 x 32 cm)*
Cézanne's work differs from that of the Impressionists in its adherence to formal traditions of painting. He was unique in his use of color and analytical approach to shapes. The warm orange-brown ground here contrasts with the cool, striking green apples.

Georgia O'Keeffe, *Red Canna,*
c.1923 *36 x 29⅞ in (91 x 76 cm)*
This is very different from the cool poise of Ruysch's work – O'Keeffe's flower is suffused with hot color and is alive with feeling. The adjacent colors are simply blended, but together they form a stunning image.

Gerhard Richter, *Betty,*
1988 *40⅛ x 28⅜ in (102 x 72 cm)*
This portrait has a forceful power and intensity. The immaculate but engaging nature of the painted surface turns this image into something precious. In a world of millions of snapshots, Richter painstakingly retrieves one of them and asks us to look at it again carefully.

OIL PAINTS

OIL PAINTS ARE MADE BY GRINDING PIGMENTS with a drying or semidrying vegetable oil such as linseed oil, walnut oil, safflower oil or poppy oil. This oil binding medium gives the paint its characteristic appearance and distinctive buttery feel. Pigments ground in oil have a particular depth and resonance of color because of the amount of light the oil reflects and absorbs. The oil also protects the pigment particles, as well as acting as an adhesive to attach the pigments to a painting surface. Commercial manufacturers add to this basic mix to give a range of stable paints with relatively consistent drying times.

Walnuts

Walnut oil
Walnut oil was more popular in the past than it is today, as it is difficult to keep fresh for any length of time. Walnuts contain about 65% oil.

Poppy seeds

Opium poppy plant

Drying and semidrying oils
The range of drying and semidrying oils used to bind pigments together are made from the crushed and pressed seeds of certain plants. The most important of these plants is linseed oil, which is a golden yellow drying oil and comes from the seeds of the flax plant. The best quality linseed oil is cold-pressed, although most modern oils are hot-pressed. Poppy oil is a semidrying oil made from the seeds of the opium poppy plant. It is a pale straw color and has long been popular as a binding medium for pale pigments that might

be affected by the more yellowing linseed oil. It is popular for alla prima work (*see* pp.316-7) as it takes a long time to dry. This means that the paint can be moved around for some time after it has been applied. Safflower oil from the seeds of the safflower plant is similarly pale and slow-drying, and it can be used in the same manner as poppy oil. Walnut oil from the nuts of the walnut tree was very popular in the past for its pale color, and it has been identified as a binding medium for white and blue pigments in many Renaissance paintings. It should be used fresh, as it goes rancid quickly.

Poppy oil
Poppy seeds contain about 50% oil. This semidrying oil is slow to dry in comparison with drying oils such as linseed oil, so to avoid any cracks appearing, ensure it is completely dry before overpainting.

Traditional and modern oil mixes
In the past, artists used a wide variety of ingredients in their painting mediums (below); some caused pictures to darken and crack. Nowadays, a mix of stand (linseed) oil and turpentine is recommended, and very little resin, if any, should be added.

Sun-bleached linseed oil

Copal oil varnish

Black oil

Orpiment pigment

Realgar pigment

Azurite pigment

Azurite

Realgar

Orpiment

Traditional pigment sources
Traditional pigments were made from natural sources. The mineral azurite was ground to powder and used as an underlayer for Ultramarine Blue. The red and yellow pigments realgar and orpiment are poisonous and no longer available. Synthetic substances now replace many natural pigments.

Oil absorption

If pigment particles were the same smooth shape, size, and weight, they would all need the same amount of oil to coat their surfaces. In fact, each pigment needs a specific amount of oil to reach a desired uniform consistency. Paint with less oil content is less flexible and is liable to crack if you paint it over a color with high oil absorption. This can be avoided using the "fat-over-lean" rule (*see* pp.322-3).

High oil content *(70% or more)* Pigments include Burnt Sienna, Raw Sienna (above), Burnt Umber, Winsor Blue and Green, Alizarin, Permanent Rose, and Cobalt.

Medium oil content *(50-70%)* Cadmium Yellow, Cadmium Red (above), Raw Umber, Oxide of Chromium, and Ivory Black are included in this category.

Low oil content *(50% or less)* Only a few pigments are included here: Ultramarine (above), Manganese Blue, and Flake White.

Mixing oil paints

Making your own oil paints is not difficult. You need a ground glass slab and a flat-bottomed glass muller (these are also available in hard stone, such as granite), a large palette knife, cold-pressed linseed oil, and some pigment powder. Avoid using toxic pigments such as Lead White or Cobalt Blue, as they are too dangerous. You should use a dust mask whenever you grind powder colors.

Materials

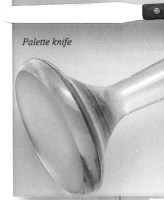

Airtight jar

Palette knife

Glass slab and muller

1 ▲ Place a small heap of pigment powder in the center of a glass slab and make a well in the middle of the powder. Then pour a small amount of linseed oil into the well.

2 ◀ Use the palette knife to mix the oil and pigment into a stiff paste. You may find this is easier to do with some pigment powders than with others.

3 ◀ Place the muller on top of the paint mixture and start to grind it with a continuous, smooth circular action. Use the palette knife to scrape any paint from the edge of the muller and the sides of the glass slab back into the middle.

4 ▲ When the paste has achieved a creamy consistency, scrape it off and store it in a small, airtight jar.

Modern commercial paints

Commercial oil paints are sold in tubes, and most manufacturers produce two lines: artists' and students'. Artists' paint is of a higher quality, as it contains the best pigments and has the highest proportion of pigment to drying oil. The price of individual colors largely depends on the cost of the raw material used to obtain that particular color. The wide range of cheap, bright, lightfast synthetic pigments now available are a good option.

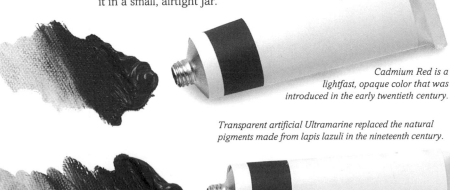

Cadmium Red is a lightfast, opaque color that was introduced in the early twentieth century.

Transparent artificial Ultramarine replaced the natural pigments made from lapis lazuli in the nineteenth century.

277

EQUIPMENT

OF THE EQUIPMENT YOU NEED for oil painting, the most important tools are your brushes, and the look of a painting depends on their quality. There are two main types of brushes: stiff hair bristle brushes made from hog hair, and soft hair brushes made from sable or synthetic material. You also need a certain amount of solvent, such as turpentine or white spirit, to dilute your oil colors and to clean off excess paint. Linseed oil, the basic binding medium for oil paint, can also be used to modify the consistency of colors. You can paint on many different surfaces and textures, but those used most frequently by oil painters are canvases and wooden panels. Keep equipment clean and always screw the lids back on bottles of solvent as they are a serious health hazard.

Bristle brushes

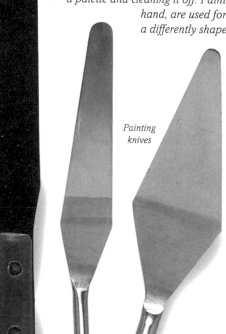

Brushes
Bristle brushes are mainly used for oil painting as they move the paint around on the textured surface of a canvas with ease. Soft hair brushes are good for small details and smooth effects. Oil painting brushes traditionally have long handles. Store your brushes safely when you aren't working with them.

Synthetic brush

Sable brush

Toe (tip) of brush

Heel of brush

Ferrule

Palette knife

Protective plastic case

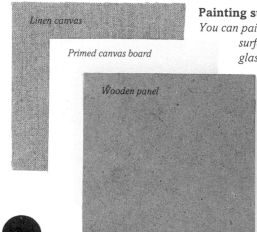

Linen canvas

Primed canvas board

Wooden panel

Painting surfaces
You can paint on almost any surface, including stone, glass, and metal. The materials most commonly used are canvases and wooden panels such as plywood, hardboard, and fibreboard. Commercially produced oil paper is good for trying out ideas and techniques.

Palette and painting knives
Palette knives are indispensable for moving paint around on a palette and cleaning it off. Painting knives, on the other hand, are used for applying paint and have a differently shaped blade and handle.

Painting knives

Dippers
These containers store small amounts of solvent and painting medium on a palette.

MAHL STICK

If you need a steady hand to work on a particular area, use a mahl stick. A mahl stick is a piece of light bamboo, about 1.25m (4ft) long, with a ball-shaped end covered in soft chamois leather. You can make your own mahl stick if you prefer.

Modern palettes
Use a palette to mix your colors. You can make your own palette from plywood by sanding it down and sealing it with linseed oil. Alternatively, you can use a glass slab over a piece of paper, or a disposable paper palette.

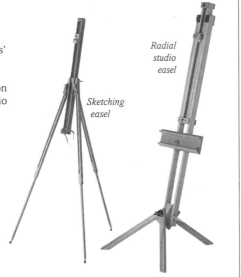

Disposable paper palettes

EASELS

There are a variety of easels available from artists' suppliers, from the simple sketching easel that folds right up for easy carrying on location, to the heavy studio easels that can hold large paintings comfortably. Some artists like to work on paintings suspended on nails on a studio wall, or propped up on a table, but it makes sense to have a good adjustable easel for your work.

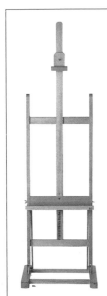

Vertical studio easel

Radial studio easel

Sketching easel

Mahogany palette
This kidney-shaped mahogany palette, with its characteristic dark red-brown color, was originally developed for artists who worked on a similarly colored painting surface. This meant colors on the palette could be seen as they would look on the painting.

HEALTH HAZARD
Solvents can damage your health – screw the lid on after use and keep your studio well ventilated.

Solvent
You need to use a certain amount of solvent to dilute your colors and clean your equipment. Use either white spirit or turpentine.

Drying oil
Linseed oil is the basic medium for binding colored pigments and drying them when painted. Use it to modify the consistency of paint.

Oil painting medium
This enhances the consistency and glossiness of oil paint. If you don't want to buy it, mix refined linseed oil, or stand oil, with turpentine.

Varnish
Varnishes are designed to protect a painting and give it a matt or a gloss finish. Dammar varnish and ketone varnish are recommended.

Choosing Colors

Most artists learn about color by discovering how it works in practice. Painting is a constant process of individual experimentation and discovery, and it is unlikely that any two artists would work with the same colors. It is, however, helpful to look at some of the basic theories of color in relation to oil painting.

Ideally, artists would need only the primary colors of red (magenta), yellow, and blue, plus white, to mix any color. In reality it can be difficult to find suitable pigments of the purity that allow, for instance, the same yellow to make a pure orange with red, and a pure green with blue. Use instead a limited palette of versatile colors.

Color wheel
This color wheel shows the three primaries – red, yellow, and blue – and the three secondary colors in between that are made by mixing two of the primaries. The wheel also shows two main methods of mixing oil color; the paint has been mixed opaquely on the outside wheel, and transparently on the inside wheel.

These colors have been painted very thinly, or transparently, over a white surface, which shows their true color, and not as they appear when squeezed out of a tube.

Opaque colors, with their rich, well-bodied appearance, conceal the surface on which they are painted. Transparent colors can be made to look opaque by adding white paint.

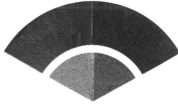

Adjacent colors
Adjacent colors have some similarity in hue (the actual color of an object or substance). Green contains blue in its mix, which gives these hues an automatic link. On a color wheel with a wider range of colors, adjacent colors are those that are positioned next to one another.

Complementary colors
Pairs of colors situated opposite each other on the color wheel give maximum contrast and enhance one another to appear brighter.

Warm and cool colors
Reds are usually thought of as warm, and blues cool. In fact, depending on their hue and context, colors can be warm or cool. Here one red (left) is cool and the other red warm. It is important to know this when mixing colors, as the cool red makes a better violet if mixed with blue.

Arranging your palette
When you choose a palette of colors, try to include both a warm and a cool color of each hue, or a versatile color such as Winsor Blue. There are no set rules for laying out your colors, but it makes sense to place adjacent colors next to one another and to keep white paint separate.

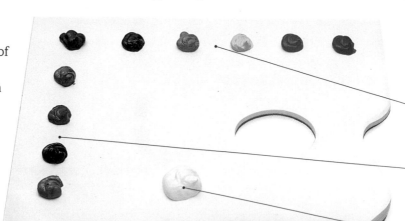

The top six colors are mainly primary colors, combining opaque and transparent paints, and placed in the order of the color spectrum.

The paints along the side include naturally opaque earth colors and more muted, low-key colors.

Keep white paint slightly separate as it will be used mainly for lightening other colors.

Transparent and opaque colors

It is important to understand the difference between opaque paint, which conceals the surface it is painted on, and transparent paint, which appears dark in a tube but transparent when painted thinly on a white surface. The transparent Permanent Rose shown here has been thinned gradually to show its true color, and then mixed with white to give opaque "tints." Black is then added to give a range of different "shades."

Permanent Rose, thinned down to its true color

If white paint is added, a range of opaque tints is produced

Touches of black mixed into the paint give dark shades

Recommended colors

The limited range of opaque [O] and transparent [T] colors (right) gives an extremely flexible palette, but add more colors if you wish. Recommended are all Cadmium and Mars colors, Light Red, Azo Red, Alizarin Crimson, Venetian Red, and Winsor Red, Arylamide or Azo Yellow, Manganese Blue, Cerulean Blue, Ultramarine Blue, Cobalt Blue, and Indanthrone Blue. Quinacridone (Violet), Dioxazine Violet, and Cobalt Violet are also good, as are Cobalt Green, Viridian, Terre Verte, Raw Sienna, Burnt Sienna, Flake White, Zinc White, Lamp Black, and Ivory Black.

Mixing primaries

It is easy to assume that a mixture of two colors will simply produce a single third color. In fact, the two colors together can produce many versions of the third color, in a wide range of tones. A useful exercise is to try painting a simple still life, such as the one below, using a range of tones in a secondary color that you have mixed from two primaries.

PURE COLORS

Use two jars of turpentine to first clean off excess paint, and then rinse the brush. This will retain the purity and strength of each color you use.

1 ▲ Before you paint these peppers, use a small scrap of posterboard and mix a range of different oranges from Permanent Rose and Cadmium Lemon (*below*). Then, with a clean medium-sized filbert bristle brush, paint the red pepper with shades of orange on a piece of oil paper.

Mix a range of orange tones before painting

Primary Peppers

These peppers look like real objects rather than flat images because a variety of different tints and shades create dimension and shape on each object. This range of clean orange tones has been achieved by carefully mixing different quantities of the primary colors red and yellow.

2 ◀ Use lighter tints of orange or yellow for highlights, and darker shades of orange or red for areas in shadow. The lightness or darkness of each orange mix creates a "tone" that models and shapes the peppers so they appear three-dimensional.

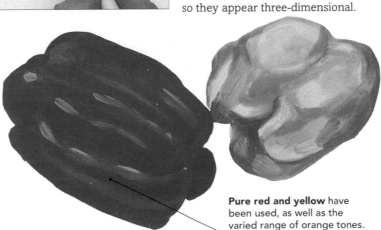

Pure red and yellow have been used, as well as the varied range of orange tones.

Permanent Rose [T]
(Quinacridone Red)

Cadmium Red [O]

Cadmium Yellow Pale [O]

Transparent Gold Ochre [T]

Winsor Green [T]
(Phthalocyanine Green)

Winsor Blue [T]
(Phthalocyanine Blue)

Titanium White [O]

Oxide of Chromium [O]

Yellow Ochre [O]

Indian Red [O]

Burnt Umber [T]

281

COLOR MIXING

WHEN YOU DECIDE to paint with a particular color, you have a choice of how you mix it and apply it to a painting surface. There are two principle ways of mixing colors. Firstly, you can mix together one color with another physically on a palette (*see below*), but you should always add small touches of the darker color to the lighter one so that you do not make more of the mixture than you need. A positive feature of oil paint is that the color you mix and apply wet has the same tone when it dries. Secondly, you can overlay one color onto another. A thin film of transparent red paint over a dry layer of yellow will give an orange color that looks quite different from a physically mixed orange. Another method of color mixing is to place small dots of pure color side by side. These appear to combine "optically," or visually, in the viewer's eye so that a third color is perceived.

Mixing clean colors

When you mix colors together, always mix them away from other paints on the palette to keep the original colors from becoming sullied. If you physically mix colors (right), use a clean palette knife or brush to transfer color each time. The brush must again be completely clean before you overlay colors (below). You can also mix colors in a "striated" brushstroke with separate colors on a brush (below right). To mix colors optically, gauge the right proportion of one color to another, or you will create something that looks gray. Allow one set of dots to dry before adding a new color.

1 ▲ Lay out the colors around the edge of your palette with a good gap between them so that they stay clean. Use a palette knife to transfer color away.

2 ▲ To physically mix green from these two colors, start with the yellow and add small dabs of the stronger blue paint to it as you mix.

3 ▲ Continue to add touches of blue to the mix until you have the right shade of green. Make sure that both paints are thoroughly mixed together.

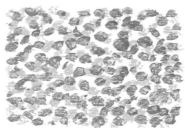

Dots of yellow and blue blend visually

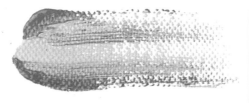

A striated brushstroke contains two separate colors that give the impression of a third

Yellow painted stiffly over blue gives a broken green

A thin glaze of yellow over blue appears green

CARE OF PAINTS

Paints are expensive, so it is worth taking care of your materials. Clean excess paint away with a tissue so that the lid screws on firmly. This also protects the strength and purity of a color, which can easily be ruined if the tube is neglected.

THE SIMPLE COLOR MIXING exercise on this page concentrates on mixing the actual color of objects in a still life. However, the colors are mixed in a variety of ways to achieve certain effects. Strokes of individual color are optically mixed or overlaid, while a touch of white added to the dark, transparent paint Winsor Blue gives a rich, deep opaque blue for the cloth.

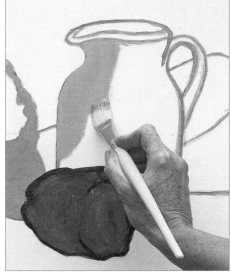

1▶ Begin by sketching the outline of each object, and then fill in the shapes with color. Paint a layer of pure Winsor Blue on the pepper, and physically mix an orange color for the onion. The jug is opaque, so add some Titanium White to this mixture.

2▲ When the blue paint on the pepper has dried, overlay it with a separate layer of pure Cadmium Yellow, dabbed on with a small clean filbert brush. You should find that although touches of blue show through, the resulting effect will make the pepper appear green.

3◀ Use a small round brush to paint strokes of Cadmium Red and Cadmium Yellow on the onion. Keep the paint quite thick so that the colors look as strong and as pure as possible.

4▶ Paint a thin mix of Winsor Blue over the cloth, so that it deepens the color of the material and describes areas of shadow.

Still-Life Study

This study shows how many options there are to mixing colors, and the different effects they make. Separate strokes of strong color on the onion appear to merge into a vivid orange, while the jug has been painted with physically mixed colors that give a more subtle appearance. Although the pepper has been overlaid with paint, any touches of individual color still visible help to establish areas of light and shadow.

This jug has been painted with a physically mixed opaque color which gives it a strong, solid look.

A layer of yellow over thin blue paint gives this pepper a fresh appearance.

A thin film of transparent blue deepens the tone of the cloth.

Individual strokes of yellow and red appear to blend optically to give an orange color.

Sharon Finmark

LOW-KEY & HIGH-KEY COLOR

LOW-KEY PAINTINGS are usually defined by their subdued tones and color mixtures that tend toward neutral browns and grays. High-key paintings are exactly the opposite, with simple mixtures of pure, bright, saturated colors, often mixed with white. The strong distinction between high- and low-key painting needs to be made to enable us to focus our use of color in terms of our approach to subject matter. Many paintings contain elements of each, but certain subjects lend themselves well to the use of high-key or low-key color. These simple exercises show how easily the mood of a subject can change.

LOW-KEY PAINTINGS are often created with tertiary colors (a mixture of three or more colors), such as the Payne's Gray above. These can produce neutral, unsaturated hues. Some artists use a small range of neutral colors that are similar in mood and tone, but their paintings can vary enormously in atmosphere. This means that a work may be low in key and somber in mood, but it can either be a quiet, reflective study suffused with a subtle atmosphere, or painted in a dramatic way on a dark ground. Some subjects are by their nature low-key, such as moonlit scenes or dimly lit interiors, but almost any subject can be treated in a low-key manner.

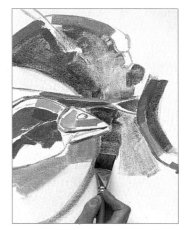

1 ▲ Block in main areas of the composition using a large brush and mixes of opaque green, blue, and Payne's Gray, thinned with turpentine. Paint with loose brushstrokes to keep the composition simple.

2 ▶ Paint over the first layers of color with thicker opaque paint that has been mixed with a little oil painting medium. Use a medium-sized flat brush to capture the shape of the fish most effectively.

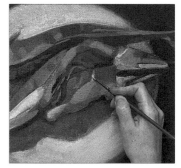

3 ◀ When the tone and depth of the composition is complete, add finer details and opaque highlights with a small round brush. Keep the highlights soft and subtle and without harsh lines.

Gutted Mackerel
This painting is composed of subdued, almost neutral colors that create a soft light and a gentle atmosphere.

A limited palette of colors keeps the work more powerful and controlled.

Opaque highlights help to create a subtle movement through the painting.

Elaine Halden

Payne's Gray

Cobalt Blue

Cerulean Blue

Cadmium Red

Burnt Umber

Yellow Ochre

Cadmium Yellow

BRIGHT, SATURATED colors such as Cerulean Blue, left, produce high-key works that are light and optimistic in tone, but which can also be richly textured. High-key scenes are usually painted on white or near-white grounds that illuminate thinly applied colors to achieve high-key effects. Transparent high-key paints can be used opaquely by adding a little white paint to bring the color out.

1 ▶ The white surface of this panel helps to keep the colors that are painted over it as bright and as luminous as possible. Paint the first coats of thin mid-toned color with a medium-sized filbert brush. Keep the colors as pure and as intense as possible.

2 ▲ Use a smaller brush and a mix of Manganese Blue, Cerulean Blue, and Viridian, together with a touch of Titanium White, to strengthen the bright but cool color of the plate.

3 ◀ Paint bright markings on top of the initial thin layers of color to give the fish better definition. The first layers of individual color should have created a sufficient sense of shape and tone on each fish.

4 ▶ As the composition is built up, less white paint is mixed into each color so that the last layers look transparent and strong. Add final highlights of thick, stiff white paint with a medium-sized or small brush.

Parrot Fish
This work has bright, saturated colors, mixed mainly from primaries and secondaries, so that they retain their purity and strength.

Strong saturated color produces a heightened, vibrant atmosphere.

Complementary colors enhance each other to make the painting appear even more luminous and strong.

Jane Gifford

Viridian Green

Ultramarine Blue

Manganese Blue

Cerulean Blue

Raw Sienna

Magenta

Permanent Rose

Cadmium Red Pale

Yellow Ochre

Cadmium Yellow

Lemon Yellow

285

GALLERY OF OIL COLORS

IF YOU TURN THE COLOR CONTROL switch on your television set, you can make an image change dramatically from black and white, through a range of color effects, to brilliant, saturated color. When you paint, you are faced with a similar range of choices and dramatic effects. Your decisions about color should be affected by the nature of your subject and by the way you see it and want to describe it. Color can convey a mood or create an area of special focus. By placing one color next to another, or choosing one particular color rather than another, you can change the visual and emotional impact of a painting. Use color to say what you want, as well as what you actually see.

Frederick Gore, RA,
Bonnieux at Cherry Time, **1989** *26 x 20 in (66 x 52 cm)*
Gore has used what seem like unnaturally bright primary and secondary colors for this study. But he has captured the presence and feel of this French village far more accurately than if he had matched the colors carefully. Bright high-key color has been used to generate a feeling of warmth and spontaneity, which gives the work a strong impact.

This detail shows how saturated yellows complement cooler lilacs and purples to heighten an effect of brilliant sunshine on the scene.

Lively, loose brushwork adds sparkle to the composition and gives the painting a more immediate quality.

Marc Chagall,
Bridges over the Seine,
1954 *44 x 64 in (112 x 163 cm)*
*Chagall's painting demonstrates
how color establishes a particular
mood or atmosphere. Above the
cool dark city hovers a magenta
and purple bird that seems to
provide a haven for the woman
and her child. The orange-red of
these figures supported within the
bird's wings generates a warm focal
point for the work. Below, in the
cool, calm blue of the foreground,
a couple sleeps beneath this bright
vision. The green goat, adjacent to
the blue and complementing the
magenta, provides a color link
between all the components of
the composition, and the harmony
of strong colors is intensified
by the dark background.*

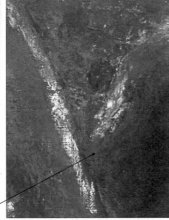

The color harmony in this
detail is created by using
colors that are adjacent to one
another on the color wheel.

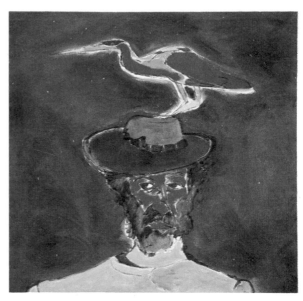

Philip Sutton, RA,
P.S. as Don Quixote, c.1989 *27 x 27 in (70 x 70 cm)*
*Sutton has retained a clarity and purity of color in this
work by having made clear decisions before painting about
where particular colors will go. The lack of overpainting
also keeps the colors clean. The painting relies on flat shapes
rather than three-dimensional forms to keep the image strong:
the bold blue shape defining the hair and beard encloses
the complementary orange-reds of the face. This intensifies
the color in the face and separates it from the background
color, making it a focal point. It also contrasts with the bird
in red and yellow, perched delicately on the man's hat.*

Elaine Halden, *Mushrooms* *18 x 20½ in (46 x 53 cm)*
*This low-key study is painted with a subdued palette, yet
it retains a fresh appearance. The vegetables are painted
sparingly, while a hint of pink in the garlic and ochre in
the mushrooms add subtlety to the color effect. The white
circle of the plate gives the work a slightly formal quality.*

Bernadette Kerr, *Scalinata* *33½ x 37¾ in (85 x 96 cm)*
*The soft, almost abstract, forms in this painting are created
with a limited range of warm ochres and terra-cottas and
cool, muted blue-greens. Colors are unsaturated and used
opaquely, and in some areas they have been mixed with
white to produce a range of pale, low-key tints.*

287

BRUSHES FOR OIL PAINTING

This special cleaner suspends brushes in turpentine

THE BRUSHES YOU USE soon become a matter of personal choice, and when you have been painting for some time, you will begin to recognize exactly which brush you need to use for a particular area of your painting. Bristle brushes are used for large-scale work, impasto work, and more vigorous techniques. They are excellent for laying in large areas of flat or blended color. Sable or synthetic soft hair brushes should be used for more precise work with oil paint mixed to a creamy consistency. As you use your brushes you will find that they often become worn in a way that suits your style. Once they lose their spring and paint-carrying capacity, they may become suitable for other techniques, such as vigorous dry brush techniques (*see* pp.290-291).

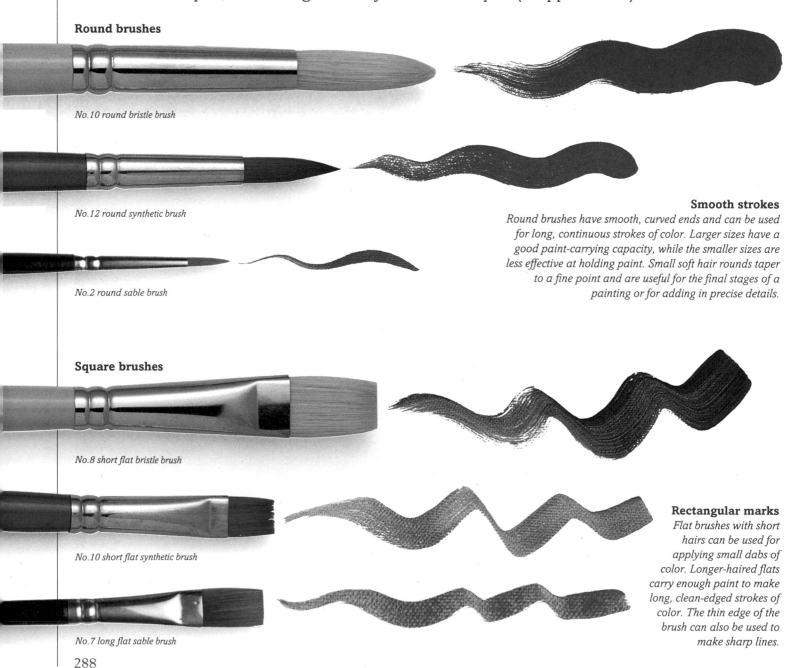

Round brushes

No.10 round bristle brush

No.12 round synthetic brush

No.2 round sable brush

Smooth strokes
Round brushes have smooth, curved ends and can be used for long, continuous strokes of color. Larger sizes have a good paint-carrying capacity, while the smaller sizes are less effective at holding paint. Small soft hair rounds taper to a fine point and are useful for the final stages of a painting or for adding in precise details.

Square brushes

No.8 short flat bristle brush

No.10 short flat synthetic brush

No.7 long flat sable brush

Rectangular marks
Flat brushes with short hairs can be used for applying small dabs of color. Longer-haired flats carry enough paint to make long, clean-edged strokes of color. The thin edge of the brush can also be used to make sharp lines.

Filbert brushes

No.10 long filbert bristle brush

No.6 long filbert bristle brush

Versatile brushwork

Filberts are made as round brushes with the ferrule, then flattened so that although the hairs are flat, they retain their rounded points. They combine some of the best features of flats and rounds, making rounded dabs of paint and strong lines of color.

No.5 short filbert synthetic brush

Specialized brushes

Bristle fan blender

Modifying the paint

A fan blender, or duster, is used for more particular techniques and to modify paint that has already been applied to a surface. The brush is used dry to soften edges or eliminate visible brushstrokes to give a very smooth appearance. It can also be used for delicate brushstrokes, such as adding highlights to hair.

BRUSH CARE

It is important to wash your brushes at the end of a painting session or they can be damaged permanently. If you leave them standing in a jar of turpentine, the pressure will distort the hair. Never use hot water to clean the brushes, as it may expand the metal ferrule and cause the hairs to fall out.

1 *Remove excess paint from the brush by cleaning it carefully with a cloth or a piece of paper towel that has been dipped in turpentine.*

2 *Dip the brush into a jar of turpentine and clean it thoroughly, pressing the tip of the brush against the base if paint still needs to be dislodged from the hairs or the ferrule.*

3 *Wipe the brush again on a clean part of the cloth to remove the last of the excess paint.*

4 *Use dishwashing liquid or soap to work up a lather with the brush in the palm of your hand.*

5 *Rinse the brush under a running tap of cold or warm water, making sure you remove all the dishwashing liquid completely and there is no trace of the pigment. Shake off the water and reshape the tip of the brush with your fingers. Store the brush upright in a suitable jar.*

BLENDING & DRY BRUSH

O IL PAINT IS ONE of the most adaptable painting mediums, and you can create many effects with it. There are several techniques for manipulating paint on a surface with a brush; blending, dry brush and scumbling, glazing, and impasto. Blending creates a smooth transition between colors, while dry brush and scumbling break up the colors to give texture.

Smooth objects
The hard, polished appearance and smoothly-rounded surface of this cup are accentuated by careful blending.

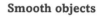

Use a clean, dry brush to blend separate colors. Make each gentle brushstroke in the same direction.

Blending

One feature that distinguishes oil paint from other painting media is its ability to be blended. Separate tones and colors can be painted onto a surface adjacent to one another and then blended by stroking a clean brush down the join between them. Blending may involve slightly softening the sharp outline of an object against a background, or working on a whole painting so that it takes on a rounded, seemingly three-dimensional effect. Use soft hair brushes for small-scale work and bristle brushes for large areas.

Realistic effects
This painting shows how oil color can be blended after it has been applied to a surface. The features of this woman's face have been modeled to give a subtle effect, shown by the smooth tonal change between the highlight on her left cheek through to her hairline and the smooth gradation of tone in her shirt sleeve. Tiny areas, such as the iris in the eye, also rely on smooth transitions between separate areas of color.

Both large and small areas of color in this painting have been blended smoothly together to create a soft, realistic sensation.

Dry brush and scumbling

Dry brush involves just a small amount of "dry" paint that is scrubbed thinly onto a surface with a bristle brush. One way of achieving this dry quality is to load a brush with color and wipe it on a rag before painting. Dry brush creates a broken color effect in which indentations or dips in the texture of a surface remain free of color while the raised areas pick it up. This gives a "halftone" effect, mingling a light tint (the white of the surface) with a darker shade (the color of the paint). Scumbling is the technique of painting over a dry layer of color using a dry brush effect, so that the color below shows through intermittently.

Scumbling is most effective when light color is laid over dark paint with a bristle brush.

Creating texture
The furry body of this teddy bear is suggested by scumbling a semi-opaque cream color over a deep shade of ochre paint.

A thin mix of blue paint over the large area of sky picks up the rough texture of this colored canvas to produce a halftone effect.

Texture in a landscape

Dry brush or scumbling can give a painting a lively appearance, accentuating the impact of colors and textures. In this work, simple mixtures of colors in different tones have been used to define the broad shapes of a landscape. These mixtures have been dry-brushed into the weave of the canvas so that the image seems almost to be imprinted onto the surface. The matte color effects in clear, slightly shaded tones heighten the simple painting style. There is a lack of extraneous detail that, together with the absence of human figures, helps to maintain the textural quality and dreamlike atmosphere of this scene.

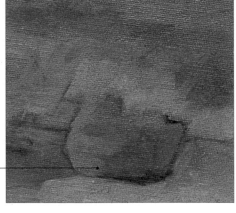

The dry brush effects in this painting create an interesting visual sensation. The canvas and the broken paint combine to produce a series of halftones that echo the rough, barren look of the landscape.

Glazing & Impasto

Glazing is a useful way of enriching or deepening the tone of a color. A glaze is a thin layer of transparent oil color that is applied over an existing area of dry paint. The color is generally mixed first with an oil painting medium, which helps to adapt its consistency and increase its transparency. A glaze can also serve as a form of color mixing (*see* p.282),

A glaze enriches another color

so that a thin red glaze over a layer of dried yellow paint produces an orange color quite different in appearance from a physically mixed orange. Impasto, on the other hand, is a technique of applying a color very thickly so that a surface retains the character and shape of each brushstroke. Oil paint has a good viscous quality suitable for impasto, so it is usually applied straight from the tube with a painting knife or a bristle brush. Impasto produces a fresh, vigorously textured look.

Glazing

Glazing can be used for a number of color effects, as its transparent quality allows the layer of paint underneath it to remain visible. Several successive layers of rich transparent glazes can achieve a wonderfully deep, luminous effect in a painting. A glaze also brings a particular unity and harmony to a work with its uniform covering. The paint should be mixed with an oil painting medium (a mixture of stand oil and white spirit or turpentine) until it forms a puree like consistency, and then applied to the surface of a painting with a soft hair or bristle brush. Once the glaze has been applied, it can be smoothed into an even layer over the surface using a clean dry round brush. For large areas, a shaving brush is useful (*see* p.322). Before glazing, always make sure the existing paint layer is dry.

The glaze is painted thinly so that the color beneath can show through.

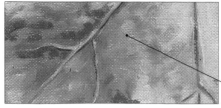

Deepening a color
The tones on this garlic are given depth, and the image greater substance, using transparent glazes.

Producing harmony
This leaf study has first been painted in a range of tones of one color, or "monochromatically," using Burnt Umber mixed with Titanium White for an opaque effect. When this was dry, a glaze of Winsor Green has been applied over the surface of the leaf, with Cadmium Lemon for the highlights.

Touches of dark transparent
Winsor Green are applied to the shadowy areas of the leaf.

Impasto

Oil paint can retain the crisp shape of a brushstroke, so it is well suited to the impasto technique. If you mix two colors together loosely and apply them with a brush, you can create a rich striated color effect with a highly textured quality. Impasto can also be useful if you need to work quickly or on a large scale so that you can cover a surface with thick, expressive brushstrokes. Impasto is a technique that relies very much upon making every brushstroke achieve exactly the right feel and sense of immediacy, so many artists who work in this way often scrape off an area that doesn't work and make the impasted brushstroke again.

Impasted brushstrokes heighten the rich, buttery quality of oil paint.

Thick paint can pick up light shining on it so that it seems to sparkle.

Retaining the shape of a brushstroke

An impasto technique can echo the appearance of the image being painted. Here the rough texture of a shell is reflected in these chunky brushstrokes. Applied wet-in-wet, the thick strokes of paint intermingle slightly so that streaks of color accentuate the textural effect of each brushtroke.

Thickly applied oil paint retains the marks or ridges left by a brush.

Loosely painted impasted brushstrokes break up the surface of a painting to create expression and vitality.

Lively brushstrokes

Painted largely with primary hues mixed with white, this image is built up with small touches of impasted high-key color. No color has been mixed with more than one other hue. Secondary blue-greens and oranges also predominate, vying with the yellows and reds. Touches of pure white have been added last for the highlights. Placed side by side, these separate brushstrokes create a lively patchwork of vibrant color.

Rich impasted colors and brushstrokes dancing in all directions are held in check within the "arrow head" composition of the two figures.

293

BRUSHWORK EFFECTS

Look for interesting textures and surfaces in familiar scenes

Picking the right brush is part of the skill of effective brushwork, and this choice takes practice. Soft hair brushes are most suitable for smooth effects and painting intricate work on a small scale. Hog hair or bristle brushes produce more "visible" brushstrokes, manipulating the oil paint into strong, vigorous shapes. Impasted strokes of thick color made with a hog hair brush can also exploit the rich texture of oil paint and give life to a work. When you paint, the amount of expression that you give to each brushstroke will determine the character and vitality of the work. Try to keep the images big and bold, working economically with large, loose brushstrokes. Remember that if you practice blending, you need to actually disguise individual brushstrokes and fuse the joins between colors and tones in order to create fully modeled images.

1 ◀ Often the most familiar scene or subject matter can reveal interesting textures and surfaces. This café has both rough and smooth surfaces and a strong light that throws some areas into dusky shadows. Sketch the composition in with a large brush, and then block in areas with color and establish patterns using a small or a medium-sized bristle brush and paint thinned with turpentine.

2 ◀ The first layers of thin paint should dry quite quickly. Drag a medium-sized bristle brush, loaded with color, over the dry surface to give a scumbled effect. The broken color should give the surface greater texture and a deeper tone.

WIPING OFF

The great advantage of oil paint is that it takes a long time to dry, so if you need to get rid of an unwanted brushstroke or color, use a piece of clean cloth to wipe off the mark carefully. Use one end of the cloth dipped in turpentine if you want to wipe the surface completely clean.

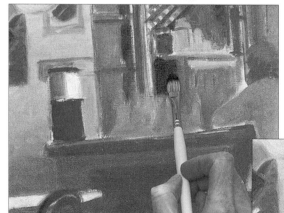

3 ▶ Overlay areas in shadow with darker tones. If you need to soften outlines or colors to give smooth gradations in tone or hue, wipe a clean finger over the paint so that the colors mingle gently.

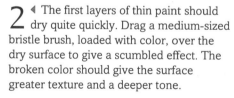

4 ◀ The marble top of this table has a cool, polished appearance, so paint a layer of violet over areas in shadow and then complement the violet with yellow highlights. Once these underlayers are dry, apply a cool mixture of Titanium White with a touch of Cerulean Blue over the table top. Use a small, clean sable brush to blend the paint to an even finish so that it looks like smooth marble. The underlayers of violet and yellow should show through faintly to suggest areas of light and shade.

5 ▶ Paint a thin transparent glaze of Alizarin Crimson over the floor area with a large synthetic wash brush to deepen the tone of the first hue. Mix the color with a little oil painting medium first if you need to make it more malleable.

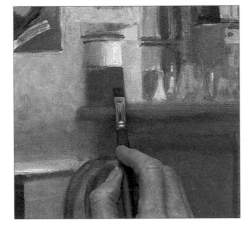

6 ▶ Paint thick impasted highlights on any bright objects with a small, round bristle brush. Keep the paint as thick and as rich as possible so that the brushstrokes look bold and eye-catching.

7 ▲ Add definition to smooth objects by using a clean, flat synthetic brush to blend the paint evenly and to create strong outlines. Paint the brushstrokes in the same direction so that the join between strokes remains invisible.

The Café Scene

Different brushstrokes give a rich variety of textures in this study. The smooth marble table catches the eye, leading it to the center of the scene. A transparent glaze on the floor creates a subtle, luminous quality, while impasted highlights stand out in relief. Scumbled walls at the back of the café create a hazy, distant feel.

A dry brush technique on these wooden chairs increases their grainy appearance.

Teacups have been blended to look like smooth china.

Sharon Finmark

Materials

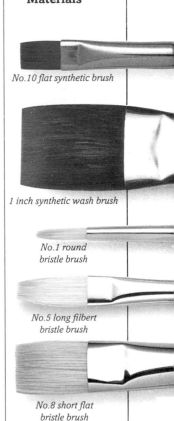

No.10 flat synthetic brush

1 inch synthetic wash brush

No.1 round bristle brush

No.5 long filbert bristle brush

No.8 short flat bristle brush

GALLERY OF BRUSHWORK

THESE PAINTINGS GIVE a good indication of the range of brushwork effects that can be achieved with oil paint, from the smoothly blended "invisible" brushwork of Meredith Frampton to the boldly impasted strokes of Emil Nolde and the beautifully loose, expressive work of Manet. An artist's brushwork is much like handwriting – it reveals the intention and perhaps the personality of its author. Paint can be dabbed tentatively onto the canvas or stirred thickly and vigorously. A brushstroke can be fluent and deft, or clumsy and heavy. It can give movement and life to an area of the canvas, or hold an image or scene with controlled precision. The particular quality of brushwork also depends on the specific brush used.

Ben Levene, RA, *Mixed Dried Flowers*, 1992 *51 x 43¾ in (130 x 111cm)*
This work subsumes a variety of different brushstrokes. Loose, scumbled brushmarks on the mirror convey a sense of distance, while objects in the foreground are painted in with careful, yet decisive small brushstrokes.

Roger Oakes,
First of Summer
48 x 48 in (122 x 122 cm)
In this lively composition, the brushwork is loose and strong, following first the diagonal line of the sea, then becoming varied and more agitated around the bird's wings. Details are also freely painted.

Daisy designs on the girl's skirt, shown clearly in this detail, are built up of particularly relaxed brushstrokes.

White highlights are sketched on loosely with opaque white paint so that they create a simple yet effective pattern.

Emil Nolde, *In the Lemon Garden*,
1933 *28¾ x 35½ in (73 x 88 cm)*
This painting carries off its mood of unabashed and tender romanticism because Nolde has painted it with such direct assurance and expression. Clear shapes of saturated color have been applied with thick, heavy brushstrokes so that solid blocks of bright yellow, red, and orange glow against the loosely painted dark greens and purples in the background. The cool blue of the woman's face and arms have also been broken up by scumbling thicker, drier paint across the canvas. Such evocative brushstrokes give a feeling of joyfulness amid the sultry perfumes of this secret arbor.

The delicate blending between individual brushstrokes gives a rounded poise to each element of the work and creates a mood of quiet stillness.

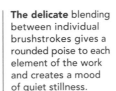

Meredith Frampton, *Portrait of a*
***Young Woman*, 1935** *42½ x 9¾ in (108 x 25 cm)*
This work is a good example of tones and colors that have been blended so perfectly that there is almost no evidence of visible brushwork. This is illusionistic painting at its most refined, and it gives the figure and the objects the rather cool quality of smooth marble.

This detail demonstrates how the edge of an area of oil paint has been smoothed where it abuts with another color so that there is no harsh edge linking the two.

Edouard Manet, *Au Bal*, c.1870-80 *22 x 14 in (56 x 36 cm)*
This loosely worked study clearly shows the marks of each brushstroke as Manet worked rapidly to capture a profile. The sense of immediacy arises from a vivacity and economy in the brushwork, with a busy cluster of horizontal strokes describing the dress and more controlled strokes for the hair.

CHOOSING A SUPPORT

A SUPPORT IS THE SURFACE that you paint on, and the type of material you choose is ultimately a personal choice. You can paint either on a rigid support, such as a board or a panel, or on a flexible support such as canvas, but within that choice there are a range of different surface textures to pick from that affect the way the paint behaves. Canvases and boards each have their own characteristic feel, and there is a big difference between the two. A hard, rigid support enables you to prepare a roughly textured surface for painting that would be quite impractical on a stretched canvas, but the flexibility and texture of canvas makes it a far more responsive surface on which to paint.

Canvas boards
These combine the rigidity of board and the texture of canvas. Although available from artists' suppliers, they are easily made by gluing linen to a piece of hardboard and then priming the entire surface.

 *Blockboard*

 *Plywood*

 *Chipboard*

 *Hardboard*

 *Medium density fiberboard*

Types of panel and canvas

Rigid supports provide a sounder and more permanent basis for painting. The advantage of using a board is that you can alter its surface texture by "priming" it roughly or smoothly (*see* p.301). Wooden panels covered with linen are particularly durable. Common materials for panels nowadays are fabricated boards such as plywood, hardboard, and fiberboard, rather than the traditional mahogany, poplar, and oak. Hardboard is a good choice, particularly for smaller panels. A recent development is honeycomb aluminum, which provides a strong support.

A traditional flexible support is linen canvas, and the flax fibers from which linen is woven are long and strong. Cotton fibers are not as strong, but some excellent cotton canvases are available in heavier weights. You should use at least a ten-ounce canvas cloth, and preferably a 12 ounce one. Weight is not so important when choosing a linen canvas. A new material, though not yet widely available, is the flexible, yet stable, polyester sailcloth.

Ready-primed canvas

Cotton duck 12oz

 *Coarse linen*

 *Fine linen*

 *Grained cotton*

 *Cotton duck 15oz*

Rough and smooth boards

A rough surface breaks up the smoothness of a brushstroke, giving it a pitted or textured appearance and producing a craggy, chunky version of an image (below). The board must be primed with loose brushstrokes to create this expressive effect, perhaps with sand in the primer to give a gravelly texture (see p.318). Use the back of a piece of hardboard if you prefer a regular texture. Bristle brushes also increase the degree of texture. On a smoothly primed board, soft hair brushes give more control for modeling and blending forms and details. Alternatively, make sweeping brushstrokes that are unimpeded by any texture on the support so that you clearly see each brushstroke (right).

The rough texture of these brushstrokes and the rugged appearance of the work is provided entirely by the nature of the ground.

This smooth ground shows up the texture of both thick and thin brushstrokes.

The energy of these brushstrokes retains a sense of freshness and immediacy.

Rough and smooth canvases

The texture of canvas can vary enormously, from the smooth, hard surface of wet-spun linen made from fine flax, to the rough texture of dry-spun coarse linen made from tow flax. Generally the finer the woven canvas, the smoother it will feel and the more refined your painting will be. A smooth canvas enables you to work with great precision and detail with soft hair brushes, while a coarse canvas encourages a more vigorous approach with bristle brushes. Try various grades and types of surface to see what kind of canvas will best suit your style of painting.

The dry brush technique on this coarse, open-weave canvas makes the work seem part of the texture of the support. The harshness of the material echoes the knotty, rough quality of fishing nets, creating a continuity from the image of fishing boats to the surface quality of the painting.

The smooth quality of this fine-weave canvas allows each small image to be painted clearly and delicately. Paint can be applied easily to this type of canvas, and the flexibility of the cloth encourages a light, refined painting style.

299

PREPARING SUPPORTS & GROUNDS

Materials

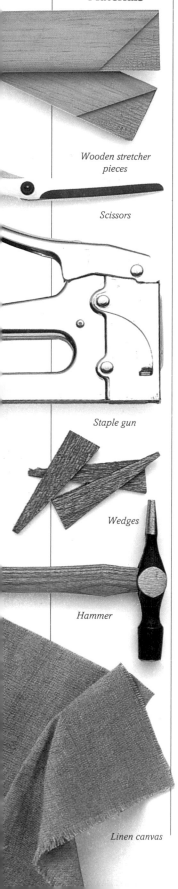

Wooden stretcher pieces

Scissors

Staple gun

Wedges

Hammer

Linen canvas

CHOOSE A SUPPORT that suits your painting style. It can be rigid and stable, such as a wooden panel made of oak or poplar, or more commonly of hardboard or plywood; or it can be flexible, made of cotton, linen, or polyester canvas. The ground is what you put on the surface of the support in order to prepare it for painting. The surface is initially sized to seal it and prevent oil from the paint from being absorbed into the wood or canvas. A primer, either toned or white, can then be applied over the dried sizing.

Stretching a canvas

1 ◀ Start by slotting the four edges of the stretcher together. Tap a rubber hammer on each corner if the pieces become stuck.

2 ▶ Lay the stretcher over a large piece of canvas and then cut around it with scissors, leaving at least 3in (8cm) of canvas clear.

3 ▶ Stretch the linen canvas over the rigid wooden frame using thick staples and a staple gun. Put a staple in the frame wherever there is a number on the diagram (*right*). Work in number order. This ensures an even tension in the taut canvas. Fold the canvas over the frame firmly rather than pulling hard; if you stretch it too tight, it may begin to strain and distort.

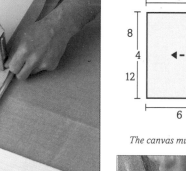

The canvas must be stapled in a specific order

4 ◀ Once the sides of the canvas have been attached securely to the frame, maintain an even tension at each corner of the support by stapling down the overlapping material. Neatly make two folds out of the canvas and then pull one fold over the other. Secure the folds to the frame with a staple.

5 ▲ Finally, tap four wedges into each corner of the frame with the hammer. These wedges help to tighten the frame a little more, making it as rigid and as taut as possible.

Sizing and priming a canvas

1 ▲ To size a canvas, heat 1 quart (1 liter) of water in a double boiler (or a pot in a saucepan) with 1oz (30 grams) of dry rabbit skin glue. Paint the mix over the canvas with a general purpose 3in (8cm) brush.

2 ▲ When the sizing has dried completely, prime the canvas by adding gesso powder – plaster of paris – to the glue size until you get the consistency of thick cream. Then cover the canvas with the white primer.

Sizing and priming a panel

1 ◄ Panels are also sized, but add 2½oz (70 grams) of rabbit skin glue to the water.

2 ▲ When the size is dry, prime all the surfaces of the panel with gesso primer.

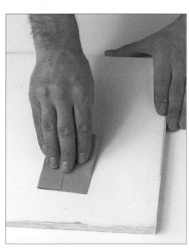

3 ◄ Once dry, sand the panel with very fine sandpaper to give it a smooth and even finish.

4 ▶ Finally, apply one more layer of glue size to the whole panel to seal the surfaces completely.

Primed canvas

Roughly primed board

Smoothly primed board

Materials

Dry rabbit skin glue

Gesso powder

Double boiler

General purpose brush

Medium density fiberboard

Sandpaper

WAYS OF WORKING WITH OIL

MOST ARTISTS BEGIN TO DEVELOP their own techniques and individual style after a long period of experimentation and discovery. For beginners, it makes sense to experiment as much as possible with many different approaches to painting so that you can build up a technical repertoire and discover ways of working that suit your own personality.

The basic art of painting

If you begin by painting small, simple objects, preferably with some sort of personal meaning, you will be able to concentrate on how you paint without worrying about extraneous details, or the initial difficulties of drawing. If you look at the work of past and present painters whose style you admire, you will see that in most cases it is largely a question of what is actually left out in the process of painting that makes their work so successful (*see* Galleries *throughout*). Simple domestic objects or toys make good subjects when you start to paint. They generally have a nice simplicity, which makes them appropriate subjects for drawing and painting. Start by painting what you see as straightforwardly as possible, and then concentrate on different ways of approaching the same subject. You may find it easier to begin working on a small scale in a rather careful style, drawing the outlines of the subject and pre-mixing a small range of tones, and then carefully filling the outlines in, stage by stage, with a soft hair or small bristle brush.

This is a good way of discovering the feel of the medium and learning how to control your brushes. After all, the basic art of painting is very much about matching what you can see, imagine, or even recall with a particular mixture of color applied in a certain way.

Developing style and technique

Painting familiar subjects will help you build up the confidence to experiment with the objects you work with. Practice laying in the shadows on a flower with a range of tones, for instance, or blending separate colors with a dry brush to achieve the smooth, rounded finish of an egg. If you choose to paint a rough-textured object, such as a piece of driftwood or a small rock, try a different technical approach and represent the crags and facets that characterize these objects with a range of different tones and loose, chunky brushstrokes.

Complex arrangements

Once you have looked at individual objects
on their own, you may decide to paint a more
complex arrangement that includes a number
of objects. Here your approach to painting can
be just the same, except that you will have to
make decisions about how you organize your
composition. Try to establish a sense of balance
between the forms. This does not mean that
what you see must be staid and solid, but that
there should be a link or a thread running
through the arrangement that binds it together.

You should also decide what kind of visual impact you want the composition to make.
A composition that fills the frame will convey a sense of boldness and generosity – or you
can create a feeling of separateness or isolation by painting gaps between the objects. This
kind of experimentation with simple, accessible forms can be invaluable in experimenting
with styles and approaches, giving you the confidence you need before you decide to tackle
the more difficult subjects of portraits and landscapes.

Visual aids

It can be helpful to use photographs for visual reference when you work on a complicated
subject such as a landscape, as you have the benefit of a three-dimensional scene or object
already transcribed into a flat, two-dimensional image. Try to paint freely and not to copy
the image exactly as it appears, or the painting may become cramped and look awkward.
 It is better to make a free transcription that leaves out all the unnecessary details and
allows you to practice looking, for example, for cooler colors and lighter tones toward
the horizon, which help to increase the sense of aerial perspective.

Working with confidence

When you come to work freely with any subject in any situation, the kinds
of simplifications that you have practiced previously are all still entirely
appropriate. When working from life, an artist needs to
make a mental synthesis of the subject being painted,
select the most interesting elements that will override
the mass of extraneous detail, and allow the
painting to develop as a succinct and
self-contained world in its
own right. In this way,
you will learn to discover
a painting style that is most
suited to you, and to adapt
techniques to create new
and unusual effects.

CREATING A COMPOSITION

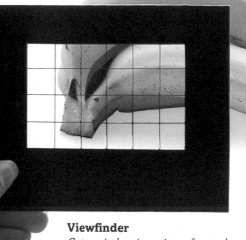

COMPOSITION IS A TERM THAT DESCRIBES the organization of space in a picture – ordering shapes, forms, and colors in a way that is appropriate to the meaning of the image. When you are putting a composition together, look for balance and a sense of appropriateness, trusting your intuition. If you are working from life, look at the image through a viewfinder. Move it closer to and then farther away from the image until you see the composition you want. If you are working from a photograph, try cropping areas of the image with small strips of paper.

Viewfinder
Cut a window in a piece of posterboard and use it to look for the best composition.

Looking for a composition
The most interesting composition is usually one that gives an image a fresh slant so that you perceive it in a new way. Arrange a still-life composition on a table top, and then sketch it from as many different angles as you can think of. Try to be adventurous, closing right in on the still-life or sketching just a few elements of the composition.

Visual impact
As you sketch, look for the way colored objects react with each other to create a subtle harmony or a vibrant contrast. You may want to rearrange objects to achieve a better visual impact.

Transferring a sketch

Once you have selected the most interesting composition, the best way of transferring it to a canvas or a board is to use a grid system (see also below right). Place a grid over the original sketch and draw a similar grid on a larger scale on the support. Transfer details from each square on the sketch using charcoal (below), or drawing directly with a brush and a thin mix of paint (right). Pencil can be used very faintly, but it is generally not recommended as it can soil the color of the paint. Some artists like to fill the outlines of shapes with light cross-hatching to determine areas of tone.

If you draw directly with a brush, use a thin mix of paint in a light or neutral color so that it does not show through the painting.

USING SLIDES

Slides can be used to transfer an image, whether it is a favorite scene or a slide of the sketch itself. Hang a panel or a canvas on a wall and shine the image onto it using a projector. You can determine very easily how large you want the image to be by moving the zoom lens on the projector. Then trace in the basic outlines of the composition with a piece of charcoal or a brush and a thin mix of paint. Polaroid pictures or photographs can also be useful for visual reference while you are painting, but you may like to crop the image first with small strips of paper to select a simplified or unusual composition.

Drawing grid

Draw a grid of squares onto a piece of tracing paper or acetate and then place it over the original sketch. This may seem like a laborious process for transferring an image, but it is a useful way to make sure the proportions of the composition remain intact.

Drawing grid

Dusting off

If you draw with charcoal, use a large soft brush or a piece of doughy bread to dust the charcoal off and leave the residual image as a guide. Another option is to seal the charcoal with a fixative.

Doughy bread

COMPOSITION

LOOKING AT A LANDSCAPE or an interior, it can be difficult to know quite where to establish the broad areas of a composition for painting. It can sometimes be helpful to think of the eye like a camera lens, zooming in on a scene to focus on just one element, or pulling back to encompass a wide viewpoint and include more visual information. You will also need to decide what the boundaries of your composition

Make several sketches to discover the most interesting composition

will be. An image can be placed partially within the frame, so that the picture seems to be part of a much larger scene, or placed centrally, so that every aspect of the scene is contained within the frame. Unusual angles and perspectives can create added interest.

1 ▶ Select the most suitable composition and transfer the sketch onto the canvas with the aid of a drawing grid. This grid system should help you retain the correct proportions of the sketch as you draw the composition out on the canvas.

2 ▶ Block in the main elements of the composition with areas of flat color, thinned with turpentine. As this interior scene has sharp distinctions of lights and darks, try to establish these areas as soon as possible so that they stay clearly defined.

3 ▲ Build up the tones and shadows on each individual object to heighten the color and establish a sense of light. The thick stroke of dark color on this jug gives it more of a three-dimensional form.

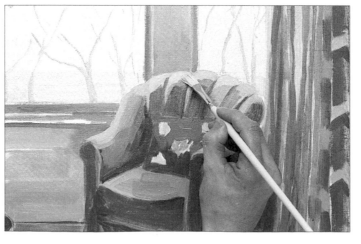

4 ◀ Mix two separate colors to build up the lights and darks on this chair. One mix of Viridian, Cadmium Yellow, Raw Sienna, and Yellow Ochre, painted on with a medium-sized bristle brush, captures the light hitting the back of the chair. A touch of Ultramarine Blue with the Viridian gives dark shadows.

6 ◀ The carpet
and curtains in
this painting play
an important part
in establishing a
strong sense of
perspective; both
carpet and curtains
recede at a sharp
angle, so patterns
or markings at the
edge of the carpet
should be painted
proportionally
smaller. Paint such
details with a fine
sable or synthetic
brush to keep the
effects soft.

5 ▲ Once an area has been built up with thin paint, overlay it
with more saturated mixes of bright color to give the effect
of strong light. When you describe the intensity of such bright light,
keep the contrast between colors as sharp and as clean as possible.
Deepen dark areas to make this contrast more dramatic.

7 ◀ The landscape
visible through the
large windows should
be painted in much
paler colors to create a
sense of distance and
aerial perspective (*see
right*). Dab touches of
color lightly over the
canvas with a medium-
sized bristle brush. A
dark glaze over the
window frame helps
it retain its rich color
and contrast with the
pale light beyond.

AERIAL PERSPECTIVE

Aerial perspective is a term
that describes the effect
of atmospheric conditions
on our perception of the
tone and color of distant
objects. As objects recede
towards the horizon they
appear to become bluer
and lighter in tone. Artists
generally work from light
tones at the back of the
composition to the darker
tones at the front.

Jude's Sitting Room

*This painting really describes
a frame within a frame. The
perspective created by the
curtains and carpet lead the
eye up into the central area
of the painting, which has
every object at an angle to
increase the degree of
interest in the composition.*

A good variation of tone and
color describes objects well
and keeps the composition lively.

Dark shadows contrast with
strong areas of light and pale
color through the windows.

Darker, stronger colors in the
foreground push the bottom of
the painting forward to catch
the eye and improve the
perspective of the painting.

Jane Gifford

Materials

*No.4 round
sable brush*

*No.1 round
bristle brush*

*No.8 round
synthetic brush*

*No.4 long flat
bristle brush*

Well-balanced colors
help to create a strong
closed composition.

GALLERY OF COMPOSITION

COMPOSITION IS ALL ABOUT establishing an appropriate relationship between various elements of your painting, such as form, tone, and color, so that together they generate the meaning you want a painting to convey. When you establish the basic structure of a composition, ask yourself whether it communicates what you want to say about your subject, or whether changing the size, position, or structure of a particular feature will make your work clearer. In these paintings, each variation creates a different impact. A low viewpoint in one painting can cause isolated objects to appear dramatically bold and create a strong psychological effect, while a high viewpoint in another work allows individual elements to become part of a broader scheme that stretches away before the viewer in a leisurely, pleasing way.

Simon Ripley, *On the Edge* *17 x 14 in (43 x 36 cm)*
Ripley's unusual composition places a vase on the far end of a table as if it is spinning off the edge. Large areas of orange-red complement the small active cool blue of the vase in this strange and evocative work.

Oskar Kokoschka, *Broad View of the Thames,* **1926**
35 x 51 in (89 x 130 cm)
Kokoschka's painting is an excellent example of the way an artist can manipulate space within a composition in order to show more of the panorama than is possible with a conventional linear perspective. Here Kokoschka has utilized a form of curvilinear perspective, pushing the painting into an all-embracing circular composition. The artist's high viewpoint also allows more of the river and ground to be included in his panoramic sweep.

Bill Jacklin, RA, *The Rink III,*
1991 *78 x 72 in (198 x 183 cm)*
This image of moving ice skaters creates a very effective open composition, a term which implies a continuation beyond the bounds of the canvas. There is a wonderful sense of swaying movement in the painting, brought about by the angle of the figures in the middle ground and foreground and their long shadows that sweep down on a diagonal, impelling the eye down and around through the moving bodies. There is also a kind of icy breathiness about the color scheme of the work that perfectly recalls the physical atmosphere of the scene.

Carel Weight, RA, *The Frustrated Tiger,* **1992**
71¼ x 59½ in (181 x 151 cm)
The two pairs of figures in this unusual composition create a strange symmetry, with curious shapes and mysterious shadows linking all the elements together. The turbulent sunset and the distant childlike image of the tiger combine to create an extraordinary atmosphere.

Sir Robin Philipson, RA, *Poppies, c.*1985
30 x 40 in (76 x 102 cm)
This study of poppies is a fine example of a closed composition, in which everything is contained within the frame. The vase and flowers fill the space generously without going beyond it. The adjacent harmony of the powerfully warm hues intensifies this small, closed world.

309

PAINTING ON A WHITE GROUND

A WHITE GROUND PROVIDES a perfect surface for reflecting the purity of a color painted over it. A transparent color that looks dark in a tube appears as a brilliant saturated hue when it is painted thinly over a white surface. Semi-opaque and even opaque colors are also given a particular clarity on a white ground, especially since there is often a variation in thickness between individual brushstrokes. Generally, more painting is required on a white ground in order to cover the white surface, while a colored or toned ground provides a useful unifying matrix between the brushstrokes of different color.

Influencing the look of a color
These examples of Permanent Rose demonstrate how easily the appearance of a color changes. The top squares, painted first thickly and then thinly, retain their brilliance and purity on a white surface. A colored ground (above) subdues the luminosity of the transparent paint.

Make a sketch on white paper to plan the color scheme

SINCE WHITE REPRESENTS the brightest highlight a painter can create, most of the white ground in this exercise has been covered to achieve a more accurate representation of tones. As you paint over the white ground, bear in mind that the colors you paint will initially look much darker on the dazzling white surface than they will when you have finished the painting and covered up most of the white ground.

1 ◀ A white ground suits this subject matter perfectly, as it can illuminate the colors painted over it to give a sensation of strong summer light. Sketch the landscape with thinned paint and a small round bristle brush, and then block in main areas of color with a clean brush.

2 ◀ This work relies on strong color to make its impact, so use pure complementary colors to achieve the maximum effect. Pick out areas of the foreground with warm colors such as orange, yellow, and red, and then complement them with cooler colors such as blue, violet, and green in the distance. Cover as much of the white surface as possible with the thin mixes of color.

3 ◀ Use a cold, clean blue, such as Cerulean Blue, for the sky. To avoid painting a heavy, flat area of color, lighten some Ultramarine Blue with touches of white and use it to break up the large expanse of sky with a long filbert bristle brush. Keep this paint dry and thick so that you can create a scumbled effect over the first layer of paint. This should give the sky a richer texture and a deeper tone.

4 ▶ Once you have covered all the white ground, you may find that some areas of color still look quite weak, so refine and strengthen the look of objects with mixes of bright, saturated color. Use a versatile green, such as Winsor Green, to increase the range of tones and emphasize the particular shape of each tree. Use a small round bristle brush for any intricate details. If the particular area you are working on is still wet with paint, maintain a steady hand by using a mahl stick (*see* p.279).

5 ▲ Apply a pale mix of Cerulean Blue, lightened with white and painted in with a fine sable brush, to provide an effective contrast with the warm orange rooftops. The coolness of the mix also increases the sense of aerial perspective in the painting.

6 ◀ Add strokes of hot color, such as pure Cadmium Red, to enliven the foreground area and contrast with the banks of green trees beyond. Use a dry brush technique and plenty of saturated paint to give both texture and brilliance to the final look of the painting.

A dry brush technique breaks up large areas of color, but the touches of white ground that show through also increase the brilliance of this blue paint.

Materials

No.2 round sable brush

No.1 round bristle brush

No.5 long filbert bristle brush

Provence Landscape

A white ground allows saturated colors to show their freshness and brilliance in this painting. The hot summer atmosphere is heightened by several complementary colors that enhance one another to look even brighter. Energetic brushstrokes and interesting texture give the scene movement and vitality.

Warm colors painted in the foreground are complemented by cool background colors that create aerial perspective.

Paula Velarde

PAINTING ON A TONED GROUND

THE GREAT ADVANTAGE of working on a toned or colored ground is the economy it can bring to your painting technique. Paint darker tones in transparent colors, which allow the ground color to show through, and lighter tones in opaque colors, which obliterate it. The mid-tones are provided by the color of the ground itself, so that you soon have a work with a very finished appearance. It would take much longer to reach the same point working on a white ground. The Yellow Ochre mid-toned ground used in the exercise below provides a warm underlying tone for the work and acts as a unifying element in the painting.

PREPARING A TONED GROUND

There are two ways of coloring a ground – either by laying a thin transparent veil of color over the white priming (this is known as an imprimatura) – or by laying an opaque layer of color over the primer. Allow plenty of time for the color to dry before painting.

1 A toned ground can be any color, but warm red ochres and browns can give more richness to a work. A thin transparent wash of imprimatura can be made by mixing Burnt Umber and Yellow Ochre and adding turpentine to reduce the paint mixture to a thin consistency. Apply the imprimatura freely and evenly over the support, in this case a panel, with a large bristle brush.

2 Let the solvent in the mixture evaporate for a few minutes, and then rub the surface with a cloth to take away the excess paint. This means that the white priming has a stain of transparent color rather than a coat of paint. The main advantage of using an imprimatura rather than a toned ground is that the film of color allows the white of the original priming to retain its reflective quality on the colors painted over it.

The opaqueness of a colored ground ensures a complete uniformity of tone over the surface of the support. A colored ground can also be laid by mixing color in with the primer itself before it is applied.

Toning a primed canvas
This canvas support has already been primed with white primer, and a colored ground made of Burnt Umber, Yellow Ochre, and Titanium White is laid over the top with a large wash brush. A colored ground will take longer to dry than an imprimatura, so ensure that it is completely dry before you begin to paint. Most colored grounds will take a few days to dry completely.

1 ◀ Sketch in the composition with a medium-sized bristle brush and a thin mix of Burnt Umber. The ground has been prepared with a mix of Yellow Ochre, Gold Ochre, and Titanium White.

2 ▶ Break up and enliven areas of the colored ground using a medium-sized bristle brush and a slightly thicker mixture of Yellow Ochre with a touch of Titanium White and Cadmium Red.

3 ▲ Once you have blocked in all the shapes and dark areas of shadow with thin color, start to build up the highlights on each figure using a thick, dry mix of Titanium White, Alizarin Crimson, and Yellow Ochre and a medium-sized filbert bristle brush.

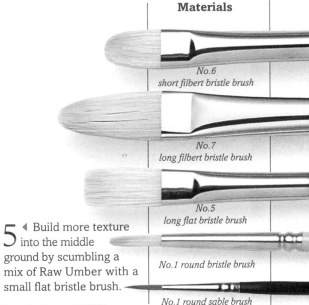

No.6
short filbert bristle brush

No.7
long filbert bristle brush

No.5
long flat bristle brush

No.1 round bristle brush

No.1 round sable brush

4 ▲ Use a small brush, such as a No.1 round bristle, to add finer details to the background and to create aerial perspective. These details should be painted over dry layers to avoid mixing paint.

5 ◀ Build more texture into the middle ground by scumbling a mix of Raw Umber with a small flat bristle brush.

6 ◀ Increase the sense of light falling across the scene with layers of light color over the initial washes. Using a cool mixture of Titanium White, Yellow Ochre, and a touch of Viridian, paint light gestural strokes over shadowed areas with a large filbert bristle brush. For warm areas add a little Alizarin Crimson instead of the Viridian.

7 ◀ Paint distant figures and objects with a cool brown, such as Raw Umber, using a fine brush, such as a No.1 sable round. When these details have dried, use even paler color in the background to increase the sense of aerial perspective and hazy light.

Indian Street Dwellers
The look of this painting is clearly affected by the warm color of the toned ground, influencing the appearance of every hue in the composition. The finished look the ground gives allows the brushstrokes to be made quite sparingly, using paint thinned with turpentine to establish the scene, and thicker highlights to finish.

Shanti Thomas

The colored ground provides an effective base for subtle juxtapositions of warm and cool color to be laid on top of it.

Dark tones have been painted with thinner transparent colors, while the lighter tones and highlights have been created with thick opaque color.

Colored grounds give a more finished effect, allowing for a much looser and relaxed style of painting.

The mid-toned ground links separate areas of color and gives an overall warmth to the painting.

313

GALLERY OF WHITE & TONED GROUNDS

THE PAINTINGS SHOWN HERE demonstrate how important the color of any ground is – from the bright clarity of color that can be produced on a white ground to the economy of painting on a subtle mid-toned ground. A toned ground not only affects the appearance of a color painted immediately on top of it, but also any successive layers of transparent and opaque paint.

Mick Rooney, RA, *Wedding Day Yalalag*, 1991 *36 x 28 in (91 x 71 cm)*
The principle of opaque highlights and transparent shadows on a dark ground is well illustrated in this painting of a village wedding. Opaque colors are worked stiffly in a scumbled dry brush technique that allows the dark ground color to show through in halftone effects.

Donald Hamilton Fraser, RA, *Grand Canal, Venice*, 1992 *30 x 23 in (76 x 58 cm)*
This is an excellent example of a painting made directly in an economical style on a white ground. The paint, applied thinly, allows the white ground to illuminate colors and give a clarity and sparkle to the quality of light in the painting. Areas of high contrast add a crisp brightness to the scene.

This detail shows how clean and strong the colors look on a white ground.

The glimpses of white ground still visible help to intensify the appearance of each color.

314

Pablo Picasso, *Head of a Sailor,*
1906-7 *15¾ x 16½ in (40 x 42 cm)*
*The pastel-like quality of this work
is due mainly to the fact that opaque
white has been painted onto a dark
ground and tinted with color. The
colored ground shows through
the brushstrokes, providing a strong
backdrop to a subtle work. The effect
of overlaying such a darkly colored
background with an opaque dry brush
technique pushes the simply styled
image forward so that we feel even
closer to the absorbed character.*

In this detail the dark
ground enhances simple
blocks of color and the
almost diagrammatical
style of painting.

Thickly painted highlights
over the dark ground make
the work look more dramatic.

Paul Lewin, *Cornish Cliffs* *17½ x 20 in (44 x 51 cm)*
*The brown mid-toned ground of this work has allowed for economy
when painting and provides a warm, unifying background color to link
the individual brushstrokes. The artist has employed thin transparent
darks for the shadows and thicker opaque colors for the lighter tones,
reserving the lightest tones and thickest paint for the breaking waves.*

Jane Gifford, *Calcutta Bus Trip* *36 x 36 in (91 x 91 cm)*
*This painting buzzes with warmth and humanity. It conveys the bustle
and excitement of a busy Indian street in a series of relatively flat planes
of bright saturated colors. Interlocking patterned shapes retain their
clarity of color, having been painted directly onto the white ground.*

ALLA PRIMA PAINTING

Establish a composition

ALSO KNOWN AS direct painting, alla prima work is usually completed in one sitting while the paint remains wet on the support. Such paintings have an expressive immediacy and freshness. It is important to bear in mind that once a color has been laid on, it will affect any color that is subsequently painted on top of it while it is still wet, so if you sketch in the broad areas of the subject first, do so with thin paint. You need a clear idea of where colors will be placed, or the painting will become muddy.

Sketching from life
Conditions constantly change when you paint from life; a landscape can alter dramatically if the sun goes behind a cloud, and people can move all too easily. Make plenty of preparatory sketches to explore your subject and collect handy reference material.

The feline characteristics of this cat have been captured with simple lines and a hint of color.

These economical studies are full of expression and interesting ideas.

1 ▲ Cats can move away instantly, so use a small support to enable you to work across the canvas as fast as possible. Outline the shape of the cat using a small brush, such as a No.1 round bristle, and Ivory Black paint thinned with plenty of turpentine. Work quickly, making a line sketch to establish the position of the cat. Look for its essential features, keeping each brushstroke as loose and as expressive as possible. If you make a mistake, use the end of a cloth dipped in turpentine to wipe away the mark.

2 ◀ Plot the relationship of the cat to the cushion and armchair so that if the cat suddenly moves, the scale of the painting has already been planned. Then return to the cat and develop it as much as possible. Look for the way the light affects its distinguishing features, and which direction its fur grows. Describe the shape of the cat with a mixture of Ivory Black and Cerulean Blue, together with a little Titanium White. Flick the brush lightly to give the impression of fur.

3 ▲ Use an orange mixed from Cadmium Yellow Deep, Cadmium Orange, and Titanium White to build up areas of the sketched cushion with light color. Avoid mixing in white paint when you fill in the darker areas of the cushion. Keep brushstrokes loose and full of expression to retain a sense of freshness.

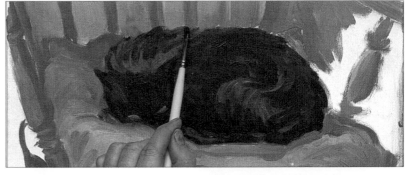

4 ◀ Use a larger bristle brush to block in the color of the armchair and the wall behind. The broken color of the background must be cool and subdued so that it does not detract from the main subject. Take time to clean your brushes thoroughly before you apply each new color – working at this speed, you should guard against mistakes such as muddying your colors. Take the paint up to the edge of each separate area of color without overpainting.

Materials

No.2 round sable brush

No.1 round bristle brush

No.5 long filbert bristle brush

5 ▶ Any gaps showing through in the canvas between broad areas of color can be covered up using a small bristle brush. Here the gaps can be covered by emphasizing the cat's wispy fur. Stroke touches of pure Cerulean Blue lightly over the first colors to give rich texture and definition to the cat.

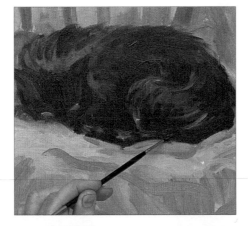

6 ▶ Take a fine brush, such as a No.2 round sable, to deepen the shadows on the cat. Using a sable brush should allow you to apply fresh color over a layer of wet paint if you want to avoid mixing the two. Mix a small amount of Cerulean Blue paint with the Ivory Black to keep the shadows cool.

7 ▶ Work up the remaining areas of the composition once you are satisfied with the look of the cat. Deepen the folds and shadows of the cushion with pure Cadmium Orange. Use simple tonal variations of Yellow Ochre and Burnt Sienna to mold the wooden armchair.

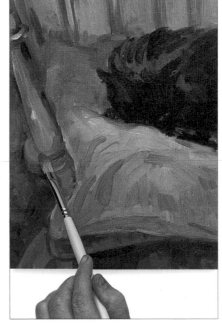

Cat on an Orange Cushion
This work has been planned in advance so that colors can be placed exactly without becoming muddy. The progress of the work has been geared around a subject that could move at any moment, without compromising the characteristic sense of immediacy associated with this style.

A strong composition is important if you are working quickly from life.

Colors are kept clean and pure, with simple variations in tone.

Sue Sareen

WORKING WITH A PAINTING KNIFE

IF YOU ARE UNACCUSTOMED to working with a painting knife, the first thing that will strike you is how different the paint feels on a knife compared to a brush. Working with a painting knife requires some delicacy, as it spreads the paint like butter onto bread; the flat surface of the painting knife seems to slice easily through the paint as you lay it onto the canvas. A paintbrush tends to come down onto the canvas vertically, while the painting knife can be applied horizontally, parallel to the surface of the painting. Painting knife studies are often made wet-in-wet, generally using more opaque colors.

Textured surfaces
A painting knife produces a variety of interesting textural effects simply by being held in different ways. If you want to increase the degree of texture on the surface of your support, mix some dry sand into the primer when you prepare the board. This builds up the surface of the support into a relief, pushing the painting into three dimensions.

Using a painting knife

A painting knife needs to be used with confidence and without hesitation, so it is worth practicing first. Use a knife both for building up final highlights in thick impasto and for a textured, lively painting. Painting knives are not the same as palette knives, which are only intended for mixing paint and cleaning palettes; painting knives have a bend in the handle so that they can be held in several different ways to manipulate the creamy paint into expressive shapes (*see below*). Many artists use their finger on the springy blade, pushing it down deliberately to control the way the paint is applied. Since paint is usually applied very thickly with a painting knife, it is sensible to work on a rigid support.

Horizontal strokes of thick, creamy paint from a loaded painting knife.

Use the length of the blade to smear paint over a surface.

Bold strokes
Grip the handle firmly, as you would a trowel, and paint decisive, vigorous strokes of color across the surface of the support.

Wrap your fingers firmly around the wooden handle.

Small dabs of color are useful for details.

Press gently into the paint with a finger on the back of the blade.

Light effects
For a lighter control of the painting knife, place your index finger on the springy part of the blade so that just the tip presses down into the paint.

Clean lines
A more common way of holding the knife is to place your index finger on the end of the wooden handle and push the metal shaft into the paint. This produces a firm imprint of the blade in the paint and is useful for making ridged lines of color.

Use this technique to build up a regular pattern of texture.

A firm but even grip gives good control.

1 ◀ This portrait is built up on a small primed panel so that the paint can be scraped easily to give a more textural study. Make a quick sketch first with thinned paint if you need to work out correct proportions. Then smooth paint over the main areas of the portrait with light strokes.

2 ◀ When you have applied different tones to the face and hair, use the edge of the painting knife, or a bit of cardboard with serrated edges, to emphasize the direction the hair grows in. These create highlights on the hair and help to break up heavy layers of paint.

3 ▶ Smooth a clean finger gently over any area where you need to blend the paint; a painting knife is effective for crisp lines of color, but it may be difficult to achieve the same degree of subtle blending that can be produced with a brush or a finger.

Materials

Diamond-shaped painting knife

Serrated edge

Paintbrush handle

4 ◀ Use the end of the painting knife, or the tip of a brush handle, if you want to make small dots of color and build up the texture of the painting. Dip the brush handle in paint and use it to suggest the pattern of this cardigan.

Textural portrait

A variety of expressive textural marks give this portrait life. A painting knife is used to apply the paint quickly and produce crisp strokes of color to establish the main features of the face. Additional techniques, such as lines and highlights made with a serrated edge and dabs of paint made with a brush handle, add to the textural surface. The painting knife has been used finally to apply thick impasted highlights.

Ridges of color made with a painting knife catch the light to give the painting a brighter quality.

Paint is both smeared over the support and laid on with strokes of thick, impasted color.

The texture of the paint gives the work an almost three-dimensional look.

Christian Furr

GALLERY OF ALLA PRIMA PAINTINGS

OIL PAINT IS SUCH a versatile and valuable material that it may be used in a variety of rich textural effects and brushstrokes. Painting from life can encourage this sense of freedom and expression when you work with oil paint, as it relies on a freshness and immediacy. Brushstrokes and marks appear more tangible if they have been painted wet-in-wet, or wiped off and reapplied, and the paintings shown here are examples of the wide-ranging results and instant appeal that can be achieved by incorporating different techniques and textural effects.

Vincent van Gogh, *The Hospital Garden at St. Rémy,* **1889** *25 x 18 in (63 x 48 cm)*
It would be difficult to make a more immediate statement in paint than this work by Van Gogh. Strong, stubby brushstrokes follow the forms of the painted objects, and the ground appears to move like a sea. The texture and rhythm of the brushstrokes across the surface of the painting give the scene an intense energy.

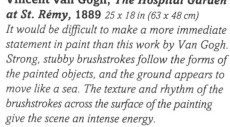

This detail shows particles of sand, blown by the wind, still embedded in the paintwork. The fluent brushwork seems to echo this tugging wind.

Claude Monet, *The Beach at Trouville,* **1870** *14¾ x 18 in (38 x 46 cm)*
This study was painted rapidly on the beach at Trouville. Built over a warm, pale gray ground, the work is striking in its immediacy and in the fluent brushwork. There is also much of the wet-in-wet work so characteristic of Monet, with fresh colors laid into one another.

Ken Howard, RA, *Blue and Gold Kimono,* 1991 *40 x 48 in (102 x 122 cm)*
The freshness of the brushwork in this scene gives a lively quality, although there is control in the painting style. The screen, for example, is carefully painted to give a loose, free impression. Broad planes of light and dark allow the artist to incorporate detail without overloading the composition. It is important to stress this idea of control in what comes across as a very spontaneous work.

The subtle pattern on this kimono is echoed in other areas of the painting.

This detail shows both the vigor and the control in the individual brushstrokes that create the pattern on the kimono.

Julian Schnabel, *The Geography Lesson,* 1980 *88 x 84 in (224 x 214cm)*
The buttery texture of oil on velvet in this work is heightened by impasted strokes of vivid color. The subject matter is perfectly matched by the painting style.

Bernard Dunstan, RA, *Piazza del Duomo, Orvieto,* c.1991 *14½ x 15¾ in (37 x 40 cm)*
This painting has an assurance of touch and economy, giving a relaxed quality and a real sense of space and light.

321

PAINTING IN LAYERS

IF YOU ARE NOT USED to building up a painting in layers, you should keep two things in mind. First, always wait until a paint layer is completely dry before overpainting it with another color, and second, add a drop or two more of your oil painting medium to your paint mixtures as you work up through the layers of color. This ensures that each layer is slightly more flexible than the one below, and is known as the "fat-over-lean" rule. Although there are many ways of painting in layers, one method is to sketch an image in diluted color and then paint in the broad areas of tone with a transparent or monochromatic technique. When this is dry, color can be added and paler tones worked in. Once these layers are dry, final applications of transparent glazes and opaque highlights can be added.

APPLYING A GLAZE

Transparent oil glazes should not simply be brushed on and left; they usually have to be manipulated with a brush on the support to give a uniformity of tone, even out the degree of color saturation, or reduce a thick glaze to a light stain. A blending brush, or a clean shaving brush, is good for dabbing and smoothing the glaze. When you mix a glaze, add a glazing or painting medium to the paint to make it more malleable. Once you have painted on the glaze, wait for a few moments so that some of the solvent in the painting medium can evaporate. Then use the shaving brush to manipulate the glaze and smooth away visible brushmarks. If you only need to glaze a small area, use a small round or flat soft hair brush instead.

1 *An underpainting in one color can be useful as it allows you to concentrate on form and tone first, rather than color.*

2 *Once the underpainting is dry, apply color over the different tones with a large bristle brush.*

3 *Smooth the glaze over the surface with a large, flat round brush, such as a shaving brush.*

Building up layers of color

A still life is a good subject to choose if you want to practice painting in layers, because you can leave the composition set up for as long as you need while you wait for individual layers of paint to dry. This study is built up over a colored ground to give the layers of color a subtle accent. A monochromatic underpainting helps to establish areas of light and dark before any colors are applied. Mix each glaze you use with a little oil painting medium.

1 ◄ Sketch the composition in with a thin mix of Burnt Umber and then use a small round bristle brush and a range of gray tones to build up a tonal picture of each object in this still life.

2 ▲ When the underpainting has dried, mix individual glazes of color and apply them with a large, flat, synthetic wash brush. If you prefer, use a new brush for every glaze so that you can retain the purity of each color.

3 ▶ When the first glazes are dry, mix a darker glaze of Permanent Red for the red stripes on the rug, adding a little more painting medium to increase the amount of oil in the next layer. Apply the deep transparent color with a medium-sized bristle brush, and as these areas of red are quite small, use a sable brush to work the glaze to a smooth finish.

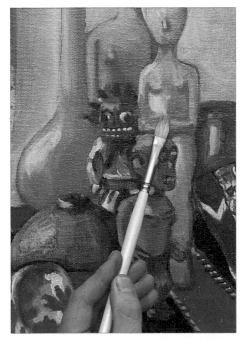

4 ◀ Add thin layers of strong color to each object using a medium-sized brush, such as a No.6 long filbert bristle. Dab the glaze gently with the round sable brush to manipulate the glaze and smooth away any uneven areas of paint. If paint builds up on the brush, wipe it off on a piece of absorbent tissue, or if you paint over any highlights, use the cloth to wipe away the unwanted paint.

5 ▲ Add a final glaze to the back wall with a large bristle brush to give a cooler, more shadowy effect. Use a clean, dry shaving brush to work the glaze in with short strokes.

Studio still life
This painting has been built up with layers of thin color. The colored ground provides a warm base for transparent glazes that are applied only after previous layers are thoroughly dry. Glazes over large areas are smoothed into a uniform tone with a shaving brush.

The tones on each object have been achieved with an underpainting.

Separate layers of transparent color together give a rich, luminous effect.

Ian McCaughrean

The large area of the back wall is glazed with cool color so that it appears to recede behind the still life.

Materials

No.1 round bristle brush

No.6 short filbert bristle brush

No.6 long flat bristle brush

1¼ in synthetic wash brush

Shaving brush

PAINTING IN STAGES

Preparatory sketch from life

THERE IS OFTEN an overlap of two or more techniques in any work. Although some paintings appear to have been painted directly from life, they may also have been built up with careful final stages to heighten the tone and effect of colors, or to increase the element of detail. The work below has all the hallmarks of a painting from life, although in fact it has been built up in a series of carefully planned stages. In this kind of transitional painting, it is usual to begin by blocking in major areas of tone and color, and then working into these with deeper glazes and more detail as the painting develops. The most important aspect of this process is that you add a new layer of paint only after the last layer is dry. A white ground retains the power and clarity of every color.

1 ▶ Make a light sketch of the composition in charcoal, working out the position of trees and plants. If the lines look too harsh, try brushing off the excess charcoal with a soft hair brush or a piece of doughy bread (*see* pp.304-305). Excess charcoal can muddy the paint if it is left lying on the surface of the canvas, so another way to protect the paint is to spray a surface coating of fixative over the charcoal outlines.

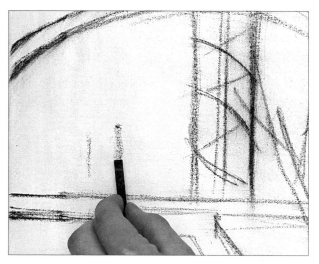

2 ▶ Block in the main areas of the painting with thin areas of pure, bright color using a large or medium-sized bristle brush. Leave these first layers to dry before adding new paint.

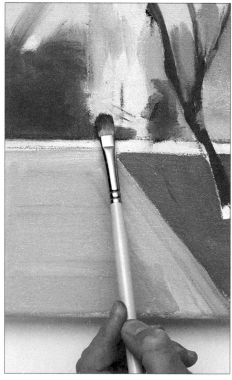

3 ▲ Once the first layers of thin paint are dry, deepen separate areas of color. Use a large synthetic wash brush to lay a thin, transparent glaze of Permanent Rose over the foreground area to deepen its tone. Mix a little oil painting medium into the Permanent Rose so that it can be manipulated more easily on the canvas. Use a clean, dry, soft hair brush to brush the glaze into a uniform consistency over the canvas.

4 ◀ Use a long filbert bristle brush to paint in branches and leaves. Use cool colors for areas in shadow and a transparent mix of Winsor Green for brighter details to create a sense of distance and capture the airy spaciousness of this conservatory.

5 ◀ Once the layers of paint are dry again, start adding in details of the foliage. This is time-consuming work, as the trees and leaves should be painted individually to create movement and depth in the painting. Emphasize bark on the tree trunks by painting cool blue shadows using a small synthetic or sable brush.

6 ▶ The ironwork across the roof and the path down the center hold the composition together, so paint them with strong, clean colors to create visual impact. Use a small flat brush to paint the gratings on the path, and a small round synthetic brush to heighten the smooth, metallic look of the ironwork beyond.

7 ▶ Finally, give the feeling of space by painting in small leaves with dabs of pale, cool blue paint over the iron arch, which should help to push it farther into the background. Darken areas in shadow if you need to increase the contrast of tones and colors that heighten the feeling of bright light in the painting.

The Palm House

The greenhouse atmosphere in this painting has been created using a white ground to keep the colors strong and retain a sense of immediacy. However, the paint has been built up in stages to increase the detailed look of the foliage and deepen the tone of transparent colors.

A white priming keeps colors strong and bright.

Touches of white paint give the impression of strong light shining through the roof.

Thick strokes of impasted color have been painted last to give texture and definition.

Thin glazes of transparent color deepen the tone of the foreground.

Ian McCaughrean

Materials

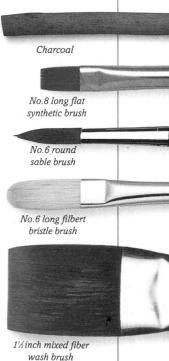

Charcoal

No.8 long flat synthetic brush

No.6 round sable brush

No.6 long filbert bristle brush

1½ inch mixed fiber wash brush

325

GALLERY OF PAINTING IN LAYERS

PAINTING IN LAYERS has been integral to the art of painting for hundreds of years, and some systematic methods have evolved. The key to this technique is that each layer of paint must be completely dry before more paint is applied. There are variations on this theme, ranging from refining a simple painting with highlights and shadows, to a more complex interweaving of transparent and opaque layers of paint to create sophisticated effects. Artists evolve their own methods of working, and the images here represent a variety of approaches.

Giovanni Moroni,
Portrait of a Widower with His Two Children, c.1565,
38½ x 49½ in (98 x 126 cm)
This painting has been layered in stages over a warm ground, and the depth of tone – so relevant to the meaning of the work – has been built up with transparent glazes. Bright pale tones are stacked up in opaque color to provide contrast with the background. A dramatic poignancy arises from the juxtaposition of pure, primary colors on the children's skirts with the widower's dark costume and background.

Shanti Thomas,
Fruit Stall, 26 x 30 in (66 x 76 cm)
This is an example of a work that gives a strong, direct, and immediate impression, but was in fact built up in stages. The painting relies on overlaid touches of transparent, semiopaque, and opaque paints in a patchwork of color to create contrasted areas of tone and rich surface effects.

Ray Smith,
Dr. McDonald,
36 x 27 in (91 x 69 cm)
Painted on a dark-toned background, the attention of this work focuses sharply on the bright, wrinkled face of the man. Dark areas have been worked up with transparent glazes and highlights with opaque color.

El Greco, ***Vision of St. John,*** **1610-14**
87½ x 76¼ in (222 x 194 cm)
El Greco may have modeled his drapery while the transparent glazes were still wet, reversing established practices and proving that there are no hard and fast rules in painting.

Sue Sareen,
Young Girl With a Cat, *36 x 28 in (91 x 71 cm)*
This painting of the artist's daughter was developed indirectly in a few simple stages. The composition was both painted from life, and worked on from four separate photographs. The image was first drawn in charcoal and then sketched on top in Burnt Umber. Colors were then blocked in thinly and left to dry. The painting was finished two weeks later when the colors were built up in a more solid application.

A large area of Cadmium Red paint on the open door is echoed in other areas of the painting. This detail shows light strokes of Cadmium Red illuminating the girl's hair.

Touches of Cerulean Blue provide cool notes throughout the painting and offset the large areas of red.

327

EXPERIMENTAL TECHNIQUES

ARTISTS HAVE ALWAYS EXPERIMENTED with different ways of working with oil paint. One traditional technique is sgraffito, in which one color is laid over another layer of dry color and then scratched through with a sharp instrument so that the color beneath is revealed as an image or pattern. Another technique is to paint or splash thick colors onto a canvas or board, lay a sheet of thin, hard paper or plastic over the top, lift some of the paint off, and use the remaining image for special textural or surreal effects. Nowadays, there are also new materials developed by manufacturers. A relatively recent product is the oil stick, which is basically oil paint in stick form. This allows you to draw with the oil paint as though it were a pastel or a piece of charcoal. It has a smooth, creamy feel and it is possible to work it into a wet color and still retain the color of the stroke you are making.

Sgraffito

Sgraffito is an old method of drawing into a layer of wet paint to produce a line drawing of an image or a detail. When you scratch through the layer of wet paint you should reveal a new color underneath, whether it is another layer of dried paint, or the canvas or board itself. Here, a thick layer of blue paint has been applied with a painting knife, and the blade of the knife then used as the drawing instrument. You can use all kinds of tools for this technique; a screwdriver, for instance, will give a line similar to that made by drawing with a carpenter's pencil. Many artists whittle the end of an old paintbrush for sgraffito effects as the softer wood is less likely to damage the canvas.

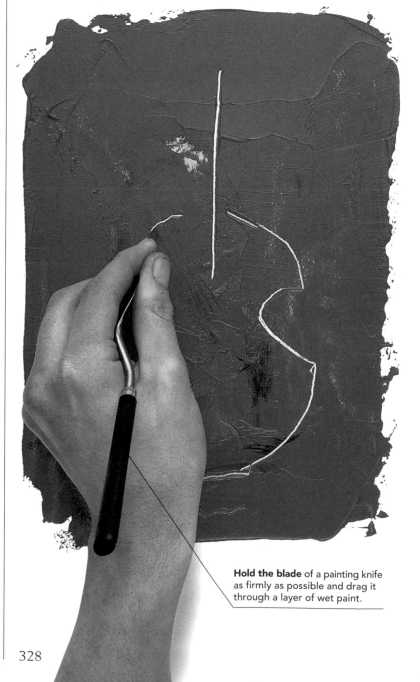

Hold the blade of a painting knife as firmly as possible and drag it through a layer of wet paint.

OIL STICKS

Oil sticks are a type of oil paint blended with waxes and applied directly onto the canvas. You can dispense with brushes entirely, modifying colors with a piece of cloth or a finger. Oil sticks are unlike other drawing materials in that they are extremely creamy in texture. They are good for working wet-in-wet, so you can apply one wet color over another without making a muddy mixture. In this study of a carnival mask, the background has been rubbed with a cloth dipped in turpentine and the other colors left unmodified.

Use a tape with a low tack adhesive, such as masking tape or drafting tape.

Masking tape
If you want to paint a very straight edge, use masking tape. Ensure that the color you lay the tape onto is dry, and that the tape is not too strong. Pull it away carefully, or it may pull off the paint beneath it.

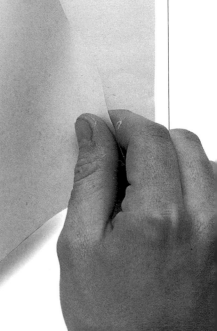

Modifying a painted surface
Modify the surface of an oil painting if you want to remove excess color or adapt the overall effect. One method, which is also a form of monoprinting, is to lay a sheet of paper over an area of paint, rub it gently with your hand, and pull it off slowly. Use a damp, absorbent paper if you want to remove plenty of paint.

If you want to make a monoprint, paint an image on a slab of glass and take a print of it using absorbent paper.

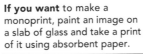

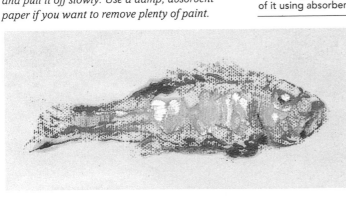

VARNISHING & FRAMING

A FILM OF VARNISH PROTECTS an oil work from atmospheric pollution and abrasion. A gloss varnish can also bring out the colors in a work, giving them a greater saturation and depth, and so heightening the impact of the picture. A varnish is actually a solution of resin in a solvent, and the resin forms a hard but flexible protective film after the solvent has evaporated.

A frame can have a significant impact on a work, giving it a focus that can either detract from its appearance, or allow it to be seen at its best. You should choose a frame with care and decide whether you make it yourself or have it made professionally; the appearance of a painting can easily be ruined by a badly made frame with its corners out of alignment.

Choosing a frame
A frame can alter the look of a painting quite significantly, so try to choose from a wide selection of frame samples.

Materials

Cotton ball

Varnish

Flat bristle brush

Tape measure

Varnishing

A painting should be completely dry before varnishing, so it is advisable to leave it for about three months. You can make an acceptable varnish by dissolving dammar resin in turpentine, but most artists buy a good quality dammar varnish for a high gloss look, or ketone varnish for a less yellowing effect. The painting must also be free from dust, dirt, and grease, which can cause the varnish to form a blotchy surface. Make sure the room you choose to work in is well ventilated and warm.

1 ▲ Lay your dry painting on a flat surface and clean it with a cotton ball moistened with saliva – an excellent cleaning agent. This should ensure that the painting is completely clear of dust and grease.

2 ◀ Apply a coat of varnish with a flat bristle brush (you can buy special varnishing brushes from artists' suppliers), making parallel strokes in one direction across the painting. When the first layer of varnish is dry, apply a second coat with the same varnishing brush, working at right angles to the first coat. This produces a fine, even film of varnish.

Framing

It can be hard to produce a well-made frame, so if you feel at all unsure about making your own, use a professional framemaker. Choose a frame that best suits the style of your painting. If the work is bright and vigorously painted, choose a bold, simple frame.

1 ◀ Measure the height and width of the painting with a tape measure. You should be as precise as possible so that the frame can then be cut to fit the painting exactly.

Materials

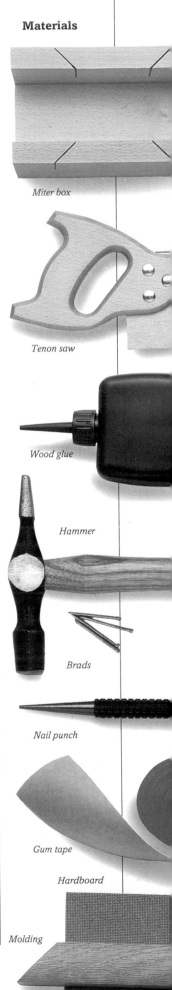

Miter box

Tenon saw

Wood glue

Hammer

Brads

Nail punch

Gum tape

Hardboard

Molding

2 ▶ The measurements of the painting form the inside lengths of the frame, so measure off the correct height and width on four pieces of molding and cut 45-degree angles at either end. You can use a special miter cutter, but this is an expensive piece of equipment, so a simple miter box is a good alternative (*right*). Fit a tenon saw into the prepared grooves of the miter box and cut the required angle.

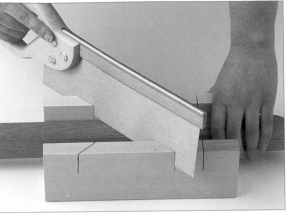

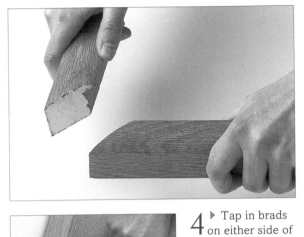

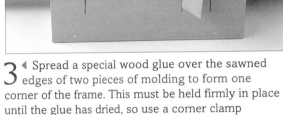

3 ◀ Spread a special wood glue over the sawned edges of two pieces of molding to form one corner of the frame. This must be held firmly in place until the glue has dried, so use a corner clamp to hold the pieces of wood in a rigid position.

4 ▶ Tap in brads on either side of the corner with a hammer, and then drive the brads right into the wood using a nail punch.

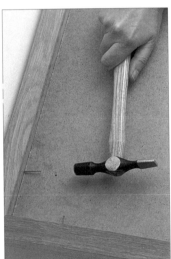

6 ◀ Finally, seal the back of the frame and cover all the brads using gum tape around the edges.

5 ▲ Once all four corners have been secured, place the painting in the frame, cut out a piece of hardboard the same size as the painting, and slot it in the back. Drive in some more brads to tighten the board.

Changing the look of a painting

This work is shown with two different moldings to illustrate how a frame changes the shape and look of a painting. Choose certain colors or textures to enhance a painting. Avoid brightly colored frames for subtle, low-key paintings.

AN INTRODUCTION TO ACRYLICS

Acrylics	334	Light, Shade, and Tone	362
History of Acrylics	336	Gallery of Composition	364
		Using Opaque Acrylic	366
MATERIALS		Opaque Portrait	368
Acrylic Paints	338	Transparent Techniques	370
Selecting Your Colors	340	Working with Washes	372
Using Colors	342	Gallery of Painting Styles	374
Color Gallery	344	Dry-brush and Scumbling	376
Brushes	346	Blending	378
Other Painting Tools	348	Glazing	380
Supports – Paper	350	The Alla Prima Approach	382
Boards and Canvases	352	Alla Prima Painting	384
Gallery of Supports		Combining Techniques	386
and Grounds	354	Gallery of Techniques	388
		Experimenting with Acrylics	390
TECHNIQUES		Exploring New Ideas	392
Ways of Working with		Gallery of Experimental	
Acrylics	356	Approaches	394
Composing Your Image	358	Presenting Your Work	396
Transferring Your Image	360		

ACRYLICS

ACRYLIC PAINT is a relative newcomer to the world of painting media. While oils have been in use for centuries, acrylics have only been available in recent decades. But they are an important addition to the repertoire of painting materials because their flexibility makes them suitable for a wide range of techniques – as the images on these pages show. Depending on how much acrylics are diluted with water, they can be used either opaquely or in a transparent watercolor style.

Thin washes of acrylic allow a textured painting surface to show through and add interest to the image

Opaque acrylic is ideal for even, flat coverage, or for much thicker effects, with highly visible brushwork. Interesting paintings can be built up easily and quickly with opaque acrylic. Because the paint takes so little time to dry, you can cover your painting surface rapidly, and any overpainting – perhaps to correct mistakes – will obscure layers underneath. If opaque and transparent methods are combined within a painting, you can incorporate the kinds of scumbles, glazes, and rich, thick impasto normally associated with oils, while acrylics are also uniquely suited to a number of much less conventional approaches.

Opaque acrylic paint creates vivid and saturated colors

Using transparent washes

Thinned acrylic washes can be applied wet-in-wet or used in many of the other methods that are common to watercolor painting. Acrylics, however, have an important advantage over watercolors. Once acrylics are dry (and they dry very quickly), they are insoluble, which means that they can be overpainted readily without disturbing the dried paint layer

Transparent washes of superimposed color produce a delicate watercolor effect

Mixing transparent washes and opaque techniques in one painting will give a creative depth and texture to your work

underneath. Try exploiting this fully by superimposing a large number of washes to create resonant color effects. Watercolor paints, however, are also associated with various ways of lifting color off the painting surface. These methods are inappropriate to the use of thinned acrylic once it has dried. Acrylics dry so rapidly that if you want to modify the color while it is wet, you must get used to working quickly.

Advantages of acrylics

One of the main advantages of acrylics is that they are largely water-based. Apart from making it easy to thin the paint, this also means that there are none of the toxicity problems linked with the kinds of solvents – such as white spirit or distilled turpentine – used with oil paints. Another plus for acrylics is that the polymer emulsions binding the pigments form very stable films when the paint dries. Acrylic film is free from the kinds of chemical changes that can take place with the more traditional painting media.

The consistency of thick acrylic lends itself well to thick, energetic impasto work

Preserving color

The only slight disadvantage with the dried acrylic film is that it is relatively soft, especially at room temperature. This can mean that acrylics attract dirt, which may become integrated into the paint film, changing the appearance of the colors so that they lose their brightness. However, this is usually a problem only when you are making your own paint and add very little pigment to an acrylic emulsion – although it can also occur if you use an acrylic medium with a small amount of pigment. You should have few problems with most of the ready-made acrylic paints that are currently available from art supply stores (*see* pp.338-339).

Acrylics are well suited to a highly experimental approach – such as this lively combination of free painting and printing techniques

335

HISTORY OF ACRYLICS

THE WIDE AND varied use of acrylics by artists in the latter part of the twentieth century shows the huge potential of the medium very clearly. From the early days of discovery and experimentation in the U.S.A. to its far more widespread use today, acrylic has become a universally accepted painting medium. Its versatility can be seen in the large and expressive abstracts by pioneers such as Morris Louis *(1912–1962)*; in the images of 1960s Pop Art and the early figurative work of David Hockney *(b. 1937)*; and in the recent, more psychological, tableaux of Paula Rego *(b. 1935)*.

ACRYLIC RESINS – originally formulated in Germany in the early 1900s – were developed in the U.S.A. during the late 1920s by the company Röhm and Haas. The discovery of a way of dissolving resins in organic solvents led to the development of an early oil-compatible form of acrylic paint.

A new medium

By the late 1940s, these early acrylics were commercially available in the U.S.A., where artists such as Helen Frankenthaler *(b. 1928)* and Morris Louis began to work with them. In the latter half of the 1950s, the water-based emulsions that we know today emerged. American artist Frank Stella *(b. 1936)* started using acrylics to explore the relationship between the canvas and marks made upon it. He moved from monochromatic work to richly colored creations.

The medium was taken up in Britain in the 1960s, notably by David Hockney, Mark Lancaster *(b. 1938)*, Richard Smith *(b. 1931)*, Bridget Riley *(b. 1931)*, and Leonard Rosoman *(b. 1912; see p.345)*.

Acrylics and Pop Art

In the 1960s, Roy Lichtenstein *(b. 1923)* and Andy Warhol *(1928–1987)* pioneered the American Pop Art movement, which related fine art to popular culture. Acrylic lent itself to the hard-edged, flat images that expressed modern life so effectively.

Morris Louis, *No. 182,* 1961 *82 x 33 in (208 x 84 cm) From 1954 until his death in 1962, Louis developed a distinctive acrylics style. Influenced by the drip paintings of Jackson Pollock (1912–1956) and by Frankenthaler's staining methods, Louis thinned acrylic with solvents and poured it onto unprimed cotton. The paint ran down the canvas, staining it with thin veils of color.*

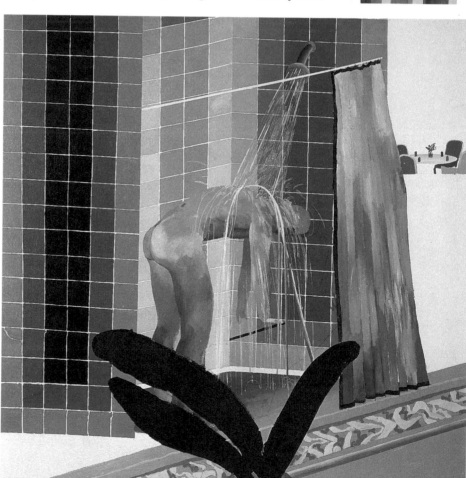

David Hockney, *Man in Shower in Beverley Hills,* 1964 *66 x 66 in (167 x 167 cm) Hockney worked with acrylics intensively for around a decade from the early 1960s, when he* moved to California. His works from that time contrast thin, flat areas of opaque color with painterly brushwork. Here, bright colors and geometric tiles provide an almost diagrammatic setting for a modern interpretation of the nude.

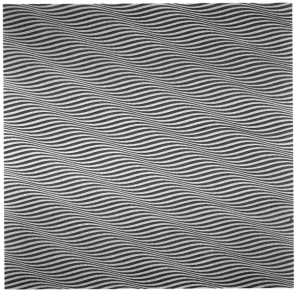

Andy Warhol, *Do-it-Yourself Landscape*, 1962 *70 x 54 in (178 x 137 cm)*
This bright, hard-edged effect was a trademark of Pop Artists such as Andy Warhol, and is particularly suited to acrylics. Employing the painting-by-numbers approach used in children's painting sets, Warhol asks questions about the decisions that artists make when creating their paintings.

Bridget Riley, *Cataracts III*, 1967
88 x 87 in (224 x 221 cm)
Riley made her name in the 1960s with her "Op Art" works, which explore surface illusionism. Working against the flat format of the canvas, she creates flowing, vibrating images. The blue wave moving across this work splits to reveal a growing band of red – the central powerhouse of the work.

Photo-realist painting

During the latter half of the 1960s and into the 1970s Americans Richard Estes *(b. 1936)* and Chuck Close *(b. 1940; see* p.388), and British artist Malcolm Morley *(b. 1931)* made acrylic works based closely on photographs. Close's huge portraits and Estes' street scenes may bear an uncanny resemblance to photographs, but the spectator becomes more actively engaged with a crafted, painted image.

The late 1970s and early 1980s saw a return to a more expressive and personal style. K.H. Hödicke *(b. 1938)* made direct works confronting the issues of recent

German history. In the U.S.A., Jim Nutt *(b. 1938)* was exploring a uniquely personal vision, and British painter Alan Charlton *(b. 1948)* found that acrylic gave his monochromatic works a flawless, matte surface.

Modern movements

The 1990s have seen a move toward more figurative paintings dealing with issues of personal, public, and artistic identity – such as the recent works by Paula Rego. There has also been a resurgence of the type of abstract forms explored by Frankenthaler in the 1950s – which she continues to evolve today.

Paula Rego, *The Dance*, 1988 *84 x 108 in (213 x 274 cm)*
The Dance *shows Rego's interest in children's fantasies and fears. This "dance of life" may spring from memories of her childhood in Portugal, showing a view over the Atlantic from her family's house on the coast outside Lisbon. The moon's cool blue light casts shadows that create a sinister undercurrent.*

ACRYLIC PAINTS

Paints on the market
Acrylics are available in tubes, jars, and tubs. They are also sold in bottles, for use with airbrushes.

ACRYLIC PAINTS REPRESENT A SIGNIFICANT advance in paint technology in this century, and are constantly improving as the medium is developed. They are water-soluble, which means that there are none of the health hazards associated with the volatile solvents used with oil paints, yet they can be used in many of the same techniques. When diluted with a lot of water, acrylics produce an effect strikingly like that of watercolor paints, yet they also have their own unique characteristics. Acrylic paints vary in consistency, depending on the manufacturer – some are flowing and liquid; others are more viscous.

WHILE OIL PAINT IS pigment bound in a drying oil, acrylic paint consists of pigment bound in an acrylic polymer or copolymer emulsion. Acrylic polymers are synthetic resins made from chemicals called monomers. The monomers are put through a polymerization process, which creates a synthetic resin with strong elastic properties. This resin is made into an emulsion consisting of particles of polymer suspended in water. The emulsion used in acrylics is normally a copolymer.

This incorporates mixed polymers specially chosen for their ability to form a good, fairly hard film. Acrylic paints dry on the painting surface – by evaporation of the water in the emulsion – to form an inert film that is water-resistant.

You can make a perfectly good oil paint by simply grinding a pigment with a drying oil, but it is more difficult to make a really reliable acrylic paint by mixing pigment with acrylic emulsion (both of which are commercially available). Ready-made paints tend to be preferable because

Thick acrylic – an effective glue

Extruded strip of dried paint

Using acrylic paint opaquely
You can use all acrylics opaquely, provided they are applied thickly – either straight out of the container or with very little water added – or mixed with white. This is important when painting on a toned ground.

Opaque paint

Note how acrylic dries to a darker color

Plastic properties
When it dries, acrylic paint takes on the tough and malleable quality of plastic. It is therefore unique among painting media because it can be extruded, knotted, or even sculpted in three dimensions.

Acrylic paint as glue
Acrylic is actually a fairly fast-drying type of glue. Because of this, it works well in collage techniques with light materials such as cardboard, provided the paint is used thickly.

they contain a specially formulated balance of additives that preserve the paint, give it body, stability, and a good consistency, and prevent it from foaming or freezing in transit.

PVA paints

In some schools, teachers make paints similar to acrylics by adding a PVA medium to a mixture of water and powdered color. PVA is another type of resin – polyvinyl acetate. Commercially available PVA paints are similar to acrylic paints, but they tend to be inconsistent in quality, sometimes producing a brittle paint film. However, there are several very high-quality makes.

Acrylic mediums and retarders

Acrylic mediums are substances that can be added to paint to adjust its consistency for special effects such as glazing or impasto, or to make it glossier or more matte. Retarder can be added to slow down the paint's drying time and keep it workable – useful for techniques like blending.

Paint mixed with texture paste

Paint mixed with gel medium and used thickly and thinly

***Above*: Paint with texture paste**
You can create highly textured effects with thick, impasted paint, by mixing special pastes into your acrylics. One very coarse paste even contains pumice.

***Left*: Paint with gel medium**
Gel medium offers you a choice of effects. A lot of gel with a little paint added can create a translucent impasto. Scraped or painted thinly across a surface, gel mixed with paint produces a transparent glaze.

Airbrushed acrylic paint

Well-diluted paint

Watered-down acrylic paint

Well-diluted acrylic can be used as an equivalent to watercolor. It has the advantage of drying insolubly, so that additional layers of color do not dissolve lower layers. Diluted acrylic also works well in an airbrush.

STORING PAINT

If you are mixing a color that you know you will need more of later, it makes sense to make up a large batch of it. Keep the mix in an airtight, screw-top jar, as acrylics dry quickly when exposed to air.

SELECTING YOUR COLORS

BECAUSE ACRYLICS are relatively new, paint manufacturers have been able to use the best new pigments, along with the reliable traditional ones. Lightfastness – a pigment's ability to withstand fading – is important. Good colors include Quinacridone violets and reds; Phthalo blues and greens; Cadmium reds and yellows (*see* p.468) and Azo Yellow; the earth colors – Ochres and Siennas; and Titanium

White. Metallic colors are also available. To understand how colors work together to create different effects, you should be aware of basic color theory. The three primary paint colors are red, yellow, and blue, and these can be set out, with related colors in between, in the form of a color wheel.

COMPLEMENTARY COLORS are those colors of maximum contrast opposite each other on the wheel. The complementary of each of the three primaries is the color you get by mixing the other two. So, the complementary of red is green (a mix of yellow and blue); the complementary of yellow is violet (red and blue); while that of blue is orange (yellow and red).

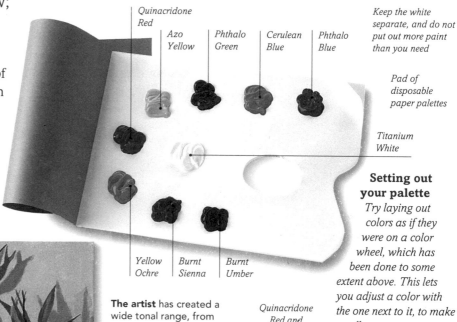

Quinacridone Red

Azo Yellow — Phthalo Green — Cerulean Blue — Phthalo Blue

Keep the white separate, and do not put out more paint than you need

Pad of disposable paper palettes

Titanium White

Yellow Ochre — Burnt Sienna — Burnt Umber

Setting out your palette
Try laying out colors as if they were on a color wheel, which has been done to some extent above. This lets you adjust a color with the one next to it, to make a yellow greener or more orange for example.

Titanium White

Cadmium Yellow

Quinacridone Red

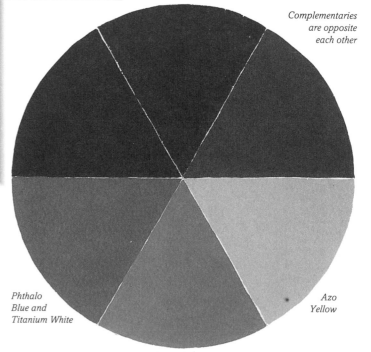

Phthalo Blue

The artist has created a wide tonal range, from dark to light, within a bold composition.

Quinacridone Red and Titanium White

Complementaries are opposite each other

Limiting your palette
Experiment with limiting your palette. This will give you the invaluable experience of mixing color and tone using just a few basic colors. The vase of flowers shown above has been painted using just the three primaries and white. The work is high in key, with opaque paint applied in bright, pure color mixes.

The color wheel
This opaquely painted color wheel shows the three primaries and the three secondaries – violet, orange, and green – obtained by mixing two primaries. The specific red and blue paints used here are naturally transparent, and so a little white was added to make them opaque. Using these fairly pure paint colors, you could mix almost any hue.

Phthalo Blue and Titanium White

Azo Yellow

Placing your colors

Every color affects the appearance of the color next to it in a painting. If you look hard at an area of strong color, and then look away, you see the complementary of the color you have been looking at. This can affect the color of whatever you look at next. So, an area of bright yellow may appear greenish after looking hard at orange-red, because you are carrying the blue after-image of the orange-red. This optical effect is known as "color irradiation," and is well worth considering when you are painting.

Bold red and green

Use complementary colors to interact with each other, producing bright contrasts and an overall color balance in your work. In this painting, the exotic red flower stands out very effectively against the lush green of the foliage.

Subtle effects

This shows how washing one complementary over another subdues the colors, as combining complementaries produces gray or black. Green washes on the red petals create rich shadows, while red touches have deepened the color of the leaves.

Adjacent colors

This afterimage effect means that if we place two complementaries right next to each other, one will reinforce the intensity of the other. Aim for balance – if a painting is predominantly blue, only a few touches of orange are needed to intensify our experience of the blue.

The term "adjacent colors" also refers to colors that are next to each other on the wheel. Use these adjacents to produce the subtle harmonies shown below.

Transparent color wheel

This wheel also shows the primaries and complementaries, but painted in thin acrylic washes. The mixes that tend to the adjacent color on each side of a wheel segment are in the outer circle. Using thin acrylic allows you to create hues not just by physically mixing colors, but by washing one color over a dried wash of another.

Red and violet

Here, a cool red is deepened in places by a further wash of the same color. The adjacent color, violet, is used for deeper shadows by washing it over the red.

Blue and violet

Delicate washes of adjacent blues and violets harmonize this image. Good wash effects rely on the luminosity of the support. Use high-quality white paper or white priming.

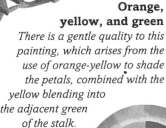

Orange, yellow, and green

There is a gentle quality to this painting, which arises from the use of orange-yellow to shade the petals, combined with the yellow blending into the adjacent green of the stalk.

USING COLORS

APPRECIATING HOW COLOR works the best in a painting – particularly in your own painting – is something that you ultimately learn by trial and error, and by looking at the work of other artists. Ask yourself certain questions about the colors you use. Is the color key appropriate for the atmosphere or mood that you want to evoke? A work can be high-key, with clean, bright primary and secondary colors used at full strength, or it may be low-key, incorporating a more subdued range of neutral tones. Mood is also established by the "temperature" of colors – if a work is mainly orange and red, it will have a different atmosphere than one painted in cool colors such as blue or green.

A GOOD OVERALL COLOR balance is essential. One important aspect of colors used next to each other in a painting is the intensity of those colors. Where you are using a particularly intense or saturated color, you may need only a small touch of it in a much larger

Above: Altering the color balance
The three paintings on this page show how the mood of a work can be altered. This first picture is basically low-key. A soft, natural light source falls from the right onto the objects. These images are created with washes of transparent acrylic paint; later changes have been superimposed with opaque paint. Throughout the painting, the colors are harmonized within a relatively subdued range of tones.

Right: Adding life
The artist has decided that he wants to start brightening the image. Changing to overhead artificial lighting gives a harsher, more even light. He has added livelier reds, such as Cadmium Red, to the pepper, lighter greens to the leeks and pears, and light shadows of Ultramarine Blue mixed with white. The striped cloth has become a white one.

area of another less intense color to achieve a good balance between the two.

We all tend to perceive some kind of balance of colors in whatever subject we choose to paint. The more we paint, the clearer it becomes that we are imitating a sense of order that we perceive in the

Left: The final image
Every tone in the painting has been livened up. Dark tones in the foreground and background of the table have been overpainted with mixes of Yellow Ochre and Cadmium Yellow and Yellow Ochre and Burnt Sienna respectively. The aubergine has been brightened by working light transparent washes into the dark areas. Yellow stripes added to the white cloth lift the whole composition.

world around us. This means that we must learn to adjust the tones and colors that we use so that we can achieve a similar color balance in our paintings.

Making adjustments

The effect of colors on each other runs through the whole course of painting, and applies to tiny paint particles just as much as it does to large areas of color. Making the slightest adjustment to a color in one part of a work can affect the whole composition – appropriate changes must be made elsewhere.

Using colors to show recession

In this landscape painting, a warm, bright yellow has been used on the fields in the foreground. Our eyes move naturally from this vivid foreground back through the cooler shades as the fields gradually recede into the hazy purple-blue used to indicate the distant horizon.

Bringing up the foreground

Bright colors tend to come forward in a painting. Here, touches of strong, bright red – to indicate poppies in the field – have been used to emphasize the foreground. Just a small amount of a bright color such as red can totally alter the perspective emphasis of a painting.

Creating specific effects

The warmth or coolness of a color affects our perception of perspective and distance in a painting. Warm colors appear to advance, and cool colors recede. Fields that are shown yellow-green in the foreground of a painting should be blue-green as they recede. This is because of the influence of aerial perspective – an effect of nature where objects in the distance take on a pale blue hue.

High-key colors

The high-key reds, oranges, and yellows that dominate this work create a light, sunny mood. Shadows are painted in light blue, rather than in black or gray. Sparkling reflections have been created either with opaque white paint, or by leaving areas of the surface of the white paper exposed.

Low-key colors

The same subject assumes a completely different, and very somber, air when painted in a low-key range of colors. Dark blues, greens, purples, and browns – colors that tend to recede – seem to push the objects farther away from us than in the high-key version.

COLOR GALLERY

COLOR IS THE KEY to establishing the mood or atmosphere of a painting. It can be high-key, in bright, saturated colors, or low-key, in subdued tones. It can rely on the harmony and balance that is set up by using colors that are adjacent to each other on the color wheel, such as reds, oranges, or yellows, or it can rely on contrasts set up between complementary colors, such as violet and yellow, for its balance. While surrounding a color with a very dark tone makes it glow, surrounding it with white makes it appear deeper in tone. Above all, it is the choice and use of color that sets the mood or tone of a painting.

John Hoyland, ARA,
Tiger Mirror, **1990**
60 x 60 in (152 x 152 cm)
A color can be made to glow and sing by being enclosed in a dark gray or black. This has the effect of isolating the color and allowing it to be perceived in all its purity. In the recent past, artists such as Léger and Rouault have exploited this technique, and long before that, such an effect could be seen in the great medieval stained glass windows. John Hoyland's snaking, dripping brushstroke in two-tone orange-red and crimson pink has a glowing lusciousness against the dark ground. The color of Tiger Mirror's *ground has the effect of pushing the brushstroke forward and adding to the immediacy of the work.*

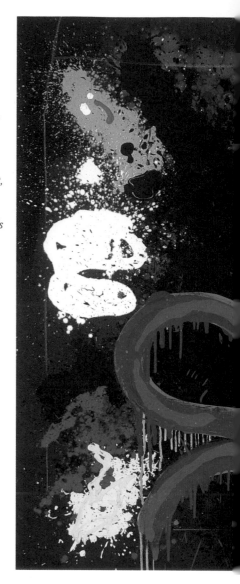

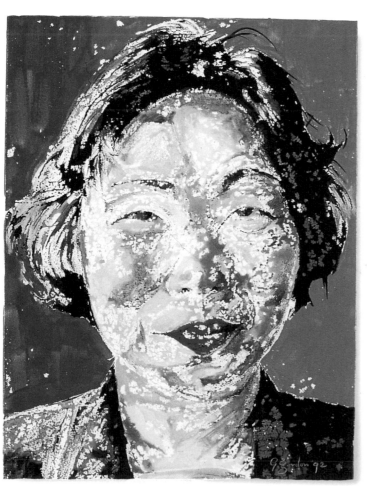

Gregory Gordon,
Portrait of the Artist's Mother-in-Law
24 x 18 in (61 x 46 cm)
Gordon's unconventional use of color lends an exuberant strength to this lively portrait. The multicolored speckled surface seems to make the image vibrate and shift slightly as we continue to look at it, bringing the subject alive. It is as though colored lights were playing in front of our eyes.

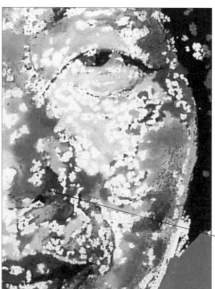

Examination of any one area of the face shows how many different colors – mainly primaries and secondaries – have been used to convey the flesh tones. Although our eyes tend to merge these different colors optically, this process is helped by the fact that the artist has worked with diluted paint, allowing colors to blend and fuse.

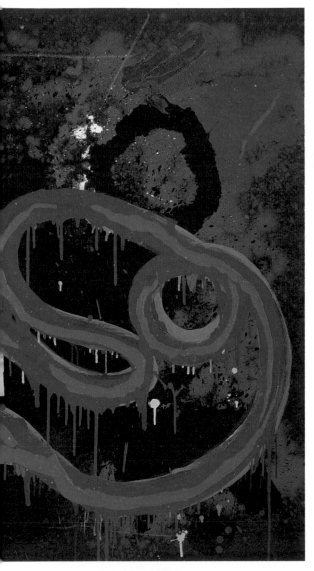

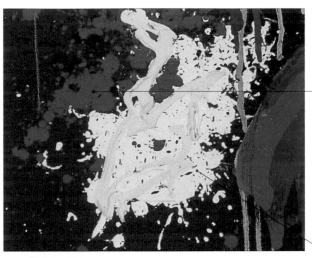

Above: **Leonard Rosoman, RA,**
The Painter Richard Eurich in His
Studio, **1988** *48 x 66 in (122 x 168 cm)*

Left: **Leonard Rosoman, RA,**
Brian and Kathleen, Elk River,
Maryland, **1990** *53 x 71 in (135 x 180 cm)*
These two portraits by Leonard Rosoman are stylistically similar but very different in their use of color, showing how the choice of key can radically affect our perception of a picture. The portrait of the painter Richard Eurich is predominantly low-key, and here Rosoman has deliberately subdued his palette to evoke the quiet atmosphere of the room and the gentle character of the sitter. The use of color reinforces the feeling of calm reflection that permeates the mood of the work. In contrast, in the double portrait, the artist has chosen a deliberately high-key approach to color. The sun shines into this large, airy room and the characters are relaxed, the bright saturated yellows and greens helping to create a mood of light and celebration.

BRUSHES

PAINTBRUSHES ARE MADE either with stiff or soft hairs. The natural hairs that are usually used are bristle for stiff brushes, and sable for softer ones. Both bristle and soft paintbrushes are also available made from synthetic fibers, and synthetic brushes are very commonly used for painting in acrylics.

Ferrule

Hairs

Toe (tip)

WHEN BUYING YOUR PAINTBRUSHES, you should bear in mind that synthetic brushes are a less expensive option – and they are perfectly adequate for all types of acrylic work. Bristle brushes are generally used for large-scale work and for broad painting techniques. Soft brushes are ideal for painting in thin washes, for watercolor-type techniques, for very small-scale work, and for achieving various other specific effects.

There are two main brush shapes: flat – in which the ferrule has been flattened – and round. Either of these can be made with long or short hairs. Another brush type, called a filbert, has a round head with a flattened ferrule, and so is effectively two brushes in one. It can be used either as a flat brush, for applying broad areas of color, or for more precise techniques, using its thin edge.

Other brushes

You can experiment with other types of brush to achieve a range of effects. For example, an ordinary shaving brush is ideal for working with thinned-down paint.

You may find that you also need a varnishing brush. This thin and flat long-haired brush is perfect for laying a smooth, thin coat of varnish over finished works (although varnishing acrylics is a controversial subject; *see* p.396).

It is essential that brushes be kept clean. Acrylics dry rapidly and are water-resistant when dry. Never leave a brush with paint on it for more than a few minutes. Always rinse a brush well after use, and clean it thoroughly at the end of a session. Never use hot water – this can harden acrylic paint on the brush. It may also expand the ferrule, causing the hairs to fall out.

BRUSH CARE

Wash your brush thoroughly at the end of a session, as shown here. Synthetic brushes are especially prone to the build-up of paint where the hairs join the ferrule, leaving the hairs splayed out and the brush ruined *(below)*.

1 *Dip the brush in a jar of cold water to loosen the paint. (Remember that hot water could damage your brush.)*

2 *Use a cloth to wipe off any excess paint. You may need to rinse the brush again in the jar or under the tap.*

3 *Rub the brush over a bar of household soap. Work up a lather in the palm of your hand. Rinse well under the cold tap.*

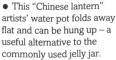

● *This "Chinese lantern" artists' water pot folds away flat and can be hung up – a useful alternative to the commonly used jelly jar.*

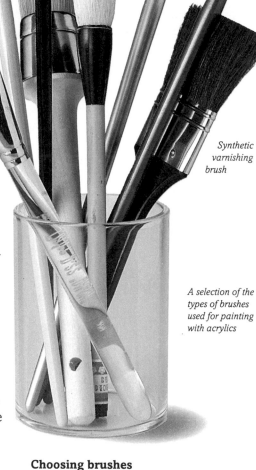

Bristle *Sable* *General-purpose brush* *Synthetic bristle* *Synthetic sable* *Japanese brush*

Sable wash brush

Synthetic varnishing brush

A selection of the types of brushes used for painting with acrylics

Choosing brushes

Experiment with different brushes to see the variety of effects that can be achieved. For example, the soft Japanese brush shown above is ideal for applying transparent washes.

Small round sable

The spring in the pointed toe of a small, round, long-haired sable lets you paint precise strokes with an easy fluency.

No.3 round sable

Larger round soft-hair brush

Larger soft round brushes have a remarkable paint-carrying capacity. Use them to make bold strokes, or to lay thin washes.

No.8 round soft synthetic

Flat soft-hair brush

Noted for their characteristically chunky, rectangular strokes, soft flats are also useful for making long, thin strokes with the edge of the brush.

No.8 flat soft synthetic

Filbert bristle brush

The filbert bristle is one of the most versatile brush shapes, with the flat/round side capable of this kind of rich stroke, and the edge suited to more careful work.

No.5 bristle

Round bristle brush

The round bristle carries a lot of paint and is a good brush to use for thick, impasted brushwork. The toe is capable of more delicate manipulations when the paint is thinned down a little.

No.5 round bristle

Flat bristle brush

Typical brushstrokes produced with a flat bristle are similar to those made with a soft flat, except that paint can be used much more thickly with the stiffer brush.

No.5 flat bristle

Sable wash brush

The flat, "one-stroke" brush is used to lay thin washes over a large area. Have the paper on a slight slope, so that each new stroke picks up paint that gathers on the lower edge of the preceding one.

1in sable wash brush

General-purpose bristle brush

This bristle brush is ideal for painting on a large scale, or for covering sizable areas of the canvas. It can also be used for applying primer. Much larger brushes, such as this, require a great deal more cleaning than smaller ones.

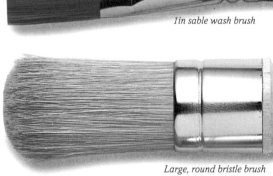

Large, round bristle brush

SPECIAL BRUSHES

There are various special brushes that are used to modify or apply paint in a particular way. Some are specifically made for this purpose, such as the fan blender and stencil brush. However, other brushes can be equally useful, for example the bristle shaving brush shown here, or a "stipple" decorating brush.

Bristle fan blender

Bristle stenciling brush

Fan blender
The fan blender is often used with oils for the delicate blending of adjoining areas of color, and large areas can be worked at one time. With faster-drying acrylics, you have to work on smaller areas while the strokes are still wet.

Stencil brush
Stencil brushes have short, stubby bristles and a flat end, so that paint can be dabbed straight down onto the surface through the stencil.

Shaving brush
A shaving brush is a handy tool for manipulating glazes of transparent paint. Is is equally valuable for rapidly working over thin, freely applied areas of wet acrylic. This can even out the tone of a transparent color, for example, leaving a uniform stain over a particular area.

Shaving brush

OTHER PAINTING TOOLS

Y OU CAN WORK OR MANIPULATE acrylic paint with a wide range of tools other than brushes. Some of these tools, such as painting knives, are traditionally associated with oil painting but work equally well with acrylics; others, such as airbrushes and plastic scrapers, are relatively new to acrylics. Use sponges to lay washes and create texture – just as in watercolor painting.

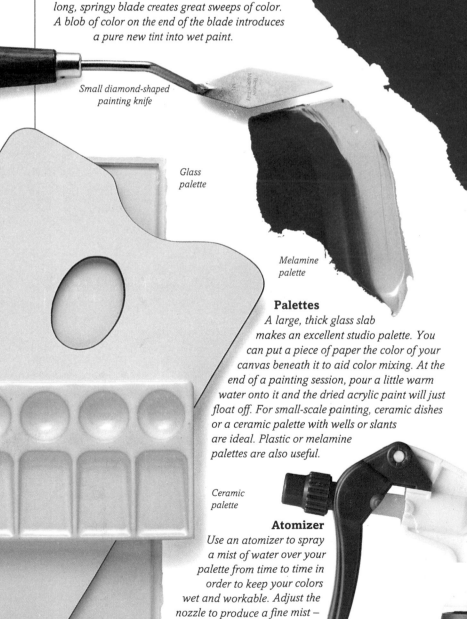

Trowel-shaped painting knife

Painting knives
Use a painting knife as if buttering bread. A short blade produces short, intense strokes; a long, springy blade creates great sweeps of color. A blob of color on the end of the blade introduces a pure new tint into wet paint.

Small diamond-shaped painting knife

Glass palette

Melamine palette

WHEN WORKING with a painting knife, palette knife, or scraper, you should work either wet-in-wet or wet-over-dry because as soon as a dried skin has begun to form over wet acrylic, any attempt to modify it or add color will usually spoil it. Acrylic paint varies in consistency according to the manufacturer. Some paints have a relatively stiff, buttery consistency straight from the container, which makes them ideal for creating textured effects, while others are much runnier and do not retain their form. The answer in this case is to use specially formulated texture mediums (*see* pp.339, 367) mixed with acrylic color to give the paint body, or used to create a textured ground.

Palettes
A large, thick glass slab makes an excellent studio palette. You can put a piece of paper the color of your canvas beneath it to aid color mixing. At the end of a painting session, pour a little warm water onto it and the dried acrylic paint will just float off. For small-scale painting, ceramic dishes or a ceramic palette with wells or slants are ideal. Plastic or melamine palettes are also useful.

Ceramic palette

Atomizer
Use an atomizer to spray a mist of water over your palette from time to time in order to keep your colors wet and workable. Adjust the nozzle to produce a fine mist – avoid drenching the palette.

Palette knives
Palette knives are indispensable for scooping up, mixing, and transferring acrylic color on the palette. Use them to mix in texture mediums, or for mixing in small quantities of ingredients on the palette if you are making your own paint (see pp.338-339). The straight knife has good leverage and a sharp end for scraping up hard color – useful for cleaning the palette.

Straight palette knife

Cranked-shank palette knife

Sponging and acrylics

Sponges are used to apply washes, create texture, and remove color. Thin the paint to a runny consistency for a wash and apply it in broad sweeps, working from top to bottom. To lift out color, press a clean damp sponge into the damp wash.

Scrapers

Scrapers are versatile tools. Use them to apply acrylic primer or straight acrylic color evenly over large or small areas of canvas, as well as to create striated, combed, and mixed color effects.

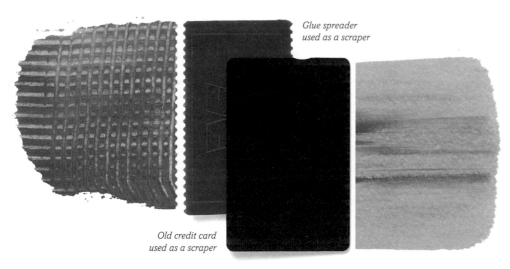

Glue spreader used as a scraper

Old credit card used as a scraper

Sponge roller

Use light pressure when taking up the paint from the palette to ensure uniformity of texture when the roller is applied to the support. Thicker paint produces a stippled effect, while thin color gives a transparent texture. Superimpose layers of paint and change the direction of the roller for a lively effect.

Sponge

A small piece of natural sponge has excellent paint-carrying capacity for laying washes and producing varied textures. Mix the color well to the required consistency before soaking the clean, damp sponge in it. Synthetic household sponges can also be used to good effect.

Airbrushes

Use airbrushes and spray guns to add small finishing touches – the glow around a lamp, for example – to a work that has been painted conventionally, or to create large areas of perfectly blended tones. You can also use them to work through stencils or to enhance textured effects. Clean airbrushes and spray guns immediately after use with clean tap water; otherwise, dry acrylic deposits will clog the nozzle and the needle.

Airbrush

Compressor

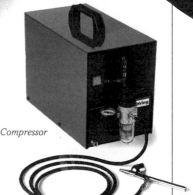

USING AN EASEL

- Easels range from solid studio items to light portable ones suitable for working outdoors. Choose one with the facility to secure the painting on it at any angle, so that you can use a wide range of techniques, such as working wet-in-wet with thin paint.

- A mahl stick helps to keep your hand steady while painting – useful while you're standing at an easel, and vital when you need to work carefully into a small area of a large canvas covered in wet paint. Available in wood or metal, the stick is screwed together in sections.

Mahl stick   *Easel*

349

SUPPORTS – PAPER

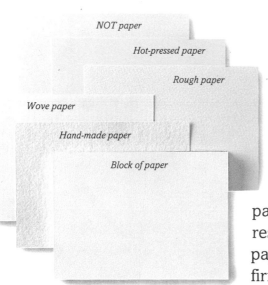

NOT paper

Hot-pressed paper

Rough paper

Wove paper

Hand-made paper

Block of paper

THE SURFACE ON WHICH YOU WORK is known as a support; the main types of support suitable for working with acrylics are paper, board, and canvas. If paper is your chosen support, look for acid-free watercolor papers. There are three main types of paper surface: Hot-pressed or HP, which is smooth, Cold-pressed or NOT (meaning not hot-pressed), which has a fine grain surface, and Rough, which is heavily textured. Paper weight varies from lightweight paper at 90lb per ream (185gsm), to 300lb (640gsm), which resembles fine board. Unless you are using a heavyweight paper, stretch watercolor paper first to ensure that it stays firm and flat when the paint is applied.

Paper selection

The surface of the paper affects the appearance of your finished painting. This is just a small selection of the large range available.

Materials

Natural sponge

Gum tape

Brushstrokes on smooth paper

When you lay a wash on smooth paper, it can be difficult to achieve an even tone. However, it will show the brushstrokes in a way that other surfaces will not, giving a crisp, delicate effect or emphasizing the fluency of the stroke.

Brushstrokes on rough paper

When washes are used on rough paper, heavier pigments settle into the hollows of the paper, creating grainy textures. If you use thicker paint and more rapid brushstrokes, the paint will miss the hollows of the paper, creating a half-tone effect.

1 ▲ To stretch paper, wet it with cold water, either by submerging it in a water bath, or by sponging the front and back with water until the fibers are fully saturated.

2 ▲ Place the wet paper onto a piece of wood an inch or two wider all around than your paper. Smooth it down with a sponge to remove excess water.

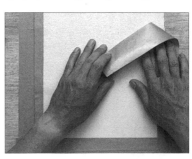

3 ▲ Cut four strips of heavy-duty gum tape, wet them and use them to stick the paper down firmly. Let the paper dry thoroughly to a hard, flat surface.

WORKING STRAIGHT onto white paper is effective when you apply thin washes that allow the luminosity of the white surface to show through. Create highlights by leaving areas of paper exposed. To tone your paper, apply an even, overall wash. Mix up a little more paint than you will need for this initial wash – you cannot afford to run out half-way through. With toned paper, use translucent darks and opaque lights to bring out the forms of your subject.

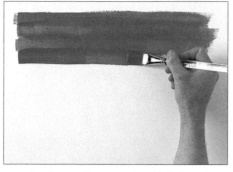

1 ▲ Apply a uniform wash which the white paper still reflects through, using well-diluted paint. Have the board at a slight angle and use a large, flat wash brush.

2 ▲ Fill the brush with color and apply it in smooth, slightly overlapping strokes from left to right. When you have finished, quickly brush out any unevenness.

South American antiquities

A mid-toned ground makes a good starting point for a work. Two of the objects are modeled using an orange-red of a deeper tone than the ground and picked out with a touch of Burnt Umber. As the overall wash obscures the white paper, opaque white paint must be used for the white highlights and the painted bird design on the right. The blue shadow here and the green body of the bird behind work well as complementaries (see pp.340-1) to the oranges and reds.

Materials

1in synthetic wash brush

Palette of dilute color

In this detail the white of the eye, and the effects of light falling on the face in the eye area, are created using the white of the paper. This draws the attention to the clear and piercing gaze of the subject.

The face is modeled with a series of overlaid brushstrokes, with very little blending. The white ground reflects the colors of each brushstroke, making it possible to read all the stages of the painting.

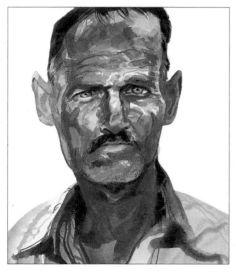

Gaucho

A good quality mold-made acid-free paper can give great clarity to a painting, a clarity which is given force by the intensity of the facial expression. In the areas in shadow the artist has worked wet-in-wet (see pp.370-1) and you can see where the pigment has settled into the grain of the paper to give a textured effect.

BOARDS AND CANVASES

MOST ARTISTS choose to paint on either a flexible material such as canvas or paper, or an inflexible one such as a wooden board. Canvas is a light, transportable, and very responsive surface and although the paint film is more vulnerable on a flexible support, acrylic paint is itself very flexible. Boards are more stable than canvas and almost any kind of rigid board or panel is suitable. Larger boards may need to be glued to a supporting wooden frame to prevent twisting.

A selection of suitable supports

HARDBOARD IS A popular support and deserves its reputation as an economical and hard-wearing material; you can paint on both the smooth side and the textured one. Thicker grades of plywood also make good, solid supports, while blockboard and chipboard are less expensive alternatives.

Medium-density fiberboard, which is used extensively in furniture manufacturing, is equally suitable and even old door panels make excellent supports. Thin cardboard or museum board can also be used, provided it is acid-free. Canvas board, combining the stability of board with the texture of the overlaid canvas, makes a very good support.

Wooden panel

Materials

Sanding block and sandpaper

Large paintbrush

Acrylic gesso primer

Blockboard

Plywood

Chipboard

Medium-density fiberboard

Hardboard – textured side

Hardboard – smooth side

Museum board

Canvas board

1 ▲ To prepare a panel for acrylic painting, cut it to the required size and sand the surface and edges smooth. Clean off all the dust before applying the primer.

2 ▲ Using a household paintbrush, apply a first coat of acrylic gesso primer, diluting it with about ten percent water to make the application easier.

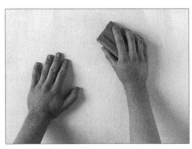

3 ▲ Sand down the panel before applying a second coat of primer. Painting the edges and the back of the panel equalizes the tension in the board, keeping it flat.

Using canvas

Most art supply stores stock prepared, stretched, and primed canvases. In the upper price ranges where properly primed fine quality linen canvas is often used, these tend to be of a reasonable quality. For acrylic painting, you must make sure that the canvas has an acrylic priming. For a sensibly priced, good quality product, buy the stretchers and canvas separately and prepare your own canvases.

Opaque paint on canvas

Canvas is a giving surface, which responds to the brush or painting knife. Where the paint is applied thickly and opaquely (left), *the effect of the brushstroke varies. The texture comes through in the center of the stroke where the paint settles into the hollows of the canvas.*

Transparent washes on canvas

Where the paint is applied in thin, transparent washes (right), *the texture of the canvas comes into its own, integrating paint and support in a unique and expressive manner.*

Materials

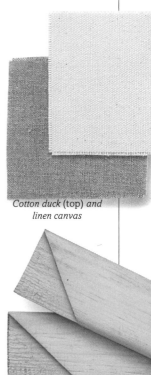

Cotton duck (top) *and* linen canvas

Stretchers

Scissors

Staple gun

Hammer

Stretcher keys

1 ▶ Assemble the frame, pushing the corner pieces together by hand. Tap with a rubber hammer (or an ordinary hammer and a block of wood), to avoid denting the frame. Check the right angles using a set square, or make sure that both diagonal measurements are equal.

2 ▶ If you are using a cotton canvas, 15oz is preferable; otherwise use linen canvas. Cut the canvas with a generous overlap around the outside edge.

3 ◀ Starting at the center of the first side, staple the canvas to the stretchers. Pull the canvas taut and repeat on the opposite side. Staple the remaining opposite sides in the same way (*see* p.465).

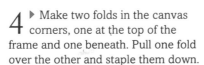

4 ▶ Make two folds in the canvas corners, one at the top of the frame and one beneath. Pull one fold over the other and staple them down.

5 ▲ Tap in the stretcher frame keys to tighten the tension in the canvas. Avoid splitting by ensuring the grain of the wood in the key is not parallel to that of the frame.

6 ◀ Prime the canvas with two coats of commercial acrylic primer. Thin the first coat, allow it to dry, sand very lightly, and apply a second, undiluted, coat. To make a tinted primer, mix a little acrylic color with water and stir it in well, or apply a thin wash of transparent color over the dry primer.

GALLERY OF SUPPORTS AND GROUNDS

YOUR CHOICE OF SUPPORT – whether it is canvas, board, or paper – will have an impact on the way you paint. For example, a rigid board will be more resistant to your brush than a flexible canvas. Whether or not you prime the surface also affects the appearance of your painting; for example, an unprimed surface absorbs more of the paint. If the ground – the surface of the support – is colored or textured, this will also dictate your painting style and the finished effect.

Louise Fox, *3333* *14 x 24 in (35 x 60 cm)*
This demonstrates extremely clearly the use of opaque acrylic on a very dark ground. The paper has been given an overall blue-black tone, so that in order for colors to show up, they need to be either opaque or mixed with white paint. For this technique, concentrate on the highlights and mid-to-light tones, so that the image emerges from the darkness. Here, combining cool blues and greens with touches of orange and warm brown creates the strange, nostalgic atmosphere that artificial light brings to an image (this train is in a museum collection).

In this detail, the shadows on the window frame were created using a thin dry-brush technique over the red ground.

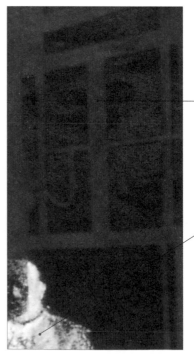

The white robes – and the light in the sky – were added in with opaque color.

Jacobo Borges, *Yesterday,* **1975** *39 x 39 in (99 x 99 cm)*
The artist has used a red ground, enabling him to paint with great economy. The painting deals with memories and dreams associated with place. In the reflection, the dawn is breaking and the image of the figure is beginning to fade. We start to question which is the "real" image and which the reflection.

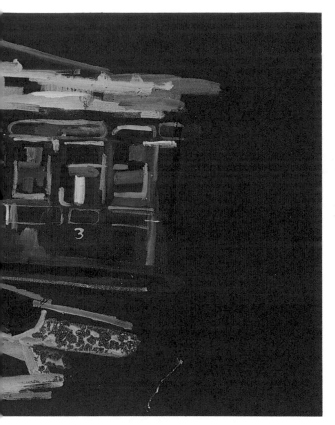

Albina Kosiec Felski, *The Circus*, 1971 *48 x 48 in (122 x 122 cm)*
The dark ground used here generates the interior, artificial light that we associate with the circus, picking out all the characters and animals with a sharp clarity against the darkness behind. The dark stripes on the zebras are the color of the ground itself, and all the other tones and details are picked out in opaque mixtures of acrylic paint. There is an overall surface quality created by the lack of conventional perspective, which, combined with the rich colors, gives the painting the feel of an embroidered textile.

Ronald Davis, *Arc Fan*

114 x 128 in (290 x 325 cm)
Light, airy effects can be achieved by applying thin acrylic to a white canvas – particularly if the canvas is unprimed, when the washes soak in like a stain on a tablecloth, becoming part of the fibers. In this finely drawn perspective study, we move between the idea of painting as illusion and as mark-making on a flat surface.

Jane Gifford, *Spitalfields Market; Four Objects*

144 x 144 in (366 x 366 cm)
These four grounds use adjacent harmonies from dark blue through blue and magenta to orange-red. The complementary colors of the pear and the peach make these objects seem to float above their grounds. Using a rigid plywood support has given an added smoothness to the paint quality.

WAYS OF WORKING IN ACRYLIC

Always keep
a sketchbook
on hand

Resist
technique

Working
with thin
acrylic washes

OVER THE FOLLOWING pages, we explore
in some detail the wide range of
techniques that you can use when working
with acrylic paints. For the sake of clarity,
we have looked at particular techniques
in isolation. These include many of the ways
of using the paint transparently in thin washes,
including working wet-in-wet and with resist
techniques, overlaying different colors, and painting
on textured grounds. We also look at opaque acrylic
techniques that range from creating flat, uniform areas of color to thick and
vigorous impasto work. However, you will find in practice that both transparent
and opaque approaches are often used in the same painting, and that
a specific area of a painting may be suited to one form of brushwork,
while another area may be worked in an
entirely different way.

The process of painting

Generally speaking, painting
should not be a cold,
mechanical process in
which you select a specific
method of working and
apply it in a rigidly fixed
manner. Try to approach painting with
acrylics in an open, organic way, so that,
having made a certain decision at one point,
you always feel perfectly free to change it quite
radically shortly afterward (a good example of this
is featured on pp.386-7). This applies just as much
to the composition of an image as it does to any
particular technique. Use the step-by-step exercises,
tip boxes, and Gallery pages in this section to build
up your repertoire of acrylic techniques. Then you
will be able to call upon them at any time that seems
appropriate during the course of working on a
painting. This way, you can expand your expressive
potential and give yourself more confidence when,
for example, you are tackling a new subject or
moving on to working on a much larger scale.

Finding your own language

After a while, painters seem to find a way of working that suits their personality and is completely appropriate to their chosen subjects. Each artist's style becomes a form of handwriting that we recognize instantly. There are many examples of this in the Gallery pages throughout this book – examples that range from the liquid economy of John McLean's work (*see* p.375) to the complex configurations created by Bernard Cohen (*see* p.389). If you are new to acrylic painting, you should not expect a uniquely personal style to develop immediately. It is not simply a question of finding a way of working with the paint itself that suits you. Painting is also about discovering an attitude or an approach that allows you to speak with your own voice. As artists, we have to learn to be less self-conscious, to trust our instincts, and to work the way we want to work, not as we imagine we ought to.

Choose the appropriate brushes and painting surface for your style and subject matter

This acrylic equipment is painted in an opaque style

Freedom and experimentation

One good way of getting to know yourself as a painter is to work out ideas as often as possible on scraps of paper or in sketchbooks. As a beginner, it can be intimidating to be faced with a large, untouched expanse of expensive watercolor paper or ready-made, primed canvas. There often tends to be a feeling that, to justify the expense, a perfectly formed painting must appear miraculously on this pristine surface. Inevitably, the result is going to be disappointing. A scrap of paper or a sketchbook, on the other hand, is not at all intimidating – you are quite free to make countless mistakes, or perhaps discover a wonderful new way of working. You will certainly develop far more quickly this way. Give yourself time to experiment with acrylic paints, to use unusual tools and surfaces, and to adopt any methods from other painting disciplines that seem suitable. You may not use any of this material in a finished painting – but you will gain a much fuller understanding of the varied ways in which acrylics work.

Acrylic's plasticity makes it uniquely suited to unusual techniques such as weaving strands of dried paint

Create this texture by lifting thick, wet acrylic off a surface with a piece of cardboard

COMPOSING YOUR IMAGE

IF YOU ARE RELATIVELY new to painting, deciding how to compose your image can seem daunting when faced with the wealth of detail in the scene before you. It is important to remember that a painting is a selective personal response to a scene and it allows you to focus on what seems important about it to you and to leave out extraneous details. How you then decide to handle your chosen subject matter in terms of color and technique will very probably relate to questions of mood and atmosphere, in addition to your own level of expertise.

Canal scene
An inner city waterway with a canalboat tied up against the bank makes a good starting point for a composition. When you come across a scene like this, your eye is going to be caught by the boat and the water rather than by the line of cars parked close by. Asked to recall the scene, you would no doubt describe those elements that set it outside of your everyday experience.

YOU DO NOT have to use a camera to record possible angles and viewpoints for your painting. It is just as good to make a series of fairly rapid pencil sketches. These automatically eliminate extraneous detail and allow you to explore the broad outlines of your subject. You will quickly begin to see whether something is going to work or not. However, if your time is limited, take photographs and make pencil sketches from them to help clarify the image in your mind.

CARDBOARD VIEWER

Use two lightweight cardboard L-shaped corners to crop into your drawing or photograph and see how the composition can be varied by focusing on a single element, and leaving others out.

A viewer gives you flexibility when composing your image

L-shaped corners

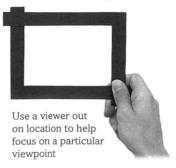

Use a viewer out on location to help focus on a particular viewpoint

Pencil sketch
This preliminary sketch concentrates on the main areas of the subject. The way it sits on the pages of the sketchbook gives the first indication of how it might look as a painting. Unless you propose to make an extremely complex painting with a great deal of fine detail, you do not need to reproduce every feature in these preliminary pencil studies.

Colored sketch
Making a few drawings in color serves as a reminder of the colors in the scene and opens your eyes to the color possibilities in your final composition. Colored pencils are easy to carry with you. The kind that are water-soluble can be dampened and used a little like watercolor if you also take along a small soft hair paintbrush.

Considering your composition

Many artists who work up paintings in the studio take a series of photographs from which they can select what seems to be the best viewpoint. If what attracts you to the image is an atmospheric quality which seems very difficult to pin down, it can be worthwhile writing a few notes to try to clarify your ideas.

When you are working on a composition, carefully consider your point of view. Are you looking down on it or up at it? How different is the subject going to be in mood and appearance according to this changing viewpoint? How much of the subject do you want to include? Do you want a panoramic view or do you want to focus in on a particular area of a scene? Make sketches from as many angles as possible. Finally, ask yourself what it is that attracts you to the image and then decide on the best way of expressing it in your work.

Sitting ducks
Three ducks in conversational mode make an interesting close-up composition drawn from the larger scene (left).

Panoramic view
The image above embraces a wide view of the scene, with the arc of the bridge spanning the composition. The scene opens out in the foreground but the water flowing into the picture draws the eye toward a distant point below and beyond the bridge, just above the center of the composition where the sides of the canal converge.

Central image
The view directly toward the stern from a standing position shows the boat foreshortened. Taken in isolation it is not clear what type of boat it is, making this a less successful composition.

View from the bridge
From a higher viewpoint, the combination of the linear perspective of the boat with the curve of the side of the canal and the standing figure creates an unusual and interesting scene.

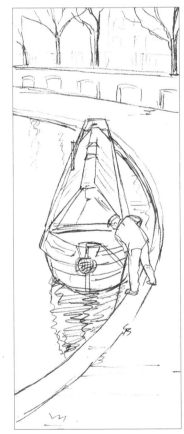

Details from the photograph opposite, such as the parked cars, have been left out so that they do not detract from the main image of the canalboat.

Placing the boat to the left of the painting establishes a proper balance in the work. Interesting reflections in the water on the right help to create a work with stillness and poise.

The finished painting is quite accurate in its depiction of the original scene although the boat has now become more of a focal point.

The finished painting
This takes in the arc of the bridge, the curve of the side of the canal, and a view of the finished boat. This demonstrates its length and also celebrates the chunky wooden rudder arrangement at the stern. It combines a close-up view with a long view, giving the boat a prominent position.

TRANSFERRING YOUR IMAGE

THERE ARE A NUMBER of ways of transferring an image onto your support before you start painting. You can, of course, start making the painting directly from life onto the canvas without producing any preliminary studies. However, many artists prefer to use a sketch or a photograph as a guide to drawing in the broad outlines of an image. It is at this point you can start to rethink the composition after consulting all your reference material. If your image is to be used at the same size, trace it onto the support in the normal way. With canvas, you can trace your sketch, run a spiked artists' wheel over the traced outline and then pounce (dab) charcoal dust through the holes in the tracing paper onto the canvas. To scale up an image, either use a grid, enlarge it with a slide projector, or judge it by eye.

Using a grid
Draw a grid of fine pencil lines over the original sketch, photograph, or postcard. Alternatively, if you do not want to draw over your image, make an acetate grid that you can use again for sketches of a similar size. Draw the lines with a permanent marker pen. Secure the grid to the sketch with masking tape. Draw a similar, but larger scale, grid onto your painting support and transfer the image square by square.

Soft pencil

Charcoal pencil

Fine round soft hair brush

Sketching with a brush
This method (below) *can be used when working from life, but is more usually used when translating the image from a sketch to the support. Sketch out the broad outlines of the image with a thin round soft hair brush and a well-diluted wash of Burnt Umber. For a large-scale work, a brush such as a filbert is preferable, used on its edge for finer lines and on the broad side for indicating broad tonal areas.*

Adding color
Show just enough of the image in the sketch to feel confident about filling in the broad areas of tone and color in the initial painting stages (above). *Keep these tones pale or even monochromatic but with sufficient tonal range to show the difference between the highlights and the areas in deepest shadow. You can either make use of the lines of the sketch in the finished work, or overpaint them.*

TRACING IS PROBABLY the easiest method of transfer, providing the reference and finished work are to be the same size. Using tracing paper, trace over the image, then draw over the lines on the back with a soft pencil. Reproduce the image on your support by shading over the top. A spiked wheel and charcoal dust makes it easier to trace onto textures such as canvas. Paint over the faint charcoal outline with dilute paint.

To scale up images by using a grid, copy the contents of each square of your grid onto the larger squares of your support. If you are enlarging by using a slide projector, work in a darkened room, with a projector that will not overheat. Project a slide of the image onto the canvas and copy it by following the projected outline.

1 ◀ If you are happy to scale up your image from the sketch onto the support by eye, then you can use a traditional method of transferring your image – drawing it with charcoal onto your support. Use either sticks of charcoal or a charcoal pencil, which is less messy.

2 ▶ Use a soft cloth to rub off the charcoal drawing, remembering to make sure that you brush off all the dust before you start to apply paint. The marks will remain as a guide, but the charcoal dust will not blacken any paint that you apply subsequently.

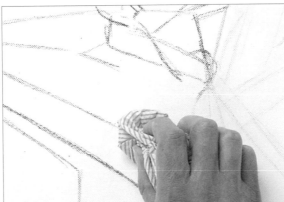

3 ▲ Using a small round soft hair brush and diluted acrylic color, paint in the outline of the image. Choose the colors that you will be using to complete the image, so that they can act as a guide while you are working.

Canalboat stern
The color guides laid down before (above right) have been worked up and now the richness of the color in the painting makes the white sing out. The finished composition – a detail of the stern of the canalboat – is so stylized as to appear almost abstract. The mooring rope leads the eye straight into the center of the painting.

Scumbles of opaque pale blue over much darker blue give solidity to the form of the boat.

Surrounding the well-defined red and blue areas with white intensifies our perception of these colors.

A transparent wash of dark blue over a lighter hue gives richness and depth to the shadows.

Materials

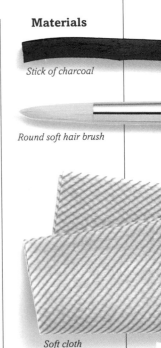

Stick of charcoal

Round soft hair brush

Soft cloth

LIGHT, SHADE, AND TONE

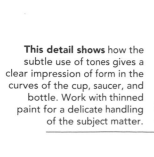

TO PAINT AN IMAGE you need to know about form. This knowledge will allow you to give depth and three-dimensional shape to your painting. Form is created by the effects of light and shade on the image. Making a monochromatic study – a painting in different tones of a single color – is a useful exercise to help you appreciate how this works. It allows you to concentrate on the lightness and darkness of tones without having to worry about getting the colors right.

Monochrome sketch
This quick sketch blocks in the tonal areas, to be re-created more subtly in further studies.

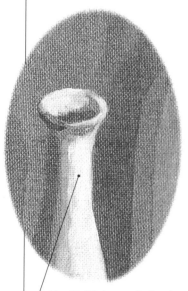

IT CAN BE DIFFICULT to separate the idea of tone from color. Take a plain sheet of white or colored paper, twist it up, and place it near a light source. Although the paper remains the same color throughout, it is broken up into a wide range of tones, from dark to light. Try making a study of it. You could also make a still life out of simple objects such as stones or old bottles. Paint the objects with white emulsion and stand them on white paper, with white paper behind them. Shine a light on them from one side, and consider how the variations in tone give you a fully three-dimensional image of the objects. Make single-color studies from this, working both on a white ground with thinned paint and on a toned ground with the addition of Titanium White.

The highlights on the bottle, indicating the direction of the light source, are created by applying Titanium White. To describe the curve of the bottle shown in this detail, make use of the full range of available tones, graduating from light through to dark.

Working on a toned ground
Prepare the canvas first with a light tone of blue, made by mixing in Titanium White. Paint in the dark tones and the light tones, allowing the toned ground to provide the mid-tones.

Working on a white ground
Produce the lighter tones by simply thinning down the paint – in this case Burnt Umber – and using the white of the ground to provide the highlights.

This detail shows how the subtle use of tones gives a clear impression of form in the curves of the cup, saucer, and bottle. Work with thinned paint for a delicate handling of the subject matter.

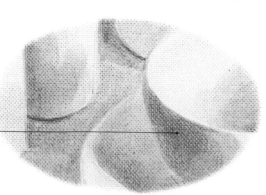

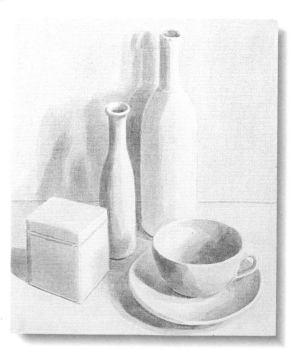

Chili peppers

Making studies in color

Learning to reproduce a solid object as an image with form on a flat surface requires practice. When you are fully confident working in monochromatic tones, move on to color, bearing in mind the lessons you have learned about the subtleties of light, shade, and tone.

1 ▶ Lay down a mid-tone of green so that you can work the color up and down to provide the highlights and shadows that will give form to the peppers. Using a violet wash for the shadows gives them a more obvious presence than in the original, enhancing the color of the green.

2 ◀ Working with transparent washes, use deeper tones of green to mold the edges and the indentations of the pepper, starting to give it form. Soften the edges with a clean, damp brush. Leave some areas of the original ground color exposed, although little of this may survive in the finished work.

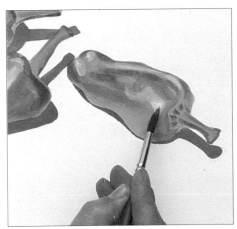

3 ▲ Mix a lighter green to give form to the stalk and use it to add to the curves of the pepper. White highlights on the upper surface of the pepper show the direction of the light source.

The use of the opaque mid-tone ground as a starting point for the painting of the chili peppers produces a substantial three-dimensional effect with only the most economical over-painting in thin washes.

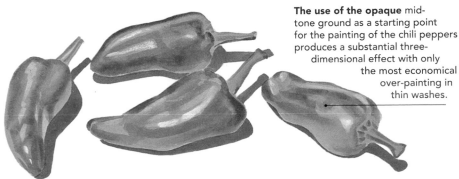

Working in monochrome
Such a range of tone is used in this work that it almost seems to be in full color. The coffeepot is especially effective, and images reflected in it help to give it form. A sense of light coming from the right is very strong.

Working in color
When you translate the same still life into color, use the monochromatic study as a guide. The tones that were dark or light now become the light or dark hues of a color, but the shadows are more subtly expressed.

GALLERY OF COMPOSITION

COMPOSITION IS THE ORGANIZATION of the pictorial space in a painting. You can organize forms in order to tell a story, create a mood, or convey a meaning. Try changing the viewpoint: looking up at an image may make it seem to loom over us; looking down on it makes it unfold like a landscape in front of our eyes. Cram things into a work to give a sense of claustrophobia, or open the space out to make it seem part of something larger. You can focus either on specific areas or on the work as a whole. Most artists strive for an overall balance, but there are no rigid rules – as these varied examples show.

Jo Kelly, *Rose Face* *36 x 36 in (91 x 91 cm)*
In this bold and striking composition, the table top dominates the canvas, pushing off the picture plane toward the viewer so that it feels as if we are actually sharing a glass of wine or a coffee with the subject.

Gillean Whitaker, *Seashells on Flower Pot* *36 x 72 in (91 x 183 cm)*
Here, the composition is contained within the frame, with the shells carefully and consciously arranged within the ellipse of the flower pot. The composition makes us look at the shells as attentively as if we were children inspecting the contents of the nature display at school. Whitaker's shells sit bright and alert in the sun, with the warm, golden yellows complementing the touches of purple. The dark shadows that the shells cast on the flat surface of the flower pot help to add to our awareness of their three-dimensional substance.

Patrick Caulfield, *Lunchtime* 1985
81 x 96 in (206 x 244 cm)
We get more of a real sense of this interior because the painting is not bounded by conventional linear perspective. Caulfield is aware that there are many ways of representing space and light. He opens up a whole series of angles and planes in a semi-symmetrical arrangement that has us looking around corners, behind walls, and through windows in sunlight and at night. The painting also manages to bring together an extraordinary range of acrylic painting styles, without appearing to be disjointed in any way.

Mike Gorman, *Flowerscape* 72 x 60 in (183 x 152 cm)
In Gorman's attractive painting, the flowers are highlighted in light, opaque tones against both the dark ground and the mid- to dark green tones of the foliage. The choice of traditional subject matter disguises an adventurous composition. The flowers are barely contained within the frame and seem to spill out on all sides. This effect owes much to the angle from which the plants are seen. It is as if we are getting right down among the flowers, much as a gardener might.

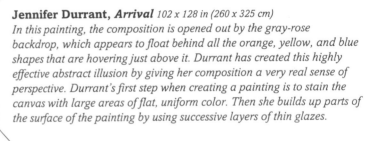

Patrick Caulfield's choice of a geranium plant for his "mini-composition" is an effective one. Using the complementaries red and green lends a strength that makes this detail perfectly self-contained.

Jennifer Durrant, *Arrival* 102 x 128 in (260 x 325 cm)
In this painting, the composition is opened out by the gray-rose backdrop, which appears to float behind all the orange, yellow, and blue shapes that are hovering just above it. Durrant has created this highly effective abstract illusion by giving her composition a very real sense of perspective. Durrant's first step when creating a painting is to stain the canvas with large areas of flat, uniform color. Then she builds up parts of the surface of the painting by using successive layers of thin glazes.

The geranium plant in Caulfield's painting is a good example of a composition within an overall composition. This detail is a closed composition in which the whole of the plant is contained within the rectangular area of the canvas on which it appears. In this carefully painted still-life detail, the effect of the light and shadow on the leaves has been precisely observed.

USING OPAQUE ACRYLIC

ARTISTS WORKING in acrylics often use the paint opaquely. This simply means that any overlaid color covers up the color underneath it. Some acrylic colors are naturally opaque – for example, Cadmium Red, Yellow Ochre, and Oxide of Chromium (a shade of green).

Transparent colors such as Quinacridone Red and Phthalo Blue can be made opaque by mixing in a little white or some other opaque color. It is common when using opaque acrylic to work on a toned ground. Areas of the ground can then provide the mid-tones, while light areas and highlights are created by obliterating parts of the ground with pale, opaque paint.

OPAQUE ACRYLIC lends itself readily to a variety of different painting styles. On the one extreme, you can make absolutely smooth, flat-toned paintings in which the actual

Seashell

This vibrant shell is painted in opaque acrylic thickened with gel medium. White highlights are added over other colors. The texture of the canvas support enhances the bold brushwork.

brushwork is invisible. Acrylic paints are particularly well-suited to this style because the medium can be applied much more evenly than other media. Using this approach, each area of color is a well-defined, hard-edged shape, filled in with a uniformly toned flat color. A number of highly influential painters have used acrylic in this way, including Andy Warhol and Bridget Riley (*see* pp.336-337).

A popular method of achieving a clean, often straight, edge, is to use masking tape. Always make sure that you rub the tape down on the canvas with a fingernail to prevent the paint from seeping underneath it.

1 ▲ Use masking tape to create a crisply outlined building standing out against a vivid sky in bright sunlight. First, paint in the broad areas of the background fairly evenly with opaque paint, and leave to dry.

2 ▲ Stick the tape down in the shape of the building. Fill this shape in with thick white paint, used straight out of the tube and brushed out flatly.

Materials

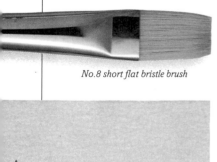

No.8 short flat bristle brush

Masking tape

3 ▲ When the white paint has dried, carefully remove the tape. If the edges of your masking tape were stuck down well, a clean-edged image should emerge.

Riviera scene

Tape was also used to add windows. Acrylic makes it easy to paint a shape opaquely over a completed backdrop, instead of having to paint carefully up to the edges of the shape.

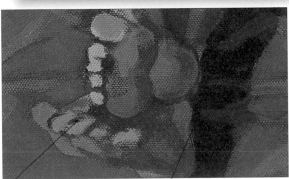

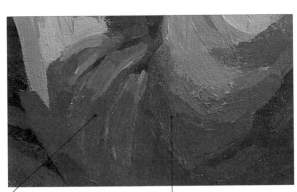

Woman sunbathing

Here, the bright, clear colors of a beach scene are painted in opaque mixtures, with the shadows provided either by superimposed dark tones, or by the color of the brown ground. When you use opaque paint on a colored or toned ground, the ground color provides an underlying structure behind the individual brushstrokes. This integrates the work and gives it a sense of cohesion. Mixing white in with the blue used for the towel and the yellow of the sand gives a striking, saturated quality to these colors, making them glow in the sun.

Impasto painting

On the other hand, acrylic is equally good for impasto techniques – highly visible brushwork used with very thick opaque color. This effect is particularly associated with oil paint, but acrylic adds a distinctive texture and color-quality of its own.

Unlike most oil colors, which dry the same color as when they were wet, acrylic tends to dry darker. This may cause color-matching problems if you return to a painting after a break. It can be worth mixing a fairly large amount of a color and keeping it in a sealed jar.

The detail of the sunbathing woman's feet shows how modeling is provided by a range of superimposed tones and areas of exposed ground.

Building up successive layers of color has created a rich, shadowed area in which the glowing red stripes on the towel are just visible.

Ridges of thick paint give an exciting texture. When oils are used like this, they may dry on the surface only, and crack. Acrylic is faster-drying and more elastic.

The highly visible brushstrokes have a thick and creamy appearance that reflects an obvious delight in both the medium and the subject matter.

Sea and sand

When you paint with opaque acrylic, you can also enjoy the fact that it can be used very effectively in a thickly textured impasto style. In this vibrant summer scene, figure, sea, and sand are integrated in a rich pattern of warm adjacent colors. When it is used very thickly, acrylic scores over oils in that it dries so quickly – oils can take months to dry.

Texture paste

Various commercial pastes can be added to acrylic to give it extra body and a range of textures. These are ideal for impasto techniques. Because acrylic is an adhesive, it can also be mixed with sand or grit.

OPAQUE PORTRAIT

Initial sketch
Carefully planned in pencil, the portrait was painted on watercolor paper.

IN OPAQUE PAINTING methods, the highlights are provided by the use of opaque white acrylic, and the paler tones by mixing colors with white. Working entirely with opaque acrylic is similar to working with gouache – an opaque form of watercolor paint. However, acrylic scores over gouache in its ability to be overpainted without dissolving the paint layer beneath. This uncompromising, bold portrait has the solid, slightly chalky feel that opaque paint brings to a work. Tonal variation is produced by separate, flat areas of uniform color. The brick wall – parallel to the picture plane and close to the viewer – has the effect of pushing the figure toward us.

1 ◄ Completing the brick background first helps you to set the tonal range of the painting. Start with areas of flat base color: Cobalt Blue, Yellow Ochre, and white for the mortar; Yellow Ochre, Ultramarine, Indian Red, and white for the bricks; darker brown for the large shadow. Now use dark mixes to tone down the mortar, to outline and add texture to the bricks, and to intensify the shadow.

2 ▶ Turning to the shirt, fill in the green stripes by adding Cadmium Yellow to the basic "mortar" color.

3 ◄ Adopt the principle used on the wall by completing the flat base colors of the shirt first. Start with the red stripes, mixing Indian and Cadmium Reds with white. For the blue, blend Cobalt Blue with white, adding a touch of Yellow Ochre to give a subtle green-blue. As with the wall, crisp definition is given by abutting rather than overlapping areas of different color.

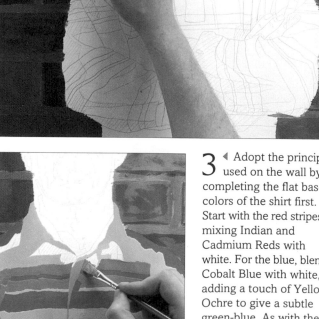

4 ▲ Switching to the ⅛in brush, create detail on the shirt by mixing dark blends for shadows and light ones for highlights. Large shadows are separate areas of color, and small ones are laid over the base colors. However, all the shadows could be overlaid because acrylics dry so rapidly. Adjust colors accordingly. For example, for the blue shadows, use less white and more Cobalt Blue, and add a little more Yellow Ochre to tone down the color.

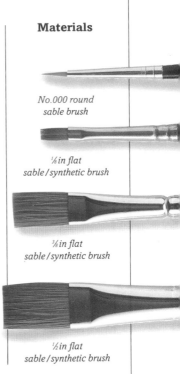

*No.000 round
sable brush*

*⅛ in flat
sable / synthetic brush*

*⅜ in flat
sable / synthetic brush*

*½ in flat
sable / synthetic brush*

5 ▶ This strong face is the focal point of the painting, so use a wide range of light, mid-, and dark tones to build up a boldly sculptural shape. Start by laying down a light overall flesh tone that mixes Cadmium Red, Cadmium Yellow, and a lot of Titanium White. Create shadow on the left-hand side of the face by adding a purple-pink mid-tone of Cobalt Blue, white, and Cadmium Red. Define the other side of the face with darker mixes of the basic flesh color.

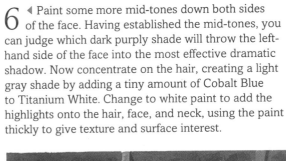

6 ◀ Paint some more mid-tones down both sides of the face. Having established the mid-tones, you can judge which dark purply shade will throw the left-hand side of the face into the most effective dramatic shadow. Now concentrate on the hair, creating a light gray shade by adding a tiny amount of Cobalt Blue to Titanium White. Change to white paint to add the highlights onto the hair, face, and neck, using the paint thickly to give texture and surface interest.

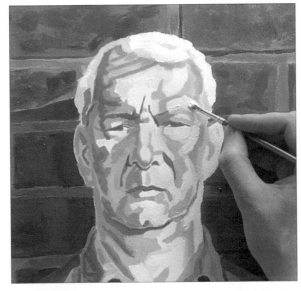

7 ▲ Finish off by bringing out details around the nose and eye area. Load the fine round brush with a dark blend of Ultramarine and a touch of Yellow Ochre – the yellow knocks back the blue, keeping it dark but not as bright. This color gives crisp definition, but is much warmer than black paint, blending in with the facial tones and bringing real strength to the face.

Portrait of the artist's father
The portrait was painted on a highly detailed pencil drawing, which is completely obliterated by the opaque paint. The dense shadow of the figure on the wall adds an element of drama, and the sharp, graphic lines make the figure "leap" forcefully out of the painting.

The shirt's simple, linear pattern brings the figure forward. The use of toned-down primary colors adds strength, but is not overpowering.

Derek Worrall

369

TRANSPARENT TECHNIQUES

MOST OF THE effects associated with watercolor painting can be created using diluted acrylic paints in a transparent technique. These effects include laying in thinned washes of uniform and varied tones, applying color wet-in-wet, and overlaying washes onto dry color to build up deep, resonant tones and colors. This is much easier using acrylic paint because it is insoluble in water when dry; overlaid colors will not disturb the ones beneath. In addition, you can use various resist techniques, including wax crayons, oil pastels, and latex masking fluid.

Transparent effects
Overlaid brushstrokes of transparent color on canvas (top) have a very different appearance to those on paper (right). The pigment particles settle into the hollows of the weave, making the texture of the fabric visible and creating expressive half-tones.

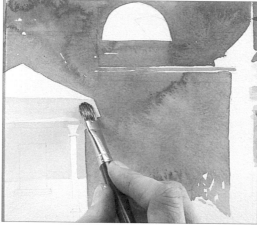

1 ▲ Lay a thin orange wash over the main area of the building, allowing the watery paint to move and flow, creating spontaneous effects. Use Cadmium Yellow Light for the portico and leave the areas to be painted in lighter tones white.

2 ▲ Add blue-gray over the white roof and window area. Use deeper washes to broaden the areas of shadow, adding depth. A blue wash over part of the orange area cools the color here, effectively creating the shadowy arch.

The special quality of transparent acrylic techniques is the beauty and subtlety of overlaid veils of thin transparent color, illuminated by the white paper.

Using deeper tones, dramatic color changes arise from simply painting one color over another.

The warm orange washes bring the wall forward, while the complementary blues make the window recede.

Sunlit window
Laying loose patches of washes in warm tones – orange, apricot, and yellow – gives the impression of a sun-dappled facade. The cool shadows within the window are achieved with blue-purple washes.

Sunlight and shadows
The finished picture (above) was built up using washes in varying strengths and mixtures of Ultramarine Blue, Burnt Sienna, purple made with Deep Brilliant Red, Phthalo Blue and Paynes Gray, and Azo Yellow Light (right).

Subdued color
The deep blue-purple background is created in the same way as the window (above), but here a low-key approach is used for the brickwork, with washes of Cerulean Blue and Burnt Sienna producing the atmospheric effects.

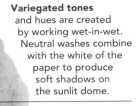

Variegated tones
and hues are created
by working wet-in-wet.
Neutral washes combine
with the white of the
paper to produce
soft shadows on
the sunlit dome.

The purple hues
of the deep shadow
on the walls contrasts
with the cool pale blue
and yellow washes,
which create subtle
greenish grays on the
right of the dome.

Working wet-in-wet

*Here, the broad area of
shadow is not painted
in one tone of a single
color as on the previous
page, but created using
the wet-in-wet technique.
Different colors are
touched into a wet
or damp area of the
painting and allowed
to mingle and fuse.*

Controlling washes

*Working successfully
with wet-in-wet
techniques relies on a balance between
control and spontaneity. Limit the effect
of the technique by wetting specific areas of
color or tone, such as the side of a column in
shadow, as here. By dealing with separate
areas in this way your paint will move freely
within them, but will not run out of control
over the work as a whole.*

Creating colors

*It is useful to know how particular colors
interact when you are working wet-in-wet.
Practice by producing some color samples
first (right). Certain color blends may give a
rather muddy result (top). Thin, pale washes
can produce an interesting feathery effect,
due to over-dilution of the pigment (bottom).*

RESIST TECHNIQUES

Because transparent techniques rely on the white of the
ground for highlights rather than the color of the paint,
you may need to protect parts of your painting to retain
highlights or pale areas when you overpaint. A good way
of doing this is to use latex masking fluid. Paint it over
the area to be protected (use an old brush and wash it
immediately). Let it dry, overpaint it, allow the paint to
dry and then rub off the masking fluid.

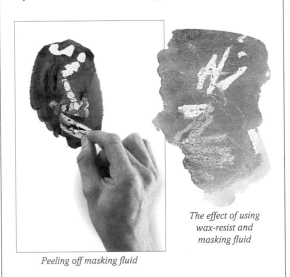

*The effect of using
wax-resist and
masking fluid*

Peeling off masking fluid

Windows and doorways

*Vibrant colors and deep shadows are typical of scenes
painted in sunny climates. Use warm oranges and yellows
for colors in sunlight – Cadmium Yellow Light alone and
mixed with Cadmium Red Light are ideal. Use cooler greens
and Phthalo Blue based purples to lay washes in the area of
shadows. Work from light to dark, overlaying washes to
deepen tones, and avoid overworking an image.*

Oil pastels and
wax candles can
also be used in resist
techniques. The acrylic
color will not be
completely repelled by
them, so they must be
incorporated into the
finished effect. This
painting uses oil pastel
on the shutters, the
arch of the door, and
in patches on the wall,
where it shows through
the transparent
washes of paint.

Masking fluid has been
used on the steps and
on the wall around the
window. When it is
removed and the white
paper is exposed, it
gives the effect of a
shaft of strong sunlight
falling on the wall.

371

WORKING WITH WASHES

PAINTING WITH ACRYLICS using a transparent technique is very similar to watercolor painting in execution and finished effect. Use the white of your paper to provide the highlights and to illuminate all the other colors and tones in the composition. For the pale tones, thin the paint with a lot of water to make fine washes of well-diluted color. Create dark tones by mixing deeper washes, or by overlaying washes.

In this painting, leave the white of the paper showing through for the areas in bright sunlight, such as the dome, the side of the building, and the foreground pavement area. Deepen the tones for the areas in shadow – warm to the left and cool to the right – to produce a convincing but still loose and relaxed impression of this city scene.

Photographic reference
When working from a photograph, there's no need to faithfully reproduce all the details; use it as a point of reference for your central image and change the details as you choose.

1 ▲ Use a large synthetic wash brush to lay a medium blue wash over part of the background. The white of the paper provides the sunlit dome; choose a No.2 round brush to work in the details. Using Raw Sienna, blending wet-in-wet with Burnt Sienna, start to lay in warm shadows on the left.

2 ◄ Mix Deep Brilliant Red and Cerulean Blue for the purple-violet shadows on the walls, which begin to give structure to the building. Lay a wash of Olive Green, French Ultramarine, and Burnt Sienna, using a flat wash brush to suggest the shadowy buildings in the background.

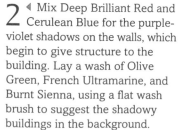

3 ▲ Deepen the shadows on the edge of the canopy of the dome with a purple made from Deep Brilliant Red and Phthalo Blue. Shade the arches and start to pick out the details of the windows using a No.6 round brush with dilute Raw Sienna. Paint in the fine architectural details above them with a No.2 round brush.

4 ◀ The facade of the building takes shape with a mixture of Phthalo Blue and Olive Green, used to add detail to the windows. Select Cadmium Red for the street sign and suggest the windows of the buildings in the background with a No. 6 round brush and a wash of Phthalo Blue.

5 ▲ The passersby appear as if by magic – start with a dab of color for the head and use Titanium White as a transparent overlaid color to build up the upper halves of the bodies. Use a selection of neutral grays, browns, and purples already mixed on your palette to add the legs. Note that Titanium White, when overpainted onto brown, has a bluish cast in comparison to the white showing through from the paper elsewhere in the painting.

Work of this kind relies on a balance between areas of free-flowing washes and finely worked details for its effects. You need just enough of the latter to define the image but not too much to crowd it.

Architectural study, Istanbul

The use of highlights from the background color of the paper gives a convincing impression of light flooding down in front of the building and reflecting back off the pavement. Overlaid transparent washes are entirely responsible for the form of the building and its surroundings; the precise architectural detail has been drawn in with a fine brush. The people are both strangely insubstantial and a powerful presence; their sense of movement is created by economic brushwork building up washes of color.

The finished background is just suggested with washes and the merest hint of detail so that the central image becomes more powerful.

The original photograph is re-interpreted, using artistic license. Notice how the people in the foreground have been dropped, and the background buildings changed subtly. Too much extraneous detail detracts from the central image and is also hard to interpret.

Materials

No.2 round sable brush

No.4 round sable brush

No.6 round squirrel brush

Synthetic wash brush

Julian Bray

GALLERY OF PAINTING STYLES

THE VERSATILITY OF ACRYLIC paint means that it can be used in a wide variety of ways. When highly diluted, acrylics produce attractive watercolor-type effects on all kinds of different painting surfaces. Acrylic paints may also be used semi-opaquely and opaquely, or very thickly – creating the kind of impasted work that is traditionally associated with oil painting. These very different paintings show how some artists working in acrylics use just one approach to great effect, while others combine several approaches in one painting.

Christopher Lenthall, *Untitled 60 x 60 in (152 x 152 cm)*
This painting has the quality of a Pop Art print and clearly demonstrates the artist's interest in typography. A bright, flat effect is achieved by applying opaque paint onto the canvas very evenly, and by using colors right out of the tube, without any mixing. The pale blue ground is actually toned primer. To create his patterns, Lenthall uses stencils to produce an outline that is then filled in with color.

Gabriella Baldwin-Purry,
Karen 21 x 29 in (53 x 74 cm)
This largely monochromatic painting is done exclusively in a transparent watercolor technique. Its immediacy arises from a loose, liquid use of the medium, with the white of the paper support illuminating the thin washes.

Jane Gifford, *Burmese Puppet 39 x 25 in (99 x 65 cm)*
Here, thin transparent preliminary washes have been combined with superimposed touches of thick, opaque color. The latter cover almost the whole surface, giving it a richness that echoes the costume's ornate decoration. The work is an unashamedly exuberant confection.

David Evans,
Pier and Old Lighthouse

3 x 4 in (8 x 10 cm)

Evans' appealing and accessible seascape is painted almost exclusively with an opaque color technique, in which colors are mixed with white to lighten the tone and the paint is applied relatively thickly. This has given the painting a solid and rather melancholy atmosphere. The work is deceptively simple; it seems almost naive. But the artist's use of color is sophisticated, with all the low-key hues enlivened by a carefully placed touch of orange-red on the lighthouse tower. Evans has achieved a sense of great breadth in what is actually a tiny work.

This detail shows how the stripes of pink, orange, pale green, apricot, and pale blue have been painted in one thick, bold brushstroke each. In doing this, the artist is exploiting the opaque possibilities of acrylic paint – the way in which it can totally obliterate colors underneath.

Albert Irvin, *Madison,* **1990**

34 x 48 in (86 x 122 cm)

Irvin's work has always celebrated the expressive possibilities of the paint itself. This painting is no exception. It gets involved with acrylic color in a vital way, combining sweeping strokes and pure color in a spirited, vigorous composition. The opacity of the color mixes allows parts of the work to be overpainted with a single brushstroke.

John McLean, *Avalanche*

58 x 91 in (146 x 231 cm)

This artist's paintings have a deceptive simplicity of appearance while showing an extraordinary control of the acrylic medium. He uses the paint in thin, transparent washes, often applied to unprimed canvas to give a soaked-in look that makes an intimate bond between paint and support. This "star-burst," in vibrant adjacent colors, has an exciting freshness and vitality.

DRY-BRUSH AND SCUMBLING

WITH DRY-BRUSH TECHNIQUES, interesting textures are created by practically scrubbing paint dryly onto your painting surface. This is often done with a bristle brush, and over a textured ground: the ridges of the surface take the paint, and the hollows are left in their original color. Dry-brushing is particularly effective over another color. Achieve the necessary "dry" brush by wiping it on a rag before painting. In scumbling, thin or thick semi-opaque color is brushed loosely over another, dried, color. The color beneath the scumble may show through in places, so that it still has a significant effect on the final result.

WHEN DRY-BRUSHING with thin acrylic, remove excess paint and moisture with an absorbent rag or paper towel. With thick paint, commonly used for dry-brushing, fill the brush with stiff paint straight from the tube before working it on your palette or on a rag. Try dry-brushing opaque light paint over a textured, colored ground, or dark color over a white ground. Halftones emerge where the paint is left on the ridges, with the ground still showing in the dips and hollows.

Pueblo village
Here, forms and shadows were painted in specific colors, and then very different colors were dry-brushed over the top. Dry-brushing a cold blue or purple over the hot yellows and oranges creates rich, deep shadows. The ladders have been added with the lightest of touches, using a very rapid dry-brush technique.

Dry-brushed cacti
The cactus above is painted on canvas board. It shows how any rough surface – paper, board, or canvas – is a very effective base for dry-brush techniques. On a smooth surface, such as the smooth paper used on the left, you will have to rely more on skillful use of a very dry brush.

Sample scumbles
A huge range of effects can be achieved with scumbling. Vermilion scumbled over Cadmium Yellow is visually different than yellow over Vermilion. Light tones scumbled over dark colors give a subtle depth.

Form and color
The rapid creation of halftones made possible with dry-brushing means that it is ideal for underpainting – for example, sketching in the basic modeling of forms.

Scumbling is important because it allows tones to be lightened and colors to be adjusted in a unique way. An effective use of scumbling is to underpaint an object in one color and then scumble the final color loosely on top. Another alternative is to underpaint in a dark color and scumble a lighter, opaque version of the same color over it.

Chameleons

This exercise shows, very clearly, the difference between scumbling opaque color loosely over a light- and dark-colored ground. On the bright yellow ground, the colors seem dark in tone, while the same colors on the dark blue ground appear lighter. The lively interaction of color that occurs within the dark outlines of the chameleons is a good example of the rich effects that can be obtained with scumbling.

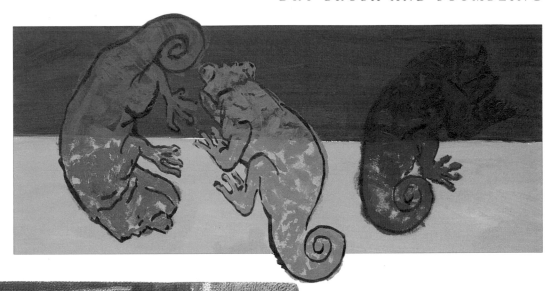

Mexican women and child

This Mexican village scene shows how well dry-brushing and scumbling can work together. Here, the rough weave of the canvas – given a warm orange-brown – provides the perfect backdrop for both the subject matter and the style used. On the dry-brushed areas, paint has been carefully stroked, rather than scrubbed, across the canvas. The shadowed areas were created with a fairly dry scumbling technique.

Dark blue scumbles create shadows on the pillars, the ground, and the women's skirts. Enough of the brown ground shows through to give the work an overall harmony.

Thick, dry opaque color, stroked across the ridges of the canvas, brings out the dazzling effects of sun on the white facade of the far building – and on the ground.

BLENDING

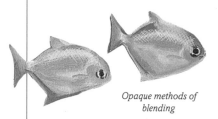

Opaque methods of blending

BLENDING IS MAKING one tone or color flow smoothly into another without an abrupt transition. You can blend colors physically or optically. With physical blending, you actually mix colors. With optical blending, colors are juxtaposed and superimposed – for example, by using dots of color or by cross-hatching – so that, visually, they appear to blend. When working with opaque color, you must work fast before the paint dries, blending with a clean, damp brush. It is easy to create smooth transitions when blending transparent color. You can apply washes to damp paper, drop color onto damp paper to create star-burst effects, or blend with a damp paintbrush.

BLENDING OPAQUE COLOR requires fast work because of the short drying time involved. With transparent color, build up tonal gradations in thin, superimposed layers of color, softening the tone each time with a clean, damp brush. Alternatively, dampen the paper so that the paint fuses into it, becoming lighter in tone.

Coral reef fish
This study incorporates all the methods of blending described here, with the soft fusion of wet areas of transparent color and the more physical blending of opaque color. Cross-hatching is shown by the plants on the left, and gradation of tone by the stippled coral.

Opaque blending
Working on canvas board, different tones of orange are applied adjacent to one another. While they are still wet, the join between them is stroked with a damp, clean brush to smooth the tonal transitions.

Cross-hatching
Applying acrylic colors in thin lines, as if shading with a pencil, is a method of blending which relates to early Renaissance techniques. You can build up tones and forms and blend colors with fine, cross-hatched strokes. Although this may seem a laborious method of working, the results are very effective.

Dabs of color applied over wet washes create the texture of the coral.

Using transparent color, blend the stripes with a damp brush.

Blending with a damp brush

Apply transparent color to one arm of the starfish, then immediately diffuse the color by running a clean, damp paintbrush along the center of the arm. Create the shadow by using a damp brush over the washed-in color in the same way.

Blending wet-in-wet

Wet the area of the shell with a damp sponge and apply the two main colors as transparent washes. When dry, dampen the paper and dab on small touches of color. These will spread, creating the characteristic cluster pattern.

Wet-in-wet blending produces subtle colors on the rocks.

Blending on wet paper

Dampen the area within the pebble with a wet sponge, and then wash in the colors so that they fuse and blend naturally. Vary the amount and dilution of the color as you apply it. Use thin lines of opaque color to create the striations on the pebble.

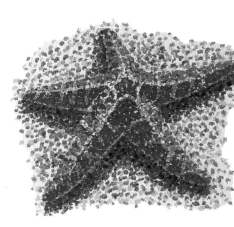

Optical blending

Apply small and uniformly sized touches of pure color straight from the tube to model the tones and colors of the starfish. Juxtaposing blues and orange-reds creates darker-toned shadows among the neutral colors.

Use a damp brush to blend the stripe of opaque color.

Optical blending creates the stippled effect of the coral.

GLAZING

GLAZING IS THE APPLICATION of a thin layer of transparent color over certain areas, or all, of a painting in order to create specific color effects. You might choose to glaze a single color over the whole surface of a work, as a way of creating a dominant overall hue. Alternatively, you could use glazes to alter the color of individual objects that have already been underpainted.

BECAUSE ACRYLIC DRIES quickly, you have only a short wait before a glaze can be applied over the top of another color. A glaze is usually modified on the painting surface, to reduce it to a thin, even stain. You must work swiftly and decisively, before the paint dries, and so it is a good idea to glaze one small area at a time. Mix the color to a thin consistency and apply with a brush. Leave it for a minute or two, and then work it over with a dry bristle brush or a shaving brush.

Changing colors
Here, bright green grass has been toned down by adding a very thin red glaze. One layer of glaze is sufficient to break the green; additional layers are too extreme.

Overall glazes
Glazing a whole painting is like putting a color filter over a camera lens. This landscape has been "cooled down" by a blue glaze, applied with a brush (left), and an airbrush (right). To prevent airbrushed paint from running, spray a fine mist in stages and allow each stage to dry.

1 ◀ This exercise shows how a painting can be subtly transformed by the application of glazes. Here, the coffeepot has been painted in a full, rich range of tones and colors and is waiting for the addition of glazes to pull the image together. Remember to keep your brush dry by wiping it off on absorbent cloth or paper each time you work over a glaze.

2 ▲ With a No.10 brush, apply a thin wash of Yellow Ochre and gloss medium as a uniform stain over the coffeepot. This enriches the color of the brass and unifies the object.

3 ◀ Create a shadow around the pot with a glaze of Ultramarine and gloss medium – applied very thinly, so that it does not kill the warmth of the red kilim.

Jane Gifford

Turkish coffeepot and kilim
In the finished work, a film of Indian Red and gloss medium has been added over all of the kilim with a flat 1in brush. This tones down the background, adds warmth and harmonizes all the colors. After glazing, the painting has a mellower, richer look that is ideally suited to the subject matter. The exotic pot and rug seem to glow, as if under artificial light.

Materials

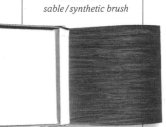

No.12 round sable/synthetic brush

1in sable/synthetic brush

Basic pointers for glazing

When you are glazing, use naturally transparent pigments (*see* p.366) or dilute more opaque ones so that they appear transparent. You can also dilute paint, without losing body, by mixing a very small amount of color with acrylic gel or gloss medium.

You do not have to use a brush. If you are glazing with a tinted acrylic gel medium, you can scrape glaze on in an even film with a piece of flexible plastic such as an old credit card.

Learning how specific colors work together will enable you to create rich, unusual effects. A blue glaze over yellow produces a green that could not be copied by physically mixing a yellow and a blue. Experiment with multi-layered glazes so that you are ready to use them when they seem appropriate to a particular work.

One interesting option is to glaze over images underpainted in mono-chrome tones such as brown and white or gray and white, or to under-paint in a paler, opaque version of the glaze color. As a general rule when glazing, your underpainting should avoid the darkest and lightest tones.

1 ▲ Use glazing to build up large areas of color and more intricate patterns. Block in the underpainting: semi-opaque Cadmium Yellow for the background; glazes of Alizarin Crimson and Cadmium Orange over the dried yellow for the rug; and a Cerulean Blue glaze for the parcel.

2 ▲ When the base colors are dry, glaze shadows over the blue parcel with a Phthalo Blue-based purple. Now build up the rug pattern, and give body to the objects, with layers of glazes.

3 ▶ Mix up highly diluted Cobalt Blue with gel medium. Using the large, flat brush, glaze this very transparently over the background yellow to produce shadows on both sides of the painting. Blue creates deeper, warmer shadows than gray or black, harmonizing well with the vivid yellow. Continue to add fine detail by layering glazes.

4 ▲ To intensify the background, add an overall glaze of Cadmium Yellow with the large brush. This now balances the saturated color of the orange foreground – created by glazing Cadmium Orange over the yellow background. With large areas of glaze, work quickly and deliberately to ensure even coverage.

Glowing glazes

The painting glows with colors built up from successive glazes. Adding an extra Cobalt Blue glaze has deepened the side shadows.

The garlic was painted by adding very fine glazes over the white priming of the board support. Letting the intense white primer shine through glazes gives the garlic a subtle translucence and a well-modeled presence.

Ian McCaughrean

Materials

¹/₂ in flat soft synthetic brush

2in bristle brush

THE ALLA PRIMA APPROACH

ALLA PRIMA – MEANING "AT FIRST" in Italian – is an approach to painting that has been popular in oil painting since the 19th century. It is equally relevant to acrylics. A painting made using this method is not generally built up in layers with long gaps between painting sessions. The work is effectively created during one continuous session, normally from life, and there may be little or no preliminary drawing. The advantage of the alla prima method is that, at its best, it conveys an immediacy of mood and style that can give it an exhilarating freshness. In practice, this does not mean that you must get it right the first time. With oil paint, you have to rub off an area before repainting. However, because acrylics dry so rapidly, you can overpaint almost immediately.

Opaque study
Here, the chair receives a chunkier, opaque treatment. Relatively stiff acrylic is applied to the paper using a dry-brush method in which the paint takes hold of the ridges of the paper but misses the hollows, giving a rich texture. As in the other study, the white ground is used as a positive element. Wipe brushes thoroughly on a rag after each rinse, so that they remain dry and the paint does not blot.

Rapid washes
This loose study, on thick watercolor paper, is a boldly direct response to the sight of a jacket casually draped over the back of a chair. The paint is used well diluted, in a watercolor-type technique – separate washes retain their shape and color but flow and blend with one another in places.

KEEPING YOUR PAINT WORKABLE

One of the problems with acrylic paints – especially when working outside or in hot weather – is that they may dry so rapidly that you do not have time to manipulate them on your painting or even on the palette. To avoid this: make sure that you only squeeze out the amount of paint you need at any one time; keep spraying the palette with water; mix a proprietary "retarder" with the paint; or use a special "stay-wet" palette *(below)*.

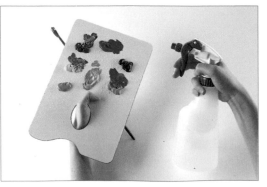 

Spraying a palette with a fine water mist to keep paint moist

Commercial "stay-wet" palette, lined with special paper that is dampened before paints are squeezed out on top

VERY OFTEN, ALLA PRIMA paintings are made outside, in the landscape. However, the alla prima approach is equally suited to any work where you want to achieve a fresh, spontaneous feel. In order to get used to this painting method, perhaps as a way of practicing before you venture outside, try doing some simple still lifes of objects around your home, like the studies shown on these pages.

If you are planning, for example, to tackle a scene featuring people, you might want to make some transitional studies of a figure, or small groups of people, such as the brisk sketch of the two flower-sellers on page 384.

Using a colored ground

You can use alla prima techniques equally effectively on a colored ground. In the painting on the left, the dark tones of the hat and shoes create a striking physical presence on the pale pink ground. The ground was painted and allowed to dry before the other main areas were blocked in roughly, in a free, abstract way. As a final step, detail was added and the boots were outlined rapidly with a mix of Burnt Umber and Ivory Black. Notice how flecks of color from one object are reflected on another object – a quick, easy touch that gives the study a satisfying unity and harmony.

A darker ground

Here, all the paper was painted with a mix of Ultramarine and Phthalo Blue first, applied flatly and evenly. This basic ground is left exposed in the top left-hand corner, and gives added depth to the yellow and pink tones, which are scumbled thickly over the top (see pp.376-7).

A study in bold brushwork

This study shows the immediacy of decisive brushwork. Mainly flat brushes were used, with their typically broad strokes. The opaque paint is creamy in texture. If just a little more water had been added, the artist would have been mixing paint on the actual painting (which is best avoided, although it has occurred in the dark beige area to the right of the hat). The work has a genuine alla prima feel; painted very rapidly, it was completed before any areas could dry. Like the other sketches, it is all about playing with abstract blocks of color before adding final defining touches – an approach that helps to prevent a "painting by numbers" effect. An exciting spontaneity arises from not quite knowing what will happen next.

Tackling figures

This slightly warm, neutral ground responds well to white at one end of the tonal scale and to black at the other. Very few swift brushstrokes are needed to convey the shape and movement of human figures – in this case, flower-sellers going about their business. The canvas board on which this was painted creates an interesting texture. It also tends to take up a lot of paint, so the color has been applied quite thickly.

ALLA PRIMA PAINTING

THE MOST SUCCESSFUL ALLA PRIMA work – also called "direct" painting – relies on a certain bravura in the brushwork and an instinct for the right tone or color. These qualities produce the sparkle

that is created by painting directly from the subject – whether working from real life or from a photograph – and by completing the work in a single session. In this alla prima painting, with its effective use of deep, dark browns and ochres, a contemporary scene at a busy café in a train station takes on an atmospheric 19th-century look. The warmth of the ochres is well complemented by the cool, pale blues.

Effective preparation
While alla prima is a very direct method, preparatory studies made to guide the choice of colors and the composition can actually free up the work and make it look more spontaneous.

1 ▷ To add a lively surface texture, work on a primed cotton canvas. The fact that acrylic dries so rapidly not only helps with overpainting, but also makes canvases easier to carry around – very useful when working outdoors. With a No.10 filbert bristle, paint in the overall background color broadly, using thick paint. Mix mainly Titanium White and Yellow Ochre with a little Azo Yellow, Cadmium Orange, and Burnt Umber for extra warmth. Think ahead – the slightly darker wedge near the center will form the basis of the floor of the café.

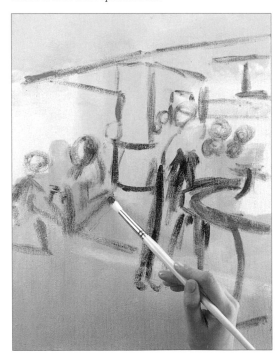

2 ▲ Now, adopting a dry-brush technique with the No.7 bristle, rapidly sketch all the main shapes in the dark colors that create the rich, inviting tones of this café interior. Use mixes of Phthalo Blue and Ivory Black, Burnt Umber and Ivory Black, and Burnt Umber and Cadmium Orange. Your brush should be very dry; use a minimum of paint and keep the pressure of the brush on the canvas light – your work at this stage should be ephemeral and open to easy alteration.

3 ◁ Turning your attention to the foreground, load the large bristle brush with a lot of Titanium White, warmed slightly by a dash of Cadmium Orange and Azo Yellow. Always mix your colors on the palette, but build up paint on the canvas progressively until you achieve the right tone. Start to block in some of the other main areas of color in a rough, free way. Although you are working very quickly, be sure to remember to wash your brushes continually and thoroughly, so that they never become clogged with dried, water-resistant paint.

5 ◀ Move on to the figures on the other side of the painting, using quite dry paint to cover areas quickly. Define shapes such as the chairs with an outline of Burnt Umber. Notice how a rapid up-and-down brushstroke on the man's trousers provides coverage and an interesting surface texture. Effective brushwork is very important – for alla prima painting, you will have to rely much more on the "autonomy" of the single brushstroke.

4 ▲ Having blocked in most of the main areas, begin to add detail to the right-hand side of the composition, as the girl and the table form the real core of the painting. When painting details, such as the girl's shoes, load a small, soft brush with thick paint and work very quickly and decisively to create a drawn effect.

6 ▶ Now that you have basically completed the central band of the composition, start work on the architectural surround. Apply the broad areas of color with a blend of Turquoise, Yellow Ochre, and Burnt Umber, tracing the light, fine lines with Burnt Umber. Once this is complete, step back and reassess the painting, adding further detail and minor alterations to every part until you are completely satisfied with it as a whole.

The whole flat area of the filbert has been used for overall coverage, and the olive and brown lines of the architecture have been made with the edge of the brush. Make sure that you use every angle of your brush – in the final picture, you can see how all kinds of different types of brushwork have been used to convey the scene effectively.

The pale color of the station platform has been intensified in places at the last minute. This anchors it properly within real space. When working alla prima, make sure that you allow yourself the vital readjustments needed to give the work unity.

Assessing the scene

The composition falls into three main blocks – the interior of the café, the architectural surround, and the foreground. When using this fast painting approach – especially if you are working outside in a busy location – it is important to assess the scene quickly. Once you come to understand the way you work and the materials, this mental editing process will become automatic.

Materials

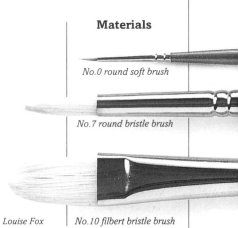

No.0 round soft brush

No.7 round bristle brush

Louise Fox | *No.10 filbert bristle brush*

COMBINING TECHNIQUES

THE GREAT VERSATILITY of acrylic paints becomes obvious when several very different techniques are brought together to function in a rich and often complex manner within the same painting. Here, washes of transparent color are combined with thicker overlaid opaque color and thin, semi-opaque scumbling, as well as various resist techniques.

A painting may go through many permutations before you are happy with the final image. In this case, although the models were outdoors, the plan was to turn the scene into an indoor one, with light flooding in from the left and a window looking out. As the work progressed, reality prevailed and, with some reworking, the scene was reinstated outdoors.

2 ▷ Create shadows on the sweater and around the face with a Phthalo Blue-based purple. A Deep Brilliant Red wash warms up the dark green of the rug. Wash in the shadows between the feet with French Ultramarine and Cerulean Blue over rust oil pastel. It is a good idea at this stage to sketch in facial details with a fine, round soft brush – use well-diluted Burnt Sienna for a very delicate feel. Add faint shadows of Burnt Sienna to the skirt. As the work progresses, it is important to achieve a balance between the broad and the detailed areas; do not leave all the detail until the end.

1 ▲ Working wet-in-wet with Raw and Burnt Sienna, lay down the initial wash for the faces, adding Phthalo Blue and Cerulean Blue to create subtle color on parts of the skirt. A Phthalo Blue wash provides the rich color of the sweater. Dry-brushing with French Ultramarine creates textures in the deep shadow on the left. Sketch in the window with neutral washes. Loosely dry-brush opaque Raw Sienna over orange oil pastel, used to add texture, on the back wall.

3 ▲ Add more of the finer details – for example, the pattern and knots on the rug and the decorative edging on the woman's skirt. An extremely faint, transparent wash of Cerulean Blue adds form to the baby's pullover. Vigorously dry-brush opaque white onto the rear wall so that it does not quite obliterate the Raw Sienna, which still comes through in areas and has a significant impact on the finished work.

4 ◁ A wash of Raw and Burnt Sienna lessens the stark effect of the white rear wall, adding subtle shadows. Stripes of Deep Brilliant Red have the effect of throwing the rug into shadow. Using a round, medium-sized brush, scumble a thin, semi-opaque lilac over the shadows on the wall. This subdues the blue, creating some textural interest, resonant tones, and depth.

OVERPAINTING

The window started as an internal window, looking out onto a scene of fields *(left)*. The artist was unhappy with the view through the window, reworking it several times. As the painting progressed, the window started to have the feel of a painting on the wall, but as soon as it was re-worked in dark shades, turning it into an external window *(right)*, the picture was transformed. The new version of the window ties in better with the blue of the shadows and the woman's clothes. It is a rather atmospheric use of thin transparent darks scumbled over opaque lights, that suggests the shadowy flower pots at the window.

The internal window, looking out

The external window, looking into the cottage

5 ◀ Crosshatching is a useful way of blending facial tones; use a mixture of Raw and Burnt Sienna and a fine brush to add detail to the baby's face. Keep adding Deep Brilliant Red, as well as Titanium White and blues, to this mix to capture the shadows on the face. Purple shadows on the skirt define the baby's hand. Add pattern to the skirt with sensitive lines and dabs of opaque color – these enhance the loose, relaxed effect of the skirt material.

6 ▲ Concentrate on the floor area – at this stage the addition of a coffee mug and the suggestion of an opened book adds foreground interest. A pale green wash gives the effect of sunlight falling across the rug, while white, orange, and rust oil pastels added to the floor area suggest stonework.

The window has been created with a rich and quite complex variety of techniques.

The bold contrasts between light and shade and between very different colors give a strong formal structure and clarity to this otherwise relaxed painting. But even heavily-worked areas such as this still retain a looseness in the brushwork and a vivacity that keeps the painting fresh. This informality is perfectly in keeping with the intimacy of the scene.

Julian Bray

Against the cottage wall

The strong colors of the first stages of the composition have been subtly transformed into an appealing study of a mother and baby. The sun pouring in from the left casts deep shadows, ranging from cool lilacs to warmer tones around the figures. The wall, having undergone several metamorphoses, now successfully recreates the texture of the whitewashed, rendered original.

Materials

White oil pastel

Orange oil pastel

Rust oil pastel

No.2 round soft synthetic brush

No.4 round squirrel brush

No.6 squirrel brush

GALLERY OF TECHNIQUES

As you get used to working with acrylics, your technical knowledge and repertoire will increase, and you will find that you are using the medium in many new ways. This process of opening out will enable you to see that there are all kinds of ways of arriving at solutions to painting problems. Acrylic paint is extremely flexible, and you can adapt it to hugely varied methods of painting. The following artists incorporate a wide range of working methods and ways of combining different techniques. William Henderson's work shows clever effects with blending; spraying and using stencils feature in Michael Andrews's painting; while Chuck Close employs photographic projection to give his subjects a remarkably powerful presence.

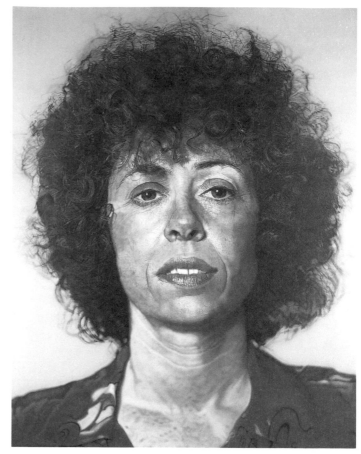

Chuck Close, *Linda, 1975–76* 108 x 84 in (274 x 213 cm)
Close works by projecting photographs onto the canvas. This may look very much like a photograph, but its huge size offers a different experience; it is clear that we are looking at the physicality of painted washes. Combining these "close-up" and "far off" aspects produces strong, bold images.

William Henderson,
Little Operas (Theme No. 2) 55 x 50 in (140 x 127 cm)
Through skillful blending, the artist has created a busy quality that gives us the sense of looking down on an insect colony. Just when one area seems to be the key to the work, our attention is drawn to another part.

Henderson has achieved his unusual effects by juxtaposing areas of blended paint. Through this technique, dimensional elements begin to appear, while the ragged edges of the brushstrokes leave the shapes unresolved, with a deliberate "out of focus" quality.

Bernard Cohen,
9 Stops
73 x 73 in (185 x 185 cm)
There is a real depth in this work, created by Cohen's special way of stenciling. A meticulous process of repeated masking out, rubbing down, repriming, and painting produces dazzling, multilayered works. While an area of one color may seem to be above another, it is often physically beneath it – Cohen rubs some areas back almost to the canvas before painting them. He views stenciling as part of the folk art tradition: his components – the stencils – are cut on a table before he assembles and uses them directly on the canvas.

Fred Pollock, *Caryatid*
80 x 66 in (203 x 168 cm)
This painting, executed in vigorous brushstrokes, illustrates the artist's breadth of knowledge: how to use shape and direction, how colors react together, and how to balance a composition.

This detail shows how the foreground has been sprayed through real grasses, held up against the canvas so that their forms appear paler than the surrounding color. This gives the effect of the sun shining on the grasses, which stand out against the warm yellows and cooler browns of the ground. Spraying the paint softens the edges where they have not been masked – evoking a sense of a heat haze.

Michael Andrews, *The Cathedral,*
The Southern Faces / Uluru (Ayers Rock),
1987 *96 x 153 in (244 x 389 cm)*
Andrews combines a high degree of technical expertise with a poetic nostalgia. His works are invariably quiet and serene, with a sense of detachment. He never allows the paint to go out of control, restraining it within a linear style in which each form is carefully observed. Here, the combination of spray painting with regular brushwork, and the deep blue sky, convey an impression of blistering heat.

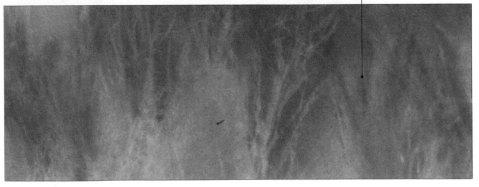

EXPERIMENTING WITH ACRYLICS

OIL PAINT has such a weight of cultural history behind it that artists new to the medium can find it intimidating. Acrylics are relatively young, so artists feel that they can experiment more freely. The fast drying times and ease of overpainting also help to build confidence – if one area of your painting is not working the first time around, you can try something else out practically right away. Also, because the dried acrylic paint film retains its plastic flexibility and stability, even in very thick applications, acrylics can be used thickly with far less fear of creating a potentially fragile work than with oils. Acrylic can be dripped, poured, sprayed, scraped, extruded – even knotted and woven. Other techniques are just waiting to be discovered.

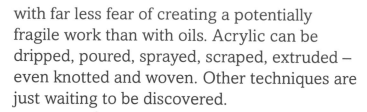

Creative sampler
These different techniques show the versatility of acrylics. Sgraffito was used here, and stripes were wiped out of the wet black paint with a damp paper tissue.

Removing paint
In this sample, the white on the right-hand black shape was applied straight out of the tube. Dabbing with a damp sponge has created dots over the main white area.

Layering paint
This was created by washing over layers of different colors with Ultramarine. Shapes were then scraped back to the brown and yellow paint underneath.

Form and texture
Forms were printed by pressing painted cardboard shapes onto a yellow ground. Sandpaper rubbed into wet yellow paint on the right produced an unusual texture.

Rough ground
Dark gray paint, applied very roughly with a toothbrush, provides the ground on which shapes were printed with thickly painted cardboard.

Sgraffito technique
Sgraffito – from the Italian for "scratching" – describes scratching through fairly thick wet or dry paint to reveal the original surface or another color underneath. Any sharp implement can be used. Here, a thumbnail scratches back to the white paper through a layer of Burnt Umber.

Inventive scraping
There are many scraping techniques (see p.349). Scrape swathes of single or combined colors across your painting surface. Scrape thin acrylic – or a glaze of gel medium and color – over a painted image. This plastic glue scraper has actually produced a type of sgraffito effect.

Rich mixtures
Achieve unusual effects by mixing thick color very loosely. A flat bristle brush was used to make these rich, impasted strokes. The outer rectangle – a loose mix of Phthalo Green and Azo Yellow – surrounds Azo Yellow combined with Cadmium Red. Because dried acrylic is so flexible, there is less chance of thick paint breaking up or flaking than with other media.

Making patterns

Develop a personal style by experimenting with any materials you have on hand. Cadmium Yellow has been allowed to dry before painting Phthalo Blue over the top. Lifting the wet blue paint off by dabbing with a dry paper tissue leaves a mottled pattern.

Rubbing through

A very different texture has been created here. Layers of colors were overpainted, allowing each to dry before applying the next. Rubbing with sandpaper has revealed colors underneath the black. Rub harder in some places to uncover deeper layers. The sandpaper lends an unusual "cross-hatched" texture of its own.

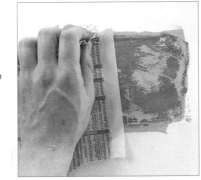

Simple scraping

This black and white sgraffito effect – using a thumbnail to scrape through black paint to a white layer beneath – is very simple, but starkly effective.

Lifting off

Cadmium Yellow has been applied to grained watercolor paper with a roller and left to dry. A mix of Cadmium Yellow and Cadmium Red has then been rolled over the top, and a scrap of newspaper pressed down lightly over the wet paint and quickly removed. The paint lifts off unevenly, and a varied overall texture emerges.

Using the ground

Layering different, semitransparent colors has produced three-dimensional forms. Good use is made of the gray with which the whole sheet was originally toned.

A working theme

Try experimenting around a theme – these samples were inspired by the shapes of fruit. Here, fingerprints give the red ground an interesting texture.

Wax resist

Here, orange and red washes have fused with each other. Paint has not "taken" where lines of wax resist were applied to the paper, creating a shimmering effect.

Wiping out

The rich yellow circle of paint was applied out of the tube. The gray crescent on the right was wiped out of the wet black paint, back to the gray-toned paper, with a damp tissue.

STENCILING AND PRINTING

Stencils are often used by artists working in acrylic. Shapes cut out of cardboard make ideal stencils, or they can be painted and pressed onto the painting surface to produce a printed image. Keep all your shapes for future use. When used repeatedly, they become attractive objects in themselves; you might incorporate some in a future collage.

1 *Paint a layer of Naphthol Crimson onto a piece of paper. Leave to dry for about 10 minutes. Holding your shape down, paint over its edges with a large brush loaded with Hooker's Green.*

2 *Now lift your stencil shape off the surface carefully but swiftly. Choosing the complementary colors red and green has made this very simple stencil exercise particularly effective.*

A selection of shapes used for stenciling and printing

EXPLORING NEW IDEAS

ONE OF THE MOST important aspects of painting in acrylics is that you should enjoy experimenting with the possibilities of the medium. If you tend to work in a close or tight style, try loosening up – even if you seem to be making a mess with your paints. It is only by trying out new things that you will add to your technical repertoire. This lively and exuberant composition is the result of a series of experiments with an image which was taken first from life.

The many methods explored on these pages include cutting up and reforming the image, stenciling, printing, and splash techniques. The image has gone through a number of permutations, but the finished result has a freshness and vivacity that reflects the pleasure that has gone into making it.

Working from life
A simplified life drawing provides the basis for the final abstract image.

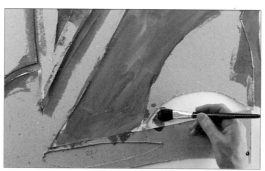

1 ◀ Copy the main shapes of the simplified sketch onto cardboard. Cut these out, number them for reference and lay them on a sheet of smooth paper.

2 ▲ Lay a wash of Ultramarine and Phthalo Blue around most of the cut-out shapes. This overall hue lends the work an air of gentle calm.

3 ▲ Carefully remove the pieces of cardboard to reveal their shapes, left as exposed white paper.

4 ▲ Paint one side of the V shape with a mix of Yellow Ochre and Raw Sienna. Leave to dry and add another coat – the first coat acts as a primer.

5 ▲ While the second coat of paint is still wet, place the shape – painted side down – onto the painting surface, in its original position.

6 ▲ Press down onto the shape with an even, sustained pressure. Use anything that is available – a rolling pin, your hands, or even your feet.

7 ▲ Remove the shape quickly but carefully. The printed impression shows the original brushstrokes made when the shape was painted.

8 ◀ Repeat this with other cut-out shapes, one at a time. To achieve varied effects, apply differing amounts of pressure, or overprint shapes to intensify the color. Note that Naphthol Crimson, with a touch of Cadmium Red, was painted between shapes in the top left to emphasize the face area.

9 ▶ With a large brush, paint black crosses freely across the bottom to bring this area forward. These touches add interest and depth – the work no longer appears to be all on the same plane.

Materials

No.4 round soft synthetic brush

No.10 round soft synthetic brush

Soft Japanese brush

³/₄ in flat soft wash brush

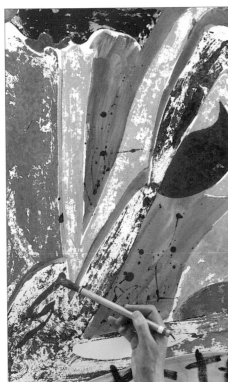

10 ◀ Replace most of the cardboard shapes, so that the printed parts are covered. Using the No.10 and 4 brushes, flick a dark mix of the basic blue wash across the central blue areas. This adds a raw, exciting energy, as well as a surface texture that gives the areas underneath greater depth.

11 ▲ Take a break to reassess your progress, perhaps looking back to the original drawings. Add touches that will bring all the elements together. Painting a bold red flourish to indicate the woman's hand complements the green underneath – bringing it forward and breaking it up slightly – and balances the red at the top. Use red sparingly – it can be overpowering.

Making marks
In the finished work, Titanium White stars have been added on the left, straight out of the tube. These provide a kind of opposite echo to the black crosses. Repeating marks across a painting – with a slight variation each time – can provide a satisfying harmony.

Burnt Umber painted on top of this yellow strip makes it recede (bright colors such as yellow tend to come forward). This strip represents the original woman's far arm. Adding brown makes it, quite rightly, appear farther away than the other yellow strip – the near arm. At first, too much brown was added, so the excess was quickly wiped off before the paint dried.

Try using one color in different ways. In this work, blue has been painted, printed, and splattered. The sense of movement and modeling created by painting blue over printed blue suggests a human form. The printed blue stands in front of the painted blue because a lot of white paper shows through the printed parts. White areas are used as a positive element in this work.

Julian Gregg

GALLERY OF EXPERIMENTAL APPROACHES

THE FACT THAT acrylic paint is a relatively new medium means that artists have felt able to experiment with it more freely than they might with traditional painting media. Morris Louis (*see* p.336) developed a staining technique, and since then other artists have explored methods that rely on the plastic qualities of acrylics. These effects simply could not be achieved with conventional media. Historically, we are still at an early stage in the development of acrylics, and further innovative techniques will evolve as our knowledge progresses.

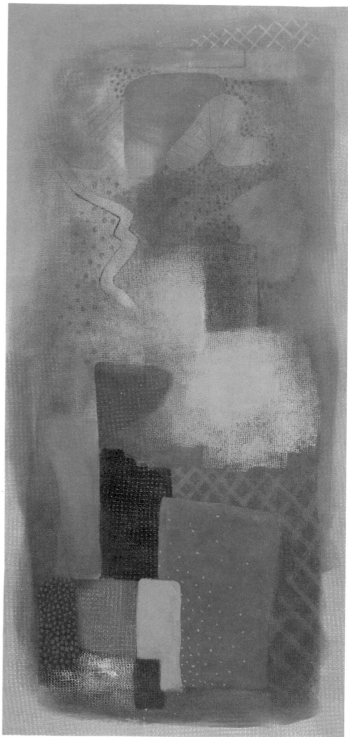

Robert Natkin, *Winchester,* **1992** *73 x 34 in (185 x 86 cm)*
Natkin's shifting layers of opaque and thin color build up a rich but delicate surface. He has developed a way of creating fabric-style textures, and an illusion of collage, through detailed brushwork and by wrapping his brush in cloth. Controlling the brush's pressure gives a range of effects.

Bruce McLean, *Untitled* *102 x 78 in (260 x 198 cm)*
This painting has all the confidence and exuberance of an artist who is happy to pull out all the stops to bring his work to life. Here, he spatters, pours, and throws the paint in thin transparent washes or in thick blobs of color. He paints black over red and scrapes through it to draw his swimming figure. Overall, the work has a refreshing vitality.

Sandra Blow, RA,
Glad Ocean
102 x 144 in (259 x 366 cm)
Sandra Blow's painting is an ambitious experiment in treading the fine line between spontaneity and control. It hinges around the massive lilac shape, which thunders across the canvas from the left and then changes direction, soaring up to the top right-hand edge. The apparent spontaneity of the purple shape is further counterbalanced by the small, hard-edged shapes. These small forms, so carefully controlled, are like tugs to a tanker. They nestle and nudge the great shape, worrying it into place. Their own position and size add a sense of scale to this powerful work.

Ray Smith, *Self-Portrait* *90 x 66 in (229 x 168 cm)*
This image brings together elements of the artist's life and work, including drawings by his children, an airplane vase by the artist Andrew Lord, and a string of illuminated red light bulbs. The face is based on a tiny brush drawing made by candlelight and then scaled up. The work incorporates the use of splashed, scraped, airbrushed, extruded, and – in the case of the socks – woven paint.

In this detail, the transparent blue has been made up from a touch of blue paint mixed with acrylic gel medium. This blue has been scraped over the splashed paint with a credit card.

The diagonal red has been extruded through a pastry bag, while the vertical red has been poured. The yellow on each side of the black line was airbrushed over white.

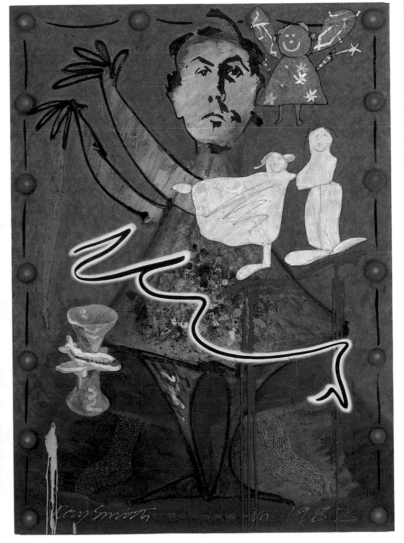

395

PRESENTING YOUR WORK

Cropping compositions
Before framing, experiment with cardboard corners to create the best composition.

THE WAY IN WHICH you choose to present your paintings can have a considerable impact on the final effect. A particularly well-chosen and well-made frame – one that does real justice to the painting – can allow a viewer to focus on the work in a clear and concentrated way. A badly made or ill-chosen frame could detract so completely from the painting that it will be impossible to appreciate it properly. Try to think about presentation as an integral part of your work – not as something that is added as a hasty afterthought.

SOME ARTISTS have a very clear idea of the way in which their work can be enhanced by its frame – for example, choosing to pick up some of the colors in a painting in the frame. Many leave their framing to a framer whose judgment they trust.

Cropping images

Another aspect of presentation is the way in which you choose to crop an image. This is especially relevant if you are working on paper, rather than on canvas or board of a fixed size.

Alternative crops
Focusing on different areas of a painting shows how a variety of totally different works can be created. Here, the slight crop has made the image a little tighter than the original. However, the woman and child are still part of a much larger image, which opens out on each side, making us curious about the world outside the frame.

APPLYING VARNISH

Many artists apply an even, overall coat of varnish over their finished paintings to protect them. Use a flat, long-haired brush – the best kind to ensure a smooth, thin coat of varnish. Most varnishes used for acrylic work contain acrylic resins but dry to a slightly harder film than acrylic paint.

There is some controversy about varnishing acrylic works. With certain varnishes, there is a small "solubility gap" between the paint and the varnish. This means that, if you want to remove the varnish with solvents – if, for example, the varnish has attracted dirt – there is a danger that some of the paint underneath could also be removed. Various new varnishes contain additives that make the varnish harder – which also means that dirt is less likely to stick – but are still removable. Time will tell whether these new types provide the answer.

2in synthetic varnishing brush

Balance and symmetry
This example closes in to establish a more precise structural balance between the window coming down from the top right-hand edge and the woman coming up from the bottom left. It creates a kind of symmetry that gives the painting a certain poise.

Mother and child
The very close crop of the third alternative focuses all our attention on the human situation of the woman and child. We become particularly aware of the extremely direct look we are getting from the young child as it eyes us from the shadow, and from the protection of its mother's lap.

Changing focus and format

Through well-judged cropping, it is possible to modify a composition quite radically before you frame it, by deciding to block some parts of it out altogether. You may wish either to leave out an area that you feel is not painted particularly well, or to focus more on a small area of your painting by making it a larger part of the whole.

By cropping, you can also change the format from landscape (horizontal) to portrait (vertical), try out alternative crops with a couple of cardboard corners.

Works on paper

Typically, a painting on paper would be framed behind a window mat and glass, backed with hardboard.

The cream mat brings the painting forward naturally because it picks up the color of the brightest highlight in the whole object – the sunlit areas of the dome. Against the cream, we are also able to focus on the depth and color of the dark tones in the image.

The dark frame has a classic simplicity that is in keeping with the relatively traditional style and subject matter of the painting.

Dark frame, light mount

The presentation of this architectural study works very well because it achieves a successful balance with the painting itself. The dark frame holds the whole work together, while the cream mat allows the image to come forward.

Light frame, dark mount

This is less successful because the contrast between the light pine frame and the mount seems more extreme. This competes with bold contrasts in the painting, making the image appear to retreat.

Mounting your paintings

When framing a painting on paper, ensure that the mat is made from acid-free cardboard. You will often find that neutral mount colors such as the ivory, pale creams, or pale grays commonly used will bring out the colors in your painting. If you are framing a canvas, attach a backing board to prevent the accumulation of dirt and damage from atmospheric changes.

Yellow frame

When framing, consider the style of your work. This kind of image benefits from a modern-looking frame, perhaps in a bright color. Here, however, the bright yellow tone is a little sickly, and competes with the rope in the painting.

White frame

This frame – like the other two, painted wood – makes the deep tones in the image too dark, so that you cannot read the painting's true colors. The intense white in the image makes the frame look slightly dirty and mismatched.

Mixed-color frame

The predominant gray tone of the frame also includes touches of colors picked up from the painting itself. It suits the work because it has a modern feel, and its mid-tone provides a balance between darks and lights in the image.

AN INTRODUCTION TO
MIXED MEDIA

Mixed Media	400	Unusual Materials	432
History	402	Gallery of Painting	434
Compatible Supports	406	Collage Materials	436
Drawing Materials	408	Printing Materials	438
Painting Materials	410	Color Collage	440
Charcoal and Black Ink	412	Photocollaging	442
Charcoal and Pastels	414	Handmade Paper	444
Line and Color	416	Creating an Image in Paper	446
Resist Techniques	418	Collage-Laminate & Frottage	448
Gallery of Drawing	420	Low Reliefs	450
Multilayered Compositions	422	Gallery of Collage	452
Oil and Soft Pastels	424	Block Printmaking	454
Experimenting with Surface	426	Monoprint	456
Adding Texture	428	Collagraph Printing	458
Gesso and Wax	430	Gallery of Monoprint	460

MIXED MEDIA

THE TERM "MIXED MEDIA" is commonly used to define works of art that combine different painting and drawing media. It is an exciting and experimental working practice that allows for the combination of likely and unlikely media. As a result it has allowed for the extension of drawing and painting techniques into areas of photography, printmaking, collage, and bas-relief construction. Combining different media has become a consistent feature of contemporary practice, and it is rare to see a group exhibition now in which there is not some use of mixed media. Most visual arts courses encourage students to focus on the use of mixed media to develop a more imaginative approach to image making and to learn more about materials. Mixing your media is an excellent way to revitalize your awareness of a familiar medium and to establish new and imaginative interpretations on familiar themes.

Charcoal, pastel and ink

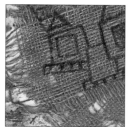

These are mixed media studies in which the artist has combined drawing media with collage materials.

Combining your materials

When developing a watercolor, it is usual to lightly sketch in pencil, then work on the image in watercolor washes, and finish by adding highlights in an opaque gouache medium. Similarly, when creating a pastel painting, charcoal is often used to establish the basic drawing, which is then overworked in pastel.

The development of mixed media as a technique has been encouraged by the relaxed attitude toward experimentation that has arisen in this century. The advent of new art materials, such as acrylics, and the development of new creative techniques in collage, print, and photographic processes has seen an increase in mixed media works not just in painting, but in all the visual

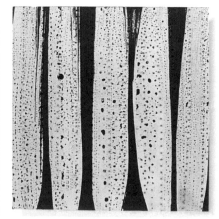

This striking tonal composition was developed using a wax resist technique. Warm liquid wax was applied to mask areas of the paper and to resist the ink.

Here a similar technique is used with the wax painted in vertical bands down a sheet of paper. Black ink was then brushed across the surface.

arts – graphics, illustration, and textiles. Looking at the breadth of materials used in combination in this century, it is exciting to realize that the expressive range of media for mixing appears to be inexhaustible. The beauty and success of many mixed media works is due to the artist's capacity for combining different media within an esthetically pleasing composition, and in the hands of an experienced artist, mundane materials such as newsprint, sandpaper, and wax crayons become vehicles of eloquent expression.

A composition based on arches has been constructed using collage. Sheets of colored tissue paper have been cut and laminated between layers of diluted PVA glue and the colors optically mixed to create new colors.

Getting started

Most of the effects and methods which will be described in the coming pages are unique to mixed media. You will be encouraged to exploit the particular qualities of different media by using them in new contexts of either juxtaposition or layering. You will be guided through the basic principles of drawing, painting, collaging, and printing, using the common range of materials carried by most art shops, alongside materials found in the home. Finally, you will experiment with less common materials and techniques.

This print was developed using a monotype process. The brown strips were printed on corrugated paper and then laminated between sheets of tissue paper.

A collage of found and cut wooden shapes has been painted using a combination of painting techniques.

HISTORY

MIXED MEDIA IS USUALLY REGARDED as an art form peculiar to the 20th century. However, throughout the history of painting, works have been produced that have successfully combined a range of the usual and more unlikely materials. There are also particular phases in Western art when mixed media works were created by using materials such as gold leaf in combination with other drawing and painting media.

FROM EARLIEST TIMES artists have created mixed media compositions by combining materials such as charcoal with earth colors and extracted minerals, such as oxides or vegetable dyes. The preparation of the ground, which is the surface to which the pigment is applied, has also led to a great deal of experimentation with materials. Artists have worked on wood, velum, and various natural fibers that have been pressed or woven into papers and textiles, and also on glass and metals such as copperplate or gold leaf.

Illuminated manuscripts and icons

Early Italian church paintings are prime examples of the beauty of combining media. Artists used underpainting and combined areas of luminous pigments and gold leaf. The splendor of the gold leaf was often heightened by a technique of embossing the gesso ground, burnishing the gold leaf and, occasionally, by the addition of precious gems. These works were created using the richest materials available. They aimed to transport the viewer from the temporal world into a state of meditation on the nature of the divine. During the 16th century, artists used sanguine (a deep blood red) earth color, with additional highlights in white chalk on colored paper, to evoke the skin

Tomasso Masaccio,
***Virgin and Child,* 1426,**
53 x 29½ in (135 x 75 cm)
Masaccio (1401–28) made a remarkable contribution to the development of Western art through the assimilation of perspective within the picture space of his compositions. The charm of this painting resides in a unique combination of treatment and materials. The use of the paint to create a naturalistic illusion of form contrasts with the abstract symbolism, the hierarchical arrangement of the figures, and the use of gold leaf in the halos.

Leonardo Da Vinci,
***Isabella d'Este,* 1500**
25 x 18 in (63 x 46 cm)
Leonardo da Vinci (1452–1519) was the archetypal Renaissance man who experimented with new approaches and materials. Leonardo was also instrumental in developing the practice of combining pastel with other drawing media. The term pastel is derived from the word "pasta," which means paste. It refers to the method of manufacture where pure pigment and chalks are mixed into a paste with a binding solution of gum and allowed to dry into crayons. In this eloquent profile of Isabella d'Este, the work has been developed in black chalk, with additional highlights visible in the use of a yellow pastel to add color to the neckline of the dress.

tones of the figure and to create warm and cool sensations of light and shadow. In 17th-century Holland, it became fashionable to heighten drawings, mainly of landscape scenes, with a limited range of tones using yellow, brown, rose madder, green, and blue watercolors. The mixed media technique of creating tinted drawings was further developed in Britain by a number of major artists, including Turner (1775–1851),

Samuel Palmer, *A Hilly Scene*, 1826,
8 x 5¼ in (20.5 x 13.5 cm)
In this visionary evocation of an idealized rustic scene, Palmer (1805–81) has loaded the painting with symbolism. Pigments mixed with gum arabic create varying areas of luminous washes and opaque color which adds to the substance of the linear drawing in pen and ink.

who lifted watercolor from the status of minor studies to complete compositions on paper that were accepted as works in their own right. Two other major British artists, William Blake (1757–1827) and his pupil Samuel Palmer, experimented with watercolor in combination with other media to create innovative mixed media works. Blake applied colored washes to his prints and along with Palmer, combined watercolor with tempera and gum to build up complex surfaces combining pen and ink with transparent and opaque layers of watercolor.

Nineteenth-century artists
An outstanding 19th-century exponent of mixed media techniques was Edgar Degas, who combined pastel with charcoal, distemper, and monotype printing techniques. Degas deliberately exploited visual tension by contrasting the varying surface qualities of the mixed media.

Edgar Degas, *Woman Arranging Her Hair*,
1895–1900, *30½ x 29½ in (77 x 75 cm)*
Toward the end of his long career, and with the failing of his eyesight, Degas worked increasingly in pastels, which he combined with charcoal, distemper paint, and monotype printing inks. He was preoccupied with the subject of the body in motion and would overlay a tonal composition in charcoal with pastels.

Gustav Klimt, *Watersnakes*, 1904–07,
19¾ x 8 in (50 x 20 cm)
Early devotional works that combined paint and gold leaf inspired Klimt to an utterly secular exploration of these mixed media. He combines the sinuous movements and sensuous forms of the body with dreamlike stylized arrangements of rhythmic patterns of embossed gold leaf and gold paint.

Adding color
There are many examples of artists who add color in a transparent or opaque form to linear drawings, using either watercolor or gouache. The sculptor August Rodin and the painters Vincent Van Gogh, Gustav Klimt, and Egon Schiele were all skilled exponents of mixed media techniques. The work of Klimt emerged out of the stylistic development of Art Nouveau, and many works combine oil paint with gold leaf in a technique that evokes the religious works of previous centuries.

THE DEVELOPMENT OF the visual arts during the 20th century has been characterized by an extraordinary diversification of approaches to both the concepts and materials of art. Two of the major protagonists of change were Georges Braque (1882–1963) and Pablo Picasso (1881–1973), who developed the use of collage by incorporating ready-made materials, such as newsprint and wallpaper, into the surface of drawing and painting compositions. The use of collage compounded a fundamental shift in awareness already developed through experiments with Cubist composition, demonstrating that the essence of a painting was in the independent arrangement of the surface shapes and textures rather than in the creation of an illusionistic view. This new development coincided with the political and social upheaval of the First World War, which stimulated a reaction against the established order. In the visual arts this reaction first manifested itself in the absurdist work of the Dada movement and was then further developed by the Surrealists. Artists such as Max Ernst (1891–1976) and Joan Miró (1893–1983) exploited the techniques of mixed media and montage by juxtaposing images in incongruous, disturbing and provocative arrangements that explored the unconscious and evoked an interior world of dreams and nightmares.

The dominant figure of this century is Pablo Picasso, who exploited an extraordinary range of materials during his long career. He proved that any material could be

Georges Braque, *Violin and Pipe,* **1913,**
29¼ x 39¾ in (75 x 101 cm)
Braque first considered the use of ready-made papers as an addition to his still-life drawings in 1912. Braque was the son of a house painter and knew how to create decorative paint effects, such as marbling and false wood grain.

He later used this experience by incorporating these techniques along with wallpaper in his paintings. In this composition the combination of collage and charcoal simultaneously emphasizes the picture surface while suggesting space through the overlapping of different media.

Max Ernst, *Katarina Ondulata,* **1920,**
12¼ x 10½ in (31 x 27 cm)
Max Ernst's early training was in philosophy, and his work as an artist can be viewed as a visual exploration of the hidden processes of the mind. Individual compositions explore the way the mind filters and retains the memory of experiences by organizing shapes and textures that act as prompts to the imagination. In the lower section of the composition, a strip of wallpaper has been collaged in juxtaposition with painted areas to evoke layers of geological strata. The surface of the upper section contains spattered ink and drawn lines, suggesting distant mountain and clouds.

Paul Klee,
***The Magic Garden*, 1926,**
19¾ x 16½in (50 x 42 cm)
Paul Klee was a master of textural control who experimented with materials and applied a diversity of techniques to create jewel-like surfaces. In his hands, mundane materials transcend their original form, turning into new creative combinations of texture and color that evoke an imaginative reverie. Here he has used a wire mesh mounted on a wooden panel as a support for an application of plaster that has then been inscribed with patterns and stylized images that float in the picture space. The surface has been stained with washes of color that are punctuated by opaque areas of impasto oil paint.

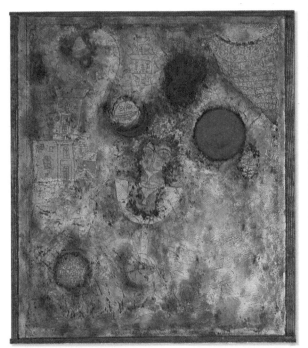

transformed into art by placing familiar materials, such as bicycle saddles in a new context. His treatment of both materials and techniques set a precedent for a level of pictorial invention for all artists in this century. Technological innovations have also provided new printing, photographic, and construction processes as well as new materials, such as acrylics, thus extending the range of pictorial effects available to artists. In the latter half of this century, abstract artists such as Robert Rauschenberg have exploited mass media processes and combined photography and found materials within their artworks.

Robert Rauschenberg, *Reservoir,* **1961,**
85½ x 62½ in (234 x 157 cm)
Rauschenberg, along with other artists who were affiliated with the Pop Art movement, chose to utilize mass media imagery in combination with found objects and traditional painting media. The relationship between the choice of found objects and the imagery does not work in the manner of a meaningful narrative but as an irrational montage held together as an abstract arrangement through the compositional skills of the artist.

Pablo Picasso, *Seated Woman,* **1938,** *30 x 21½ in (76.5 x 55 cm)*
This composition has been energized by an insistent rhythmic line in pen and ink that gives the forms volume and creates contrasting areas of patterning across the surface of the work. Pastel has been used to create large areas of color that add luminosity to the figure.

COMPATIBLE SUPPORTS

THE SURFACE YOU CHOOSE to work on is called a support, and its texture, color, and absorbency will influence the techniques you use to develop a mixed media composition. There is a huge variety of supports for you to explore in combination with mixed media. Try a selection of ready-made supports first and note the different ways your chosen media interact with each one. You can then experiment and create your own supports through a simple process of "priming" and adding a variety of textures and colors to the different surfaces.

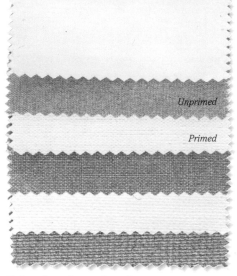

Unprimed

Primed

Primed and unprimed canvas
There are two types of canvas available in various weights and widths: artist's linen, made from flax, and cotton duck. You can purchase preprimed canvases or prepare your own.

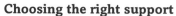

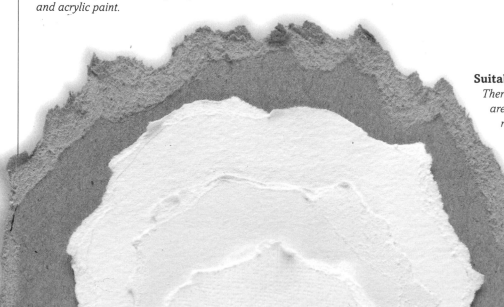

Commercially prepared boards
"Art boards," which have been prepared with either a surface of artists' quality paper or fine textured linen canvas, are suitable for both wet and dry techniques using media such as watercolor and pastel. Precolored art board has a stiff surface and does not buckle when wet. Oil board is primed as a surface for oil and acrylic paint.

Choosing the right support

There are a few simple rules to follow to guarantee the life of a mixed media work. Dry drawing media such as charcoal, chalks, and pastels need a support with sufficient tooth to hold the particles of pigment in the surface. Paper, cardboard, and linen supports have a distinct tooth which is ideal for dry media. For this reason, shiny and very smooth surfaces, such as hot pressed paper, are less suitable for extensive working in dry media.

Particle board

Blockboard

Plywood

Suitable wood
The most common wood supports for mixed media works are particle board, plywood and blockboard (a type of plywood). These are made from compressed wood dust or layers of wood bonded by glue. Wood panels are the most suitable for building bas-relief surfaces.

Suitable paper grounds
There is now a huge variety of papers available that are suitable for mixed media compositions. These range from artists' quality paper to handmade colored papers and cardboard. The artists' quality papers are more expensive, but, they can sustain prolonged applications and have a guaranteed longevity.
These papers are available in various thicknesses, weights, and textures and are made from 100 percent cotton rag, which does not become brittle and yellow with age. The three standard grades of surface for watercolor papers are Hot-pressed (smooth), NOT (Cold-pressed, semirough), and Rough.

Water and oil-based media

The main criteria to bear in mind when choosing supports is whether they are suitable for wet or dry media. Water-based media require a support of sufficient absorbency to hold the liquid but not so absorbent that the color sinks and loses its brilliance. For this reason manufacturers add size to paper to reduce its absorbency. Water-based media will cause a support to buckle as the surface absorbs the water, so the thicker the paper you choose the less dramatic the buckling will be and the more capable it will be of weathering heavy treatment.

When working with oil-based media, it is generally recommended that you prepare the surface of your support with an acrylic primer because the oil will damage the surface of unprimed paper, board, or canvas. Priming also reduces the absorbency of the support and stops acrylics and oil-based media from sinking into the surface and losing brilliance. A colored support will interact with overlaid pigments and when combined with a textured surface the result will be attractive broken color effect on the surface of the paper or canvas.

Handmade and manufactured papers

There is a vast range of colored and textured papers for you to use available from art and paper stores in single sheets, pads, and rolls. An increasingly diverse selection of papers are now being made which incorporate various plant fibers such as flax, onion skin, and bracken. These papers make highly attractive and surprising supports for mixed media work and are used to create a dominant texture in a collage or print work.

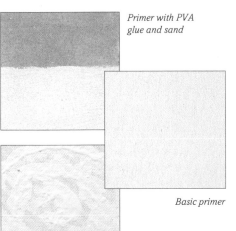

Primer with PVA glue and sand

Basic primer

Thickly primed board

Gesso

When applied to a surface, acrylic gesso can be manipulated to create a range of textures that can make the basic support more interesting.

Sandpaper

You can buy sand-papers or make your own rough surfaces by mixing sand into or sprinkling sand on top of the gesso.

Primed Boards

To create a luminous background, boards need to be primed with a suitable primer, such as acrylic primer or gesso, before paint is applied. Boards can also be primed with colored gessos made by adding acrylic paint, or they can be primed with PVA and sand to create texture.

Using gesso with additives

Various materials can be added to gesso to create an exciting textured or colored surface in bas-relief. Sand, string, dried grasses, and grains will all create interesting surfaces. You can also add sawdust, stone dust, or any other inert powdered material to PVA glue, acrylic primer, or gesso to create an interesting diversity of textures to work on. By adding a water-based paint or dried pigment, such as charcoal dust or crushed chalk pastel, you can tint the primer to any color. Additional materials can be applied in several ways: you can sprinkle or embed them in the wet surface of the gesso so that the color and tone of the materials remains evident, or you can mix the materials into the gesso so that they all become the same color.

DRAWING MATERIALS

A NUMBER OF DRAWING MATERIALS are suitable for mixed media, and they can be used in almost any combination. Since each drawing medium will produce a range of marks of a different density, tone, and texture, it is a good idea to explore the scope of line and tone that each produces before you experiment with them in combination. It is also important to find sympathetic combinations of drawing media that will enhance rather than detract from each other. Drawing media that are alike, such as charcoal and chalks, will work unobtrusively together, whereas media with disimilar qualities such as wax crayons and inks will create dramatic qualities of contrast. This is because the water and the wax resist each other and create distinctive patterns.

DRAWING MEDIA can be categorized into those that share similar characteristics (watercolor and ink are both wet) and those that use a common method of application (pastel and chalk are both rubbed on the support). Dry media are those that can be applied without a brush for example charcoal, pastels, and crayons. Wet drawing media are those that are either suspended in a liquid medium or require diluting before use.

Colored charcoal pencils
Colored charcoal pencils are the same as pastel crayons, only they are slightly harder and encased in wood. Their chalky constitution makes them more suitable for subtle blending techniques and ideal for very fine detailed work.

Felt-tip pens
Felt-tip pens are a relatively recent addition to the repertoire of drawing materials. The range of marks they produce is limited but they are popular for techniques requiring a bold line and strong color saturation.

Sharpening
Hard pastels and charcoal can be sharpened using a pencil sharpener or sharp blade to gently pare the end to a point.

Pencil sharpener and blades

Graphite pencil

Kneaded eraser

Kneaded erasers
Kneaded erasers are suitable for erasing a range of dry drawing media. They can be pulled and kneaded into a fine point for detailed work. You can effectively use this type of eraser as a drawing tool, creating highlights in a work as you remove the pigment and reveal the surface of the support below.

Water-soluble pencils
Water-soluble pencils are used in the same manner as other pencils to create a linear drawing and areas of shading. The drawing is then washed over with a wet brush. This transforms the linear marks by dispersing the color to create a wash drawing. Rich color effects can also be achieved by drawing directly on a damp surface to disperse the pigment.

Fixatives

The surface of a mixed media work that incorporates dry media like charcoal and pastel is easily spoiled by smudging. You can avoid this by giving the work a light spray of fixative to fix the particles of pigment to the paper. Fixative is also used to build up a work in layers of different dry pigments by spraying and fixing each successive layer of color. The fixative will alter the work by slightly darkening some of the tones. With pastel work it is very important not to overspray since this will destroy the inherent "bloom" of the pastels. For this reason some artists do not fix the last layer, or else choose to spray only the back of their work.

Wax crayons

Wax crayons are popular for resist techniques where a drawing is first developed in wax crayon and then worked over with a wash of watercolor or ink. The wax repels the water-based medium and shows through the layer in striking contrast. Crayons can also be overlaid on top of each other and scratched off to reveal the layers below.

Willow charcoal and charcoal pencil

Charcoal is carbonated wood that comes in various thicknesses. Paper which will readily accept charcoal is easy to erase and alter. Charcoal can be pared and filed to a point with a blade or by rubbing its edge on glass paper. Charcoal also comes compressed in stick and pencil form that produces a dense, velvet black.

Types of charcoal

Reed pen

Technical pen

Pen and ink

There is a variety of inks available, the main types being the water- and shellac-based inks. Shellac-based inks are waterproof when dry and are suitable for techniques of overpainting when you do not want the ink line to spread and bleed into subsequent washes of color. Inks also come in a full range of colors from black to the full spectrum of luminous primaries and secondaries. Inks can be worked with different tools including nib pens, reed pens, and sable, bristle, or synthetic brushes. A particular advantage of inks is their ability to be worked in dilutions of water, making it possible to produce monochrome works in a subtle gradation of tones.

Chinese inks are sold in either sticks or bottles. The ink can then be diluted with water in a small stone well. The art of using a Chinese brush is to hold the brush vertically or diagonally so that you can vary the thickness of the line from a delicate trace, using the tip, to a full broad stroke, using the heel of the brush.

Chinese block ink

Soft pastels

Soft pastels and Conté crayons

Soft pastels are essentially pure pigment held lightly in a gum solution. The soft-grained texture produced is ideal for painting because of its ease of application and blending qualities. Conté crayons are basically harder pastels with a denser texture and they are ideal for detailed work. Both types of pastel are available in a huge range of colors.

Colored Conté crayons

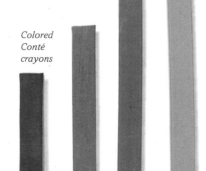

Chinese brushes

Basic pen and ink

PAINTING MATERIALS

EVERY PAINTING MEDIUM has particular qualities of texture and color, and all are suitable for mixed media techniques. Painting media can be broadly classified as water-based and oil-based. Water-based media include watercolors, gouache, tempera, poster colors, and acrylics. Oil-based colors include oil paint, oil bars, pastels, and wax encaustic, which is thinned using turpentine or mineral spirits. Media that share similar qualities, such as watercolor and gouache, are readily used in any combination. Mixing oil- and water-based paints requires more careful consideration.

Oil bars
Oil bars are applied in the manner of an oil pastel, by rubbing the medium into the support. They can be further diluted on the support using a brush and turpentine.

Crushed chalk pastels

Fine hog hair oil brush (No. 10)

Fine hog hair oil brush (No. 12)

ALL PAINTS ARE MADE from colored pigments suspended in a medium. This allows the pigment to be controlled in a fluid state and to dry to form a durable surface. Each type of paint has a distinct quality of handling and will have an advantage over other painting media for certain techniques. The advantage of water-based paints is that they generally dry quickly, allowing for speed of application and ease of alteration. The acacia gum used in watercolor and gouache paints allows you to over-paint in layers without picking up the dried underlying color. The gum also allows you to make alterations by simply wetting and lifting the color from the support

using a sponge or tissue. Acrylic paints are also water soluble but, unlike watercolor, they dry to an insoluble plastic film. Acrylics can be used in transparent washes, but they are also suitable for using in impasto to add texture. Manufacturers have developed a range of additives, which you can add to alter the paint or retard the drying time to allow for more

Palette knives and scrapers
Palette knives are used for mixing paint on a palette. Painting knives are similar, but they are specifically shaped and angled to apply the paint to the support. Scrapers are used to drag and scrape paint across the surface of a wide support and to create linear patterns.

Brushes and palettes
Oil paint can be mixed on either a hand-held palette or on a smooth impermeable sheet of board or glass. There is a specialist palette for acrylics – a tray that keeps the paints moist to prolong mixing time. Both oils and acrylic paints can be used with a range of brushes.

Alizarin Crimson (oil)

Cadmium Yellow (oil)

Phthalo Blue (oil)

Phthalo Green (acrylic)

Titanium White (acrylic)

Painting knife and scrapers

Ultramarine Blue (acrylic)

controlled blending of colors. All water-based media are suitable for overlayering in different drawing and oil-based media.

Oil paints

Oil paint is a popular medium because of its ease of manipulation. Combined with its scope of color and texture, it generally surpasses water-based media. Oil paint dries slowly and is most commonly used in the "a la prima" technique of painting wet-in-wet. When used in a wash (or impasto), oil paint is suitable for receiving oil pastels and oil bars, but it will repel water-based media. It is very important to use artists'-quality paints where possible, since the pigments used in the paints have been tested and are known to be of a highly durable nature.

Watercolor brushes: mixed sable Nos. 12 and 8

Gamboge

Resist technique

The simplest way to create a resist technique is to apply an application of an oil-based medium such as wax crayon, grease pencils, or oil pastel to a composition. These media repel water and show through the subsequent watercolor wash. Another excellent resist medium is masking fluid, which can be used to create subtle color variations.

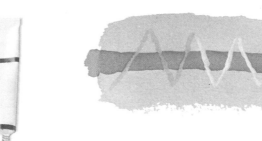

Masking fluid

Watercolor

Watercolors are made of pigment suspended in gum solution and have different degrees of lightfastness, depending on the type of pigment. Watercolors can be built up in layers of transparent washes. They can also be lifted from the support by wetting and wiping away with a sponge.

Windsor Green

Cerulean Blue

Tortillons

Scarlet Lake

Sponges and tortillons

Sponges are used for lifting water from the surface, but they can also be used to apply paint. Tortillons can be used to blend details in pastel works.

Natural sponge

Coarse sponge

Sponge rollers

Rollers are useful for applying liquid paint to a support. You can use small foam rollers, which are suitable for watercolor, or decorators' rollers for larger works in acrylics and oils. Rollers can either amplify or unify the texture of a support.

Roller

Oil pastels

Oil pastel is bound by oil, providing a rich depth of tone and a distinct degree of transparency. Oil pastels are not readily displaced and, as a consequence, do not require the use of fixative. They can be used in impasto and, when diluted with spirits, moved around on the support as a wash of color.

CHARCOAL AND BLACK INK

CHARCOAL AND BLACK INK are two tonal drawing media whose contrasting qualities of wet and dry create exciting mixed media combinations. The dry nature of charcoal produces a delightful range of tones and marks – from faint delicate traces and scumbled broken applications to a rich velvet black. The density of ink can be altered by adding water and can be applied with a range of tools from sable and Chinese brushes, to reed and metal-nib pens. Using these two media together, you will have the freedom to exploit drawing to its optimum tonal range.

Texture and pattern

This drawing demonstrates the contrasting qualities of charcoal and ink and the expressive range of marks that both media can produce. There is a contrived tension in the composition achieved by the close arrangement of the foreground figures and the dramatic shift in scale of figures in the background. The artist has used various techniques to emphasize the textures and features of the women's clothing. In contrast to the subtle areas of tone created by the charcoal, the artist has blocked in the dense area of black using a brush and ink in the jumper of the figure on the right.

Frottage
Frottage is the technique of using the side or blunt end of a stick of charcoal, crayon, or graphite to take a rubbing off a textured surface. This shows the texture of the wooden grain of a drawing board, but you can also take rubbings from stone and artificial materials.

By drawing charcoal across the paper around the woman's collar, the artist has utilized the grain of the paper to amplify the texture of the support, giving the clothing a realistic appearance.

Hilary Rosen, *Cafe*, 1989, charcoal and ink

Ink and charcoal
Ink and charcoal react in contrasting ways with the paper support. Whereas the charcoal is effectively filed away by the tooth of the paper, creating a grainy texture, the ink soaks into the surface of the paper. This absorption produces a wet effect known as bleeding, where the ink is dispersed across the paper surface.

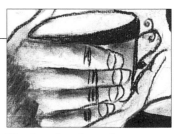

The hand and cup have a clearly defined contour with the fingers, created by variations in light and shade and outlined in ink. The artist has blended the charcoal into the paper with her fingers, creating areas of depth and lighter touches.

Contrasting effects

The abstract image below also concentrates on the creative possibilities of line and tone. Two contrasting qualities of tone are created by using similar media with diffferent methods of application. The ink is applied with a brush to contrast with areas of tone created by the use of spray paint. The recurrent use of cellular shapes evokes a feeling of organic growth rather than describing any specific plant form.

The artist has created an ambiguously witty play of lines and patterns that draws the viewer into translating this abstract arrangement. In the construction of this imaginative work, the flow of the rhythmical marks is uninterrupted by any hesitation or correction, creating an air of confident improvisation. Looking carefully into the compostion you can see the way the artist has developed complex relationships between the shapes. Some are enclosed cells, others are open, some contain nuclei and others appear to be gyrating, bending, or splitting. Each delineated shape has its own unique character while maintaining a general resemblance to the other shapes.

CHINESE INK

Chinese ink is a very expressive medium which requires disciplined control. The great Chinese masters of this medium would first study their subject for long periods of time until they understood its form. Working on a roll of rice paper, they would lay on diluted washes and marks in undiluted black. The art of controlling a Chinese brush is to vary the angle of the brush to the support, holding the brush vertically using the tip and at an angle using the heel of the brush. By pressing and lifting the brush you can vary the line from thin traces to broad expressive sweeps.

Fine Chinese brush

Reed pen

Chinese brush

Chinese block and ink

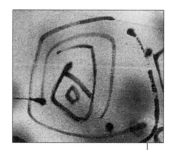

The linen texture of the support creates a broken line as the ink is drawn across the absorbent surface.

Marks retain the echo of the action that created them and in this example the quality of the line reflects an angular wrist action. This is in direct contrast with the diffuse and erratic character of the spray paint.

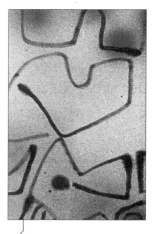

USING A DIFFUSER

A mouth diffuser is used by holding the two tubes at right angles to each other and immersing the end of the longer tube in the paint. Holding the shorter end, with the plastic mouthpiece between your lips, blow firmly; your breath will draw the fluid up the longer tube and atomize the liquid into a fine spray. You can vary the spray you produce by altering the pressure of your breath and the distance and angle at which you hold the diffuser from the support.

Hold the spray in a single stationary position to create a starlike explosion of ink, or sweep the diffuser across the page to give a wider and finer coverage.

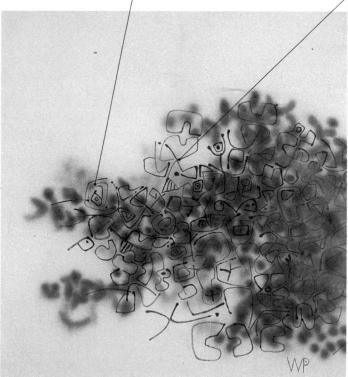

Wendy Pasmore, RA, *Untitled*, 1991, spray paint and ink

Visual invention
In contrast with the complexity of the shapes, defined by the ink lines, a unifying tone has been created using spray paint. The beauty of this work lies in the clarity and simplicity of its construction, which echoes the principles of Chinese painting. Artworks such as this simply evoke the energy of nature in just the same way that the rhythm and structure of music evoke the natural harmonies and movements of the elements.

CHARCOAL AND PASTELS

CHARCOAL IS A HIGHLY VERSATILE drawing medium. Its inert nature makes it highly suitable for laying down a drawing design before over-painting in a water- or oil-based medium. As a tonal drawing medium, charcoal is commonly overworked with additional dry coloring media such as chalks and pastels. Esthetically, charcoal and pastel work well together, and by using the two media, you can achieve subtle traces of line, delicate transitions of blended tone, and dense applications of bold marks. A considerable advantage of these media is that they are easily erased and manipulated, which allows for great freedom of compositional movement. Because of this, it is necessary to preserve your work carefully by fixing the surface with a light spray of fixative (see p.409).

Pastel and charcoal
The responsive nature of these media encourages a sensitivity of touch and subtlety of manipulation. You can work pastel and charcoal either as lines or as areas of tone by altering their angle to the support and by working with either the edge or the side of the media.

Pigments
Both charcoal and pastel are capable of an exciting array of marks, depending on the action of the hand and how much pressure is applied. With all dry drawing media it is the raised tooth of the support that files away the particles of pigment, so the harder you press, the more pigment is deposited on the surface.

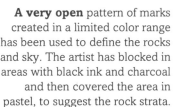

A very open pattern of marks created in a limited color range has been used to define the rocks and sky. The artist has blocked in areas with black ink and charcoal and then covered the area in pastel, to suggest the rock strata.

To emphasize the dramatic movement of the waves and wind against the weathered form of the rock, the artist has overlaid linear traces of white and ochre pastel onto blended sweeps of pink and gray. These colorful patterns give the whole piece a sense of movement.

Michael Wright, *Mullion Cove Rocks*, 1994, charcoal, ink, and pastel

Female head

In this image, in contrast with the previous painting, the charcoal has been very subtly blended with the pastel to create a blurred effect. The simplified form and full frontal angle of vision produce an eerie stillness. Paradoxically, the apparent symmetry of the composition amplifies all the nuances of asymmetry contained within the features of the face. This means that our attention is focused on the slight shifts and movements in the form of the features. This is an emotionally taut image, full of a subtle pathos that is expressed in the physical working of the surface. Nervous touches of pastel which have been swept across the woman's features, simultaneously emphasize her emotional intensity and blur the details of her features.

Creating details

To produce facial details in charcoal and pastel, you should aim to combine the two mediums with confident subtlety. To create these lips, a rich vermilion pastel has been streaked across a line of charcoal. In the image below the smudged lipstick effect amplifies the masklike appearance of the woman.

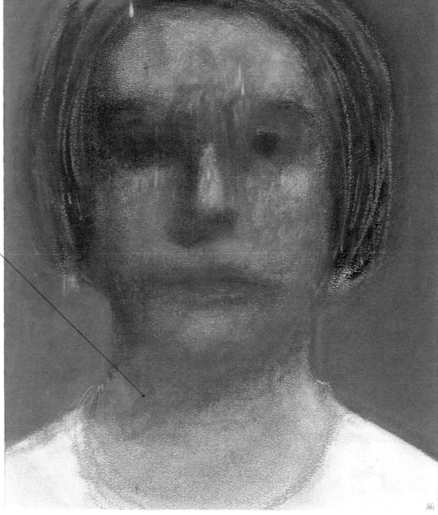

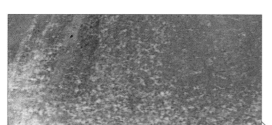

A technique of subtle blending has been used in this detail of the neck. Pastel has been worked into the surface of the support with a finger in order to merge the pastel powder with the previous application of charcoal.

Soft pastels

Used in their full strength, colored pastels are an extremely powerful coloring medium. However, immensely subtle modeling can be achieved by using the wide range of subtle tints that are available in each of the colors.

Robert Clatworthy, *Female head II,* 1993, charcoal and pastel

Pastel dust

Soft pastels are pure pigment, bound in a light solution of gum with the addition of chalk to create subtle tints. Pastel can easily be reduced to dust by paring it with a knife. The dust can then be applied to a composition using a brush or cotton ball to create a dry wash of color.

LINE AND COLOR

THE MOST COMMON TECHNIQUE for combining line and color is to
add a watercolor wash to a linear drawing medium. The outline is
established in graphite, charcoal, or ink to create a strong linear arrangement.
Once you are satisfied with the organization of line, you can apply washes
of watercolor in increasing strength to add body to the linear structure.

Combining colors

In this expressive rendition of a familiar
subject, the artist has created strong linear
movements and patterns in charcoal to
contrast with vibrant washes of watercolor.
The weight of the sunflower heads and
compact foliage have been amplified by the
application of dense line and saturated
color. The work has been completed
using a delicate linear drawing in chalk
to define the texture of the curling leaves.
The artist has successfully combined an
analysis of the plant itself with an
experiment in mark-making.

Surface interaction

*Wet media in the form of
watercolor will interact with
the surface texture of the support
very differently from an
application of a dry medium
such as charcoal or chalk. The
watercolor will retain the shape
of the brushstroke and will settle
into the pitted hollows of the
surface in tiny pools of pigment –
a dry medium will catch in the
raised surface.*

The benefit of using charcoal
as a drawing media is that it can
be easily manipulated, allowing
for alterations before adding a
watercolor wash. Charcoal has
been used here to create a linear
pattern over a watercolor wash
that points up the texture and
form of the sunflower.

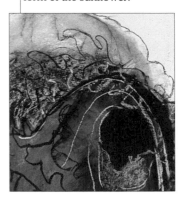

Wet and dry media used in
combination create areas of
textural contrast. Here the
saturated areas of color, created
by watercolor, contrast with the
dry texture of the white pastel
which has been overlaid in
broken lines. The areas of
charcoal have been created to
give the piece a strong linear
structure and added definition.

Susan Lloyd, *The Sunflower Bed,* **1990,
charcoal and watercolor**

Ink and wash

*Watercolor and inks can be used
in different combinations to create
effects of either a clear line or
bleeding. Here a sepia line was
drawn across a watercolor
wash while the wash
was still wet.*

416

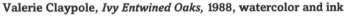

Valerie Claypole, *Ivy Entwined Oaks,* 1988, watercolor and ink

Controlled color

This is a subtle and complex work in which the artist has painstakingly observed the growth of ivy as it envelops the gnarled forms of the oak trees. The linear composition has been developed first in pencil and then in clear unbroken line using pen and sepia ink. Delicately controlled washes have been carefully applied to add color to the composition. The artist has strived to establish a balance between line and color throughout the composition without obscuring the linear work. The color key to this composition is a harmony of greens that serves to highlight the parasitic colorless form of the ivy embracing the central tree.

Using color as shape

Bob Baggaley's semiabstract work is based on memories of traveling through the Cumbrian landscape. The linear drawing was established using a fountain pen. It was subsequently overworked in saturated washes of watercolor. The striking arrangement of washes evokes the drama of a moonlit night. The light areas of the composition are amplified by the deep blue of the surrounding border that frames the scene in the manner of a window. Baggaley trained during the sixties and assimilated the Pop Art and abstract influences of this period into a later preoccupation with landscape imagery. These influences can be seen in the deliberate play of positive and negative shape, in the use of the white of the paper, and in the artist's evident delight in the abstract emphasis of the paint surface.

Bob Baggaley, *Westward,* 1989, watercolor and ink

The washes of color have been loosely applied wet-into-wet, allowing the colors to run and create secondary mixtures of color. The overworking of watercolor on ink has caused the ink to lift and bleed into the colors of the washes.

WATERCOLOR TECHNIQUES

Watercolor is an ideal medium to use in combination with drawing media, to either add tone in a monochrome wash or add color in the full range of hues and tints. Depending on the texture of the support and the technique of application, it is possible to achieve a wide range of expressive qualities of wash. You can create dramatically different effects by working wet-over-dry or wet-into-wet, or by combinations of these two techniques.

Wash on dry wash
By laying a wash, allowing it to dry, and applying subsequent washes in confident single applications, you can achieve the effect of distinct overlapping layers of color. Where the layers overlap, the colors will mix optically to create a secondary color.

Bleeding wet-into-wet
By applying a wash of color to a wet area of the support or to a previous wash in a wet state, you can explore dramatic and spontaneous color effects. The colors will run and merge into each other, creating new colors and feathering movements in the paint.

Scumbling
Use the side of a semidry brush to drag a light trace of pigment across the raised tooth of artist's textured watercolor paper. The effect created is one of a broken surface of color that allows the previous wash or tone of the support to show through in sparkling flecks of light.

RESIST TECHNIQUES

Oil pastels

Watercolor brushes

ONE INTERESTING MIXED MEDIA EFFECT is created using resist techniques, which capitalize on the tendency of oil to repel water. There is a wide range of oil-based media suitable for resist techniques, including oil paint, oil pastels, and wax crayons. Another useful resist medium is masking fluid. A design is created using the fluid and overpainting in a wash of watercolor or ink. The resist medium adheres to the support and shows through the subsequent wash of water-based media. Experimenting with resist techniques allows you to exploit bold contrasts of color or to work with a more subtle range of contrasts with a closer range of tones. You can use an opaque oil-based color to contrast with a subsequent wash, or you can apply a transparent oil or wax medium that will allow the tone of the support or prior layer of color to show through.

Using wax resist

The master British sculptor Henry Moore consistently used resist techniques in his drawings. In this small sketchbook composition he has pursued a sculptural theme of interior and exterior form by using transparent white and yellow wax crayons to portray a wire armature sculptors use as a support for plaster or clay. This technique defines the inner structure of the head. The abstract network of wax lines glows through the subsequent wash of dark gray watercolor. The final details of human features have been achieved with a cursive stroke of black chalk on the contour of the head, and brushstrokes of black India ink to define the nose, mouth, and eyes.

It is possible to clearly see the way in which the wax repels and causes the watercolor to collect in little spots on the surface of the wax crayon. The density of the shellac-based India-ink drawing has allowed the black line to partially cover the wax crayon in a broken line and magnifies the resist effect on the surface.

Henry Moore, *Female head,* 1958, wax crayon, watercolor and ink

Lifting and patterning

The artist chose "Mirage" as the title of this work because the quality of the light and color suggests the presence of a landscape suffused in a shimmering heat. The work has been developed using an original approach to watercolor.

The bands of watercolor that wash across the upper section of the painting have been patterned using plastic bubble wrap. The bubble wrap has partly displaced and partly lifted the watercolor from the surface of the support, leaving a distinct pattern. This process was repeated using crumpled foil to overlay the middle section, creating a complex overlayering of the two patterns.

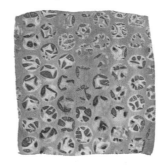

Masking fluid

This is a latex liquid which is applied with a brush or dip pen to mask out areas of an artwork. After a subsequent wash has dried, the masking fluid can be gently rubbed away to reveal the underlying color.

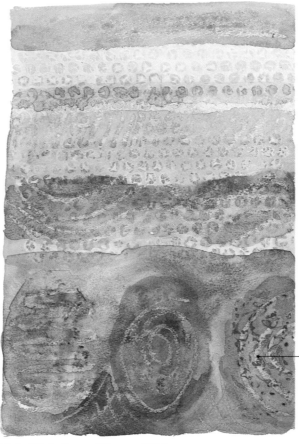

Kate Nicholson, *Mirage*, 1994, wax crayon and watercolor

Washes of saturated

colors have been bled into each other over concentric circles of pink wax resist line. Before the watercolor dried, the artist pressed a crumpled sheet of aluminum foil into the surface using a book as a weight to displace some of the color.

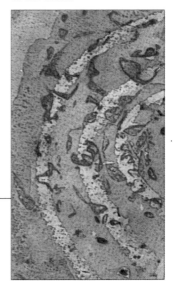

TECHNIQUES FOR LIFTING AND PATTERNING WATERCOLOR

An exciting variety of textures can be created within the surface of water-based media by pressing materials into the wet paint. Choose nonabsorbent materials that have either a distinct texture such as bubble wrap, or materials that can be folded and crumpled to create a texture, such as foil or grease-proof paper.

You can also experiment using thin wire, string, and grasses. Place the material onto a wash of color while it is still wet and then apply pressure using a book or board. Lift the material away from the painting as the paint is close to drying and a distinct pattern will remain.

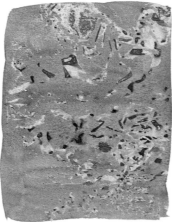

Creased aluminum foil

In this watercolor wash you can see the patterning created by the use of the foil. The foil has displaced the watercolor into pools of deep color and the result is similar to light playing on water.

Bubble plastic

The bubble wrap has been applied in the same manner as the foil, left. The uniform orange wash has been drawn in a cellular pattern that has effectively taken a print of the surface of the bubbles in the wrap.

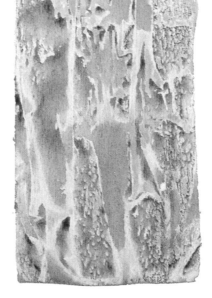

Plastic wrap

Placed in contact with the watercolor, the surface of the plastic wrap has created a complex pattern akin to marbling.

Materials

Crumpled paper

Crumpled foil

Plastic wrap

Acrylic paint

GALLERY OF DRAWING

D RAWING IS THE MOST fundamental language of visual expression and employs the simplest of media in the forms of graphite, charcoal, ink, and chalk. The directness of application when using drawing media allows the artist to develop a composition rapidly in line and tone and to focus on the primary task of organizing a meaningful design. There are many examples of drawings in which artists have enhanced their work using either watercolor, chalks, or pastel.

Henry Moore, *Row of Sleepers,* 1941, pen, ink, chalk, crayon, and watercolor *21½ x 12½ in (54.5 x 32 cm)*
Henry Moore (1898–1986) is best known for his international work as a sculptor and his monumental treatment of form was profoundly influenced by pre-Columbian and Romanesque carving. He was commissioned as a war artist during the Second World War and made a series of moving studies of people taking refuge in the London subway. This composition, which has religious associations with the Madonna and Child, was developed using his unique technique of overlaying wax lines and ink with watercolor.

Egon Schiele, *Adele Harms Seated in a Striped Dress,* 1917, gouache, watercolor, and pencil on paper *7 x 4½ in (17.5 x 11 cm)*
Egon Schiele's (1890–1918) distinctive style was influenced by and partly developed as a reaction to the rhythmical patterns and decorative use of color in the Art Nouveau movement. In this beautifully observed study Schiele's economical control of line, using graphite, is complimented by a limited palette of warm and cool colors applied in a scumbled application of gouache adding volume to the figures.

David Jones, *Flora in Calix Light,* 1950,
pencil and watercolor *22¼ x 30¼ in (56.5 x 76.5 cm)*
David Jones (1895–1974) was both an artist and a poet. In this luminous reverie on light playing through delicate forms of flowers and glass bowls, he creates a flux of rhythmic movements that lead the eye on a spiraling journey through the composition. The substance of matter is tranformed and replaced by transparent veils of light and shadow created through the delicate use of line and nervous touches of watercolor.

Jones is a supremely sensitive draftsman who amplifies and embellishes the details of his observations of the external world with the imaginative imagery of his internal world. His heightened sensitivity to the rhythms of form and to the illuminating nuances of light produces a heady intensity of movement that contradicts the static nature of the still life.

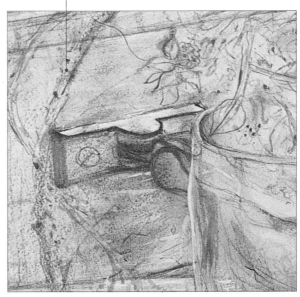

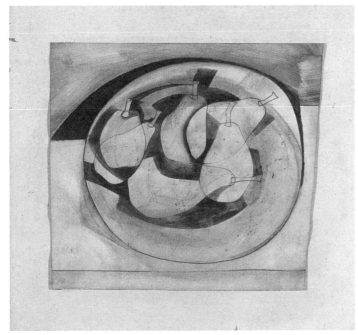

Ben Nicholson, *Plate of Pears,* 1955,
pencil and oil wash on paper *12 x 13⅜ in (30.5 x 33 cm)*
The drawing's flat surface is emphasized by hatching (closely spaced parallel lines) on the stained surface. An illusion of form is created by overlapping the shapes to create silhouettes.

Peter Coker RA, *Le Peintre au Travail,*
1994, mixed media *31 x 22 in (76 x 56 cm)*
In this drawing, Coker uses chalk and pastel in a limited palette of black and somber earth colors, creating a tension between the presence of the figure and the surrounding structure of the room.

421

MULTILAYERED COMPOSITIONS

Water-based media can be used in combination with a range of other paints to create works of multiple layers. One of the best media to use for multilayered compositions is acrylic. This is because the rapid drying time of acrylic paint allows overworking without disturbing the previous application of color. Watercolor and gouache can be transformed into paints with acrylic qualities by adding PVA (polyvinyl acetate) to the pigment. You can also paint layers of PVA over water-based washes to effectively seal the paint and allow a subtle build up of colored layers.

Using PVA glue

This artist has developed a technique of building up an image in layers of gouache and PVA, adding passages of ink to define the strata and texture of the forms in the landscape. By mixing PVA with the gouache or applying it in a wash, the PVA soaks into the pigment, giving the chalky gouache a depth and richness of color. PVA in a liquid state is opaque white, but it dries into a transparent plastic film, sealing the absorbent gouache and stopping the ink from sinking into the surface. The effect of combining the black ink and gouache washes is akin to the contrast created by the leadwork surrounding luminous areas of stained glass.

Craig Peacock's paintings are lyrical interpretations of landscape and his work is in the tradition of the British Neoromantics, echoing the work of artists such as Graham Sutherland in his concern with the way the imagination transforms the memory of landscape.

Craig Peacock, *Landscape Cumbria*, 1993, acrylic and gouache

In this part of the composition the artist has overlaid a thin pale wash of gouache and PVA to push back the underlying black ink lines. This has created a quality of mist in contrast with the more strident tones lower down in the composition.

WET-ON-DRY TECHNIQUE

A richly varied and textured quality of color can be created in a painting by working layers of color over each other, using the different qualities of both wet and dry mixed media. You can create the effects of layers of transparent, semitransparent, and opaque color by overlaying acrylics and gouache and using a technique of wet-on-dry.

Suspension
The black ink line is suspended between two semitransparent layers of color by a wash of diluted PVA applied between each wash of pigment.

Optical mixing
A wash of vermilion acrylic has had an application of saturated red and magenta gouache dragged across it to create the broken effect of optical mixture.

Complementary colors
Turquoise and ochre oil pastels have resisted a wash of orange acrylic and magenta gouache to create a surface of flecks of complementary colors.

Building up the layers

1 ◀ Begin by grouping a small collection of objects, such as pitchers, fruit, and leaves, then set the arrangement against tissue paper of a complementary color. Looking carefully at your still life, roughly sketch in the outlines of the various objects with a soft, pastel pencil on a sheet of handmade watercolor paper.

2 ▲ Develop the composition by building up the image with a variety of oil pastels to create areas of vivid and intense color.

3 ▶ Using a wash brush for the larger areas, and a fine brush for the details, paint over the oil pastel with washes of acrylic. To add more depth you can vary the thickness of the application of acrylic paint. Here a bright pink has been used on the pitcher.

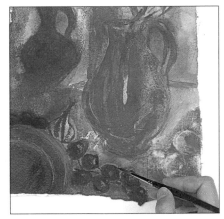

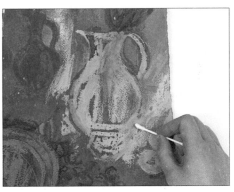

4 ▲ Make subtle alterations to the surface by overworking with a cotton ball to remove pastel, adding texture and detail.

Still life

Lucinda Cobley trained as an illustrator and her work, like much contemporary illustration, crosses the boundaries between design and fine art. She uses a variety of mixed media techniques, and here she has chosen to work on handmade paper and use the torn edge to interact with the forms in the composition. The surface treatment and the rough edging encourages us to view the work as a surface of beauty rather than a simple view of objects. To fully exploit the contrasting textures and colors of the different media, an open treatment of mark-making is used in preference to detailed observations.

A rich turquoise oil pastel has been overlaid by saturated washes of violet gouache and vermilion acrylic paint. The overall effect is one of a rich layering by working colors over each other using various broken-color techniques. One of the most effective of these methods is scumbling, which involves dragging dry paint across the raised tooth of the support.

Materials

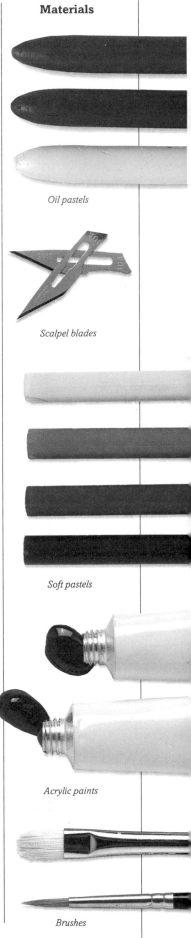

Oil pastels

Scalpel blades

Soft pastels

Acrylic paints

Brushes

OIL AND SOFT PASTELS

PASTELS ARE MADE from pure pigment bound by gum, to form soft pastels or by oil to form oil pastels. Oil pastels have a rich, luxurious texture, whereas soft pastels have a subtle powdery bloom. Each type of pastel can be mixed with other media, but one of the most expressive combinations is to mix and work the two forms of pastel together. The variations in the surface qualities of opacity and transparency are dependent upon the contrasting adhesive and blending qualities of each type of pastel.

Combining pastels

Both of the compositions examined here in detail are the work of a superlative contemporary pastelist. Ken Draper is a British artist and an associate Royal Academician who has extended the expressive potential of soft and oil pastel by using these media in combination. Due to the absence of a liquid medium, soft pastels have the highest degree of luminosity of all the painting media. The expressive power of soft pastels is created by the sensation of pure pigment-reflecting light, but the presence of the oil imparts a

In this composition the artist has achieved a luminous evocation of light playing on the contrasting textures of a shoreline. The interactions of light upon water are created by alternating applications of pastel, powdered and blended in a dry wash, and oil pastel, applied in dense impasto.

You can alternate between line and tone using either the tip or the side of your pastel. The more pressure is applied the more of the medium will be filed away and held by the tooth of the support. The artist has used the texture of the support to create a grainy line in contrast with the smooth blending of the violet tone of the sand.

Ken Draper, *Recollections,* **1994, oil and soft pastel**

saturated depth of tone to the darker colors. Combining these media creates a visual tension of contrasting degrees of luminosity and surface texture. To achieve the most subtle transitions of tone, a range of similar hues in soft pastels can be crushed into the surface of the support and blended in the manner of a dry wash. In contrast, the artist uses oil pastels to create abrupt passages of bas-relief impasto.

The physicality of the landscape

A miner's son, Draper shows in his work a heightened awareness of the physical strata of rocks and the power of the landscape. These works are not realistic views but pictorial reconstructions of the forces and substance of earth. Draper's work is characterized by an intense awareness and subtle manipulation of surface qualities both as texture and as a vehicle for color. The elemental forces of nature in the form of matter are reconstituted in an inventive control of pigment that celebrates the interactions of form and light.

Unlike other painting media, which are controlled with the aid of brushes and thinners, pastel is generally applied directly onto the surface of the support without any tools. There is a freedom and spontaneity in the directness of pastels that encourages an intensity of involvement in the physical handling. Here, pulling an oil pastel across the raised texture of the support with variable pressure causes it to adhere unevenly, creating a broken surface texture.

Ken Draper, *Autumn Drift,* 1993, oil and soft pastel

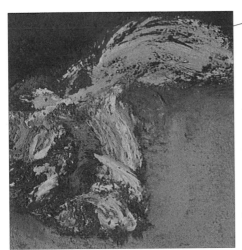

Oil and soft pastels have differing degrees of adhesion. The powder of soft pastels can be displaced and blended into the fibers of the support very easily. In contrast, oil pastel vigorously adheres to the support. When dragged, oil pastels become more fluid as they are warmed by the heat of your hand or by the air temperature.

In this lower section of the painting, the artist has alternated bold strokes of oil impasto, evoking seaweed, with a subtle blending of soft pastel, overlaid by areas of scumbling and stippling.

EXPERIMENTING WITH SURFACE

AN EXCITING DIVERSITY of surfaces can be created by using watercolor, gouache, and acrylic paints in combination. Depending on the degree of paint dilution and the texture of the support, you can vary the power of the paint from a transparent wash to a full opaque impasto. Acrylics are designed to work in the widest range of painting techniques, and there are additives that are manufactured to give different qualities of bulk, transparency, or luster to the paint. In addition to the inherent qualities in the paint, there are tools available, including brushes and rollers, that can determine the character of the paint surface.

Broken surface

The nature of your support will have a fundamental effect on the surface of the paint. This broken surface effect was made by scraping the paint across a heavily textured paper using a metal painting knife. The paint has been forced into the pitted surface of the support, leaving the raised tooth of the paper free of paint.

Gouache impasto
Gouache has been applied in impasto over a water-color wash in which two colors were blended wet-into-wet.

The renowned British artist John Piper has engaged in a "tour de force" of texturing and markmaking in this painting. Washes of gray, blue, and green evoke the airy sensations of a landscape in the shadow of dusk against which patterns appear to dance in the space of the composition.

John Piper, *Landscape*, 1968, watercolor, ink and gouache

The surface of the composition has been built up in successive layers of paint. The orange pattern on the left has been washed over and dispersed into a subtle warm gray wash by mixing with the underlying blue. Blue is the complementary color to orange and on the right-hand, side the artist has superimposed scumbled patches of orange in strident contrast with the underlying turquoise blue.

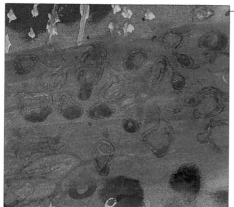

Creating an illusion

The range of painting techniques, from watercolor washes to opaque mark-making, can also be achieved in acrylic. Whereas Piper has used overlaid washes as a base for a rhythmical counterfoil of irregular and linear marks in gouache and ink, Boyd has capitalized on the properties of acrylic to create areas of dense impasto. Both artists have layered paint, causing the marks to appear to advance and recede as though suspended in space.

Texturing with acrylics

This artist engages in an experimental approach exploring the plasticity of acrylics and placing particular emphasis on the rich texturing properties of impasto that can be achieved using this medium. This abstract work was developed from studies of the forces and actions of the sea against coastal rocks that the artist has expressed in an equivalent painterly form through the gestural treatment of the paint surface.

Areas of deep pink, ochre, and a tint of ultramarine blue were laid onto a dried gray surface in loose impasto. While the paint was still wet, a large decorator's roller was used to roll the colors across the support. A splash of white paint was then pushed across the surface, and the blunt end of a brush was used to score lines in the pink and ochre sections. Lastly a strip of painted paper was collaged into the wet surface.

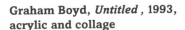

Graham Boyd, *Untitled* , 1993, **acrylic and collage**

Wet-into-wet

Acrylic paint can be worked either wet-into-wet or wet-on-dry. In this example paint has been applied wet-into-wet. Red and yellow have been mixed together to create a rust orange. The colors were worked into each other on the support, and an application of yellow was dribbled and brushed into the orange. Lastly strokes of green and red were laid in single movements to avoid mixing with the underlying colors.

Black paint was laid on the wet surface of the underlying paint, and a large brush was used to pull the fresh application of paint across the surface. A composition that has been worked in impasto will record, in a precise imprint, the actions of the hand, which in turn reflect the thoughts of the artist.

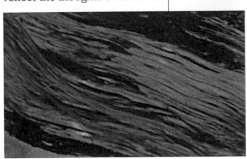

Iridescent acrylics

Blue acrylic paint has been mixed with gel medium and applied with a painting knife to create a passage of impasto. The paint was allowed to dry, and then a dilution of gold acrylic was applied over the impasto surface to imbue the surface of the blue paint with a metal luster.

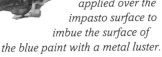

427

ADDING TEXTURE

PAINT IS USED PRIMARILY as a coloring medium, but it also has a texture, which can be manipulated in different ways. You can explore an extensive range of surface textures by adding various materials to the paint, including coarse sand, synthetic fibres or even by gluing additional sheets of paper to the support. Irregular textures create a visual disturbance that will significantly affect your perception of the color because of the way the light is reflected from the textured paint surface.

Choosing your materials

A diversity of texture can be created by using different materials and methods in your composition. You can work onto a uniformly textured ready-made support such as a rough paper or canvas, or create areas of contrasting texture by gluing thin sheets of flexible materials, such as cloth or paper, between the layers of paint as shown here.

The artist has laminated shapes (cut out of sheets of tissue paper) to the support not only to suggest natural forms, but also to intensify the expressive quality of the paint surface of the composition. The creases and edges of the tissue paper have created a heightened sense of surface texture as well as amplifying the feeling of the movement of shapes across the picture surface. By applying tissue paper with PVA glue the paper is turned into a semitransparent film and, after being laid over an existing wash, it will modify the underlying color in the manner of a watercolor.

Craig Peacock, *Rite of Spring*, 1993, mixed media

Using tissue paper and glue

The textural range of your surface can be changed by laminating tissue paper onto the support using PVA glue. You can either use cut shapes, or fold and corrugate the paper to create a bas-relief surface texture that can be regular and rhythmical or random and erratic.

Once you have glued a sheet of tissue to your support, you can paint over it using any type of paint to emphasize the texture of the tissue.

Sonia Lawson RA, *Seashore*, 1994, gesso, pigment and linseed paste

Powdered pigment

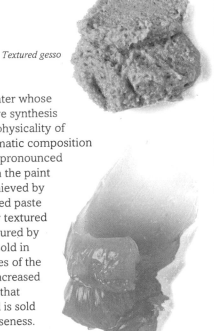

Textured gesso

Amplifying the surface

Sonia Lawson RA is a painter whose work epitomizes expressive synthesis of color and texture. The physicality of the forms within this enigmatic composition has been amplified by the pronounced granular textural quality in the paint surface. This has been achieved by mixing pigment with linseed paste to produce a more heavily textured paint than those manufactured by artists' color makers and sold in tubes. The textural qualities of the paint surface can also be increased by using a textured gesso that contains carborundum and is sold in different grades of coarseness.

Linseed paste

ADDING TEXTURES

Gesso can be used to create a textured surface or, you can add inert materials such as sand to either the gesso or the paint. Recently some manufacturers have produced textured acrylic media that contain fibers that impart a distinctive irregular texture to the paint.

Fine sand
Sands come in different grades from fine to coarse. You can also use a sand that contains different granules to create an uneven texture.

Acrylic media
Acrylic media contain either granular or stringy fibers. In the example (right) a stringy fiber medium has been added to acrylic color whereas on the left a more granular fiber mixed with turquoise pigment has created a more pronounced texture.

Color and texture

In this heavily textured composition, the artist has deliberately arranged different collected grades of canvas supports into a pattern of contrasting surface textures. Depending on their degree of intensity and their proximity to a neighboring color, all colors will either advance or recede in the picture space. The use of primary and secondary colors results in the colors pushing and pulling against the surface texture of the collaged materials.

GESSO AND WAX

A PAINTING IS FIRST and foremost a surface of texture and color. Irrespective of whether a work is abstract or figurative, its power relies on the skill and care with which the surface of the work has been developed. Gesso and wax, used separately or in combination, are two media that produce an interesting array of surface qualities.

Gesso is commonly used to prime a board or canvas in preparation for the application of a paint medium. It is normally applied on an even, flat surface, but it can also be used creatively to develop a bas-relief design within the surface of a composition. Beeswax is a semitransparent medium that produces unique surfaces of paint texture.

GESSO IS AN ANCIENT preparation for priming a painting surface in readiness for paint. Originally gesso was made from chalk and glue, with the addition of small amounts of oil to add flexibility. Manufacturers now produce an excellent modern gesso that is highly flexible and made from acrylic, titanium, and chalk.

Drawing into gesso
A design has been drawn into the surface of the gesso using the end of a brush. You can also add materials to create more texture.

WAX ENCAUSTIC PREPARATION

Wax encaustic is made from beeswax that has been gently melted to a liquid state in a double boiler. This warm wax then has powdered pigment added. The mixture can be used as a medium when the wax is still warm. A little dammar varnish can be added to strengthen the medium. It causes the wax to set on the support within seconds, forming a durable surface.

Solid beeswax
Beeswax is one of the oldest painting mediums known – wax paintings have survived since the Egyptians. Wax does not crack, flake, or darken with age.

Turpentine
Another wax encaustic technique involves blending turpentine and warm wax in a 50-50 ratio. This mixture should set to a buttery consistency.

Melting wax
Place the wax in a can in a pan of hot water.

The final mixture
When the wax is mixed in equal quantities with turpentine, it forms a soft paste that will impart the characteristics of wax to the oil paint. It must be kept in a sealed container to stop the wax from hardening.

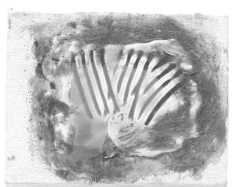

Applying the wax
Here the gesso has had an application of orange wax encaustic scraped across the surface, depositing the color in the indentations.

A layer of purple and orange wax encaustic has been scraped across gesso. An impasto layer of beeswax without pigment has then been applied with a knife.

Wax encaustic

Texture and geometry

In this powerful composition, the artist has created a beautiful surface using wax over four square panels. The surface was constructed using layers of crepe paper and liquid wax. Afterwards color was added using oil paint and a metallic pigment. The work intends to inspire religious meditation. It was designed to be housed in a large space, with the symbolic positioning of the four squares forming a single square to give the piece a sense of sacred symbolism. The artist has developed a complex textural surface as a source of reverie to complement the severity of the geometry.

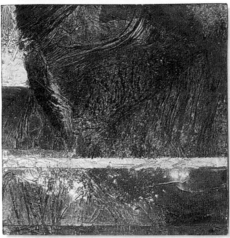

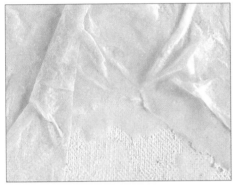

Wax and tissue

Poured wax sets in different thicknesses over tissue paper that has been soaked and draped over the surface of the canvas board.

Maureen Wilkinson, *Revelation,* **1992, collage and encaustic on wood**

Suspending materials in wax

Wax can be used to separate and suspend materials. To create an opaque wax medium, you can apply layers of paint within semitransparent layers of wax or add pigment. Here a sheet of tissue paper was soaked in warm wax. A layer of metallic pigment was brushed into the surface and a thin wash of blue oil paint applied to the surrounding area.

Barbara Freeman, *Arachne,* **1993, oil, wax and tissue paper**

The webs of gesso evoke the myth of Arachne, a weaver who is turned into a spider as revenge by the Greek gods.

UNUSUAL MATERIALS

CONTEMPORARY ARTISTS are often concerned with testing and extending the bounds of visual expression to incorporate unusual materials in the creation of their mixed media compositions. This originality has occurred as artists have searched for materials to fulfill a particular quality of color or texture that is usually outside the scope of more orthodox materials. As a result, the conventional formats have been challenged as artists find alternative shapes to use instead of the familiar rectangle of paper or canvas.

Using the landscape

Tessa Maiden was raised in a farming community, and her choice of materials and work reflects her awareness of the structure of the landscape. In the two paintings on this page, she has used a highly unusual and inventive arrangement of natural, artificial, regular, and irregular forms. These two pieces were originally part of a vertical arrangement of eight subtly different canvases.

In contrast with the regular pattern of the empty tea bags, the artist has created a visual nucleus in each composition by using the contrasting textures of a patch of canvas and radiating lines of string. In the lower half of the canvas, a mixture of button polish and linseed oil has coagulated into patterns on the surface.

Tessa Maiden, *Tissue Culture No.1*, button polish, tea bags, linseed oil and string

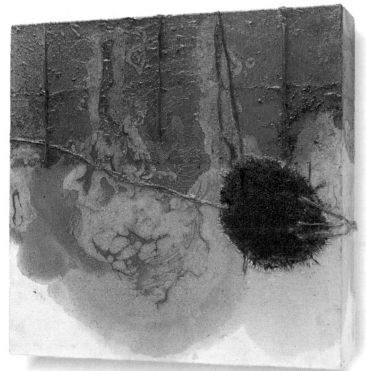

Tessa Maiden, *Tissue Culture No.1*, button polish, tea bags, linseed oil and string

Using tea bags

The artist has used the tea bags to represent the division of land into fields.

Tea bags

432

Using metals and wax

The circle is a very pleasing format to work with. Free from the constraints of verticals, horizontals, and right-angled corners, the imagination can explore another world of associations. In this composition, the artist has beaten a thin sheet of copper over a wooden panel and coated the copper surface with a layer of melted wax. The wax was darkened with the addition of pigment, and areas of the impasto wax surface have been scraped away to reveal the uneven texture and reflective surface of the beaten copper.

The qualities of wax

Wax is a versatile medium that can be used to alter the qualities of a surface. A light application of wax thinned with turpentine will deepen the tone of wood or stone and will also add transparency to a paper surface.

Rowena Dring,
Untitled, 1993,
tempera, pigment, and wax

Rowena Dring,
***Diskworld,* slate and plastic padding**

Using slate

Slate is an ancient building material and would normally be associated with sculpture rather than painting. Here the artist has used slate to create a work that could be defined as a wall sculpture, but whose surface is read in the manner of a painting. A shape that is evocative of land mass has been created by carving into the edges of the slate, then a subtly texturing the surface.

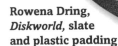

Natural slate

433

GALLERY OF PAINTING

PAINTINGS CREATED BEFORE the 20th century were largely figurative – using artistic conventions such as perspective, they offered convincing pictures of the world as we knew it. Contemporary art is often more abstract, emphasizing colors, shapes and textures, which results in more attention being focused on the picture surface itself. This has resulted in an extraordinary period of experimentation in which artists have used a huge range of materials to produce an exciting array of mixed media works. Artists have concentrated on generating a new awareness of surface and have succeeded by adding materials, by using impasto techniques, and by scraping and inscribing a surface to amplify the characteristics of each medium.

Nicholson has used an unusual vertical, double square format for this large canvas. He has worked the surface in colors and textures that are similar to weathered stone. A definite structure of shapes within the piece complements the diffuse texture of the paint surface. The finely scraped layers of gray paint reveal previous applications of color and create the sense of an underlying strucure being rediscovered.

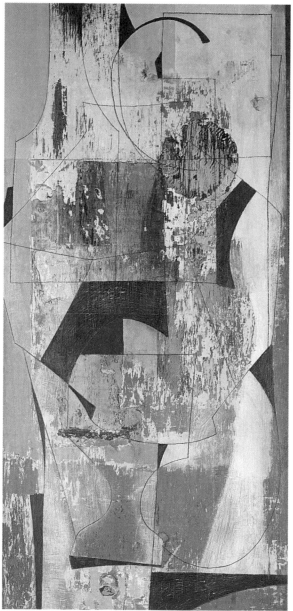

Ben Nicholson, *August 1952 (Palimpsest),* **(detail) oil and pencil** *42 x 21 in (107 x 53 cm)*
A "palimpsest" is a piece of paper or parchment on which the original text has been obliterated to make room for other writing. Nicholson has built up subtle layers of paint by wiping and then scraping back the pigment on a textured surface.

Joan Miró, *Morning Star,* **1940, tempera, oil, and pastel** *15 x 18 in (38 x 46 cm)*
Joan Miró (1893–1983) was one of the major Surrealists, and here he employs a perennial surrealist device – the juxtaposition of incongruous subjects to disturb our normal perception. In this piece, Miró demonstrates the combination of wet and dry painting materials by rubbing pastel into the support to amplify the texture of the surface and contrast with the opaque painted shapes. A menagerie of beasts linked by a linear framework forms a dreamlike constellation that floats against the nebulous vapors implied by the pastel wash. Miró was profoundly influenced by his Catalan roots, as shown by his strident patterns and his inventive use of textured materials.

Agar has taken meticulous care in the organization of the design by manipulating pastel in careful transitions to retain the purity and saturation of the colors. Particular attention has been given to the edge of the forms to achieve distinct shapes. There is a careful avoidance of casual gesture and a deliberate flattening of shapes into silhouettes.

Eileen Agar, *Orpheus*, 1991, pastel and chalk
33 x 24 in (84 x 61 cm)
Eileen Agar's use of vibrant colored chalks and pastels evokes the beguiling power of music and prompts an imaginative reading of the head in profile as the entrance to an underworld of dreams. The image, imbued with a visual lyricism and the inventive use of organic shapes, evokes a pastoral theme.

Ken Draper, *Light Fall*, 1993, oil and pigment on wood *48 x 42 in (122 x 107 cm)*
In this startling mixed media composition, the artist has employed an innovative combination of oil paints with pure pigment in powder form. The wood grain has been stained using oil paint to emphasize the support. Rectilinear shapes have been delineated in masking tape. Draper has created extremes of texture by blending pigment into the smooth surface of the wooden panel as a foil to the bas-relief surface in oil paint. The painting is a compelling allusion to the structure of the earth's crust.

The artist has scraped through the layer of gold in a sgraffito technique to create an inscribed pattern of foliage. The allusion to vegetation has been amplified by the use of a Viridian green that has been glazed over the gold. This detailing highlights the monumental scale of the towering gold edifice.

Barbara Rae, *Field Altandhu*, 1994, oil or acrylic with gold paint *67 x 76 in (170 x 194 cm)*
In this large-scale work, the artist has evoked an exotic night through a sumptuous combination of iridescent gold pigment and saturated colors. The surface of the support has been textured and reworked in layers of pigment that can be seen in the shimmering surface of the area in gold. The deep blue unifies the broken surface and throws the iridescent gold and luminous red band into high relief.

435

COLLAGE MATERIALS

COLLAGE, LIKE ANY OTHER ART FORM, needs to be held together with a visual theme, either by a dominant color, an emphasis on contrasting textures, or a linking concept such as landscape. Once you have established a theme, you can experiment with collaging almost any inert material that you can stick to a sheet of paper or a board. Any light material such as plastic or cloth can be attached to a heavyweight paper support using glue. Heavier wood and metal materials are best attached to a stronger support of either a board or panel.

THERE IS AN INEXHAUSTIBLE wealth of colored and textured materials to be found for collaging, including, tissue papers, newspaper imagery, magazines, posters, books, wallpaper, packing materials, and cardboard. An experienced collagist soon learns that "junk" can be rearranged to form a compelling artwork and develops the habit of collecting and storing found materials to form a storehouse of stimuli for the imagination. Suitable materials for bas-relief collages are light metal sheeting, aluminum foil, thin plywood, and veneers. You can also use flexible linear materials like string and wire to add curvilinear shape to your composition.

The average home is a great source of materials, not only for the wide selection of disposable cardboard, plastic, and paper that accumulates in the home, but also for the range of dried foods to be found in the kitchen, such as grains, beans, and pastas. However, it is important to use only food materials that will not disintegrate when exposed to the air.

Printed material
Newspapers, magazines, and brochures provide a surfeit of disposable printed material and imagery. The fonts and scales of the letter forms are particularly useful.

Old photographs
Most vacations and events result in a number of unwanted photographs. These can be filed into subjects and used to form collages on different themes, and they can also inspire a color theme.

Assorted fabrics
The delightful and seemingly endless diversity of natural and synthetic fabrics is highly suitable for collage. Fabrics can be grouped and organized in a composition according to texture and color. You may wish to begin with contrasting patterns of printed cotton or the different weaves and textures of canvas and burlap.

Burned tin can

Found objects
Discarded items and broken household appliances can be dismantled to retrieve small machine parts that inspire ideas. Complex electrical parts, along with broken toys, provide a ready supply of diverse shapes and forms that can suggest themes to explore in collage.

Discarded toys & shapes

Copper wire

Pumice stone

Tinfoil pie-case

Glue gun & glue sticks

Wood glue

PVA glue

Found natural objects
A walk through a garden will provide many natural, beautifully textured leaves, twigs, seeds, grasses, and barks, which are very suitable for collaging. Beaches are good hunting grounds for artists, and works can be developed from weathered fragments of rope, driftwood, and stones. The beauty of these fragments is that they are textured from the action of the sea.

Found objects

Adhesives
For light paper and fabric materials a PVA glue is ideal. There is a range of wood glues that are suitable for plywood, veneers, and driftwood, but they take some time to dry. A helpful tool for bas-relief collage is an electric glue gun, which heats the glue and squeezes it through a nozzle onto the support. This is particularly useful for metal and stone.

Cutting implements
Paper and cardboard are quickly cut to shape using either a sharp craft knife or a pair of scissors. A useful addition to your tool kit is a pair of wire cutters which can cut thin sheets of metal and mesh.

Wire cutters

Fretsaw
The fretsaw is a saw that is designed to allow for the cutting of complex shapes from thin sheets of wood. The thin saw blade is held in tension and can easily cut and form curves.

PRINTING MATERIALS

PRINTMAKING MAY SEEM a forbidding prospect, requiring access to presses and a printmaking studio. However, it is possible to create a range of fascinating and creative prints without the necessity for expensive machinery. Printing is basically the process of lifting an impression from a surface that has been inked or, instead, pressing painted shapes onto a paper surface. There are many materials that are suitable for printmaking. It is a simple process to develop works of striking texture and color using inexpensive tools.

Roller with ink

Wooden spoon

Palette knife

THE MOST POPULAR method of creating a print is by relief printmaking. This involves either cutting into or building up a printing surface into a pattern of raised shapes. Ink is then rolled over the surface of the printing block and a sheet of smooth paper placed on the inked surface. Even pressure is then applied to transfer the design onto the paper. Pressure is best applied by either using a roller or rubbing the back of a wooden spoon across the back of the paper. Another highly creative process for you to explore is monoprint. This involves painting a design onto a sheet of smooth impermeable material such as acetate or glass. Again, make a print by rubbing the back of the paper with a roller or spoon.

Ink and surfaces
Inks should be mixed with a spatula on a palette of either plate glass or, as a safer alternative, a sheet of acetate or plastic. The ink should be taken up with a roller, which should lift enough ink to coat the printing block evenly. As you roll, you can control the thickness of the ink to create either a transparent or opaque application.

Brushes
Different-sized brushes are used in monotype printing to apply and move the ink around on the plate, creating areas of line or tone. Brushes are also used as an alternative to the uniform application achieved by rollers.

Masking out
Masking tape is designed for blocking out areas of a composition before an application of paint or ink. The tape is then peeled away from the surface, allowing the underlying tone to show through. Masking tape is also essential for securing the paper to prevent movement when making a print.

Scalpel
Scalpels are useful for carving patterns into sheets of paper and card for printing.

Printing inks
Printing inks are made of finely ground pigments suspended in a transparent drying medium. Inks come in an extensive range of colors, but by mixing the three primary colors of magenta, cyan, and yellow, along with black and white, you can create a full palette of colors. Most commercial inks are oil based and are thinned with mineral spirits. You can also buy water-based inks. Manufacturers make an extending medium for oil-based inks that can be added to create transparent tints.

Shellac

Shellac is a resin-based varnish. It can be used to seal the surface of a bas-relief work or collagraph. The dried application of shellac stops the cardboard from absorbing water- and oil-based inks. Without the layer of shellac, the surface of a bas-relief cardboard print will deteriorate in contact with the ink, allowing only a few impressions to be taken.

Shellac

Turpentine

Linseed oil and turpentine

Linseed oil is used as an extending medium for printing ink and oil paint and will increase the transparency of the colors. Turpentine is used to clean the roller after a printing session.

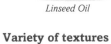

Linseed Oil

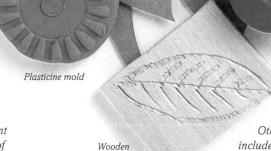

Rubber stamp

Positive and negative card cutouts

A piece of jigsaw puzzle

Plasticine mold

Plasticine mold

Wooden stamp

Printing blocks

Cardboard is easily cut with a craft knife or scissors to form a printing block. Rigid shapes can also be cut from hardboard or plywood using a fretsaw. Other more easily cut materials include balsa wood and polystyrene. You can also take impressions from surfaces using plasticine, which can then be used as a short-term printing block.

Variety of textures

There is a wide selection of synthetic materials that can be either cut or crumpled to create a textured surface. Each material is capable of different patterns by either folding to create regular creases or crumpling to create irregular patterns in the folds. There are other interesting textures in products that have been made with a bas-relief surface, such as certain wallpapers, bubble wrap, and woven fibers.

Plastic wrap

Using found objects

Collagraphs can be made from a diversity of materials, including string and thin wire, which are ideal for creating curved lines. These shapes can be used in contrast with the more regular weaves of gauze and other heavily textured fabrics. Grains such as rice can be used to create a pattern of small marks.

Aluminum foil

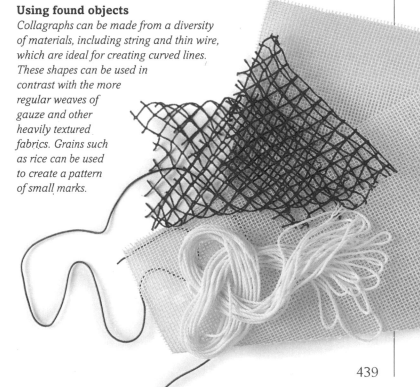

Bubble wrap

Tracing paper

COLOR COLLAGE

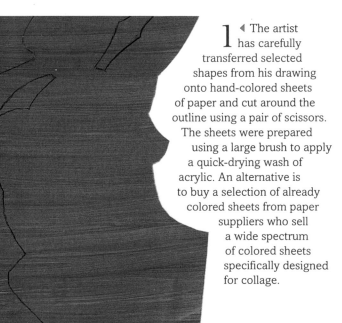

C OLLAGE IS A TECHNIQUE of cutting and arranging colored or toned materials to form a composition of shapes. This allows for extensive exploration of possible arrangements and affords scope for many adjustments before fixing the shapes in place. A major advantage of collage is that you can build an arrangement rapidly, which encourages a confident and inventive treatment. A color collage also makes an excellent base for additional mixed media techniques using paint and found objects.

Using your sketches

The artist has developed a dynamic compositional theme based on life drawings of the figure in motion. The implications of translating the drawing into collage are that the shape becomes the sole means of expression as the process of collage reduces the figure to flat shapes. The artist has selected angular and curved shapes from his sketches to emphasize movement.

A collection of sketches

By placing a number of studies on the same sheet, interactions of positive and negative shapes occur, acting as a prompt to the imagination.

1 ◀ The artist has carefully transferred selected shapes from his drawing onto hand-colored sheets of paper and cut around the outline using a pair of scissors. The sheets were prepared using a large brush to apply a quick-drying wash of acrylic. An alternative is to buy a selection of already colored sheets from paper suppliers who sell a wide spectrum of colored sheets specifically designed for collage.

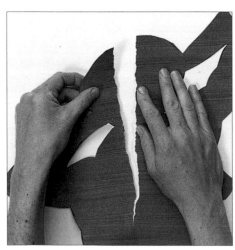

2 ◀ The dominant concern of collage is forming and arranging expressive shapes. As a means of intensifying the character of the shapes, the artist has chosen to vary the texture of the edges of the forms by alternating between the sharp edge of a shape cut with scissors and the ragged edge created by tearing the paper.

NEGATIVE SPACE

Composition is profoundly affected by having to translate a three-dimensional world of forms onto a two-dimensional surface. This process creates new shapes in the subject, but they only come into existence on the picture surface. They are the negative shapes that are created between the positive form of the subject and other areas of the composition. The negative shapes are as important as the positive shapes, and it is in collage that this awareness of composition can be most fully developed to create a a range of interesting images.

Maximum effect
The cut shapes have been shifted in this collage arrangement until the maximum interaction between the positive cut shapes and the negative shapes of the remaining areas of the support has been achieved.

Overlapping
The original leaf design has been transformed into a complex interaction of positive and negative shapes by the simple process of overlapping.

Scale and format
It is vital to consider the relationship between the position of the positive shape and the scale and format of the support. Here the shape is placed in an uninteresting static position, creating no interaction.

Positioning the shapes
The positive white shapes have been carefully positioned to touch the edge of the support and each other, creating dynamic negative red shapes among the positive shapes.

3 ▲ Where the shapes overlap, contrasting areas of primary and secondary color create a tension of positive and negative shapes in the composition.

Making connections
In the final composition there are two movements leading the eye through the artwork in different ways – through the recurrence of curved lines and the repetition of colors, which create alternative sets of connections.

PHOTO-COLLAGING

COLLAGING PHOTOGRAPHIC IMAGERY has become a mainstream contemporary art form that is both a product and mirror of our technological age. Technology now provides us with a perpetually renewed fund of ready-made printed imagery in the form of magazines, advertising, posters, and newspapers. We also create personal imagery using our own cameras. The essential principle of collage is the arrangement of cut shapes on an esthetic or a conceptual theme. Imagery for the collage can also be manipulated by using either a photocopier or a computer.

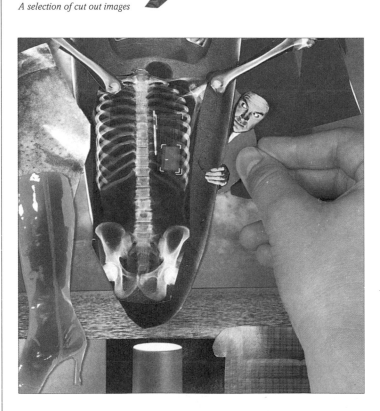

A selection of cut out images

Choosing a theme

Through selection and organization, collaging can result in powerful contrasting visual qualities of form. This can be seen here in the surreal photographic montage by Ed Smy. The artist's working method is to select and store imagery by themes – for example, machines, organic forms, and faces. The stored images are used as a fund of potential collage imagery. This collage was created by carefully arranging areas of color to create a dominant color key and a stage-like illusion of space. As a sculptor, Ed Smy is interested in the expressive power of combining familiar forms in a new context.

Ed Smy *Vaudeville*, 1994, photo-collage

Composing your collage

Collage can be used to draw images from our unconscious and to create compositions that reflect the incongruous juxtapositions that confront us daily. In the home, magazines and television flood our minds with imagery. In the street, billboards jostle for attention among the multitudes of items displayed in store windows. This bombardment of visual stimuli gives modern life a surreal quality that is strikingly mirrored by this witty collage.

Reduction and enlargement

The photocopier has given the contemporary artist exciting new effects to exploit in collage. New artistic possibilities are generated through the ease with which these machines reduce and enlarge printed imagery in both color and monotone. The photocopier, like all print forms, has its own particular quality of tone and texture, exaggerating the tone to either black or white.

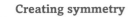

Creating symmetry

In this unusual arrangement, an image has been repeated and cut into irregular shapes. The cropped image of the front of a building has been given a new reading as a symmetrical abstract design of black and white textured shapes.

Architectural patterns

In this collage, the artist has used a photocopier to enlarge and reduce original photographs to the scale necessary for the composition. Images of architectural structure have been repeated and collaged over textured and painted papers to create an inventive painting.

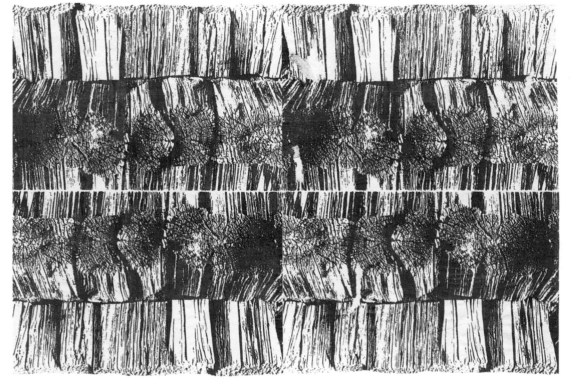

Repeat patterns

Any image can be constructed into a repeat pattern within minutes, allowing the artist to make rapid decisions and significant changes without difficulty. Here, a photograph of heavily textured stacks of wood has been repeated, using four sheets to create a single composition. It can also work as a textile design.

HANDMADE PAPER

Materials

Mixing bowl

Measuring cup

Plastic bowl

Shredded paper

Blender

MAKING YOUR OWN PAPER is a surprisingly simple process and a useful skill to master for creating unusual mixed media pieces. A number of qualities of surface can only be created by making your own paper. To do this you will need to buy some basic materials including a mold and deckle, which is a fine mesh stretched over a frame to catch a thin layer of pulp. The simple process of soaking and shredding existing paper into a pulp can allow you to create a raw mixture that you can work in many ways. You can either add pigments or dyes to create color or blend in a range of other fibers.

Making your own paper

2 ▶ The presoaked paper mixture needs to be pureed to reduce it to a pulp. This can be done in an ordinary blender in about 30 seconds. If you want to create a coarse pulp, puree for only 10–15 seconds in short bursts.

1 ▲ Tear up old paper and place the shreds in a bucket. Add enough hot water to make sure you fully submerge all the paper. Leave the paper to soak for at least an hour or, ideally, overnight.

3 ◀ Fill a plastic bowl half full with tepid water and pour in the pulp mixture from the blender. A half-full bowl of water should only take one load of pulp. Stir the mixture to disperse the pulp.

5 ▶ It is important to get an even covering of pulp on the mesh. The mold and deckle should then be lifted out horizontally, allowing the excess water to drain off.

4 ▲ Before lifting out the pulp you should prepare a board by placing felts over wet newspaper laid over a wooden board. Submerge the mold and deckle into the mixture, mesh side up, at a 45° angle.

6 ◀ Making sure the prepared surface is very even and moist, quickly flip the mold and deckle over and place the frame face down onto the felt.

7▲ Stroke the surface of the mesh to sponge off some of the excess liquid and flatten the pulp onto the felt. You can build up layers of paper by placing a wet felt between each layer of pulp.

8▶ It is extremely important to bounce off the mold and deckle in a quick clean movement. This is done by holding one end firmly and bouncing off the opposite side. This should leave the layer of pulp on the board.

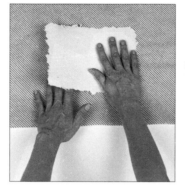

Materials

Felts

Mold and deckle

9◀ The pulp should be left to dry into sheets of paper. This can be done by leaving the layers of pulp to dry together in a pile or by taking each piece of felt and hanging it up to dry on a line. The paper should only take a couple of hours to dry into a sheet. Once dry, the paper should be carefully peeled off and sealed using starch, gelatin, or PVA glue.

USING ADDITIVES

Natural additives

Give interest and texture to your paper by adding all kinds of material to the paper pulp, ranging from dried grasses, leaves, petals, seeds, and thin bark to different grades of textured and colored papers, threads, cottons, string, and nylon netting. There are different ways in which you can add your collected materials to the prepared paper pulp. You can break up plant and paper fibers by pureeing them into your paper pulp. This will create flecks of various colors and textures in the paper. This is an excellent method for creating sheets of paper of a uniform texture with subtle variations of color. The size of the additional fibers can be varied by the amount of shredding the fibers undergo in the blender and you can create a surface with more contrast by blending in larger fibers or simply by pressing material such as small petals into the surface of a sheet of wet pulp. You can make some very unusual papers out of a range of plant fibers such as the leaves of the iris plant, which can be used as an alternative to paper pulp. The cellulose in the leaves needs to be broken down first by soaking the leaves in a solution of sodium hydroxide and then washing the fibers to remove any trace of chemicals. The fibers are then blended and pressed in the same manner as other pulps.

Laminating

Laminating is a process that involves pressing long fibers such as string and netting between two or more layers of wet pulp. This method of constructing paper allows you to experiment, creating some very original shapes. You can either sandwich the string between two layers of paper pulp or use the string or netting as a structure on which to press broken areas of pulp into irregular shapes.

Natural objects

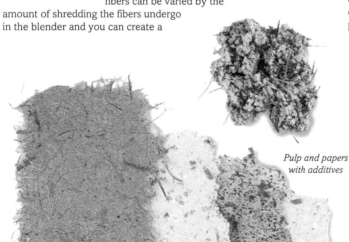

Pulp and papers with additives

String and coloured threads

CREATING AN IMAGE IN PAPER

Having explored the process of making paper, you can now adapt this technique to create your own imagery. The raw pulp can be colored most effectively by adding dyes, but you can also use water-based paint. The different colors of pulp can then be manipulated into shapes to form a composition of varied areas of color. An excellent way to create an image in your handmade paper is to use sheets of aluminum mesh (available where autoparts are sold and in some hardware stores) that can be cut into templates and used to create precise shapes of color.

Handmade paper overworked with crayons and paints

Colored pulps

To create an exciting image using handmade papers, you can experiment by overlaying complex arrangements of different colors and textures of pulp and later rework the surface of the dry paper with different materials. The design of your sheet of handmade paper can be as simple or intricate as you desire. The piece above uses different colors of pulp for the basic shape of the horses and then uses gold pastels and paint to create the highlights and embossed patterns.

DYEING PULP

To dye pulp ideally you should use procion dyes. Place two handfuls of strained paper in a saucepan. Add one gallon of water, a cup of salt as a fixing agent, half a cup of household soda, which helps the pulp absorb the dye, and a cup of dye. Simmer for 10 minutes over a low heat. Rinse the pulp in cold water and put it through a strainer to ensure that the color will not bleed out of the pulp. You can keep the dyed pulps for future use by sealing them in bags and storing them in a refrigerator.

Sea salt

Red

Yellow

Brown

1 ▲ Make yourself some stencils by cutting fine aluminum mesh into your chosen shape. It is important to choose your shapes carefully and to practice some layouts before you start.

2 ▲ Place your chosen color of base layer onto the prepared board. Submerge the stencil in a different color of pulp, then place the shape on the base layer and lift off in the usual way.

3 ▲ After you have created the basic layout, you can add highlights to the images by simply submerging small areas of the stencils in contrasting colors of pulp and placing these on top.

4 ▲ You can use any shape of stencil to build up your image, and you can add many subtle variations of color. Leave the pulp to dry in the usual way before applying any other media.

Working with handmade papers

Working with handmade papers is very satisfying, since the addition of color pigments emphasizes the color and texture of the paper. You can exploit the texture of the paper surface using a selection of dry drawing and painting media. A light application of charcoal or soft pastels will leave a grainy textured area of pigment through which the color of the paper will sparkle. Oil pastels have a stickier quality, and you can experiment melting the pastels into the paper using a warm iron on a sheet of paper placed over the work. It is also worth experimenting with blades, sandpaper, and steel wool to scratch through the layers of pigment. An interesting way of removing the color of the dye in the paper and of any other subsequent application of ink is to use household bleach to take out the color and leave a faded white pattern on the surface. You can work the surface of the paper even more by tearing and cutting additional pieces of paper and gluing these and other light objects, such as feathers and string, to the surface. You can also print patterns on the surface using painted shapes of cardboard and plastic erasers.

Various handmade colored papers

Building up color

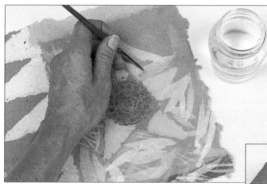

1 ◀ Once finished a piece of patterned handmade paper can be overworked using a variety of media. In this piece the artist starts by using bleach to produce white marks on the paper.

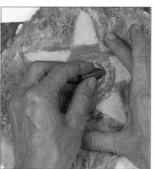

2 ▶ This particular piece has been overworked using soft pastels and crayons of various colors, but you can overwork your paper with any kind of media you find suitable.

3 ▲ An embossed design is created in the center of the star by rubbing a metallic pastel over a textured surface. Here the artist has used a patterned wooden board for the rubbing.

Materials

Steel wool

Gold crayons and paint

Wax crayons

4 ▲ The metallic wax crayon can be overworked and emphasized using gold poster paint or gouache.

5 ▲ The distressed effect is created by scratching off areas of the crayon and paint with steel wool.

This piece shows the level to which these handmade papers can be overworked using a variety of different techniques.

Brush and bleach

COLLAGE-LAMINATE & FROTTAGE

FROTTAGE IS THE TECHNIQUE of taking a rubbing from a textured surface. These rubbings can be developed into sophisticated designs by collaging the different patterns into a composition. Laminating is an extension of collage. It is produced by gluing thin sheets of tissue paper together, which effectively causes the sheets to become transparent layers of color. These two techniques can be explored and used together.

TO CREATE A FROTTAGE, the side of a wax crayon or chalk is rubbed evenly across a thin sheet of paper placed over the surface of any textured form. This process can be developed into complex layers of patterns by taking a rubbing of a surface and then using the same sheet to take a rubbing from another surface. There is a multitude of patterns to be found, including wall and floor surfaces, grid patterns on metal castings, and the bark of trees. A collection of patterns can be employed as a palette of textures for future collages.

Strips of frottage

Composing with patterns

You can overlay different patterns of the same or contrasting colors using a wax crayon, an oil pastel, or a water-soluble pastel. You can also take a rubbing and then shift the paper to another angle and take another rubbing so that the overlaid rubbing runs in a direction counter to the first impression. Intriguing and dynamic designs can be composed by cutting the frottaged sheets into shapes and placing the different textured areas into a composition, thus capitalizing on the contrasting textures and directions of the marks.

Detailing your work

The artist has contrasted the delicate monochrome rhythms of the frottage by laminating additional bands of a darker tone and colored string and feathers into the surface of the composition.

Laminating paper step-by-step

1 ▲ Place tissue paper over your chosen textured surface and rub with the side of a wax crayon or pastel to reveal a pattern. You can also use white and metallic crayons on colored paper.

2 ▲ Place the frottaged tissue over a sheet of plain tissue that has been coated with diluted PVA glue. Flatten out the paper using a printmaking roller.

3 ▲ Build up your laminated frottage using different pieces of tissue paper. You can use store-bought colored tissue or create your own colors by using washes of thinned acrylic paint on top of each glued layer.

4 ▲ A variety of objects can be added to the laminating process, including string (coiled into shapes) and metallic papers. Simply place them onto the paper and paste another sheet on top.

Working onto your lamination

Here the artist has created a *"tour de force,"* exploring the possibilities of combining frottage and lamination. Frottaging has been used to lift a pattern from the weathered surface of a stone, creating a snakelike movement through the composition. Sheets of tissue paper have been prepared by painting on patterns of bleach with a brush, thereby bleaching out the color of the paper.

Patterns have been printed onto tissue paper using corrugated cardboard. The overlaid sheets of tissue paper have been transformed by the diluted washes of PVA into transparent veils of color that contrast with the opaque forms of the feathers and string embedded between the tinted layers of tissue paper. Another way to develop your laminated frottage is to use an oil-based medium for the frottage and overlay a wash of watercolor on top. This will create a striking resist technique.

Creating details

The ochre tissue paper creates a golden glow that contrasts with the texture of the stone design and twists of string. Ink from a fresh photocopy can be transferred onto another sheet by placing the photocopy face down, dampening the back with a solution of detergent, water, and solvent and then rubbing hard.

BAS-RELIEFS

THE VISUAL QUALITIES required for a good collage are shape, tone, color, and texture. As you start to use materials with a more pronounced texture, you will inevitably begin to explore bas-relief form. You can create these forms out of cardboard, wood, and paper. Paper is a highly versatile medium and not immediately associated with bas-relief, but it can be used to create striking bas-relief forms by cutting, folding, gluing, and weaving. There is also a diversity of suitable bas-relief materials provided by objects found in nature and the discarded products of a consumer society.

Fretsaw and wood

Found objects

A BAS-RELIEF COLLAGE requires a unifying theme and so simply by using the right natural objects you can produce harmonies of textures and forms. You can see the natural harmony in the common characteristics of weathered fragments such as driftwood, rope, bits of corroded metals and plastics. In addition to collecting materials, you can develop bas-relief works in prepared wood, sheets of cardboard, plywood, and hardboard. You can then paint and stain them to form a colored bas-relief composition. Thin wood can be sawed into complex shapes using a fretsaw and glued in place using a glue gun.

Dick Lee, RA, *In a Persian Garden,* **1994, found object collage**

The intense hot colors of the base of the work amplify the enclosed green area, giving this space the impression of verdant coolness and calm. The scale of the paper figure forces the fir cone and the metal cast to be reread as ornamental bushes. This inventive use of materials epitomizes the creative skill of making a prosaic object appear poetic by allowing the object to evoke other forms.

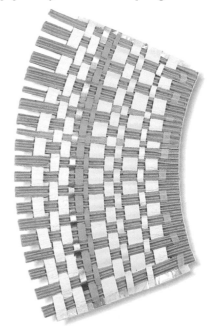

Weaving paper
You can either use a single type of paper or alternate different-toned and textured papers as you weave the strips together.

Experimenting with shapes
The artist has created a diversity of bas-relief forms by experimenting with folding, pleating, curling, crumpling, and twisting paper. Another technique is to laminate by gluing layers of paper together to create thicker forms, which can be carved and cut into in the manner of cardboard.

Tonal collage
A simple means of altering the perception of objects in a bas-relief collage is to change their natural color, or to reproduce their form in another material, such as plaster (as seen in the child's hand at the bottom of this composition).The forms, by being sprayed white, have taken on the characteristic qualities of a sculptural arrangement. In the absence of color the qualities of form and texture are amplified and produce contrasts of light and shadow.

Working in paper
By working with paper, you can create complex bas-relief collages that explore folding, cutting, and weaving techniques. The advantage of using paper for construction is the ease with which you can fashion and glue shapes in any position. Initially, you should use neutral-toned papers, so that you will be able to see clearly and exploit the tonal play of shadows created by the folds in the paper.

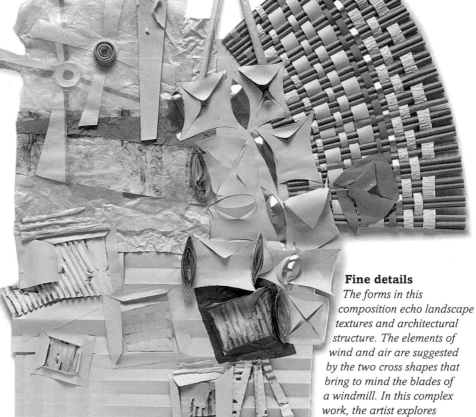

Fine details
The forms in this composition echo landscape textures and architectural structure. The elements of wind and air are suggested by the two cross shapes that bring to mind the blades of a windmill. In this complex work, the artist explores the illusion of space by over lapping the forms to create the sensation of recession.

451

GALLERY OF COLLAGE

COLLAGE IS AN ESSENTIALLY modern technique. Its unique feature is that it allows artists to explore arrangements of printed materials and found objects as ready-made imagery. By composing these items into harmonious arrangements and unlikely juxtapositions, artists challenge our perception of the familiar and create a new visual language.

In this deliberate pastiche of children's art, Dubuffet has combined the complex, natural texture of dried leaves with a quirky use of imagery in the form of a stray donkey. There is no attempt to force the material to look like the subject; rather he relies on the title to prompt an imaginative reading of the materials.

Max Ernst, *Dadaville*, 1924, painted plaster and cork on canvas
26 x 22 in (66 x 56 cm)
Max Ernst's (1891–1976) collage work is characterized by the diversity of found materials. As a soldier in World War I he was radically affected by the absurd waste and destruction he witnessed. This led to a profound skepticism about the establishment in life and art. In this work, Ernst creates an illusion of city structure by juxtaposing and transforming found materials into an arrangement with new meaning.

Jean Dubuffet, *L'âne égaré*, 1959, leaves and bark *27 x 20 in (68 x 51 cm)*
Jean Dubuffet trained as a painter, but he is also noted for his unconventional use of materials in the creation of "Art Brut" (raw art) imagery. Dubuffet experimented extensively with heavily textured surfaces by adding sand to paint and collaging with found materials. He would use textures as diverse as printed images and butterfly wings. The artist deliberately combines contradictory qualities, bringing together an esthetically refined and subtle control of texture.

Peter Blake, CBE, RA
Manhattan Boogie Woogie,
1994 photo-collage
12½ x 12½ in (32 x 32 cm)
*Along with David Hockney and
Richard Hamilton, Peter Blake
was a key figure in the Pop Art
movement. His originality lies
in the deliberate use of the
transient imagery of advertising
and mass culture that had
previously been regarded as
outside the bounds of fine art.*

Blake creates a rhythm of
negative shapes, produced
by a deliberate arrangement
of cut forms, using only
found imagery.

Anneli Boon,
Untitled, **1994, paper,**
photocopies and
emulsion paint
18 x 13 in (45 x 33 cm)
*Anneli Boon has used photo-
graphs of architectural forms that
have then been reproduced using a
photocopier. The modern process
of photocopying, with its
additional facilities for enlarging
and reducing the scale of the
image, produces a large range of
material for the artist. Here,
several copies of the same image,
in different ratios of scale, have
been cut out and then pasted onto
a textured sheet of paper that has
been distressed by staining and
crumpling the surface.*

453

Block Printmaking

Basic print shape

BLOCK PRINTMAKING IS A TECHNIQUE of relief printing that involves cutting a design into a block. Traditionally, wood blocks and linoleum are used, but there is a wide selection of alternative materials that can be carved or cut into without using carving chisels. A sharp craft knife can be used to carve printing blocks from thick sheets of cardboard, root vegetables, erasers, polystyrene, and plaster of paris. Where the surface of the block has been cut away, the ink will not be absorbed and the area will appear as white in the final printed image.

Cardboard cutouts to use as printing shapes

THE SIMPLEST way to block print is to cut shapes out of a thick piece of cardboard, paint them with a water-based paint, and press the cardboard, paint side down, onto a sheet of paper. Making a print using small blocks involves pressing the block onto a pad of printing ink or brushing paint onto the raised surface of the block. The block is then positioned and pressed onto the paper, leaving a print of its cut shape. You can create

Using found prints

Block printing is an excellent technique to use in combination with collage. Here the artist has used a combination of media with a selection of found materials. A sheet of brown paper has been treated with a broken application of white paint to create a surface suggesting a weathered wall. Sections of printed materials, including musical manuscripts and images of palmists' hands, have been incorporated into the printwork.

The artist has built up this design in a limited color range to focus our attention on the rich variety of textures in the work. The gold border has been printed from an eraser cut into the shape of a star. The gold paint has been applied to the handmade block and carefully repeated diagonally across the composition.

Flea Cooke, *Ancient Signs*, **1993, Collage and prints**

A sheet of brown paper was textured with white gouache using a sponge. The artist then collaged sections of a musical score, hand-painted strips of paper, gauze, string, and feathers to contrast with the underlying texture of the paper.

Dream garden

This composition was developed using broad applications of violet, green, and yellow ink to evoke the images and colors of a garden. The pattern of parallel lines, evocative of garden fencing, were produced by bleaching out the ink using a fine brush.

The pressure of the print block squeezes the paint towards the edges of the cut shape. As a result, the printed shape will look slightly transparent and will have a distinct raised edge of opaque color.

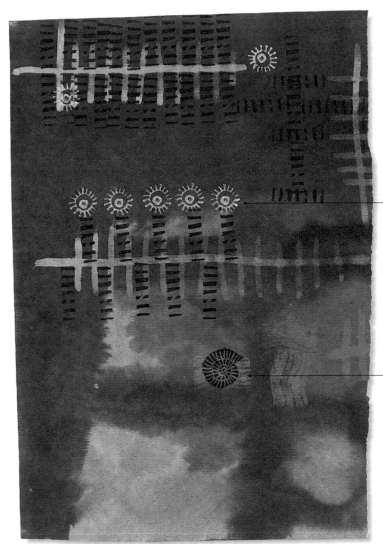

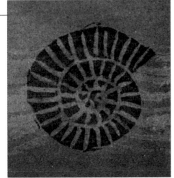

The isolated location of this single block print (representing a snail) has given the composition a point of focus away from the repetition of shapes in the upper section. The design in the block was created by cutting a spiral line, then superimposing a series of lines radiating from the center of the shape.

Flea Cooke, _The garden_, 1993, block printing and bleach

a repeat print using this method by reinking and applying the same block several times to create a recurring pattern. In the case of larger block prints, the block is inked with a roller, which will apply the ink evenly to the raised surface of the block. A sheet of smooth paper is carefully placed on the inked surface, and even pressure should then be applied to the surface of the paper to lift an impression onto the paper. Pressure can be applied by either using a roller or rubbing the back of a large wooden spoon across the back of the paper. It is neccessary to stop at intervals while rubbing and lift one corner of the paper at a time to check that the rubbing has evenly lifted the ink onto the paper.

EASY-TO-MAKE BLOCKS FOR PRINTING

This selection of small blocks are all carved from plastic erasers. The erasers had a design drawn in ballpoint pen, and the negative shapes were cut away using a craft knife. You can either press the cut block onto an inked printing pad or use a brush to apply paint to the raised areas of the block. Delightful repeat patterns can be created by reinking and printing the same block across different areas of the artwork.

MONOPRINT

Materials

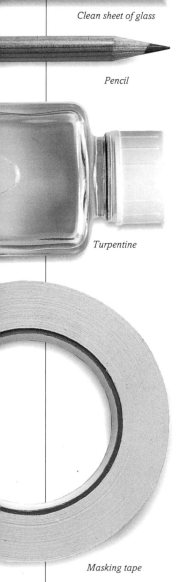

Clean sheet of glass

Pencil

Turpentine

Masking tape

MONOPRINT IS A SIMPLE and manageable printmaking technique that gives exciting results particularly in the texture of the printed surface. It is so named because it is a method of printing that produces a single print from a smooth sheet of metal, glass, or acetate, any of which can be used as the printing plate. The plate can be worked on in a number of ways – by painting and wiping ink into a design or by using stencils to create shapes. A monotype print is an ideal base for a mixed media composition since you can overwork the print with pastels or paints.

1 ◀ To ink the roller, squeeze a line of ink from the tube at the top of the plate and roll the ink so that it is evenly distributed over the plate.

2 ▶ Place a sheet of paper onto the plate, avoiding movement. Draw a design onto the paper using a pencil. Avoid touching the paper with your hand.

3 ◀ You can create areas of tone by gently pressing your finger onto the back of the paper. This will lift ink from the plate onto the paper surface.

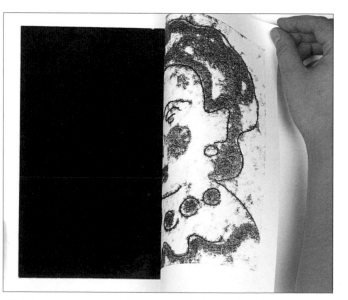

4 ▶ Again, being careful not to touch the back of the paper, in contact with the plate, lift the paper from the plate by pulling away from one corner. The print will be a mirror image of the original drawing.

Alternative method

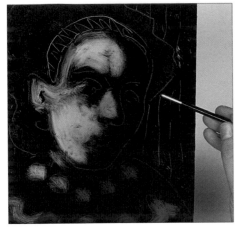

1 ▲ Another technique is to roll ink onto
the plate and then wipe and scrape lines
into the ink to create areas of white.

Small brush

Rubber roller

2 ◀ Place a large sheet
of paper on the plate,
and tape down securely.
Use a roller to apply
pressure and lift the
image from the plate.

3 ▲ In the final print, you can
see how the details, added
using a fine brush with diluted
ink, create a striking positive
and negative tonal image.

Tubes of ink

USING STENCILS AND OVERWORKING

Monoprints can be developed into sophisticated images
by building up the print using stencils. A shape is drawn
onto a sheeet of paper or cardboard and cut out. The
printing plate is then inked in the normal way and the
paper stencil laid on the plate. The stencil masks out
areas of the plate, and when the printing paper is placed

and the impression is lifted off, the stencil shape
remains untouched by the ink. By using stencils of
different shapes, a complex design of superimposed
shapes can be built up into a multilayered print. Once
a monoprint has been produced you can overwork
the basic shapes with pastels, paint, or crayons.

Any suitable paper

1 *The plate was inked and two
stencils were applied to the
plate – one for the silhouette of
the figure and one for the shape
of the face. Lines were inscribed
into areas of ink to add detail
and then a print was lifted.*

2 *The finished print can
be worked on in a range
of mixed media. You can
overwork the print with soft
pastel to add color or even
watercolor that will be
resisted by the oil-based ink.*

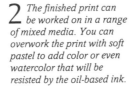

COLLAGRAPH PRINTING

COLLAGRAPH IS A PRINTING TECHNIQUE that involves building up, rather than cutting away, a bas-relief surface. The name collagraph is a derivative of collage, as a collagraph is a technique of collaging materials to create a print. A bas-relief design is created by gluing materials to a stiff sheet of cardboard. A great variety of textured materials can be used, from coarse cloth, sand, and string to grasses and grains. The textured collagraph produces a print with an embossed surface that mirrors the bas-relief surface of the original collagraph.

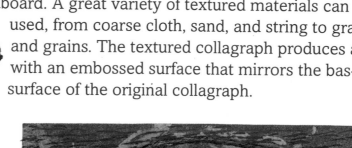

String

Collagraphs can be displayed as works of art in their own right.

Basic collagraph

In this collagraph a sheet of stiff cardboard has been used as a base for an interesting diversity of bas-relief textures. A pattern has been created by gluing string to the surface to form a linear design. Using a craft knife a pattern of marks has been scored into the cardboard and other shapes cut from paper to create contrasting areas of texture. A collagraph can also be constructed purely from PVA glue by dribbling the glue across the cardboard or by laying down a thick area of glue and drawing into the wet surface to create negative lines.

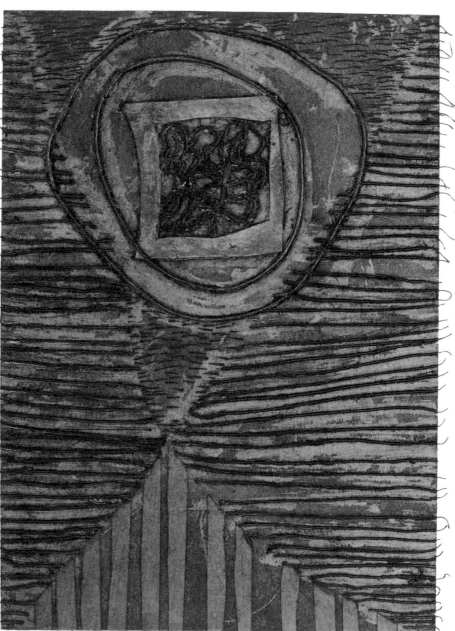

In this composition a linear design has been created by using string, and additional textures have been produced by cutting into the cardboard. A unique feature of collagraph printing is that the collagraph itself acquires a subtle beauty by being constantly inked, wiped, and reinked in different colors. Many collagraphs are kept and framed as bas-relief works.

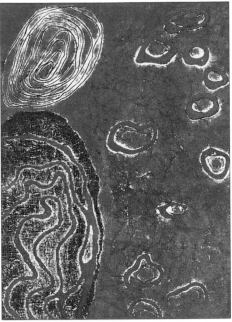

Monotone print

In this first print taken from the original collagraph (see left), there is a surprisingly different appearance. The artist used a roller to ink the collagraph in a single dark blue color. The raised surface of the materials has created a striking white halo around the textured forms in the print.

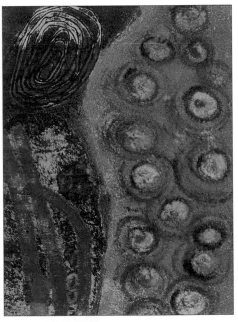

Multicolored print

In this second impression from the same collagraph, the composition is radically altered by the application of different colors. The artist has carefully painted different colors on various parts of the print to create two contrasting halves to the composition and to amplify the circular forms.

To BUILD UP up a collagraph, you can use many materials, including wallpaper, fine and coarse cloths, netting, and light metals such as foil. When the design is finished the surface should be sealed with PVA glue or shellac. After the surface has dried the collagraph is inked using a roller or a brush. A sheet of paper is laid face down on the print and the back of the paper rubbed in the same manner as block printing. If you dampen the surface of the paper it will accept the ink more readily.

Original collagraph

Anneli Boon is a Finnish artist who has explored the patterns in the strata of weathered rock formations as a source for her collagraph compositions. She has created this collagraph using a combination of fine gauze, a sheet of foil, string, and dribbled glue. The design was painted over in a coat of shellac to seal the surface, allowed to dry, and inked using a roller. A sheet of paper was laid on the print and held in place with masking tape. The back of the paper was then rubbed to lift an impression from the collagraph.

GALLERY OF MONOPRINT

THE SIMPLE TECHNIQUE of monoprint has been used by these artists to create a remarkably diverse range of visual imagery, from monochrome prints that have the quality of tonal drawing to complex multilayered color compositions. Printmaking is normally associated with multiple editions of the same image. However, monoprint, as the name implies, involves building up a single print surface and in this sense is closer to the process of creating a painting. Monoprints can be produced either by transferring a painting on a plate to paper or by using a roller to impart a uniform texture onto the printed image. Artists who work in monoprint frequently overwork the print using paints or pastels.

Tom Wood, *Monoprint II,* 1991, monoprint
42 x 63½ in (106.5 x 160.5 cm)
Tom Wood has developed a complex surface of overlaid colors in a monoprint based on a still life. The surface of the print has been built up through multiple layers of colored ink. Cut paper stencils were used to mask areas of the plate, creating the shapes within the composition.

The artist has cut leaf shapes out of paper and laid them onto the printed surface of the paper. Where these stencil shapes have been applied to the print, the subsequent application of white ink has been masked from the paper. The stencil was then pulled away from the paper, revealing the color and texture of the previous layer of ink.

Edgar Degas, *Woman Leaving Her Bath,* 1876–77, monotype and pastel
6¼ x 8½ in (16 x 21.5 cm)
Degas was a master draftsman who obsessively explored the theme of the body in movement. He contributed greatly to the development of monoprint. Here the image has been developed by brushing and wiping black ink onto a plate, and this can be seen in the gray areas of the wall. The print was overworked in pastel to add color and more texture.

Bob Baggaley, *Avebury Rd,* **1993, monotype**
16 x 20 in (40.5 x 51 cm)
Bob Baggaley combines different print processes to create monoprints based on a landscape theme. An image is printed using either silkscreen or lithography, and individual prints are then overworked using a monoprint process. The artist has experimented with the surface by dissolving the top layer of the ink with a thinner to reveal the previous layers of color.

Bill Jacklin, RA, *Untitled,* **1993, monotype**
40 x 48 in (101.5 x 121.5 cm)
In this energetic monoprint of figures bathing, the artist has used the pronounced texture of sweeping brushstrokes in blue and green ink to evoke the motion of the waves. He then dropped thinner onto the plate in spots to displace the ink and create the effect of foam. A small brush has been used for the fine details of the figures in motion.

PRESERVING AND STORING

PRESERVING AND STORING finished works requires careful consideration since mixed media surfaces are easily spoiled by careless handling. Framing under glass is the best solution for preserving bas-relief work, because this isolates the artwork's surface from air pollution. Works can also be stored in a portfolio with a covering sheet of tissue paper.

Box frame

In this assemblage a box frame has been specifically designed to provide adequate clearance for the different elements that make up the bas-relief. This type of framing enables the irregular format of the composition to be seen clearly and gives the artwork a more interesting perspective.

THE BEST METHOD FOR preserving your work depends on the size of the piece and the nature of the materials used in the composition. As a general rule it is recommended that oil- and acrylic-based paintings be given a coat of picture varnish to preserve the surface of the work from airborne pollution. This is sufficient protection as it is expensive to frame large works under glass. You can store works on canvas and board by wrapping them in polyethylene or bubble wrap when transporting the work. Encaustic painting, heavily textured, and bas-relief surfaces along with collage and works on paper will absorb dust and moisture from the surrounding atmosphere. Since these surfaces are not recommended for varnishing, they are best framed under glass.

Cross-section of the box frame

In this cross-sectional view of the box frame, you can see that this design of frame is deep enough to allow adequate clearance for the bas-relief forms in the composition.

Corner view

A box frame differs from other frames in that the glass and the base are held apart by slotting into recesses that are cut into the inner edge of the molding.

Framing under glass

There are many different frames. The best way to choose a suitable one is to visit a contemporary gallery or a professional picture framer to see the various types available. Some wooden frames have molding that is stained or coated in gesso or gilt to form a more elaborate surface. Aluminum frames can also be purchased in kits. In some cases you may need to have glass cut to size. Framing has a tremendous effect on the appearance of a work and will greatly enhance its presence and value. Choose a frame that allows for a border of at least 2-3 in (5-7 cm) around a work. Test the color of the frame against the artwork so that you can see if the color goes with the composition. Usually, works on paper are mounted on cardboard and a mat placed over the work. If you choose this method of framing it is essential that the color of the mat works with the key colors of the composition.

Handmade frame

In this inventive frame scraps from a sawmill have been used to create a frame that has the particularly original feature of string linking the corners.

FIXING AND STORING

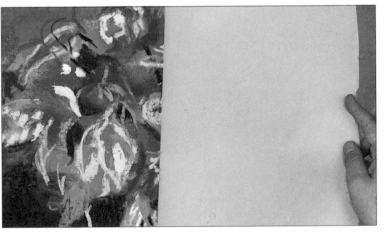

1 *Dry media are easily spoiled and need to be preserved by a light spray of fixative to fix the pigment to the support. Do not overspray the surface as this can darken or displace the pigment.*

2 *When storing artwork, be sure to cover the surface and to avoid friction that displaces the surface pigment. Make a cover by taping a sheet of tissue, greaseproof or tracing paper to a piece of cardboard and place the artwork underneath.*

GLOSSARY

ABSORBENCY The degree to which the paper absorbs the paint, often due to the amount of surface sizing.

ACCELERATED PERSPECTIVE Sometimes used in stage and film sets and occasionally in architecture. It exaggerates the effects of perspective, so that a shallow stage, for example, can be made to look deeper.

ACID-FREE PAPER Paper with a neutral pH that will not darken excessively with age.

ACRYLIC Synthetic resin used in an emulsion as the binding medium for artists' acrylic colors.

ACRYLIC PAINTS These are bound by an acrylic and are water-soluble but, unlike watercolor and gouache, they dry to an insoluble plastic film. Acrylic is ideal for creating surface texture in a painting, since it can be worked in thick impasto or with added texturing. Manufacturers have developed a variety of additives that can be added to alter the texture of the paint or retard the drying time. This allows for more controlled blending of colors.

ADJACENT COLORS Literally, those colors closest to each other on the color wheel, but also used to describe colors that lie next to each other in a painting. Adjacent complementary colors appear brighter because each reinforces the effect of the other.

ADVANCING COLOR The perception of a color, usually a warm (orange/red) color, as being close to the viewer.

AERIAL PERSPECTIVE The effect of atmospheric conditions on our perception of the tone and color of distant objects. As objects recede toward the horizon, they appear lighter in tone and more blue.

AFTERIMAGE In painting, the visual effect that results from looking at a strong color, *i.e.,* perceiving the complementary color of the color we have just been looking at. If, for example, we look hard at an orange-red area and then look at a bright yellow, we might see the yellow as green because we are carrying a blue afterimage of the orange-red. This effect is known as color irradiation.

ALLA PRIMA Literally means "at first" and is a direct form of painting made in one session or while the colors remain wet. (As opposed to "indirect" painting in which the painting is built up in layers). This is the technique employed by artists when they want to paint spontaneously. It is, however, a difficult style to master as it requires fluent brushstrokes and a skillful manipulation of the paint.

ANAMORPHOSIS The distortion of an image by transferring it from a regular rectangular grid to a stretched perspective grid, so that when it is seen from an oblique angle, it reverts to its original appearance.

ART BOARD Artists' quality paper mounted on cardboard. It gives the support a stiffness that reduces the incidences of pastel loss caused by the flexing of the paper surface.

ARTISTS' QUALITY PAINT These paints are labeled with information on the nature of the pigment and lightfastness of the color.

ARTISTS' QUALITY PAPER Paper with a neutral pH balance and a high rag content that does not yellow and become brittle with age

ARTISTS'-QUALITY WATERCOLOR PAINTS The best-quality paints, with high pigment loading and strong colors.

ASCENDING VANISHING POINT A point above the horizon line to which two or more parallel lines in the same plane and receding away from the viewer appear to converge. For example, in a sloping roof.

ATMOSPHERIC (OR AERIAL) PERSPECTIVE The effect of the atmosphere on the way we perceive tones and colors as they recede toward the horizon. Tones lighten and colors become cooler or more blue.

AXONOMETRIC PROJECTION A system where a plan is set up at a fixed angle to the horizontal, such as 45 degrees, and verticals are drawn true to scale to show the sides of the object.

BINDER In a paint, this is the substance that holds the pigment particles together and that allows them to attach to the support. In the case of watercolor, the binder is water-soluble gum.

BINDING MEDIUM The substance that holds pigment particles together and attaches them to a surface. Water-soluble gum is used for soft pastels, wax for crayons, and oil for oil pastels.

BLEEDING The tendency of some organic pigments to migrate through a superimposed layer of paint.

BLENDING A soft, gradual transition from one color or tone to another.

BLOCKING IN Laying in a broad area of color.

BLOCK PRINTING A technique of relief printing that involves cutting a design into a block. Traditionally, woodblocks or linoleum are used but there is a wide selection of other materials, such as thick sheets of cardboard, root vegetables, plastic erasers,

Alla prima

Texture paste

Gel medium for impasto

Working wet-in-wet

Glazing

polystyrene, and plaster of paris, which can be carved or cut using either wood-carving chisels or a sharp craft knife. The surface of the block is inked and a print taken by applying pressure to the back of a sheet of paper placed on the inked block. The areas where the surface of the block is cut away appear as white lines or negative shapes in the printed image.

BLOOM This refers to the characteristic powdery brilliance of the surface of an application of soft pastel.

BODYCOLOR Also called gouache. A type of paint or painting technique characterized by its opacity.

BRACELET SHADING A form of shading in which semi-circular lines are repeatedly drawn close to one another.

BRISTLE BRUSHES Hog hair or bristle brushes are used extensively in oil painting. They have coarse hairs which hold plenty of thick paint and yet retain their shape. Bristle brushes are useful for covering large areas with a uniform tone and for blending.

BROKEN COLOR A light application of color that allows the underlying color to show through in an irregular pattern.

BURNISHER Traditionally, a piece of polished stone such as agate has been used to burnish gold leaf and similar materials. In watercolor painting, a burnisher is used to smooth down the fibers of the paper when these have been raised by vigorous handling. Some artists use the back of a fingernail for this purpose.

CAMERA LUCIDA A drawing aid invented in the early 19th century and still used by some artists. This is a simple prism with a lens and eyepiece on a stand. With this instrument it is possible to see the subject of a painting directed down onto the watercolor paper. The artist can then draw the outlines.

CAMERA OBSCURA A development of the pinhole camera effect in which an inverted image is formed when rays of light pass through a tiny aperture. By substituting the pinhole for a lens, and using a portable screen for viewing an image, artists found that they could transcribe a scene accurately onto their drawing paper.

CANNON A cylindrical container used to measure the hairs for brushes.

CANVAS There are two main types of canvas: artists' linen, made from flax, and cotton duck. You can purchase preprimed canvases on stretchers of various sizes or prepare your own.

CARBORUNDUM PASTEL BOARD Board coated in a fine dusting of powdered carborundum. This creates an exceptional degree of tooth that can hold a thick application of pastel.

CENTER LINE OF VISION (LINE OF SIGHT) An imaginary line from the artist's eye to the horizon, bisecting the angle of the cone of vision and at 90 degrees to the picture plane. It intersects the horizon line on the picture plane at the center of vision.

CENTER OF VISION The point on the horizon line at the intersection with the center line of vision. It is the point we are directly looking at and the single vanishing point in one-point perspective.

CHALK Natural calcium carbonate, used in the preparation of chalk/glue grounds for its whiteness and opacity and as a cheap extender in oil-based paints in which it is translucent. "Chalking" is the powdering of the paint surface due to the breakdown of the binder as a result of ultraviolet radiation.

CHALK (PRECIPITATED) A very fine grade of chalk used in the manufacture of pastels to create paler colors, called tints, of the original pigment.

CHARCOAL Carbonized wood made by charring willow, vine, or other twigs in airtight containers. Charcoal is one of the oldest drawing materials.

CHROMA The intensity or saturation of a color.

CHROMATIC Drawn or painted in a range of colors.

CLAUDE GLASS *see* Reducing glass

COLLAGRAPH PRINT Collagraph is a printing technique that involves building up a bas-relief surface using light materials that are arranged and glued onto a stiff sheet of cardboard in the manner of a collage. The raised surface is inked and a print is taken by applying pressure to the back of a sheet of paper placed on the inked surface. Collagraph prints have a characteristically embossed surface that mirrors the bas-relief forms of the original materials.

COLOR IRRADIATION The aftereffect that results from looking at a very strong color in which you perceive its complementary color. *See also* Afterimage

COLOR TEMPERATURE A measurement of color in degrees Kelvin. This is of importance to photographers who need to correlate the color temperature of a light source with the type of film they use. As artists, we are aware that the color temperature of a room illuminated by electric light is significantly different from (yellower than) that of daylight.

COLOR WHEEL The primary, secondary, and tertiary colors arranged in a circle as colors are refracted in a rainbow: red, red/orange, orange, orange/yellow, yellow, yellow/green, green, green/blue, blue, blue/violet, violet, violet/red.

COLORED PENCILS Wax-based crayons in a pencil format and available in a wide selection of colors.

COMPLEMENTARY COLORS Those colors of maximum contrast, opposite each other on the color wheel. For example, the complementary color of a primary color is the mixture of the other two primaries, i.e., green is the complementary of red because it is made up of yellow and blue, and purple is the complementary of yellow because it is made up of red and blue.

CONE OF VISION A cone of up to 60 degrees, within which a subject can be comfortably represented without perceived distortion.

CONTÉ CRAYON A commercial drawing stick in varying degrees of hardness and in a range of black, white, and red earth colors.

Pigment

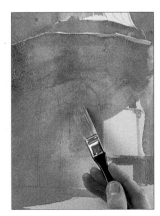

Laying in wash

Resist techniques

CONVERGENCE the apparent coming together of parallel lines receding from the viewer toward a fixed point.

COOL COLORS Generally, a color such as blue is considered cool. Distant colors appear more blue because of atmospheric effects and cool colors are therefore said to appear to recede.

COUNTER PERSPECTIVE In counter perspective, if lettering or relief at different levels on a building is to appear the same size when seen from the ground, it must be carved or painted at a larger scale higher up than lower down.

CROSS-HATCHING Parallel marks overlaid roughly at right angles to another set of parallel marks.

CURVILINEAR PERSPECTIVE A perspective system in which lines that may in reality be straight appear curved. It applies particularly when an image is seen from close up or with a wide angle of vision.

DAMMAR A soft resin that is soluble in turpentine and used to make a gloss varnish. You can make an acceptable varnish by dissolving some dammar resin in a jar of turpentine or mineral spirits.

DARKS Those parts of a painting that are in shadow.

DESCENDING VANISHING POINT A point below the horizon line to which two or more parallel lines in the same plane and receding away from the viewer appear to converge - as in a sloping street.

DEXTRIN Starch made water-soluble by heating. It is used as an inexpensive alternative binder to gum arabic.

DIAGONAL VANISHING POINT The vanishing point for lines receding at 45 degrees from the picture plane.

DIFFUSER A spray diffuser is a tool for spraying either a liquid pigment or fixative in atomized droplets onto the surface of a support. Two small hinged metal tubes are opened at right angles to each other, with the end of the longer tube immersed in the medium. Hold the shorter end with the plastic mouth piece between your lips and blow firmly. The action of your breath will cause the fluid to rise up the longer tube and atomize the liquid into a fine spray. You can vary the density of the spray according to the pressure of your breath and the distance you hold the diffuser from the support.

DIRECT PAINTING *See* alla prima

DISTANCE POINT A point on the horizon line from which a line is drawn to establish the intersection points of transversals with orthogonals. In one-point perspective, it corresponds to a diagonal vanishing point.

DRAGGED Describes brushstrokes that are made across the textured surface of canvas or paint or at a shallow angle into wet paint.

DRAWING GRID A drawing grid is made up of a series of squares that enable an artist to transfer a sketch proportionately onto a large-scale support. The grid can easily be produced by drawing squares onto a piece of acetate or tracing paper and then laid over the sketch.

DRY BRUSH TECHNIQUE A painting method in which paint of a dry or stiff consistency is stroked or rubbed across the canvas, producing a broken color effect.

DRY WASH The technique of working pastel powder into the support to create even areas of color. Soft pastels are pared with a knife or crushed to create a powder.

DURABILITY RATING *see* Lightfastness

EASEL A frame for holding a painting while the artist works on it. Watercolor painters tend to use sketching easels of light construction. A good sketching easel allows the painting to be held securely in any position from vertical to horizontal.

ELEVATION A two-dimensional scale drawing of the side of a building.

ELLIPSEL A circle whose apparent height appears to diminish the farther it tilts away from you.

EMULSION In acrylics, a stable suspension of acrylic resin particles in water.

ENDERS A pigment which has a limited effect on a color. It may be added to control the properties of a paint or to reduce the cost. Examples are chalk and china clay.

ERASER A tool for removing pencil and other marks. In the past, artists used rolled bits of bread, or feathers. More recently, artists have used standard rubber erasers, soft putty rubbers, or artgum erasers, although the new plastic erasers are extremely clean and versatile.

EYE LEVEL The distance from the ground line to the eye of the viewer establishes the eye-level. It is the same line as the horizon line.

FAT-OVER-LEAN The rule applying to oil painting in layers, in which each superimposed layer should have a little more oil in the paint than the one beneath. This ensures that each layer is more flexible as a dried film than the one below it, with less risk of the paint cracking.

Two-point painting

Atmospheric perspective

Three-point painting

FEATHERING Laying roughly parallel strokes of pastel, usually over a previous area of color, to modify the original strength or tone. Also used to create atmosphere.

FELTING In paper manufacturing, the process by which plant fibers mat together.

FERRULE The metal part of a brush, which surrounds and retains the hairs.

FINDER A rectangular hole to the scale of the artist's paper cut in a small piece of cardboard to act as a framing device. This is held up at arm's length, and the scene to be drawn or painted is viewed through it.

FIXATIVE A surface coating that prevents charcoal, chalk, and conté crayon from becoming dusty and from mixing with overlaid color.

FLAT COLOR An area of matte color of uniform tone and hue.

FLAT WASH An application of an even and uniform area of tone and color.

FLOCCULATION Like granulation in appearance, but the result of pigment particles coming together as a result of electrical charges rather than the coarseness of the pigment.

FLOCKED PAPER A pastel paper or board that is sprayed with a fine coating of cloth fibers and grips the pastel pigment.

FLOTATION The streaky effect made by lighter pigments as they disperse unevenly on the paper.

FOCAL POINT In a painting, the main area of visual interest.

FORESHORTENING If you are looking across a courtyard of square pavement slabs in which two parallel sides of the slabs recede directly away from you in a straight line towards a central vanishing point and the others recede horizontally, the distance between the lateral or horizontal edges will get progressively smaller. This is foreshortening. The degree of foreshortening depends on the angle at which you view an object.

FORM The shape of a three-dimensional object, usually represented by line or tone in a two-dimensional drawing.

FROTTAGE A technique of taking a rubbing from a textured surface. A sheet of thin paper is placed onto the textured surface and the side or blunt end of a stick of charcoal or crayon is rubbed vigorously over the back of the paper. The crayon will impart pigment to the paper only where the raised areas of the textured surface are in contact with the paper.

FUGITIVE Colors that are not lightfast and will fade over a period of time.

GLASSINE A paper with a smooth, shiny surface, used to protect a pastel work from smudging or accidental loss of pastel dust.

GLAZE Applying a transparent layer of paint over all, or part, of a painting to modify the effect of the color.

GLYCERIN The syrupy ingredient of watercolor paints, used as a humectant or moisture absorber in order to keep them moist.

GOUACHE A type of watercolor paint which is characterized by its opacity.

GOUACHE RESIST Using gouache paint or bodycolor to protect areas of your paper or paint film from further applications of paint. The gouache is subsequently washed off.

GRADED WASH A wash in which the tones move smoothly from dark to light or from light to dark.

GRANULATION The mottled effect made by heavy coarse pigments as they settle into the hollows of the paper. It may be caused by flocculation or by differences in the specific gravity of the pigments.

GRAPHITE PENCIL Standard pencil leads are made from a mixture of graphite and clay. The mixture is fired and subsequently impregnated with molten wax. The proportion of graphite to clay varies, and it is this which determines the hardness or softness of the pencil.

GRAPHITE STICK A large-scale pencil lead used for drawing.

GRID SYSTEM A method of putting objects into perspective in relation to a drawn perspective grid of rectangles.

GROUND The surface on which color is applied. This is usually the coating rather than the support. A colored ground is useful for paintings where the ground provides the halftones and the unifying element for the different colors. A colored ground can also be applied as a translucent stain over a white priming, or as a primer that has been colored.

GROUND LINE The bottom edge of the picture plane where it cuts the ground plane. It is parallel to the horizon line.

GROUND PLANE The level ground upon which the artist is imagined to be standing in order to view a scene and which stretches to the horizon. The ground plane is in reality uneven and we are able to take account of its ascending and descending planes and uneven contours when making perspective drawings.

GUM ARABIC Gum from the acacia tree used as a binding material in the manufacture of watercolor paints. Kordofan gum arabic, which takes its name from the region in Sudan from which it comes, is the main type used nowadays.

GUM ARABIC RESIST Covering details of your painting with gum arabic solution to protect the paper or paint film from further applications of paint. The gum arabic is subsequently washed off. Alternatively, mixing gum arabic with paint allows you to lift the paint off more easily later.

GUM SOLUTION A dilution of gum in water used as a binder to hold the pastel pigment in stick form. The greater the gum content, the harder the pastel.

Anamorphosis

Architectural sketch

467

HALF TONES Transitional tones between the highlights and the darks.

HARD PASTEL A pastel with a high gum content, which produces a hard texture, suitable to preliminary drawing and detailed work. Hard pastels can be sharpened to a fine point and come up in 80 colors.

"HARD" WATERCOLORS Blocks of straight pigment and gum mixes with no added plasticizer or humectant (such as honey or glycerin), which were used by early watercolor artists. The blocks had to be scrubbed to get the color out but, once the paint had dried, it could be painted over with little danger of dissolving the paint film.

HATCHING Making tonal gradations by shading with long, thin brushstrokes. Often used in underpainting.

HEIGHT LINE (MEASURE LINE) A vertical line on the picture plane with heights marked to scale of objects that may be behind or in front of the picture plane.

HEEL OF BRUSH The base of the hairs, near the ferrule.

HIGH-KEY COLOR Brilliant and saturated color. High-key paintings are usually painted on white or near-white backgrounds.

HIGHLIGHT The lightest tone in drawing or painting.

HORIZON LINE The line where the sea and the sky appear to meet. The horizon line is always at your eye level and is the location of horizontal vanishing points.

HP OR HOT-PRESSED Paper with a very smooth surface.

HUE Describes the actual color of an object or substance as it would appear on the color wheel.

HUMECTANT A moisture-absorbing additive, such as glycerin, which is added to watercolors to keep them moist.

IMPASTO A thick layer of paint, often applied with a painting knife or a bristle brush, which is heaped up in ridges to create a heavily textured surface and a look of fresh immediacy.

IMPRIMATURA A thin overall film or stain of translucent color over a white priming. This is applied before the artist begins to paint. It does not affect the reflective qualities of the ground, but it provides a useful background color and makes it easier to paint between the lights and darks. It also allows for an economical style.

INKS The main types are water-based and shellac-based inks. Shellac inks are waterproof when dry and are suitable for overpainting.

INTERNAL SIZING A means of reducing the natural absorbency of paper by adding sizing at the pulp stage. *See also* Sizing and Surface sizing

ISOMETRIC PROJECTION A form of axonometric projection that denies the apparent convergence of receding lines. Height lines are true and to scale. The angle of receding lines relates to the angles at which the planes of the cube meet.

LAID PAPER Paper in which you can detect a ladderlike horizontal and vertical pattern due to the pattern of the wire mold on which it was made.

LAMINATING An extension of collage. It is a process of gluing thin sheets of tissue paper over each other between layers of PVA (polyvinyl acetate) glue. The glue transforms the tissue paper into transparent sheets of color.

LATEX *see* Masking fluid

LAY IN The initial painting stage over a preliminary drawing where the colors are applied as broad areas of flat color. This technique is also known as blocking in.

LIFTING OUT The technique used to modify color and create highlights by taking color off the paper using a brush or sponge.

LIGHTFASTNESS Permanence (or durability) of a color measured by the American Standard Test Measure (ASTM) in the United States, in which the most permanent colors rate 1 or 2. The equivalent institute in Great Britain, the Blue Wool Scale, rates the most permanent colors at 7 or 8.

LINEAR (ARTIFICIAL) PERSPECTIVE A system of representing space on a two-dimensional surface by recording the intersection on the picture plane of rays of light from an object as they converge on the eye of the viewer.

LINSEED OIL A vegetable drying oil from the seeds of the flax plant used as a binding material in oil color. Linseed oil is the most commonly used oil and it dries more quickly than semidrying oils. The oil does not dry by evaporation but forms a solid film.

LOW-KEY COLOR Subdued, unsaturated color that tends toward brown and gray. *See also* High-key Color

MAHL STICK A bamboo or aluminum stick about 4ft (1.23m) long with a ball-shaped end. If you paint with your right hand, the stick is held with the left hand, with the ball end touching the canvas so that the right hand can rest on the stick while painting. This helps hold your hand steady if you need to work on a particular area.

MASKING FLUID This is a latex liquid that can be applied with a brush or dip pen to mask out areas of an artwork before applying another wash.

Mixture for texturing paper

Treatment of different surfaces

Form and color

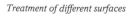

MASKING OUT The technique of using masking fluid or other materials to protect areas of the watercolor paper while adding washes. With masking fluid, the solution is allowed to dry, paint is applied over it and once that has dried, the masking fluid is gently peeled off.

MASKING TAPE Pressure-sensitive tape used to protect areas from paint.

MEASURING POINT A point for each vanishing point on the horizon line obtained by describing an arc, with the vanishing point as center, from the station point to intersect the picture plane on the horizon line. A measuring point provides a simple means of locating the position of objects behind or in front of the picture plane by reference to scale measurements on the picture plane.

MEDIUM The binding material in paint in which the pigment is suspended.

MODELING Describing the form of a solid object using solid shading or linear marks.

MOLD-MADE PAPER The most common form of high-quality watercolor paper is made on a cylinder mold machine. The more random arrangement of the fibers in this process as compared with that on commercial machine-made paper gives far greater strength and dimensional stability to the paper.

MONOCHROMATIC Drawn or painted in shades of one color.

MONOFILAMENTS Individual strands of manufactured fiber.

MONOPRINT A unique print taken from a work created on a slab of glass or laminate.

MONOTYPE A form of monoprint that involves applying ink to a plate in a design and taking a print. The process of inking the plate can be repeated and applied to the same paper so that an image is built up in layers. Stencils cut from paper can be used to mask out areas and create shapes in the design of the print.

MORTAR AND PESTLE A bowl and grinding tool used to reduce pastel sticks to a powder for reconstituting pastel fragments into new pastels and for dry wash techniques.

NICKEL TITANATE A modern inorganic yellow pigment of great permanence.

NOT OR COLD-PRESSED Paper with a fine grain or semi-rough surface.

OAK GALL INK Ink made by crushing and boiling oak galls. The galls are formed by parasitic insects living off oak trees and tend to appear in autumn.

OBLIQUE PROJECTION In oblique projection, an elevation is drawn and receding lines are added all at the same angle, for example 45 degrees to the horizontal. The length of these receding lines is reduced by the same ratio of the 90-degree angle to the angle of the elevation that the receding line represents (i.e., if it is 45 degrees, it is half as long).

OIL PAPER Textured paper coated with an oil-resistant primer, used for oil pastel work. Particularly suitable when white spirits of turpentine are used, as the primer protects the paper from their detrimental effects.

OIL PAINT Paint bound by poppy or linseed oil. It is the most popular medium for easel painting because of its ease of manipulation and saturated colors. With the addition of resin such as dammar varnish or gel medium, it is possible to glaze washes of color in oil paint.

OIL PASTEL Pastel bound by oil as opposed to gum. The oil gives this type of pastel a slight transparency and a strong adherence to the support. It comes in a less extensive range of colors than soft pastels.

OIL STICKS A type of oil paint blended with waxes in the form of sticks and applied directly to the canvas. Colors can be modified with a piece of cloth or a finger. Oil sticks, unlike other drawing materials, are extremely creamy in texture and are good for working wet-in-wet.

ONE-POINT PERSPECTIVE The simplest linear perspective construction where all parallel lines at right angles to the picture plane and parallel with the ground plane appear to converge at the same vanishing point on the horizon.

OPAQUE COLOR *See* Body color.

OPAQUE PAINTING Paintings that use predominantly opaque paints and the techniques associated with them.

OPTICAL MIX This occurs when small areas of colors next to each other appear to the eye, at a certain distance, to merge and become a third color - red and yellow dots will mix and become orange.

Pigment, chalk, and tragacanth

ORIENTAL PAPER Highly absorbent, handmade paper with no internal or surface sizing. Some Japanese papers can weigh as little as 12 gsm.

ORTHOGONALS Lines that recede at right angles from the picture plane to a vanishing point on the horizon.

ORTHOGRAPHIC PROJECTION The standard method of showing a plan and elevation.

OVERLAYING WASHES The technique of painting one wash over another in order to build up a depth of color or tone.

OXGALL A wetting agent that helps the paint flow more easily on the paper.

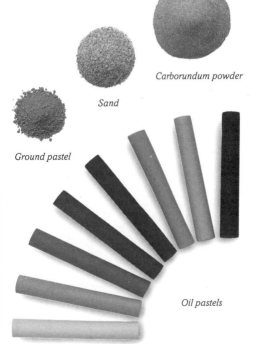

Carborundum powder

Sand

Ground pastel

Oil pastels

Art Deco teapot in pastel pencil

469

PASTEL PENCILS Similar to soft pastels only slightly harder and encased in wood. Suitable to drawing and detailed work. Also known as colored charcoal pencils.

PERSPECTIVE The method of representing three dimensions on a two-dimensional surface. Linear perspective makes objects appear smaller as they get farther away by means of a geometric system of measurement.

PHTHALOCYANINE Modern organic transparent blue and green (chlorinated copper phthalocynine) pigments of high tinting strengths and excellent lightfastness. Also known by trade names.

PHYSICAL MIX When a color is arrived at by mixing together several colors on the palette before applying it to the paper.

PICTURE PLANE The imaginary plane on which we make an image of the scene we see through it, representing the point of intersection of rays of light from objects in the scene to the artist's eye. It is normally set at 90 degrees to the ground plane, but it can be tilted if we are looking up or down.

PIGMENT Solid-colored material in the form of discrete particles that form the basic component of all types of paint.

PLAN A two-dimensional scale drawing of a horizontal section of an object, such as a building.

PLEIN AIR This term refers to painting in the open air. Alla prima techniques are normally used in this situation.

POLYMER A chainlike molecule of which the individual links or units are known as monomers. Acrylic polymers form the basic binding medium for acrylic paint.

PRESERVATIVE Substance added to painting materials to act as a fungicide and bactericide. This is particularly important in watercolor because the paints are prone to microbiological growth.

PRIMARY COLORS The three colors, red, blue, and yellow, which cannot be produced by mixing other colors and which, in different combinations, form the basis of all the other colors.

PRIMING This refers to the preliminary coating that is laid onto the support prior to painting. Priming provides the surface with the right key, absorbency, and color before painting.

PROJECTION In linear perspective, carrying lines from the station point to points on the plan and thereafter to the picture plane where the points of intersection are marked.

PVA Polyvinyl acetate is a glue medium used for gluing paper and binding pigments to the surface of the support.

QUINACRIDONE A modern organic transparent red pigment with very good lightfastness.

RECEDING COLOR The perception of a color, usually a cool (blue), as being distant from the viewer.

REDUCING GLASS A drawing aid, also known as a Claude glass, used extensively in the 18th and 19th centuries. A small tinted convex mirror reflects a reduced and largely monochromatic image of the landscape.

REFRACTIVE INDEX A measure of the degree of refraction of a substance. The ratio between the angle of the incident ray in air with that of the refracted ray in the substance produces this measure.

RESIST A method of preventing the paint from coming into contact with the paper or the layer of paint film by interposing a protective coating. Used to preserve highlights, for example, or to retain a particular color.

RETARDER Added to acrylic paint to delay the drying process. If over-used, the quality of the paint can be impaired.

ROUGH OR COLD-PRESSED Paper with a rough surface.

SABLE Mink tail hair used to make fine watercolor brushes.

SATURATION The degree of intensity of a color. Colors can be saturated, i.e., vivid and of intense hue, or unsaturated, i.e., dull, tending toward gray.

SCRATCHING OUT Similar to sgraffito, the process of scratching the surface of the paint (wet or dry) to reveal the paint film or paper that lies below. Can be done with a blade or, in wet paint, with the handle of the brush.

SCUMBLING Semi-opaque or thin opaque colors loosely brushed over an under-painted area so that patches of the color beneath show through.

SECONDARY COLORS Green, orange, and purple, the colors arrived at by mixing two primaries and which lie between them on the color wheel.

SECTION A scale drawing showing a two-dimensional slice through an object, such as a building, in the vertical or horizontal plane.

SGRAFFITO A technique, usually involving a scalpel or sharp knife, in which dried paint is scraped off of the painted surface. Often used for textural effects.

SHADE Color mixed with black.

SHADING Usually refers to the way areas of shadow are represented in a drawing and is invariably linked with tone.

SIGHT SIZE The measurement of the size of a distant object as you see it, which is then transferred exactly to the paper.

Ready-primed canvas

Alla prima

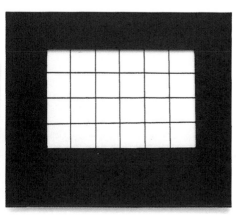

Viewfinder

SILVERPOINT A method of drawing whereby a fine piece of silver is dragged over a piece of prepared paper: Chinese White watercolor provides a matte surface to which the tiny particles of silver adhere.

SIZE Rabbit skin or other glue used to protect canvas from the potentially damaging effects of oil in the paint before priming and to seal or reduce the absorbency of wooden panels. The binding material for gesso.

SIZING The coating, either internal or external, of paper. Prepared size usually contains a mixture of gelatin, water, and a preservative. The sizing affects the hardness and absorbency of the paper and consequently the way in which the paint will react on it.

SIZING, NEUTRAL A modern size with a neutral pH that replaces the earlier, more acidic, sizing materials.

SKETCHING UMBRELLA A large umbrella designed to provide shade and shelter for the artist when working outdoors. It has a spiked handle, so that it can be stuck into the ground firmly.

SOFT HAIR BRUSHES These are used mainly in watercolor painting but are also suitable for precise brushwork in oil painting. They can hold a great deal of thin paint while still retaining their shape.

SOFT PASTEL The original and most common form of pastel. The weak solution of gum used in their manufacturing ensures a very soft texture.

SPARKLE The term used to describe the effect of an irregular, broken application of pastel on a support that contrasts with the tone or hue of the applied pastel.

SPATTERING A technique that involves flicking paint off of the hairs of a bristle brush or a toothbrush with your nail to create an irregular pattern of paint.

SPIRITS White spirits or turpentine are used to dissolve oil pastels to create a wash.

Working on a white ground

SPONGING OUT The technique of soaking up paint with a sponge or paper towel so that areas of pigment are lightened or removed from the paper. Can be used to rectify mistakes or to create particular effects.

SQUARING UP A grid system used to transfer a sketch or other image accurately to the painting surface. A square grid is superimposed onto the sketch and replicated on the painting surface – often on a larger scale. Complicated areas, as in the girls' faces below, can be given a more detailed grid. The image is then copied square by square from the original image onto the painting surface.

STAINING POWER The degree to which a pigment stains the paper and resists being washed off or scrubbed out. *See also* Tinting Strength

STATION POINT The position on the ground plane from which the artist views the subject.

STENCIL An image cut out of cardboard or another material. Paint can be sponged or sprayed through the cutout.

STIPPLING A method of painting involving the application of tiny dots of color with the tip of the brush.

STRETCHER The wooden frame on which a canvas is stretched.

STRETCHING PAPER The process by which watercolor paper is stretched to prevent it from buckling when paint is applied. The paper is wetted by sponging or dipping briefly in water, attached to a board with masking tape, and allowed to dry.

Proportion of oil to pigment

SUBDIVISION A method of putting images into perspective by subdividing within shapes such as simple rectangles, the outlines of which have been put into perspective.

SUPPORT The material on which a painting is made. Almost any surface can be used, but artists tend to use paper, a wooden panel, or a canvas to work on.

SURFACE The texture of the paper. In Western papers – as opposed to Oriental – the three standard grades of surface are Rough, Hot-pressed (smooth) and NOT or Cold-pressed (semi-rough).

SURFACE SIZING A means of decreasing the absorbency of a painting surface. Commercially available artists' quality watercolor paints are invariably surface-sized in warm gelatin to allow the paper to withstand vigorous treatment.

TECHNICAL PEN A relatively recent innovation in which the tip of the pen is hard and inflexible and designed to give a consistent width of line regardless of the pressure placed on it.

TERTIARY COLORS Colors that contain all three primaries.

THREE-POINT PERSPECTIVE Perspective in which the object is at an angle vertically to the picture plane in addition to the horizontal plane. An additional vanishing point for the third (vertical) plane will be required.

TINT Color mixed with white.

TINTING STRENGTH The strength of a particular color or pigment.

TOE OF BRUSH The tip of the hairs.

TONAL KEY The degree of reduction of a color toward white as chalk is added to the original coloring pigment. Soft pastels have up to eight tints of any one color.

TONE The degree of darkness or lightness of a color. Crumpling a piece of white paper allows you to see a range of tonal contrast.

Bristle brushes

Protective case

471

TONED GROUND Also called a colored ground. An opaque layer of colored paint of uniform tone applied over the priming before starting the painting.

TOOTH OF PAPER Paper, when examined under a microscope, appears as a felted weave of fibers, which trap the particles of color from a dry medium. The coarser the texture of the paper the more tooth and the more medium is retained by the paper surface.

TRANSPARENT PAINTING A painting technique that relies on the transparency of the paints used.

TRANSVERSALS Receding horizontal lines parallel to the picture plane.

TURPENTINE (DISTILLED) Used to thin oil color and to make resin varnishes such as dammar varnish. Turpentine is also used as an ingredient in a number of oil painting mediums. White spirit can be used instead of turpentine.

TWO-POINT PERSPECTIVE A perspective construction where the object has its vertical edges parallel with the picture plane, but with its sides set at any angle to it. There will be two vanishing points, both on the horizon line.

UNDERPAINTING Preliminary painting, over which other colors are applied.

UNSATURATED COLOR Sometimes known as desaturated color. A pure, saturated color becomes unsaturated when mixed with another color into a tint or a shade. When three colors are mixed together in unequal amounts, the resultant color can be called a colored neutral.

VALUE The extent to which a color reflects or transmits light.

VANISHING AXIS A vertical axis at right angles to the horizon line. Descending or ascending parallel lines in the same plane will have their vanishing points on this axis.

VANISHING LINE A line that converges on a vanishing point.

VANISHING POINT The point at which any two or more parallel lines in the same plane and receding from the viewer appear to converge.

VARIEGATED WASH A wash in which different colors have been applied in such a way that they run into one another.

VARNISH Protective surface over a finished painting imparting a glossy or matte surface appearance to a painting.

VIEWER *see* Finder

VIEWFINDER Two L-shaped pieces of cardboard that form a framing device. This is usually held at arm's length and the scene to be drawn can be seen through it.

VIEWPOINT The point, particularly the height, from which the artist sees the scene. It will determine the height of the horizon line and the nature of the composition.

VISCOSITY A measure of the flow characteristic of a color or medium (e.g., stand oil is more viscous than alkali-refined linseed oil). Oil paint with some viscosity is described as having body.

WARM COLOR Generally, a color such as orange-red is considered warm. In accordance with atmospheric or aerial perspective, warm colors appear to advance toward the viewer, whereas cool colors appear to recede.

WASH A layer of color, often uniform in tone, applied across the paper with a brush.

WASHING OFF The process of dislodging an area of paint, possible with a bristle brush dipped in water, or a damp sponge.

WATERCOLOR A quick-drying paint made from ground pigments and a water-soluble binding medium such as gum arabic. The medium is characterized by its luminosity.

WATERLEAF A paper with no internal sizing, and which is consequently highly absorbent.

WATER-SOLUBLE PASTEL A recent innovation, this type of pastel functions like an oil pastel in a dry state and is then reworked using a brush and water to convert the pastel lines into a wash of color.

WAX ENCAUSTIC A painting medium made by mixing powdered pigments into melted beeswax. The advantage of wax is that it is a very stable coloring medium - it does not darken with age in the manner of oil paint. It is more complicated to use because, to keep the medium in a liquid state, the pigment is manipulated using heat. The melted wax can also be thinned to a maleable paste by adding turpentine. When the mixture is set, it is mixed with oil paint.

WAX RESIST The process by which wax crayons or a sliver of a candle are used to protect areas of the paper or paint film from further applications of paint.

Sgraffito

Drawing grid

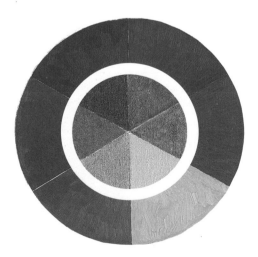

Color wheel

WEIGHT Watercolor paper is measured in lbs (pounds per ream) or gsm (grams per square meter). It comes in a large range of weights, although the standard machine-made ones are 90 lb (190 gsm), 140 lb (300 gsm), 260 lb (356 gsm), and 300 lb (638 gsm). The heavier papers, 260lb and over, generally do not need stretching.

WET-IN-WET Working with wet paint into wet paint on the surface of the paper.

WET-ON-DRY Applying a layer of wet paint onto a dry surface.

WOOD-FREE PAPER Good-quality paper made from purified, acid-free wood pulp that does not yellow with age.

WOVE PAPER Paper in which you can detect the pattern of the wire mold on which it was made, giving it a woven appearance.

A NOTE ON COLORS AND PIGMENTS

In recommending Winsor Blue and Winsor Green (which are trade names of the Winsor & Newton Company), we are recommending "phthalocyanine" pigments; other artists' material manufacturers refer to them by their own trade names. These include Phthalo Blue and Green, Monestial Blue and Green, and so on. Similarly, in recommending Permanent Rose, we are recommending a "quinacridone" pigment. Lemon Yellow Hue, another of our recommended pigments, is also known as Nickel Titanate Yellow. If you have any doubts about which pigment you are buying, refer to the manufacturer's literature.

We have tried to avoid recommending pigments, such as the Chrome colors, which carry a significant health risk. In the case of colors such as the Cadmiums, however, there is nothing commercially available that matches them for color and permanence. But there is no danger in their use nor in that of other pigments provided artists take sensible precautions and avoid licking brushes with paint on them.

A NOTE ON PAPERS

The surfaces of papers – Rough, Hot-pressed, and NOT (semi-rough) – vary noticeably from one manufacturer to another so it is worth considering several before deciding which to buy.

A NOTE ON TOXICITY

• When using and combining a wide selection of materials it is important to be aware of the health hazards.

All art materials are required by law to label clearly their chemical contents and levels of toxicity. You should avoid inhaling the dust from powder pigments and fumes from thinners, glues, and fixative sprays. It is also important to be aware that pigments and thinners can be absorbed through the skin; therefore prolonged contact should be avoided. Always keep the lids of solvent jars screwed on tight and only use as much as you need at any one time. Artists should also make sure they avoid licking brushes with paint on them. If you are in any doubt about the toxicity of a product, contact the manufacturer directly.

A NOTE ON MATERIALS

• Avoid using Chrome colors when you work with watercolor as they carry a significant health risk. There is no danger with any other pigments, provided artists take sensible precautions and avoid licking brushes with paint on them.

• Soft pastels generate a good deal of dust, so it is best to avoid inhaling the pigment powder as much as possible. If you are working indoors, make sure the room is well ventilated.

• The brush sizes given in this book refer to Winsor & Newton brushes. They may vary slightly from those of other manufacturers.

High-key color

Low-key color

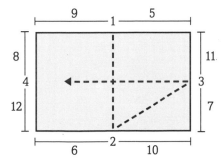

Stretching a canvas

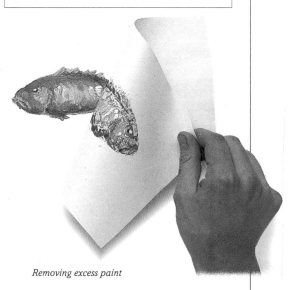

Removing excess paint

INDEX

A

Aboriginal art, 76
absorbency, paper, 167, 464
accelerated perspective, 128, 464
acetate, 264
acid-free paper, 26, 167, 223, 464
acrylic, 464
  chapter on, 332-397
acrylic gesso, 28, 226
acrylic paints, 169, 262, 410-1, 464
  experimenting with surfaces, 426
  multilayered compositions, 422-3
  textured, 429
acrylic primer, 227
acrylic washes, 111, 117
adhesives, see glue
adjacent colors, 152-3, 341, 280, 464
advancing colors, 155, 464
aerial perspective, 32, 49 92-7, 307, 343, 464
aerial views, 108
after-image, 152, 464
Aghajanian, Sophie, 255
airbrushing, 339, 249
  blending, 379
  glazing, 380
Alberti, Leon Battista, 78, 88, 128
alla prima, 270, 382-5, 464
  gallery, 320-1
  oils, 276
  techniques, 316-7
aluminum mesh, 446
anamorphosis, 128-9, 464
Andrews, Michael, 389
angle of incidence, 116, 117
animals, 52
architecture,
  gallery, perspective 114-5
  one-point perspective, 89
  plans and elevations, 106-7
  three-point perspective, 87, 108-13
architectural drawings, 46-7
Armfield, Diana, 67, 229
art board, 406, 464
artificial light, 120-1
artists' quality paints, 147, 277, 411, 464
artists' quality papers, 222-3, 225, 464
artists' quality pastels, 210
ascending vanishing point, 104, 464
atmosphere, portraits, 62
atmospheric perspective, 92-97, 464
axonometric projection, 77, 464
azurite, 276

B

bas-reliefs,
  collage, 450-1
  collagraph printing, 458-9
backgrounds, 32
  firgure drawing, 64-5
balance, color, 342-3
balance, composition, 176-7, 235
Baldwin-Purry, Bagriella, 334, 374
bamboo brushes, 159, 162
bamboo pens, 16
Baroque, 42
Bartlett, Paul, 220
Bassano, Jacopo, 206
beachcombing, 52
beeswax, 430
Bell, Richard, 53, 56
Bellini, Giovanni, 272
binder, 464
  acrylics, 335, 338
  oil, 216
  reconstituting pastels, 251
  soft pastels, 210
binding medium, 464
bird's-eye view, 108
black chalk, 206
black oil, 276
Blackburn, David, 236
Blake, Peter, 453
Blake, William, 403
Blamey, RA, Norman, 67
bleeding, 412, 416, 417, 464
blending, 464
  pastels, 242-3
  acrylics, 378-9, 389
  brushes, 215, 322
  dry wash, 250-1
  gallery, 254
  hard pastels, 213
  oil, 290
  oil pastels, 216, 217
  tools, 21, 215, 242
block printing, 454-5, 465
blockboard, 298, 352
blocking in, 233, 465
blocks, paper, 167
bloom, 465
blotting paper, 162, 191
Blow, Sandra, 395
boards, 298-9, 352, 406-7
Boccioni, Umberto, 136
body color, 22, 465
Borges, Jacobo, 354
Boucher, François, 207
Boudin, Eugène, 51, 208
Bowyer, RA, William, 123
box frames, 462
boxed grid construction, 102-3
boxed sets, 210, 218-9
bracelet shading, 38, 39, 465
Braque, Georges, 274, 404
bread, erasers, 215
Breugel, Pieter the Elder, 10, 11
bristle brushes, 158, 159, 278, 346, 347, 465
broken color, 208, 246, 465
Brunelleschi, Filippo, 78
brush strokes
  watercolor, 160-5
  oil painting, 294
brushes, 22, 215, 410, 438
  acrylic, 346-7

applying glazes, 322, 323
architectural drawings, 47
blending, 242
cleaning, 158
dry brush, 291
line drawings, 36
masking fluid, 195
oil painting, 288-9
texturing supports, 226
types, 158-9, 278, 288-9
washes, 183
watercolor, 158-9
  gallery, 164-5
brushwork:
  alla prima, 383
  boards, 299
  effects, 294-5
  gallery, oil, 296-7
  impasto, 293, 367
  paper surface and, 350
  sketching, 360
  transparent acrylic, 370
bubble wrap, 419, 439
buildings, 46-7
burnishers, 193, 465
Butlin, Anne-Marie, 51
Byzantine art, 77

C

camera lucida, 124, 465
camera obscura, 124, 126, 465
cameras 174-5
  lenses, 124
Canaletto, 11, 126
candles, resist techniques, 371
cannon, 465
Canson paper, 222, 223, 224
canvas, 465
canvas boards, 226, 227, 298, 352
canvas rolls, 23
canvases, 406
  acrylic, 352, 353
  framing, 397
  oil, 278
  stretching, 300
  textures, 299
  working alla prima, 384
Caravaggio, 11, 273
carbon paper, 71
carborundum pastel board, 226, 227, 465
card, 222, 352
cardboard, 162
Carline, Sydney, 114
Carriera, Rosalba, 206, 207
cartridge paper, 26, 30, 37
Cartwright, Richard, 228
Cassatt, Mary, 208
Caulfield, Patrick, 364-5
cave paintings, 10
center of vision, 84, 465
center line of vision, 84, 465
Cézanne, Paul, 24, 144-5, 275
Chagall, Marc, 287
chalk pastels, 20
chalk, precipitated, 465
chalks, 18-9, 210, 465
  gallery, 25, 221
  history, 206

keeping work clean, 49
paper, 28
characteristics of oil paint, 270-1
charcoal, 18, 178, 260-1, 262, 360, 361, 400-9, 465
  and black ink, 412-3
  capturing a mood, 62
  colored pencils, 408
  fixatives, 409, 463
  line drawings, 36
  and pastels, 414-5
  pencils, 409
  sketches, 305, 324
  and watercolor washes, 416
charcoal pencils, 18
Chardin, Jean-Baptiste-Siméon, 207
Charlton, Alan, 337
children's drawings, 75
chipboard, 298
Chinese brushes, 409, 412
Chinese ink, 17, 409, 413
chroma, 465
chromatic, 465
circles, 90-1
Clatworthy, Robert, 415
Claude glass, 465
Claude Lorrain, 142, 274
cleaning brushes, 158, 289, 346
cleaning pastels, 211
Clemente, Francesco, 275
Close, Chuck, 337, 388
closed composition, 177
clothes, 58-9
cloths, blending, 242
clouds, 95
Cobley, Lucinda, 262
cockling, 168
Cohen, Bernard, 357, 389
Coker, Peter, 421
Cold-pressed paper, 167
collage, 338, 400, 401
  color collage, 440-1
  gallery, 452-3
  history, 404
  laminating, 448-9
  bas reliefs, 450-1
  materials, 436-7
  photo-collaging, 436, 442
  texture, 429
  and wax encaustic, 431
collagraph print, 465
collagraphs, 439, 458-9
color: 92-3
  adjacent, 152-3, 280
  advancing, 155,
  aerial perspective, 32
  alla prima, 316-7
  and form, 244-5
  and light, 154-5
  blending, 242-3, 378-9, 380-1
  broken color, 208
  chosing, 280-1, 340-1
  "color irradiation", 341, 465
  color wheel, 148, 218, 280, 340-1
  complementary, 152-3, 248, 280
  composition, 44-5, 235
  cool colors, 155, 218, 244-5, 280, 342-3

depth of, 271
drawing for painting, 70-1
dry-brushing, 376-7
dry wash, 250-1
drying, acrylic, 367
dyeing paper pulp, 446
feathering, 248-9
figures in a setting, 64-5
frames, 397
fugitive, 467
gallery
  acrylic, 344-5
  oil painting, 286-7
  watercolor, 156-7
gouache, 199
glazing, 292
hard pastels, 212-3
harmony, 152-3
high-key, 150, 152, 284-5
impasto, 293
interiors, 48-9
irradiation, isolated, 153
landscapes, 54-5
line and, 416-7
local color, 244
low-key, 150, 152-3, 284-5
mixing, 148-151, 281, 282-3
monochrome, 362-3
oil pastels, 216
opaque, 284, 366
optical mixing, 15, 38
overlaying, 150-1, 187-9
painting in layers, 322-3
papers, 224-5
primary, 148, 150-1, 218, 280-281
receding, 155
saturation, 470
scumbling, 246-7, 376-7
secondary, 148, 150, 218
selecting, 218-9
sgraffito, 328
sketches, 238, 239, 358, 360
soft pastels, 210, 211
swatches, 146, 150-1
temperature, 465
tertiary, 148, 150, 284
toned grounds, 312-3, 314-5
tones, 186-7
transparent, 281
  acrylic, 370
varnishing, 330
warm, 155, 218, 244-5, 280, 342-3
wet-in-wet, 371
white grounds, 310-11, 314-5
see also mixing colors
colored charcoal pencils, 408
colored inks, 17
colored grounds, 362, 383
colored paper, 26, 29
colored pencils, 14-5, 38, 465
combing, 163
combining techniques,

acrylic, 386-7
complementary colors, 152-3, 189, 248, 280, 340-1, 466
composition,
  acrylic, 358-9
  drawing, gallery, 50-1
  mixed media, 422-3
  oil paintings, 304-9
  pastels, 234-7
  watercolors, 176-7
compressed charcoal, 260
computer generated images, 125
cone of vision, 79, 80-1, 85, 466
Constable, John, 12, 143, 144
Conté crayons, 18, 19, 178, 212, 409, 466
convergence, 88, 466
cool colors, 155, 218, 244-5, 280, 466
copal oil varnish, 276
copolymer emulsion, 338
copying sketches, 233
cotton balls, 215, 250, 257
cotton swabs, 212
Cotman, John Sell, 144
Cotman, Miles E., 184
counter perspective, 128, 466
cow gum erasers, 162, 172-3
Cox, David, 144
craft knives, 15, 193
crayons, 18-9, 21, 212
cropping, 208, 232, 396-7
cross-hatching, 15, 38, 69, 213, 378, 379, 466
crustaceans, 52-3
cubes, 34
cubism, 79, 274
Cucchi, Enzo, 275
curves, 90-1
curvilinear perspective, 79, 130-5, 466

D

Dada, 404
Dali, Salvador, 274
dammar, 279, 330, 466
darks, 466
Davis, Ronald, 355
deconstructing images, 45
Degas, Edgar, 12, 13, 122, 208, 403, 460
descending vanishing point, 466
Delacroix, Eugène, 12, 208
detail, 94-5
devices, 124-7
dextrin, 146-7, 466
diagonal vanishing point, 88-9, 466
Dibbets, Jan, 79
diffusers, 214, 413, 466
dip pens, 16, 173
dippers, 278
direct painting, 384-5
distance point, 466
distortion, 84-5, 128
dragged, 466
Draper, Ken, 255,
drapery, 58-9
drawing, 141, 178-9

chapter on, 6-71
gallery, 420-1
materials, 408-9
drawing, hard pastels, 212
drawing boards, 23
drawing chalks, 18
drawing clips, 23
drawing frames, 124, 174-5
drawing grids, 264, 466
transferring sketches, 305, 306
drawing nibs, 179
dry brush, 270, 295
acrylic, 376-7, 384
supports, 299
techniques, 291, 466
texture, 271, 291
white grounds, 311
dry scrubbing, 215
dry wash, 214, 250-1, 466
Dubuffet, Jean, 452
Dufy, Raoul, 165
Dunstan, Bernard, 321
durability rating, 149, 199, 466
Dürer, Albrecht, 79, 142, 175
Durrant, Jennifer, 365
dust, 211
dry wash, 214, 250-1
safety, 230
dyeing paper pulp, 446

E

easels, 231, 279, 348, 466
Edholm, Felicity, 231, 251
egg tempera, 272
Egypt, ancient, 74, 77
elevations, 466
computer-generated images, 125
two-point perspective, 86-7, 98-9, 106-7
ellipsel, 466
ellipses, 34-5, 90-1
emery boards, 212
enlargement, 99, 124
enlarging sketches, 360-1
equipment,
drawing, 15
pastels, 214-5,
oil, 278-9
erasers, 15, 40-1, 215, 466
block printmaking, 455
cow gum, 162, 172-3
kneaded, 408
Ernst, Max, 274, 404, 452
Estes, Richard, 337
Evans, David, 375
experimental techniques,
acrylic, 390-5
oil, 328-9
Expressionism, 274
extender, 467
extruded paint, 338
eye level, 33, 46, 84-5, 99, 467

F

fabrics, collage, 436
fan blenders, 289, 347
"fat-over-lean", 277, 322, 467
feathering, 38. 39, 213, 467
gallery, 254
techniques, 248-9
Felski, Albina Kosiec, 355
felting, 467
felt-tip pens, 17, 263, 408
ferrule, brushes, 158, 278, 467
fiberboard, 298, 352
figure drawing:
drapery, 58-9

drawing for painting, 70-71
gallery, 66-7
life room, 60-1
movements and gestures, 68-9
setting, 64-5
filbert brushes, 289, 346, 347
finders, 124, 467
Finmark, Sharon, 242-3, 244-5, 249
fixatives, 178, 214, 324, 409, 463, 467
flat brushes, 159, 193, 346, 347
flat color, 467
flat washes, 180
flocculation, 467
flocked paper, 467
flocked pastel board, 222, 223, 224
flotation, 148, 467
focal points, 64, 176-7, 467
foil, 418, 439
foreground, 32
colors, 343
foreshortening, 34, 77, 79, 467
one-point perspective, 88
two-point perspective, 87
form: 362-3, 376, 467
and color, 244-5
gallery, 42-3
sketches, 238, 239
tonal drawing, 40-1
tone, 240-1
format, supports, 235
Foster, Norman, 75
found objects, 437, 434, 450
fountain pens, 16
Fouquet, Jean, 14, 79
frames, 124, 396-7
framing, 266-7, 330-1, 462-3
Frampton, Meredith, 297
Frankenthaler, Helen, 336
Fraser, RA, Donald Hamilton, 43, 314
fretsaws
Freud, Lucian, 275
Friederich, Caspar David, 97
frottage, 227, 412, 448-9, 467
fugitive colors, 199, 467
futurism, 79, 136

G

Gainsborough, Thomas, 143, 274
Gallwey, Kay, 29
Gauguin, Paul, 144, 274
gel medium, 339, 381, 427
gesso, 226
with additives, 407
textured, 429
and wax, 430-1
gesso primer, 28, 352
gestures, 68-9
Gifford, Jane, 224-5, 234-5, 252-3, 264-5
Gilbert and George, 136, 137
gelatin size, 167
Girtin, Thomas, 143-4
Girvin, Joy, 236,
glasses,
reducing, 124
sketching, 82-3
Glass, Margaret, 229
glass, painting, 252
glass paper (pastel board),

224
glassine, 467
in pads and books, 223
protecting work with, 215, 266
glaze, 188, 270, 380-1, 467
applying, 322-3
uses, 292, 295
gloss medium, 381
glue, 226, 227
acrylics as, 338
adding texture, 428
collage, 437
collagraph printing, 458-9
multilayered compositions, 422
glycerine, 146, 147, 467
gold leaf, 402
gouache, 410
impasto, 426
multilayered compositions, 422-3
Gordon, Gregory, 344
Gore, Frederick, 286
Gorman, Mike 365
gouache, 22, 29, 140, 147, 201, 368, 467
highlights, 169, 198
overlaying, 198
resist techniques, 196-7, 467
using, 198-9
graded washes, 180-1, 467
granulation, 148, 467
graphite pencils, 14, 467
graphite sticks, 14, 178, 467
El Greco, 327
Greece, ancient, 77, 128
Green, RA, Anthony, 79, 137
grey, mixing, 149
grids, 264
scaling up, 360, 361
grit supports, 226, 227
grid system, 78, 175, 467
anamorphosis, 128-9
drawing frames, 124
one-point perspective, 88-9, 102-3
two-point perspective, 98
ground line, 467
ground plane, 84, 467
grounds, 467
colored, 362, 383
textured, 226
sizing and priming, 300-1
toned, 312-3, 314-5
white, 310-1, 314-5
guidelines, 35
gum arabic, 17, 146-7, 467
resist techniques, 196-7, 468
gum solution, 468

H

half pastels, 211
half tones, 290, 376, 468
hard pastels, 212, 468
erasing, 215
hard watercolors, 147, 468
hardboard, 298-9, 352
harmony, color, 152-3
Harris, Jon 50
hatching, 38, 39, 69, 248, 254, 468
heel of brush, 278, 468
Helmholtz, Hermann von, 131
Henderson, William, 388
high-key colors, 150, 152, 284-5, 343, 468

highlights, 40-41, 468
gouache, 169, 198
masking, 194
opaque acrylic, 368
resist techniques, 371
scratching out, 192
washes, 351, 372, 373
history,
acrylic, 336-7
drawing, 10-13
oil, 272-5
mixed media, 402-5
pastels, 206-9
perspective, 76-9
watercolors, 142-5
Hockney, RA, David, 13, 79, 126-7, 132, 336
Hodgkin, Howard, 275
Hödicke, K.H., 337
hog hair brushes, 159, 215, 226, 294
Holbein, Hans, 10
Hollar, Wnceslas, 142
Homer, Winslow, 145
Hopper, Edward, 145
horizon line, 33, 84-5, 176-7, 468
box grid construction, 102-3
inclined planes, 104-5
Horton, James, 47, 49, 69
Horton, Percy, 29, 57
Hot-pressed paper (HP), 167, 468
Howard, Ken, 321
Hoyland, John, 344
hue, 210, 468
human body see
figure drawing
humectant, 468

I

icons, 402
illuminated manuscripts, 402
illusionism, 79, 128
impasto, 390, 468
acrylic paints, 427
glass paper, 223
gouache, 426
painting knives, 318
oils, 270
oil pastels, 217, 255, 257
soft pastels and water, 258
techniques, 292-3, 295
texture paste, 339, 367
watercolor, 199
Impressionism, 208, 274
imprimatura, 312, 468
inclined planes, 91, 104-5
Indian ink, 17
Ingres, Jean-Auguste Dominique, 12
Ingres paper, 222, 224
inks, 468
block printmaking, 454-5
charcoal and, 412-3
monoprints, 456-7
printing, 438
and watercolor washes, 416
ink drawings, 179
interiors, 48-9, 70-1
internal sizing, 468
Irvin, Albert, 375
isolated colors, 153
isometric projection, 77, 125, 468
italic nibs, 179

J

Jacklin, RA, Bill, 97, 309, 461

John, Augustus, 13
Jones, David, 421

K

Kandinsky, Wassily, 145
Kelly, Jo, 364
ketone varnishes, 279, 330
Kitaj, R.B., 208, 262
Kirchner, Ernst, 274
Klee, Paul, 145, 170, 405
Klimt, Gustav, 403
Kneaded erasers, 215, 242, 405, 408
knives, 15
acrylic painting, 348
oil painting, 278, 318-9
palette, 348
scratching out, 192
Kokoschka, Oskar, 308
Kordofan gum arabic, 146

L

La Tour, Maurice Quentin de, 207
laid paper, 167, 468
laminating, 468
collage, 448-9
paper, 445
Lancaster, Mark, 336
landscapes, 54-7
atmospheric perspective, 92-7
colors, 219
gallery, 114-5
texture, oil, 291
three-point perspective, 108-9
large pastels, 211
latex, see masking fluid
Lawson, Sonia, 429
lay in, 468
layering paint, acrylic, 390, 391
layers, painting in, 322-3, 326-7
laying a wash, 216
layout, 44-5
"lead" pencils, 12, 14
Lear, Edward, 132
Lebrun, Charles, 206
Lebrun, Christopher, 275
Lee, Dick, 450
Leger, Fernand, 79
Lenthall, Christopher, 374
Leonardo da Vinci, 56, 79, 130, 206, 402
Levene, RA, Ben, 123, 296
Lewin, Paul, 43, 57, 263
Lichtenstein, Roy, 336
life drawing, 60-1
lifting out, 191, 391, 468
light:
and color, 154-5, 235, 244-5
and tone, 240-1
angle of incidence, 116, 117
architectural drawings, 46
artificial, 120-1
changing effects of, 32
drawing for painting, 70
interiors, 48-9
modeling, 38
portraits, 62
sunlight, 118-9
tonal drawing, 40-1
working areas, 230
lightfastness, 340, 468
linear drawing, 36-7, 94
linear perspective, 33, 74-5, 468
line, sketches, 238, 239
line and color, 416-7
line and wash, 213

linen, 222
linen canvas, 298
linseed oil, 271, 429, 439, 468
as medium, 278, 279
types, 276
Liotard, Jean Etienne, 207
local color, 244
Louis, Morris, 336, 394
low-key colors, 150, 152-3, 284, 343, 468
low reliefs:
collage, 450-1
collagraph printing, 458-9

M

McCaughrean, Ian, 220, 233
McCrum, Bridget, 237
McLean, Bruce, 394
McLean, John, 357, 475
Macke, August, 145
mahl sticks, 279, 311, 349, 468
Malangi, David, 76
Manet, Edouard, 208, 228, 297
mapping nibs, 179
Marc, Franz, 145
Martin, John, 79
Masaccio, 402
masking, 389
masking fluid, 163, 173, 194-5, 201, 371, 418, 419, 469
masking out, 174, 439, 469
masking tape, 71, 214, 329, 366, 438, 469
mat, 266-7
materials, 408-11
Matisse, Henri, 12
measuring, 44, 83
measuring point, 469
mechanical devices, 174-5,
Michelangelo, 10, 42
middleground, 32
medium, 279, 338, 348, 469
metallic colors, 340
metals, 433
Millet, Jean François, 207
Miró, Joan, 404, 434
mirrors, self portraits, 63
miter boxes, 331
mixed media, 24, 31, 262-3
chapter on, 398-463
mixing colors, 148-51, 204
hard pastels, 213
optical mix, 211, 217
soft pastels, 211
stippling, 217
see also blending
modeling, 38-9, 469
moldings, frames, 331
mold-made paper, 166, 469
Monet, Claude, 123, 208, 274, 320
monochromatic, 469
monochrome, 40, 155, 186
glazing, 381
studies, 362-3
underpainting, 322
monofilaments, 159, 469
monomers, 338
monoprints, 438, 456-7, 469
gallery, 460-1
monotypes, 401, 439, 469

montages, 130-1, 132
mood, portraits, 62
Moore, Henry, 418, 419
Morisot, Berthe, 208
Morley, Malcolm, 337
Moroni, Giovanni, 326
mortar and pestle, 469
mounts, 266-7, 397
mouth diffusers, 214
movement, 68-9, 239
Mughal paintings, 77
multilayered
  compositions,
  422-3
Museum board, 266, 352
muslin boards, 226, 227

N

Natkin, Robert, 394
natural forms, 52-3, 56-7
natural found objects,
  437, 450
negative space, 441
Newbolt, Thomas, 42, 50
newspaper, collage, 436
nibs, 16-7
Nicholson, Ben 421, 434
Nickel Titanate, 469
Nolde, Emil, 274, 296,
  297
Nutt, Jim, 337

O

oak gall ink, 17, 469
oblique projection, 77,
  469
observation, 32
oil bars, 410
oil-based media, 407
oil board, 216
oil paints, 411, 469
oil paper, 216, 469
oil pastels, 21, 411, 469
  erasing, 215, 216
  gallery, 221
  mixed media, 262, 263
  resist techniques, 262,
    371, 418
  techniques, 216-7,
    256-7
  with soft pastels, 424-5
oil sticks, 328, 329, 469
oil painting,
  chapter on, 268-331
oils, 276,7
O'Keeffe, Georgia, 275
one-point perspective,
  74, 86, 469
  box grid construction,
    102-3
  principles, 88-9
opaque acrylic, 338
  alla prima 382
  blending, 378
  on canvas, 353
  combining techniques,
    386-7
  techniques, 366-7
opaque colors, 281, 469
opaque painting, 469
open composition, 177
optical mix, 15, 211, 217,
  282-3, 378, 379, 469
Oriental papers, 166,
  167, 469
orpiment, 276
orthogonals, 88, 469
orthographic projection,
  77, 469
outdoor drawing, 23
overlaying gouache, 198
overlaying washes,
  150-1, 187-9, 469
overpainting, 334-5, 387
ox gall, 146, 469

P

pads, 223
Paine, Ken, 254
painting, drawing for,
  70-1
painting knives
  acrylic 348
  oils, 278
  sgraffito, 328
  techniques, 318-9
painting materials,
  410-11
paints,
  color mixing, 148-51
  pigments, 146-7
  watercolor, 22-3
Paladino, Mimmo, 275
palette knives, 278, 348,
  410
palettes, 147, 279, 280,
  348, 410
  setting out, 340
  "stay wet", 382
  "palimpsests", 434
Palmer, Samuel, 144, 403
pan colors, 146-7
panels, 298, 352
  preparing, 30
paper:
  acrylic, 350-1
  absorbency, 167
  acidity, 167
  bas reliefs, 450
  blocks, 167
  burnishing, 193
  choosing, 30-1
  collage, 436
  colors, 224-5
  creating an image in,
    446-7
  frottage, 227
  gallery, 28-9
  hand-made, 444-5
  hard pastels, 213
  low reliefs, 450
  manufacture, 166-7
  oil pastels, 216
  pastels, 222-3
  sketchbooks, 27
  stretching, 168
  supports, 406, 407
  surface, 167
  texture, 170, 182, 224,
    428
  texturing, 226-7
  transporting, 23
  toning, 168-9
  tooth, 222
  tortillons, 214, 242
  types, for drawing, 26-9
  washes, 182
  watercolor, 166-71
  weaving, 451
  weight, 167
paper towels, 191
parallel lines, 86-8
pastel board, 222, 223,
  224
pastel pencils, 470
Pastel Society, 209
pastello, 210
pastels, 20-1, 120-1,
  and charcoal, 414-5
  chapter on, 202-267
  fixatives, 409
  gallery, 24, 220-1
  keeping work clean, 49
  multilayered
    compositions, 423
  oil pastels, 411, 418,
    424-5
  paper, 26, 28
  shading, 38
  soft pastels, 409, 424-5
pattern, 200

pavements, 88
pen and ink, 16-7, 409
  architectural drawings,
    46-7
  capturing a mood, 62
  charcoal and, 412-3
  line drawings 36, 37
  mixed media, 22, 31
  paper, 28
  shading, 39
  techniques, 30
pen drawings, 179
pencil drawings, 141,
  178-9
pencil sketches, 358
pencils, 83
  capturing a mood, 62
  charcoal, 18
  gallery, 220, 221
  history, 12
  mixed media, 31
  pastel, 20, 213
  techniques, 30
  water-soluble, 408
penknives, scratching
  out, 192
pens, 173
Perréal, Jean, 206
Perroneau, Jean-Baptiste,
  207
perspective, 470
  aerial, 32, 49, 307, 343
  buildings, 46
  chapter on, 72-137
  composition, 45, 176-7
  foreshortening, 238
  landscapes, 54
  linear, 33
Perugino, 272
Philipson, Sir Robin, 309
photocopies, 174-5, 443,
  453
photographs: 79, 124,
  128, 134, 174, 305
  cropping, 208, 232
  references, 232, 264,
    372, 373
Photo-collaging, 436,
  442-3
Photo-Realism, 337
Phthalocyanine, 470
physical mix, 282-3, 378,
  470
Picasso, Pablo, 209, 274,
  315, 404-5
picture plane, 82-3, 84,
  470
  curvilinear perspective,
    130
  projecting plans, 104
  three-point perspective
    108
  two-point perspective,
    98-9
Piero della Francesca, 75,
  78, 272
pigments, 210, 270,
  276-7, 338, 470
Piper, John, 426-7
Pissarro, Camille, 144,
  208
Place, Francis, 142
plan, 470
  computer-generated
    images, 125
  two-point perspective,
    98, 106-7
plants, 52
plastic wrap, 419, 439
plein air, 470
plum line, 45
plywood, 298, 352
Pollock, Fred, 389
Pollock, Jackson, 336
polymer emulsion, 335,
  338, 470

polyester sailcloth, 298
Pontormo, Jacopo da, 10
Pop Art, 336, 337
poppy oil, 276
portraits, 11, 12, 62-3
portraits, colors, 219
Post-impressionism, 274
pounce, 360
Poussin, Nicolas, 96, 142
Prentice, David, 237
presentation, 396-7
preservatives, 147, 470
preserving pastels, 266
preserving works, 462-3
preparatory drawings,
  70-1
primary colors, 148, 218,
  280, 281, 340-1, 470
  mixing, 150-1
primed boards, 407
primer, 28, 227, 352-3,
  354
priming, 301, 470
  boards, 299
  texture, 318
  toned grounds, 312
printed material, collage,
  436, 442
printing,
  acrylic, 390, 391
  block printmaking,
    454-5
  collagraph, 458-9
  materials, 438-9
  monoprints, 456-7,
    460-1
  monotype, 401, 439
prints, mono, 329
projection, 470
  axonometric, 77
  isometric, 77, 125
  orthographic, 77
  plans and elevations,
    104
  three-point
    perspective,
    108
  two-point perspective,
    98-99
proportion:
  buildings, 46
  portraits, 62
putty erasers, 15, 40-1,
  408
PVA, in acrylics, 339
PVA glue, 226, 227, 422,
  428, 470
  adding texture, 428
  collage, 437
  collagraph printing,
    458-9
  multilayered
    compositions, 422

Q

quill pens, 16
quinacridone, 470

R

Raphael, 272
Raney, Karen, 24, 28
Rauschenberg, Robert,
  405
Ravilious, Eric, 201
raw sienna ink, 17
realgar, 276
realism, 79
receding colors, 92-3,
  155, 343, 470
recession, 46, 77
reconstituting pastels,
  251
Redon, Odilon, 209, 221
reducing glasses, 124,
  470
reed pens, 16

reflections, 116-7
refractive index, 271, 470
Rego, Paula, 336, 337
reliefs, bas, 450-1
relief printmaking, 438,
  454
Rembrandt, 10, 11, 28,
  30, 273
Renaissance, 10, 14, 42,
  79, 128
Renoir, Pierre-Auguste,
  209, 274
resin, fixatives, 214
resin, varnishes, 330
resist, 470
resist techniques,
  acrylic, 371, 391
  pastels, 262
  mixed media, 400, 409,
    411, 418-9
  watercolor, 173, 194-7,
    201
retarder, 339, 382, 470
Reynolds, Sir Joshua,
  274
rice, cleaning pastels,
  211
rice paper, 266
Richter, Gerhard, 126,
  127, 275
rigger brushes, 163
Riley, Bridget, 336, 337,
  366
ripples, 117
Rodin, August, 403
Röhm and Haas, 336
rollerball pens, 17
rollers, 411, 427
  sponge, 349
Roman art, 77
Rooney, RA, Mick, 136,
  314
Rosoman, Leonard, 336,
  345
Rough paper, 167, 470
round brushes, 346, 347
rubbing, frottage, 448-9
rubbing through, 391
Rubens, Peter Paul, 11,
  66, 273
Ruisdael, Jacob van, 96
rulers, 83
Ruysch, Rachel, 273

S

sable, 470
sable brushes, 22, 47,
  158-9, 163, 164, 278,
  288, 346, 347
safety, 230
safflower oil, 276
sand, 429
  priming boards, 318
sand supports, 226
Sandby, Paul, 142
Sandby, Thomas, 142
sandpaper, 214, 390, 391,
  407
  scratching out, 192-3
sanguine, 402
  chalk, 18, 206
saturation, 470
Saul, Rosemary, 221, 257
Sareen, Sue, 59, 66
scale, 264-5
scalpels, 214
Schiele, Egon, 402
Schnabel, Julian, 321
scrapers, 348, 349, 410
scratching out, 192-3,
  214, 390-1, 470
script nibs, 179
scumbling, 246-7, 270,
  376-7, 417, 470
  techniques, 291, 294
secondary colors, 148,

150, 218, 340, 470
section, 470
self portraits, 63
sepia ink, 17, 416, 417
sfumato, 255
sgraffito, 38, 435,
  471
  acrylic, 390, 391
  oil, 271, 328
  pastels, 217, 257
  watercolor, 192-3
shade, 471
shading, 471
shadows, 118-9, 120,
  122-3, 154, 235
  modeling, 38-9
  tonal drawing, 40-1
shapes, 34-5
  architectural drawings,
    46
  form and modeling, 38-
    9
  tonal drawing, 40-1
sharpeners, 15
sharpening hard pastels,
  212
shaving brush, 322, 323,
  346, 347
shellac, 17, 439
"sight size" technique,
  44, 471
silverpoint, 14, 471
size, 301, 471
sizing, 166-7, 471
sizing, neutral, 471
sketchbooks, 32, 33,223
  figure drawing, 58
  making, 26
  watercolor, 22
sketches, 178-9, 232, 238-
  9
  alla prima painting,
    316, 384
  blocking in, 233
  brush, 360
  charcoal, 260-1
  composition, 306, 358
  copying, 233
  dry-brushing, 376
  monochrome, 362
  oil pastels, 256
  pens, 17
  tone, 240-1
  transfering, 305, 360
sketching glass, 82-3
sketching umbrella, 471
slate, 433
slide projectors, 124
slides, 305
Smith, Ray, 395
Smith, Richard, 336
Société de Pastellistes,
  209
soft hair brushes, 471
soft pastels, 210-1, 409,
  424-5, 471
  erasing, 215
  gallery, 221
  texture, 252-3
  and water, 258-9
solvents, 278, 279
sparkle, 471
spattering, 471
Spencer, Stanley, 13, 133
spheres, curvilinear, 131
spirits, 471
splayed brushes, 163
sponge rollers, 349
sponges, 19, 162, 163,
  172-3, 183, 349, 390,
  411
sponging out, 190-1, 471
spray diffusers, 413
spray painting, acrylic,
  see airbrushing
square brushes, 288

LEDGEMENTS

or: Emma Foa; Project
teel, Ann Kay, Lynne
es, Joanna Warwick; Senior
nds; Assistant editors:
il Lockley; Art editors:
Claire Legemah, Brian Rust,
Gurinder Purewall; Designers:
n Morris; Assistant Designer:
DTP manager: Joanna Figg-
er: Zirrinia Austin;
rs: Helen Creeke, Meryl
archer: Jo Walton;
atward, Steve Gorton,
e Streeter, Tim Ridley,
dy Crawford.

edgements

like to thank Sean Moore and
on the DK Art School series;
for providing valuable
many artists and illustrators
awings, and photoworks
ecial thanks to everyone at
associated with the DK Art

so like to thank Alun Foster
an of Winsor and Newton
advice.
ld like to thank the staff and
ol of Art and Design from
ertfordshire who have
f the works illustrated in
ction of the book.

c=center, l=left, r=right,
= Royal Academy of Arts
l Arts Library, London, all

Sarah Holliday; p4: Philip
rd, RA, RAAL; pp 8/9: a/w
Pontormo, Uffizi;
lbein, Staatliche
resden; p 11: c Canaletto,
alleries; t Breughel, Hamburger
dt, Albertina Graphische
table, Victoria and Albert
Art Library; c Delacroix,
n des Musées Nationaux; p13:
London; bl Van Gogh, Gift of
1960-232-1, Courtesy of
nal Museum of Design,
n/Art Resource, NY; br
of the National Portrait
tate of Stanley Spencer 1994 all
p14: Fouquet, New York
/ Visual Arts Library; p22: a/w
Karen Raney; b Cézanne,
: t John Ward, RA, RAAL; b
Rembrandt, The British
ey; t Kay Gallwey; b Percy
owyer; cl Percy Horton; br
William Wood; b Neale
le Worley; pp34/35: all James
reen; c Neale Worley; b
orman Blamey, RA; br James
n Finmark; p42: Michelangelo,
Albertina, Vienna; b Thomas
ewin; b Donald Hamilton
4: all James Horton; p 46: a/w

James Horton; p50: t Thomas Newbolt; b Jon Harris;
p50/51: Boudin, Marmotton Museum/Dorling
Kindersley; p51: tr Jane Stanton; c l Anne-Marie
Butlin; p56: b Richard Bell; p56/57 Van Dyck, The
British Museum; p57: t Percy Horton; b Paul Lewin;
p58: a/w James Horton; pp 60/61: all Neale Worley;
p62: tl Karen Raney; rest William Wood; p64: tl a/w
Richard Bell; p66: t Rubens, The British Museum; b
Sue Sareen; p67: t Diana Armfield, RA; b Norman
Blamey, RA; p68: a/w James Horton; p70: t John
Ward, RA; rest James Horton; p71: bl James Horton;
p72: Ray Smith; p74: tr The Trustees of the British
Museum, London; b Turner, Tate Gallery, London;
p75: t Ben Johnson; c Camilla Smith; b Norman
Foster Associates; p76: t David Malangi, Founding
Donor Fund 1984, (Ex Karel Kupka Collection),
Collection: National Gallery of Australia, Canberra; b
The Trustees of the British Museum, London;
p 77: t Miniature from the Akbarnarma, By courtesy
of the Trustees of the Victoria and Albert Museum,
London; b Entertainments in Kyoto, By permission of
the British Library; p78: t Uccello, Chiesa di Santa
Maria Novella, Florence/ Bridgeman Art Library; b
De Witte, Museum Boymans-van Beuningen/ Visual
Arts Library; p79: t Tiepolo, Chiesa dei Gesuati,
Venice/ Scala; c Dibbets, Castello di Rivoli,
Museo d'Arte Contemporanea/ Photo Paolo
Pellion di Persano/Ikona/ © ARS, NY and DACS,
London 1995; b Léger, Solomon R. Guggenheim
Museum, New York/ Photo AKG London/ © DACS
1995; p80: tl Martin Roche; br Sue Sareen; p81: all Ray
Smith; pp82/83: all Ray Smith except sketches p.83 b
Sue Sareen; p84: tl Martin Roche; bl, br Ray Smith;
p85: t: Martin Roche; bl, br Ray Smith; pp86/87:
diagrams Martin Roche; p87 clb Image Bank;
pp88/89: Guy Marsden/Mark Annison; p90: tl, br
Ray Smith/ Mark Annison; bl, br Julian Bray; p91: tl
Julian Bray; b Ray Smith; p92: all Ray Smith; p93: tr
Ray Smith; rest Julian Gregg; p94: b Ray Smith; p95: t
Julian Gregg; br Ray Smith; p96: t Poussin, The Earl
of Plymouth, National Museum of Wales; b Van
Ruisdael, Kimbell Art Museum, Fort Worth, Texas;
p97: t Friedrich, Hermitage, St. Petersburg/
Bridgeman Art Library; b Bill Jacklin, RA, RAAL;
pp98/99: Ray Smith/Dinwiddie McClaren;
pp102/103: Guy Marsden; p104: Ray Smith/ Mark
Annison; p105: Noel McCready; pp106/107: Guy
Marsden; p108: Dinwiddie McClaren; p109: Julian
Bray; p114: tr Michael Smith; bl Sydney Carline,
Imperial War Museum, London; p115: t Ben Johnson;
b David Prentice; p116: all Ray Smith; p117: tr Ray
Smith/ Martin Roche; rest Jane Gifford; pp118/119:
diagrams Guy Marsden; a/w Sue Sareen; p122: tr
Degas, Musée D'Orsay, Paris; bl Ian Cook; 122/123:
c Ben Levene RA, RAAL; p123: tr William Bowyer
RA, RAAL; b Monet, Orangerie, Paris; p124: all
Ray Smith; p125: Guy Marsden/ Henry Newton
Dunn; p126 tr Vermeer, Bridgeman Art Library/
Giraudon; bl Canaletto, Reproduced by courtesy of the
Trustees, The National Gallery, London; p127: t ©
David Hockney; br Richter, Courtesy: Anthony
d'Offay Gallery, London; p130: l Ray Smith/ Mark
Annison; r S.J. Cappleman; p131: t Tabitha Sims; b
Ray Smith/ Mark Annison after Helmholtz/
Lawrence Wright; p132: tr Lear, The Trustees of the
British Museum, London; bl © David Hockney; p133: t
Spencer, National Trust Photographic Library/ Roy
Fox/ © Estate of Stanley Spencer 1995/ All right
reserved DACS; b Carel Weight RA, City of
Nottingham Museums; Castle Museum and Art
Gallery; p136: tr Mick Rooney RA, RAAL; bl Boccioni,
Museum of Modern Art, New York/ Photo AKG,
London; p137: t Gilbert and George, Courtesy:
Anthony d'Offay Gallery, London; b Anthony
Green RA, RAAL; p138 Philip O'Reilly; p139:
Gabriella Baldwin-Purry; pp140/141: carnations
Sharon Finmark; others Gabriella Baldwin-Purry;

pp142/143: Dürer, British Museum/Bridgeman Art
Library; Girtin, Tate Gallery/Bridgeman Art Library;
Turner, British Museum/Bridgeman Art Library;
Cozens; Private Collection/Bridgeman Art Library;
Constable, by Courtesy of the Board of Trustees of
the V & A/ Bridgeman Art Library; pp144/145:
Pissarro, British Museum/Bridgeman Art Library;
Cotman, Bonhams/Bridgeman Art Library; Sargent,
by Courtesy of the Board of Trustees of the V &
A/Bridgeman Art Library; Hopper, Whitney
Museum of American Art, New York/Bridgeman Art
Library; Palmer, Odham Art Gallery, Oldham;
pp146/147: all, Winsor & Newton; pp148/149: color
wheel and boxed swatches, Ray Smith; others
Sharon Finmark; pp150/151: all, Ray Smith;
pp152/153: all, Sharon Finmark; p154: Will Adams;
p155: t Sharon Finmark; b Jane Gifford; p157: Nolde
(attr.), Ruttebüll Tief, Christie's, London/Bridgman
Art Library, © Nolde-Stiftung Seebüll; p158: Winsor
& Newton; p159: Ray Smith; pp160/161: all, Jane
Gifford; pp162/163: all, Julia Rowntree; p165: Dufy,
Visual Art Library, London; p166: sketchbook Jane
Gifford; cylinder mold machine and Bockingford
tinted paper, Inveresk, St.Cuthberts Paper Mill;
p168: t Sharon Finmark; p169: Jane Gifford;
pp170/171: Klee, Christie's, London/Bridgeman Art
Library; pp172/173: portrait, Ray Smith; others,
Julia Rowntree; p174: t Julia Rowntree; p175: Maria
D'Orsi; pp176/177: all, Sharon Finmark; p178: Ray
Smith; p179: t Sharon Finmark; b Jane Gifford;
pp180/181: all, Sharon Finmark; pp182/183: beach
scenes, Julian Gregg; others, Ray Smith; p184:
Cotman, Oldham Art Gallery, Oldham; pp186/189:
all, Sharon Finmark; pp190/197: all, Julia Rowntree;
p198: t Ray Smith; bl&r Sharon Finmark; p199: t
Sharon Finmark; b William Ireland; pp200/201:
Ravilious, Private Collection/Bridgeman Art
Library; p202: Paul Lewin, Cape Coast; pp204/205:
all, Sue Sareen; pp206/207: Bassano, Louvre,
Paris/Réunion des Musées Nationaux; Carriera,
Academia Venezia/ Scala; La Tour, Louvre, Paris;
Chardin, Louvre, Paris; Millet, Glasgow Museums:
The Burrell Collection; pp208/209: Degas, Louvre,
Paris; Cassatt, Museum of Art, Dallas/Visual Arts
Library; Redon, reproduced by courtesy of the
Trustees, The National Gallery, London; Picasso,
Musée Picasso, Paris, Réunion des Musées
Nationaux, © DACS 1993; Kitaj, Marlborough Fine
Arts; pp216/217: all, Rosemary Saul; p219: a/w
Sharon Finmark; p221: Redon, Private
Collection/Visual Arts Library; pp224/225: a/w
Jane Gifford; p228: Manet, Ancienne Collection
Brame et Lorenceau/Giraudon; pp232/233: a/w Ian
McCaughrean; pp234/235: all, Jane Gifford;
pp238/239: all Ian McCaughrean; p255 Aghajanian,
The Kerlin Gallery, Belfast; pp262: Kitaj,
Marlborough Fine Arts; pp268: ©Howard RA;
pp272/273: van Eyck, Rembrandt, Ruysch, Tura,
reproduced by courtesy of the Trustees, The National
Gallery, London; Titian, Isabella Stewart Gardner
Museum, Boston; pp274/275: Claude, reproduced by
courtesy of the Trustees, The National Gallery,
London; Monet, The Brooklyn Museum 20.634 Gift
of A. Augustus Healy; Cézanne, Louvre/Réunion des
Musées Nationaux; O'Keeffe, Collection of the
University of Arizona Museum of Art, Gift of Oliver
James, ©1993 The Georgia O'Keeffe
Foundation/ARS, New York; ©Richter, Anthony
d'Offay Gallery; pp280/281: all, Ray Smith;
pp286/287: Chagall, Kunsthalle Museum, Hamburg,
ADAGP, Paris and DACS, London 1993; ©Gore RA,
©Sutton RA, Royal Academy of Arts Library; p290:
bl Ray Smith; r Jane Gifford; p291: t Jane Gifford; b
Ray Smith; p292 t Jane Gifford; b Ray Smith; p293 t
Jane Gifford; b Ray Smith; pp296/297: ©Levene RA,
Royal Academy of Arts Library; Frampton, all rights
reserved/The Tate Gallery, London, Nolde,

square pastels, 211
squaring up, 471
squinting, 233
stages, painting in, 324-5
"stay-wet" palettes, 382
staining power, 471
stand oil, 292
Stanton, Jane, 25, 51
station point, 84, 471
Stella, Frank, 336
stencil brushes, 347
stenciling, 389, 391
stencils, monoprints, 457, 471
still life, 234-5
  forms, 35
  linear drawing, 37
  tonal drawing, 40
stippling, 38, 379, 471
  oil pastels, 217, 257
  textured grounds, 226
stools, 23
stopping out, 173, 194-7
storage: 462-3
  paint, acrylic, 339
  paintings, 231, 266
  pastels, 210
Strand, Sally, 254
stretchers, 300, 471
stretching canvases, 300, 353
stretching paper, 168, 350, 471
Strother, Jane, 221
Stubbs, Geroge, 274
students' paints, 277
subdivision, 471
sunlight, 118-9
supports, 402, 406-7, 471
  chosing, 298-9
  gallery, 228-9
  papers, 222-3
  preparing, 300-1
  textures and colors, 224-5
  texturing, 226-7, 428
surface, paper, 167, 471
surface sizing, 471
surfaces, experimenting with, 426-7
Surrealism, 404, 434
Surrealists, 209, 274
Sutherland, Graham, 422
Sutton, Philip, 287
synthetic brushes, 346

T
tea bags, 432
technical pens, 16, 17, 471
techniques:
  acrylics, 356-97
  drawing, 30-71
  oils, 302-331
  pastels, 230-267
  watercolor, 172-201
Teiger, Tamar, 247
tempera, 272
temperature, color,
tertiary colors, 148, 150, 284, 471
texture: 200-1, 390, 428-9
  architectural drawings, 46
  brushstrokes, 295
  collagraph printing, 458-9
  dry brush, 291
  impasto, 367
  exploring, 252-3
  frottage, 448
  gesso, 407
  hand-made paper, 445, 447
  low reliefs, 450-1
  painting knives, 318, 319

papers, 26, 28, 31, 170, 182, 224
printing, 439
supports, 298, 299
texturing paper, 226-7
texture paste, 339, 367
Thomas, Shanti, 229
"three crayon technique, "206
three-point perspective, 86, 108-113, 471
thumbnail sketches, 239
Tiepolo, Giambattista, 11, 79
tint, 472
tinting strength, 472
Tintoretto, 273
tissue paper, 231
  laminating, 448-9
  texture, 428, 431
Titian, 273, 274
toe of brush, 472
tonal drawing, 40-1
tonal key, 240, 472
tone, 92-3, 94, 472
  acrylics, 362-3
  hard pastels, 213
  sketches, 240-1
  soft pastels, 210
  softening, 379
  washes, 372
  watercolor, 186-7
toned grounds, 312-3, 472
  acrylic, 362, 383
  gallery, oil, 314-5
  preparing, 312
toned paper, 26, 28, 29
  gouache, 198
tones, modeling, 38
toning paper, 168-9
tooth of paper, 222, 472
tortillons, 21, 214, 242, 411
Tosa-Sumiyoshi School, 77
Toulouse Lautrec, Henri de, 209
Towne, Francis, 143
tracing paper, 20, 71, 214, 231, 266
tracing sketches, 360, 361
tragacanth, 210
transferring sketches, 305, 360-1
transparency, 140, 252
transparent acrylic:
  alla prima, 382
  blending, 378-9, 380-1
  on canvas, 353
  combining techniques, 386-7
  techniques, 370-1
transparent colors, 281
transparent painting, 472
transversals, 88, 472
Treanor, Frances, 263
tube colors, 146-7
Tura, Cosima, 272
Turner, J.M.W., 12, 74, 79, 142, 143-4, 147, 403
turpentine, 216, 257, 278 430, 439, 472
  cleaning brushes, 289
  glazing, 292
  as medium, 270
  wiping off, 294
two-point perspective, 86-7, 98-9, 100-1, 472
  box grid construction, 103
  plans and elevations, 106-7

U
Uccello, Paolo, 78
Umbrellas, sketching,

underpainting, 322, 376, 472
  glazing, 381
unsaturated color, 472
unusual materials, 432-3

V
value, 472
Van Dyck, Sir Anthony, 56, 175
Van Eyck, Jan, 272
Van Gogh, Vincent, 13, 79, 274, 320, 403
vanishing axis, 472
vanishing line, 472
vanishing point, 33, 46, 472
  box grid construction, 102-3
  diagonal, 88-9
  horizon line, 85
  inclined planes, 104-5
  non-linear perspective, 77
  one-point perspective, 74, 86, 88-9
  shadows, 118, 120
  sunlight, 118
  three-point perspective, 87, 108-9, 110
  two-point perspective, 86-7, 98
variegated washes, 181, 472
varnish, 279, 330, 396, 462, 472
varnishing brushes, 346, 396
Vasari, Giorgio, 78
Velázquez, Diego, 11, 79, 273
Vermeer, Jan, 11, 126
vertical format, 235
video cameras, 175
viewfinders, 44, 54, 174, 232, 305, 358, 472
viewpoint, 84-5, 472
  bird's-eye view, 108
  ellipses, 91
  high, 84, 99, 107
  horizon line, 84
  linear perspective, 74
  low, 85, 99, 107
  worm's-eye view, 108
Vigée-Lebrun, Marie-Louise, 207
viscosity, 472
Vitruvius, 77
Vivian, Joseph, 206
Vuillard, Edouard, 209

W
walnut oil, 272, 276
Warhol, Andy, 336, 337, 366
warm colors, 155, 218, 244-5, 280, 472
wash brushes, 159, 323
washes, 141, 180-5, 472
  color mixing, 150-1
  dry wash, 250-1
  gallery, 184-5
  gouache, 199
  laying, 180-1, 216
  on canvas, 353
  overlaying, 182-3, 187-9
  paper surface and, 350-1
  sponging, 183
  techniques, 372-3
  transparent acrylic, 370-1
  warm and cool colors, 155

washing off, 182, 196-7, 472
Ward, RA, John, 25, 70
washes, watercolor, 22
water, soft pastels and, 258-9
water-based media, 407, 410
  multilayered compositions, 422-3
  gallery, 220
watercolors, 22-3, 95, 472
  chapter on, 138-201
  effects, 339, 370-1
  experimenting with surfaces, 426
  gallery, 24-5
  landscapes, 54
  mixed media, 31, 263
  monoprints, 67
  paper, 26, 28-9
  shading, 38
  techniques, 30, 31, 417
  toned grounds, 50
  washes, 416
  wax resist, 196-7, 418-9
watercolor brushes, 158-9, 215
watercolor papers, 166-71, 222-3, 224, 350
waterleaf, 167, 472
water-soluble pastels, 21, 213, 472
water-soluble pencils, 14, 15
wax, 433
wax crayons, 409, 448
wax encaustic, 430-1, 472
wax resist, 472
wax resist trechniques, acrylic, 371, 391
  mixed media, 400, 409, 418-9
  watercolor, 196-7, 201
weaving paper, 451
weight, paper, 167, 472
Weight, RA, Carel, 132, 133, 309
wet-in-wet, 371, 417, 427, 473
  blending, acrylics, 379
wet-over-dry, 348, 422, 473
wet wipes, 215
wetting agents, 146
Whistler, James, 209
white chalk, 206
white grounds, 310-1, 314-5
white spirit, 216, 217
Whittaker, Gillean, 364
wide-angle views, 81
willow charcoal, 260
window mounts, 266-7
wiping off, 294, 391
wire cutters, 437
Witte, Emanuel de, 78
wooden panels, 278, 352
Wood, Tom, 460
wood supports, 406
wood-free paper, 473
work surfaces, 231
wove paper, 167, 473
Wright, Michael, 259

ACKNO

Credits: Series e
  editors: Susanna
  Nazareth, Peter J
  editor: Gwen Edr
  Margaret Chang,
  Heather McCarry
  Spencer Holbroo
  Dawn Terrey, Ste
  Stephen Crouche
  Latham; DTP des
  Production contro
  Silbert; Picture re
  Photography: Phi
  Jeremy Hopley, C
  Susannah Price, A

Authors acknow
The authors woul
the managing tea
the Royal Academ
assistance; and th
whose paintings,
enrich the book. S
Dorling Kindersle
School project.
Ray Smith would
and Richard Good
Ltd. for their expe
Michael Wright w
students of the Sc
the University of I
contributed many
the Mixed Media s

Picture credits
Key: t=top, b=botton
a/w=artworks, RAA
Library, VAL = Vis
rights reserved

p2: Martin Taylor; p
O'Reilly; p6: John V
James Horton; p10:
Florence/Ikona; b H
Kunstsammlungen I
Courtauld Institute (
Kunsthalle; b Rembra
Sannlung; p12: t Cor
Museum/ Bridgema
Louvre, Paris/ Réun
t Degas, Tate Galler
Miss Edith Wetmor
Cooper-Hewitt, Nati
Smithsonian Institu
Spencer, by courtes
Gallery, London, © F
rights reserved DAC
Metropolitan Museu
James Horton; p24:
Kunsthaus Zurich; p
Jane Stanton; p28: t
Museum; b Karen Ra
Horton; p30: t Jason
Neale Worley; p31: tr
Worley; p33: a/w Ne
Horton; p36: tr Sue S
Richard Bell; p38: tl I
Horton; p39: all Shar
Graphische Sammlur
Newbolt; p43: t Paul
Fraser, RA, RAAL; p4

Staatsgalerie, Stuttgart, ©Nolde-Stiftung Seebüll/Arthothek Kunstdia-Archiv; *p299 tl* Ray Smith; *tr, b* Trevor Chamberlain; *bl* Lance Beeke; *pp302/303* all, Ian McCaughrean; *pp304/305 a/w*, Jane Gifford; *pp308/309:* Kokoschka, Albright Knox, Atkins Museum/Visual Arts Library ©DACS 1993; ©Jacklin RA, ©Weight RA, ©Philipson RA, The Royal Academy of Arts Library; *pp314/315:* Hamilton-Fraser RA, Rooney RA, Royal Academy of Arts Library; Picasso, Private Collection/Visual Arts Library, ©DACS 1993; *pp320/321:* van Gogh, Musée d'Orsay, Paris; Monet, reproduced by courtesy of the Trustees, The National Gallery, London; ©Howard RA, ©Dunstan RA, Royal Academy of Arts Library; Schnabel, Courtesy of Galerie Bruno Bischofberger, Zurich, all rights reserved; *pp326/327:* Moroni, The National Gallery of Ireland; El Greco, Metropolitan Museum of Art, New York/Visual Arts Library; *p328:* Ian McCaughrean; *p329: tl* Ray Smith; rest, Ian McCaughrean.*tr* Ray Smith; *br* Louise Fox; *cl* Ian McCaughrean; *p332:* Julian Bray; *p334: tl* Jane Gifford; *cr* Jane Gifford; *bl* Gabriella Baldwin-Purry; *p335: tl* Jane Gifford; *cr* Jane Gifford; *bl* Julian Gregg; *p336: tr* Morris Louis, The Phillips Collection, Washington, DC, © Marcella Louis Brenner; *br* David Hockney, The Tate Gallery, London, © David Hockney 1965; *p337: tl* Andy Warhol, Museum Ludwig, Cologne, © 1993 The Andy Warhol Foundation for the Visual Arts, Inc.; *tr* Bridget Riley, Private Collection /Bridgeman Art Library, © 1993 Bridget Riley, Courtesy Karsten Schubert Ltd., London; *b* Paula Rego, The Tate Gallery, London, © Paula Rego; *p340: cl* Jane Gifford; *br* Ray Smith; *p341:* all Jane Gifford except *c* Ray Smith; *p342:* all Julian Bray; *p343: tl* and *tr* Sue Sharples; *bl* and *br* Julian Bray; *pp344/345: c* John Hoyland ARA, RAAL; *p344: bl* Gregory Gordon; *p345: r* and *b* Leonard Rosoman RA, RAAL; *p351: c* Ian McCaughrean; *b* Julian Bray; *pp 354/355: c* Louise Fox; *p354: b* Jacobo Borges, Private Collection, Caracas/Courtesy of CDS Gallery, N.Y./VAL; *p355: tr* Albina Kosiec Felski, National Museum of American Art, Smithsonian Institute/Bridgeman Art Library; *cl* Ronald Davis, Private Collection/VAL; *br* Jane Gifford; *p356: tl* Jane Gifford; *br* Julian Bray; *p357: tr* and *c* Jane Gifford; *b* Ray Smith; *p358: c* and *b* Jane Gifford; *p359:* all Jane Gifford; *pp360/361:* all Jane Gifford; *p362:* all Jane Gifford; *p363: t* and *c* Ray Smith; *b* Jane Gifford; *p364: tr* Jo Kelly; *cl* Gillean Whitaker, RAAL; *pp364/365: b* Patrick Caulfield, The Saatchi Collection, London, © Waddington Galleries Ltd, London; *p365: tl* Mike Gorman, Private Collection/VAL; *tr* Jennifer Durrant, RAAL; *p366: tl* Jane Gifford; *c* and *b* Ian McCaughrean; *p367:* all Jane Gifford; *p368/369:* Derek Worrall; *pp370/371:* all Julian Bray; *pp 372/373:* all Julian Bray; *p374: tr* Christopher Lenthall; *bl* Gabriella Baldwin-Purry; *br* Jane Gifford; *p375: tl* Albert Irvin; *tr* David Evans; *br* John McLean, Art For Sale/Francis Graham Dixon Gallery; *p376:* all Ian McCaughrean; *p377: tr* Ian McCaughrean; *c* and *b* Jane Gifford; *p378/379:* all Jane Gifford; *p380: tl* and *tr* Sue Sharples; *c* and *b* Jane Gifford; *p381:* Ian McCaughrean; *pp382/383:* Louise Fox; *pp384/385:* Louise Fox; *pp386/387:* Julian Bray; *p388: tr* Chuck Close, Akron Art Museum, Akron, Ohio/Courtesy Pace Gallery /VAL; *b* William Henderson, RAAL; *p389: tl* Bernard Cohen, RAAL; *tr* Fred Pollock, RAAL; *c* and *b* Michael Andrews, Anthony d'Offay Gallery, London; *pp390/391:* Julian Gregg; *p390: cl* Julian Gregg; *cr* Ian McCaughrean; *bl* Ray Smith; *p391: tl* and *c* Ian McCaughrean; *tr* and *b* Julian Gregg *pp392/393:* Julian Gregg; *p394: r* Robert Natkin, Gimpel Fils Gallery; *bl* Bruce McLean, Anthony d'Offay Gallery/VAL; *p395: t* Sandra Blow RA; *b* Ray Smith; *p396:* Julian Bray; *p397: t* Julian Bray; *b*

Jane Gifford; *p398:* Flea Cooke; *p400: cl,* Angela Gaye Mallory, *bl* Flea Cooke, *p401: cl, tr* Anneli Boon, *b* Janet Nathan, *p402: tr* Reproduced by Courtesy of the Trustees of The National Gallery, London, *b* Musée du Louvre, Paris/Flammarion-Giraudon, *p403: tl* Tate Gallery, London, *cl* Musée Cantonal des Beaux-Arts, Lausanne, *br* Osterreichische Galerie, Vienna/Bridgeman-Giraudon, *p404: t* Musée National d'Art Moderne/Lauros-Giraudon/© ADAGP, Paris and DACS, London 1995, *b* Private Collection, England (on loan to the Scottish National Gallery of Modern Art, Edinburgh)/ Penrose Film Productions/ © SPADEM/ADAGP, Paris and DACS, London 1995, *p405: t* Guggenheim Collection, Venice/Bridgeman Art Library/© DACS 1995, *bl* National Museum of American Art, Smithsonian/Art Resource/Bridgeman Art Library/© Robert Rauschenberg /DACS, London/VAGA, New York 1995, *br* © DACS 1995, *p412:* Hilary Rosen, *p413:* Wendy Pasmore, *p414:* Michael Wright, *p415:* Robert Clatworthy RA, RAAL *p416:* Susan Lloyd, *p417: tl* Valerie Claypole, *cr* Bob Baggaley, *p418:* © The Henry Moore Foundation, *p419:* Kate Nicholson, *p420: br* Graphische Sammlung Albertina, Vienna, *tr* © The Henry Moore Foundation, *p421: t* Kettle's Yard, University of Cambridge/The Trustees of the David Jones Estate, *cl* Private Collection/© Estate of Ben Nicholson 1995 All Rights Reserved DACS, *br* Peter Coker RA, RAAL,*bl* © Angela Verren – Taunt 1995, All rights reserved DACS, *p422:* Craig Peacock, *p423:* Lucinda Cobley, *p424/425:* Ken Draper, *p426:* Estate of the Artist, Courtesy of Waddington Galleries, London, *p427:* Graham Boyd, *p428:* Craig Peacock, *p429: tr* Sonia Lawson RA, RAAL, *br* Kate Nicholson, *p431: t* Maureen Wilkinson, *br* Barbara Freeman, *p432:* Tessa Maiden, *p433:* Rowena Dring, *p434: l* Fundació Joan Miró, Barcelona/ ADAGP, Paris and DACS, London 1995 *r* Private Collection/ © Angela Verren-Taunt 1995 All Rights Reserved DACS, *p435: t* Eileen Agar RAAL, *cr* Ken Draper, *b* Barbara Rae RAAL, *p440/441:* Julian Gregg, *p442: br* Ed Smy, *p443:* Angela Gaye Mallory, *p444/447:* Flea Cooke, *p448/449:* Anneli Boon, *p450:* Dick Lee RA, RAAL, *p451:* Angela Gaye Mallory, *p452: b* Musée des Arts Décoratifs, L.Sully Jaulmes, Paris, All Rights Reserved/© ADAGP, Paris and DACS, London 1995, *r* Tate Gallery London/©SPADEM/ADAGP, Paris and DACS, London 1995, *p453: t* Peter Blake RA, RAAL, *b* Anneli Boon, *p454/455:* Flea Cooke, *p456/457:* Michael Wright, *p458/459:* Anneli Boon, *p460: bl* Musée d'Orsay, Paris/Photo: Philippe Sebert, *tl* Bob Bagalley, *p461: b* Marlborough Graphics Ltd, *t* TomWood, *p462:* Michael Wright; *p463: tr* Flea Cooke, *b* Michael Wright.

Additional photography:
Julian Bray: *p110;* Jane Gifford: *p117; p134;* Susanna Price: *p123: b;* Tim Ridley: *p80; p94 c; p116; p120;* Philippe Sebert: *p122: tr;* Ray Smith: *p83, p84; pp86/87:* all except *p87: clb; pp92/93; p94: tl; p95; p124 cl* Philippe Sebert: *p207: tl, c; p208: t.* The Dorling Kindersley Studio and Karl Adamson.

Dorling Kindersley would like to thank:
Paintworks, Cornellison & Son Ltd., and Winsor & Newton Ltd. for kindly supplying the artists' materials used in the book.